OZ CLARKE'S
# WINE
# GUIDE
# 1993
## NINTH EDITION

## Contributors to *Oz Clarke's Wine Guide 1993*

**Nicholas Faith** is a financial journalist and the author of books on Champagne and Cognac as well as the classic study of the Bordeaux wine trade, *The Wine Masters*. Historian and food and wine writer **Giles MacDonogh**'s latest books are a biography of Brillat-Savarin and *The Wine and Food of Austria*; soon to be published is his book on *Syrah, Grenache, Mourvèdre*. He also writes on food and drinks for the weekend *Financial Times*. **Tom Stevenson** is the author of the invaluable *World Wine Encyclopedia* and a book on Champagne; he also writes a regular column on Champagne for *Wine* magazine. **Stephen Brook** writes on wine for *Vogue* and other magazines as well as writing on travel; his two latest books are one on Sauvignon Blanc and a travel book on Los Angeles, *LA Lore*. **Andrew Jefford** has written an award-winning book on Champagne and one on port, and writes regularly for the London *Evening Standard*. **Gordon Brown** writes a regular column on spirits for *The Guardian*, and contributes to many other publications on wine. **Jim Ainsworth** writes on wine for *Wine, Elle* and many other magazines and is the author of the Mitchell Beazley pocket guides to *Red Wines* and *White Wines*. **Richard Mayson** has written a book on the wines of Portugal, and **Anthony Rose** is the award-winning wine correspondent for *The Independent*.

## Reviews of previous editions

'Packed with insider information and opinion, and worth every penny.' Derek Cooper

'...the guide gets better with every vintage. Clarke writes with enthusiasm virtually steaming off the page. Here is someone who loves wine.' *The Guardian*

'If you haven't bought a copy, there is little hope for you.' *The Sunday Telegraph*

'An enthusiastic, opinionated and entertaining survey of the world's wines and a price guide to wines on the shelves of Britain.' *The Sunday Times*

'... typically up-to-date, irreverent but informative.' *The Independent*

'Scholarly, funny and thought-provoking.' Robert Parker

'*Webster's Wine Guide* is both passionate and quite unpretentious, in true Oz Clarke fashion.' *The Newcastle Journal*

# OZ CLARKE'S
# WINE GUIDE
# 1993
## NINTH EDITION

'WEBSTER'S'
THE COMPLETE WINE
BUYER'S HANDBOOK

WEBSTERS
MITCHELL BEAZLEY
LONDON

*Editorial Director* Sandy Carr
*General Editor* Margaret Rand
*Art Editor* Jason Vrakas
*Price Guides Editors* Siobhan Bremner,
Lorna Bateson
*Editorial Assistant* Gemma Hancock
*Indexer* Naomi Good
*Cover photograph* James Merrell
*Art Director* Douglas Wilson
*Editorial Consultant* Rosemary George

Created and designed by
Webster's Wine Price Guide Limited,
Axe and Bottle Court, 70 Newcomen Street,
London SE1 1YT
in association with Mitchell Beazley
International Limited, Michelin House,
81 Fulham Road, London SW3 6RB

Oz Clarke's Wine Guide 1993 Edition
© Websters International Publishers
and Mitchell Beazley Publishers 1992

ISBN 1 85732 932 5

Printed and bound in the UK by
Cox & Wyman, Reading

# CONTENTS

# INTRODUCTION

And here is a health warning. To all those winemakers who look backwards rather than forwards. To all those cynical producers who foist stale, unsulphured, washed-out rubbish on to an unwilling populace. To all those complacent ladies and gentlemen who believe that they know best because they and their kith and kin have been making wine for a thousand years and consequently they couldn't be less interested when we, the consumers say – excuse me, we don't like the taste of your wine – never did, actually, but we couldn't find any alternative at the price – oh, and the price, er, why does it keep doubling? To all those, I say – take cover. The Australians are coming.

Not Australian wines. Sure, they're still coming over on to our shelves in bigger volumes than ever, and so long as they keep the quality up and the price fair there's no reason why they shouldn't double their sales virtually every year. No, I mean Australians themselves. Flesh and blood ockers with a funny way of speaking English and an enormous capacity for beer. They have the best training the world has to offer in how to make wine and in particular how to take a whole pile of sows' ears and turn them into silk purses. And they're pouring into Europe – not into Bordeaux and Burgundy, Champagne and the Rhine, but rather the unheralded, often despised vinelands of the South and the East condemned for generations to be producers of the most basic of table wines.

Well, the sprawling vineyards south and east of Lisbon, the vines that carpet the tired, rutted fields of southern France, and the mile upon mile of centrally farmed vines in Hungary, Moldova, the Ukraine, Crimea and Czechoslovakia will continue to fill that rôle – providing us with our basic drinking wine. The thing is that most of it used to be unutterable filth, and now it's going to be fresh, bright, packed with interesting flavours – and affordable. And the chief reason is the bands of roaming Australians who increasingly consult or actually make the wines in these many corners of Europe.

### Cuvée Earls Court

I'll just take three examples. Firstly, close to home. Thames Valley vineyards – owned by an Aussie, employing an Aussie winemaker. I don't understand half the jargon John Worontschak spouts, but his wines sing a tune I find thrilling, especially so since it's happening in our own backyard. The Thames Valley Fumé is the finest oak-aged white yet produced in Britain, and its sweet wine is the finest botrytized sticky. Hidden Springs Pinot Noir 1990 is Britain's best Pinot so far – and Worontschak made that too. Sorry, I forgot. Despite the name, Worontschak of Thames Valley and Hidden Springs is Australian and he is rapidly becoming the most influential wine-maker in the kingdom, making world class wine out of our proud old English fruit. God bless 'im. I hope they don't revoke his work permit too soon.

Less close to home – Portugal. Peter Bright is another Aussie, the guy who created João Pires dry Muscat, a delicious, fragrant dry white that sent the traditional Portuguese wine world into a state of shock. But that's nothing to what he does now. He's producing remarkable reds from local grapes as well as Cabernet and Merlot; a Chardonnay simply light years ahead of anything Portugal has come up with in the dry white stakes so far; and he's even found time to produce the first exciting Setúbal fortified wine anyone can remember –

as well as splashing in 77 per cent alcohol spirit to fortify it, he threw great wodges of dates and sultanas in and then stored the whole gooey mess in whisky barrels for five years.

Sounds original? It is. Overrides the traditions and breaks the rules? It does. But that is why the Aussie revolution is so important. The third example is English – Hugh Ryman – but his whole philosophy is based on what he learnt from Brian Croser in Australia. Now he is the star producer of the south-west of France, has shocked everybody by his 1991 creations in Hungary and is set to shock us all still further by what he can weave out of the tangled webs of potential brilliance in the newly independent ex-communist states that circle the Black Sea. He has a lieutenant, a Croser-trained Australian, and a roving team of winery and vineyard workers – Australians – all trained in the art of the possible, all with one thought drummed into their heads – there's no point in making a wine unless it's going to give pleasure to the person who drinks it.

### Two per cent claret

If the writing is on the wall in the unheralded regions of the wine world, the message has to be taken on board in the traditional areas too. I went to one supermarket tasting and out of a hundred wines there were only two Bordeaux. Why so few, I asked. Who's drinking Bordeaux? was their reply. Another big supermarket range. No Beaujolais. Why, I asked? Because they couldn't sell it, no-one liked the flavour, no-one liked the price. A high street giant showed off their range – but minus Muscadet. They'd delisted it except in a selection of their shops because the price was too high and the flavour too poor.

Now, in all these areas there are intelligent, go-ahead producers. These are the ones who will try to argue for flexibility and innovation against their many colleagues who prefer to bury their heads in the sand and hide behind their *Appellation Contrôlées* and their dwindling reputations. If the *Appellation* areas of France, and the *Denominacion* regions of Italy and Spain in particular are to keep their meaning they must welcome that kind of change into their musty cellars. I don't want them all to start making one international style of wine, I just want them to make the best wine they can from the grapes that they grow.

There's no question that Cabernet and Chardonnay, Syrah and Sauvignon can produce highly attractive international flavours. In traditional areas where the grape varieties are pathetic then the authorities must either allow improving grape varieties into the blends or accept that their farmers and their successors are doomed. In areas with good grapes – Mourvèdre, Nebbiolo, Tempranillo, Periquita – they must encourage the best wine-making practices to draw out the best flavours the grape can give, not blindly force upon eager and talented producers the half-baked dictates of a bygone era.

This is what we stand for at the *Guide*. We want to show you where the best flavours are, where the best prices are, which men and women are breaking out of a hidebound past and rejoicing in offering us pleasure at a price we can afford, and which merchants and supermarkets up and down the land are stocking such wines and at what cost to you, the consumer. Since our very first issue we have had as our guiding light the consumers' interest. We fear no reputations, we kowtow to no worthless traditions, but we do laud excellence wherever it occurs, and we do try to give you, the consumer, the inside track knowledge that will enable you to buy better wine, at better prices – and be part of the surge that is bringing Britain greater variety and greater quality than ever before.

# 100 BEST BUYS

How do you know a bargain when you see one? Answer: you leave it to *Webster's*, because we've sought them out for you. On these two pages are listed, country by country, 100 star bargains. These are the best of the best: our pick of this year's *Guide*. Many are mature vintages at bargain prices, and each is specific to the merchant and the vintage listed here. A word of warning: the prices quoted were those in force in early summer 1992. We cannot guarantee that those prices will still hold by the time this guide is published.

**Red Bordeaux**
1988 Ch. Domaine la Grave, Graves (GE) £6.50
1988 Ch. la Tour-de-By, Médoc (GRE) £6.95
1985 Ch. d'Angludet, Margaux (CV) £9.20
1983 Ch. Citran, Haut-Médoc (BYR) £6.85
1983 Ch. la Tour-de-Mons, Margaux (HOG) £8.16

**White Bordeaux**
1990 Ch. Thieuley (AD) £4.95
1990 Clos St-Georges, Graves (SAI) £6.29

**Burgundy**
1991 Sauvignon de St-Bris, Brocard (CH) £5.65
1990 Bourgogne Aligoté Brocard (WAI) £4.89
Crémant de Bourgogne Cave de Lugny (WAI) £5.95
1989 Bourgogne Pinot Noir Cave de Buxy (OD, WAI) £4.99
1988 Bourgogne Irancy, Bienvenu (HAU) £6.95
1988 Bourgogne la Digoine Villaine (AD) £7.20

**Beaujolais**
1991 Juliénas Pelletier (EL) £4.99
1990 Morgon Domaine Jean Descombes, Duboeuf (BEK) £5.83

**Rhône Red**
1990 Côtes du Rhône Parallèle 45, Jaboulet (NI) £4.60
1988 Côtes du Rhône Guigal (BO, HAY) c. £4.80
1988 Côtes du Ventoux Jaboulet (HOG, OD) £3.66
1988 Crozes-Hermitage Domaine de Thalabert, Jaboulet (LOE) £6.66
1983 St-Joseph Clos de l'Arbalestrier, Florentin (WCL) £8.99

**Loire**
Crémant de Loire Brut, Gratien & Meyer (WS) (sparkling) £7.95
1990 Chardonnay du Haut Poitou Cave Co-op (WAI) £3.99
1990 Sauvignon du Haut Poitou, Cave Co-op (WAI) £3.69

1990 Quincy Domaine de la Maison Blanche (ASD, SAI) c. £4.75
1990 Sauvignon de Touraine Confrerie d'Oisly et Thesée (WW) £4.99
1990 Savennières Clos du Papillon, Baumard (HOG) £6.67
1989 Bourgueil la Hurolaie Caslot-Galbrun (TES) £5.59
1989 Chinon Domaine Morin (BYR) £4.99
1988 Coteaux du Layon Clos de Ste-Catherine, Baumard (HOG) £5.96
1985 Montlouis Sec Deletang (RAE) £5.15
1982 Vouvray Clos du Bourg, Huet (BOR) £6.64
1976 Vouvray Château de Vaudenuits (UN) £8.49
1975 Anjou Moulin Touchais (EL) £10.05

**Alsace**
1990 Pinot Blanc Cave Co-op, Turckheim (THR, NI) £3.99
1989 Riesling Turckheim, Zind-Humbrecht (VIC) £4.69
1983 Gewürztraminer Vendange Tardive, Muré (BU) £7.95
1979 Riesling Frederic Emile, Trimbach (FA) £7.83

**South of France**
Sainsbury's Muscat de St-Jean de Minervois 1/2 bottle (SAI) £2.79
1990 Minervois Domaine de Ste-Eulalie (DAV) £3.99
1989 Bergerac Château la Jaubertie (NI) £4.75

> *The codes given in brackets after the wine names indicate the merchants stocking the wines at these prices in the summer of 1992. The same codes are used in the price guides which begin on page 246. The key to the codes will be found on page 247.*

1989 Corbières Château de Cabriac (EL, NI) c. £3.70

1989 Safeway Corbières, Château de Caraguilhes (SAF) £3.94

1988 Fitou Caves du Mont Tauch (HOG) £3.22

1988 Jurançon Sec Domaine Cauhapé (NI) £6.99

1988 La Clape Domaine de Pech Celeyran (AD) £3.95

1987 Coteaux d'Aix-en-Provence Mas de la Dame (AUG) £4.55

1983 Bandol Château Vannières (BUT) £6.85

## Germany

Rheingau Riesling, Schloss Reinhartshausen (GA) £2.99

1990 Niersteiner Spiegelberg Riesling Kab., Rudolf Müller (TAN) £3.60

1988 Schloss Böckelheimer Kupfergrube Riesling Aus., Staatsdomäne (GE) £5.25

1988 Wachenheimer Rechbachel Riesling Kab., Bürklin-Wolf (ASD) £5.99

1983 Niederhauser Hermannsberg Riesling Kab., Staatsdomäne (LOE) £5.87

1983 Oestricher Doosberg Riesling Kab., Schonborn (GA) £4.99

1981 Scharzhofberger Riesling Kab., Hövel (THR) £5.79

1975 Forster Freundstuck Riesling Spät., Buhl (LOE) £6.76

## Italy

1991 Moscato d'Asti Viticoltori dell'Acquese (WCL) £2.49

1991 Soave Classico Zenato (ASD) £4.25

1991 Vermentino di Sardegna C.S. di Dolianova (WCL) £3.59

1990 Chianti Rufina Villa di Vetrice (SOM) £3.45

1990 Dolcetto d'Acqui Viticoltori dell'Acquese (VIC) £3.59

1990 Soave Classico, Monte Tenda, Tedeschi (OD) £3.99

1989 Bardolino Classico Superiore Rizzardi (HOG) £4.10

1989 Rosso di Montalcino Campo ai Sassi, Frescobaldi (WAI) £4.79

1988 Chardonnay Lageder, Alto Adige (AUG) £3.99

1988 Chianti Classico Isole e Olena (SOM) £6.70

1983 Recioto Amarone Riserva Tommasi (CH) £7.70

1982 Barolo Riserva Fontanafredda (OD) £6.99

1982 Chianti Classico Riserva Montagliari (GE) £6.25

1978 Barbaresco Marchesi di Barolo (HOG) £7.79

## Spain – Table Wine

Co-op. del Ribeiro Pazo Ribeiro Blanco (WCL) £3.99

Don Darias (SAF, TES) c. £2.65

1986 Felix Solis Viña Albali Reserva, Rioja (THR) £3.49

1986 La Rioja Alta Vina Alberdi (SOM) £4.95

1985 Faustino V Reserva, Rioja (WHI) £5.79

1984 Contino Reserva, Rioja (CV) £7.05

1975 Castillo de Tiebas Reserva (PEN) £5.91

1966 Bodegas Riojanas Monte Real (BUT) £6.08

## Sherry

Manzanilla de Sanlúcar, Barbadillo (OD,CE) £4.50

Tio Guillermo Amontillado, Garvey (CV) £8.54

## Portugal

Sainsbury's Arruda (SAI) £2.69

1987 Dry Palmela Moscato, João Pires (ASK) £3.87

1986 Planalto Reserva (GRG) £3.49

1982 Dão Grão Vasco Garrafeira (GRG) £3.99

1975 Barraida Frei João (ASK) £7.96

## Australia

Angas Brut (SOM) £5.00

1991 Coldstream Hills Pinot Noir (CV) £7.93

1991 Hill-Smith Old Triangle Riesling (BYR, WAI, GRE, ASD) c. £3.90

1991 Yalumba Oxford Landing Chardonnay (HUN) £4.75

1990 Orlando RF Chardonnay (HOG) £4.46

1990 Penfolds Cabernet Sauvignon/Shiraz Bin 389 (OD) £6.99

1990 Tim Adams Sémillon (BO) £5.70

1989 Mitchelton Wood-Matured Marsanne (WAI, MAJ) c. £5.95

1988 Hungerford Hill Coonawarra Cabernet Sauvignon (CB) £7.21

1988 Yalumba Oxford Landing Cabernet Sauvignon/Shiraz (AUS) £4.79

1985 Penfolds Kalimna Shiraz Bin 28 (OD) £4.69

1985 Rouge Homme Shiraz/Cabernet Sauvignon (BYR) £4.79

## New Zealand

1991 Montana Marlborough Sauvignon Blanc (VIC, THR) £4.99

## Other Regions

1987 Hamilton Russell Pinot Noir, South Africa (HOG) £5.96

1985 Chateau Carras Côtes de Meliton, Greece (CV) £5.64

1985 Chateau Musar, Lebanon (GA) £6.25

# KEEP THE <u>RED FLAG</u> FLYING

We're going to have to learn a whole new language. Or rather several new languages; and the trouble is, they're going to keep changing. Start learning now, and they'll be different again by the time we're halfway through; but put it off, and we'll be left behind, floundering in the shallows of basic Cabernet while everyone else has moved on to wineries and wine regions of which, a fortnight ago, we had barely heard.

What I'm talking about is, of course, Eastern Europe, which we decided to make the subject of this year's *Webster's* tasting. When we first started thinking about this tasting it involved around half a dozen countries; now any count is likely to be outdated pretty quickly. They mostly have designated wine regions (there were 41 different regions represented in this tasting); most have systems of quality classification with which as the wines available here increase from a river to a flood we are going to have to become familiar. But lest this all appear too daunting, remember there is one bright spot: they all grow Cabernet Sauvignon, the world's greatest red wine grape.

Learning about Eastern European wines – even tasting 127 of them, as we did for this year's *Webster's* – is thus not quite such an alarming exercise as it might at first appear. A lot of the tastes are familiar, albeit with a national twist, but that is as it should be: this tasting would have been miserable if Romanian Cabernet had been indistinguishable from Bulgarian. No, what we are going to have to learn are the native grapes – the white Irsay Oliver, the red Frankovka – and the regions. Places like Nitra or Nagyréde do not as yet slip easily off the average British tongue. But they will, they will. In time we'll learn to sort them out, and compare them – but, as I say, they're all going to be changing so much in the next few years that the wineries and regions that seem best now could slip behind or surge ahead – I'm making no predictions.

In 127 wines you'd expect some variation, especially when the vintages ranged from 1960 to 1991 (and the 1960 was a revelation: try suggesting a Romanian dessert wine to your wine-snobbier friends and see what reaction you get). The styles ran the gamut from sticky whites (there's a new company, Schlumberger, beginning to show what should be done with Tokaji: they bought certain vats of wine from the Hungarian government, blended and bottled them and they're head and shoulders above the Hungarovin versions) to dry whites (pick your producer carefully here; state boundaries mean little, since it takes wine-makers, not politicians, to make good white) to decent rosés and masses and masses of reds. Sixty-seven reds, in fact, and I have to admit that once I'd escaped the whites my spirits rose. Here was fruit, at last, and balance, and flavour. Jamminess, too, quite often, and the fruit might be stewed-tasting, or just downright peculiar. But they were better; overall, the reds were a helluva lot more fun. Not only did reds dominate my top 30 wines, Cabernet dominated the reds, with the odd streak of Merlot and only the occasional indigenous grape like Feteasca Neagra to prove that Eastern Europe won't always have to play so safe. At the moment, though, I'd stick to Cabernet, if in doubt: just under half of the reds in the tasting were Cabernet or mostly Cabernet, compared to over three-quarters of the reds in my top 30.

The whites? Well. To be positive, it's here that we're going to see the greatest improvement over the next few years. At the moment they're too unpredictable:

some Chardonnays taste like Chardonnay, some more like old socks, and the label won't tell you which is which. All the faults are curable, though: principally by a change of attitude. These countries need hard currency, and they're going to have to get it by means of elbow grease – scrubbing those barrels, selecting the grapes, cleaning up the wineries. And here's one prediction I will make – hold this tasting again in five years' time, and the results will be quite different. The wines will be better, and there'll be more of them. They'll be more international in style – and then, in a few years after that, they'll swing back to more national and regional styles, but they'll do it better. There'll be more crisp, fruity Pinot Blanc and Riesling, as well as Chardonnay. And one more thing – we'll all be able to pronounce Nagyréde.

## BULGARIA

Bulgaria has had such a success that her problem is really, what now? So far her attempts to diversify away from Cabernet have met with mixed results; and the area she most wants to succeed in – the globally popular, highly priced Chardonnay and Sauvignon – are almost total flops so far. Many tasted as though they'd been drunk before; I'll leave it to you to decide of exactly which kind of re-incarnation the flavours in the glass reminded me.

It's a pity, because we could do with more good, tasty inexpensive whites, but apart from one or two vaguely perfumy cheap country whites at well below £3 a bottle, the standard of Chardonnay and Sauvignon here was a disgrace, with sulphur levels that I'd have thought you'd need to measure by the shovelful per bottle rather than the usual parts per million. Our advice? Steer well clear.

The reds were a different matter. These are still Bulgaria's strong suit. Even so, some wineries have become too popular – Bulgarian Cabernet in one form or another is the most popular red wine in Britain – and the easy, unassuming ripe berry blackcurrant flavour can frequently end up tasting thin and cooked and fruitless. Luckily, as one winery hits the down slope, another hits form and since, despite an ever expanding assortment of titles, most of them still aspire to tasting pretty similar, our tasting shows which are best at the *moment*.

The extremely cheap Mehana range was always supposed to be an easy introduction to Bulgarian wine. In fact, the wines were so poor they probably served a better purpose introducing people to the joys of Alka Seltzer. But the new 'Country' range of reds really do serve as good introductions. Not *all* are good, and some wineries like Russe seem consistently better than others, but the Cabernet and Merlot based reds are generally juicy and enjoyable. Indeed I like them so much I don't see any need to trade up, and this is a common trend throughout the Eastern Bloc: cheapest is often best, youngest is often best.

## CZECHOSLOVAKIA

What do I call this state? Or these states? Slovakia, Moravia, or what? Let's stick with Czechoslovakia just at the moment. Now, I'm not suggesting that Czechoslovakia is a major player in the wine world. Beer world, yes, wine no. But in the context of Eastern Europe it does produce styles that the others (with the occasional exception) have so far completely failed to match. Cool climate is one answer; acidity and perfume and sharply focussed fruit of the sort that Germany at her best produces are the natural flavours of Czechoslovakia.

Ah, but there's more. Although the Sunday Times Wine Club has been pushing Czech wines for several years, they've almost all been rather cloddish (the Traminer excepted) and generally a bit musty, as well as costing rather a lot for an experimental tot. But last year a bustling, hustling dynamo of an English wine merchant called Angela Muir began creating mayhem in the comatose co-operative wineries of Slovakia, in particular Nitra, north east of Bratislava.

It was the quality of fruit that sparked off an idea in her brain. So she went out there herself and virtually single handedly began to browbeat the sullen crew of grape-growers and wine-makers who for 40 years had never once either been asked for a good wine or been criticized for a bad one. Slovenly disinterest in the winery and a total disregard for hygiene were the enemies, allied to a tortuous system of post-communist red tape. The first vintage she tried to influence she reckons one wine in nine was any good. But that one wine in nine was bought and paid for in hard currency. The last vintage she reckons she got the success rate of her vats up to one in three, and the woman they began by insolently nicknaming the 'Sergeant Major' is now called 'The General'.

Victoria Wine has them; so do I, in my top 30. The prices are low, around the £3 mark, and they produced some high points in the line-up of dull, poorly-made whites I'd inflicted on myself.

## HUNGARY

Hungary's wine traditions go back for aeons, but hoary traditions are more likely to destroy any chance of competing nowadays than enhance it. All the splendid strong Magyar whites and reds that used to appear over here in the 60s and early 70s have disappeared. The Kéknyelüs and Szurkebarats from Balaton and Mount Badacsony, though not in this tasting, are stale and flat and lifeless. And Tokaji, once a genuine contender in the 'great wines of the world' stakes, has for decades been decaying into turgid oxidized mediocrity, though there are signs here of improvement.

But, but, but... Hungary does have an established range of good vineyard regions, so it is possible for talented winemakers to transform an area from backwater to buzzing commercial and quality success in a single vintage. An interventionist assault on The Gyöngyös Estate north-east of Budapest has given us one of the best and fairest-priced Sauvignon Blancs we've seen for many a year. A similar mood looks to be catching hold in the moribund but potentially superb Tokay cellars: the Schlumberger Tokajis here were actually clean. Extraordinary. The red wine areas of Sopron and Villany also come up trumps with a brilliant aptitude for young juicy reds that I am sure we shall lap up so long as the quality stays high and the price stays fair.

## MOLDOVA

I do hope the Russian Wine Company's bright start is not going to be blotted out before it properly gets going. The old Moldovan Roche Purkar and Negru Purkar wines that we discovered last year were a revelation. Unbelievably good deep, dry, cedary wines of quite brilliant quality – they tasted like really high quality old Bordeaux reds, maybe even as good as fine but old-fashioned Pauillacs from the 1950s – and all this for less than £10 a bottle.

We were supposed to have seen a whole new wave of such delights by now, but all that has so far been forthcoming for this tasting from this corner of old Russia on the northern borders of Romania were much younger wines of an acceptable but less thrilling style. Even so, they made the top 30. But Moldova's potential is enormous. Romania's famous sweet wines are in fact from the part of Moldova the USSR didn't sequester, and if common sense and stability return, we shall not only see more of the great old treasures, like Negru Purkar, but a new generation of wines as good as almost any in Europe.

## ROMANIA

The remarkable thing about Romania is that despite all her upheavals it is clear from this tasting that her best wines have continued to be made in a virtually unchanged style, and at a barely increased price. These are her delicious sweet wines from the east of the country – Cotnari and Murfatlar – and their survival is partly explained by the fact that right through communist times a considerable proportion of vineyards remained in private hands. These gently syrupy wines are outstanding value.

The rest of Romania's so-called 'modern' whites in this line-up – Chardonnay and Sauvignon – were as bad as the general run of these trendy varieties. But reds are safer in badly-equipped wineries so long as the fruit is good, and there were some marvellous reds here – from the bad old days too. Merlots weren't bad, but Cabernets were really attractive, original wines – but avoid the Pinot Noirs which used to be pretty tasty but have obviously got too popular for their own good.

## YUGOSLAVIA

Or rather, Bosnia, Croatia, Kosovo, Macedonia, Vojvoldina and Montenegro. It is still impossible to tell how much the 1992 harvest has been affected but, casting sentiment aside, I must regretfully state that long before the fighting began, Yugoslavian wines seemed to be in terminal decline. Yugoslavia was the first Eastern European country to seek out our market. My very first mouthful of wine was Ljutomer Laski Rizling, and I bet for millions of others it was too. I can't exactly give you a full tasting note on it, but I do remember it was soft, not quite dry, with a mildly pear-like flavour. Pretty decent grog for an eight-year old. Indeed Ljutomer Laski Rizling was Britain's biggest wine brand at one time, and my father, for one, regarded it as the perfect everyday white wine.

He wouldn't think so today. Despite its origins in good traditional vineyards in Slovenia, when I look at my tasting note for this one time trusty warhorse, I see – nothing. I remember tasting it – wine number 44 – and I remember thinking, why bother to make a note? On some of the other wines from Ljutomer, I did make a bit more effort, but never to their advantage. Pinot Blanc is a good grape, but from Ljutomer it is flat, dull and sulphurous. Chardonnay is a better grape, though not from Ljutomer it isn't – yucky, thick stale stuff without the slightest resemblance to Chardonnay. And Gewürztraminer: a lovely spicy musk-scented grape is here so sulphur-smothered it makes you want to gag.

There are some drinkable reds – light Merlots from Istria, adequate but rather unripe Pinot Noir and a few sabre-rattling southern reds like Vranaç, but the general picture is one of miserable decline. Try looking for a Yugoslav wine in our top 30. There isn't one. In our top 60 one single Istrian Merlot would scrape in. My advice has to be: avoid until further notice.

# OZ CLARKE'S TOP THIRTY

| WINE | RATING | SAMPLE PRICES |
|---|---|---|
| 1988 Cabernet Sauvignon, Russe, Bulgaria | ★★★ | £2.69 |
| Country Wine, Cabernet Sauvignon and Cinsaut Russe, Bulgaria | ★★★ | £2.70 |
| 1989 Cabernet Franc, Sopron, Hungary | ★★★ | £2.45 |
| 1990 Cabernet Sauvignon, Kiskórös, Hungary | ★★★ | £3.45 |
| 1986 Sakar Mountain Cabernet, Strandja,Bulgaria | ★★★ | £3.95 |
| 1985 Cabernet Sauvignon Reserve, Suhindol, Bulgaria | ★★★ | £3.50 |
| 1983 Cabernet Sauvignon, Villany, Hungary | ★★★ | £3.50 |
| 1991 Sauvignon Blanc, Gyöngyös Estate, Hungary | ★★★ | £3.19 |
| Merlot, Villany, Hungary | ★★ | £2.45 |
| 1991 Merlot, Villany, Hungary | ★★ | £2.59 |
| 1991 Cabernet Sauvignon Rosé, Nagyréde, Hungary | ★★ | £2.79 |
| 1991 Cabernet Sauvignon, Villany, Hungary | ★★ | £2.59 |
| 1987 Cabernet Sauvignon, Plovdiv, Bulgaria | ★★ | £3.00 |
| 1987 Kodru, Krikova Winery, Moldova | ★★ | £4.50-£5.30 |
| 1986 Directors' Reserve, Cuvée Kamrat, Koshushny Winery, Moldova | ★★ | £6.50-£6.90 |
| Feteasca Neagra & Cabernet Sauvignon, Romanian Cellars | ★★ | £2.39-£2.69 |
| 1990 Pinot Blanc, Dunavár, Hungary | ★★ | £2.59 |
| 1991 Chardonnay, Gyöngyös Estate, Hungary | ★★ | £3.19 |
| 1991 Traminer, Moravenka, Czechoslovakia | ★★ | £4.75 |
| 1986 Tamaioasa, Pietroasele,Romania (sweet) | ★★ | £3.39 |
| 1960 Tamaioasa Romaneasca, Murfatlar, Romania (sweet) | ★★ | £6.99 |
| 1981 Tokaji Aszú, 3 Putts, Schlumberger, Hungary | ★★ | £6.05-£9.25 |
| 1981 Tokaji Aszú, 5 Putts, Schlumberger, Hungary | ★★ | £7.71-14.75 |
| 1988 Cabernet Sauvignon, Korten, Bulgaria | ★ | £3.00 |
| 1985 Vinenka Cabernet Sauvignon, Bulgaria | ★ | £3.95 |
| 1985 Cabernet Sauvignon & Merlot, Oriachovitza, Bulgaria | ★ | £5.00 |
| 1982 Cabernet Sauvignon, Svischtov, Bulgarian Estate Selection | ★ | £5.00 |
| 1987 Bulls Blood of Eger, Hungary | ★ | £3.69-£4.19 |
| 1990 Irsay Oliver, Nitra, Czechoslovakia | ★ | £2.99 |
| Czechoslovakian Gewürztraminer | ★ | £2.99 |

*Prices are as supplied to us by merchants in June 1992.*

# EASTERN EUROPEAN WINES

| TASTING NOTES | STOCKISTS |
|---|---|
| Blackberries, blackcurrants, damsons... mmm, yummy. | MAJ |
| Attractive, easy, gentle wine full of sweetish blackcurrant fruit tempered by an attractive cattiness. | SAI, TES, ROB, THR, WIW |
| Rich and plummy, gentle mint perfume. Soft yet strong – a Kleenex wine. | WIW |
| Low tannin, gluggable blackcurrant and blackberry fruit gum flavours. | UN |
| Full, minty, with soft creamy oak, blackcurrant fruit, a bit of tannin. | TES, WHI, WIW |
| Rich, almost creamy texture; blackcurrant fruit and coconut and mint spice plus a streak of mineral dryness. | SAI, SAF |
| Grassy, blackcurrant fruit balanced by soft, earthy tannin. | WIW |
| Gooseberry and nettles dry white, real Sauvignon zing, yet not aggressive. | MAJ |
| Fruitcake and cream cut through with green pepper bite. Fresh young red. | WIW |
| Bright plum and raspberry fruit, a whiff of pepper, lovely fresh earthiness. | ASD |
| Fresh, not quite dry rosé, peppery with attractive apple fruit and a hint of tobacco. | VIC |
| Grassy, a bit earthy, but with attractive raspberry fruit. | ASD, SAF |
| Rich, old-style stuff; thick currant and sultana fruit, a sprinkling of dust. | THR |
| Deep, raisiny and tough, but should develop cedar perfume in a few years. | VIG,BAR |
| Worth ageing: has an almost raisiny tannic quality, but attractive with quite a bit of soft, dry blackcurrant fruit lurking in there. | AN,AD,VIG |
| A curious strawberry and white peaches flavour that is strangely beguiling. | ASD |
| Full, round, slightly honeyed, fairly dry; attractive, easy white. | ASD |
| Very nice, slightly grapy Chardonnay, a streak of lemon, mild peach fruit. | MAJ |
| Gradually reveals a yeasty softness, a touch of acid, a nice musky nose. | WIC |
| Very good rich, sweet peach syrup/greengage fruit. Bargain pudding wine. | SAF,TES |
| And here's more. Again the greengage edge, again this deep, satisfying richness of peaches in syrup and honey. All this, and maturity too. | BU |
| Full, sweet, surprisingly youthful; peaches and syrup, yet lacks extra oomph. | ROB,LAY |
| Deeper, richer, sweet raisin concentration, a little cedarwood perfume. | ROB,LAY |
| Plums and cooked cherries fruit in a pleasant, solid mouthful. | WIW |
| Gentle texture of fruitcake and plums, then a little earth, or dirt maybe; soft, easy, mature red. | WIW |
| Deep old-style soupy mix of meat and long, stewed-blackcurrant fruit with mushrooms and mint to follow. Perfect for a mid-winter Sunday lunch. | WIW |
| Mature, that meat is there again, but there's still some grassy freshness, and pleasant blackcurrant and green pepper too. | WIW |
| Distinctly non-mainstream: green pepper, radish, celery; pretty good. | ASD, BO, UN |
| Weird but exciting: meaty, musky, grapy, rose-like nose like air freshener. | ASD, VIC |
| The exact opposite: fresh, lighter, slightly peppery. | THR |

*For a key to stockists and codes, see page 249. (Shipments may vary.)*

# IDEAL CELLARS

Right, now it's fantasy time. This is when I hand out three cheques to wine merchants and a writer for them to splurge as they want. Well, on wine, that is. I get three cheques, too – I'm not stupid. And what have we all come up with? Enough bargains and oddities to keep your recession-battered budgets happy for a whole year, that's what. Even if you're a millionaire.

## JULIAN BRIND MW

### *WAITROSE*

The wines in these cellars come from all over the world, and show the fascinating differences to be found. All the prices quoted would be subject to a 5 per cent discount on purchases of more than £100.

### £100

*With £100 to spend, I have picked a straightforward selection of red, white and dry sparkling wines, all good quality and all ideal for entertaining.*

Crémant de Bourgogne Blanc, Lugny *A fresh, crisp, dry sparkler made the same way as Champagne, from the same grapes, but at half the price.* **6 for £35.70**

1991 Sauvignon Blanc, Michelton, Victoria, Australia *Dry, full-flavoured and herbaceous. Unoaked.* **6 for £29.94**

1989 Château Mont Belair, St-Émilion *Smooth, soft fruit, some maturity, made from mainly Merlot grapes.* **6 for £32.70**

**Total cost: £98.34**

### £500

*Everything here except the Champagne is under £6 a bottle, so I can indulge myself with a pud wine and an Alsace Gewürz.*

Waitrose Champagne NV Brut *Simply because there is nothing quite like a glass of chilled Champagne.* **12 for £135**

Angas Brut Rosé *Dry, fruity, soft, sparkling and reliable. One of South Australia's greatest hits.* **12 for £65.40**

1990 Mâcon Lugny Les Charmes *An unoaked Chardonnay from the Mâconnais, dry and quite delicate.* **12 for £63.00**

1990 Waitrose Alsace Gewürztraminer *A spicy, dry, elegant wine that goes perfectly with smoked salmon.* **12 for £59.40**

1988 Château de Berbec, Premières Côtes de Bordeaux *Sweet, luscious and mature, sip on its own, with puddings or, even better, with foie gras.* **12 for £59.40**

1988 Médoc, Oak Aged *Full of fruit and still youthful. Indeed, it will get better over the next two or three years.* **12 for £47.88**

1989 Moncenay, Vin de Pays de la Côte d'Or *Pinot Noir from just outside the Côte d'Or; lookalike red Burgundy.* **12 for £47.88**

1987 Cabernet Sauvignon, Concha y Toro, Chile *Lovely intense blackcurrant. The '87 will be followed by the 1989.* **12 for £40.68**

**Total cost: £518.64**

### £1000

*With £1000 I can afford to be a bit more extravagant here – but I'm still going for a good variety of affordable tastes from around the world.*

1983 Waitrose Extra Dry Champagne *Good bottle age and refinement. The 1983 will be followed by the 1986.* **12 for £165.00**

Crémant de Bourgogne, Lugny *I couldn't resist this again. For lesser celebrations – every day, for example!* **12 for £71.40**

Crémant de Bourgogne Rosé, Lugny *The pink version of the above.* **12 for £81.00**

1990 Chablis Premier Cru, Beauroy *Crisp, elegant Chardonnay from one of the best sites in Chablis.* **12 for £107.40**

1983 Château des Coulinats, St Croix du Mont *Wonderful full, rich, sweet wine with good acidity and bottle age.* **12 for £87.00**

1989 Santa Cristina Chardonnay, Zenato, *Fine balance from Italy.* **12 for £71.40**

1991 Sauvignon Blanc, Villa Maria, Marlborough, New Zealand *Intense flavour from the South Island.* **12 for £59.88**

1989 Chorey-les-Beaune, Maillard, Burgundy *Smooth, rich, classic Pinot, drinking well now.* **12 for £83.40**

1986 Château d'Agassac, Haut Médoc *Typically dry Médoc to drink now or keep for several years.* **12 for £99.00**

1988 St-Joseph, Cave de Saint Désirat *Great warmth and weight from the Syrah from this area of the Rhône.* **12 for £83.40**

1989 Campo ai Sassi, Rossi di Montalcino *Great Tuscan fruit and depth of flavour.*
**12 for £57.438**

**Total cost: £966.36**

## STEPHEN BROWETT

### *FARR VINTNERS*

I hope my large budgets (specially increased by the editor) won't make me look too élitist. We deal in fine and rare wines, but are certainly not snobbish. To prove it, all these wines are ready to drink. I'm too impatient to spend money on something I can't touch for years.

### £1000

*£1000 spread sensibly on a broad range of wines such as these provides 84 marvellous bottles, all classic examples of their type.*

1989 Tokay/Pinot Gris Vieilles Vignes, Zind Humbrecht, Alsace *A more exciting aperitif than non-vintage Champagne. The '89 is packed with ripe fruit.* **12 for £135**

1991 Sauvignon Blanc,Wairau River Marlborough, New Zealand *Clean, sharp and fresh with a hint of pineapple, lychees and grapefruit. A classic.* **12 for £76**

1989 Kumeu River Chardonnay, New Zealand *Premier-cru-Burgundy quality with a balance of acidity, fruit and oak that few in the New World can match.* **12 for £153**

1982 Clos du Marquis, Bordeaux *Léoville-Las-Cases' second wine, with that unique '82 ripeness and soft tannin.* **12 for £170**

1989 Coudoulet de Beaucastel *A Rhône second wine. Its big brother, Château de Beaucastel, needs a decade. Big, thick red for chilly winter evenings.* **12 for £65**

1985 Côte Rôtie Brune et Blonde, Guigal, Rhône *Mediterranean flavours of black olives and rosemary.* **12 for £161**

1985 Morey St-Denis Domaine Dujac, Burgundy *Light colour, but what a nose. This is what Pinot is all about.* **12 for £247**

**Total cost: £1007**

# Around the world in 400 way
## One man's joyful romp through the Sainsbury's Wine Department.

Do you believe there is life beyond the borders of Bordeaux?

Are you one of those adventurous souls who thinks that Burgundy is not the be-all and end-all?

Splendid.

Then you'll enjoy reading the following few hundred words as much as I enjoyed writing them.

Over the years, Sainsbury's buyers have built up a list of more than 400 wines from 20 countries.

All have much to recommend them, but there are some areas in particular where Sainsbury's have excelled themselves.

Either because they've brought a deserving but hitherto unknown wine to the public's attention.

Or simply because of the sheer value for money.

Or, indeed, both.

**Thirsty? Try Hungary.**

Although famous for their lusty Bull's Blood, the Hungarians are capable of making wines of rather more subtlety and finesse.

Witness Sainsbury's Hungarian Merlot and Pinot Blanc.

The former is soft and fruity

with a hint of spice on the nose.

The latter, crisp, dry and fragrant, with a lively acidity.

And at Sainsbury's prices they as easy on the pocket as they are the palate.

**A Brave New World.**

The Appellation Contrôlée law in France were a fine and splendid thing when first brought in.

However, with their strict rule on methodology, they have some what stifled the urge and ability French growers to experiment.

No such red tape has hinder the free spirits of the New World.

In Australia, New Zealand, C fornia and South America, they' had great fun exploring single gra varieties and modern techniqu such as maturation in new oak a so forth.

Two good things have resul from this liberated attitude.

Some great wines, which a now finding their way over here increasing numbers. And a chan of heart by some French grow who are now producing wines Sainsbury's specific requirements.

To pick just three from many, try the Hunter Valley Shiraz from Australia and the Sainsbury's Selection Cabernet Sauvignon and Chardonnay.

You won't be disappointed.

### Drink Germany dry.

For too long, German wines have been regarded as suitable only for those with a sweet tooth.

Go back far enough in German wine-making history, however, and you'll find some delightfully dry, crisp white wines.

Go into Sainsbury's today and you'll find these self-same wines just waiting to leap into your fridge.

Amongst many fond memories, I can recall the Trocken and Baden Dry and the Morio-Muskat, a grape variety more usually found in a blend.

This is a great shame, as when vinified in its own right it makes a superb medium dry wine; light, fragrant and perfect as an aperitif.

### Second wines from first rate châteaux.

Once known and drunk by a select few wine buffs, second wines from famous châteaux such as Margaux are now much more widely available, thanks to shrewd buyers such as Sainsbury's. And with good reason.

They're made with the same loving care as their more illustrious brothers, but differ in quality and price only because the wines are younger or taken from a different part of the vineyard.

Sainsbury's have managed to get their hands on quite a few of these little gems and three in particular stand out.

To wit, Artigues Arnaud 1988, from Château Grand Puy Ducasse at around £8, Mondot 1989 from Château Troplong-Mondot at around £10 and the Pavillion Rouge du Château Margaux 1988 at around £18. Second wines they may be, second rate they are not.

### And now, a little something to finish.

A friend of mine had never before tried a dessert wine until, one day, he was lucky enough to be offered a glass of the incomparable Château Yquem.

It changed his life, turning him from being comfortably off to contentedly broke, but thanks to Sainsbury's, we needn't take out a mortgage to enjoy a fine dessert wine at the end of a meal.

For the proof of the pudding wine, try their Muscat de Beaumes de Venise, their Château Mayne des Carmes 1989 Sauternes or their excellent Auslese.

They even do a few in half bottles, but if you're anything like me, it just means twice as much work with the corkscrew.

## Good wine costs less at Sainsbury's.

## £5000

*With £5000 in your pocket you can pick one case from every region of your fantasies.*

1975 Louis Roederer Cristal *Vintage Champagne doesn't come better than this, yet it doesn't increase in price with age to the same extent as great red.*   **12 for £720**

1985 Bâtard Montrachet Domaine Jean-Noël Gagnard, Burgundy *Nowhere else in the world is Chardonnay of this depth and intensity produced.*   **12 for £540**

1981 Château de Beaucastel, Rhône *Now reaching full maturity, this is earthy, complex and powerful.*   **12 for £259**

1966 Clos de la Roche, Domaine Armand Rousseau, Burgundy *Mature Pinot at its best. A stunning nose.*   **12 for £600**

1964 Château La Mission-Haut-Brion *La Mission made claret of First Growth quality in '64: the essence of Graves.*   **12 for £1000**

1964 Cheval Blanc, Bordeaux *Gorgeous; on a par with the great 1961. A fascinating comparison with the La Mission. This is rich, smooth and silky.*   **12 for £1100**

1967 Château Gilette Crème de Tête *This incredibly rich Sauternes can equal Yquem '67, at a fifth of the price.*   **12 for £822**

1966 Fonseca Vintage Port *Even bigger than the more famous '63.*   **12 for £410**

**Total cost: £5451**

## £10,000

*I could blow the whole lot on the ultimate: a case of Mouton Rothschild 1945 — but perhaps I'd better not.*

1971 Corton Charlemagne, Louis Latour, Burgundy *As great as its reputation.*   **12 for £1410**

1962 Château Mouton Rothschild *Not far behind the '61 and '59 in quality. The wine of the vintage and surprisingly good value.*   **12 for £1410**

1959 Château Latour, Bordeaux *Black, concentrated and magnificent. Half the price of the 1961 and nearly as good.*   **12 for £2350**

1971 La Tâche, Domaine de la Romanée Conti, Burgundy *Marvellous Pinot character and great depth.*   **12 for £2820**

1959 Château d'Yquem, Sauternes *My favourite year (and my birth year, if anyone is stuck for what to give me).*   **12 halves for £2100**

**Total cost: £10,090**

# ANDREW BYRNE

## D BYRNE & CO

I have become three different people for the purposes of this cellar. The first is used to entertaining umpteen members of my family; the second likes searching for good wines at middling prices; the third knows that the moment he opens anything really good his family is likely to want some too. Some, therefore, can be locked safely in the cellar until the coast is clear.

## £100

*Being the eldest of 14 children, I am aware that when entertaining I need quantity as well as quality.*

Cuvée Jean-Paul, Rouge *A consistently good medium-weight fruity French table wine.*   **6 litre bottles for £21.90**

1991 Domaine de Perras, Vin de Pays des Côtes de Gascogne *Fresh, light, fruity: ideal on a warm summer's evening.* **6 for £21.14**

1990 Domaine Bouchard, Vin de Pays du Thongue *An easy-drinking fruity red from the south of France.* **6 for £18.54**

1991 Rosemount Shiraz-Cabernet Sauvignon *Of the cheaper Aussies this is my favourite. Fresh, bags of fruit.* **6 for £25.14**

Muscat de Rivesaltes, Mimosas *Perfect to finish the meal; luscious, sweet and grapey. Rivesaltes is Clitheroe's twin town, so I feel a certain loyalty.* **6 halves for £14.84**

**Total cost: £101.56**

## £500

*These wines were chosen from about 700 on our list in this mid-price category, which I consider to be our great strength.*

1986 Gran Sangredetoro, Miguel Torres, Spain *For value this takes some beating. Big, rich and rounded with nice oak.* **12 for £94.68**

1986 Château de Fonsalette, Côtes du Rhône *Expensive for the AC but worth it: full, rounded, very stylish.* **12 for £124.68**

1988 Penfolds Bin 389 Cabernet-Shiraz *Characterful, lots of fruit, nice wood: one of the best Aussies at this price.* **12 for £83.40**

1990 Juliénas, Domaine de la Seigneurie, Georges Duboeuf *One of the best Beaujolais. Quite serious, deep-coloured, loads of fruit and a nice dry, clean finish.* **6 for £35.34**

1989 Berri Estate wood-aged Chardonnay *Rounded, rich, oaky, full-flavoured Aussie. Excellent value.* **12 for £62.58**

1991 Pallister Estate NZ Sauvignon Blanc, Martinborough *Rich, full of exotic ripe mango flavours. Lovely stuff.* **6 for £41.70**

1991 Weltevrede Gewürztraminer, South Africa *A very full-flavoured medium-dry wine which finishes slightly sweet.*

**6 for £28.74**

**Total cost: £471.12**

## £1000

*My final selection contains some to drink now and and some to look forward to.*

Don Zoilo Fino *A pale, very old, nutty dry sherry – the perfect aperitif.* **6 for £97.08**

1986 Château Haut Marbuzet, St-Estèphe *The first of two contrasting clarets. This is big, blackcurranty, with hints of cedar and nice tannins.* **12 for £158.40**

1988 Château Haut Bages Liberal, Pauillac *Underrated and under-priced claret. Medium weight, very stylish, with a dry elegant finish.* **12 for £122.28**

1987 Echèzeaux Vieilles Vignes, Mongeard Mugneret *An outstanding red Burgundy from a lesser vintage.* **6 for £131.94**

1989 Chardonnay, Hamilton Russell *Well-made South African, not too heavy. Nice oak hints; clean, dry finish.* **12 for £76.20**

1988 Tinto Pesquera Cosecha Especial *One of Spain's best wines, nicely rounded with lots of plummy fruit.* **12 for £125.88**

1985 Barberesco Asili, B&M Ceretto, Italy *Multi-layered wine with hints of truffles and exotic spices.* **12 for £153.48**

1986 Churchill's Crusted Port *Half the cost of vintage, many of the same characteristics. Lovely and rounded.* **6 for £61.74**

*To finish, two bottles of* Billecart-Salmon Rosé *with the change to me. This is what good fizz is all about.* **2 for £52.00**

**Total cost: £979.00**

# ANTHONY BYRNE

## *ANTHONY BYRNE FINE WINES*

I've concentrated on France in my cellars – well, I make no apology. France has some of the greatest most surprising, complex, subtle wines in the world.

### £100

*In this cellar I have chosen wines to drink now and over the next 12 months with the emphasis on quality and value for money.*

1990 Pinot Blanc d'Alsace, Domaine Materne Haegelin, Alsace *A 50/50 blend of Pinot Blanc and Pinot Klevner, making for freshness with depth.*          **6 for £29.32**

1991 Côtes des Gascogne Colombelle, André Daguin *Clean, fresh, fruity dry white from the south-west of France. A good light, all-round wine to drink at any time.*          **6 for £20.65**

1989 Château La Gravette, Bordeaux *The large percentage of Merlot in this vineyard produces a soft, approachable claret.*
          **6 for £22.28**

1990 Morgon Domaine St Vincent, Cellier des Samsons *The cherryish, juicy fruit of this Beaujolais cru is now more affordable, thankfully.*          **6 for £26.79**

          **Total cost: £92.04**

### £500

*Here I have concentrated on wines and growers that have impressed me with their quality over the years. One way and another, there's quite a lot of Chardonnay in this case – but it's a wonderful grape.*

1990 St-Véran Cuvée Classique, Cellier des Samsons *Creamy unoaked Chardonnay from the Mâconnais; rich fruit and depth of flavour.*          **12 for £71.42**

1990 Bourgogne Rouge, Cuvée Jeune Vignes Clos des Forêts, Domaine de L'Arlot *Classic Pinot Noir with vanilla oak flavours made by Jean-Pierre Desmet from his excellent vineyards.*          **12 for £71.88**

1988 Cuvaison Chardonnay, Napa Valley, California *Four hundred acres of vineyard in the Carneros region is one reason why Cuvaison continues to produce excellent wines. The other is John Thacher, one of Napa's most talented winemakers.*
          **12 for £128.32**

1987 Delatite Devil's River Cabernet Merlot, Victoria, Australia *A well-structured but not austere red, balanced with superb berry fruit flavours; still improving.*          **12 for £97**

Champagne Drappier Récamier Brut NV *Affordable Champagne from a young talented wine-maker – Michel Drappier. Good biscuity nose, fruity and rounded.*
          **12 for £131.40**

          **Total cost: £500.02**

### £1000

*For £1000 I'd have a balance of maturing wines and those that are drinking now – and rather than have umpteen different wines, I'd go for just half a dozen top quality classics from some of the world's best growers.*

1985 Auxey-Duresses Rouge, Domaine Lafouge *Lingering flavours of Pinot Noir; beautifully balanced Burgundy from this great vintage.*          **12 for £155.64**

1988 Carraudes de Lafite Rothschild *The second wine of Château Lafite in Bordeaux. Classic claret: full, rich, well-balanced and with great potential.*          **12 for £190.80**

1990 Pouilly Fumé Pur Sang, Domaine Didier Dagueneau *A remarkable Loire Sauvignon Blanc, matured but not fermented in new oak to produce a unique harmony of flavours. Dagueneau is a cult figure in the Loire.* **12 for £167.22**

1985 Hermitage, Domaine Etienne Guigal *Another keeper, but just beginning to show well. An extraordinary wine capturing all the depth of flavour and finesse of the Syrah grape – rich and concentrated.*
**12 for £222**

1990 Gewürztraminer Herrenweg, Domaine Zind Humbrecht *The essence of the Gewürztraminer grape, beautifully balanced, combining delicacy, freshness and great depth.* **12 for £131.88**

1990 Chablis Vigne de la Reine, Château Maligny *One of the best vineyards of this Chablis estate has produced a clean, fresh, non-oaked Chablis typical of the appellation.* **12 for £104.28**

**Total cost: £972.34**

## ROSEMARY GEORGE MW

I have opted for a purely South African cellar this year. The wines will improve still further in years to come, and at the moment the best are remarkably good value.

### £100

*A straightforward bargain white and a red from a grape found only in South Africa.*

1989 Simonsig Pinotage *SA's original grape, a cross between Pinot Noir and Cinsaut. Firm, spicy fruit.* **12 for £60.00**

1992 Chenin Blanc Simonsvlei Co-op *Soft, ripe, fresh and very gulpable.* **12 for £36.00**

**Total cost: £96.00**

1991 Rustenberg Chardonnay *Elegant,with just a touch of oak; should develop well, if you can bear to let it.* **12 for £72.00**

1990 Paradise Vale Pinotage *Spicy, peppery flavour, made by an ex-Springbok.*
**12 for £60.00**

1989 Hamilton Russell Pinot Noir *The leading Cape Pinot and from the southernmost vineyard of Africa. Should mature nicely.* **12 for £84.00**

1987 Klein Constantia Cabernet Sauvignon *Stylish blackcurrant fruit, with a hint of mint.* **12 for £96.00**

**Total cost: £487.00**

### £500

*For £500 I can have a good spread of the Cape's grape varieties.*

1991 Neil Ellis Sauvignon Blanc *Grassy and soft, from a top wine-maker.* **12 for £60.00**

1991 Thelema Sauvignon Blanc *A Crisp, pungent example of the grape.* **12 for £60.00**

Van Loveren Pinot Gris *Lovely ripe, spicy, varietal fruit.* **12 for £55.00**

### £1000

*South Africa is producing some excellent Bordeaux blends to add to its traditional wines like Constancia. And, of course, I must have some fizz.*

1987 Vin de Constance *The traditional dessert wine of the Cape; deliciously marmaladey Muscat.* **12 for £132.00**

Tradition de Charles de Fere *Quite full fizz, lightly bready.* **12 for £108.00**

1991 Hamilton Russell Chardonnay *Lightly oaked and very stylish.*   **12 for £84.00**

1990 Overgaauw Chardonnay *Some nutty fruit, with good acidity.*   **12 for £81.00**

1990 Klein Constantia Sauvignon Blanc *Crisp, pithy fruit and fresh balancing acidity from a grape that is more difficult to get right than Chardonnay.***12 for £69.80**

1991 Weltevrede Gewürztraminer *Ripe spicy, varietal fruit with a hint of orange pith. An attractive example of a grape that can easily get too fat.*   **12 for £60.00**

1989 Warwick Trilogy *An elegant red Bordeaux blend; still needs bottle age; really worthwhile locking away.*   **12 for £132.00**

1989 Rustenberg Gold *Bordeaux mix red, a hint of new oak. Needs time.* **12 for £115.76**

1989 Talana Hill Royale *Full claret-style red with staying power.*   **12 for £114.00**

1989 Vriesenhof Cabernet Sauvignon *Elegant cedarwood fruit. Leave it for a while yet, though.*   **12 for £108.00**

**Total cost: £1010.55**

# TREVOR HUGHES

## *T & W WINES*

I have put together my cellars together on the desert island principle: wines I would want to drink day-in, day-out and never tire of, that would brighten my long days. How well they would go with the local food is another matter: what does one eat on desert islands, anyway? Coconuts?

### £100

1988 Chianti Classico, Assolo, Villa Vistarenni *Wonderful depth of rich flavour with real grip on the finish.*   **6 for £51.00**

1989 Mâcon Clessé, Domaine Guillemot-Michel *Superb Chardonnay from producers Marc and Pierrette Guillemot whose wines just get better every year. Lovely balance of fruit and weight, perfect with the fish I hope to catch.*   **6 for £48.90**

**Total cost £99.90**

### £500

*This was the most difficult selection – what, oh what, could I leave out? In the end I chose six wines that I hope will cover most eventualities.*

1989 Sauvignon de Saint Bris, Domaine Luc Sorin *A delightful Sauvignon from the village of St Bris Vineaux, deep in the heart of Chablis country. Wonderfully fresh and clean with great depth of Sauvignon flavour.*   **12 for £89.53**

1990 Fleurie, La Madone, Domaine Chaintreuil *Fabulously vibrant and alive Fleurie. Packed with rich, ripe Gamay fruit and a mouthwatering nose.*   **12 for £112.10**

1990 Moscato d'Asti, Bava *Irresistible grapy Muscat aromas that leap from the glass. A soft, creamy sparkle and loads of upfront flavours on the palate.*   **12 for £95.17**

1991 Beaujolais Rosé, Domaine des Sables d'Or *Perfect summer afternoon wine, dark rosé and plenty of depth.*   **12 for £80.10**

1985 Château Respide Médeville, Graves *This is from the Médevilles who also own the cult Sauternes, Château Gilette. Plummy and vibrant with rich, ripe Cabernet, on the offchance that there may be pheasants on the island.*   **12 for £123.37**

**Total cost: £500.27**

## £1000

*I did consider blowing my £1000 on Yquem or Montrachet, but would I really be happy with only four bottles? No, I would not.*

1986 Silver Oak, Cabernet Sauvignon, Alexander Valley *Superb, ripe, voluptuous, packed with rich, full fruit.* **12 for £224.90**

1989 Ruche di Castagnole Monferrato, Bava *The most un-Italian Italian ever, all soft fruit and violets.* **12 for £140.30**

Champagne Andre Clouet Rosé *Masses of raspberry aromas, wonderfully clean and alive on the palate.* **12 for £207.27**

1983 Late Harvest Gewürztraminer, Costello, Napa Valley *Seriously sweet wine in half bottles is a must; intense flavours and a hint of citrus to accompany all that tropical fruit.* **12 halves for £109.28**

1985 Riesling Cuvée Frederic Emile, Trimbach, Alsace *Trimbach produces great Riesling full of exotic fruits with petrolly undertones.* **12 for £177.66**

1958 Tokaji Muskotaly
1957 Tokaji 6 Puttonos *Two sublime Tokajis to be saved for the day I find my Ms Friday.* **2 half-litres for £141.00**

**Total cost: £1000.41**

## TIM JACKSON

### *HALVES*

All my cellars consist of half bottles – well, you might have guessed. Wine in half bottles matures slightly faster than it does in full bottles, but not alarmingly so – and it's the only way to drink Manzanilla.

## £100

*The problem here is what to exclude. So much in halves is so special that it would be easy to have too many different ones.*

Manzanilla la Gitana, Hidalgo *Serve it cold with some Bresaola sprinkled with a little ripe Parmesan. Ooooh...* **6 for £19.44**

1987 Muscadet Château la Berrière *Some will say this is too old. Try it and see. Rich, balanced and steely.* **6 for £17.58**

1989 Domaine Jean Cros Rouge, Gaillac *Rich, peppery and mulberryish. Good long, positive fruit at the finish.* **6 for £18.30**

1989 Château de Gaudou, Cahors *Deep intense fruit, complex, rich, soft and supple, at an extraordinary price.* **6 for £19.86**

1990 Bianco di Custoza, Cavachina, Verona *Fuller and better value than Soave and with a greater depth of fruit with good soft acidity on the finish.* **6 for £24**

**Total cost: £99.18**

## £500

*Five hundred pounds will bring so many goodies in halves; enough to suit all manner of tastes and food. Halves are perfect for food. They are not glugging wines; instead it's so much fun to sit down and try lots with dinner.*

*More sherry to start. Half a bottle is the perfect size for this much abused wine. Hands up those who have been given a fresh glass of sherry, be it dry or sweet, in any restaurant or hotel in the past umpteen years. Not many, I'm sure.*

Fino Especial, Hidalgo **6 for £25.92**
Amontillado Seco, Hidalgo **6 for £20.94**
Oloroso Especial Seco, Hidalgo *Try it with cheese.* **6 for £24.00**

1990 Château de Tracy, Pouilly Fumé, Loire *Wonderful balance of ripe juicy fruit and soft acidity. Much the best vintage from Pouilly for a while.*    **12 for £68.52**

1988 Chablis Premier Cru Montée de Tonnerre, Louis Michel *Honeyed and big, showing well, but will improve. This wine sees no oak.*    **12 for £76.08**

1990 Château de Chorey les Beaunes, Jacques Germain *Classic Burgundian Pinot showing intense raspberry fruit, not that thick, chewy style so often seen in the past. Lovely balance.*    **12 for £82.08**

1985 Château Sénéjac, Haut Médoc *Epitomises the best of Bordeaux at the moment. Velvety, concentrated, raisiny fruit with enormous depth and class. Really great wine-making.*    **12 for £69.24**

1990 Quivira Sauvignon Blanc, Dry Creek Valley, Sonoma *Rich, ripe, melony fruit and a good balance of acidity.*    **12 for £60.12**

1986 Freinzheimer Goldberg Riesling Auslese, Lingenfelder, Rheinpfalz *Lingenfelder is one of the best growers in Germany. Rich ripe fruit, showing the Riesling at its best, affected by noble rot and beautifully balanced.*    **6 for £63.78**

1980 Taylor Vintage Port *Just to top off the evening. Now drinking superbly in a half bottle.*    **Just the one for £12.08**

**Total cost: £502.76**

### £1000

*Oh, to have this to put down in a cellar. Perfect wine-making, lots of fruit, and never too much to drink at a sitting.*

Champagne Bruno Paillard Rosé Premier Cuvée *A bit of Champagne to start. This wine is aged for three to four years on the first cork and is wonderfully soft and indulgent.*    **12 for £125.40**

Manzanilla Pasada, Hidalgo; Jerez Cortado, Hidalgo *Intense, rich and with a depth of flavour seldom seen in sherry. Try the Jerez Cortado with Italian salami, served hot with olive bread. Oh, calories...*    **6 of each for £55.56**

1990 Condrieu, Vernay, Rhône *The fragrance of hedgerows, apricots and almonds. A half bottle is enough for four, or two people as greedy as me. Condrieu should not be aged. It needs to be drunk like this.*    **12 for £150**

1989 Pernand Vergelesses Blanc, Jacques Germain, Burgundy *Utterly delicious, rich, honeyed and with a hint of cinnamon. Superb value.*    **12 for £89.64**

1990 Gevrey Chambertin Vieilles Vignes, Alain Burguet, Burgundy *The wines reflect the man – big and powerful. Needs a bit of time, but rich, ripe fruit from old vines make this quite stunning Gevrey.*    **12 for £129.84**

1985 Château Pichon-Longueville-Baron *Softness, class, concentrated blackcurrant and some cedar make this one of the best Bordeaux tasted recently.*    **12 for £132.12**

1989 Mantanzas Creek Chardonnay, Sonoma *True Chardonnay without overt oakiness. Some pineapply fruit with a soft buttery finish distinguish the wines of Matanzas Creek.*    **12 for £95.04**

1989 Tokay Grand Cru Furstentum, Sélection de Grains Nobles, Blanck, Alsace *A real stunner. Lovely depth of fruit and weight with good firm acidity. Needs a bit of time and will become a classic.*    **12 for £156**

1970 Taylor Vintage Port *Perfect. Long gone are the days when one could down two bottles of vintage at lunch. A half isn't so serious on the pocket, either.*    **3 for £66.75**

**Total cost: £1000.35**

# MICHAEL ROMER

## *PETER GREEN & CO*

Wine merchants are not as purposeful as your average MW, but the idea of choosing purely for pleasure is quite disturbing. Still, I'll do my best to get used to it.

### £100

*Here I'll opt for flavour from underrated areas – even Touraine was underrated until Sancerre prices went through the roof.*

1990 Pinot Blanc, Dopff au Moulin, Alsace *Sometimes I prefer the Schlumberger one, sometimes this. I'll keep running the tests.* **6 for £28.40**

1990 Sauvignon de Touraine Comte d' Ormont, Saget, *With just six, I'll stick to the classic Loire cat's pee.* **6 for £24.20**

1990 Côtes du Ventoux, La Vieille Ferme *Plenty of Rhône weight and character in this blend of half Grenache with Syrah and Cinsaut.* **6 for £23.90**

Bulgarian Merlot & Gamza Country Red *Odd how interesting this wine is. Great for economical evenings at home, or feeding to people who hose it down.* **6 for £15.30**

**Total cost: £91.80**

### £500

*There used to be a danger in the wine trade of becoming a bore who drank nothing but claret, or a jaded roué who drank nothing but fizz. Some people managed to alternate the roles for variety. At least the wines are more exciting these days.*

Castellblanch Cristal, Cava *This is dry, but with an apparently low acidity that makes your friends drink the stuff too quickly. It can be quite hard to stay one glass ahead of them.* **12 for £67.10**

1990 Bourgogne Aligoté, Ropiteau *The days have gone when Aligoté was fit only to be drunk as kir.* **12 for £64.40**

1990 Savennières, Clos du Papillon, Baumard, Loire *Dry Chenin Blanc needs to be well-made. QED.* **12 for £82.60**

1991 Orvieto Abboccato, Antinori *This wine has a lovely fresh apple fruitiness and is only slightly sweet.* **12 for £51.30**

1989 Valpolicella Classico, Guerrieri-Rizzardi *The eponymous Contessa (and she's not called Val) produces an excellent organic range. Medium-weight, with character.* **12 for £52.40**

1988 Château de Terrefort-Quancard, Bordeaux *A good dose of Merlot gets it drinking well, but it will still improve for a year or two.* **12 for £67.80**

1987 Gran Sangredetoro, Torres, Penedès *A blend of Garnacha and Cariñena has good weight and depth, enhanced by 18 months in oak.* **12 for £62.10**

1986 Cabernet Sauvignon Antiquas Reservas *Good wines are often spotted before their areas become fashionable, and this Chilean has been available in Britain at least since its 1976 vintage. It has not too much new oak, and lots of interest. It has developed nicely in the six years since the vintage.* **12 for £59.80**

**Total cost: £507.50**

### £1000

Time for both indulgence and deferred gratification; I can't drink it all at once.

Barbadillo Manzanilla Sherry *Ideally, I'd like a bottle as needed; that way, it would always be fresh.* **12 for £56.40**

Pol Roger Champagne *Pol Roger is never less than three years old.*   **12 for £205.00**

1985 Marqués de Murrieta Rioja, Blanco Reserva *Dry, honeyed. I prefer this to the 1970, which sells at £25.35. It's so nice to have simple tastes.*   **12 for £79.60**

1989 Nobilo, Tietjen Chardonnay, NZ *Full, with eight months' oak.*   **12 for £97.40**

1988 Schloss Vollrads Riesling Kabinett *A Rheingau to lose for a while.*   **12 for £90.60**

1986 Châteauneuf-du-Pape, Domaine de Nalys *A red Rhône just coming round. Fair weight, lots of velvety fruit.*   **12 for £107.70**

1985 Château Haut Marbuzet, Bordeaux *Good now, but it had better go in the same dark corner as the Vollrads.*   **12 for £170.40**

1989 Quarts-de-Chaume, Baumard, Loire *I'd drink this every second Christmas – or perhaps every third.*   **12 for £191.50**

**Total cost: £998.60**

## HELEN THOMSON

### O W LOEB

These are perhaps *kellerei* rather than cellars, with lots from Germany and Alsace. Both make some of the finest whites in the world. Give them time to age, and they have flavours like no other.

### £100

*Just two wines, both delicious now, but I'll keep them – if I can resist the temptation.*

1989 Gigondas Pierre Aiguille, Paul Jaboulet Aîné *A sensational Rhône made from 100 per cent Grenache.*   **6 for £44.06**

1989 Tokay Tradition, Hugel et Fils, Alsace *An underrated grape, and very food-friendly.*   **6 for £44.65**

**Total cost: £88.71**

### £500

*What I saved before I am overspending here on the Riesling at its finest.*

1989 Riesling Schlossberg Grand Cru, Mme Théo Faller, Alsace.   **12 for £119.85**

1988 Riesling Jubilee, Hugel *Two brilliant expressions of the Riesling grape as grown*

*in Alsace. I want to have them both in my cellar.*   **12 for £128.07**

1990 Josephshöfer Riesling Kabinett, Reichsgraf von Kesselstatt   **12 for £74.02**

1990 Oberemmeler Hütte Riesling Spätlese, von Hövel   **12 for £88.12**

1989 Hochheimer Domdechaney Riesling Spätlese, Aschrott'sche Gutsverwaltung *Two Moselles and one Rhine. The Hochheimer is the fullest.*   **12 for £106.92**

**Total cost: £516.98**

### £1000

*These are to be hidden away, even the '83.*

1983 Crozes Hermitage Domaine de Thalabert, Jaboulet Aîné   **12 for £138.65**

1988 Châteauneuf-du-Pape Pignan, J Reynaud *The little brothers of La Chapelle and Château Rayas, wonderful wines and unrivalled value.*   **12 for £123.37**

1990 Maximin Grünhauser Herrenberg Riesling Auslese, von Schubert
   **12 for £196.22**

1990 Eitelsbacher Karthäuserhofberg Riesling Auslese, Rautenstrauch'sche Gutsverwaltung *From either side of the Ruwer, benchmark Riesling.* **12 for £179**

1989 Vouvray Clos Naudin Moelleux, Foreau *In 1989, Foreau had the chance of a lifetime to make* moelleux. **12 for £155.10**

Riesling, Tokay and Gewürztraminer Quintessence Sélection de Grains Nobles, Mme Théo Faller, *I still have some money left over and it is going on just three halves from Alsace. At the time of writing, Mme Faller has yet to set a price, but I know I will have enough.* **Total cost: £1000**

## TIM WATERS

### THRESHER

**£100**

*Sometimes it takes a wine-maker in an unlikely region to remind us all of just what can be done with a familiar grape variety.*

Gyongyos Estate Sauvignon Blanc, Hungary *Characterful (and cheap). It's pronounced 'Join-Josh'.* **6 for £19.50**

1989 Domaine du Tariquet, Cuvée Bois *Yves Grassa's oak-aged Côtes de Gascogne has shot to fame.* **6 for £29.94**

1990 Tollana Shiraz Cabernet, Australia *Big, broad aromas, lovely warm, round, spicy flavours, some tannin.* **6 for £22.14**

Great Western Imperial Reserve *A good honest Aussie fizz to lift the heart and freshen the palate.* **6 for £29.94**

**Total cost: £101.52**

**£500**

Condé de Valdemar Rioja Sin Crianza *This wine sprang out at us with its light, fresh, clean flavours.* **12 for £52.68**

1990 Château Valoux, Graves *A thoroughly modern white Bordeaux.* **12 for £91.08**

1986 Carmignano, Villa di Capezzana, Italy *Spicy, ripe Sangiovese plus some Cabernet.* **12 for £83.88**

1989 Marsannay, Louis Jadot, Burgundy *Honeyed, buttery-woody.* **12 for £119.88**

1988 Clos de Marquis, St-Julien, Bordeaux *The second wine of Léoville-Las-Cases. Leave it a year, if you can.* **12 for £155.40**

**Total cost: £502.92**

**£1000**

Cava Reserva de la Familia, Juvé y Camps *Every household should have some: elegant, dry and long.* **12 for £97.20**

1980 Condé de Valdemar Gran Reserva, Rioja *First class: clean, well-structured and enough wood on the nose.* **12 for £91.32**

1986 Penfolds Bin 95 Grange, Australia *Rich, concentrated and firm. Splendid wine with years ahead of it.* **12 for £297.00**

1991 Wairau River Sauvignon Blanc New Zealand *A stunner, with almost dreamy fruit and a long, long finish.* **12 for £75.12**

1986 Corton-Pougets, Louis Jadot *A tricky year in Burgundy, yet this is strawberryish with good chewy fruit.* **12 for £274.92**

1986 Tignanello, Antinori, Italy *Antinori's classy first experiment in Cabernet / Sangiovese blends.* **12 for £226.32**

**Total cost: £1061.88**

# OZ CLARKE

I'm after fruit, fruit and more fruit. And I'm not prepared to pay more than bargain basement prices to ease my recession blues. So where do I go, what do I get? Hold on to your seats, because my first stop is South Africa!

## £100

1991 Far Enough Pinot Noir, South Africa *A brilliant slug of sweet chewy fruit. Worth double.*                    **6 for £18**

1991 Far Enough Sauvignon *Tangy, lemon-sharp, apple-fresh white. If South Africa can make more like these, look out.*   **6 for £18**

Leziria Tinto, Almeirim, Portugal *So easy, such sheer gluggable happy juice, all damsons and raspberries, a hint of apple skins.*                          **6 for £14**

1988 Señorio de Val, Valdepenas, Spain *This fruit's a bit bruised – apples and apricots from the bottom of the barrow – but lovely big soft, rich stuff.*        **6 for £19**

1991 Hungarian Cabernet Sauvignon, Villány *Unbeatable soft, blackcurrant and fresh earth – the kind of wine you wish Bordeaux made now and then.* **6 for £15.50**

1986 Tamaioasa, Romania *Who said you couldn't make a good cheap dessert wine? This is a cracker; goldengage, peach and the syrup from the tin, too.*   **6 for £22**

*So where am I? Hell – £106.50. OK, let's make it 5 only of those last two.*

## £500

*If this cellar is all about the middle price range, there is brilliant stuff around at the moment – so long as we don't want famous names on the label. Doesn't worry me. I drink wine for the taste; I never did go for the flavour of ink, paper and glue.*

*A couple of Chardonnays first.* Koonunga Hill, South Australia.                **6 for £30**

Domaine de Bellevue, Vin de Pays des Côtes de Thongue, France *If the Aussies keep on turning out heavenly ripe, peachy, spicy stuff like Koonunga Hill, the rest of the world might as well pack up and go home. Then you taste the Bellevue from the middle of nowhere in Southern France, soft and perfumed, the peaches a little whiter, the spice more delicate – and you realize there's everything to play for.*   **6 for £28**

Cova du Ursa, Portugal *I'll stick on Chardonnay for a bit; this is fantastic. Made by an Aussie, but there you go.*
**6 for £38**

Bairrada Reserva, Sogrape, Portugal *All toast and nuts, this would fool me into calling it ace Chardie any day.*  **6 for £37**

1991 Rothbury Sémillon, Australia *I keep coming across this, and its shocking flavour of lime peel, whitewash and putty helps knock me groggy. Knock on. I'll have*
**6 for £36**

Yalumba D, Australia *To clean my palate and brain and bring me back into the mainstream: Now this is really classy fizz, toasty and creamy enough to make a Champenois quake in his swimming pool.*
**6 for £56**

*And I'm **still** in white mood. 1990 brought great German wine-makers out of the woodwork, especially the brilliant* Muller-Cattoir. *I want his* Muskateller, *his* Müller-Thurgau *and his heavenly* Scheurebe. *And I'll pay on the nail.*            **12 for £88**

*I've got to have something red.* Vacqueyras *made wonderful pine-scented Rhônes in 1990, packed with juicy rich red raspberry fruit. I'll have* Domaine Fourmone *and* Domaine Vieux Clocher.        **12 for £66**

Stratford and Cartlidge Zinfandel, California *Marvellously fruity, bramble bush stuff.*

Errázuriz Chilean Merlot *Sheer blackcurrant bliss.* **6 of each for £51.50**

Muscat de Rivesaltes, Cazes and Chateau de Jau *Two different producers, both making raisin-sweet wine, perfumed with honeysuckle.* **12 halves for£48**

Seppelt's Sparkling Shiraz: *mad, not a bit nice to know and an irresistibly strange fizzy red. Aaaah.* **3 for £24.50**

**Total cost: £503**

## £1000

*I always get this nervous sense that I'm going to be terribly serious and grown-up when it comes to the £1000 cellar, and I start flicking through my lists of vintage port, Classed Growth claret and vintage Champagne. Well, I can flick away to my heart's content, but I'm not buying! OK? Classics, yes, but ones to warm my heart and make my feet tap. Do I smell Australia? Do I smell Shiraz? I certainly do.*

Coriole Shiraz, Australia *There's some startlingly good Shiraz being grown in Oz right now; this is unprintably magnificent.*

Mount Langhi Ghiran Shiraz, Australia *An amazing soup of pepper and loganberry and chocolate.*

Dalwhinnie Shiraz, Australia *More of the unforgettable same.*

Briagolong Pinot Noir *A great undiscovered Pinot Noir made on the last bit of land before the Antarctic.* **6 of each for what, £170? It's a steal**

*And since I'm over in the Southern Seas – the 1991 vintages produced some sensational stuff in New Zealand.* Wairau River Sauvignon, Vavasour Reserve Wooded Sauvignon, Giesen Riesling *and* Waipara Springs Chardonnay *These are the star names of the future.* **6 of each for £180**

1991 La Morandium Bric Puju, Italy *One of the finest Chardonnays anywhere, and from one of the young turks of Piedmont.*

1988 Barolo La Serra, Voerzio, Piedmont *Magical richness,depth and perfume from this single vineyard, and a demonstration that of all the world Barolo and Côte d'Or Burgundy are likely to be the spots where vineyard site is most crucial to personality.*

1988 Barolo, Clerico *Fabulously scented, honey-warm, chocolate-deep wine.*

1991 Barolo Giacomo Conterno, Serralunga *If this keeps its perfume and fruit when it's bottled we're talking celestial stuff. These wines are so exciting that just for once I'm prepared to spend this kind of money.* **6 of each for £350, maybe £400**

*I've got about £250 left, and I've just remembered the 1990 red Burgundies. What a combination – the greatest of the new wave in Piedmont and Burgundy. But I can probably only afford single bottles.* 1990 Clos de la Roche, Castagnier-Vadey

1990 Charmes-Chambertin, Perrot-Minot

1990 Latricières-Chambertin, Chapelle-Chambertin and Chambertin, Rossignol-Trapet *Triumphant vindication of the new Trapet generation.*

1990 Clos de Vougeot, Aimé and Francois Gros *Succulent stuff.* **1 of each for £200**

*All I can manage now is the only five bottles in the UK of one of Australia's most brilliant, whacky creations, even more off the wall than Seppelt's version*: Rockford's sparkling Black Shiraz. *And I mean sparkling – and I mean black.* **5 for £50**

**Total cost: £1000**

# FRANCE

After the year of the frost comes the year of plenty – or at least that's what it looks like as the grapes settle down to the slow business of ripening in preparation for the harvest of 1992. Last year the Loire, Bordeaux, Burgundy and almost every major region of France was devastated by April frosts that made every *vigneron's* worst nightmares come true. This year those same vines have shrugged off their troubles and produced a bumper crop.

Not that it was an ideal spring for vines. Perfect weather for flowering would consist of a succession of warm, calm, sunny days with rain in due measure once the flowers had set; a steady progression from the cold of January to the heat of July, with no nasty hiccups. None of this happened in 1992. The flowering was early in many places, which was just as well, because June was ushered in by rain, ushered out by rain and had nothing much else in the middle. In the South-West the rain started on 1 June and barely stopped until 12 July; in Bordeaux the flowering was chaotic, with heat, wind and storms; in Burgundy the Côte de Beaune had a relatively easy time, but the Côte de Nuits fared less well.

Yet in spite of all these metereological fireworks, there are an awful lot of grapes. In Burgundy they've been 'green pruning', removing some of the young grapes to give the rest more chance of concentration and flavour, and taking the risk that storms and hail later this summer could reduce still further what they've left. In Bordeaux the weather during flowering meant that the Merlot got through less well than the Cabernets – but there'll still be plenty. Champagne looks due for a bumper crop, and it all promises to be early. Whether it will be good is another matter: ask me that once the grapes are safely in the cellars. On second thoughts ask me later than that: it looks as though the cellars are going to be so packed with grapes there'll be no room for me.

## QUALITY CONTROL

The French have the most far-reaching system of wine quality control of any nation. The key factors are the 'origin' of the wine, its historic method of production and the use of the correct grape types. There are three defined levels of quality control – AC, VDQS, and *Vin de Pays*.

**Appellation d'Origine Contrôlée (AC, AOC)** To qualify for AC a wine must meet seven requirements:
**Land** Suitable vineyard land is minutely defined. **Grape** Only those grapes traditionally regarded as suitable can be used. **Degree of alcohol** Wines must reach a minimum (or maximum) degree of natural alcohol. **Yield** A basic permitted yield is set for each AC, but the figure may be increased or decreased year by year after consultation between the growers of each AC region and the Institut National des Appellations d'Origine (INAO).

**Vineyard practice** AC wines must follow rules about pruning methods and density of planting. **Wine-making practice** Each AC wine has its own regulations as to what is allowed. Typically, chaptalization – adding sugar during fermentation to increase alcoholic strength – is accepted in the north, but not in the south. **Tasting and analysis** Since 1979 wines must pass a tasting panel.

**Vin Délimité de Qualité Supérieure (VDQS)** This second group is, in general, slightly less reliable in quality. It is in the process of being phased out. No more *vins de pays* are being upgraded to VDQS but there is still no news on when existing ones will be upgraded to AC (or downgraded to *vin de pays*).

**Vin de Pays** The third category gives a regional definition to France's basic blending wines. The rules are similar to AC, but allow a good deal more flexibility and some wonderful cheap wines can be found which may well surprise. Don't expect stunning quality, but do expect fruit, value and competent wine-making.

**Vin de Table** 'Table wine' is the title for the rest. No quality control except as far as basic public health regulations demand. *Vins de pays* are always available for approximately the same price, and offer a far more interesting drink. Many Vins de Table here are dull and poorly made.

# RED BORDEAUX

First the bad news, for British drinkers anyway. In the eyes of Bordeaux we don't matter much any more. Over the past three decades our supremacy had already been dented by the Americans. But now the French themselves have become the star buyers of claret and this is having a considerable and unhealthy impact on the Bordeaux market.

For, whatever one might think, the French know very little about wine. They assume that they're born with all the knowledge they'll ever need; even if they do try and educate themselves they have problems, because their supermarkets buy (and sell) purely on price, and there are virtually no specialist wine merchants.

More seriously for us, the French buy and drink claret young and cheap. Example: a large French chain, Intermarche, hoovered up most of the spare '87s hanging around Bordeaux and sold them as Christmas drinks in 1990. Result: we must not delude ourselves that the present soft (not to say miserable) market for claret means that we can hang back and wait to buy the superb vintages of the late '80s – and the few decent 1991s. By the time we have sufficiently recovered from the recession to think of indulging, we will find that the French will have drunk virtually the whole 1988 vintage – already to be seen on many a wine list, even Classed Growths in the best restaurants – and will be starting on the 1989s and even the 1990s.

This may sound a rather extraordinary view, especially as every wine-merchant in Britain seems to be having a permanent sale to get rid of the wines he can't afford to finance and can't sell at his original prices. In Bordeaux, the situation is even worse, with every month producing another crop of rumours that a major merchant or two is going under. Even without any dramatic bankruptcies, the present depression – and the increasing power of the French supermarket chains – is putting an unprecedented strain on the market. The smaller merchants without a solid export trade look particularly vulnerable, and the brokers may even start to sell directly to customers outside the Gironde.

### Château car-boot sales?

All these developments are likely to confuse the historic route by which claret has been imported into Britain. But the urgency to buy now while stocks last is due directly to the new French demand. The growers will have to sell off their latest vintages, because they have neither the storage space nor the finance to house more than two vintages, in the same way they did the 1987s, suddenly and cheaply. So the time to buy is now, while prices are lower than they have been for years.

The same argument applies to older wines. These, as always, are both cheaper and more plentiful here than in France, and although there is a fair supply of the finer wines being re-exported to Europe from the US much of it is being absorbed by the Swiss and other well-heeled Continental drinkers.

But enough of the economics: back to the wine, or rather the lack of it following the extraordinary events of 1991. Weather-wise this was one of the most tumultuous years Bordeaux has seen. 'In 1991,' wrote Peter Sichel of Château Palmer, 'Bordeaux's climate was more temperamental than temperate. Excessive cold, excessive heat and some excessive rain played a part in providing conditions that, as every year, made it not quite like any other.'

First was the Great Frost, and even that was different from other Great Frosts. It came in spring, but it wasn't a 'spring frost'. These tend to hit the less-favoured vineyards, especially those in the lee of woods. The result of the night of 20-21 April is best described by Sichel: 'When Bordeaux woke up on 21 April the sky was blue and the ground was white. Stunned, the shoots were still green, but by lunch-time they were limp and by the evening they had withered.'

For the 1991 frost was a winter frost in spring, more severe and all-embracing in its effects than lesser ones. Many vines in what are considered 'frost pockets' survived, sheltered by the trees. But, as so often with spring frosts, it was the early-budding Merlot which suffered the worst: Pomerol and St-Émilion produced barely a tenth of a normal crop.

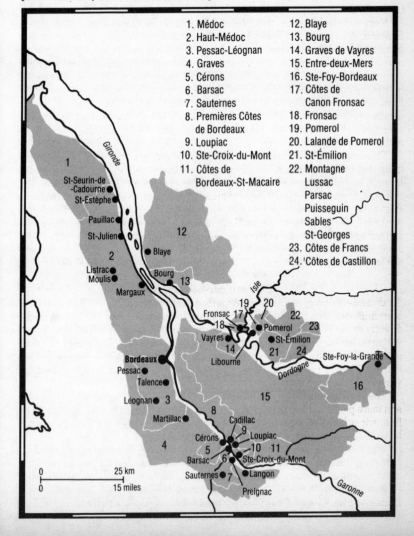

1. Médoc
2. Haut-Médoc
3. Pessac-Léognan
4. Graves
5. Cérons
6. Barsac
7. Sauternes
8. Premières Côtes de Bordeaux
9. Loupiac
10. Ste-Croix-du-Mont
11. Côtes de Bordeaux-St-Macaire
12. Blaye
13. Bourg
14. Graves de Vayres
15. Entre-deux-Mers
16. Ste-Foy-Bordeaux
17. Côtes de Canon Fronsac
18. Fronsac
19. Pomerol
20. Lalande de Pomerol
21. St-Émilion
22. Montagne Lussac Parsac Puisseguin Sables St-Georges
23. Côtes de Francs
24. Côtes de Castillon

Spring frosts, being less severe and usually later, do not allow the vines to produce the 'second crop' which further bedevilled life in 1991. Each bud has a double, a second bud that is normally dormant, but which can, if necessary, provide a second chance for the plant to produce fruit. Such second buds never provide as generously, but growers consoled themselves with the hope that at least some of the lost volume might be recuperated in this way.

## Rushing not to buy

For what happened then you will have to turn to page 57 and read about the rest of the year. But one funny thing happened after the Great Frost had guaranteed a shortage of wine. No-one rushed in to buy the better wines – although prices of basic Bordeaux Rouge, which had stagnated for years, rose slightly, albeit not enough to make the stuff too expensive for normal drinking. But the absence of demand for earlier vintages has lulled buyers – wrongly, I believe – into assuming that the lake of fine claret is a permanent one.

In the vineyards early fears that the vines themselves – and not just the buds – would be damaged have proved unfounded and 1992 seems to be developing into a more ordinary year than the Gironde has seen for some time. Indeed without the Great Frost Bordeaux would have had little to gossip about. Only two major estates changed hands: significantly Smith-Haut-Lafitte was the first major property for years not to be sold to an institutional investor. Instead it went to the Cathiars, ski champions, reinvesting the money from the sale of a supermarket chain. Like all the best new owners they are dedicated to improving what was already a very decent wine.

The Cathiars succeeded against a number of institutional bids because they came up with the cash faster than their rivals. Château Suduiraut in Sauternes, too, was sold, at least in part: Axa, the insurance group who already own five Bordeaux châteaux, bought 51 per cent for FF108m. Otherwise the institutions have remained quiescent, refusing to pay the outrageous sums demanded for properties like Rausan-Ségla, which is known to be on the market. In fact the estate-mania appears to have passed, with the Japanese in no state to lash out, and the French institutions realising that in many cases they paid over the odds. As a result the fear that there wouldn't be more than a handful of family-owned major estates left in the Gironde by the year 2000 has gone the way of similar attacks of hysteria in the past. The Bordelais can console themselves with their latest, and unhappily well-founded, fear, that the whole structure of the trade is about to change.                                                    NICHOLAS FAITH

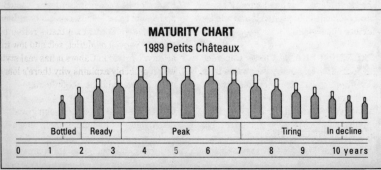

**MATURITY CHART**
1989 Petits Châteaux

| | | | | | | | |
|---|---|---|---|---|---|---|---|
| Bottled | Ready | | Peak | | | Tiring | In decline |
| 0 | 1 | 2 | 3 | 4 | 5 | 6 | 7 | 8 | 9 | 10 years |

## GRAPES & FLAVOURS

Fine claret has the most tantalizing and unlikely combination of flavours of any red wine. There's the blast of pure, fragrant blackcurrant essence of the basic fruit, and then the exotic, dry perfumes of lead pencil shavings, fresh-wrapped cigars and the intense smell of cedar resin to weave an endlessly fascinating balance of sweet and dry tastes. Increasingly nowadays this is also blended with the buttersweet overlay of new oak barrels, the whole adding up to one of the most absorbing tastes the world possesses.

Bordeaux's vineyards are so poised on the knife-edge of being able to ripen their grapes or failing to do so that every vintage is fascinatingly, absorbingly different. The relatively temperate air in this coastal region is a crucial factor in the quality of the wine. In all but the very hottest years, the sunshine is tempered by cool breezes off the Atlantic. If the year nevertheless gets too hot, as in 1959 and 1976, and in some cases 1982, 1989 and 1990, the flavour can be rich, strong and burnt, more like the Californian or Italian attempts at claret. If the summer rains and autumn gales roll in off the Bay of Biscay and the grapes can't ripen, then the taste may be thin and green, resembling the Cabernets of the Loire valley. But in the years of balance, like 1966, '70, '78, '83, '85, '86,'88,'89 and '90 those astonishing sweet and dry, fruity and tannic flavours mix to produce the glory that is claret.

**CABERNET SAUVIGNON** It comes as a surprise that this world-famous Bordeaux grape covers only a fifth of the vineyard. In the Médoc and Pessac-Léognan, however, more than half the vines are Cabernet Sauvignon, and the grape has a greater influence on flavour here than elsewhere in Bordeaux. Crucially, a wine built to age needs tannin and acidity, and the fruit and extract to keep up with them. Cabernet Sauvignon has all these in abundance. It gives dark, tannic wine with a strong initial acid attack, and a stark, pure blackcurrant fruit. When aged in new oak, it can be stunning. It's the main grape of the Haut-Médoc, but other varieties are always blended in to soften it and add a further dimension.

**CABERNET FRANC** A lesser Cabernet, giving lighter-coloured, softer wines than Cabernet Sauvignon, sometimes slightly earthy but with good, blackcurranty fruit. It's always blended in Bordeaux. In St-Émilion and Pomerol it can give very fine flavours and is widely planted. Château Cheval Blanc in St-Émilion is two-thirds Cabernet Franc.

**MERLOT** Bordeaux has more Merlot than Cabernet Sauvignon. It covers almost a third of the vineyard, and is the main grape in St-Émilion and Pomerol, whereas in the Médoc and Graves it's used to soften and enrich the Cabernet. It ripens early and gives a gorgeous, succulent, minty, blackcurrant- or plum-flavoured wine, which explains why Pomerols and St-Émilions take less effort to enjoy than Médocs. It also makes less long-lived wine than Cabernet, which are likely to peak and fade sooner.

**MALBEC** A rather bloated, juicy grape, little seen nowadays in Bordeaux, though it appears in some blends, especially in Bourg and Blaye. In Bordeaux it tastes rather like a weedy version of Merlot, soft and low in acidity. Upriver in Cahors it has real style, which probably explains why there's lots of it in Cahors and little in Bordeaux.

**PETIT VERDOT** A dark, tough grape with a liquorice and plums taste, and a violet perfume, used for colour. Little planted in the past but on the increase now because it adds quality in a late, ripe year.

# WINES & WINE REGIONS

**BORDEAUX ROUGE, AC** Unless qualified by one of the other ACs below, this is the everyday wine of Bordeaux, either from co-ops, from properties in undistinguished localities, or wine disqualified from one of the better ACs. It can come from anywhere in Bordeaux. Still reasonably priced, for drinking young, it is a delicious, appetizing meal-time red when good, and a miserable palate-puckering disappointment when bad.

**BORDEAUX SUPÉRIEUR, AC** Similar to Bordeaux Rouge but, in theory, a bit more interesting. It must have a little more alcohol and be produced from vines with a slightly lower yield. The same comments on quality apply, but from a well-run estate the wines can be delicious – and age for a number of years. Best results increasingly come from properties producing white Entre-Deux-Mers and from the Premières Côtes on the right bank of the Garonne river. Best châteaux: *Brethous, Cayla, Domaine de Terrefort, Fayau, la Gabory, le Gay, Grand-Moüeys, Gromel Bel-Air, Jalousie-Beaulieu, Jonqueyres, du Juge, Lacombe, Méaume, Peyrat, Pierredon, Reynon, la Roche, Tanesse, Thieuley, de Toutigeac, de la Vieille Tour*.

**CÔTES DE BOURG, AC** A reasonable-sized area across the river to the east of the Médoc, with its best vineyards looking directly across the Gironde to Margaux. Their rather full, savoury style is backed up by sweet Merlot fruit and occasionally a touch of new oak. As Médoc and St-Émilion prices spiral, Bourg wines are slowly coming into their own. Best châteaux: *de Barbe, du Bousquet, Brûle-Sécaille, la Croix, Dupeyrat, Grolet, Guionne, Haut-Guiraud, Haut-Rousset, de Millorit* and wines from the co-op at *Tauriac*.

**CÔTES DE CASTILLON, AC** and **CÔTES DE FRANCS, AC** Two small regions east of St-Émilion on the road towards Bergerac, which are turning out an increasing number of exciting wines. They can be a little too earthy, but at their best they combine a grassy Cabernet Franc freshness with a gorgeous, juicy, minty Merlot sweetness, even honeyed in the best châteaux. Best châteaux: *Beau-Séjour, Belcier, Brisson, Canon-Monségur, Ferrasses, Fonds Rondes, Grand Taillac, les Hauts-de-Grange, Lessacques, Moulin-Rouge, Parenchère, Pitray, Rocher-Bellevue*. On the extreme eastern edge of the Gironde is the department's latest rising star. The scions of a number of well-known wine-making families are producing fruity, light, delicious wines to drink early, using a lot of Cabernet Franc. Best châteaux: *la Claverie, de Francs, Lauriol, du Moulin-la-Pitié, la Prade, Puygueraud*.

**CÔTES DE FRONSAC, AC** (now usually called simply Fronsac) with the (in theory) superior **CANON-FRONSAC, AC**, is a small area just west of Pomerol. The wines can be a bit grassy and tannic, but they can also be excellent, often having the sweet fruit of St-Émilion, the mineral depth of Pomerol, and a slightly cedary perfume. Nevertheless the general standard has been increasing recently, greatly helped by the interest shown by the firm and family of *Jean-Pierre Moueix*, the best merchants in Libourne. Best châteaux: *Canon-de-Brem, Canon-Moueix, Cassagne Haut-Canon, Dalem, de la Dauphine, Fonteuil, Mayne-Vieil, Mazeris, Moulin Haut-Laroque, Plain Point, la Rivière, la Truffière* (super since 1985), *Toumalin, la Valade*.

**GRAVES, AC** Since 1987 the Graves, the vast region south of Bordeaux town, has been deprived of its most prestigious properties, the ones nearest the city, and

The price guides for this section begin on page 249.

now grouped in a separate AC, Pessac-Léognan. The southern two-thirds had a bad reputation as a semi-sweet white area, which it has taken a decade to overcome. These efforts have been intensified by the lopping off of Pessac-Léognan.

Red Graves run the gamut of claret flavours, and are less easy to sum up than others. There are various different soils, and though the Cabernet Sauvignon is the dominant grape in the North, as in the Médoc, there's a little less stress on Cabernet, a little more on Merlot, which makes for slightly softer wines. They tend to have some of the blackcurrant and cedar of the Médoc, but without the sheer size of, say, Pauillac: they have some of the full, plummy richness of St-Émilion yet it never dominates; and there is a slightly gravelly quality in many of them, too. The less well-known châteaux are cheapish, and pretty good. Local merchant Pierre Coste has developed a style of young-drinking Graves which is deliciously drinkable (available in Britain at Adnams, Haynes, Hanson & Clark, Tanners and others).

**HAUT-MÉDOC, AC** Geographically, the prestigious southern part of the Médoc, nearest Bordeaux – from Blanquefort in the South to St-Seurin de Cadourne in the North. The AC covers the less exciting vineyards in between because there are six separate ACs within the region where the really juicy business gets done. These are Margaux, St-Julien, Pauillac, St-Estèphe, Listrac and Moulis. Even so, the AC Haut-Médoc has five Classed Growths including two superb ones – *Cantemerle* and *la Lagune* – and an increasing number of fine *bourgeois* properties like *Beaumont, de Castillon, Cissac, Hanteillan, Lamarque, Lanessan, Liversan, Pichon, Sociando-Mallet* and *la Tour-du-Haut-Moulin* – plus lots of lesser properties, such as châteaux *Bernadotte, Cambon-la-Pelouse, Coufran, le Fournas, Grandis, du Junca, Larose-Trintaudon, Malescasse, Maucamps, Moulin de Labarde, Quimper, Sénéjac* and *Verdignan.*

**LALANDE-DE-POMEROL, AC** Pomerol's northern neighbour, a region as tiny as Pomerol itself, is often accused of being overpriced, but since it can produce rich, plummy wines with a distinct resemblance to those of Pomerol at a distinctly less painful price, this criticism is not entirely justified. The best châteaux are *Annereaux, Bel-Air, Belles-Graves, Bertineau-St-Vincent, Clos des Moines, Clos des Templiers, la Croix Bellevue, la Fleur St-Georges, Grand Ormeau, Haut-Ballet, les Hauts-Tuileries, Lavaud-la-Maréchaude, Siaurac, les Templiers, Tournefeuille.*

**LISTRAC, AC** One of the less prestigious communes of the Haut-Médoc, just to the west of Margaux. Grown on clay-dominated soils, the wines contain a higher proportion of Merlot. They are generally tough, rather charmless, only slightly perfumed wines, lacking the complexity of the best villages, but the meteoric rise in quality amongst the *bourgeois* wines since the '82 and '83 vintages has made its mark, though without quite the same show of fireworks. But some properties rise above this such as *Clarke, la Bécade, Cap-Léon-Veyrin, Fonréaud* (since 1988), *Fourcas-Dupré, Fourcas-Hosten, Fourcaud, Lestage* and the *Grand Listrac* co-op.

**MARGAUX, AC** Of the famous Haut-Médoc communes, this is the nearest to Bordeaux, covering various villages making rather sludgy, solid wines at one extreme, and at the other extreme the most fragrant, perfumed red wines France has yet dreamed up. The great wines come from round the village of Margaux itself. People pay high prices for them and still get a bargain. The best châteaux include: *d'Angludet, la Gurgue, d'Issan, Labégorce-Zédé, Margaux, Monbrison, Palmer, Prieuré-Lichine, Rausan-Ségla, du Tertre.* Among the next best are châteaux *Durfort-Vivens, Giscours, Marquis d'Alesme-Becker, Marquis de Terme, Siran* and *la Tour-de-Mons.*

**MÉDOC, AC** This name covers the whole of the long (80km) tongue of land north of Bordeaux town, between the Gironde river and the sea, including the Haut-Médoc and all its famous communes. As an AC, it refers to the less regarded but important lower-lying northern part of the area, traditionally known as the Bas-Médoc. AC Médoc reds, with a high proportion of Merlot grapes, are drinkable more quickly than Haut-Médocs and the best have a refreshing, grassy, juicy fruit, backed up by just enough tannin and acidity. Easily the best property is *Potensac*, where Michel Delon of Léoville-Las-Cases makes wine of Classed Growth standard. Other good wines are *le Bernadot, Cardonne, Cassan d'Estevil, David, d'Escot, la Gorce, Greysac, Grivière, Haut-Canteloup, Lacombe-Noaillac, Noaillac, Ormes-Sorbet, Patache d'Aux, la Tour-de-By, la Tour-St-Bonnet, Loudenne, Vieux-Château-Landon*. Most of the co-ops – especially *Bégadan, Ordornac* and *St-Yzans* – make good fruity stuff.

**MOULIS, AC** Another lesser commune of the Haut-Médoc next door to, and similar to, Listrac, but with more potentially outstanding properties and a softer, more perfumed style in the best which can equal Classed Growths. Best are *Bel Air Lagrave, Brillette, Chasse-Spleen, Duplessis-Fabre, Dutruch-Grand-Poujeaux, Grand-Poujeaux, Gressier-Grand-Poujeaux, Maucaillou, Moulin-à-Vent, Poujeaux*.

**PAUILLAC, AC** The most famous of the Haut-Médoc communes, Pauillac has three of the world's greatest red wines sitting inside its boundaries, *Latour, Lafite* and *Mouton-Rothschild*. This is where the blackcurrant really comes into its own. The best wines are almost painfully intense, a mixture of blackcurrant and celestial lead pencil sharpenings that sends well-heeled cognoscenti leaping for their cheque books. Best: *D'Armailhacq (*formerly known as *Mouton-Baronne-Philippe), Grand-Puy-Lacoste, Haut-Bages-Avérous, Haut-Bages-Libéral, Lafite-Rothschild, Latour, Lynch-*

*Bages, Mouton-Rothschild, Pichon-Baron, Pichon-Lalande*. Next best: *Batailley, Clerc-Milon-Rothschild, Duhart-Milon, Grand-Puy-Ducasse, Haut-Bages-Monpelou*.

**PESSAC-LÉOGNAN, AC** An AC in its own right since September 1987 for the area traditionally the Graves' best and containing all the *crus classés*. The AC covers ten communes but only 55 châteaux. In recent years the growers have fought back with increasing success against the tide of suburbia, replanting and improving their wines, above all the whites which, at their best, offer a depth surpassed only by the best Burgundies. The reds have a biscuity, bricky warmth. Best: *Carmes-Haut-Brion, Cabannieux, Cruzeau, Domaine de Chevalier, Domaine de Gaillat, Domaine la Grave, Ferrande, de Fieuzal, Haut-Bailly, Haut-Brion, Haut-Portets, la Louvière, Malartic-Lagravière, la Mission-Haut-Brion, Pape-Clément* (since 1985), *Rahoul Rochemorin, de St-Pierre, Smith-Haut-Lafitte* (since 1988), *Roquetaillade-la-Grange, la Tour Martillac, Tourteau-Chollet*.

**POMEROL, AC** Tiny top-class area inland from Bordeaux, clustered round the town of Libourne. The Merlot grape is even more dominant in Pomerol than in St-Émilion, and most Pomerols have a deeper, rounder flavour, the plummy fruit going as dark as prunes in great years, but with the mineral backbone of toughness preserving it for a very long time. Pomerol has no classification, but it harbours the world's greatest red wine, *Château Pétrus*. Any vineyard that has been picked out by *Jean-Pierre Moueix* or influenced by oenologist *Michel Rolland*, can be regarded as being of good Classed Growth standard. Best châteaux: *le Bon Pasteur, Bourgneuf-Vayron, Certan-de-May, Certan-Giraud, Clinet, Clos René, Clos du Clocher, Clos l'Église, la Conseillante, la Croix de Gay, l'Église Clinet, l'Évangile, le Gay, la Grave-Trigant-de-Boisset, Lafleur, Lafleur-Gazin,*

*La Fleur Pétrus, Lagrange à Pomerol, Latour-à-Pomerol, Petit-Village, Pétrus, le Pin, Trotanoy, Vieux-Château-Certan.*

## PREMIÈRES CÔTES DE BLAYE, AC

There is a shift to red in this historically white area across the river from the Médoc. The wines are too often a little 'cooked' in taste and slightly jammy-sweet. They're cheap, but have a lot more improving to do. Good names: *Bas Vallon, Bourdieu, Charron, Crusquet-Sabourin, l'Escadre, Fontblanche, Grand Barail, Haut-Sociando, Jonqueyres, Peybonhomme.*

## PREMIÈRES CÔTES DE BORDEAUX,

**AC** This long, south-facing slope stands opposite Bordeaux town and slides down the river Garonne to about opposite Barsac. In spite of its rather grand name, its only claim to fame until recently has been the production of rather half-baked Sauternes look-alikes. But it is now producing some very attractive reds. The 1985, '88 and '89 vintages produced numerous wines with a surprising amount of soft fruit and durability. Best châteaux: *de Berbec, Brethous, Cayla, Fayau, Grands-Moüeys, du Juge, Lamothe, de Lucat, Peyrat, la Roche, Reynon, Tanesse.*

## ST-ÉMILION, AC

Soft, round, and rather generous wines, because the main grape is the Merlot, aided by Cabernet Franc and Malbec, and only slightly by Cabernet Sauvignon. St-Émilions don't always have Pomerol's minerally backbone, and the sweetness is usually less plummy and more buttery, toffee'd or raisiny. Top wines add to this a blackcurranty, minty depth. It's a well-known name, yet with few famous châteaux. It has its own classification, but it is very sprawling, and it has two top châteaux, *Cheval-Blanc* and *Ausone*, plus a dozen excellent ones. Some areas also annex the name, like St-Georges-St-Émilion or Puisseguin-St-Émilion. They're often OK, but would be better value if they didn't trade greedily on the St-Émilion handle. Best in satellites: *St-Georges,*

*Montaiguillon, Tour du Pas St-Georges* (St-Georges-St-Émilion)*; Haut-Gillet, de Maison Neuve* (Montagne-St-Émilion)*; Bel Air, la Croix-de-Berny* (Puisseguin-St-Émilion)*; Lyonnat* (since 1983) (Lussac-St-Émilion*). Best châteaux: *l'Angélus, l'Arrosée, Ausone, Balestard-la-Tonnelle, Beauséjour-Duffau-Lagarosse, Canon, Canon-la-Gaffelière, Cheval-Blanc, Clos des Jacobins, la Dominique, Figeac, Fonroque, Larmande, Magdelaine, Pavie, Pavie Decesse, Soutard, Tertre-Rôteboeuf, Troplong-Mondot.* Next best: *Belair,Cadet-Piola, Berliquet, Cap de Mourlin, Cardinal Villemaurine, Carteau, Côtes Daugay, Clos Fourtet, Corbin-Michotte, Couvent des Jacobins, Destieux, de Ferrand, Trappaud, Fombrauge, Franc-Mayne, la Gaffelière, Grand-Mayne, Gravet, Villemaurine, Magnan-la-Gaffelière, Mauvezin, la-Tour-du-Pin Figeac, Monbousquet, Pavie-Macquin, Rolland-Maillet, Tour-des-Combes, Trottevieille.*

## ST-ESTÈPHE, AC

This northernmost of the great Haut-Médoc communes is a more everyday performer. There aren't many famous names, and most of the wines are relatively cheap. Best châteaux: *Calon-Ségur, Chambert-Marbuzet, Cos d'Estournel, Haut-Marbuzet, Lafon-Rochet, Marbuzet, Meyney, Montrose, les Ormes-de-Pez, de Pez.* Next best: *Andron-Blanquet, Beausite, du Boscq, Cos Labory, le Crock, Lavillotte, Phélan-Ségur.*

## ST-JULIEN, AC

There are two main styles. One is almost honeyed, a rather gentle, round, wonderfully easy-to-love claret. The other has glorious cedar-cigar-box fragrance mixed with just enough fruit to make it satisfying as well as exciting. Best châteaux to look for: *Beychevelle, Ducru-Beaucaillou, Gruaud-Larose, Lagrange* (in recent vintages especially), *Lalande-Borie, Langoa-Barton, Léoville-Barton, Léoville-Las-Cases, St-Pierre, Talbot.* Next best: *Branaire-Ducru, Gloria, Hortevie, Léoville-Poyferré* and *Terrey-Gros-Caillou.*

# THE 1855 CLASSIFICATION

This is the most famous and enduring wine classification in the world – but it was never intended as such, merely as a one-off guide to the different Bordeaux wines entered for the Great Paris Exhibition of 1855, made up by various local brokers and based on the prices the wines had obtained over the previous century or so. Those brokers would be dumbfounded if they returned today to find we still revered their rather impromptu classification.

An interesting point to note is that the wine name was classified, not the vineyard it came from. Some of the vineyards that make up a wine are now completely different from those of 1855, yet, because the name got into the lists, the level of classification remains. There are endless arguments about the quality ratings – which châteaux deserve promotion, which ones should be demoted and so on, but the only change so far occurred in 1973, when Mouton-Rothschild got promoted from Second to First Growth level after 50 years of lobbying by its late owner. In general, those properties which are classified do deserve their status, but that's never yet stopped anyone from arguing about it.

### First Growths (1ers Crus)

Latour, *Pauillac*; Lafite-Rothschild, *Pauillac*; Margaux, *Margaux*; Haut-Brion, *Pessac-Léognan* (formerly Graves); Mouton-Rothschild, *Pauillac* (promoted in 1973).

### Second Growths (2èmes Crus)

Rausan-Ségla, *Margaux*; Rauzan-Gassies, *Margaux*; Léoville-Las-Cases, *St-Julien*; Léoville-Poyferré, *St-Julien*; Léoville-Barton, *St-Julien*; Durfort-Vivens, *Margaux*; Lascombes, *Margaux*; Gruaud-Larose, *St-Julien*; Brane-Cantenac, *Cantenac-Margaux*; Pichon-Longueville, *Pauillac*; Pichon-Lalande, *Pauillac*; Ducru-Beaucaillou, *St-Julien*; Cos d'Estournel, *St-Estèphe*; Montrose, *St-Estèphe*.

### Third Growths (3èmes Crus)

Giscours, *Labarde-Margaux*; Kirwan, *Cantenac-Margaux*; d'Issan, *Cantenac-Margaux*; Lagrange, *St-Julien*; Langoa-Barton, *St-Julien*; Malescot-St-Exupéry, *Margaux*; Cantenac-Brown, *Cantenac-Margaux*; Palmer, *Cantenac-Margaux*; la Lagune, *Ludon-Haut-Médoc*; Desmirail, *Margaux*; Calon-Ségur, *St-Estèphe*; Ferrière, *Margaux*; Marquis d'Alesme-Becker, *Margaux*; Boyd-Cantenac, *Cantenac-Margaux*.

### Fourth Growths (4èmes Crus)

St-Pierre, *St-Julien*; Branaire-Ducru, *St-Julien*; Talbot, *St-Julien*; Duhart-Milon-Rothschild, *Pauillac*; Pouget, *Cantenac-Margaux*; la Tour-Carnet, *St-Laurent-Haut-Médoc*; Lafon-Rochet, *St-Estèphe*; Beychevelle, *St-Julien*; Prieuré-Lichine, *Cantenac-Margaux*; Marquis-de-Terme, *Margaux*.

### Fifth Growths (5èmes Crus)

Pontet-Canet, *Pauillac*; Batailley, *Pauillac*; Grand-Puy-Lacoste, *Pauillac*; Grand-Puy-Ducasse, *Pauillac*; Haut-Batailley, *Pauillac*; Lynch-Bages, *Pauillac*; Lynch-Moussas, *Pauillac*; Dauzac, *Labarde-Margaux*; d'Armailhacq, *Pauillac* (formerly known as Mouton-Baronne-Philippe); du Tertre, *Arsac-Margaux*; Haut-Bages-Libéral, *Pauillac*; Pédesclaux, *Pauillac*; Belgrave, *St-Laurent-Haut Médoc*; de Camensac, *St-Laurent-Haut-Médoc*; Cos Labory, *St-Estèphe*; Clerc-Milon-Rothschild, *Pauillac*; Croizet-Bages, *Pauillac*; Cantemerle, *Macau-Haut-Médoc*.

*Webster's* is an annual publication. We welcome your suggestions for next year's edition.

# CHÂTEAUX PROFILES

These properties are valued according to how they are currently performing; a five-star rating means you are getting a top-line taste – not just a well-known label. Some big names have been downgraded, some lesser-known properties are promoted – solely on the quality of the wine inside the bottle. A star in brackets shows that the wine can achieve the higher rating but does not always do so.

The £ sign shows which are offering particularly good value – that does not mean any of these wines will be cheap but look for recessionary price reductions.

**L'ANGÉLUS** *grand cru classé St-Émilion* ★★★★ One of the biggest and best known *grands crus classés*. A lot of Cabernet in the vineyard makes for a reasonably gutsy wine, although rich and soft. Since 1979 new barrels have helped the flavour. The 1985 and 1986 are, by a street, the finest yet, with excellent '87, '88 and '89.

**D'ANGLUDET** *cru bourgeois Margaux* ★★★ £ *Bourgeois* easily attaining Classed Growth standards. Owned by an Englishman, Peter Allan Sichel, the wine has much of the perfume of good Margaux without ever going through the traditional tough, lean period. Fairly priced. Tremendous value. The 1980s have seen Angludet on a hot streak. The '83 and '90 are the property's finest wines *ever*, and the '85, '86, '88 and '89 are big and classy.

**D'ARMAILHACQ** *5ème cru classé Pauillac* ★★★(★) (Formerly known as Mouton-Baronne-Philippe) A wine of very good balance for a Fifth Growth, with the perfume particularly marked, this obviously benefits from having the same ownership as Mouton-Rothschild. 1986 and '83 are very good, with '82 not bad either.

**AUSONE** *1er grand cru classé St-Émilion* ★★★★(★) The phoenix rises from the ashes. For many years, people have been referring to Ausone as they would to a slightly mad and distinctly embarrassing maiden aunt, who then marries the most popular boy in town. The boy in question is Pascal Delbeck, who has been at the château since 1976 and has worked at returning Ausone to its proper position as one of St-Émilion's two First Growths. Potentially great wine at its best and very expensive. The 1985, '86, '89 and above all the '90, should be especially good.

**BATAILLEY** *5ème cru classé Pauillac* ★★★ £ Batailley's reputation has been of the squat, solid sort rather than elegant and refined, but recently the wines have performed that extremely difficult Pauillac magician's trick – they've been getting a lot better, and the price has remained reasonable. Drinkable young, they age well too. The 1983, '85, '86, '88, '89 and '90 are excellent, available – and affordable.

**BELAIR** *1er cru classé St-Émilion* ★★★ The arrival of Pascal Delbeck at Ausone had a dramatic effect on Belair too, since it's under the same ownership. It looked as though it was rapidly returning to a top position as a finely balanced, stylish St-Émilion, but some recent bottles have been strangely unconvincing.

**BEYCHEVELLE** *4ème cru classé St-Julien* ★★★★ Certainly the most expensive Fourth Growth, but deservedly so, since traditional quality puts it alongside the top Seconds. It takes time to mature to a scented, blackcurrant, beautifully balanced – and expensive – wine. At the end of the 1970s and beginning of the 1980s the wines were rather unconvincing, but the sale of the château (to a civil servants' pension fund) in 1985 dramatically improved matters through greater selectivity. 1989 and 1990 sublime.

**BRANAIRE-DUCRU** *4ème cru classé St-Julien* ★★★ Used to be soft, smooth wine with a flavour of plums and chocolate, gradually achieving a classic, cedary St-Julien dry perfume in maturity. The 1981, '82, '85 and '86 are good. But the 1980s have been very erratic, with rather dilute flavours and unclean fruit. '82, '85 and '86 were clean and fruity, but '83, '87 and '88 were strangely insubstantial. 1989 and '90 saw a welcome return to form, thanks to a change of ownership, with wine of sturdy fruit and backbone.

**BRANE-CANTENAC** *2ème cru classé Margaux* ★★(★) This is a big and famous property which has been underachieving, when most of the other Second Growths are shooting ahead. It has had chances in the last eight years to prove its greatness, but in spite of some improvements remains well behind the rest of the field. Even its supposedly inferior stable-mate Durfort-Vivens has produced better wine in recent years.

**CALON-SÉGUR** *3ème cru classé St-Estèphe* ★★★(★) The château with the heart on its label. This is because the former owner, Marquis de Ségur, though he owned such estates as Lafite and Latour, declared 'my heart belongs to Calon'. An intensely traditional claret, it's certainly good on present showing, but doesn't set many hearts a-flutter. '86 and '88 were promising though.

**CANON** *1er grand cru classé St-Émilion* ★★★★(★) Mature Canon reeks of the soft, buttery Merlot grape as only a top St-Émilion can. Recently, it has been getting deeper and tougher, and although we'll probably miss that juicy, sweet mouthful of young Merlot, the end result will be even deeper and more exciting. The wines seem to get better and better; marvellous 1982s and '83s were followed by a stunning '85 and a thoroughly impressive '86. 1988 was excellent. '89 and '90 are keeping up this high standard.

**CANTEMERLE** *5ème cru classé Haut-Médoc* ★★★(★) Since 1983 the Cordier company has controlled this Fifth Growth and the wine is now often up to Second Growth standards, although sometimes a little light. The 1988 and '89 are the best recent vintages by a long way, and the '83 was really good, but though the '85, '86 and '90 are beautifully perfumed, they are a little loose-knit. Interestingly, the perfumed style quite suits the '87.

**CHASSE-SPLEEN** *cru bourgeois Moulis* ★★★(★) A tremendously consistent wine, at the top of the *bourgeois* tree, and a prime candidate for elevation in any new classification. The wines have been impressive, chunky and beautifully made right through the 1980s, except for a rather 'over-elegant' 1985. Choose 1982 and '86, followed by lovely '87 and tip-top '88. The 1989 is a bit fierce, but the '90 is first class, with lots of blackberry fruit backed by a firm structure.

**CHEVAL-BLANC** *1er grand cru classé St-Émilion* ★★★★★ The property stands on an outcrop right next to Pomerol, and seems to share some of its sturdy richness, but adds extra spice and fruit that is impressively, recognizably unique, perhaps due to the very high proportion of Cabernet Franc. Good years are succulently good. Lesser years like 1980 can be great successes too, and only 1984 and 1987 haven't worked here recently. The 1982 is unbelievably good, and the '81, '83, '85 and '86 are not far behind. '88 is one of the top wines of the vintage, but '89 and '90 are not quite of the intensity I would want.

**CISSAC** *cru grand bourgeois Haut-Médoc* ★★★ £ Traditionalists' delight! This is one of the best known *bourgeois* growths, dark, dry and slow to mature with lots of oak influence, too – the oak perhaps a little more apparent than the fruit. It is best in richly ripe years like 1982 and '85, and can be a little lean in years like '86. '88, '89 and '90 were very good indeed.

**COS D'ESTOURNEL** *2ème cru classé St-Estèphe* ★★★★(★) £ Now the undoubted leader of St-Estèphe in quality terms, this property has rapidly acquired much of the fame of the top Pauillacs. The wines are dark, tannic and oaky – classically made for long ageing despite a high percentage of Merlot. They are deservedly among the most expensive Second Growths. The quality was so good in '85, '88 and '89 that they are probably undervalued. Second label Château Marbuzet is good.

**DOMAINE DE CHEVALIER** *cru classé Pessac-Léognan* ★★★★(★) The red and white are equally brilliant. The red has a superb balance of fruit and oak, and the white is simply one of France's greatest. You have to book ahead even to see a bottle of the white but you might find some red. Buy it. It's expensive and worth every penny. The hottest years are not always the best here, and despite an impressive richness in 1982, the '81, '83, '85, '86 and '88 may yet turn out better. 1987 is a resounding success in a light vintage, as is 1984. 1989 and 1990 were classy in an area of Bordeaux where results seem uneven.

**DUCRU-BEAUCAILLOU** *2ème cru classé St-Julien* ★★★★(★) One of the glories of the Médoc. It has now distanced itself from most other Second Growths in price and quality, yet the flavour is so deep and warm, and the balance so good, it's still worth the money. With its relatively high yields, it has a less startling quality when young than its near rivals Léoville-Las-Cases and Pichon-Lalande, but if the balance is right, the wine can age impressively and beautifully without extra concentration. 1982, '85, '86, '88, '89 and '90 are all top drawer and marvellously complex, while '81, '79 and '78 are also remarkably good and fit for the long haul.

**L'EVANGILE** *Pomerol* ★★★(★) Top-line Pomerol, lacking the sheer intensity of its neighbour Pétrus, but perfumed and rich in a most irresistible way. Output isn't excessive, demand is. 1982, '85, and '88 are delicious, with first-rate '87 too. '89 is packed with multi-layered, firm, luscious fruit, and '90 is another blockbuster.

**DE FIEUZAL** *cru classé Pessac-Léognan* ★★★★ Now one of the stars of Pessac-Léognan. The red starts plum-rich and buttery, but soon develops typical earthiness and cedar perfume allied to lovely fruit. It made one of the finest 1984s, outstanding '85s and '86s as well as lovely '87s and thrilling '88s. '89 was absolutely top-notch, and '90 very good. The white, though unclassified, is scented, complex, deep and exciting. One to watch.

**FIGEAC** *1er grand cru classé St-Émilion* ★★★★(★) Figeac shares many of the qualities of Cheval-Blanc (rare gravelly soil, for a start) but it's always ranked as the – ever-reliable – star of the second team. A pity, because the wine has a beauty and a blackcurranty, minty fragrance not common in St-Émilion. High quality. High(ish) price. Figeac is always easy to drink young, but really deserves proper ageing. The excellent 1978 is just opening out, and the lovely '82, '85 and '86 wines will all take at least as long. '89 and '90 are already marvellously seductive.

**LA FLEUR-PÉTRUS** *Pomerol* ★★★★ This wine is in the top flight, having some of the mineral roughness of much Pomerol, but also tremendous perfume and length. Real class. We don't see much of this in the UK since the Americans got their teeth into it, but the 1982 and '89 are without doubt the best recent wines; the '85 and '86 seem to lack that little 'extra' class.

**GAZIN** *Pomerol* ★★★ This can produce the extra sweetness and perfume Nenin usually lacks. Although fairly common on the British market, it wasn't that great up to about 1985. Now controlled by Moueix, '87 and '88 are an improvement, and '89 and '90 are really very fine, so we can all start buying it again.

**GISCOURS** *3ème cru classé Margaux*
★★★ This property excelled right through the 1970s and into the 1980s, and made some of Bordeaux's best wines in years like '75, '78 and '80. But something's gone wrong since 1982. Although 1986 is good, and '87 is reasonable for the year, '83, '85 and '88 are really not up to par. 1989 and '90 showed a welcome return to form.

**GLORIA** *cru bourgeois St-Julien* ★★(★)
Owing to the high-profile lobbying of its late owner, Henri Martin, Gloria became expensive and renowned. The quality of this quick-maturing wine has not always been faithful to the quality of the rhetoric. 1986, '88 and '89 show some signs that the wine is becoming worthy of the price.

**GRAND-PUY-DUCASSE** *5ème cru classé Pauillac* ★★★ £ Every recent vintage has been a success, and, with a price that is not excessive, its slightly gentle but tasty Pauillac style is one to buy. The 1979 is lovely now, and the '82 and '83 are very nice without causing the hand to tremble in anticipation. Since 1984 there has been a discernible rise in tempo and '85 and '86 look to be the best wines yet.

**GRAND-PUY-LACOSTE** *5ème cru classé Pauillac* ★★★★ £ This wine manages to combine perfume, power and consistency in a way that shows top Pauillac at its brilliant best. The blackcurrant and the cigar-box perfume are rarely in better harmony than here. Not cheap but worth it for a classic. The 1978 is sheer class, the '82, '83, '86 and '88 top wines, and the '84, though very light, is gentle and delicious. 1989 is deliciously perfumed with robust fruit – a real star.

**GRUAUD-LAROSE** *2ème cru classé St-Julien* ★★★★(★) Another St-Julien that often starts rich, chunky and sweetish but will achieve its full cedary glory if given time, while still retaining a lovely sweet centre, typical of the wines (like Talbot) owned by the Cordier family. The

remarkable run of 1982, '83, '84 and '85 continued with a great '86, an attractive '87, exceptionally impressive '88 and '89 and, keeping up the standards, almost unnervingly juicy, ripe '90.

**HAUT-BAILLY** *cru classé Pessac-Léognan* ★★★★ Haut-Bailly tastes sweet, rich and perfumed from its earliest youth, and the high percentage of new oak adds to this impression even further. But the wines do age well and, though expensive, are of a high class. 1981, '82, '85, '86, '88 and '89 are the best recently.

**HAUT-BATAILLEY** *5ème cru classé Pauillac* ★★★ Once dark, plummy and slow to sweeten, Haut-Batailley is now a somewhat lighter, more charming wine. In some years this has meant it was somehow less satisfying, but 1989 is the best yet, marvellously concentrated. 1986 and '88 are the best of earlier wines, with '82, '83 and '85 all good, but just a touch too diffuse and soft.

**HAUT-BRION** *1er cru classé Pessac-Léognan* ★★★★★ The only non-Médoc red to be classified in 1855. The wines are not big, but are almost creamy in their gorgeous ripe taste, deliciously so. If anything, they slightly resemble the great Médocs. Although 1982 is strangely insubstantial, the next four vintages are all very fine and '88 and '89 are outstanding, while the 1990, although worthy of the château, could not quite compete with its predessors. There is also a delicious white Haut-Brion – the 1985 is spectacular.

**D'ISSAN** *3ème cru classé Margaux* ★★★★
One of the truest Margaux wines, hard when young (though more use of new oak recently has sweetened things up a bit), but perfumed and deep-flavoured after ten to 12 years. Fabulous in 1983, '88 and '90, first rate in '85 and '86, with a good '87 too. 1989 has excellent fruit, while 1990 is a star, rich and concentrated, with lots of liquorice fruit on the palate.

**LAFITE-ROTHSCHILD** *1er cru classé Pauillac* ★★★★(★) The most difficult of all the great Médocs to get to know and understand. It doesn't stand for power like Latour, or overwhelming perfume like Mouton. No, it stands for balance, for the elegant, restrained balance that is the perfection of great claret. And yet, till its day comes, Lafite can seem curiously unsatisfying. I keep looking for that day. I keep being unsatisfied. 1989 and '88 are undoubtedly the best recent vintages, followed by 1982 and '86, but this fabled estate does seem to be dishing up fairy tales in the place of the real stuff that dreams are made of.

**LAFLEUR** *Pomerol* ★★★★★ This tiny property is regarded as the only Pomerol with the potential to be as great as Pétrus. So far, they couldn't be further apart in style, and Lafleur is marked out by an astonishing austere concentration of dark fruit and an intense tobacco spice perfume. The 1982 almost knocks you sideways with its naked power, and the '83 and '85 are also remarkable. 1989 is superbly fruity and displays tremendous finesse already. It should be a good buy.

**LAFON-ROCHET** *4ème cru classé St-Estèphe* ★★★(★) Since the 1970s, an improving St-Estèphe, having as much body, but a little more perfume than most of them. 1982, '83 and '85 are all good, though none of them stunning, while '86, '87, '88, '89 and '90 show lots of class and a welcome consistency of style.

**LAGRANGE** *3ème cru classé St-Julien* ★★★★Until its purchase by the Japanese Suntory whisky group in 1984, Lagrange had always lacked real class, though '82 and '83 were reasonable. But the vineyard always had great potential, even when the wine was below par, and investment is making its presence felt; '85, '86, '88, '89 and '90 are impressive and '87 was good too. Another bandwagon is rolling. Make sure you concentrate on newer vintages.

**LA LAGUNE** *3ème cru classé Haut-Médoc* ★★★★ Certainly making Second Growth standard wine, with a rich, soft intensity. It is now becoming more expensive, but the wine gets better and better. The 1982 is a wonderful rich, juicy wine, with '85 and '88 not far behind, and '83 not far behind that. 1986 is burly but brilliant stuff, as is '89. 1987 is more delicate but good.

**LANESSAN** *cru bourgeois Haut-Médoc* ★★★ 'Grand Cru Hors Classe' is how Lanessan describes itself. This could be a timeless reminder of the fact that a previous owner felt it unnecessary to submit samples for the 1855 Classification, and so its traditional ranking as a Fourth Growth was never ratified. Nowadays, the wine is always incredibly correct. But this may be because the owner resolutely refuses to use new oak and therefore his wines *are* more discreet when tasted young. The '82 and '83 are both exhibiting classic claret flavours now, '88 looks set for the same path and first tastings of '90 reveal a wine of balance and depth.

**LANGOA-BARTON** *3ème cru classé St-Julien* ★★★★ £ This wine is very good. It is in the dry, cedary style, and although sometimes regarded as a lesser version of Léoville-Barton, this is patently unfair since the wine has exceptional character and style of its own, and is reasonably priced. '82 and '85 are exciting, '86 and '87 very typical, but the '88 may be the best for 30 years. The '89 almost matched Léoville for elegance and the '90 was fully its equal.

**LASCOMBES** *2ème cru classé Margaux* ★★★ Lascombes made its reputation in America, and that's where it still likes to be drunk. Very attractive early on, but the wine can gain flesh and character as it ages. It's been a little inconsistent recently, but the 1985 and '83 are good, and the '86 is the most serious effort for a long time. '87 is also good, but '88 is so light you'd think they'd included every grape on the property. The '89 and '90 are more hopeful.

**LATOUR** *1er cru classé Pauillac* ★★★★★
This is the easiest of all the First Growths
to understand. You may not always like it,
but you understand it because it is a
massive, dark, hard brute when young,
calming down when it ages and eventually
spreading out to a superb, big,
blackcurrant and cedar flavour. It used to
take absolutely ages to come round, but
some recent vintages have seemed a little
softer and lighter, yet usually retaining
their tremendous core of fruit. Let's hope
they age as well as the previous ones,
because the 1984 was more true to type
than the '85! And though the '82 is a
classic, both '83 and '81 are very definitely
not. '86 and '88 seem to be back on course,
and '89 looks splendidly powerful. With the
'89 and '90 the new management showed
that power and richness were part of their
inheritance. The second wine, Les Forts de
Latour, is getting better and better, while
the third wine, Pauillac de Latour, is now
made in most years to preserve the quality
of the two greater wines.

**LÉOVILLE-BARTON** *2ème cru classé St-
Julien* ★★★★(★) £ The traditionalist's
dream. Whoever described claret as a dry,
demanding wine must have been thinking
of Léoville-Barton. Despite all the new
fashions and trends in Bordeaux, Anthony
Barton simply goes on making superlative,
old-fashioned wine for long ageing, and
resolutely charging a non-inflated price for
it. All the vintages of the 1980s have been
attractive, but the 1982, '83, '85 and '86 are
outstanding, the '87 delicious, and the '88
and '90 are two of the best wines of the
Médoc. 1989 keeps up the standard. All are
*wonderfully* fairly priced.

**LÉOVILLE-LAS-CASES** *2ème cru classé
St-Julien* ★★★★★ Because of the owner's
super-selectivity, this is the most brilliant
of the St-Juliens, combining all the sweet,
honeyed St-Julien ripeness with strong,
dry, cedary perfume. The wine is justly
famous, and despite a very large
production, the whole crop is snapped up at
some of the Médoc's highest prices. The
1982 is more exciting every time a bottle is
broached, and all the vintages of the 1980s
are top examples of their year. The second
wine, Clos du Marquis, is better than the
majority of Classed Growths, if only
because Michel Delon puts into it wines
which any other owner would put into his
*grand vin.*

**LÉOVILLE-POYFERRÉ** *2ème cru classé
St-Julien* ★★★ The Léoville that got left
behind, not only in its unfashionable
reputation, but also in the quality of the
wine, which until recently had a dull,
indistinct flavour and an unbalancing
dryness compared with other top St-
Juliens. Things are now looking up with
new investment and new commitment and
I feel more confident about this property
with every vintage. The 1982, '85, '86 and
even the '87 are considerable
improvements, and '88, '89 and '90
continue the progress, but it still has some
way to catch up in terms of power and
concentration with its peer group.

**LOUDENNE** *cru bourgeois Médoc* ★(★)
The château is owned by Gilbey's and the
wine is seen a lot in such chains as Peter
Dominic. The red has a lot of Merlot and is
always fruity and agreeable, but
unmemorable and a little too soft to lay
down for long.

**LYNCH-BAGES** *5ème cru classé Pauillac*
★★★★(★) This château is so well known
that familiarity can breed contempt, and
its considerable quality be underestimated.
It is astonishingly soft and drinkable when
very young, and yet it ages brilliantly, and
has one of the most beautiful scents of
minty blackcurrant in all Bordeaux. The
most likely to show that character are the
1986 and '83 and, remarkably, the '87, but
for sheer exuberant starry-eyed brilliance,
the '88, '85 and particularly the '82 are the
ones. '89 is unusually big and powerful,
while the '90 is a more restrained and
classic wine.

**MAGDELAINE** *1er grand cru classé St-Émilion* ★★★★ A great St-Émilion, combining the soft richness of Merlot with the sturdiness needed to age. They pick very late to maximize ripeness, and the wine is made with the usual care by Jean-Pierre Moueix of Libourne. Expensive, but one of the best. 1982 and 1985 are both classics, '88 and '89 tremendously good.

**MALARTIC-LAGRAVIÈRE** *cru classé Pessac-Léognan* ★★★ £ While its near neighbour, Domaine de Chevalier, hardly ever produces its allowed crop, this property frequently has to declassify its excess. Even so, the quality is good, sometimes excellent, and while the white is very attractive young, the red is capable of long ageing. 1987, '86, '85, '83 and '82 are all successful, with '88 and '89 the finest yet, but the '90s are disappointing.The red, in particular, is rather wishy-washy.

**MALESCOT-ST-EXUPÉRY** *3ème cru classé Margaux* ★★(★) A property which seems to have lost its way. Traditionally it started out quite lean and hard and difficult to taste, but after ten years or so it began to display the perfume and delicate fruit only bettered by such wines as Palmer and Margaux. Yet after tasting and re-tasting the wines of the 1980s, sadly the conclusion is that they are now being made too light and lacking in depth for this thrilling perfume ever to develop. The 1990 may prove me wrong. I hope so.

**MARGAUX** *1er cru classé Margaux* ★★★★★ Since 1978 a succession of great wines have set Margaux back on the pedestal of fragrance, refinement and sheer, ravishing perfume from which it had slipped a dozen or so years before. The new Margaux is weightier than before, yet with all its beauty intact. 1978 and 1979 were the exciting harbingers of this new 'Mentzelopoulos era', the '80 was startlingly good in a tricky vintage, and '82, '83 and '86 are just about as brilliant as claret can be, while the '88 may well be the wine of the vintage. The deep, concentrated '89 doesn't seem to match up to the '88, but the 1990 is as fragrant and powerful as the 1986 – which is saying a lot.

**MEYNEY** *cru bourgeois St-Estèphe* ★★★(★) £ This epitomizes the reliability of St-Estèphe, yet is better than that. The wine is big, meaty and strong, but never harsh. Vintages in the 1970s lacked personality, but recent wines are increasingly impressive and although the wine is difficult to taste young, the '82, '83, '85, '86, '88 and '89 are remarkable and the '84, '87 and '90 good.

**LA MISSION-HAUT-BRION** *cru classé Pessac-Léognan* ★★★(★) La Mission likes to put itself in a class apart, between Haut-Brion and the rest. Yet one often feels this relies more on weight and massive, dark fruit and oak flavours than on any great subtleties. For those, you go to Haut-Brion or Domaine de Chevalier. '82, '85 or '86 are recommendable of recent vintages.

**MONTROSE** *2ème cru classé St-Estèphe* ★★★★ Traditionally famous for its dark, tannic character, and its slow, ponderous march to maturity. For a wine with such a sturdy reputation, some recent vintages have seemed faintly hollow. 1986 made amends with a really chewy, long-distance number, and '87 was densely structured, if hardly classic, but it's taken until '89 and '90 for the wine to really return to form. The château, which tends to pick rather early, came into its own in '89 and '90, and even made a decent '91. The second wine, Dame de Montrose, has been a bargain these past four years.

**MOUTON-ROTHSCHILD** *1er cru classé Pauillac* ★★★★★ After 50 years of well-orchestrated lobbying, Baron Philippe de Rothschild managed to raise Mouton to First Growth status in 1973. Of course it should be a First Growth. But then several Fifths should probably be Seconds. The wine does have an astonishing flavour, piling an intense cigar-box and lead-pencil perfume on to the rich blackcurrant fruit. The 1982 is already a legend, the '86 and '89 are likely to join '82, and the '85, '84 and '83 are well worth the asking price.

**NENIN** *Pomerol* ★★ A thoroughly old-fashioned wine. It quite rightly pleases the royal family, who order rather a lot of it. But in fact it is rather chunky and solid and has quite a tough core for a Pomerol, which doesn't always disperse into mellow fruitfulness. The 1985 and '86 aren't bad, but, really, the '82, the '83 and the '88, all good vintages, were pretty feeble.

**PALMER** *3ème cru classé Margaux* ★★★★ 'Most expensive of the Third Growths?' asks one of Palmer's owners. 'No. Cheapest of the Firsts.' There's (some) truth in that. Until 1978 Palmer used to out-Margaux Margaux for sheer beauty and perfume. And it still can occasionally out-perform some of the First Growths in tastings. It was consistently brilliant in the 1960s and 1970s (excepting '64), but the 1980s have seen it lose some of its sure touch, and the '83 lacks some of its neighbours' class. '87 and '88 are very good too, but are closer in style to out-Beychevelling Beychevelle. '89 is cedary and elegant, rich but tannic, in a year when not all Margaux wines had great depth of fruit. In 1990 Palmer was better than most, but not all, of its neighbours.

**PAPE-CLÉMENT** *cru classé Pessac-Léognan* ★★★★★ One of the top properties in Pessac-Léognan, capable of mixing a considerable sweetness from ripe fruit and new oak with a good deal of tough structure. 1975 was great, but then we had a very poor decade until 1985. The last five vintages are outstanding, with the 1990 an example of Pessac-Léognan at its best.

**PAVIE** *1er grand cru St-Émilion* ★★★★ The biggest major property in St-Émilion, with high yields, too. Until recently good without being wonderful, stylish without being grand. Still, Pavie does have the true

gentle flavours of good St-Émilion and recent releases are showing a deeper, more passionate style which puts it into the top flight. 1990, '89, '88, '87, '86 and '85 are good examples of the new, '82 of the old.

**PETIT-VILLAGE** *Pomerol* ★★★★ A fairly pricy wine, it is not one of the soft, plummy Pomerols, and until recently there was a fair amount of Cabernet giving backbone. The wine is worth laying down, but the price is always high. 1985, '83 and the absurdly juicy '82 are all very good, but the '88 and '89 look likely to be the best yet.

**PÉTRUS** *Pomerol* ★★★★★ One of the world's most expensive reds, and often one of the greatest. Astonishingly, its reputation, though surfacing briefly in 1878, has only been made since World War Two, and in particular since 1962, when the firm of Jean-Pierre Moueix took a half-share in the property. This firm has given the kiss of life to many Pomerol properties, turning potential into achievement, and with Pétrus it has a supreme creation. Christian Moueix says his intention is to ensure no bottle of Pétrus ever disappoints. 1982 and 1989 were stupendously great. 1985 isn't far off it, nor is '81 and the only example from the last 20 years which seemed atypical is the rather Médoc-like 1978. Can they keep it up in the face of blistering world demand?

**DE PEZ** *cru bourgeois St-Estèphe* ★★★ One of the most famous *bourgeois* châteaux, the wine is almost always of Classed Growth standard, big, rather plummy and not too harsh. 1982 and '83 were very attractive, though some prefer the more unashamedly St-Estèphe wines made during the 1970s, which saw a bit of a comeback with the excellent '86.

**PICHON-LONGUEVILLE** *2ème cru classé Pauillac* ★★★★(★) (since 1987) Often described as more masculine than its 'sister', Pichon-Lalande, this tremendously correct but diffident Pauillac (formerly

Pichon-Longueville-Baron) was until 1987 only hinting at its potential. Drier and lighter than Lalande, it was also less immediately impressive, despite ageing well. 1987 saw the property being bought by the Axa insurance company and the supremely talented Jean-Michel Cazes of Lynch-Bages being brought in to run it. The '87 was very good, the '88 superb, the '89 *tremendous*, broodingly intense, while the '90 is one of the Médoc's greatest wines.

**PICHON-LALANDE** *2ème cru classé Pauillac* ★★★★★ Pichon-Lalande announced its intentions with a stunning 1970, and since then has been making a rich, oaky, concentrated wine of tremendous quality. Its price has climbed inexorably and it wishes to be seen as the equal partner of St-Julien's leading pair, Léoville-Las-Cases and Ducru-Beaucaillou. 1982, '83 and '85 all brim with exciting flavours, and they think '86 is even better. '87 doesn't quite reach the same standards, but '88 does, and '89 is velvety, elegant and seductively fruity. With the revival of Pichon-Longueville over the road, the rivalry between these properties has produced some stunning twins, notably in 1990, when there were virtually identical.

**PONTET-CANET** *5ème cru classé Pauillac* ★★(★) The biggest Classed Growth. Famous but unpredictable, and still trying to find its traditionally reliable form. 1985 and '86 are hopeful, '87 and '88 less so, '90 hopeful again as the owners become more selective.

**POTENSAC** *cru bourgeois Médoc* ★★★(★) £ The most exciting of the Bas-Médoc properties, since it is owned by Michel Delon of Léoville-Las-Cases, and a broadly similar style of wine-making is pursued. This gives wines with a delicious, blackcurrant fruit, greatly improved by a strong taste of oak from once-used Las-Cases barrels. Not expensive for the quality. Beats many *crus classés* every year for sheer flavour.

**PRIEURÉ-LICHINE** *4ème cru classé Margaux* ★★★ One of the more reliable Margaux wines, and in years like 1970, 1971 and 1975 it excelled. Recently it has been fairly priced and although not that perfumed, a good, sound Margaux. 1983, '86, '88 and '89 are all good, but '90 is the first really exciting wine for some time.

**RAUSAN-SÉGLA** *2ème cru classé Margaux* ★★★★(★) Up to and including the 1982 vintage this lovely property, rated second only to Mouton-Rothschild in the 1855 Second Growths, had been woefully underachieving for a couple of generations. But a dynamic change of ownership in 1983 saw a triumphant return to quality – in the very first year! Many proprietors moan that it takes ten or 20 years to improve a property's performance. 1983, '85 and '86 were triumphs. 1987 was declassified as Château Lamouroux but is still delicious. The '88 is a supreme achievement which the '89 matches and the '90 surpasses.

**RAUZAN-GASSIES** *2ème cru classé Margaux* ★★ Right behind Rausan-Ségla, but the wine is leagues below most Second and Third Growths in quality, and so far hasn't taken the hint from Ségla that quality pays in the end.

**ST-PIERRE** *4ème cru classé Médoc* ★★★★ Small St-Julien property producing superb, underrated, old-fashioned claret. Once under-priced, but the image-conscious Henri Martin of Gloria put paid to that when he took over in 1982. Still, the quality has been worth the asking price, and while the 1970 and '75 were underrated stars, the wines of the 1980s are possibly even better. Since Martin's death in 1991, the future is uncertain.

**DE SALES** *Pomerol* ★★★ £ An enormous estate, the biggest in Pomerol by a street. This vastness may show a little in a wine, which, though it is good round claret, doesn't often excite. The 1985 is very nice, the '83 and '82 are very nice.

**SIRAN** *cru bourgeois Margaux* ★★★★
This château is sometimes mistaken for a
Classed Growth in blind tastings, this
property is indeed mostly made up from
the land of Châteaux Dauzac and Giscours.
The '85 and '83 are the most successful
wines of recent years, but all vintages have
been good lately. The '88 was a bit clumsy,
but the '89 and '90 vintages are showing
well, hence its extra (bracketed) star this
year.

**TALBOT** *4ème cru classé St-Julien* ★★★★
One of the most carefully made and
reliable of the fleshier St-Juliens, suffering
only in comparison with its sister château
in the former Cordier stable, Gruaud-
Larose, and always offering value for
money and tremendous consistency. Maybe
the name Talbot just lacks the right ring?
Whatever the reason, you must seek out
the exciting 1986, the super-classy '85, '83
and '82 and the ultra-stylish '84, as well as
the lovely '87, the impressive '88 and the
big, rich '89. The '90, however, seems to
lack something in the way of
concentration.

**DU TERTRE** *5ème cru classé Margaux*
★★★(★) This wine is unusually good, with
a lot of body for a Margaux, but that weight
is all ripe, strong fruit and the flavour is
direct and pure. Funnily enough, it's not
cheap for a relative unknown but neither is
it expensive for the quality. The '85 is rich
and dense and yet keeps its perfume intact,
while the '86, '83 and '82 are rich and
blackcurranty – already good and sure to
improve for ten years more. '88 was not
quite so good, for some reason, but '89 was
back to normal.

**TROTANOY** *Pomerol* ★★★★ If you didn't
know Château Pétrus existed, you'd say
this had to be the perfect Pomerol – rich,
plummy, chocolaty fruit, some mineral
hardness, and tremendous fat perfume. It's
very, very good, and makes Pétrus'
achievement in eclipsing it (in a friendly
way) all the more amazing. The '82 is
brilliant, and although the '85 is also
wonderfully good, the vintages of the mid
and late 1980s haven't been quite as
thrilling as have previous examples of this
château.

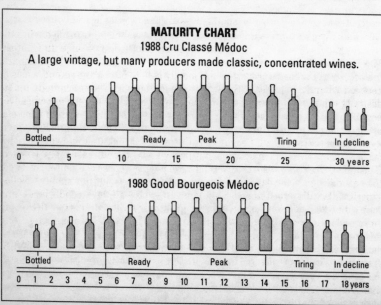

**MATURITY CHART**
### 1988 Cru Classé Médoc
A large vintage, but many producers made classic, concentrated wines.

| Bottled | | Ready | Peak | | Tiring | In decline |
|---|---|---|---|---|---|---|
| 0 | 5 | 10 | 15 | 20 | 25 | 30 years |

### 1988 Good Bourgeois Médoc

| Bottled | | | | | Ready | | | | Peak | | | | | Tiring | | | In decline |
|---|---|---|---|---|---|---|---|---|---|---|---|---|---|---|---|---|---|
| 0 | 1 | 2 | 3 | 4 | 5 | 6 | 7 | 8 | 9 | 10 | 11 | 12 | 13 | 14 | 15 | 16 | 17 | 18 years |

# SECOND WINES

The second wines from the major Bordeaux châteaux can be defined, broadly, as being wines from the same vineyard as the *grand vin* (the wine with the château name) which, for quality reasons, have been 'selected out' of the top wine. Legally they could be included, but maintaining the *grand vin*'s quality is vital.

These may be the produce of particularly young vines, which won't have the concentration and staying power demanded from an expensive Classed Growth. They may be from sections of the vineyard that, owing to the vagaries of the weather, didn't produce quite the right style, or that are just traditionally less good. Or they may include first-class wine from mature vines and good parts of the vineyard that just doesn't fit into this particular vintage of the *grand vin* style. For example, if the Merlot grape produces an enormous crop and the tougher Cabernet falls a bit short on quantity, then a winemaker may decide to use less Merlot, so as to preserve the balance he wants.

Then there is another form of second wine. Sometimes a major château buys up a lesser property nearby, and begins to use its label for its second wine. Since it is in the same appellation this is perfectly legal. Cos d'Estournel uses the seven-hectare vineyard of Château Marbuzet like this, and Lynch-Bages uses Haut-Bages-Avérous in the same way.

If you talk to retailers about the Bordeaux market in Britain, more and more will tell you that sales of remotely ready to drink Classed Growths are gradually becoming almost irrelevant to their business. Apart from a few old-established companies and one or two new up-market specialists, very few retailers now sell more than token amounts of mature *grand vin* claret. But the desire to trade up is as strong as ever. It's just the ridiculous price which people balk at.

### Declassified class

And that's where the second wines have made phenomenal inroads during the last couple of years. If we leave out wine such as Pavillon Rouge du Château Margaux and Les Forts de Latour, which are usually priced at the £15 plus mark, the other top Bordeaux properties are mostly able to offer their second wines at between £8 and £10 a bottle. Sure, that is a lot, but given the seemingly innate desire of the British to drink decent claret as their 'high days' wine whenever possible, and given the fact that at three to four years old, the second wine of a property like Léoville-Barton, Pichon-Longueville, Pichon-Lalande, Palmer, Lynch-Bages or, above all, Léoville-Las-Cases can be outstandingly attractive – far less tannic than the main wine, but fleshy and soft and reasonably oaky too. Consumers can really taste the class they are buying. Marks & Spencer really got the ball rolling a few years ago with its smartly turned out but simply labelled generics – Pauillac, St-Estèphe, St-Julien and so on – all top second wines – and they sold like hot cakes, especially at Christmas. As top properties declassify more and more of their wine to maintain the densely structured, dark, long distance style which is popular with the château owners and the trade at the moment, the second wines will play a bigger and bigger part in our market. In years like '85, '86, '88, '89 and '90 top properties might declassify as much as 40 per cent. Twenty years ago many of them wouldn't declassify at all, and more than ten per cent was very rare. But recently, as prices have risen, the owners have realized that to justify the price, the quality has to be something special.

We should take immediate advantage. Not only to drink now, but also to lay down. Good second wines do have a ten year life expectancy from the good vintages of the '80s, although there are lighter styles – like some of the AC Margaux properties, and the delicious but delicate wines of a label like Lacoste-Borie (Grand-Puy-Lacoste) which are so good at five years old it seems a pity to wait. But if you've got the wherewithal – try a bottle of the *grand vin* next to a bottle of the second wine. This is a wine lover's game we'll also see a lot more of in the next decade or so. There's no question of not being able to tell them apart. The second wine almost always lacks a little of the drive, a little of the lingering, tantalizing flavour of the *grand vin*. The flavours that shout at you in the *grand vin* are more likely to whisper in the second wine. Well, that's as it should be: if you buy the *grand vin*, that's what you're paying for. But they'll be ready to drink much more quickly, and that is often their chief virtue. They give you a suggestion, within four or five years of the vintage, of the glorious flavours the *grand vin* may take 20 years to achieve.

## Reading the small print

Just one word of caution. The number of second wines appearing on the market has mushroomed. If you see an unfamiliar name on a bottle with a familiar *appellation contrôlée*, look at the small print on the bottom of the label. If it's a real château it'll just say something like 'Propriétaire M Major et Fils' or something like 'Société Civile' of the main name on the label. But it may also say 'Société Civile' of one of the well-known properties in the AC. In which case it is almost certain to be a second wine of that property. Some proprietors own more than one property in the AC – Jacques Lurton of Brane Cantenac and Durfort Vivens is an example – in which case it may say something like 'Domaine Lurton' on the second wine label.

And another cautionary note. There are a lot of ambitious properties in lesser ACs – like Listrac, Moulis, Haut-Médoc, St-Émilion, Lalande-de-Pomerol, even Côtes de Francs. Many of these are starting to utilize second labels for their lesser *cuvées*. That's fine; the wine can be good and not expensive. But make a rule – don't buy the second wine of a property you don't think is up to much in the first place. It'll just be a worse example of a not very good wine. And, despite the pronouncements of one or two leading Bordeaux figures about '87 being the year for second wines – don't buy second wines from indifferent vintages. To take 1987 as an example, the properties who cared to make fine wine in 1987 did so because they declassified as much as half their wine. Almost all of this would be the unripe Cabernet Sauvignon hit by vintage-time rains. There is nothing less likely to give you drinking pleasure in the short term than unripe, dilute Cabernet Sauvignon. So don't touch it. (The exception I would make is Château Lamouroux which is the declassified Rausan-Ségla – but they declassified all their wine and the result is delicious. And Palmer and Angludet sold some extremely attractive wine to large groups in the UK for drinking at less than two years old which was also a delight.) Anyway, 1987 is the year we can afford to buy the *grand vin* – so whatever the Bordelais try to tell us, what we don't want is their '87 slops. 1985 was basically a year when Merlot and Cabernet both overproduced and the second wines are absolutely lovely for now and to keep. A 1987 Classed Growth *grand vin* should be better than '86 *grand vin* and not necessarily much more expensive, but there should be some good '89s and '90s to look forward to, and '88s to keep us going until then.

# RECOMMENDED WINES

Most of these (and we have starred the ones we feel are the best bets) are from the Haut-Médoc, since properties there are larger and the opportunities for selection much greater. Some retail chains are now doing 'generic' wines which are in fact classy second wines. These are usually very good buys. And don't feel you're buying a second rate modern invention. Château Margaux produced its first Pavillon Rouge du Château Margaux in 1908, and Léoville-Las-Cases created its second label, Clos du Marquis, in 1904. But the habit faded in the 1930s as the owners rushed to sell everything as *grand vin* simply to survive. Only recently has it been revived.

## Haut-Médoc

*1st Growth*: ★les Forts-de-Latour (Latour), Moulin-des-Carruades (Lafite), ★Pavillon-Rouge-du-Château Margaux (Margaux).

*2nd Growth*: ★le Baronnet-de-Pichon (Pichon-Longueville), ★Clos du Marquis (Léoville-Las-Cases), ★la Croix (Ducru-Beaucaillou), la Dame de Montrose (Montrose), Domaine de Curebourse (Durfort-Vivens), ★Lamouroux (Rausan-Ségla), ★Marbuzet (Cos d'Estournel), Moulin-Riche (Léoville-Poyferré), Notton (Brane-Cantenac), ★Réserve de la Comtesse (Pichon-Lalande), ★St-Julien (Léoville-Barton), ★Sarget de Gruaud-Larose (Gruaud-Larose), ★les Tourelles-de-Pichon (Pichon-Longueville).

*3rd Growths*: ★Fiefs de Lagrange (Lagrange), ★St-Julien (Langoa), de Loyac (Malescot St-Exupéry), Ludon-Pomies-Agassac (la Lagune), Marquis-de-Ségur (Calon-Ségur), ★Réserve du Général (Palmer).

*4th Growths*: de Clairefont (Prieuré-Lichine), Connétable-Talbot (Talbot), des Goudat (Marquis de Terme), Moulin-de-Duhart (Duhart-Milon-Rothschild), ★Réserve de l'Amiral (Beychevelle), St-Louis-le-Bosq (St-Pierre).

*5th Growths*: Artigue-Arnaud (Grand-Puy-Ducasse), Enclos de Moncabon (Croizet-Bages), ★Haut-Bages-Avérous (Lynch-Bages), les Hauts-de-Pontet (PontetCanet), ★Lacoste-Borie (Grand-Puy-Lacoste), ★Villeneuve-de-Cantemerle (Cantemerle).

*Good Bourgeois Châteaux*: Abiet (Cissac), ★Admiral (Labégorce-Zédé), Bellegarde (Siran), Bory (Angludet), ★Clos Cordat (Monbrison), Domaine de Martiny (Cissac), Domaine Zédé (Labégorce-Zédé), Ermitage de Chasse-Spleen (Chasse-Spleen), Labat (Caronne-Ste-Gemme), Granges-de-Clarke (Clarke), ★Lartigue-de-Brochon (Sociando-Mallet), ★Lassalle (Potensac), Moulin d'Arrigny (Beaumont), Prieur de Meyney (Meyney), Réserve du Marquis d'Evry (Lamarque), ★Tour de Marbuzet (Haut-Marbuzet) ★Salle-de-Poujeaux (Poujeaux).

## Graves, Pessac-Léognan

★Abeille de Fieuzal (Fieuzal), Bahans-Haut-Brion (Haut-Brion), ★Batard-Chevalier (Domaine de Chevalier), ★Coucheroy (la Louvière), ★Hauts de Smith-Haut-Lafitte (Smith-Haut-Lafitte), ★la Parde-de-Haut-Bailly (Haut-Bailly).

## St Emilion

Beau-Mayne (Couvent des Jacobins), ★Domaine de Martialis (Clos Fourtet), ★Franc-Grace-Dieu (Canon), Jean du Nayne (Angelus),Grangeneuve-de-Figeac (Figeac), ★des Templiers (Larmande).

## Pomerol

Chantalouette (de Sales), Clos Toulifaut (Taillefer), ★Fleur de Clinet (Clinet), la Gravette-de-Certan (Vieux-Château-Certan), Monregard-Lacroix (Clos du Clocher), ★la Petite Église (l'Église Clinet).

## Bordeaux Supérieur Côtes de Francs,

les Douves de Francs (de Francs), ★Lauriol (Puygueraud).

# CLARETS OUT OF THEIR CLASS

Trying to rearrange the Classification of 1855 is a regional pastime. These days there is many a Fifth Growth that should perhaps be a Second or Third, and some Seconds or Thirds that should be Fourths or Fifths.

One of the most exciting things for a claret devotee is to catch a château at the beginning of a revival in its fortunes. While a reputation is being built or re-built, the quality will keep ahead of the price. However, the price will rise – and while in the old days it might have taken a painstaking decade or two, nowadays you can go from mediocrity to magnificence in a bare two or three years.

The problem for the drinker is complicated by the competitive nature of the growers who, naturally, see price as a yardstick of quality. In the late 1970s, there was a handful of Second Growths – most obviously Ducru-Beaucaillou, Pichon-Lalande and Léoville-Las-Cases – which rose above their peers, in price and quality, while others – notably Cos d'Estournel and Léoville-Barton – kept quality up and prices (relatively) down. The same process was repeated in the late 1980s with the emergence of some excellent but over-priced 'super' *crus bourgeois*. Monbrison, Poujeaux-Thiel, Chasse-Spleen, Sociando-Malet, all got above themselves. Fortunately 1991 sobered them up.

### Médoc

*Minor châteaux performing like top* bourgeois *wines:* Andron-Blanquet, Cartillon, le Fournas Bernadotte, de Junca, Lamothe, Malescasse, Maucamps, Moulin-de-Laborde, Patache-d'Aux, Peyrabon, Ramage-la-Bâtisse, la Tour-de-By, la Tour-du-Haut-Moulin, la Tour-Pibran, la Tour-St-Joseph, Victoria.

*Top* bourgeois *performing like Classed Growths:* d'Angludet, Brillette, Chasse-Spleen, Chambert-Marbuzet, Cissac, la Gurgue, Hanteillan, Haut-Marbuzet, Gressier-Grand-Poujeaux, Hortevie, Labégorce-Zédé, Lanessan, Maucaillou, Meyney, Monbrison, les Ormes-de-Pez, de Pez, Potensac, Poujeaux, Siran, Sociando-Mallet, la Tour-de-Mons.

*Classed Growths outperforming their classification:* Camensac, Cantemerle, Clerc-Milon-Rothschild, Grand-Puy-Lacoste, Haut-Bages-Libéral, d'Issan, Lagrange, la Lagune, Langoa-Barton, Léoville-Barton, Lynch-Bages, Marquis d'Alesme-Becker, Rausan-Ségla, St-Pierre, du Tertre, la Tour-Carnet. Since 1987 Pichon-Longueville has been top flight.

### Graves

*Outperformers:* Cabannieux (white), Domaine la Grave (white), Montalivet (red and white), Rahoul (red), Roquetaillade-la-Grange (red and white), Cardaillan.

### Pessac-Léognan

*Outperformers:* Carbonnieux (white), Couhins-Lurton (white), Cruzeau, de Fieuzal (red and white), la Louvière (red and white), Malartic-Lagravière (red and white), Rochemorin, Smith-Haut-Lafitte (white, and red since 1988), la Tour-Martillac.

### Pomerol

*Outperformers:* Bertineau St-Vincent (Lalande-de-Pomerol), Belles Graves (Lalande-de-Pomerol), le Bon-Pasteur, Bourgneuf-Vayron, Certan de May, Clinet, Clos du Clocher, Clos René, L'Eglise Clinet, Feytit-Clinet, la Fleur-St-Georges (Lalande-de-Pomerol), Franc-Maillet, Grand Ormeau (Lalande-de-Pomerol), la Grave-Trigant-de-Boisset, les Hautes-Tuileries (Lalande-de-Pomerol), Latour-à-Pomerol, Lavaud la Maréchaude (Lalande-de-Pomerol), Siaurac (Lalande-de-Pomerol), les Templiers (Lalande-de-Pomerol).

| **St-Émilion** | **Sauternes** |
|---|---|
| *Outperformers:* l'Arrosée, Balestard-la-Tonnelle, Bellefont-Belcier, Berliquet, Cadet-Piola, Cardinal-Villemaurine, la Dominique, de Ferrand, Fombrauge, Larmande, Monbousquet, Montlabert, Pavie-Decesse, St-Georges, la Serre, Tertre-Rôteboeuf, Troplong-Mondot, Vieux-Château-Mazerat. | *Outperformers non-classed:* Bastor-Lamontagne, Chartreuse, de Fargues, Gilette, Guiteronde, les Justices, Liot, Menota, Raymond-Lafon, St-Amand.<br><br>*Outperforming Classed Growths:* d'Arche, Doisy-Daëne, Doisy-Védrines, de Malle, Nairac. |

## CLARET VINTAGES

Claret vintages are accorded more importance than those of any other wine; so much so that good wine from a less popular vintage can get swamped under all the brouhaha. We have had a parade of 'vintages of the century', although the noise and fuss more often start in Bordeaux itself or on the volatile American market than in more cautious – or more cynical – Britain.

Wines age at different rates according to their vintage. They may get more delicious or less so as they mature; some may be at their best before they are fully mature, because, although their balance may not be terribly impressive, at least they've got a good splash of young fruit. Wines also mature differently according to the quality of the property.

The generic *appellations* – like Bordeaux Supérieur – rarely need any ageing. So a 1985, for instance, from a *premier cru*, might take twenty years to be at its best, a good *bourgeois* might take ten, and a *petit château* might take five years.

The grape variety is also important. Wines based on the Cabernet Sauvignon and/or Cabernet Franc (many of the Médocs and the Graves) will mature more slowly than wines based on the Merlot (most Pomerols and St-Émilions).

In the following tables, A = quality; B = value for money; C = drink now; D = lay down.

**1991** After the Great Frost, a miserable May and June did not help matters, though hopes rose after an August which was the hottest on record. The more optimistic growers started to talk of a repeat of 1961, when a spring frost produced a small but perfectly formed vintage.

Trouble restarted in late September, just as the harvest was beginning in the Médoc. Rain fell heavily and the growers, faced with the usual problem of rot after late rains, had to decide whether to try and harvest both generations of grapes. Although the second crop (formed after frost damage to the first) was still relatively unripe the two were virtually indistinguishable (especially to mechanical harvesters) since by that time all the grapes were their normal purple-black. Only a separate analysis of each grape could tell the two generations apart.

Those growers who waited a few days for the grapes to ripen but managed to pick before 14 October stood the best chance of making decent wines. At that point the rain started in earnest and all hope for improvement had to be abandoned. The result was a small and wildly variable vintage, but not as small as has been suggested by merchants anxious to dispose of their stocks of earlier years. As far as red wines were concerned it was less than half the amount made in the two previous vintages, but the region has become so used to record crops that everyone has forgotten how much more wine is now being made than even a few years ago. In fact in 1991 a tenth more claret was made than in 1984, and in the 1970s it would have been considered a perfectly decent crop, at least in size.

Naturally the best wines were made by the handful of châteaux nearest the Gironde, some of which (like Margaux) went through the vineyard in July getting rid of the still-green second generation of grapes while the first crop was starting to change colour. In other cases (like Cos) the new and the old were in clearly distinguishable plots. But elsewhere there was a lot of confusion, so 1991 is one of those difficult years (like 1987) when you stick to the very best estates, stars like Margaux, Latour, Ducru-Beaucaillou and Léoville-Las-Cases. Montrose also stood out: its vines face the river and were little affected, and Jean-Louis Charmolue is famous for picking early, so he got his grapes in before the rains. So even his second wine (Dame de Montrose) is good value. Among the *crus bourgeois* reliable estates like Chasse-Spleen and Sociando-Malet came up to scratch. In the Graves a few estates like Smith-Haut-Lafitte and La Tour Martillac made decent wines.

But all the growers faced the problem of the mixture of grapes from both generations and the lightness of late-picked wines diluted by the rains. I agree with merchants Lay & Wheeler that 'the best are fragrant and attractive, but they are not wines to lay down'. In the Libournais the situation was already worse, with nine-tenths of most crops simply wiped out in the frost. The combination of second-crop grapes and the rain means that few reputable growers are marketing 1991 wines under their château labels, instead usually shipping the little wine they did make under a generic label, although there were a few more-than-acceptable wines, notably Gazin.

And the prices? Happily, unlike in 1984, they reflect the lower quality of the wine. The first-growths dropped FF40 to a mere FF160 (Haut Brion sold at FF150) and there has been a corresponding 20 per cent drop elsewhere, bringing an excellent wine like Haut-Bages-Liberal down to a mere FF32. But, frankly, stick to the bargains. These will never be great wines.

Instead they will be agreeable, light, easier to drink than the 1987s but, like that other vintage which was damned at first, very decent in four or five years' time, if you can find the right wine at the right price.

**1990** (AD) For the third consecutive year and for the eighth time in a decade, the harvest was excellent if not superlative. If statistics alone were sufficient to create good wine, 1990 would certainly make well-justified claims to being one of the best of the century: the sum of average temperatures was higher than in any year since 1947 and there were more hours of sunshine than in any year since 1949. There was also a far from contemptible amount of rainfall; albeit chiefly falling in two great bucketfuls at the end of August and in the fourth week of September. August was hotter than in 1989: only those notable scorchers 1947 and 1949 had the edge on it.

The freak weather conditions began even before the buds appeared on the vines. The winter was not only mild, there were periods when it might have put an English summer to shame. There was rain in spring and a little frost during the often bitter period of late April; flowering, however, took place during the hot spell in May. This was especially true of the earlier ripening Merlot and Cabernet Franc; some of the Cabernet Sauvignon vines didn't flower until June.

With an abundant vintage in sight the better estates began to prune bunches from the vines to concentrate the goodness in a very small number. The hot weather lasted, only briefly broken, from the second week in July until October. A little rain fell during the picking of the Cabernet Sauvignon in the first half of October, but not enough to affect the quality seriously.

Bordeaux is a hot, dry place; but by anyone's description, 1990 was an exceptionally hot year. That might not have been so important as far as the vines were concerned if it had not been for the fact that 1989 had been similar; and that there had been virtually no winter in which to recuperate . As the heat set in, the vines became severely stressed. In these circumstances it is generally the old vines which cope best, as their roots have pushed their way into every nook and cranny where they know water can be found. In a very hot year a water-collecting, clay-based subsoil is an advantage: those vines grown on well-drained pebbles (chiefly Cabernet Sauvignon) were in for a hard time in 1990.

With some notable exceptions, the Merlot-based wines did better than those primarily made from Cabernet Sauvignon. Some Médoc properties (Latour is unusual in this) have a subsoil of clay.

On the whole the very hot summer and lack of rain during the ripening season meant that the acidity was low and the alcohol high. Some vats were recorded with an alcohol content of over 14 degrees which is hardly a manifestation of the elegance so often vaunted in Bordeaux. The lack of acidity will also mean that the wines are not destined for the longest shelflife. Some may be very good and exceptionally ripe; but they were not made to be stashed into the furthest corner of your cellar or laying down for your first-born's 21st.

The quality has been widely reported as uneven. In the very north of the Médoc (the area that used to be called the Bas Médoc), the wines fared well. Also good were St-Estèphes from the most northerly of the Médoc Classed Growths; as you go further south, however, through Pauillac, St-Julien and Margaux, quality is far more variable: some very nice wines, yes, but to be chosen with care. Across the Gironde where the Merlot dominates the mix, the alcohol in the wines tends to be too high to produce wines of the elegance which is meant to typify Bordeaux in a good year.

Following the traumas of 1991 it is now clear that 1990 was the last of the 'trois glorieuses' along with 1988 and 1989. Of the three it now seems clear that anyone looking for a classic Bordeaux vintage (albeit a tough and tannic one) should opt for the 1988; the last two vintages having

been too unusual to produce wines in the old claret mould, though many were splendid, if richer and fruitier than old-style claret buffs would like. Modern drinkers, immersed in rich Australian reds, will lap them up.

**1989** (AD) For those who like to designate a Bordeaux vintage as either a Merlot year or a Cabernet year, this was one in which the Cabernet Sauvignon couldn't fail to ripen well, and in fact most of the Cabernet grapes brought in were deliciously, juicily ripe. Merlot was more of a problem. Grown to add ripeness and fatness to a possibly lean Cabernet, in 1989 the Merlot grapes were in most cases fully ripe at the beginning of September. It became a balancing act, attempting to catch the grapes *before* acidity got too low but *after* the tannins were ripe.

1989 will become known as a year when the decisions of the winemaker were particularly crucial. When it came to assessing vats for the final blend, some of the early-picked wines were found to be far too 'green-tasting'. The better châteaux will have eliminated these batches from the *grand vin*, but there will still be a fair number of rawish-tasting wines around. *Petits châteaux* looked disappointing early.

Prices, needless to say, went up, even though this was a gigantic crop and a record for AC reds was reached at nearly five million hectolitres. But the growers claimed that the 1988 First Growths increased in value by 50 per cent within a year of picking; they felt little pressure on them to keep prices down.

So to specifics. In the Haut-Médoc, Cantemerle stood out from others, followed by La Tour de By, Coufran, Citran and Lanessan. Rausan-Ségla in Margaux is back on form. Giscours, d'Issan, du Tertre, Lascombes and Cantenac-Brown were very successful, but overall it may not prove to be a Margaux year.

Elsewhere in the Haut-Médoc the wines seem juicier, fruitier, better constructed for the long haul. In St-Julien,

Langoa-Barton, Léoville-Barton, Beychevelle, Gruaud-Larose, Talbot, Branaire-Ducru were all excellent with Ducru-Beaucaillou a notch above. In Pauillac, Haut-Batailley looks back on form, sturdy, rich Pichon-Longueville a lovely counterpoint to the elegance of Pichon-Lalande, Latour impressively magnificent, combining power with finesse.

In St-Estèphe Montrose attracted attention with a triumphant return to the top, and also successful were Cos Labory, Meyney and Lafon-Rochet.

Over on the right bank, St Émilion and Pomerol defied attempts to call this a Cabernet year by producing Merlot wines of great richness and charm, from First Growths down. Best so far seem to be Canon-la-Gaffelière, Balestard la Tonnelle, Larmande, Cap-de-Moulin, Troplong-Mondot among the good value ranks, elsewhere there is Canon, La Conseillante, Gazin, Clinet, L'Evangile, Clos Fourtet, Pavie, an especially powerful L'Angélus, and a Cheval-Blanc of tremendous concentration and fragrance.

The Graves and Pessac-Léognan produced more uneven levels of quality on the whole, and although Domaine de Chevalier and Pape Clément are as classy as you would hope, only de Fieuzal, La Louvière and Haut-Bailly stood out from the rest.

**1988** (AD) A difficult year, saved by a long warm summer – a vintage which could yield the most classically balanced claret of the '80s.

Graves/Pessac-Léognan yielded a remarkable range of wines, and it really showed how they are getting their act together down there. Special efforts from La Louvière, Larrivet-Haut-Brion, de France, Smith-Haut-Lafitte (a joyous return to the top rank), Fieuzal, Olivier (another wine coming out of the shadows), La Tour-Martillac, Malartic-Lagravière, Pape-Clément, Haut-Bailly and Domaine de Chevalier. In the Médoc, La Lagune was good and Cantemerle as good as the

inspiring '83. Margaux was less exciting, but there were good wines from Angludet, d'Issan, Tertre, Prieuré-Lichine, Palmer, Durfort-Vivens (at last) and superb efforts from Monbrison, Rausan-Ségla and Margaux. Chasse-Spleen and Poujeaux were the best of the Moulis while St-Julien had beautiful wines from Beychevelle, Gloria, St-Pierre, Talbot, Gruaud, Ducru-Beaucaillou, Langoa-Barton and Léoville-Barton. Pauillac did very well, with Lafite, Grand-Puy-Lacoste, Haut-Bages-Libéral and Pichon-Lalande all excellent, and tip-top Lynch-Bages and the triumphantly resurrected Pichon-Longueville. St-Estèphe made its best vintage for several years, with consistently high quality from Cos d'Estournel, Calon-Ségur, Les Ormes-de-Pez, Meyney, Cos Labory and Lafon Rochet. The northern Médoc was a success too, in particular at Cissac, Hanteillan, Sociando-Mallet, La Tour-de-By, Potensac.

Pomerol made some excellent wines, and should have made more, but overproduction diluted the quality in many cases and they taste rather one-dimensional. Best so far seem to be Clinet, Beauregard, Évangile, Moulinet, l'Enclos, Vieux-Château-Certan, with improved efforts from La Croix-de-Gay and La Pointe. St-Émilion made superb wines, as good as 1985 and '82. Cheval-Blanc and Figeac lead the way, followed by Canon, Pavie, L'Angélus, Larmande, Fonplégade, Canon-la-Gaffelière, Balestard-la-Tonnelle, Couvent-des-Jacobins and Clos des Jacobins.

**1987** (BCD) There *are* lean, unbalanced edgy wines in 1987 – often made by the same uninspired proprietors who made mediocre '88s. But the overall style of the vintage is wonderfully soft and ridiculously drinkable, the soft Merlot fruit combining with good new oak to produce light but positively lush reds, totally unlike the other two vintages it tends to be bracketed with, 1984 and 1980. These will happily last up to ten years, but you can start really enjoying them *now*.

## MATURITY CHART
### 1985 Cru Classé Médoc
### Although delicious young, these wines will repay keeping

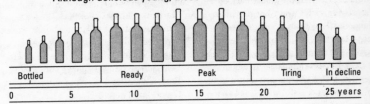

| Bottled | Ready | Peak | Tiring | In decline |
|---|---|---|---|---|

0      5      10      15      20      25 years

### 1985 Good Bourgeois Médoc

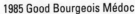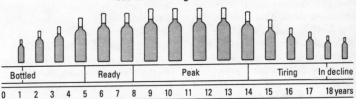

| Bottled | Ready | Peak | Tiring | In decline |
|---|---|---|---|---|

0   1   2   3   4   5   6   7   8   9   10   11   12   13   14   15   16   17   18 years

### 1986 Cru Classé Médoc
### A great vintage that requires patience

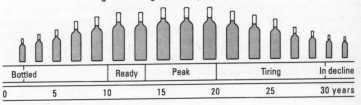

| Bottled | Ready | Peak | Tiring | In decline |
|---|---|---|---|---|

0      5      10      15      20      25      30 years

### 1986 Good Bourgeois Médoc

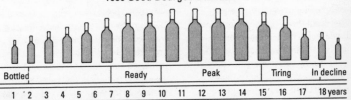

| Bottled | Ready | Peak | Tiring | In decline |
|---|---|---|---|---|

0   1   2   3   4   5   6   7   8   9   10   11   12   13   14   15   16   17   18 years

**1986** (AD) These wines are not in general heavyweight brutes; if anything inclining to the lean and austere in style, but the fruit does seem to be developing a vintage style in a surprising number of wines – and it is a rather thick and jammy, allied to a slight rasp like the flavour of the grape skin itself. That said, the wines are good, sometimes very good, and mostly for the 10 to 20 year haul, though some will be attractive in about five years' time. I think you should have some in your cellar, but if I had only one fistful of £5 notes and '86 and '88 to choose between, I'd choose '88.

**1985** (ACD) These are so delicious you can drink them now – even the top wines. The top wines will age as long as any sensible person wants to age them – but like, I'm told, 1953, they'll *always* be good to drink. The *petits châteaux* are still gorgeous if you can find them, the *bourgeois* probably the best ever on many properties and most of the Classed Growths and Graves/Pessac-Léognans are soft, and deep and ravishing.

**1984** I downgrade this every time I drink an example. What seemed to be quite light, dry – and grossly overpriced – Cabernet clarets are, at present, mostly short, fruitless and tough. They *may* improve.

**1983** (ABD) A true Bordeaux classic, still relatively well-priced. Though tannic now, the wines will flower into a lovely dry cedar and blackcurrant maturity – but it'll take another five to ten years. AC Margaux made its best wines for a generation.

**1982** (ACD) Fabulous year, unbelievably ripe, fat, juicy and rich. They're going to make great drinking right to their peak in ten to 20 years' time, although some of the lesser wines, while marvellous now, are not likely to last over five years.

**1981** (BCD) Good vintage, but not spectacular. Quite light, but classic flavours from top properties which should still age a bit.

**1980** (BC) Nice light, grassy claret, which needs drinking up.

**1979** (ABCD) Many of these wines demand another five years at least. Keep your top wines, and hurry up with the lesser ones.

**1978** (ACD) Some of the tip-top wines are a bit tough still, but most Classed Growths are lovely now, and many lesser wines are still good. Graves and St-Émilions are ready, although Graves will hold.

**1976** (C) Rather soft and sweet on the whole. Not inspiring, apart from a few exceptions in St-Émilion and Pomerol. Drink up.

**1975** (A) A difficult vintage. The very harsh tannins frequently didn't have ripe enough fruit to mesh with, and the flavour went stale and brown before the wine had time to soften.

**1970** (ACD) Now re-emerging with the fruit intact to make lovely current drinking – but the top wines will age a decade yet.

**1966** (AC) Some say they're tiring, some say they aren't quite ready yet. I say *all* the wines are ready, with many at their peak now. Yet some lesser wines which seemed to be dying out have taken on a new lease of life.

**1961** (AC) Still wonderful. I marvel at how great claret can match richness and perfume with a bone-dry structure of tannin and acidity.

Most other vintages of the 1960s will now be risks; '69 and '67 are basically past it, '64 can still be good, rather big, solid wines, and '62, one of the most gorgeous, fragrant vintages since the war, is just beginning to show the ladders in its stockings. If your godfather's treating you, and offers '59, '55 or '53, accept with enthusiasm. If he offers you '49, '47 or '45, get it in writing before he changes his mind.

# WHITE BORDEAUX

Twenty years ago, there were only half a dozen dry white wines made in Bordeaux worth a moment's consideration. Moreover, the tiny quantities of the dry whites made at Haut Brion or the Domaine de Chevalier, combined with their inordinately high prices, made them irrelevant to the vast majority of wine drinkers. As far as these were concerned, white Bordeaux meant either Sauternes or a vast mass of mediocre, muddy, sulphurous sludge indifferently labelled Graves or Entre-Deux-Mers.

It is important to rub in this point – familiar, though I am sure it is, to readers of *Webster's* – simply to appreciate the scale of the revolution of these past two decades. Now there is a mass of delicious dry white available from Bordeaux, the Sauvignon crisper (and thus more to my taste) than many of the fashionable wines made from the same grape by the New Zealanders, while at a higher level the traditional Bordeaux blend of Sémillon and Sauvignon provides a depth, and an ageing potential, matched only by a handful of other dry whites. It can be surpassed only by the Burgundians, and then only at their best.

The revolution came about at a time when the total production of non-botrytized white wines in the Gironde was static. For, just as demand for dry whites started to soar the world over, Bordeaux's growers were responding to an earlier market preference for reds (and to an increasing incapacity to sell their existing wines). So the Dry White Revolution was the result of a combination of simple greed, mutual emulation, market forces and the spread of scientific knowledge amongst the whole wine-making community.

The revolution is symbolized by two men: André Lurton and Denis Dubordieu. Lurton, a typically obstinate, bloody-minded but dedicated and immensely talented wine-maker, was a pioneer in making good-value, fruity but clean dry whites on a large scale at Château Bonnet, his estate in the Entre-Deux-Mers. He was also one of the first to start the reconquest of the historic heart of the Graves round Léognan, where the vines had been sidelined by the spread of suburbia (and the pine forest), so that in 1970 they covered only 100 hectares. Hence the rebuilding of La Louvière and the reclamation of Rochemarine and other estates from the pine forest. Lurton's obstinacy was also responsible for the creation of a separate appellation, Pessac-Léognan, covering the northern Graves nearest to Bordeaux, in 1987.

### White socks

This was bitterly opposed (some timid souls ventured to suggest that Bordeaux's existing ACs, some 50 or more, were enough) but has had two beneficial results. The wines of the new appellation (especially the lesser-known whites) have benefitted from the increased publicity; and – a much more surprising result – the mass of wine-growers left as makers of simple Graves have no longer been able to benefit from the renown of their better-known brethren. So they have pulled up their socks and are now producing a mass of perfectly decent dry whites.

They have done so largely thanks to Dubordieu. His father owns Doisy-Daëne in Barsac, where he has been making a distinguished dry white since 1950, and the family also owned Château Reynon in the Premières Côtes south-east of Bordeaux and Clos Floridene in the Graves. These estates served as pilot plants for the new techniques Dubordieu developed at the Institute Oenologique, which had already revolutionized the making of claret. Dubordieu started by assuming that better wine demanded only a certain discipline (for example, no rot, and the installation of modern temperature-controlled vats) but in the early 1980s undertook a proper research programme which resulted in further refinements, notably an even more rigorous elimination of even slightly rotten grapes (and thus the abandonment of mechanical harvesting) a limited skin contact, and strict control of the pre-fermentation process by which the juice is allowed to settle, to provide the proper balance between cleanliness and the development of more interesting aromas.

The progress he engendered is now general, but unfortunately just as the techniques were becoming more widespread, the weather took an unkind turn. While 1988 was a splendid year for making crisp, well-balanced dry whites, the very warmth and sunshine which made the two following vintages so remarkable for claret merely ensured that only a minority of dry whites had the combination of crispness and fruity depth required. So you have to shop around far more than with claret, or Sauternes for that matter. And as for 1991? A disaster, but, given the new-found pride of the wine-makers they are only releasing wines worthy of the appellation – and then only in tiny quantities so they are worth sampling.

But if Bordeaux's dry whites have been a revolution, the story of Sauternes over the past 15 years has been a fairy-tale. The 1980s saw a series of vintages ranging from the excellent to the superb, culminating in one of the most extraordinary years of the century in 1990, when the weather was almost tropical and the resulting wines so complex, rich and varied that it will be years before their qualities can be properly appreciated. Nature's generosity was matched by that of wine drinkers, who, for the first time for a generation, were prepared to pay a proper price for wines which are among the most expensive in the world to produce. The minimal yields, a mere quarter of those achieved with Bordeaux's other wines, are summed up at Yquem, where each vine yields a glass of wine. In the Médoc each vine yields a bottle.

## First freeze your grapes

When I first went to the region in 1978, a well-made Sauternes, free from sulphur and matured in clean (let alone new) wood was the exception, with only a handful of conscientious owners losing money every year by producing decent wines, and a group of newcomers, like Tom and Nicole Heeter at Château Guiraud, following in the same honourable but financially unrewarding path.

Fourteen years on there has been a revolution: well-made wines are now the rule, not the exception. The price is being paid by the consumer: and if the price of a classed-growth Sauternes is 50 per cent higher than that of a claret of similar rank, that only provides partial compensation for the sheer chanciness of producing Sauternes. For the noble rot that is essential for these wines does not develop every year: and the season in which the grapes are picked is so late (except in that breathtaking year 1990 when they were picked before those in the Médoc) that every vintage remains a gamble.

Fortunately the Sauternais now have a powerful scientific weapon to help: cryoextraction. This simply means bunging the grapes into a large 'fridge and taking them down to well below freezing. At that point, with the water content frozen, the only juice that will run will be one desirably full of sugar, so this simple technique provides a degree of selectivity which does not affect the chemical content of the juice except to concentrate it. It would come in handy under a variety of the difficult conditions in which the Sauternais habitually find themselves, above all when late rains swell the grapes and produce grey rot.

Ironically, since they all equipped themselves with the 'fridges in 1987-1988 they haven't needed them, since the next three vintages were all so extraordinary – and in 1991 not even the most elaborate equipment could have allowed them to produce much wine, although the 'cryo' did help. But they do guarantee that in future Sauternes vintages will be much less irregular, in both quantity and quality – which, together with a slow-down in demand, should lead to some downward adjustment in prices.

Even before the arrival of 'le cryo' the owners and wine-makers had invested heavily in better presses and vats and in new oak as part of the region's resurrection. The process was helped, not only by new owners, but, as so often in France, by a new generation of better-trained wine-makers, and the results can be seen in the entries for individual châteaux.

The results can also be seen in the lesser appellations also producing sweet wines, formerly known by the unfortunate name of 'petits liquoreux.' In despair the growers in Cadillac, Sainte Croix du Mont and Loupiac, on the lovely banks of the Garonne opposite Sauternes, and in Cérons north of Barsac, had turned to making (generally indifferent) red and dry white wines. But increasingly, they too are making wines to sell under their château names. This is splendid news for drinkers wanting lighter, less expensive sweet wines, light lemon-honey glassfuls for any time between tea and dinner.     NICHOLAS FAITH

## GRAPES & FLAVOURS

**SAUVIGNON BLANC** There has been a rush to plant more of this fashionable grape in Bordeaux in recent years, but with a couple of exceptions, such as Malartic-Lagravière, Couhins-Lurton and Smith-Haut-Lafitte, Sauvignon by itself here often gives rather muddy, tough wine. Even so, many dry white Bordeaux *are* entirely Sauvignon, particularly at the cheaper end, and *can* be fresh and flowery if made by careful wine-makers like Mau, Dourthe, Ginestet and Coste, but the best are almost always blended with Sémillon. A little Sauvignon adds acidity and freshness to Sauternes and other sweet whites, too.

**SÉMILLON** The most important grape of Sauternes, and very susceptible to noble rot. Sémillon is vital to the best dry wines, too, though it has become unfashionable. With modern techniques one can hardly tell a good dry Sémillon from a Sauvignon, except that it's a little fuller. But ideally they should be blended, with Sémillon the main variety. It gives a big, round dry wine, slightly creamy but with an exciting aroma of fresh apples and leaving a lanolin smoothness in the mouth. From the top properties, fermented cool and aged in oak barrels, the result is a wonderful, soft, nutty dry white, often going honeyed and smoky as it ages to a maturity of 7 to 15 years, as one of France's great white wines.

**MUSCADELLE** A very little, up to five per cent, of this headily perfumed grape often goes into the Sauternes blend and has proved particularly good in wines from Loupiac and Ste Croix du Mont. In dry white blends a few per cent can add a very welcome honeyed softness. It is now being produced in small quantities as a single varietal, dry, lean, but perfumed.

*The price guides for this section begin on page 273.*

# WINES & WINE REGIONS

**BARSAC, AC** (sweet) The only one of the Sauternes villages with the right to use its own name as an official *appellation* (it may also call itself Sauternes – or Sauternes-Barsac for that matter). Barsac has chalkier soils than the other Sauternes villages, and tends to make lighter wines. Even so, wines from good properties are marvellously rich despite a certain delicacy of texture.

**BORDEAUX BLANC, AC** (dry) This AC covers a multitude of sins. It is the catch-all name for all white Bordeaux, and as such is the label on some of France's dullest medium-to-dry whites, as well as on many fresh, simple well-made wines. With the sudden surge of interest in Bordeaux's dry whites spurred on by the idiotic pricing shenanigans of its rivals in the Loire and Burgundy, there is simply no excuse for the – happily decreasing – amounts of over-sulphured sludge still coming on to the market. Thank goodness every year sees another surge of good guys beating back the bad. Château wines are usually the best and should generally be drunk as young as possible. Recommended names include: *Birot, Grand-Mouëys, du Juge, Lamothe, Reynon*. Good blends are possible from *Coste, Dourthe, Dubroca, Ginestet, Joanne, Lurton, Mau, Sichel* and *Univitis*. Some classy properties in red areas make good, dry white which is only allowed the AC Bordeaux. Château Margaux's white, for instance, is a simple AC Bordeaux. Many great Sauternes châteaux have started to make a dry wine from the grapes unsuitable for Sauternes. These use the 'Bordeaux Blanc' AC and often their initial letter – as in 'G' of Guiraud, 'R' of Rieussec and 'Y' of Yquem. 'Y' can really be spectacular.

**BORDEAUX BLANC SUPÉRIEUR, AC** (dry) Rarely used, but requires higher basic strength and lower vineyard yield than Bordeaux Blanc AC.

**CADILLAC, AC** (sweet) In the south of the Premières Côtes de Bordeaux, just across the river from Barsac; can produce attractive sweet whites, but since the price is low, many properties now produce dry white and red – which do *not* qualify for the AC Cadillac. The AC is in any case so involved that few growers bother with it.

**CÉRONS, AC** (sweet) Enclave in the Graves butting on to Barsac, producing good, fairly sweet whites, but many growers now prefer to produce dry whites, which can sell as Graves. *Château Archambeau* is a typical example, producing tiny amounts of very good Cérons and much larger amounts of good, fresh dry Graves. *Château Cérons* makes splendidly complex sweet whites worthy of the AC of Barsac. Other good properties: *Grand Enclos du Château Cérons, Haura*.

**ENTRE-DEUX-MERS, AC** (dry) Large Bordeaux area between the Garonne and Dordogne rivers. The AC is for dry whites, which are of varying quality, but every vintage produces more examples of good, fresh, grassy whites. Many properties make red, and these can only be Bordeaux or Bordeaux Supérieur. Best: *Bonnet, Ducla, de Florin, Fondarzac, Moulin-de-Launay, Tertre du Moulin, Thieuley, Union des Producteurs de Rauzan*.

**GRAVES, AC** (dry) Famous, or perhaps infamous area south of Bordeaux, on the left bank of the Garonne. The infamy is the result of the endless turgid stream of sulphurous, flabby, off-dry white that *used* to flow out of the region. However, modern Graves is a dramatic improvement. Even at the level of commercial blends it can be sharply fruity and full in style, while at the best properties, with some oak ageing employed, the wines are some of the most delicious dry whites in France. As from the 1987 vintage the wines from the northern Graves bear the *appellation* 'Pessac-

Léognan'. Best châteaux: *Archambeau, Bouscaut, Cabannieux, Carbonnieux, Domaine de Chevalier, Couhins-Lurton, de Cruzeau, Domaine la Grave, de Fieuzal, la Garance, la Garde, Haut-Brion, Landiras, Laville Haut-Brion, la Louvière, Malartic-Lagravière, Montalivet, Rahoul, Respide, Rochemorin, Roquetaillade-la-Grange, Smith-Haut-Lafitte* and *la Tour-Martillac*.

**GRAVES SUPÉRIEURES, AC** (sweet or dry) White Graves with a minimum natural alcohol of 12 degrees. Often made sweet. Best property: *Clos St-Georges*.

**LOUPIAC, AC** (sweet) These white wines from the lovely area of Bordeaux looking across the Garonne to Barsac are not as sweet as Sauternes, and many properties until recently made dry white and red without the Loupiac AC because of difficulties in selling sweet whites.With rising prices has come a welcome flood of lemony-honeyed Barsac styles. Best châteaux: *Domaine du Noble, Loupiac-Gaudiet, Ricaud*.

**PESSAC-LÉOGNAN, AC** (dry) The AC for reds and whites declared in 1987 and created out of the best and northernmost part of Graves. Fifty-five estates are involved, including all the *crus classés*, so quality ought to be high. Yields are lower than for Graves and the percentage of Sauvignon is higher (at least a quarter of the grapes used). This might change the style of some estates, but the crucial point is that the new AC will be further motivation for improvement in what is rapidly becoming one of France's most exciting white areas. The best wines start out with a blast of apricot, peach and cream ripeness and slowly mature to a superb nutty richness with a dry savoury finish. Best châteaux: *Bouscaut, Carbonnieux* (from 1988), *Couhins-Lurton, Domaine de Chevalier, de Fieuzal, Haut-Brion, la Louvière, Malartic-Lagravière, Rochemorin, Smith-Haut-Lafitte* and *la Tour Martillac*.

**PREMIÈRES CÔTES DE BORDEAUX, AC** Some very attractive reds and excellent dry whites from the right bank of the Garonne opposite Graves and Sauternes in the bang-up-to-date, fruit-all-the-way style as well as some reasonable sweetish wines. The sweet wines can now take the AC Cadillac, but you still get some under the Premières Côtes mantle, sometimes with their village name added, as in *Château de Berbec*, Premières-Côtes-Gabarnac.

**STE-CROIX-DU-MONT, AC** (sweet) The leading sweet white AC of the Premières Côtes de Bordeaux. Can be very attractive when properly made. *Château Loubens* is the best-known wine, but *Lousteau-Vieil* is producing better wine every year, and *Domaine du Tich, La Grave, la Rame, des Tours*, and the sadly minuscule *de Tastes* are also good.

**SAUTERNES, AC** (sweet) The overall *appellation* for a group of five villages in the south of the Graves region, Sauternes, Bommes, Fargues, Preignac and Barsac. (Barsac wines may use their own village name if they wish.) Concentrated by noble

---

**1855 CLASSIFICATION OF SAUTERNES**
**Grand premier cru** Yquem (Sauternes).

**Premiers crus** Climens (Barsac); Coutet (Barsac); Guiraud (Sauternes); Haut-Peyraguey (Bommes); Lafaurie-Peyraguey (Bommes); Rabaud-Promis (Bommes); Rayne-Vigneau (Bommes); Rieussec (Fargues); Sigalas-Rabaud (Bommes); Suduiraut (Preignac); la Tour-Blanche (Bommes).

**Deuxièmes crus** d'Arche (Sauternes); Broustet (Barsac); Caillou (Barsac); Doisy-Daëne (Barsac); Doisy-Dubroca (Barsac); Doisy-Védrines (Barsac); Filhot (Sauternes); Lamothe (Sauternes), Lamothe-Guignard (Sauternes); de Myrat (Barsac) (now extinct); Nairac (Barsac); Romer-du-Hayot (Fargues); Suau (Barsac); de Malle (Preignac).

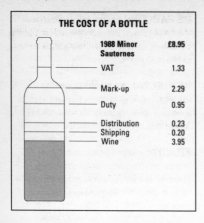

**THE COST OF A BOTTLE**

| 1988 Minor Sauternes | £8.95 |
|---|---|
| VAT | 1.33 |
| Mark-up | 2.29 |
| Duty | 0.95 |
| Distribution | 0.23 |
| Shipping | 0.20 |
| Wine | 3.95 |

rot, the Sémillon, along with a little Sauvignon and Muscadelle, produces at its glorious best a wine that is brilliantly rich and glyceriny, combining honey and cream, pineapple and nuts when young, with something oily and penetrating as it ages and the sweetness begins to have an intensity of volatile flavours, rather like a peach, bruised and browned in the sun, then steeped in the sweetest of syrups. These are the fine wines. Sadly, owing to economic pressures, much Sauternes outside the top Growths used to be made sweet simply by adding sugar to the juice and the brutal arrest of the fermentation with a massive slug of sulphur. In recent years the average quality has soared, and the wines are infinitely less turgid and sulphury, as indeed they ought to be given their rising prices. And in bad years those châteaux that can afford it can now practise cryoextraction – which isn't some form of torture but a method of freezing the grapes before fermentation which can increase the richness of the juice pressed out. Best châteaux: *Bastor-Lamontagne, Climens, Doisy-Daëne, Doisy-Védrines, de Fargues, Gilette, Guiraud, Lafaurie-Peyraguey, Lamothe-Guignard, Rabaud-Promis, Raymond-Lafon, Rayne-Vigneau, Rieussec, St-Amand, Suduiraut, La Tour Blanche, d'Yquem.*

# CHÂTEAUX PROFILES

I have valued these properties according to how they are currently performing; a five-star rating means you are getting a top-line taste – not just a well-known label. Some big names have been downgraded, some lesser-known properties are promoted – solely on the quality of the wine inside the bottle. A star in brackets shows that the wine can achieve the higher rating but does not always do so.

The £ sign shows which wines are offering particularly good value for money – although that does not mean any of these wines will exactly be cheap.

**D'ARCHE** *2ème cru Sauternes* ★★★(★)
A little-known Sauternes property now beginning to make exciting wine after a long period of mediocrity. 1983, '86, '88, '89 and '90 are particularly good and show great promise for the future

**BASTOR-LAMONTAGNE** *cru bourgeois Sauternes* ★★★ £ Unclassified property making marvellous, widely available and easily affordable wines, as rich as many Classed Growths. 1981, '82, '83 and '86 epitomize high quality Sauternes at a remarkably fair price.

**BROUSTET** *2ème cru classé Barsac* ★★(★) A reliable, fairly rich wine, not often seen, but worth trying. The '88 and '90 are especially good, the dry white disappointing.

**CABANNIEUX** *Graves* ★★★ £ One of the new wave of non-classified Graves which is radically improving its white wine by the use of new oak barrels. The red is good, too. 1986, '88 and '89 show the way.

**CARBONNIEUX** *cru classé Pessac-Léognan* ★★★(★) This large property used to make decent enough old-style white that aged surprisingly well, but since 1988 they have been using 50 per cent new oak – and can you taste the difference! The 1990 is the best yet.

**CLIMENS** *1er cru Barsac* ★★★★(★)
Undoubtedly the best property in Barsac, making some of the most consistently fine sweet wines in France. 1983, '86, '88 and '89 are all excellent. It also makes a delicious second wine called Les Cèdres that is well worth seeking out.

**COUHINS-LURTON** *cru classé Pessac-Léognan* ★★★★ 100 per cent Sauvignon dry white fermented in new oak barrels, producing a successful blend of grassy fruit and oaky spice. Recent vintages have been excellent.

**COUTET** *1er cru Barsac* ★★★ A great property which in recent years has not been living up to its previous exacting standards.

**DOISY-DAËNE** *2ème cru Barsac* ★★★(★)
A very good, consistent property providing relatively light, but extremely attractive sweet wine. Doisy-Daëne Sec is a particularly good dry white.

**DOISY-VÉDRINES** *2ème cru Barsac* ★★★★ £ A rich, concentrated wine, which is usually good value. 1980, '83, '86 and '89 are very good.

**DOMAINE DE CHEVALIER** ★★★★★ (for white). See Red Bordeaux.

**DE FARGUES** *cru bourgeois Sauternes* ★★★★(★) Small property owned by Yquem, capable of producing stunning, rich wines in the best years.

**DE FIEUZAL** ★★★★(★) The white is unclassified, but, with its burst of apricot fruit and spice, is one of Bordeaux's leading dry whites. See Red Bordeaux.

**FILHOT** *2ème cru Sauternes* ★★(★) Well-known Sauternes property producing pleasant but hardly memorable wines, though the 1988 effort looks a bit more hopeful.

**GILETTE** *cru bourgeois Sauternes* ★★★★ Remarkable property which ages its wines in concrete tanks for 20 to 30 years before releasing them. Usually delicious, with a dry richness unique in Sauternes thanks to long maturation and absence of wood. The 1955 and 1959 are heavenly, and only just released. Seriously!

**GUIRAUD** *1er cru Sauternes* ★★★★(★)
Fine property owned since 1981 by a Canadian who has revolutionized the estate and brought the wines back to peak, and pricy, form. The wines are difficult to taste when young but are very special, and the 1983, '86, '88, '89 and '90 are going to be outstanding.

**HAUT-BRION** *cru classé Pessac-Léognan* ★★★★(★) Small quantities of very fine, long-lived wine, also appealing when young. See Red Bordeaux.

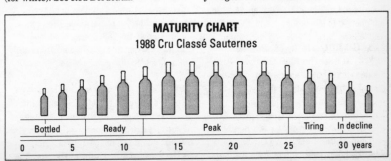

**MATURITY CHART**
1988 Cru Classé Sauternes

| Bottled | Ready | Peak | Tiring | In decline |

| 0 | 5 | 10 | 15 | 20 | 25 | 30 years |

**LAFAURIE-PEYRAGUEY** *1er cru Sauternes* ★★★★(★) Fine property, returning to top form after a dull period in the 1960s and '70s. Remarkably good in the difficult years of '82, '84 and '85, it is stunning in '83, '86, '88, '89 and '90.

**LAMOTHE-GUIGNARD** *2ème cru Sauternes* ★★★ Since 1981 this previously undistinguished wine has dramatically improved. 1983, '86 and '88 will show the improvement as do '89 and '90.

**LAVILLE-HAUT-BRION** *cru classé Pessac-Léognan* ★★★★ This should be one of the greatest of all white Pessac-Léognan, since it is owned by Haut-Brion, but despite some great successes, the general effect is patchy – especially given the crazy prices.

**LA LOUVIÈRE** *cru bourgeois Pessac-Léognan* ★★★★ This property has been making lovely, modern, oak-aged whites since the mid-70s but is only now achieving the acclaim it deserves. Since 1987, the quality has climbed even higher.

**MALARTIC-LAGRAVIÈRE** *cru classé Pessac-Léognan* ★★★(★) £ Tiny quantities of perfumed Sauvignon wine; recently more variable.

**DE MALLE** *2ème cru Sauternes* ★★★(★) Good, relatively light wine from a very beautiful property set partly in the Graves and partly in Sauternes. It went through a bad patch in the early and mid-'80s when the owner died after a long illness, but since '88 his widow has been making wines fully worthy of the name.

**RABAUD-PROMIS** *1er cru Sauternes* ★★★(★) At last! The 1986, '88 and '89 are excellent and show a long-awaited return to First Growth quality.

**RAHOUL** *cru bourgeois Graves* ★★★ A leader of the new wave of cool-fermented, oak-aged whites among the Graves properties, having an effect not only on the *bourgeois* properties, but on the Classed Growths as well. Also increasingly good red. Ownership changes are worrying, though, and the '88, '89 and '90 were not as special as previous vintages, though still good. Domaine Benoit and Château Constantin also good in the same stable.

**RAYMOND LAFON** *cru bourgeois Sauternes* ★★★★ Owned by the former manager of neighbouring Yquem, this is fine wine but not quite as fine as the increasingly daunting price would imply.

**RIEUSSEC** *1er cru Sauternes* ★★★★(★) One of the richest, most exotic Sauternes, and particularly good wines during the 1980s. The 1982 is good, the '83, '86 and '88 really special, the '89 and '90 wonderful.

**ST-AMAND** *cru bourgeois Sauternes* ★★★(★) £ Splendid property making truly rich wines that age well, at an affordable price. Also seen as Château de la Chartreuse. Since the 1970s each decent vintage has produced a delicious example.

**SMITH-HAUT-LAFITTE** *cru classé Pessac-Léognan* ★★★★ A late convert to cool fermentation and oak-barrel ageing, but since 1985 there have been superb wines in this new mode. Also increasingly good, and better-known, reds.

**SUDUIRAUT** *1er cru Sauternes* ★★★★ Rich, exciting wines, frequently deeper and more intensely perfumed than any other Sauternes – except for its neighbour, d'Yquem, but unfortunately not as reliable as it should be. A remarkable 1982 was followed by a fine '83, a very good '85 but slightly disappointing '86 and ditto in 1988. '89 was a leap up again though.

**D'YQUEM** *1er grand cru classé Sauternes* ★★★★★ The pinnacle of achievement in great sweet wines. Almost every vintage is a masterpiece and its outlandish price is almost justified, since d'Yquem at its best is the greatest sweet wine in the world.

## SWEET WHITE BORDEAUX VINTAGES

The 1980s brought Sauternes a share in the good fortune that was drenching the red wines of Bordeaux with great vintages. About time too, because 1983 created a much needed surge of interest in these remarkable, super-sweet wines and 1986, '88, '89 and '90 can continue it. The astonishing run of Indian summer vintages that saved red Bordeaux year after year from 1977 was not always so kind to Sauternes. In 1978 and 1981, the botrytis just didn't quite develop, and in 1982 the rains came at exactly the wrong time, diluting potentially perfect grapes. But the vintages of the late 1980s are more than making amends. It's worth remembering that Sauternes can be drunk very young or very old, depending entirely on whether you like the startlingly sweet shock of young wine or the deep, nutty, golden honey of older wines. The best can last a very long time. The *en primeur* prices have the wine merchants listing the best Barsac at around £250 a case and the finest Sauternes at over £300. But you can still find super 1983 and 1986 wines for half that price, so it's worth shopping around.

**1991** A very difficult year, in Sauternes as in the rest of Bordeaux. In Sauternes the impact of the frost was greatest on the Sémillon, leaving yet another source of imbalance in an overly high proportion of Sauvignon. Moreover there was a high degree of differential ripeness when the few remaining grapes were harvested. Such wines as are being let onto the market are correct or better, but only Climens seems to have produced a stunner.

**1990** The most extraordinary year in Sauternes since 1893. The weather was tropical, and the grapes were so ripe that when it rained heavily in late August the botrytis really took off, and there was no stopping it. Almost everybody (including Yquem, most traditional and cautious of châteaux) started to pick in early September, earlier than in any year since – 1893.

By that time the grapes were absurdly full of sugar, with a potential of 26 per cent alcohol, a fifth more than port. But they would never have fermented properly, so the locals mixed in with them a judicious proportion of grapes that were not *botrytisés* but merely *passerrillés,* ripe and juicy but unaffected by the noble rot and therefore containing (in 1990 anyway) a mere 15 per cent potential alcohol. They probably helped the balance, too.

As can be imagined, the result was wines which are so big and so varied, even within the same estate, as to be almost impossible to judge young — because no-one, even in Sauternes, has any point of comparison. Whether they will remain too big, rich and heavy to be truly enjoyable is possible, but I doubt it: they should all, the lesser wines as well as the classed growths, be treated as if they were old-style claret, to be left for a decade before being sampled. Then, I believe, they will prove to be the treat (though not, alas, the bargain) of a lifetime.

**1989** A superlative vintage. Not only did the sun shine so perfectly that the white grapes all ripened beautifully, but the early days of September also brought those early morning mists that noble rot enjoys so much and thrives on. The growers who waited for the botrytis to spread, praying rain would hold off, made richly succulent wines of great character. Comparing 1989s with '88s is going to be one of life's more indulgent pleasures in years to come.

**1988** In 1988 every Sauternes and Barsac château and many in Cadillac, Loupiac and Ste-Croix-du-Mont, had the chance to make the greatest wine in a generation. It all depended on each individual's desire to excel, his pride, his passion. It was a dry year and patience was needed while botrytis developed. Sadly, one or two leading properties were seen harvesting long before noble rot had run its full course. Many other producers went through the vines again and again, picking only the well rotted grapes: the wines are already destined to be classics.    ▷

**1987** The rains came far too early this year, long before noble rot could get going on the grapes. Even so some pleasant, light wines were made, especially by those properties who used the cryoextraction method of freezing the grapes to concentrate what sugar there was. But some estates bottled no wine from this vintage.

**1986** Another marvellous year, when noble rot swept through the vineyards, and any proprietor who cared to could make great sweet wines. At the moment the best wines seem to be even better than 1983 and 1988 but it is notoriously difficult to judge young Sauternes, so I could well reverse my opinion in a year or two. By which time the '89s and '90s can join the debate.

**1985** Quite pleasant lightish wines, but only a handful of outstanding wines from estates with the courage to wait for botrytis in a very dry year.

**1983** Superbly rich, exciting wines to be ranked alongside 1986 and 1988, 1989 and 1990. Which vintage will finally turn out best is going to entail a large amount of comparative tasting over the next decade. What a jolly thought.

**1981/80/79** Three attractive mid-weight vintages. The 1981s are a touch graceless, but the best 1980s have been underrated and will still improve.

**1976** Fat, hefty, rich. Some haven't quite developed as hoped, but lots of 'lanolin' oiliness and lusciousness in those that have.

**1975** Another lovely year. Not quite so utterly indulgent as 1976 but perhaps a little better balanced.

**1971/70** Two fine years which need drinking up.

## DRY WHITE BORDEAUX VINTAGES

Using cool fermentation, and a greater percentage of Sauvignon Blanc, many white Bordeaux are not now being made to age, but all Graves/Pessac-Léognan should be kept for at least two to three years, and the best 10 to 20 years.

**1991** The April frost that damaged just about the whole of Bordeaux hit the Graves particularly badly, so there simply won't be much dry white from that region in 1991. There'll be a bit, though, and what this is looks as though it could be rather good: concentrated by the frost damage, and well-balanced. Try and get somebody else to buy it for you, though: it won't be cheap.

**1990** Even hotter and drier than 1989, and considerably less successful. The Graves seems especially disappointing. No doubt there will be some good wines, but consumers will need to be very selective.

**1989** Unlike 1988, the problem was with overripe rather than underripe grapes. Growers who picked early made crisp wines, but those who didn't will provide us with some flabby drinking. In years to come the dry wines will inevitably be overshadowed by the sweet ones.

**1988** Some of the 1988 dry whites lack a little oomph. The excessively dry summer retarded ripening and some producers picked grapes which were not totally ripe. Even so, most 1988s from good producers are delicious, and some are outstandingly good.

**1987** All the grapes were safely in before the rains arrived which lashed Bordeaux's vineyards and threatened the red harvest. A slight lack of acidity has meant they have aged quite fast and even the top wines are already drinking well, although those from Pessac-Léognan can happily take further ageing.

**1986** Basic wines now tiring. Top line properties made outstanding wines which will last.

# BURGUNDY

Recessions have a way of bringing chickens home to roost. When times were good everybody wanted fine Burgundy: the British, the Americans, the Japanese, everybody. Even inadequate Burgundy sold. Burgundy, in fact, had it very easy.

What the recession has done is make customers choosier – to the extent of not buying Burgundy at all. In the year from September-August 1990-91, sales of Burgundy in some of the main export markets dropped dramatically – 37 per cent in the US, 31 per cent in Britain and 45 per cent in Japan. Figures like that will concentrate the collective mind of any region.

Wine merchant and Burgundy specialist Jasper Morris of Morris & Verdin sums up the current market thus: 'In a recession, a wine has to be exactly right for people to buy. If it's not quite right, then nobody will buy. It's a question of the best wine or the best buy; nothing else will do. It's the middle ground (by which I do not mean the middle appellations) that has suffered.'

With sales falling, the logical thing for Burgundy to do would be to reduce its prices, and indeed they did fall at the 1991 Hospices de Beaune auction. The Hospices sale does not fix the prices for the ensuing months, but it is taken as an indication, and in 1991 the price of red wines at the auction dropped by 25 per cent and that for white wines by 44 per cent. This followed on a fall of 24.5 per cent and 37 per cent respectively at the 1990 auction. So can we expect to see decent Burgundy at affordable prices this year?

Jasper Morris points out that 'the *négociants* have been doing one thing on prices and the growers another. That is to generalize, of course; to generalize still more, if one takes 1983 as a base year, then *négociants'* prices have been zigzagging up and down, while growers' prices have been more gently and steadily rising. Now the *négociants* have slashed their prices and are still not selling, while the growers have maintained or even increased theirs, and are selling.'

## Over-mortgaged '89s

The market has taken its toll: the *négociants* bought heavily of the 1989 vintage, and buying a lot of '89 Burgundy was akin to buying a house in Britain at the height of the boom. The '89s were terrifically expensive, and no sooner had they been paid for than the American dollar started heading the wrong way against the franc. North America is a vital market for white Burgundy – or was. No doubt it will be again, but at the moment the *négociants* are much in the position of someone who bought a bigger house than they needed with money they couldn't afford, and now can't sell it. There are rumours that many of the *négociant* firms themselves are up for sale, including several of the best ones.

The '89s were good, yes, but the 1990s were as good if not better – more concentrated and better balanced – and in 1991 the frost damage, though considerable, was less than in Bordeaux. The quantity was about 15 per cent down, and affected the best vineyards least; though quality was not helped by the rain, which began on the eve of the vintage (and some grapes, certainly, were picked in the rain) some concentration was restored to the wine by the low yields. So the 1991s should not be written off, especially since the barrel prices were half those of the 1989s.

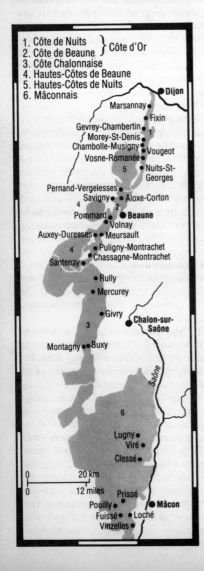

1. Côte de Nuits ⎫
2. Côte de Beaune ⎬ Côte d'Or
3. Côte Chalonnaise
4. Hautes-Côtes de Beaune
5. Hautes-Côtes de Nuits
6. Mâconnais

## CLASSIFICATIONS

Burgundy has five different levels of classification:

**Non-specific regional appellations** with no geographical definition, e.g. Bourgogne, which may come from inferior land or young vines.

**Specific regional appellations**, e.g. Côte de Beaune-Villages, generally a merchant's blend of wines from one or more villages. Côte de Nuits-Villages is usually better.

**Village commune wines** Each village has its vineyards legally defined. The village names are traditionally used for vineyards with no special reputation, which are thus usually blended together under the village name. But there is a growing move towards even relatively unknown vineyards appearing on the label. These unclassified vineyards are called *lieux-dits* or 'stated places'. They can only appear on the label in letters half the size of the village name.

**Premier cru** It's typical of Burgundy that *premier cru* or 'First Growth' actually means 'Second Growth', because these are the second best vineyard sites. Even so, they contain some of Burgundy's finest wines. They are classified by both village and vineyard names, e.g. Gevrey-Chambertin, Combe-aux-Moines. The vineyard name must follow the village name on the label, and it may be in the same size print. Confusingly, some growers use smaller print, but the appellation should make it clear whether it is a *premier cru* or a *lieu-dit*.

**Grand cru** These are the real top growths. Not every village has one. The reds are mostly in the Côte de Nuits, the whites in the Côte de Beaune. A *grand cru* vineyard name can stand alone on the label without the village – for example, Chambertin from the village of Gevrey-Chambertin. (By long tradition, a Burgundy village is allowed to tack on the name of its *grand cru* vineyard, and use the compound name for wines that have nothing to do with *grand cru*, for instance Puligny-Montrachet.)

That disparity is unlikely to be maintained all the way to the shop shelves. Even so, there should be some good buys among the 1991s, and the not-unusual advice to go to a specialist Burgundy merchant like Haynes Hanson & Clark or Morris & Verdin, and take their advice about growers, applies. At the lower end, basic Bourgogne Rouge or Blanc from a good grower in a good village is a good bet. If his village wine is good, then the same sort of care has probably been taken with his plain Bourgogne.

If falling sales and falling prices are one part of the Burgundian picture at the moment, then the other part is an increasing, though still patchy, insistence on good wine-making. For some years now a younger generation of wine-makers has been heralded as revolutionizing the heavy, soupy, often less than clean styles of yore. But it is a very gradual process indeed. 'A lot of growers liked those old-fashioned wines,' points out Jasper Morris. 'They thought that was how the wines from their village were supposed to taste. But now the idea is getting across that if you consistently make good wine you will get a better price' – and hard cash will change ideas a great deal faster than mere theories.

## Opening the Côte d'Or

In addition, Burgundy has traditionally not exactly been a hotbed of discussion about wine. It has not been the habit of Burgundian growers to spend their spare time seeing how other regions, other countries do things; they didn't even make a habit of tasting in the next village. Secrecy ruled; outsiders were treated with suspicion and their views (especially if they were unfavourable) were not countenanced. So when Burgundy announced that in March 1992 it would hold open house for ten days; that merchants and journalists would be welcome to taste and chat to their hearts' content; that there would be a comparative tasting of Burgundy versus the New World, you could have knocked most wine merchants down with the proverbial feather.

Burgundy christened the beano the Grands Jours de Bourgogne, and promised it would hold a repeat two years' hence. So was this just the recession talking? It would be easy to think so. Burgundy had it easy for years, and was capable of treating even its admirers pretty gracelessly. Then sales plummet, and hey presto! Suddenly it's out there wooing the world.

But let's not be cynical. Let's say that it's the influence of a new generation that has proved that it wants to make good wine for good wine's sake; that has travelled to Australia, to California, to Oregon, that has even ventured down the road to the next village; that has seen that Pinot Noir can be one of the most wonderful grapes in the world, but is not so automatically; and that has realized that any wine-maker who expects the world to queue to pay £30 a bottle for sloppily-made, over-chaptalized soup from vines that cropped too heavily and were picked in the rain is, sooner or later, going to be on to a loser.

Actually, £30 a bottle doesn't look a lot against the three figure sum you'd have to fork out for a bottle of Romanée Conti from the domaine of that name. Nobody would accuse Domaine de la Romanée Conti wines of being sloppily-made, though; what most people who aspire to drink them object to is their price.

Now, though, there has been a dramatic change of management. Co-director Lalou Bize-Leroy has been ousted after a massive row, and the apparent reason – the reason given, anyway – is the way the domaine has lost control of part of its distribution, and that is a result of its sales policy.

The DRC wine most in demand, and most highly priced, is Romanée Conti itself. But in order to obtain any, the DRC's official agents had to buy a fixed amount of the domaine's other wines. What happened then was that the wine, once on the open market, would be sent in different directions, taking advantage of the fact that the DRC sold its wines at different prices in different markets. The Romanée Conti could be sold to, say, Japan for a vast profit; the other wines could then be sold around the world, often for less than the official DRC price. The result was a very unhappy DRC and very unhappy official agents.

What direction the DRC will take under its new management is, at the time of writing, not yet clear. Aubert de Villaine, the other co-director, remains in place, but Lalou Bize-Leroy's nephew and successor at the domaine was killed in a car crash only a few weeks after taking over. One thing does, however, seem certain: if you have to ask the price, you still won't be able to afford it.

# RED WINES

It is here that much of the excitement is to be found in Burgundy at the moment. But the excitement is not universal: standards vary not just between *négociants* and growers, which is the usual gripe in Burgundy (the growers usually being the ones with the Avis, we-try-harder mentality), but between grower and grower, as well.

As ever, the Burgundian picture is patchy. A wine from a good *négociant* – and they do exist – can be infinitely better than one from a grower who doesn't know what he's doing. They exist, too. And complacency in Burgundy is by no means confined to the merchant houses.

It has been easy to be complacent while it was clear that the rest of the world had not mastered the art of making Pinot Noir. For the rest of us, though, the efforts of Pinot novices to handle the grape can be instructive: unlike, for example, Cabernet Sauvignon, which seems to taste pretty much like itself no matter what you do to it, most early efforts with Pinot Noir underline the skill the grape needs. Taste experimental samples from Australia or California or Oregon – or even Baden in Germany, where they have been making it for years — and you will find wines that are too soft and jammy, or too hard and tannic, or wines that simply lack any of the seductiveness that makes great Burgundy so irresistible.

Those New World cellars have had an effect on Burgundy, though. Some of the faults of Burgundy, past and present, amount to good old-fashioned dirt and sloppiness. Get rid of those, plunge into a recession, and suddenly the scene is set for some bargains. We're not talking about top vineyards here, you understand; we're not even talking about tremendously low prices – only lowish, and then only by Burgundian standards. Take a crisp tenner, or maybe even half that, into your local supermarket this year and you should be able to swap it for a bottle of silky, fruity red Burgundy. Okay, that's up to twice the price of a top Bulgarian Cabernet, but how much good Eastern European Pinot Noir have you tasted recently?

Sainsbury's have an Hautes Côtes de Beaune; Tesco a Bourgogne Rouge called Clos de Chenôves; M&S a Bourgogne Epineuil; Oddbins a 1989 Rully from Joseph Drouhin; Waitrose and Gateway wines from the Buxy co-op. Or look for basic red Burgundy from the best growers and *négociants*; we recommend some in the following pages.                                  **MARGARET RAND**

## GRAPES & FLAVOURS

**PINOT NOIR** The sulkiest, trickiest, most tempestuous fine wine grape in the world is the exclusive grape in all but a tiny proportion of red Burgundies. It needs a more delicate balance of spring, summer and autumn climate than any other variety to achieve greatness, and one Burgundian maxim is that you must have unripe grapes, ripe grapes and rotten grapes in equal quantities to achieve that astonishing part-rotted, part-perfumed, and part-ethereal flavour.

It used to be true to say that no other part of the world could produce a Pinot Noir to match those of Burgundy. But isolated growers in Oregon, California, New Zealand, Australia and South Africa are now making very fine examples. Even so, Burgundy is still the only place on earth where fine Pinot Noirs abound. The problem is, awful Pinot Noirs abound too, heavy, chewy and sweet-fruited or thin and pallid. Good Burgundian Pinot Noir should generally be *light*, fragrant, marvellously perfumed with cherry and strawberry fruit, sometimes meatier, sometimes intensely spicy, but, as a rule, *light*. It needs time to mature, but it can be delicious young.

**GAMAY** Most Burgundy has by law to be 100 per cent Pinot Noir, but the Gamay (the Beaujolais grape) can be used in wines labelled 'Burgundy' or 'Bourgogne' which come from the Mâconnais and the Beaujolais regions, or from elsewhere in Burgundy in wines labelled 'Bourgogne Passe-Tout-Grain', 'Bourgogne Grand Ordinaire' or 'Mâcon'.

## WINES & WINE REGIONS

**ALOXE-CORTON, AC** (Côte de Beaune) Ten years ago, this village at the northern end of the Côte de Beaune was the best of all buys for full-flavoured, balanced Burgundy. Most recent Aloxe-Corton has been pale stuff indeed. Its production is overwhelmingly red, and it has the only red *grand cru* in the Côte de Beaune, Le Corton, which is also sold under various subdivisions like Corton-Bressandes, Corton Clos du Roi and so forth, and is seen on the market rather more frequently than one might expect a *grand cru* to be. Go for *Jadot, Drouhin, Jaffelin, Tollot-Beaut*. Also good: *Chandon de Briailles, Dubreuil Fontaine, Faiveley, Juillot, Daniel Senard, Michel Voarick*.

**AUXEY-DURESSES, AC** (Côte de Beaune) Backwoods village with a reputation for full, but fairly gentle, nicely fruity reds, though there seems to have been a slump in quality, the wines often tasting rather lumpish. However, don't let this hiccup put you off. There are a handful of good growers which includes *Ampeau,*

*Diconne, Duc de Magenta, Leroy, Roy, Prunier* and *Thévenin*. They have made excellent wines in 1987, '88 and '89.

**BEAUNE, AC** (Côte de Beaune) One of the few reliable commune wines, usually quite light, with a soft, 'red fruits' sweetness and a flicker of something minerally to smarten it up nicely. The wines are nearly all red. Beaune has the largest acreage of vines of any Côte d'Or commune, and they are mostly owned by merchants. It has no *grands crus* but many excellent *premiers crus*, for example, Grèves, Marconnets, Teurons, Boucherottes, Vignes Franches and Cent Vignes. In general, the 1983s were better than elsewhere, the 1986s a bit light but the 1987s much better and the '88s and '89s outstanding. The best growers are *Lafarge* and *Morot,* and good wines are made by *Besancenot-Mathouillet, Drouhin, Germain, Jadot, Jaffelin, Tollot-Beaut*.

**BLAGNY, AC** (Côte de Beaune) Tiny hamlet on the boundary between Meursault and Puligny-Montrachet. The red wine is usually a bit fierce, but then this is white wine heartland, so I'm a bit surprised they grow any red at all. Best producers: *Leflaive, Matrot*.

**BONNES-MARES, AC** (Côte de Nuits) *Grand cru* of 15.54 hectares mostly in Chambolle-Musigny, with a little in Morey-St-Denis. Usually one of the most – or should I say one of the very few – reliable *grands crus*, which ages extremely well over 10 to 20 years to a lovely smoky, chocolate and prunes richness. Best producers: *Domaine des Varoilles, Drouhin, Dujac, Groffier, Jadot, Roumier, de Vogüé*.

**BOURGOGNE GRAND ORDINAIRE, AC** Très Ordinaire. Pas Très Grand. Rarely seen outside Burgundy, this is the bottom of the Burgundy barrel. It may be made from Pinot Noir and Gamay, and even a couple of obscure grapes, the Tressot and César, as well.

**BOURGOGNE PASSE-TOUT-GRAIN, AC** Often excellent value, lightish Burgundy made usually in the Côte d'Or or the Côte Chalonnaise from Gamay blended with a minimum of one-third Pinot Noir. In some years it may well be mostly Pinot. *Rodet* and *Chanson* make it well, but as usual, the growers make it best, particularly in the less famous Côte d'Or and Hautes-Côtes villages; *Rion* in Nuits-St-Georges, *Léni-Volpato* in Chambolle-Musigny, *Henri Jayer* in Vosne-Romanée, *Thomas* in St-Aubin, *Chaley* or *Cornu* in the Hautes-Côtes, and many others like them.

**BOURGOGNE ROUGE, AC** The basic red AC for the Burgundy region from Chablis in the North to the Beaujolais *cru* villages in the South. Unknown Bourgogne Rouge is best avoided – much of it is very basic indeed. Most of Burgundy has to make its Bourgogne Rouge exclusively from the Pinot Noir, but Gamay can be used in the Beaujolais (if declassified from

one of the ten *crus*) and Mâconnais, and the César and Tressot are permitted in the Yonne around Chablis. Wine from the ten Beaujolais *crus* can be declassified and sold as Bourgogne – and *that* should generally be from the Gamay grape alone. Domaine-bottled Bourgogne Rouge from good growers can be excellent value. Look out for those of *Bourgeon, Coche Dury, Germain, d'Heuilly-Huberdeau, Henri Jayer, Juillot, Lafarge, Mortet, Parent, Pousse d'Or, Rion* and *Rossignol*. Good merchants include *Drouhin, Faiveley, Jadot, Jaffelin, Labouré-Roi, Latour, Olivier Leflaive, Leroy, Rodet, Vallet*. The co-op at *Buxy* is also good as is the *Caves des Hautes-Côtes*. Their 1987s are good now; their 1988s and 1989s will be even better.

**CHAMBERTIN, AC** (Côte de Nuits) Most famous of the eight *grands crus* of Gevrey-Chambertin, this 13-hectare vineyard should make wines that are big, strong and intense in their youth, mellowing to a complex, perfumed, plummy richness as they mature. Good ones need ten to 15 years' ageing. Best producers: *Drouhin, Faiveley, Leroy, Mortet, Ponsot, Rebourseau, Rousseau, Tortochot*.

**CHAMBERTIN CLOS-DE-BÈZE, AC** (Côte de Nuits) *Grand cru* in the village of Gevrey-Chambertin next door to Chambertin both geographically and in quality. Can keep ten years in a good vintage. The wines may also be sold as Chambertin. Best producers: *Drouhin, Faiveley, Gelin, Rousseau*.

**CHAMBOLLE-MUSIGNY, AC** (Côte de Nuits) This village towards the southern end of the Côte de Nuits can make light, cherry-sweet, intensely perfumed, 'beautiful' Burgundy, but sadly most commercial Chambolle will be too sweet and gooey to retain much perfume. The best producer is *Georges Roumier,* with wonderful wines in every vintage since 1985. For other producers the years to go for are 1988 and '89: *Barthod-Noëllat, Château de Chambolle-Musigny, Drouhin, Dujac, Groffier, Hudelot-Noëllat, Rion, Serveau, Volpato-Costaille, de Vogüé*.

**CHAPELLE-CHAMBERTIN, AC** (Côte de Nuits) Small *grand cru* vineyard (5.4 hectares) just south of the Clos-de-Bèze in Gevrey-Chambertin. Typically lighter and more delicate than the other *grands crus*. But over-lightness – from over-production – is their curse. Best producer: *Jadot*.

**CHARMES-CHAMBERTIN, AC** (Côte de Nuits) At 31.6 hectares, this is the biggest of the *grands crus* of Gevrey-Chambertin. It can be fine, strong, sensuous wine, but as with all the Gevrey-Chambertin *grands crus*, it can also, sadly, sometimes be disgracefully light. Best producers: *Bachelet, Drouhin, Rebourseau, Roty, Rousseau, Tortochot*.

**CHASSAGNE-MONTRACHET, AC** (Côte de Beaune) Down in the south of the Côte de Beaune, about half the wine Chassagne-Montrachet produces is red, even though its fame lies in its large share of the white *grand cru* Le Montrachet. The reds are a puzzle. I'm frequently disappointed by their rather hot plum-skins and chewy earth flavours, yet because the price is keen, I do keep coming back for more! Best producers: *Bachelet-Ramonet, Carillon, Colin, Jean-Noël Gagnard, Duc de Magenta, Gagnard-Delagrange, Albert Morey, Moreau, Fernand Pillot, Ramonet-Prudhon*.

**CHOREY-LÈS-BEAUNE, AC** (Côte de Beaune) Good lesser village near Beaune, not expensive for soft, fruity reds. Because the village isn't popular, these are some of the few affordable wines in top vintages such as 1988 and 1989. *Germain* and *Tollot-Beaut* are the best producers.

**CLOS DE LA ROCHE, AC** (Côte de Nuits) Largest and finest *grand cru* of Morey-St-Denis, on the border with

Gevrey-Chambertin. When not made too lightweight, this can be a splendid wine, full of redcurrant and strawberry richness when young, but coming to resemble a pretty good Chambertin after ten years or so. Best producers: *Amiot, Dujac, Leroy*, both *Hubert* and *Georges Lignier, Ponsot, Rousseau*.

**CLOS DES LAMBRAYS, AC** (Côte de Nuits) A *grand cru* only since 1981, this nine-hectare vineyard in Morey-St-Denis belongs to a single family (*Saier*), unusual in Burgundy. In the 1970s the estate became very run down and the wines were not only very rare but also not very tasty. Wholesale replanting in 1979 means that no real style has yet emerged, but old-timers say that the Clos des Lambrays could potentially make one of Burgundy's finest, most fragrant reds.

**CLOS DE TART, AC** (Côte de Nuits) *Grand cru* of Morey-St-Denis wholly owned by Beaujolais merchants *Mommessin*. At its best Clos de Tart is a light but intense wine which lasts a surprisingly long time.

**CLOS DE VOUGEOT, AC** (Côte de Nuits) This 50-hectare vineyard completely dominates the village of Vougeot. Over 80 growers share the enclosure and, while the land at the top is very fine, the land by the road is not. That rare thing, a good bottle of Clos de Vougeot, is a wonderful fat Burgundy, rich, strong, thick with the sweetness of perfumed plums and honey, unsubtle, but exciting. It can only be found in top vintages, like 1988. Best producers: *Arnoux, Château de la Tour, Jacky Confuron, Drouhin-Laroze, Engel, Grivot, Gros, Hudelot-Noëllat, Jadot, Lamarche, Leroy, Mugneret, Raphet, Rebourseau*.

**CLOS ST-DENIS, AC** (Côte de Nuits) The village of Morey-St-Denis gets its name from this *grand cru* but the villagers probably should have chosen another *grand cru* – like the much better known Clos de la Roche – because this small 6.5

hectare vineyard has rarely achieved great heights and is probably the least known of all the *grands crus*. I'd give my vote to *Georges* or *Hubert Lignier* or *Ponsot*, though *Dujac* is the best known.

**LE CORTON, AC** (Côte de Beaune) The only red *grand cru* in the Côte de Beaune, on the upper slopes of the famous dome-shaped hill of Corton. Ideally, Corton should have something of the savoury strength of Vosne-Romanée to the north, and something of the mouth-watering, caressing sweetness of Beaune to the south, but the wines labelled Corton have been strangely insubstantial in recent vintages, and wines from subdivisions of Le Corton such as Corton-Pougets, Corton-Bressandes and Corton Clos du Roi more regularly reach this ideal. Best producers: *Chandon de Briailles, Dubreuil-Fontaine, Faiveley, Gaunoux, Laleur-Piot, Maldant, Prince de Mérode, Quenot, Rapet, Ravaux, Reine Pédauque, Daniel Senard, Tollot-Beaut, Michel Voarick*.

**CÔTE CHALONNAISE, AC** The area immediately south of the Côte d'Or, the full name of which is Bourgogne Rouge (or Blanc) Côte Chalonnaise. The vineyards come in pockets rather than in one long swathe, but the top three villages of Rully, Mercurey and Givry all produce good wines, with a lovely, simple strawberry and cherry fruit.

**CÔTE DE BEAUNE** The southern part of the Côte d'Or, fairly evenly divided between red and white wines. There is a tiny AC Côte de Beaune which can produce light but tasty reds in warm years. Best producers: *Bouchard Père et Fils, René Manuel, J Alexant*.

**CÔTE DE BEAUNE-VILLAGES, AC** Catch-all red wine *appellation* for 16 villages on the Côte de Beaune. Only Aloxe-Corton, Beaune, Volnay and Pommard cannot use the *appellation*. Rarely seen nowadays and rarely exciting, it used to be the source of much excellent soft red, as many lesser-known but good villages would blend their wines together. Still, it *is* worth checking out the wines of *Jaffelin, Lequin-Roussot* and *Bachelet.*

**CÔTE DE NUITS** The northern part of the Côte d'Or, theoretically producing the biggest wines. Frequently it doesn't and many of Burgundy's most disappointing bottles come from the top Côte de Nuits communes. It is almost entirely devoted to Pinot Noir.

**CÔTE DE NUITS-VILLAGES, AC** An *appellation* covering the three southernmost villages of Prissey, Comblanchien and Corgoloin, plus Fixin and Brochon in the North. Usually fairly light and dry, they can have good cherry fruit and the slightly rotting veg delicious decay of good Côte de Nuits red. Look out for the wines of *Durand, Rion, Rossignol* and *Tollot-Voarick*, and especially *Chopin-Groffier.*

**CÔTE D'OR** The source of Burgundy's fame – a thin sliver of land only 30 miles long, and often less than a mile wide, running from Dijon to Chagny. It has two halves, the Côte de Nuits in the North and the Côte de Beaune in the South.

**ÉCHÉZEAUX, AC** (Côte de Nuits) Large, (relatively) unexciting *grand cru* of Vosne-Romanée. Best producers: *Domaine de la Romanée-Conti, Engel, Faiveley, Louis Gouroux, Grivot, Henri Jayer, Lamarche, Mongeard-Mugneret, René Mugneret.*

**EPINEUIL , AC** Tiny region near Tonnerre, producing light but fragrant styles of Pinot Noir.

**FIXIN, AC** (Côte de Nuits) A suburb of Dijon, Fixin can make some of Burgundy's sturdiest reds, deep, strong, tough but plummy when young, but capable of mellowing with age. Such wines are slowly reappearing. If you want to feel you're

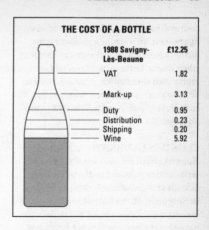

**THE COST OF A BOTTLE**

| | | |
|---|---|---|
| **1988 Savigny-Lès-Beaune** | | **£12.25** |
| VAT | | 1.82 |
| Mark-up | | 3.13 |
| Duty | | 0.95 |
| Distribution | | 0.23 |
| Shipping | | 0.20 |
| Wine | | 5.92 |

drinking Gevrey-Chambertin without shouldering the cost, Fixin from the following producers could fit the bill: *Bordet, Charlopin-Parizot, Bruno Clair, Fougeray, Gelin, Joliet, Moillard, Guyard.*

**FLAGEY-ÉCHÉZEAUX, AC** (Côte de Nuits) Commune that sells its basic wines as Vosne-Romanée but, in Échézeaux and Grands-Échézeaux, has two *grands crus.*

**GEVREY-CHAMBERTIN, AC** (Côte de Nuits) The start of the big time for reds. Gevrey-Chambertin has eight *grands crus,* and two of them, Chambertin and Chambertin Clos-de-Bèze can be some of the world's greatest wines. They should have rough, plum-skins and damson strength, fierce when young, but assuming a brilliant, wafting perfume and intense, plummy richness when mature. Many of the best wines are made by young growers who do not own as much land in the top vineyards as the larger, old-established estates, but whose commitment to quality shines through. *Bachelet, Boillot, Burguet, Michel Esmonin, Philippe Leclerc, Mortet, Naddef* and *Rossignol* are the names to look out for. Of the old estates, *Rousseau* is best but *Domaine des Varoilles* is also good. Also look out for *Frédéric Esmonin, René Leclerc, Maume* and *Roty,* and for the merchants' bottlings, *Drouhin, Jadot, Faiveley* and *Jaffelin.*

**GIVRY, AC** (Côte Chalonnaise) Small but important red wine village. At its best, deliciously warm and cherry-chewy with a slightly smoky fragrance but there are too many mediocre bottles around, especially from *négociants*. *Baron Thénard* is the best estate, but *Chofflet, Clos Salomon, Joblot, Mouton* and *Ragot* are also worth investigating.

**LA GRANDE RUE, AC** (Côte de Nuits) Wholly owned by the Lamarche family. Elevated to *grand cru* status in 1990, more because of its potential – it is situated between La Tâche and La Romanée-Conti, the two greatest vineyards in Burgundy – than because of the wines it has recently produced.

**GRANDS ÉCHÉZEAUX, AC** (Côte de Nuits) A slightly second-line *grand cru*, but capable of delicately scented, plum-and-wood-smoke flavoured wine which will go rich and chocolaty with age. Best names: *Domaine de la Romanée-Conti, Drouhin, Engel, Lamarche, Mongeard-Mugneret*.

**GRIOTTE-CHAMBERTIN, AC** (Côte de Nuits) One of the smallest *grands crus* of Gevrey-Chambertin – 5.58 hectares. Best producers: *Drouhin, Ponsot, Roty*.

**HAUTES-CÔTES DE BEAUNE** and **HAUTES-CÔTES DE NUITS** A happy hunting ground, this hilly backwater behind the line of famous villages and vineyards on the Côte d'Or. The 28 Hautes-Côtes villages make some fairly good, light, strawberry-like Pinot at a decent price. The grapes do not always ripen fully every year, but they had no problems in 1988 or '89. Look out in the Hautes-Côtes de Nuits for the wines of *Cornu, Domaine des Mouchottes, Jayer-Gilles, Thévenet* and *Verdet* and in the Hautes-Côtes de Beaune for such growers as *Bouley, Capron Manieux, Chalet, Guillemard, Joliot, Mazilly* and *Plait*. The *Caves des Hautes-Côtes* is beginning to produce some of the best value reds in the whole of Burgundy.

**IRANCY, AC** Wines made mostly from Pinot Noir from vineyards just to the south-west of Chablis, sometimes with a little of the darker, tougher local grape, the César. Rarely deep in colour, but always perfumed, slightly plummy and attractive, good at two years old and usually capable of ageing several years more. It must legally be labelled 'Bourgogne Irancy'. Good producers: *Léon & Serge Bienvenu, Bernard Cantin, André & Roger Delaloge, Gabriel Delaloge, Jean Renaud, Simmonet-Febvre, Luc Sorin*.

**LADOIX-SERRIGNY, AC** (Côte de Beaune) An obscure village, overshadowed by Aloxe-Corton next door. Worth looking out for though, as *Capitain, Cornu, Prince de Mérode, Chevalier* and *Ravaut* all make decent, crisp wines at very fair prices.

**LATRICIÈRES-CHAMBERTIN, AC** (Côte de Nuits) Small *grand cru* vineyard in Gevrey-Chambertin and very similar in style to Chambertin though without the power. So long as the producer hasn't pushed the yields too high, it is at its best at ten to 15 years. Best producers: *Camus, Ponsot, Leroy*.

**MÂCON ROUGE, AC** There's a lot of red wine made in the Mâconnais but it's usually fairly lean, earthy Gamay without the spark of Beaujolais' fruit. If you like that sort of thing, try the wines of *Igé* and *Mancey*, or *Lafarge*'s wine from *Bray*. *Lassarat* is improving things by using new oak, and I'm sure more will follow.

**MARSANNAY, AC** (Côte de Nuits) This used to produce mostly pink wines, under the name Bourgogne Rosé de Marsannay, but the introduction of an *appellation* for red wines in 1987 has encouraged growers to switch from pink to red. The first results of this new seriousness are most encouraging and some lovely wines are already emerging, usually quite dry and cherry-perfumed, sometimes much more full-blown and exciting. One to watch. Best producers: *Bouvier, Charlopin-Parizot, Bruno Clair, Collotte, Fougeray, Fournier, Geantet-Pansiot, Huguenot, Jadot, Naddef.*

**MAZIS-CHAMBERTIN, AC** (Côte de Nuits) 12.5 hectare *grand cru* in Gevrey-Chambertin, far more reliable than most of the neighbouring *grands crus*. Mazis wines can have a superb deep blackberry-pip, damson-skin and blackcurrant fruit which gets deeper and more exciting after six to 12 years. Best producers: *Faiveley, Hospices de Beaune, Maume, Rebourseau, Roty, Rousseau, Tortochot.*

**MAZOYÈRES-CHAMBERTIN, AC** (Côte de Nuits) *Grand cru* of Gevrey-Chambertin, rarely seen since producers generally take up the option of using the *grand cru* Charmes-Chambertin instead.

**MERCUREY, AC** (Côte Chalonnaise) The biggest Chalonnais village, producing half the region's wines. Indeed many people call the Côte Chalonnaise the 'région de Mercurey'. It's mostly red wines, and these are often fairly full, with a most attractive strawberry fruit and a little smoky fragrance. As with the other Chalonnais reds, Mercurey's problems are infuriating inconsistency of quality, allied to callous exploitation of the name by some *négociants*. *Château de Chamirey, Chandesais, Chanzy, Domaine La Marche, Dufouleur, Faiveley, Jacqueson, Juillot, de Launay, Antonin Rodet, Saier* and *de Suremain* are all good.

**MONTHÉLIE, AC** (Côte de Beaune) Monthélie shares borders with Volnay and Meursault, but fame with neither. It's a red wine village, and the wines deserve recognition, because they're full, dry, rather herby or piney, but with a satisfying rough fruit. Often a good buy but beware the insidious growth of *négociants'* labels from firms who never traditionally noticed the AC. Best producers: *Boussey, Caves des Hautes-Côtes, Deschamps, Doreau, Garaudet, Château de Monthélie,*

*Monthélie-Douhairet, Potinet-Ampeau, de Suremain, Thévenin-Monthélie.*

**MOREY-ST-DENIS, AC** (Côte de Nuits) Once obscure and good value, the wines of Morey-St-Denis are now expensive and in general suffer badly from overproduction and over-sugaring. They should be wines with less body and more perfume than Gevrey-Chambertin, and a slight savouriness blending with a rich, chocolaty fruit as they age. Most are far too light, but there is a small number of outstanding growers. *Pierre Amiot, Bryczek, Dujac, Georges* and *Hubert Lignier, Marchand, Ponsot, Serveau, Charloppin, Perrot-Minot* and *Vadey-Castagnier.* Their 1987s, '88s, '89s and '90s are all excellent.

**MUSIGNY, AC** (Côte de Nuits) Extremely fine *grand cru* which gave its name to Chambolle-Musigny. All but a third of a hectare of the 10.65 hectare vineyard is red, capable of producing Burgundy's most heavenly-scented wine, but few recent offerings have had my hand lunging for the cheque book. Best names include: *Château de Chambolle-Musigny, Jadot, Leroy, Jacques Prieur, Georges Roumier, de Vogüé.*

**NUITS-ST-GEORGES, AC** (Côte de Nuits) When it's good, this has an enthralling decayed – rotting even – brown richness of chocolate and prunes rising out of a fairly light, plum-sweet fruit – quite gorgeous, whatever it sounds like. It used to be one of the most abused of all Burgundy's names and virtually disappeared from the export markets, but is now fairly common, expensive but immeasurably better, and increasingly reliable. From companies such as *Jadot, Jaffelin, Labouré-Roi* and *Moillard*, it's even becoming possible to buy good merchants' Nuits once more. *Labouré-Roi*

*The price guides for this section begin on page 278.*

is the most consistent merchant, although *Moillard* and *Jadot* are increasingly good particularly at *premier cru* level. The most famous growers are *Robert Chaillon, Gouges, Michelot* and *Daniel Rion*, but excellent wines are also made by *Domaine de l'Arlot, Ambroise, Chicotot, Jean-Jacques Confuron* and the amazing (and amazingly expensive) *Leroy*. There were problems with rot in 1986 and with hail in 1987 so it is best to stick to top vintages such as 1985, '88, '89 and '90.

**PERNAND-VERGELESSES, AC** (Côte de Beaune) Little-known village round the back of the hill of Corton. Some quite attractive, softly earthy reds, mostly on the lean side. *Besancenot-Mathouillet, Caves des Hautes-Côtes, Chandon des Briailles, Delarche, Dubreuil-Fontaine, Laleure-Piot, Pavelot, Rapet* and *Rollin* are the best producers.

**POMMARD, AC** (Côte de Beaune) From good producers, Pommard can have a strong, meaty sturdiness, backed by slightly jammy but attractively plummy fruit. Not subtle, but many people's idea of what red Burgundy should be. The most consistently fine wines are made by *de Courcel* and *de Montille*, but also look out for the wines of *Billard-Gonnet, Boillot, Château de Pommard, Girardin, Lahaye, Lejeune, Jean Monnier, Mussy, Parent, Pothier* and *Pousse d'Or*.

**RICHEBOURG, AC** (Côte de Nuits) Exceptional *grand cru* at the northern end of the commune of Vosne-Romanée. It's a wonderful name for a wine – Richebourg – and, at its best, it manages to be fleshy to the point of fatness, yet filled with spice and perfume and the clinging richness of chocolate and figs. Best producers: *Domaine de la Romanée-Conti, Gros, Henri Jayer, Leroy, Méo-Camuzet*.

**LA ROMANÉE, AC** (Côte de Nuits) This *grand cru* is the smallest AC in France, solely owned by the Liger-Belair family

and sold by *Bouchard Père et Fils*. It is usually adequate, but nowhere near the quality of the next-door vineyards owned by the *Domaine de la Romanée-Conti*.

**LA ROMANÉE-CONTI, AC** (Côte de Nuits) This tiny *grand cru* of almost two hectares is capable of a more startling brilliance than any other Burgundy. The 7,000 or so bottles it produces per year are seized on by the super-rich before we mere mortals can even get our tasting sheets out. It is wholly owned by the *Domaine de la Romanée-Conti*.

**LA ROMANÉE-ST-VIVANT, AC** (Côte de Nuits) 9.54 hectare *grand cru* in the village of Vosne-Romanée. Much less easy to taste when young than its neighbouring *grands crus* and needing a good dozen years to show what can be a dazzlingly delicious, savoury yet sweet personality. Best producers: *Arnoux, Domaine de la Romanée-Conti, Latour, Leroy*.

**RUCHOTTES-CHAMBERTIN, AC** (Côte de Nuits) The smallest *grand cru* of Gevrey-Chambertin at 3.1 hectares, making wines of deeper colour and longer-lasting perfumed richness than most of the village's other *grands crus*. Best producers: *Georges Mugneret, Roumier, Rousseau*.

**RULLY, AC** (Côte Chalonnaise) Village just a couple of miles below Santenay, initially known for its sparkling wine, but gradually gaining a reputation for light but tasty reds and whites. Best producers: *Chanzy, Château de Rully, Delorme, Domaine de la Folie, Duvernay, Faiveley, Jacqueson, Jaffelin*.

**ST-AUBIN, AC** (Côte de Beaune) Some of Burgundy's best value wines, especially from *Bachelet, Clerget, Lamy, Prudhon, Thomas* and *Roux*. The 1985s, 1988s and 1989s are delicious and reasonably priced.

**ST-ROMAIN, AC** (Côte de Beaune) Even more out of the way than St-Aubin. Full, rather broad-flavoured, cherry-stone dry reds. On the whole sold cheaper than they deserve. Look for *Bazenet, Buisson, Gras, Thévenin* and *Thévenin-Monthélie*. Go for top vintages such as 1985, '88 and '90.

**SANTENAY, AC** (Côte de Beaune) Rough and ready red. At its best, with a strong, savoury flavour and good strawberry fruit, though frequently nowadays rather lean and mean. Best producers include: *Belland, Girardin, Lequin-Roussot, Morey, Pousse d'Or, Prieur-Bonnet, Roux*. Even here, there can be a lot of variation.

**SAVIGNY-LÈS-BEAUNE, AC** (Côte de Beaune) Not renowned, but pretty reliable reds. Rarely very full, but with an attractive earthiness backing up strawberry fruit. Often good quality at a fair price. Look out for *Bize, Camus-Bruchon, Capron-Manieux, Chandon de Briailles, Ecard-Guyot, de Fougeray, Girard-Vollot, Guillemot, Pavelot-Glantenay* and *Tollot-Beaut*. The 1985s, '87s and even some 1989s are drinking deliciously now; the 1988s need a while longer.

**LA TÂCHE, AC** (Côte de Nuits) Another *grand cru* monopoly of the *Domaine de la Romanée-Conti*. As famous as Romanée-Conti, but not so totally unobtainable, since the 6.06 hectare vineyard can produce all of 24,000 bottles a year – that's two bottles each for the world's 12,000 richest people. The wine is heavenly, so

rich and heady the perfumes are sometimes closer to age-old brandy than table wine and the flavour loaded with spice and dark autumn-mellow fruits and the acrid richness of dark chocolate.

**VOLNAY, AC** (Côte de Beaune) Volnay is one of the most perfumed red Burgundies, with a memorable cherry and strawberry spice, but also, in its *premiers crus*, able to turn on a big, meaty style without losing the perfume. The best at the moment are *Lafarge* and *de Montille*. Their 1985s, '88s and '89s are superb. Other good names: *Ampeau, Blain-Gagnard, Boillot, Bouley, Clerget, Comtes Lafon, Delagrange, Glantenay, Lafon, Marquis d'Angerville, Pousse d'Or, Vaudoisey-Mutin, Voillot*.

**VOSNE-ROMANÉE, AC** (Côte de Nuits) The greatest Côte de Nuits village, right in the south of the Côte. Its *grands crus* sell for more money than any red wine on earth, except for Château Pétrus in Bordeaux, and, remarkably for Burgundy, they are dominated by a single estate, *Domaine de la Romanée Conti*. These vineyards make wines capable of more startling brilliance than any other red wine in France, with flavours as disparate yet as intense as the overpowering, creamy savouriness of fresh *foie gras* and the deep, sweet scent of ripe plums and prunes in brandy. You may need to re-mortgage your house in order to experience this though. There are also fine *premiers crus*, and the village wines, though not so reliable as

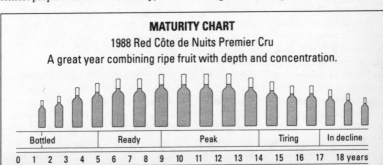

**MATURITY CHART**
1988 Red Côte de Nuits Premier Cru
A great year combining ripe fruit with depth and concentration.

| Bottled | | Ready | | Peak | | Tiring | | In decline |
|---|---|---|---|---|---|---|---|---|

0   1   2   3   4   5   6   7   8   9   10   11   12   13   14   15   16   17   18 years

they once were, can sometimes reflect their leaders. The 1987s and 1989s are particularly good here; the 1985s and '88s are unutterably great. Apart from the Domaine, good producers include *Arnoux, Sylvain Cathiard, Confuron-Coteditot, Engel, Grivot, Jean Gros, Hudelot-Noëllat, Georges Jayer, Henri Jayer, Henri Lamarche, Leroy, Méo-Camuzet, Mongeard-Mugneret, Georges Mugneret,* *Pernin-Rossin, Rouget, Daniel Rion* and *Jean Tardy.*

**VOUGEOT, AC** (Côte de Nuits) A village famous only because of its *grand cru* Clos de Vougeot, which at its best is plummy and broad. However, there are some decent wines made outside the hallowed walls of the Clos – notably from *Bertagna* and *Clerget.*

---

### RED CÔTE D'OR VINTAGES

**1991** A small crop, partly because of hail damage, though it would have been small even without that, and it would have been outstanding had not rain at vintage time come along and spoilt things. Even so, there were some very good reds made – and with some yields as low as 10 hectolitres per hectare, they can have extraordinary concentration. It's a patchy vintage, but the good wines will be ones to keep, because of that concentration.

**1990** Despite uneven flowering, the long, warm summer produced yet another large crop, so once again there will be plenty of wine around. The best of the 1990s are brilliantly coloured and brilliantly fruity, naturally high in sugars. Producers who attempted to restrict the crop will have made the best wines, with good concentration and balance; others will have produced less concentrated drinking for the medium term.

**1989** The warm season produced a large crop of healthy, ripe grapes pretty well everywhere. It shouldn't have been necessary to chaptalize and the better growers held back. A lot of good wines were made, but only a few that might be regarded as exceptional. The wines are softer than the 1988s, and some commentators view them as a kind of cross between 1982 and 1985 in style. Though, having said that, there are some superbly concentrated wines, particularly in the Côte de Beaune, destined to rival the 1988s and, dare I suggest it, surpass them in some cases.

**1988** There was potential to make great wine in 1988, though it was hardly a textbook year. There was serious drought during the summer, and some may have ended up with grapes rather short on sugar. Those who waited to pick, however, were walloped by the rain. But throughout the Côte d'Or a surprising number of growers did not overproduce, did pick fully ripe grapes before the rains came, and have made delicious wines – more joyously fruity than 1987, and quite a bit deeper and riper than 1986.

**1987** It didn't start out with much of a reputation because no-one was enthusiastic about Bordeaux '87s and this impression travelled. The good producers made quite small amounts of well coloured, concentrated wine which in some cases is better than their 1985s. The best '87s are very good indeed, Côte de Beaune having the edge over Côte de Nuits. Further down the scale the wines aren't as good as '85, but are better than '86.

**1986** Over the last year the wines have been shedding toughness, and now exhibit their best feature, perfume. Stick to decent producers, because there was some rot .

**1985** When the 1985s were young, they were terrific. Some have gone from strength to strength. Some seem stuck in a 'dumb' phase. Some shot their bolt early.

**1983** The best wines display impressive flavour. If you can wait another decade you may have the most impressive old-style Burgundies made in the last 20 years, but I'd avoid Vosne-Romanée, Chambolle-Musigny and Morey-Saint-Denis.

**1982** Ridiculously over-praised to start with. The best wines are from the Côte de Beaune and are delicate, perfumed, nicely balanced.

# WHITE WINES

Sometimes it is red Burgundy that is criticised for poor winemaking, high prices and deadening complacency, while white Burgundy seems to be rising to the challenge of the New World with clean new oak and temperature-controlled fermentation. However, with red-wine makers putting their house in order it's becoming horribly obvious that the whites are making a less exciting job of it; that all that New World inspired cleanliness has not taken root very deeply.

You can, in fact, be too clean. To make good wine, white or red, you need to play safe, with minimal oxidation, scrupulous hygiene and absolute reliability in the cellar. Making great wine is another matter. Here you need to take chances: you are walking a tightrope, and on one side lies disaster, on the other, boredom. But if you keep your balance...

Not all wine of course has the capacity to be great; the same applies to wine-makers. Very few wine-makers, in fact, make great red and white; this is true everywhere, not just in Burgundy. Some manage to pull it off, but not many.

In Burgundy, some of the faults stem from large yields from the vineyards; large harvests are likely to mean less concentration in the wine. Leflaive, in particular, has been criticized in the past for huge yields; Vincent Leflaive used to claim that he could make great wine every year under such conditions. Now Vincent has retired, and while there has been nothing so inelegant as a U-turn, the new co-manager, his daughter Anne-Claude Leflaive, has let the world know that yields may well be lower as a result of the organic viticulture which the domaine is now practising.

## Green Chardonnay

These organic methods are still only experimental at Domaine Leflaive and are being used on just 2.5 acres at the moment, but they involve the use of natural fertilizers rather than chemical ones, and the shunning of chemical pesticides and fungicides. Organic viticulture is more familiar in the hot, dry vineyards of Provence, where it is relatively problem-free; in the cool northern rot-prone climes of Burgundy to embark on such a programme is to make life very difficult indeed for yourself.

Whether such methods will be used in Domaine Leflaive's new baby is not yet clear. The new baby is an expensive acquisition: a tiny sliver, no more than a fifth of an acre, of the finest and most expensive of all Burgundian white wine vineyards, Le Montrachet. It's the sort of thing lovers of white Burgundy dream about: the elegant Leflaive style being applied to the greatest Chardonnay site on the Côte d'Or. Not that there'll be much to go round. The 1991 crop amounted to around 30 cases and will sell to a few very lucky – or very wealthy – people at about £200 a bottle.

It was the first time in 15 years that a plot of Le Montrachet had come up for sale – and it is an indication of the value of this particular patch of earth that even at that rather high price per bottle (put your name down now, if you want one), it will be around 15 years before the domaine starts making a profit on its sales of Le Montrachet. The domaine is in fact believed to have paid at least £600,000 for its fifth of an acre.

Now, it is possible to buy white Burgundy at less than £200 a bottle. It's even possible to buy very good white Burgundy for less than that. But in Burgundy it is all too easy to lose touch with reality; to suppose that if Le Montrachet is worth £200 a bottle (and somebody must think it is, or how could such a price even be contemplated?) then £15 for a village Meursault must be stunning value indeed. But for £15 I expect a wine to be very good quality; anything less is not just poor value, it's a rip-off. And it has to be said that an awful lot of white Burgundy comes into that bracket.

Yes, there are examples from all over the world, of course; it's not just Burgundy. It's hard to suppress a sceptical yawn when a California grower prices his top Cabernet at US$150 a bottle (Diamond Creek Vineyards 1987 Lake Cabernet, in case you want to start saving) while claiming that this price was set by the market.

I haven't tasted the wine; it may be an extraordinary experience. Paying for it certainly must be. But if I expect very good quality for £15, what can I expect for £150? Or £200?

Am I misjudging them? Or the market? I compare Burgundy to other wine regions and I compare its white wines of village quality to good estate Chardonnays from Australia or California – I'm not talking about Le Montrachet here, nor about basic Bourgogne Blanc – and I find more reliability, more clean fruit, in the New World examples. I also find better value. The Burgundians might say that the New World examples lack complexity and will not age, but then village Burgundy has never been intended to be cellared for years either.

## Burgundy with L-plates

The crucial point is reliability. Burgundy is in many ways not a wine for the novice buyer because it is so complex: leaving aside the system of communes, *premiers crus* and *grands crus*, the consumer must find his way through a maze of growers and *négociants*. There are no quick *aides memoires*; you have to know your producers. If you don't, you will find yourself on a roller-coaster of quality, up one moment, plunging down the next and nearly always spending a lot of money. The New World, by contrast, offers a smooth path. Sure, some New World Chardonnays are over-priced; particularly in California. But go into a shop here, pick up an unknown New World Chardonnay and you can have a reasonable idea of what sort of quality you can expect within a price range. That's as specific as anyone needs to be: buying wine is not like buying eggs or milk.

Buying great wines, or potentially great wines, is different. Here the gamble, the excitement of seeing how they turn out years hence, is part of the fun. At the very top level it is very hard indeed to beat Burgundy – so perhaps that £200 a bottle has some justification.

One could argue that the reliability of the New World imposes a uniformity; that the very openness that means that customers take an educated interest in winemaking techniques leads to all producers doing the same thing. Up to a point, it's true. The mere fact that they're all growing Chardonnay indicates a certain similarity of approach.

Nobody, surely, wants to see uniformity in Burgundy. Nobody is likely to: it's a region of individuals who don't take kindly to being told what to do. But wouldn't it be nice if the attack of openness suffered by the region this year turned out to be permanent? If, in five years' time, one could buy white Burgundy, not quibbling about the price because, yes, it's in short supply and high demand – but know that, whatever the price, it was good value. Wouldn't that be nice? **MARGARET RAND**

# GRAPES & FLAVOURS

**CHARDONNAY** In a world panting for Chardonnay, Burgundy makes the most famous Chardonnay of all. Even in the decidedly dicky Burgundian climate, it produces a fair to considerable amount of good to excellent wine almost every year. Its flavour depends on where it is grown, and how the wine is made. Chardonnays made without the use of oak barrels for ageing will taste very different from barrel-aged wines. A Mâcon produced in stainless steel will have rather appley fruit as well as something slightly fat and yeasty or, in a hot year, a slightly exotic peachiness. Côte Chalonnaise Chardonnay is in general rather taut and chalky-dry, but given a little oak, it can become delicate and nutty. Chablis, too, generally produces lean wine, but in riper years and with some oak treatment it can get much rounder and mouth-filling. The Côte d'Or is the peak of achievement for Chardonnay, and a top wine from the Côte de Beaune manages to be luscious, creamy, honeyed yet totally dry, the rich, ripe fruit intertwined with the scents of new oak into a memorable, and surprisingly powerful wine – from the right producer, the world's greatest dry white wine. It is this outstanding accolade that has so enticed the New World wineries – and quite a few in the Old World, too, outside France – into trying to mimic the success of the Burgundian grape with their own examples of fine wine.

**ALIGOTÉ** Not planted in the best sites – though there are a few vines in Corton-Charlemagne. Aligoté used to be merely sharp, spritzy café wine, but from old vines it can produce a lovely, refreshing wine, scented like buttermilk soap yet as sharp and palate-cleansing as a squeeze of lemon juice.

**PINOT BEUROT** Known elsewhere as Pinot Gris. Rare in Burgundy, but it produces rich, buttery wine usually blended in to soften the Chardonnay. There is a little unblended Pinot Beurot in the Hautes-Côtes.

**PINOT BLANC** There is a little of this about in the Côte d'Or – in Aloxe-Corton, for instance, where it makes a soft, rather unctuous, quick-maturing wine. Rully in the Côte Chalonnaise has a good deal and it ripens well in the Hautes-Côtes. There is also an odd white mutation of Pinot Noir – as at Nuits-St-Georges where the *premier cru* La Perrière produces a very savoury white, and in the Monts Luisants vineyard in Morey-St-Denis.

# WINES & WINE REGIONS

**ALOXE-CORTON, AC** (Côte de Beaune) This most northerly village of the Côte de Beaune has one of the Côte's most famous *grands crus*, Corton-Charlemagne. It can be a magnificent, blasting wall of flavour, not big on nuance, but strong, buttery and ripe, which traditionally is supposed to require long ageing to show its full potential. Do not expect this sort of quality from the simple village wine, however, recent vintages of Corton-Charlemagne have mostly been strangely disappointing and one is left wondering if they're not trying to produce too much wine.

**AUXEY-DURESSES, AC** (Côte de Beaune) Tucked away in the folds of the hill rather than on the main Côte de Beaune slope, Auxey-Duresses has never been well known, but has always had some reputation for soft, nutty whites. Recently, though, too many have been disappointingly soft and flabby, but the new confidence of the lesser villages is evident here too and 1990, '89, '88 and '87 have all produced good wine. Producers like *Ampeau, Diconne, Duc de Magenta, Jadot, Leroy* and *Prunier* are still producing pretty decent stuff.

**BÂTARD-MONTRACHET, AC** (Côte de Beaune) *Grand cru* of Chassagne and Puligny lying just below Le Montrachet and, from a good producer, displaying a good deal of its dramatic flavour, almost thick in the mouth, all roast nuts, butter, toast and honey. Exciting stuff, costing rather more than the national average wage – per bottle, that is – in the few restaurants that stock it. Good names: *Blain-Gagnard, Clerc, Jean-Noël Gagnard, Leflaive, Bernard Morey, Pierre Morey, Michel Niellon, Pernot, Poirier, Claude Ramonet, Ramonet-Prudhon, Sauzet*.

**BIENVENUES-BÂTARD-MONTRACHET, AC** (Côte de Beaune) Tiny *grand cru* in Puligny below Le Montrachet, and inside the larger Bâtard-Montrachet – whose wines are similar though the Bienvenues wines are often lighter, more elegant and may lack a tiny bit of Bâtard's drive. Producers: *Carillon, Clerc, Leflaive, Pernot, Ramonet-Prudhon*.

**BOURGOGNE ALIGOTÉ, AC** Usually rather sharp and green except for vineyards near Pernand-Vergelesses where old vines can make exciting wine, but the Burgundians usually add Crème de Cassis to it to make Kir – which tells you quite a lot about its usual character. Look out for *Coche-Dury, Confuron, Diconne, Jobard, Monthélie-Douhairet, Rion, Rollin*.

**BOURGOGNE ALIGOTÉ DE BOUZERON, AC** (Côte Chalonnaise) The white wine pride of the Côte Chalonnaise is made not from Chardonnay but from Aligoté in the village of Bouzeron. The vines are frequently old – more crucial for Aligoté than for most other wines – and the buttermilk soap nose is followed by a very dry, slightly lemony, pepper-sharp wine, too good to mix with Cassis. It got its own AC in 1979. It owes its sudden fame to the interest of the *de Villaine* family, who own a substantial estate there making fairly good, oaked Aligoté. *Chanzy* and *Bouchard Père et Fils* are also good.

**BOURGOGNE BLANC** This can mean almost anything – from a basic Burgundy grown in the less good vineyards of anywhere between Chablis and the Mâconnais to a carefully matured wine from a serious producer, either from young vines or from parts of his vineyard that just miss a superior AC, especially on the borders of Meursault. Best producers: *Boisson-Vadot, Boyer-Martenot, Boisson-Morey, Henri Clerc, Coche-Dury, Dussort, Jadot, Javillier, Jobard, Labouré-Roi, René Manuel, Millot-Battault*, and *Buxy co-op (Clos de Chenoves)*.

**CHABLIS, AC** Simple Chablis, mostly soft, sometimes acidic, covers the widest area of the *appellation*. Well it would, wouldn't it? They've included most of what used to be Petit Chablis for a start. But at the rate they're now extending the *premier cru* status to virtually anything that moves, maybe *premiers crus* will soon overtake Chablis in acreage. Chablis covers a multitude of sins, with a lot of wine going under *négociants'* labels, and a lot being sold by the co-op – they make most of the *négociants'* stuff too. Some of the co-op's best *cuvées* are outstandingly good, but many of the cheaper *cuvées* are too bland and soft. A good grower is more likely to give you something steely and traditional. Good producers: *Christian Adine, Jean-Marc Brocard, La Chablisienne, Jean Collet, René Dauvissat, Defaix, Jean-Paul Droin, Joseph Drouhin, Jean Durup, William Fèvre, Vincent Gallois, Alain Geoffroy, Jean-Pierre Grossot, Michel Laroche, Bernard Légland, Louis Michel, Guy Mothe, François & Jean-Marie Raveneau, Regnard, Simmonet-Fèbvre, Philippe Testut, Robert Vocoret*.

**CHABLIS GRAND CRU** The seven *grands crus* (Blanchots, Preuses, Bougros, Grenouilles, Valmur, Vaudésir and Les Clos) come from a small patch of land just outside the town of Chablis, on a single slope rising from the banks of the river Serein. The wines *can* be outstanding, though still unlikely to rival the *grands cru* of the Côte de Beaune. To get the best out of them, you need to age them, preferably after oaking, although *Louis Michel's* oak-free wines age superbly. The last three vintages have seen a considerable increase in the use of oak by the better producers, and the results are much deeper, more exciting wine which may well benefit from six to ten years' ageing in bottle.

**CHABLIS PREMIER CRU** Some 30 names, rationalized into 12 main vineyards. Once upon a time, this used to be a very reliable classification for good, characterful dry white, if less intense than *grand cru*, but again, there has been this expansion mania, meaning that many hardly suitable pieces of vineyard are now accorded *premier cru* status. Given that there is a price difference of £3 to £4 a bottle between Chablis and *premier cru* Chablis, the quality difference should be plain as a pikestaff. Sadly it rarely is. However, since 1986 there has been a definite move towards quality by the better growers and *La Chablisienne* co-op.

**CHASSAGNE-MONTRACHET, AC** (Côte de Beaune) Only half the production of this famous vineyard at the south of the Côte de Beaune is white, but that does include a chunk of the great Montrachet vineyard. The *grands crus* are excellent, but the *premiers crus* rarely dazzle quite like those of nearby Puligny-Montrachet. The Chassagne '86s are mostly at their best now, and should be drunk; the 1989s are wonderfully ripe and concentrated and can be drunk now or kept for years. Best producers: *Blain-Gagnard, Carillon, Chartron et Trebuchet, Colin, Duc de Magenta, Fontaine-Gagnard, Jean-Noël Gagnard, Gagnard-Delagrange, Génot-Boulanger, Lamy-Pillot, Laguiche, Château de la Maltroye, Moreau, Albert Morey, Bernard Morey, Niellon, Fernand Pillot, Ramonet.*

---

**CHABLIS VINEYARDS**
**Grands Crus**

Blanchots, Bougros, Les Clos, Grenouilles, Preuses, Valmur, Vaudésir.

**Premiers Crus**

Fourchaume (including Fourchaume, Vaupulent, Côte de Fontenay, Vaulorent, l'Homme Mort); Montée de Tonnerre (including Montée de Tonnerre, Chapelot, Pied d'Aloup); Monts de Milieu; Vaucoupin; Les Fourneaux (including Les Fourneaux, Morein, Côte des Prés-Girots); Beauroy (including Beauroy, Troesmes); Côte de Léchet; Vaillons (including Vaillons, Châtains, Séché, Beugnons, Les Lys); Mélinots (including Mélinots, Roncières, Les Epinottes); Montmains (including Montmains, Forêts, Butteaux); Vosgros (including Vosgros and Vaugiraut); Vaudevey.

---

**CHEVALIER-MONTRACHET, AC** (Côte de Beaune) *Grand cru* vineyard of Puligny, directly above Le Montrachet. The higher elevation gives a leaner wine than Le Montrachet, but one with a fabulous deep flavour as rich and satisfying as a dry white wine can get. Good examples will last 20 years. Best producers: *Bouchard Père et Fils, Clerc, Jadot, Latour, Leflaive, Niellon.*

**CORTON, AC** (Côte de Beaune) Corton-Charlemagne is the white *grand cru* here in Aloxe-Corton, but tiny patches of the Corton *grand cru* grow Chardonnay and Pinot Blanc. The finest wine, the *Hospices de Beaune's* Corton-Vergennes, is all Pinot, and *Chandon de Briailles* makes Corton-Bressandes, half from Pinot Blanc, half from Chardonnay.

**CORTON-CHARLEMAGNE, AC** (Côte de Beaune) This famous *grand cru* of Aloxe-Corton and Pernand-Vergelesses occupies the upper half of the dome-shaped hill of Corton, where the first of the Côte de Beaune's limestone outcrops becomes apparent. It is planted almost entirely with

Chardonnay, but a little Pinot Blanc or Pinot Beurot can add an intriguing fatness to the wine. Good producers: *Bonneau du Martray, Chandon de Briailles, Chapuis, Dubreuil-Fontaine, Hospices de Beaune, Laleure Piot, Latour, Rapet*.

**CÔTE CHALONNAISE, AC** As the ordered vineyards of the Côte de Beaune swing away and dwindle to the west, the higgledy-piggledy vineyards of the Côte Chalonnaise hiccup and splutter into life as a patchwork of south- and east-facing outcrops. Light, usually clean-tasting Chardonnay predominates among the whites – although at long last the idea of oak-ageing is catching on. But the Côte Chalonnaise has one star that cannot be overshadowed by the famous Côte d'Or: the village of Bouzeron makes the most famous, if not quite the finest Aligoté in all France.

**CÔTE D'OR** This famous strip of vineyard, running south-west from Dijon for 30 miles, sprouts famous names right along its length, with a fine crop of illustrious whites in the southern portion. But in fact it produces only about 16 per cent of Burgundy's white. (Mâconnais is the chief white producer, with the Côte Chalonnaise chipping in a bit.) Price lunacy for whites has become a fairly common phenomenon in all the Côte d'Or villages, as has complete absence of the wines from many British wine-lovers' cellars, including mine.

**CRÉMANT DE BOURGOGNE, AC** What used to be simple, pleasantly tart Burgundian fizz, based on slightly green Chardonnay and Aligoté grapes, excellent for mixing with cassis, is beginning to sharpen up its act. Competition from other wine-producing regions and from neighbouring countries, added to the increase in Champagne prices, has led to co-operatives, such as the *caves* of Viré or St-Gengoux-Clessé in the Mâconnais, and the *Cave de Bailly* in the Yonne and

*Delorme* in Rully, producing excellent, eminently affordable fizz, increasingly from 100 per cent Chardonnay. Crémant de Bourgogne is becoming a wine that no longer needs disguising.

**CRIOTS-BÂTARD-MONTRACHET, AC** (Côte de Beaune) Tiny 1.6 hectare *grand cru* in Chassagne-Montrachet nuzzled up against the edge of Bâtard itself. Hardly ever seen but the wines are similar to Bâtard, full, strong, packed with flavour, perhaps a little leaner. Best producers: *Blain-Gagnard, Fontaine-Gagnard*.

**HAUTES-CÔTES DE BEAUNE, AC** and **HAUTES-CÔTES DE NUITS, AC** A lot of reasonably good, light, dry Chardonnay from the hill country behind the Côte de Beaune and Côte de Nuits. Best producers: *Caves des Hautes-Côtes, Chalet, Cornu, Goubard, Jayer-Gilles, Alain Verdet* (organic).

**MÂCON BLANC, AC** It seemed, a few years ago, that the spiralling price of Pouilly-Fuissé – the region's only white wine star – was acting as a spur for the producers to improve quality. As Pouilly-Fuissé came spinning back to earth – a wiser but better, and cheaper, wine – upping the price of Mâcon to patently unrealistic levels seemed to have been the only effect. Now prices are back down again, and quality has yet to show any great improvement.

**MÂCON BLANC-VILLAGES, AC** One step up from basic Mâcon Blanc, this must come from the 43 Mâcon communes with the best land. The rare good ones show the signs of honey and fresh apples and some of the nutty, yeasty depth associated with fine Chardonnay. You can expect the better wines from those villages, notably **Viré, Clessé, Prissé** and **Lugny**, that add their own village names (Mâcon-Viré, etc). Full, buttery yet fresh, sometimes spicy: look for that and, if you find it, consider paying the price. You will find it occasionally in the

1989s and 1990s – but only rarely in other vintages. Prices went silly in the mid-1980s but are now merely too high, and have stopped being an insult to our intelligence. Best producers: *Bicheron, Bonhomme, Danauchet, Goyard, Josserand, Lassarat, Manciat-Poncet, Merlin, Signoret, Thévenet-Wicart*.

**MERCUREY, AC** (Côte Chalonnaise)
Village making over half the wine of the Côte Chalonnaise. Most of the production is red – the whites used to be rather flaccid afterthoughts from the less good land, but as the price of white shifts upwards in the Côte de Beaune, several producers have started making a bigger effort with interesting results. Good examples come from *Chartron et Trebuchet, Château de Chamirey, Faiveley, Genot* and *Boulanger*.

**MEURSAULT, AC** (Côte de Beaune)
Halfway down the Côte de Beaune, this village is the first, working southwards, of the great white wine villages. It has by far the largest white production of any Côte d'Or village, and this is one of several reasons why its traditionally high overall standard is gradually being eroded. The wines should be big and nutty and have a delicious, gentle lusciousness, and sometimes even peachy, honeyed flavours. Meursault has more producers bottling their own wine than any other village. These are some of the best: *Ampeau, Pierre Boillot, Boisson-Vadot, Boyer-Martenot, Buisson-Battault, Coche-Debord, Coche-*

*Dury, Comte Lafon, Gauffroy, Henri-Germain, Jean Germain, Grivault, Jobard, René Manuel, Matrot, Michelot-Buisson, Millot-Battault, Pierre Morey, Prieur, Roulot.*

**MONTAGNY, AC** (Côte Chalonnaise)
White-only AC in the south of the Côte Chalonnaise. In general the wines are a bit lean and chalky-dry, but now that the use of oak is creeping in, some much more interesting wines will appear. Best producers: *Arnoux*, co-op at *Buxy, Latour, B Michel, de Montorge, Alain Roy*.

**LE MONTRACHET, AC** (Côte de Beaune)
Finest of fine white *grands crus* in the villages of Puligny and Chassagne. Does it mean most enjoyable, most happy-making? Not really. In fact the flavours in Montrachet can be so intense it's difficult sometimes to know if you're having fun drinking it or merely giving your wine vocabulary an end of term examination. So be brave if someone opens a bottle of Montrachet for you and let the incredible blend of spice and smoke, honey and ripeness flow over your senses. Good producers: *Amiot-Bonfils, Bouchard Père et Fils, Domaine de la Romanée-Conti, Jadot, Comtes Lafon, Laguiche, Pierre Morey, Prieur, Thénard*. Presumably *Leflaive* too, though 1991 was its first vintage.

**MUSIGNY, AC** (Côte de Nuits) Just 0.3 hectares of this predominantly red *grand cru* of Chambolle-Musigny are planted

---

**MATURITY CHART**
1989 White Côte de Beaune Premier Cru
Generally fairly rich but beautifully balanced wines.

| Bottled | Ready | | Peak | | | Tiring | In decline |
|---|---|---|---|---|---|---|---|
| 0   1   2 | 3   4 | 5 | 6   7   8 | 9 | 10 | 11 | 12 years |

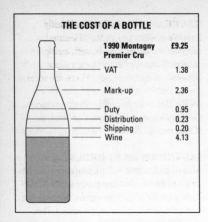

**THE COST OF A BOTTLE**

| | 1990 Montagny Premier Cru | £9.25 |
|---|---|---|
| | VAT | 1.38 |
| | Mark-up | 2.36 |
| | Duty | 0.95 |
| | Distribution | 0.23 |
| | Shipping | 0.20 |
| | Wine | 4.13 |

with Chardonnay, owned by the *Domaine de Vogüé*, and most of it seems to be consumed on the premises.

**PERNAND-VERGELESSES, AC** (Côte de Beaune). The village wines can be good, – with the best Aligoté in Burgundy, while the Chardonnays are generally fairly lean and need time to soften, but can be gently nutty and very enjoyable from a good producer. Can also be very good value. Best names: *Dubreuil-Fontaine, Laleure-Piot, Pavelot, Rapet, Rollin*.

**PETIT CHABLIS** There used to be lots of this grown on the least good slopes. But the growers objected that it made it sound as though their wine was a lesser form of Chablis. Nowadays, of course, pretty well the whole lot is called 'Chablis' – so *we* can't tell what's what, *they're* all richer, they're happy, we're not... I give up.

**POUILLY-FUISSÉ, AC** (Mâconnais) This once ridiculously overpriced white has more than halved its price in the last couple of years; and you can find parcels of Pouilly-Fuissé here and there for as little as a fiver. This tumble in price came about partly because the Americans stopped buying, although they were the ones who made it famous in the first place, and partly because the general quality from this co-op-monopolized, *négociant*-abused

AC was a disgrace. So the price slid. But snap up any bargains you see; they won't be there for long. Best producers: *Béranger, Corsin, Duboeuf*'s top selections, *Ferret, Guffens-Heynen, Leger-Plumet, Loron's les Vieux Murs, Manciat-Poncet, Noblet, Vincent* at *Château Fuissé*. Adjoining villages **Pouilly-Loché, AC** and **Pouilly-Vinzelles, AC** have borrowed the name and make similar wines at half the price.

**PULIGNY-MONTRACHET, AC** (Côte de Beaune) The peak of great white pleasure is to be found in the various Montrachet *grands crus*. Le Montrachet is peerless, showing how humble words like honey, nuts, cream, smoke, perfume and all the rest do no honest service to a white wine that seems to combine every memory of ripe fruit and subtly worn scent with a dry, penetrating savouriness. There are several other *grands crus*, less intense, but whose wines buzz with the mingling opposites of coffee and honey, and smoke and cream. There are *premiers crus* as well. While 'village' Meursault may be good, it's always worth buying a single vineyard wine in Puligny-Montrachet. Much of the wine is sold in bulk to *négociants* whose offerings vary between the delicious and the disgraceful, but look for the wines of *Amiot-Bonfils, Boyer-Devèze, Carillon, Chartron et Trebuchet, Clerc, Drouhin, Jadot, Labouré-Roi, Laguiche*, both *Domaine Leflaive* and *Olivier Leflaive, Pernot, Ramonet-Prudhon, Antonin Rodet, Sauzet, Thénard*.

**RULLY, AC** (Côte Chalonnaise) This village gets my vote for the most improved AC in Burgundy. Originally best known for fizz, then for pale, nutty, dull Chardonnay, the use of oak to ferment and age the wine has turned a lot into wonderfully soft, spicy Burgundies of good quality – and low price. Best names: *Bêtes, Chanzy, Cogny, Delorme, Dury, Duvernay, Domaine de la Folie, Jacqueson, Jaffelin, Rodet*.

**ST-AUBIN, AC** (Côte de Beaune) Some of Burgundy's best value white wines, full and racy, come from this tiny, forgotten Côte de Beaune village behind the far more famous Puligny-Montrachet and Meursault. Two-thirds of the vineyards are *premiers crus* and it really shows. Starting with 1982 it became clear that St-Aubin's *premiers crus* could rival the more famous wines of Meursault and Puligny-Montrachet. The 1986s from *Prudhon, Roux, Albert Morey* and *Jadot* were both delicious and affordable but need drinking. But grab any that you see on sale. The 1989s are better and richer but not such good value. Other good producers in the commune are *Bachelet, Bouton, Clerget, Colin, Delaunay, Duvernay, Jadot, Jaffelin, Lamy, Albert Morey, Prudhon, Roux* and *Thomas*.

**ST-ROMAIN, AC** (Côte de Beaune) The flinty, dry whites that emerge from this out of the way Côte de Beaune village right up near the Hautes-Côtes are often decent quality and pretty good value. Best are: *Bazenet, Buisson, Germain, Gras, Thévenin, Thévenin-Monthélie*.

**ST-VÉRAN, AC** (Mâconnais) Pouilly-Fuissé's understudy in the Mâconnais, capable of making simple, soft, quick-maturing but very attractive, rather honeyed white Burgundy. There are some great 1989s but, like their predecessors, they will tire very quickly. Best producers: *Corsin, Duboeuf, Grégoire, Lassarat, de Montferrand, Thibert, Vincent*.

**SAUVIGNON DE ST-BRIS, VDQS** A wine of undoubted AC quality grown south-west of Chablis that languishes as a VDQS merely because the Sauvignon Blanc is not a permitted AC grape in the area. Often one of the most stingingly nettly, most greeny gooseberryish of all France's Sauvignons, but recent ones have been more expensive and less exciting. Ah well, New Zealand has some nice Sauvignon, and Bordeaux Blanc is really tasty right now, so perhaps I'll drink those instead. Producers take note. Good names: *Louis Bersan, Jean-Marc Brocard, Robert & Philippe Defrance, Michel Esclavy, André Sorin, Luc Sorin*.

## WHITE BURGUNDY VINTAGES

White Burgundy is far less prone to vintage fluctuation than red, and in most years can produce a fair amount of pretty good wine.

**1991** Like the reds, the 1991 white Burgundies look patchy in quality, though without the reds' occasional brilliance. That vintage-time rain did more damage to the Chardonnay than to the Pinot Noir, in terms of rot, and some of the picking had to be pretty hasty. The whites certainly won't match up to the previous three vintages in quality; prices should ease a bit, but in Burgundy, who can say?

**1990** Though the growing season was in many ways similar to 1989 the 1990s have some of the structure of the '88s and some of the richness of the '89s. They are less austere than the '88s and probably won't last as long.The Chardonnay crop was very large, so the whites are likely to be inferior to the reds. A good rather than a great vintage for white Burgundy.

**1989** An outstanding year for white Burgundy, in the hands of competent winemakers. Hailed as the best white vintage of the 1980s, almost all the best growers' wines are beautifully balanced, despite their richness. Just a few lack acidity. As one Burgundy importer put it: 'a richer version of the structured and seriously undervalued 1985s'. The best news of all is that individual vineyard characteristics seem particularly pronounced in 1989.

**1988** The fruit was, if anything, a little cleaner and fresher than in 1987 and the wines may yet turn out like those of 1982. Which would be very nice – but remember 1982 was a year of record yield and the wines never attained real complexity. Numbers of Mâconnais wines have a bright fresh fruit not seen down that way for a few years. Chablis prices went up by 10 to 15 per cent, but you couldn't honestly say that its quality went up in parallel.

**1987** Good producers made attractive, quite light wines, sometimes with a slightly lean streak of acidity. Try the exciting new growers in the Côte Chalonnaise and Mâconnais. The Côte d'Or produced wines that were often frankly dull, but with time, Chablis is turning out to be good.

**1986** There's an interesting debate over the relative qualities of '86 and '85. Initially 1986 was given a better reception even than '85 because, whereas the former seemed to rely on sheer power, 1986 seemed to have finer acidity, a more focussed fruit and even a hint of richness. The balance has redressed a bit now. The good 1985s have proved to be much better balanced than previously thought, and the '86s have closed up somewhat. Whether they finally outshine the '85s will make for some interesting tasting over the years – if we can a) find, and b) afford any of the wines. Chablis had that classic blend of leanness and restrained ripeness which can make it the logical, if not the emotional choice for so many fish dishes. *Grands crus* still need several years. The Mâconnais promised so much, but few bottles really delivered much.

**1985** This is on the way back. Along with the strength are increasing signs of a proper acid balance and an outstanding concentration of fruit. Pity nobody waited to find out because most '85s were consumed long ago. If you do see one from a good producer, go for it – well, perhaps not, I've just remembered the price it'll be. Chablis started out with a lesser reputation, but wines from good producers can still improve. Mâconnais 1985s never really fulfilled their potential.

**1983** In 1983 there was a serious rot problem and a lot of grapes were also seriously overripe. The result is frequently heavy, rather unrefreshing, soggy-flavoured wines which rapidly lost their fruit. Some rare examples may turn out to be wonderful, but they aren't ready yet.

**1982** Easy, outgoing, clean-flavoured wines, almost entirely drunk by now.

# BEAUJOLAIS

The Beaujolais region was in luck last year: it was one of the very few parts of France to escape the full force of the spring frosts. Not only was the damage minimal during those late April days, but the region had a second lucky escape at vintage time: the grapes were perfectly ripe, and ready to pick a good week before the cold, wet weather arrived at the end of September. All but a handful of growers managed to get in their crop before the problems began.

But a fourth fine vintage in succession was perhaps less of a godsend for the growers than you might imagine. Beaujolais has been going through some rough times recently as a result of unrealistic pricing. An easy-drinking, commercial vintage might have been the perfect solution, but this was not to be, because 1991 is a genuinely fine year. The wines have body and tannin, yet also have a gorgeous concentration of fruit. They aren't what we nowadays think of as typical gluggers, but maybe they are more typical of the kind of Beaujolais we'd have seen in the days when yields were half as high as they are now, and the ripeness and the concentration were consequently much more marked.

Price has been the major worry for a few years now. In last year's *Webster's*, Gordon Brown took a hard look at the unremitting hikes which have frightened off a great many Beaujolais drinkers. This year, for the first time in ages, there is some good news: few growers have increased their prices, while in London, according to Jacquie Kay of Berkmann Wine Cellars (Duboeuf's UK agents) prices have 'dropped dramatically'.

'Beaujolais is back in business,' says Jacquie. 'Prices went through the roof with the 1989 vintage, but everywhere the shippers encountered resistance from the traditional market.' With 1991, she says, 'Prices have returned to normal with Brouilly selling to the trade at under £50 a case.' When you see Sainsburys lopping two quid off the price of their Fleurie, maybe it really is the time to take a sniff round the shelves at the off-licence.

It wasn't just the prices, though, which caused some of us to fall out with Beaujolais; it was the change in the nature of the beast. One problem was increasingly sugar-happy growers who chaptalized their musts by two degrees and more as a matter of course. Pierre-Marie Chermette, whose Domaine des Vissoux is in the south of the Beaujolais, says that the local *comité* is now trying to bring the growers to heel by telling them to pick just under-ripe and chaptalize the musts by one degree only: from 11.5 Baumé to 12.5. Jean Foillard points out that the purpose of chaptalizing the musts in the Beaujolais was not just to achieve higher alcoholic strength, but also to spin out the fermentation time to obtain greater extraction of colour and flavour from the fruit. Smaller yields, though, would give more sugar, plus the extra colour and flavour so frequently missing in modern Beaujolais, but evident in a fair number of 1991s.

Another problem has been a growing tendency to use new oak with Beaujolais. I am certainly not alone in regretting this trend, which appears to be little more than the expression of an inferiority complex among growers, heartbroken that they do not have the right to replant with Chardonnay or Cabernet Sauvignon: grapes more appropriate to the *barrique* treatment. Beaujolais all too easily loses its charm with new oak; possibly only Moulin-à-Vent has the weight to take the extra tannins. A couple of years ago a grower from Morgon was claiming to get round that problem by putting his wines into new casks for just two weeks! It gave him the oak flavouring without the tannin; and he could limit himself to buying only a few barrels, with the real maturation taking place in his concrete vats.

Two-week *barrique*-ageing is simply a joke, but other growers and merchants take the thing increasingly seriously: Georges Duboeuf buys new casks and rents them out to his growers with the result that more and more of his *cru* wines have oaky tastes. In general these are not over-popular here in Britain, but the Americans, they say, take to them like ducks to water.

A third misgiving about Beaujolais has been the advent of fashion when it comes to the *crus*. In the old days Moulin-à-Vent was the most expensive and the longest-lasting wine in the region. Now we are expected to pay the highest prices for Fleurie. In France it looks as though Fleurie has had its day: Chiroubles and Chénas are the thing. Meanwhile Regnié, the much heralded tenth *cru,* so far seems to be something of a dead duck, and no better than the rest of the wines from the Villages.

Still, it has to be said, the odd bottle of unchaptalized, unoaked, unhyped Beaujolais which comes my way can be one of the great experiences of the year. The best of the '91s which I have tasted have been the Morgon and the Moulin-à-Vent from Jacky Janodet (shipped by Thorman Hunt). But I should be equally happy with any '91 from Foillard, Lapierre or Breton, and I intend to make sure I find some.                                      GILES MACDONOGH

## GRAPES & FLAVOURS

**CHARDONNAY** Chardonnay does make some white Beaujolais, and it's usually quite good. Grown in the North, it has a stony dryness closer in style to Chablis. In the South it is much nearer to the fatter, softer, wines of southern Burgundy.

**GAMAY** The Gamay grape produces pretty dull or tart stuff in most places. But somehow, on these granite slopes, it gives one of the juiciest, most gulpable, gurgling wines the world has to offer. The Gamay has no pretensions. Ideally Beaujolais is simple, cherry-sharp, with candy-like fruit, sometimes with hints of raspberry or strawberry. The wines from the *crus* go further, but in the main the similarity they share through the Gamay grape is more important than the differences in the places they come from. All but the wines of the top villages should be drunk as young as you can find them, although years like 1988, '89 and '90 have produced wines at *cru* levels that are now ageing well. 1990s and 1991s still need another year or two for the best wines to come round.

**BEAUJOLAIS, AC** This covers *all* the basic wines, the produce of the flatter, southern part of Beaujolais, stretching down towards Lyon. Most of the best is now sold as Nouveau. Run-of-the-mill Beaujolais, apart from Nouveau, is likely to be pretty thin stuff, or beefed up illegally with something altogether different. In fact, since you're allowed to re-label Nouveau as 'Beaujolais', some of the best wine in the new year (much appreciated by those who scoff at Nouveau) will be none other than re-labelled Nouveau. Good producers include *Blaise, Carron, Charmet, Château de la Plume,* co-op at *Bully, Duboeuf Bouteille Cristal, Garlon, Labruyère, Loron, Pierre-Marie Chermette* of the *Domaine des Vissoux.*

**BEAUJOLAIS BLANC, AC** To be honest, Beaujolais Blanc is usually quite expensive and in its rather firm, stony-dry way is rarely as enjoyable as a good Mâcon-Villages. Most of the examples we see come from the North, often bordering on St-Véran in the Mâconnais, so despite being rather closed in, you expect it to blossom sometime – but it doesn't. I'd plant Gamay instead if I were them. *Charmet* is the most interesting producer, but his vineyards are in the South. *Tête* is good.

**BEAUJOLAIS ROSÉ, AC** I never thought I'd waste space on this apology for a wine – but a couple of years ago I came across an absolute stunner from *M Bernard* of Leynes – one of the best pinks I'd had all year. The co-op at *Bois d'Oingt* has also shown that it can make exciting Beaujolais rosé.

**BEAUJOLAIS NOUVEAU** (or **PRIMEUR**), **AC** The new vintage wine of Beaujolais, released in the same year as the grapes are gathered, at midnight on the third Wednesday in November. It is usually the best of the simple wine, and will normally improve for several months in bottle, but in good Nouveau vintages like 1989, '88 and '85 it can improve for years. I always keep a bottle or two to fool my wine-buff friends – and it always does – they're usually in the Côte de Beaune at about £12 a bottle. I'm sniggering in the kitchen.

**BEAUJOLAIS SUPÉRIEUR, AC** Superior means that the basic alcoholic degree is higher. It doesn't ensure a better wine, and is in any case rarely even seen on the label.

**BEAUJOLAIS-VILLAGES, AC** Thirty-five villages can use this title. They're mostly in the north of the region and reckoned to make better than average wines, with some justification because there are quite major soil differences that account for the demarcation of Beaujolais and Beaujolais-Villages. The wines are certainly better than basic Beaujolais, a little fuller and deeper, and the cherry-sharp fruit of the Gamay is usually more marked. However, look for a wine bottled in the region, and preferably from a single vineyard, because an anonymous blend of Beaujolais-Villages may simply mean a

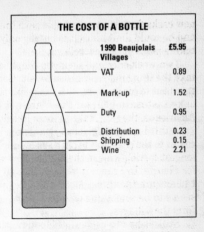

**THE COST OF A BOTTLE**

| 1990 Beaujolais Villages | £5.95 |
| --- | --- |
| VAT | 0.89 |
| Mark-up | 1.52 |
| Duty | 0.95 |
| Distribution | 0.23 |
| Shipping | 0.15 |
| Wine | 2.21 |

heftier version of an ordinary Beaujolais. *Noël Aucoeur, Domaine de la Brasse, Domaine de la Chapelle de Vatre (Sarrau), Jacques Dépagneux, de Flammerécourt, Château Gaillard, Gutty Père et Fils, André Large, Château des Loges, Jean-Charles Pivot, Jean-Luc Tissier, Trichard,* and *Château des Vergers* are good local producers, but most domaines are bottled by one of the merchants in the region. Labelling by the domaine is on the increase.

**BROUILLY, AC** Southernmost and largest of the Beaujolais *crus*, Brouilly has the flattest of the *cru* vineyards, and usually makes one of the lightest *cru* wines. There is some variation in style between the more northerly villages and those in the South where granite produces a deeper, fuller wine, but in general Brouilly rarely improves much with keeping. In fact, it makes a very good Nouveau! A few properties make a bigger wine to age – but even then, nine months to a year is quite enough. Good names include *Château de la Chaize, Domaine Crêt des Garanches, Château de Fouilloux, Hospices de Belleville, Château de Pierreux, Domaine de Combillaty (Duboeuf)* and *Domaine de Garanches, André Large, Château de Nevers. Château des Tours,* although lovely young, can age much longer.

**CHÉNAS, AC** This second-smallest *cru*, from between St-Amour and Moulin-à-Vent, makes strong, dark wines, sometimes a bit tough, that can be drunk a year after the harvest, or aged to take on a Pinot Noir-like flavour. Exceedingly fashionable in France. Look out for the wines of *Louis Champagnon, Charvet, Château de Chénas, Domaines des Brureaux, Domaine Chassignon, Domaine de la Combe Remont (Duboeuf), Pierre Perrachon, Emile Robin.*

**CHIROUBLES, AC** Another *cru* for early drinking, grown on hillsides south-west of Fleurie, towards the southern end of the Beaujolais *crus*. The wines are naturally light, similar to Beaujolais-Villages in weight, but with a perfumed, cherry fragrance that makes Chiroubles France's favourite Beaujolais *cru*. Good producers include *René Brouillard, Cheysson, Château Javernand, Château de Raousset, Jean-Pierre Desvignes, Duboeuf, Méziat* and *Georges Passot.*

**CÔTE DE BROUILLY, AC** The slopes in the centre of the Brouilly area make fuller wines than straight Brouilly, since they come largely from exposed slopes and have lapped up the sun. Best producers include: *Château Thivin, Conroy, Claude Geoffray, Jean Sanvers, Lucien Verger.*

**CRU** The ten *crus* or growths (Fleurie, Moulin-à-Vent, Brouilly, Chénas, Côte de Brouilly, Chiroubles, Juliénas, St-Amour, Morgon, Regnié) are the top villages in the steeply hilly, northern part of Beaujolais. All *should* have definable characteristics, but the produce of different vineyards and growers is all too often blended to a mean by merchants based anywhere in France. Always buy either a single estate wine, or one from a good local merchant like *Chanut Frères, Duboeuf, Dépagneux, Ferraud, Sarrau, Thomas la Chevalière, Trenel.*

**FLEURIE, AC** Often the most delicious of the *crus*, gentle and round, its sweet cherry and chocolate fruit just held firm by a touch of tannin and acid. Very popular in Britain and the US: I used to be prepared to pay, but now the wine has to be *very* special for me to shell out. Try *Château de Fleurie (Loron), Chauvet, Chignard, Colonge, Domaine de la Grand, Grand Pré (Sarrau), Domaine de la Presle, Domaine des Quatre Vents, Duboeuf's la Madone, Bernard Paul, Verpoix,* the Fleurie co-op.

**JULIÉNAS, AC** Juliénas *can* be big wine, with tannin and acidity, but many of the best more closely resemble the mixture of fresh red fruit and soft, chocolaty warmth that makes for good Fleurie. Good ones include *Château du Bois de la Salle, Domaine des Bucherats, Château des Capitans, Château de Juliénas, Domaine de la Dîme* and *Domaine de la Vieille Eglise.* Also good: *Pelletier* and *Duboeuf.*

**MORGON, AC** The wines of this southern *cru* can be glorious. They can start out thick and dark, and age to a sumptuous, chocolaty, plummy depth with an amazing smell of cherries, not unlike Côte de Nuits Burgundy, and yet still Beaujolais. *Jacky Janodet's* is unusually intense. Look also for *Aucoeur, Château de Pizay, Château de Raousset, Descombes, Desvignes, Domaine de la Chanaise, Domaine de Ruyère, Drouhin, Gobet, Lapierre, Félix Longepierre* and *Georges Vincent.*

**MOULIN-À-VENT, AC** Enter the heavy brigade. These *cru* wines should be solid, and should age for three to five years, and more from years like 1985 and '88. The best have a big, plummy, Burgundian style,and the toughness of a young Moulin-à-Vent doesn't give you much option but to wait. It rarely resembles anyone's view of straight Beaujolais – it takes itself far too seriously – but quite a few of the 1988s are already very good. *Louis Champagnon's* is good, as

The price guides for this section begin on page 295.

is *Brugne, Charvet, Château des Jacques, Château du Moulin-à-Vent, Château Portier, Domaine de la Tour de Bief, Jacky Janodet, Raymond Siffert* and *Héritiers Maillard* (formerly *Héritiers Tagent*). *Duboeuf* is experimenting with new oak barrel-ageing.

**REGNIÉ, AC** Since the 1988 vintage, Beaujolais' tenth *cru*. Makes wine quite similar to Brouilly in ripe vintages but a bit weedy when the sun doesn't shine. *Duboeuf Bouteille Cristal* the best so far.

**ST-AMOUR, AC** Among the most perfect Beaujolais, this pink-red wine from one of the least spoilt villages usually has freshness and peachy perfume and good, ripe fruit all at once. It isn't that common here (though the French love it), and yet it is frequently the most reliable and most enjoyable *cru*. Sadly, the news has leaked out and prices are leaping up. Look out for *Château de St-Amour, Domaine des Billards (Loron), Domaine des Ducs, Domaine du Paradis, André Poitevin, Francis Saillant.*

---

## BEAUJOLAIS VINTAGES

With most Beaujolais the rule is, drink it as young as possible. Only the top wines from the best villages will benefit much from ageing, although Nouveau can benefit from a month or two's rest.

**1991** Unlike most of France, Beaujolais had an excellent year in 1991. Largely spared the April frosts, the grapes were ripe two weeks before the cold wet weather which set in in the last week of September. Beaujolais from the 1991 vintage has good colour and relatively high tannin levels. Most of the *crus* will only just be coming round at Christmas 1992. The best wines will need longer still.

**1990** Yet another corker of a vintage – very good quality and plenty of it. The harvest yielded very fruity, typical Beaujolais with rich, authentic Gamay character. Easy-drinking but full flavours reach right across the board, with the ordinary Beaujolais, the Villages and all of the *crus* emerging well. Nouveau prices were high but resistance to the high prices of the other names and widespread slump conditions slowed sales right down and prices began to fall.

**1989** Along with other vineyard areas of France, and indeed Europe, the 1989 vintage in Beaujolais was one of the earliest ever. Picking of the grapes, which had been sunning themselves under a blazing sky all summer, started on 3 September. The heat meant that colour was unusually deep, but along with this the aromas were much more pungently fruity than expected after the hot and dusty summer season. Dry weather meant there were few problems with rot or mildew, and the crop came in in healthy condition. But this was the year higher prices really started to bite. In terms of value for money, the less well-known *cru* names like Chénas and Côte de Brouilly look worth a try.

**1988** There's no doubt that 1988 was a lovely year in Beaujolais. There is a marvellous quality of luscious, clear, ripe fruit about the best wines. Even the Nouveaus were terrific. I remember a string of delicious Beaujolais-Villages. And some delightful St-Amour and Brouilly. Pressure on supply meant overproduction in some quarters, though. So I'm going to say – 1988 was an exceptional year. Make sure you grab hold of the good examples.

**1987** Many are still drinking well, although this was a vintage best enjoyed in its youth. Some of the sturdier *crus* produced wines with the class and stamina to survive – Moulin-à-Vent can be delicious. But the lighter wines are fading already.

**1986** Started mean and the few remaining bottles won't excite anyone.

**1985** No vintage has ever given so much sheer pleasure as 1985 with its riot of fruit and spice. Many of the wines are still excellent – but they've grown up, become serious. Many will be enjoyable, but the days when they made you dance with delight are over.

# CHAMPAGNE

It may be conditioning or it may be taste, but it is still difficult for regular drinkers of good Champagne to be satisfied with anything else. There are, to my mind, only a handful of alternatives to compare with Champagne when it is good, although about a dozen others are on the verge of joining them.

Not all Champagne comes up to the mark either, although its pricing never seems to reflect this. Since last year the average age of Champagne on the shelf has increased, simply because sales have dropped; for the same reason, the Champenois have improved their stocks. In 1991 they had no difficulty in buying grapes, and all of this should add up to quality waiting in the wings.

And not, one might say, before time. The recent decline in Champagne quality and its plummeting sales have, it seems, been a lesson to the Champenois. So what happened? Well, although the unique combination of Champagne's climate and soil is its blessing, it is also its curse. This lean, uncertain, northern climate is responsible for Champagne's quantity, quality and price going up and down like a yo-yo. When a run of poor or small vintages puts pressure on stocks, the fallibility of Champagne's situation is exposed. When this pressure is at odds with market pressures, chaos ensues.

The origins of Champagne's most recent bout of chaos can be traced back to a conscious decision made by some larger *grande marque* houses in the mid-1980s. Until then Champagne was quality-led. Not only did Champagne houses believe their reputations were worth protecting, but there wasn't enough Champagne around to satisfy demand, and little temptation to drop either quality or price. And yet, in the mid-1980s, a decision was made by these houses to go for volume.

Demand seemed to be insatiable and the profits, for many, were irresistible. Accordingly, they opted for selling as much as possible. That retail sales spiralled was not a direct result of the houses' decision, but it was certainly connected. Retailer after retailer shaved its prices to grab some of the action and by late 1986 the cheapest supermarket Champagne was £6.99. Even some famous *grandes marques* now joined in the price-cutting game.

The market, already soaring, went through the stratosphere, increasing existing stock and supply difficulties. Exacerbating this suicidal course of events was the problem of the interprofessional contract. This, a contract between the houses who blend and sell the wine, and the growers who own the vineyards was, by the mid-1980s, supposed to ensure that each house, including the smallest and least powerful, received an adequate supply of grapes (the houses sell 67 per cent of the Champagne, but own just 12 per cent of the vineyards).

## Growers' home wine-making

That share, however, was restricted to a percentage of its previous year's sales. The quantity therefore rose or fell according to its sales, and the size of the cake as a whole varied according to the size of the harvest. In theory this sounds fine, but in practice the demand for Champagne was shooting off the graph at a time when more and more growers were beginning to make their own Champagne. And although they were not actually selling much more, they were removing a large and and growing chunk of the crop from the market. What was left was simply inadequate to meet the houses' needs. The houses' vital stocks dwindled and quality and maturity began to evaporate. The irony was that those houses which tried to conserve stocks in order to maintain quality were punished because the system gave them fewer grapes the following year.

I might be wrong, but I cannot think of one house that claimed to have declining sales during this period, although some did have the discipline to restrict their growth. As a whole, the Champagne trade went through a boom period, even though the houses had insufficient grapes for their current needs, let alone higher sales. The answer to the riddle is simple: on average the houses had just 1.9 years' of stock, not the three years that was claimed. The region as a whole had three years' stocks, but a lot of that was in the cellars of growers and co-operatives. These stocks were being used by the houses, who were buying bottles of ready-made Champagne (at the stage, before disgorgement, when the wines are stored *sur-lattes*), slapping on labels and selling them as their own. Not very moral or very fair to the consumer (unless they were being sold as own-label Champagnes or secondary *marques*), but perfectly legal. As consumers we were left with an invidious choice: immature, green Champagne of reasonable quality, or poor quality mature wine.

### The price of folly

Things should never have got into that state. It was folly to start a price-war with something, like Champagne, that must always be in restricted supply. Over in the region itself, the contract should have been altered or torn up ages ago and the *sur-lattes* facility should never have been legal for the principal *marque* of any house. Champagne had dug itself into a hole, and the solution had to include a dramatic increase in price and a reversal of the interprofessional contract.

What happened was that the contract was not signed in 1990, and the free market prices for grapes shot up by between 30 and 56 per cent. Prices in 1991 were just as high, but each house was able to purchase as much as it needed from both vintages. The *sur-lattes* trade is dead except for own-label Champagnes, which is what it should be used for.

This rise in grape prices did not in itself cause the dramatic increase in retail prices that Oz bemoaned in *Webster's* last year, because they started going up before a single grape was purchased in the free market of 1990. The Champenois were attempting to ration us by price, and although it was not well-planned, it was necessary.

All previous attempts to solve stock shortages, which are usually caused by the vagaries of Champagne's climate, and only more rarely aggravated by the Champenois themselves, have failed. The normal solution is for some houses (not all) to promise to ration certain markets by, say, ten per cent, and then produce export figures for the year which reveal an increase instead.

In 1990, when supply and demand were so much out of control, more drastic action was needed. Average annual output had risen by 42 per cent over the previous 15 years, while the vineyards had expanded by only 25 per cent, yet even pumping-up production like that could not cope with the demand: sales had risen by a massive 104 per cent in the same period. The Champenois were scraping the very bottom of the growers' vat, where there was nothing but rubbish left. Demand had to be controlled, and fast.

In the long run, however, the Champenois cannot dictate prices. Champagne will find its own level because, in the end, the consumer votes with his or her wallet. If that is insufficient for the Champenois to make a profit, then it will cease to exist, but I doubt that will ever happen.          TOM STEVENSON

## GRAPES & FLAVOURS

**CHARDONNAY** The grape of white Burgundy fame here tends to produce a lighter, fresher juice, and the resulting Champagnes are certainly the most perfumed and honeyed. They have been criticized for lacking depth and ageing potential. Not true. Good Blancs de Blancs have a superb, exciting flavour that is improved by ageing, especially those from the southern end of the Côte des Blancs.

**PINOT NOIR** The grape that makes all the finest red Burgundies also makes white Champagne. Pinot Noir has enough difficulty in ripening in Burgundy, and further north in Champagne it almost never attains any great depth and strength of colour or alcohol, which is fair enough since the general idea here is to produce a *white* wine. Very careful pressing of the grapes in traditional vertical presses is the best way to draw off the juice with as little colour as possible, and the rest of the reddish tinge generally precipitates out naturally during fermentation. Even so, the juice does feel quite big: a Champagne relying largely on Pinot Noir is certain to be heavier and take longer to mature.

**PINOT MEUNIER** The other black grape, making a softer, fruitier style of wine, important for producing easy wines for drinking young, and crucial for toning down the assertive flavours of Pinot Noir.

## WINES & WINE STYLES

**BLANC DE BLANCS** An increasingly common style from Chardonnay grapes. Usually fresh and bright with a soothing, creamy texture. Many de luxe Champagnes are now labelled Blanc de Blancs, but they rarely have the added nuances the much increased price would suggest. Best producers: *Avize* co-op, *Billecart-Salmon, Henriot, Lassalle, Pol Roger, Louis Roederer, Dom Ruinart, Sézanne* co-op, *Taittinger Comtes de Champagne, Krug Clos de Mesnil, Salon, Charbaut Certificate.*

**BLANC DE NOIRS** This white style is made 100 per cent from black grapes and is commonly made throughout the Marne Valley. Few have the quality and longevity of *Bollinger*, but none are even half as expensive. Most are rather solid. *Pierre Vaudon* from the Avize co-op is good; *Barancourt* is more expensive, and beefy.

**BRUT** Very dry.

**BUYER'S OWN BRAND (BOB)** A wine blended to a buyer's specification, or more probably, to a price limit. The grapes are of lesser quality, the wines usually younger, and cheaper. *Maison Royale (Victoria Wine), Sainsbury, Tesco, Waitrose* are consistent, *M&S* less so but can be best.

**CM** In the small print on the label, this means *co-opérative-manipulant* and shows that the wine comes from a co-op.

**COTEAUX CHAMPENOIS** Still wines, red or white. Overpriced, rather acid. A village name, such as Cramant (white) or Bouzy (red) may appear. *Alain Vesselle*'s Bouzy is one of the few exciting reds.

**CRÉMANT** A half-sparkling Champagne. If the base wine is good, that's still enough. Best: *Besserat de Bellefon, Alfred Gratien, Abel Lepitre, Mumm Crémant de Cramant.*

**DE LUXE/CUVÉE DE PRESTIGE/ CUVÉE DE LUXE** A special, highly prized, highly priced blend, mostly vintage. Some great wines and some gaudy coat-

The price guides for this section begin on page 299.

trailers. Most come in silly bottles, and are overpriced, but a few do deliver. In general drunk *far* too young. Most need ten years to shine. Best: *Bollinger RD, Dom Pérignon, Dom Ruinart, Krug Grande Cuvée, Laurent Perrier Grand Siècle, Pol Roger Cuvée Sir Winston Churchill, Roederer Cristal, Taittinger Comtes de Champagne, Cuvée NF Billecart, Cattier Clos du Moulin, Philipponnat Clos des Egoïsses, Perrier-Jouët Belle Epoque, Vilmart Grand Cellier.*

**DEMI-SEC** Medium sweet. Rarely very nice, but *Louis Roederer* is outstanding, and *Mercier* is surprisingly fresh and floral.

**DOUX** Sweet. *Louis Roederer* is excellent.

**EXTRA DRY** Confusingly, this is less dry than 'Brut', but drier than 'Sec'.

**GRANDE MARQUE** Ambiguous term meaning 'great brand'. It's a self-styled grouping of, at the last count, 28 houses, including the 15 or so best known. The term *should* be synonymous with quality – more expensive grapes, older reserve wines and more rigid selection. But the pressure for market share has been taking its toll.

**MA** Label code meaning *marque auxiliare*, implying a subsidiary brand or a secondary label. Any Champagne selling for a quid less than you expect is likely to be one.

**NM** In the code on the label, this means *négociant-manipulant* (merchant-handler)

and may show that the wine was bottle-fermented by the house on the label; but buying wine *sur-lattes* is still legal.

**NON-DOSAGE** Most Champagne has a little sweetness – a 'dosage' – added just before the final cork. A few are sold bone-dry and will have names like Brut Zero, implying a totally dry wine. Best are *Laurent Perrier, Piper-Heidsieck*.

**NON-VINTAGE** The ordinary, most basic blend. Many houses used take pride in a house style achieved by blending various vintages. Some would even occasionally go to the extent of not declaring a vintage in a good year if they wanted to use the wine to keep up the standard of their non-vintage. Sadly, this happens far less nowadays. Although a little older reserve wine is added to smooth out the edges when the blend is being put together, most non-vintages are now released 'ready' for drinking, heavily dependent on a single year's harvest of perhaps two or three years' age, and some producers will offer wine not much more than 18 months old. The current blends are based on excellent vintages but are often released much too young to justify fully the scary prices. Best are *Alfred Gratien, Billecart-Salmon, Gosset, Charles Heidsieck, Duval-Leroy, Jacquesson, Henriot, Lanson, Laurent Perrier, Mercier, Bruno Paillard, Pol Roger, Louis Roederer, Veuve Clicquot Vilmart*. All improve greatly if laid down for even a few months between buying and drinking.

**MATURITY CHART**
1985 Champagne
1985 is a ripe, forward year in Champagne, but the wines will still age well

| Bottled | Disgorged | Ready | Peak | Tiring | In decline |
|---|---|---|---|---|---|

| 0 | 1 | 2 | 3 | 4 | 5 | 6 | 7 | 8 | 9 | 10 | 11 | 12 years |

**RC** A new designation indicating *récoltant-co-opérateur* – for a grower selling wine produced at a co-operative. It should stop growers pretending they've made it themselves.

**RECENTLY DISGORGED** A term used for Champagnes that have been left in the cellars, drawing flavour from their yeast deposits, for much longer than usual before disgorging. The wines can happily rest for 20 to 30 years on the lees but are usually released after seven to ten years. *Bollinger RD* is the most famous; wines also from *Deutz, Alfred Gratien* and *Laurent Perrier*.

**RICH** The sweetest Champagne.

**RM** Indicates that the wine comes from a single grower, a *récoltant-manipulant*, literally harvester-handler. Since 1989 RM should indicate a grower who's made his Champagne himself, rather than taking it to the local co-op. Good results come from *Bara, Beerens, Billiot, Bonnaire, Brice, Cattier, Clouet, Fliniaux, Michel Gonet, André Jacquart, Lassalle, Albert Lebrun, Leclerc-Briant, Legras, Vesselle, Vilmart*.

**ROSÉ** Traditionally, the pink colour is gained by a short, careful maceration of the black Pinot Noir and Pinot Meunier skins with the juice. Other producers add a little red Bouzy wine to white Champagne before bottling. Ideally rosés are aromatic, fruity wines, with a delicious strawberry or cherry flavour. Sadly, many are virtually indistinguishable from white. Most should be drunk young. Best producers: *Besserat de Bellefon, Boizel, Bollinger,Charbaut Certificate, Dom Ruinart, Alfred Gratien, Jacquart la Renommée, Lassalle, Laurent Perrier, Moët et Chandon,Louise Pommery, Roederer* and *Roedererer Cristal, Taittinger Comtes de Champagne. Krug rosé* is in a class of its own, and so it should be at the price.

**SEC** Literally 'dry', but actually medium dry.

**SR** Société de Récoltants. Label code for a family company of growers.

**VINTAGE** Wine of a single, good quality year, generally fuller than non-vintage, but almost without exception nowadays released too young. Best producers: *Billecart-Salmon, Bollinger, Gosset Grande Millésime, Alfred Gratien, Henriot, Krug, Lanson, Bruno Paillard, Joseph Perrier, Perrier-Jouët, Pol Roger, Louis Roederer, Ruinart, Veuve Clicquot.*

---

### CLASSIFICATIONS

The classification system in Champagne is based on vineyards. The approved areas for vineyards are strictly demarcated and the vineyard land graded according to suitability for black and white grapes, going from 100 per cent for the finest *grand cru* villages through 90–99 per cent for the 41 *premier cru* villages and on to 80 per cent for the least favoured.

If the guideline price is 20 francs per kilo of grapes, a 100 per cent village grower receives the full 20 francs. An 80 per cent grower will receive only 80 per cent – 16 francs – and so on, it's all quite simple. The whole system is now less rigorous than it was 50 years ago, when percentages ranged from 50 to 100.

Champagne houses boast about how high their 'average percentage' of grapes is. Some Champagne labels will say either '100 per cent Grand Cru' or 'Premier Cru' and even a village name as well, Avize, for example, if the wine comes entirely from one single top village.

Hardly surprisingly, no one ever bothers to declare on the label percentages in the 80s or lower 90s, but in actual fact many of the best value Champagnes on the UK market come from these so-called 'lowly' villages. There is no reason why careful vineyard managment and vinification should not produce good results.

# CHAMPAGNE HOUSE PROFILES

**BILLECART-SALMON** ★★★★
Terrifically elegant Champagne from a
family-owned house. Very refined, delicate
wines and a lovely rosé. Its vintage, Cuvée
NF Billecart, is also excellent.

**BOLLINGER** ★★★(★) Like Krug, makes
'English-style' Champagnes, warm, rich,
oaky. Reputation slightly marred in recent
years because the wines were released too
young. RD, for *Récemment Dégorgé*, its
luxury *cuvée*, is kept on its lees until just
before sale. Also *Vieilles Vignes*.

**ALFRED GRATIEN** ★★★★ Serious, oak-
fermented wine at a much lower price than
Krug. Very long-lived vintage.

**KRUG** ★★★★★ The classic heavy, serious
Champagne. Grande Cuvée, oak-fermented
is outstandingly good, and weightier than
any competitor. Expensive rosé has an
incomparable Pinot Noir cherry-fruitiness.
Even more expensive Clos de Mesnil is a
delicate, single vineyard Blanc de Blancs.

**LANSON** ★★★(★) Until recently had
(well-deserved) reputation for excessive
acidity. Under new ownership it is ageing
wine longer, for a light, quaffable style.
Classic, long-maturing vintage.

**LAURENT PERRIER** ★★★★ Possibly the
most reliable of all the non-vintage blends.
Excellent, reasonably-priced rosé. Prestige
brand Grand Siècle is (sensibly) blend of
several vintages. Good value.

**MOËT & CHANDON** ★★(★) Brut
Imperial infuriatingly unreliable –
sometimes as good as any NV, at other
times hardly tasting like Champagne at
all. Vintages usually show well but are
released far too young.

**MUMM** ★(★) Traditionally rich wine, but
all too frequently the least impressive of

the famous names. Delicate, creamy
Crémant from south-facing slopes in
Cramant. I wish some of the Crémant's
class would rub off on the NV and vintage.

**PERRIER-JOUËT** ★★★ Reputedly the
brand most respected by the wine-makers,
who drink it if they can't get their own.
Best known for Belle Époque in a pretty
bottle, all flowery elegance, echoed in fresh,
slightly unripe-cherry feel of the wine.

**POL ROGER** ★★★★ Model family firm,
producer of Churchill's favourite fizz.
Delicious, delicate Blanc de Blancs. NV,
vintage and Cuvée Sir Winston Churchill
all top class. New are vintage Blanc de
Chardonnay, vintage rosé and a Demi-sec.

**POMMERY** ★★ Despite ownership
changes, Pommery is still rather too bland.
The wine can be exciting, when it tries.

**LOUIS ROEDERER** ★★★★(★) Most
profitable drinks firm in the world. Most
famous for Cristal, invented to satisfy
sweet tooths of Russian Tsars. Now the
most natural of all the prestige *cuvées*,
reflecting the quality of individual
vintages. Cristal is made (in small
quantities) even in theoretically bad years
– like 1974 and 1977 – when its almost
vegetal sweetness comes through. NV
usually one of the best despite needing
more maturity. Good Demi-sec and Doux.

**TAITTINGER** ★★★(★) Splendidly light,
modern, Chardonnayish style, carried
through in its model Blanc de Blancs,
Comtes de Champagne.

**VEUVE CLICQUOT** ★★★★ For a century
and a half greatly loved by the British. The
NV still has the rich, warm style first made
famous by the formidable Madame Veuve
Clicquot-Ponsardin. Prestige *cuvée* La
Grande Dame almost chocolate-rich.

## CHAMPAGNE VINTAGES

A vintage table for Champagne is not straightforward since so much is blended without vintage designation. Also, vintage wines released and sold very young, while good for laying down, are unlikely to give any more immediate pleasure than good non-vintage. Most Champagne can do with ageing; vintage demands it. Historically, a vintage was 'declared' by the houses after an exceptional year, and then released at six to seven years old when reasonably mature. There has been a trend recently  for some vintage wine to appear almost every year, and at only four to five years old. Moët is often guilty of infanticide and released its 1985, in particular, far too young. Its excellent '79 is now coming into its own, yet most of it has already been drunk. But some of the 1982s, released at only six years old, were immediately delicious.

**1991** Like 1986, a vintage declared by a few houses only. A large harvest, despite spring frosts taking their toll. Should be  useful for blending good non-vintage.

**1990** A second, late crop produced the third largest harvest recorded in Champagne, helped by late sunshine. The wines are of fairly good quality, but are unfortunately unlikely to be cheap.

**1989** For once an enormous, much-hyped vintage is turning out to be as good as the Champenois thought it would be. But I suppose they'll inevitably release the wines far too young.

**1988** The harvest started on 19 September – weeks before supposedly warmer areas. But the vines had flowered incredibly early – around 12 June – and the grapes were ripe. In ten years' time there could be some memorable bottles of 1988. Try to be patient and not open them until then.

**1987** I can say precisely one thing in favour of the 1987 Champagne harvest – there's lots of it. 1987 produced some of the blandest, least memorable wine I can ever remember tasting. What they should do is to use it to make lots of pleasant, fairly-priced non-vintage Some hope.

**1986** Useful wines of reasonable quality, but the yield was rather spoiled by rot. Mostly good for blending into non-vintage, but the way the Champagne hounds are all rushing headlong into the more expensive styles, you're sure to see 1986 vintage labels peeking out in a few years.

**1985** Well, after all the gloom and despondency when the Champagne guys were wringing their bejewelled hands and crying 'no wine, no wine', 1985 produced a fair amount; much of it good to excellent. Most have launched their 1985s, but you could keep them for a few years yet.

**1984** A very feeble year. Anyone who produced a vintage  could probably turn water into wine. The one exception was Waitrose – who found a producer making his wine in fresh new wood.

**1983** The second of the record-breaking vintages which sent fizz prices plunging in the UK and dramatically increased the amount of Champagne we all drank – remember? There are still some 1983 wines around and they are extremely good, a little leaner than 1982, but  high-quality.

**1982** Not so long ago I castigated houses like Bollinger and Veuve Clicquot for wantonly releasing their vintage wines at five years old.  Well, the '82s  were sheer bliss. They were ready at five years old – in fact the Bollinger '82 tasted readier to drink than its non-vintage.

**1979** This is an excellent vintage: it yielded beautifully soft, balanced wines only now hitting their  peak .

# RHÔNE

On 15 May 1992 the small town of Tain-l'Hermitage in the northern Rhône played host to the first ever 'World Syrah Day.' Interested viticulturalists poured in from the southern half of France; a few even came from abroad. It was hot as only the Rhône Valley can be. As temperatures rose, the morning was taken up with highly cogent lectures relating to the history, geography and adaptability of the Syrah grape in different parts of the world. Some of this was fairly arid and a percentage of the growers nodded off in their seats. They woke up for two forbiddingly technical talks on rootstocks and clones, at which point the majority of the English sloped off to the local câfé. So far we had heard next to nothing about the nature of the wine itself: that was left to the afternoon and a tutored tasting of the world's greatest Syrahs to be held in the town Gymnasium.

At lunch we received our first inkling of the sort of political problems likely to beset these shindigs in the Rhône Valley: no-one was allowed to know the identity of the wines served with the meal because the growers, we were told, would never have consented to the conference if anyone was to be able to leave with a clear idea of who among them made good wine and who did not.

This problem was to dominate events at the Gymnasium. At first, however, the organisation was faultless: the Syrah wines were well able to overcome any residual smell of sweaty gym-shoes; the trainee sommeliers from the local hotel school were put through their paces with military precision, and, to our relief, the 'world's best' Syrahs were offered from their original bottles without any attempt being made to conceal their identity. Except that they were not the world's best: a Brazilian wine no-one knew for certain to be Syrah, since it could have been Durif; a trio of Californians; two Australians (Penfolds had not been asked to send Grange, the finest of Australian Shiraz); a brace of South Africans; an Italian and two Swiss. Of these only the Jasper Hill from Australia and the Swiss from Pierre-Luc Remondeulaz-Michellod took us by surprise.

These wines appeared naked before us; not so the French. Every effort was made to conceal the identities of the three Hermitages which followed. The committee had made its decision and it was not going back on it.

## Dining blind

Thirteen more bottles of white and red Hermitage were served with dinner. In every case the authorship of the wine was concealed from us. By this stage discovering which was which had become an enjoyable game conducted by bribes, generous glass-filling and subterfuge: tactics which revealed names for 80 per cent of the wines. We slept relatively easy.

What the World Syrah Day overwhelmingly proved was that Tain-l'Hermitage remains in the deepest folds of *la France profonde* despite a decade of courtship by the world's richest wine buyers. Money was not lacking, but the northern Rhône has yet to assume the degree of openness present even in Burgundy, let alone the spirit of fair-play that one encounters in the New World.

I suspect that this might be even more true of Hermitage than it is of the other main *crus* of the Rhône Valley, because Hermitage is sewn up by its *négociants* in a way that the others no longer are. Moreover, quite unlike most parts of France, the *négociants* of Hermitage are still responsible for nine-tenths of the best wine. Chapoutier is up this year with a quite superb 1990 Pavillon;

Jaboulet's La Chapelle '90 was also a model of concentration. Gérard Chave remains the one grower with a sizable estate and his wines are as good as ever.

Much like Cornas to the South, Hermitage growers had a tricky time in 1989 which has left the wines tasting ungainly and surprisingly light. I suspect that the drought led to problems of maturity which would have been most keenly felt in the younger vines. From this point of view the 1991s may well prove a better bet. This was certainly the case in Côte Rôtie, where the drought affected the 1990 vintage more than the '89. If you are looking to buy some 1990 Côte Rôtie, you should opt for those growers who have old vines.

### New star formations

A few new stars have emerged in the region over the past 18 months, but with the possible exception of Albert Belle, none of these is in Hermitage itself. Alain Graillot goes from strength to strength in Crozes-Hermitage, outdistancing Etienne Pochon's Château de Curson with his top La Gueraude wine. Another name to watch in Crozes Hermitage is Stephane Cornu of the Domaine du Pavillion in Mercurol. His 1990 is a wonderfully intense Syrah brew.

In Cornas two new men stand out: Jacques Demenicier, who made a lovely 1988 and followed up with an excellent '88 and '90,and Thierry Lallemand, whose '90 is currently on sale from Bibendum in London.

In Côte Rôtie both Albert Dervieux and Marius Gentaz have retired. In the case of the former, the vines have gone to his son-in-law, René Rostaing, currently the greatest attraction in Côte Rôtie.

In St-Joseph a team of growers continues to clear the slopes in the locality of St-Joseph and Tournon themselves: these are Jean-Louis Grippat, Bernard Gripa and the Coursodon family. Maurice Courbis has done similar work to the South around Châteaubourg, and the St Desirat co-op has re-created steep terraces to the North. When these vines come into production we should see some big changes in St-Joseph: for the first time in some 50 years the wine will be coming from the slopes and not from the muddy plains.

But the Rhône is not just the Syrah-dominated North, it is also the South with its Grenache. Châteauneuf-du-Pape did not fare as well in 1991 as the northern Rhône. If, like the North, the region was largely spared the frosts which ravaged other parts of France, the cold, damp weather which followed resulted in *coulure*, the vine disease which prevents the flowers from setting on the vine. Normally *coulure* in Châteauneuf hits the sensitive Grenache, but this year it had a go at the varieties which give the wine its tannins and aromas: Syrah and Mourvèdre. The result is minute quantities of fairly mediocre wine; the growers were lucky to harvest 25 hectolitres per hectare.

The 1991 will be a little like the '84, not disgusting (like so many of the '87s) but short-lived, with a tendency to gaminess. A small, average-quality vintage like 1991 does not come at a bad time: Châteauneuf-du-Pape is not the world's most fashionable wine just now and the three preceding years produced such wonderful things that most of the faithful must have stuffed their cellars to the oesophagi. The '90s are just coming on to the market as I write: wines of enormous power made in a vintage when some vats of Grenache topped 16 per cent alcohol and when the need for the lightening touch of the other varieties was keenly felt. If you are buying '90s you'd be as well to put your faith in the tried and trusted: Clos des Papes, Domaine du Grand Tinel, Château Rayas, Domaine de Vieux Télégraphe and Château de Beaucastel.            GILES MACDONAGH

# RED WINES

Northern Rhône reds are really the different manifestations of a single grape variety – the Syrah. It is virtually the only red grape grown in the North, and certainly the only one tolerated for the various *appellations contrôlées*. Syrah can range from light, juicy and simple in the more basic St-Joseph and Crozes-Hermitage offerings, to something rich, extravagant and wonderfully challenging in the top wines of Hermitage, Côte-Rôtie and Cornas.

Southern Rhône reds are usually made from a range of grape varieties, none of which, except the Syrah and very occasionally the Grenache are able to produce wine of dramatic individuality on its own, and that means basic fruit flavours across the whole area are very similar. These are usually raspberry-strawberry, often attractively spicy, slightly dusty, and sometimes livened up with some blackcurrant sweetness or wild herb dryness. The introduction of *macération carbonique* – the Beaujolais-type method of vinification – in the Rhône has meant that many wines, even at the cheapest level, can have a deliciously drinkable fruit; but with a certain uniformity of style.

## GRAPES & FLAVOURS

**CARIGNAN** This grape is much maligned because in the far South it produces tough, raw, fruitless wines in big volumes which frequently form the bulk of France's red contribution to the wine lake. Old vines can produce big, strong but very tasty wines that age well.

**CINSAUT** Another gentle grape, giving acidity and freshness but little fruit to the reds and rosés of the southern Rhône.

**GRENACHE** The most important red grape in the southern Rhône, because it gives loads of alcoholic strength and a gentle, juicy, spicy fruit perked up by a whiff of pepper, ideal for rosés and easy-going reds. So what's the problem? Well, it keeps failing to flower properly and the crop can be ruined. On the other hand, a little *coulure* or *millérandage* could have been an advantage in a year like 1982, when huge quantities of Grenache almost flooded the valley.

**MOURVÈDRE** An old-fashioned, highly flavoured wine, low in alcohol, which doesn't usually ripen fully (its home base is Bandol, right on the Mediterranean). But it

has an excellent, rather berryish taste, and a strong whiff of tobacco spice that is making it increasingly popular with the more imaginative growers.

**SYRAH** Wine-making in the northern Rhône is dominated by this one red grape variety. Along with Cabernet Sauvignon, Bordeaux's great grape, the Syrah makes the blackest, most startling, pungent red wine in France, and, although it is grown elsewhere, it is here that it is at its most brilliant. From Hermitage and Cornas, it rasps with tannin and tar and woodsmoke, backed by the deep, ungainly sweetness of black treacle. But give it five or ten years, and those raw fumes will have become sweet, pungent, full of raspberries, brambles and *cassis*. Syrah is less prevalent than the Grenache in the southern Rhône, but as more is planted, the standard of southern Rhône reds is sure to rise.

**VIOGNIER** This aromatic white grape can be used as up to 20 per cent of the blend of red Côte-Rôtie to add fragrance, and it really does: Côte-Rôtie made purely of Syrah lacks the haunting beauty of one blended with Viognier.

# WINES & WINE REGIONS

**CHÂTEAUNEUF-DU-PAPE, AC** The largest of the ACs of the Côtes du Rhône, this can be quite delicious, deep, dusty red, almost sweet and fat, low in acidity, but kept appetizing by back-room tannin. *Can* be. It can also be fruit-pastilly and pointless, or dark, tough and stringy. Thirteen different red and white grapes are permitted, and the resulting flavour is usually slightly indistinct, varying from one property to another. The occasional 'super-vintage' like 1978 gives wines that can stay stunning for ten years and more. Around one-third of the growers make good wine – and as much as two-thirds of the wine sold probably exceeds the permitted yields. So it makes sense always to go for a domaine wine and certainly not to buy one bottled away from the region of production. Good, full Châteauneufs include: *Château de Beaucastel, Château Rayas* and *Clos du Mont-Olivet, Château Fortia, Château St-André, La Nerthe, Chante Cigale, Clos des Papes, Chante-Perdrix, Le Vieux Donjon, la Jacquinotte, Font de Michelle, Font du Loup, Clos du Mont Olivet, Brunel, Quiot, Domaine du Grand Tinel, Domaine de Mont-Redon, Domaine du Vieux Télégraphe, Domaine Durieu, Bosquet des Papes, Lucien Gabriel Barrot, Les Clefs d'Or, Fabrice Mouisset, Chapoutier's La Bernadine, Henri Bonnot*.

**CORNAS, AC** Black and tarry tooth-stainers, from the right bank of the Rhône, opposite Valence. Usually rather hefty, jammy even, and lacking some of the fresh fruit that makes Hermitage so remarkable, yet at ten years old this is impressive wine. There have been quite big price rises in recent years, but then quality seems to improve year by year, too. Really excellent blockbusters are made by *Auguste Clape, Robert Michel* and *Noël Verset*. It's also worth looking out for the wines of *de Barjac, Colombo, Delas, Juge, Lemenicier, Lallemand, Maurice Courbis, Jean Lionnet* and *Michel*.

**COTEAUX DU TRICASTIN, AC** Constantly improving spicy, fruity reds from this large *appellation* east of the Rhône. Good value. Best producers: *Domaine de Grangeneuve, Tour d'Elyssas* (especially its 100 per cent Syrah), *Producteurs Réunis Ardéchois* (co-op).

**CÔTE-RÔTIE, AC** The admixture of the white Viognier grape makes this one of France's most scented reds when properly made. But the AC has been extended on to the plateau above the traditional 'roasted slope', and unless something is done to differentiate the two, the reputation of this highly prized, highly priced vineyard will be in tatters. At best, from *Gentaz-Dervieux, Jamet, Guigal* and *René Rostaing*, Côte-Rôtie is rare and delicious. Look also for *Gilles* and *Pierre Barge, Bernard Burgaud, Jasmin Dervieux-Thaize, Vidal-Fleury* and *Delas Cuvée Seigneur de Maugiron*.

**CÔTES DU LUBÉRON, AC** Upgraded from VDQS in 1987, Lubéron makes some decent reds, usually rather light, but capable of stronger personality. The Val Joanis rosé is one of the best in the South. Try also *Château de Canorgue, Château de l'Isolette, Mas du Peyroulet, Val Joanis* (also to be seen under own label as *Domaines Chancel* or *Domaine de la Panisse), Vieille Ferme*.

**CÔTES DU RHÔNE, AC** This huge *appellation* covers 80 per cent of all Rhône wines, from Vienne to Avignon. Well-made basic Côtes du Rhônes are quite delicious when young, wonderfully fresh and fruity, like a rather softer version of Beaujolais. Or they can be fierce, black, grape-skins-and-alcohol monsters. Since the label gives no clue, it's trial and error, or merchants'

*The price guides for this section begin on page 305.*

recommendations. *Coudoulet de Beaucastel* (formerly Cru de Coudoulet) is a particularly beefy version from the family who own Beaucastel, and many of the weightiest are made by Châteauneuf or northern Rhône producers like *Guigal*. *Château du Grand Moulas* is spicy and attractive, with plenty of body. Also good: *Caves C.N. Jaume, Château de Deurre, Château de Fonsalette, Château de Ruth, Château de Goudray, Clos du Père Clément, Dom de Bel Air, Dom de la Cantharide, Dom de St-Estève, Domaine des Aussellons.*

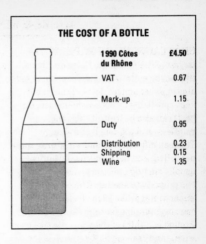

**THE COST OF A BOTTLE**

| | 1990 Côtes du Rhône | £4.50 |
|---|---|---|
| | VAT | 0.67 |
| | Mark-up | 1.15 |
| | Duty | 0.95 |
| | Distribution | 0.23 |
| | Shipping | 0.15 |
| | Wine | 1.35 |

## CÔTES DU RHÔNE-VILLAGES, AC
One of the best areas for good, full reds that can also age, combining earthy, dusty southern heat with spicy, raspberry fruit. They come from higher quality villages, 17 of which can add their names on the label, including Vacqueyras, Cairanne, Chusclan, Valréas, Beaumes-de-Venise and Rasteau. Good growers: (Laudun) *Domaine Pelaquié;* (Rasteau) *Domaine de Grangeneuve;* (Sablet) *Jean-Pierre Cartier, Château de Trignon, Domaine de Boisson, Domaine St-Antoine, Domaine de Verquière;* (Cairanne) *Domaine de l'Ameillaud, Dom Brusset, Dom l'Oratoire St-Martin, Dom de la Présidente, Dom Rabasse-Charavin;* (St-Gervais) *Dom Ste-Anne;* (Séguret) *Dom Courançonne, Dom de Cabasse;* (Valréas) *Roger Combe, Dom des Grands Devers, Le Val des Rois;* (Vacqueyras) *Château de Montmirail, Clos des Cazaux, Dom la Fourmone, Dom des Lambertins, Le Sang des Cailloux.*

## CÔTES DU VENTOUX, AC
Rather good area just to the east of the Rhône producing lots of fresh, juicy wine, of which the red is the best. Can occasionally be quite special. Best: *Domaine des Anges, Jaboulet, Pascal* as well as *Vieille Ferme* and *Vieux Lazaret.*

## CROZES-HERMITAGE, AC
A large *appellation* providing a lot of fairly strong and slightly tough and smoky Hermitage-type wine which at its best has a lovely juicy fruit as well. *Etienne Pochon (Château de Curson), Graillot's La*

*Guérande* and *Jaboulet's Thalabert* brand are outstanding; also good are *Desmeures, Ferraton, Albert Belle, Stephane Cornu* and *Tardy & Ange.* The *Tain* co-op is also finally producing some decent stuff.

**GIGONDAS, AC** Red and rosé wine from the village of Gigondas, west of Orange. Not the most immediately attractive of reds – a bit ragged at the edges – but nonetheless consistent, big, plummy and rather solid. *Domaine de St-Gayan* is very good, as are *Château de Montmirail, Clos des Cazaux, Château du Trignon, Domaine les Gouberts, Domaine de Longue-Toque, Domaine l'Oustau Fauquet, Domaine les Pallières, Domaine Raspail-Ay.*

**HERMITAGE, AC** One of France's burliest, grandest reds, from a small, precipitous vineyard area around the hill of Hermitage. Strong and fierily tough when young, it matures to a rich, brooding magnificence. There is always a stern, vaguely medicinal or smoky edge to it, and an unmatchable depth of raspberry and blackcurrant fruit. Although a number of people produce Hermitage of sorts, there have traditionally been only two stars, the low-key but marvellously good *Chave*, who produces small amounts of impeccable wine, and the ebullient, export-orientated *Paul Jaboulet Aîné*, who produces larger amounts of more variable wine. To them should be added *Chapoutier's Le Pavillon.* Other good producers: *Delas Cuvée Marquise de la Tourette, Desmeure, B. Faurie, Guigal, Sorrel, Belle, Faurie* and *Jean-Louis Grippat.*

**LIRAC, AC** An excellent and often underrated area just south-west of Châteauneuf whose wines it can frequently equal. The reds are packed with fruit, often tinged with a not unwelcome mineral edge. The rosés are remarkably fresh for so far south. And they're cheap. Whites can be first-class if caught young. Best: *Domaine de Château St-Roch, Domaine des Causses et St-Eymes, Domaine les Garrigues, Domaine la Fermade, Domaine de la Tour.*

**ST-JOSEPH, AC** Almost smooth and sweet by comparison with their tougher neighbours, these reds, especially those from the hillsides between Condrieu and Cornas, can be fairly big, fine wines, stacked with blackcurrant in a good year. There has been some expansion of the AC wine into unsuitable terrain, but the quality is mostly high, and though there have been hefty price rises, the wines *were* undervalued. *Chave, Coursodon, Florentin, Gripa, Grippat, Jaboulet, Maurice Courbis and Trollat* are leading names. The co-op at *St-Désirat Champagne* makes 'Beaujolais-type' St-Joseph; not traditional, but lovely.

**TAVEL, AC** The AC only applies to one colour of wine – pink! The wines are quite

expensive, certainly tasty, but too big and alcoholic to be very refreshing. Any of the Rhône grapes will do, but generally it's Grenache-dominated, with the addition of a little Cinsaut. Best producers: *Château d'Aqueria, Château de Trinquevedel, Domaine de la Forcadière, Domaine de la Génestière.*

**VIN DE PAYS DES COLLINES RHODANIENNES** A usually impressive and expanding northern Rhône area, particularly for inexpensive, strongly flavoured Syrah reds, though Gamay can also be good.

**VIN DE PAYS DES COTEAUX DE L'ARDÈCHE** This straggly, upland Rhône *département* puts into a nutshell what the *vins de pays* should be trying to achieve. Not content with the usual mishmash of southern grapes, a mixture of go-ahead co-ops and outside influences decided to plant grapes to make wine that would *sell*: delicious Nouveau-style Gamay, first class Syrah, good Cabernet, and they've planted Sauvignon Blanc, Pinot Noir – and Chardonnay. *Louis Latour*, one of the largest sellers of Burgundian Chardonnay, has inspired much of the Chardonnay planting here for his Chardonnay de l'Ardèche. Sixty local growers have planted Chardonnay and are contracted to Latour. That's good news. But the news that the local co-ops are already producing higher quality wines at far lower prices – without his help – is much better!

**MATURITY CHART**
1988 Côte-Rôtie
Côte-Rôtie from an excellent vintage like this repays keeping

| Bottled | Ready | Peak | Tiring | In decline |
|---------|-------|------|--------|------------|

| 0 | 5 | 10 | 15 | 20 | 25 years |

# WHITE WINES

The two main styles of northern Rhône white could hardly be more different. The wines based on Marsanne and Roussanne – Hermitage, Crozes-Hermitage, St-Joseph and St-Péray – are in general weighty, strong, initially lacking in perfume and charm, but capable of a great, opulent, Lord Mayor-like, broad richness, given the decade or so they need to mature. Some modern versions, like those of Jaboulet, are less ambitious but ready within the year. The wines based on the Viognier are heavenly – totally different in style, bursting with the fruit flavours of apricots and pears and a mad, heady perfume like flower gardens in spring. Very special.

The interest in southern Rhône whites is fairly recent because it had always been assumed, with justification, that white wine from the region's non-aromatic grapes, produced on parched vineyards in the baking summer heat, could not possibly be anything but dull and flabby and fruitless. Now that many leading producers have invested in refrigerated equipment, and adopted cool fermentation techniques, it is quite remarkable what delicious flavours are beginning to appear. The vintage of 1989 was particularly good and 1990 looks like matching that quality – where growers were careful not to overproduce.

## GRAPES & FLAVOURS

**CLAIRETTE** Makes sparkling Clairette de Die, but is a bit dull unless livened up with the aromatic Muscat. In the South it makes rather big, strong whites, occasionally creamy, but more often dull and nutty. Needs careful handling and early drinking.

**GRENACHE BLANC** A widely planted variety in the southern Rhône producing appley wines with a strong whiff of aniseed. Good, but soft, so drink young.

**MARSANNE** The dominant of the two grapes that go to make white Hermitage and Crozes-Hermitage, as well as white St-Joseph and St-Péray. Its wine is big and weighty but with a rather good, rich, sweet scent. Further south it makes big, burly wine, fat, lanoliny, but capable of rich exotic peach and toffee flavours, too. A good quality producer.

**MUSCAT** Used to great effect blended with Clairette to make the sparkling Clairette de Die Tradition, but more famous for Muscat de Beaumes de Venise.

**ROUSSANNE** An altogether more delicate and fragrant grape than the Marsanne, but it is inconveniently prone to disease and also a low yielder, so it is increasingly losing ground to Marsanne. Found chiefly in Hermitage and St-Péray in the northern Rhône, though it also produces light, fragrant wines further south in Châteauneuf-du-Pape.

**UGNI BLANC** Boring workhorse grape planted all over the South to produce basic gulping stuff. The same as the Trebbiano of Italy, where it is hardly more exciting.

**VIOGNIER** The grape of Condrieu and Château Grillet. It has one of the most memorable flavours of any white grape because it manages to blend the rich, musky scent of an overripe apricot with the breeze-blown perfume of springtime orchard flowers. Autumn and spring in one glass. The wine is made dry, but it is so rich you hardly believe it! The rarest of the world's great white grapes, though interest in planting it is growing, even as far afield as Australia.

# WINES & WINE REGIONS

**CHÂTEAU GRILLET, AC** A single property in the far North-west of the northern Rhône, and the smallest individual *appellation contrôlée* in France at only three hectares, excepting a couple of Vosne-Romanée *grands crus* in Burgundy. This wine should have that magic reek of orchard fruit and harvest bloom about it. Sometimes it does.

**CHÂTEAUNEUF-DU-PAPE BLANC, AC** Only three per cent of the AC is white, but the wines can be outstandingly perfumed with a delicious nip of acidity, leaving you wondering how on earth such aromatic wines could come from such a hot, arid region. Magic or technology; or it might be such delights as the Roussanne, Picpoul and Picardan varieties adding something to the base of Grenache Blanc, Clairette and Bourboulenc. Wonderful wines can be produced in the most unlikely places – and this just happens to be one of them. Although the wine can age, you lose that perfumed rush of springtime madness after a year. Best producers: *Beaucastel* (especially their pure Roussanne *Vieille Vigne* – and the new Viognier white), *Clefs d'Or, Clos des Papes, Font de Michelle, Grand Tinel, Mont-Redon, Nalys, Rayas, Vieux Télégraphe*.

**CLAIRETTE DE DIE BRUT, AC** Adequate fizz from the Clairette grape grown in the beautiful Drôme valley, east of the Rhône.

**CLAIRETTE DE DIE TRADITION, AC** Delicious, light, off-dry, grapy fizz made half from Clairette, half from Muscat.

**CONDRIEU, AC** From a small vineyard area at the northern end of the northern Rhône, this is wonderful white when made properly, with apricot scent that leaps out of the glass, and an exciting balance of succulent fruit and gentle, nipping acidity. But its sudden popularity has led to great replanting, sometimes by people concerned more with high prices than high quality. But the potential quality is so stunning, that hopefully the *arrivistes* will realize that the real thing is worth striving for. The potential area is 200 hectares, but with only just over 20 planted, there's very little wine; and it's expensive, though less than half the price of Château Grillet. A recent departure has been the release of *cépage* Viognier wine (the grape used in Château Grillet), which will show what the fuss is about – at half the Condrieu price. (Yapp has one.) Very good names include *Château du Rozay, Delas, Dumazet, Guigal, Jean Pinchon* and *Georges Vernay*.

**COTEAUX DU TRICASTIN, AC** Fresh, fruity and quite full-flavoured southerly whites, not as exciting as the reds. Best bet: *Producteurs Réunis Ardéchois*.

**CÔTES DU LUBÉRON, AC** Usually pleasant and light southern wine but little more, though recent innovations have started to produce much more fragrant, interesting styles at such properties as *Château de l'Isolette, Mas du Peyroulet, Val Joanis* and *Vieille Ferme*.

**CÔTES DU RHÔNE BLANC, AC; CÔTES DU RHÔNE-VILLAGES BLANC, AC** Increasingly fresh, fruity and gulpable especially from the villages of Laudun and Chusclan. *Domaine Pelaquié* at Laudun is the leading estate, and *Domaine Ste-Anne* at St-Gervais is good.

**CROZES-HERMITAGE, AC** Generally a rather dull, strong northern Rhône white, but there are good ones from *Desmeure, Fayolle, Jaboulet* and *Pradelle*.

**HERMITAGE, AC** Often a bit heavy and dull, but curiously it ages tremendously well to a soft, rich nuttiness. Some of the finest is made by *Chapoutier, Chave, Desmeure, Ferraton, Grippat* and *Sorrel*.

**LIRAC, AC** The whites can be good young. Can resemble a less exotic Châteauneuf: less exotic flavour; less exotic price.

**ST-JOSEPH, AC** Northern AC with some fair, nutty white and better red. *Grippat* is good. *Florentin* does an intense old-style headbanging white unlike any other.

**ST-PÉRAY, AC** Made in the southern bit of the northern Rhône, this was once France's most famous sparkling wine after Champagne. Not any more. It tends to be rather stolid and short of freshness. And the still whites are just dull. The occasional better bottle will come from *Chaboud, Clape, Grippat, Juge* or *Voge*.

# FORTIFIED WINES

**MUSCAT DE BEAUMES DE VENISE, AC** This Côtes du Rhône village is the only place in the Rhône to grow the Muscat grape. The golden sweet wine – a *vin doux naturel* – has become a real fad drink, but for once the fad is a good one, because it's supremely delicious! Grapy, fresh, rich but not cloying. Look for *Domaine de Coyeux, Domaine Durban, Jaboulet* and the *Beaumes de Venise* co-op.

**RASTEAU, AC** The Côtes du Rhône village of Rasteau also makes a few big, port-like fortified wines – *vins doux naturels* – both red and off-white. Young ones can have a delightful raspberry scent from the Grenache Noir. The whites are made from Grenache Blanc and can be frankly unpleasant. Production is pretty small. Try *Domaine de la Soumade, Co-opérative de Rasteau.*

---

### RHÔNE VINTAGES

**1991** Many northern Rhône growers had their fourth very good year in succession. Most were spared spring frosts and in Côte Rôtie at least the wines are generally better than the 1990s. In the South the crop was severely reduced by *coulure* in the spring; yields were tiny, and the wine only moderately good.

**1990** Another long, warm summer led to drought and uneven ripening. On the whole the northern Rhône survived better than the South though rain affected picking in Côte-Rôtie. Choose 1990 for the northern Rhône (though Côte Rôtie is dodgy); 1989 for the South.

**1989** Drought affected much of the region, and some poor Hermitage and Cornas was made by growers who were unable to master it. But small crops meant concentrated Châteauneuf for keeping. Trust your wine merchant.

**1988** There is certainly *some* great 1988, mostly in Côte-Rôtie, Hermitage and Châteauneuf-du-Pape. There is a fair amount which is far too tannic for its own good.

**1987** White Châteauneuf was actually rather good, but the red isn't special. Drink now and don't buy any more. Côtes du Rhône reds and northern Rhônes can be good.

**1986** A rather joyless vintage for reds. Some very good Châteauneuf and Hermitage but the ambitious Côtes du Rhône names made some of the best. Some white still improving.

**1985** Brilliant Côte-Rôtie, St-Joseph and Cornas. Hermitage could have been as good if its leading producers had tried a bit harder. Châteauneuf is delicious and juicy.

**1983** Outstanding dark, rich, complex Hermitage and very good Côte-Rôtie for keeping. Southern reds are good, but the failure of the Grenache left some a bit tough.

**1982** Good, rather simple northern reds; a difficult, hot vintage in the South.

**1980** Underrated but high quality in North and South.

**1978** The best vintage since 1961. Drink now — if you can find any.

# LOIRE

I was sitting in the offices of an Austrian wine estate in the spring of 1992 when the telephone rang. Afterwards the owner explained: 'That was a call from a *négociant* in the Loire. He wanted to know if I could sell him some wine.'

This brought home to me how devastating were the consequences of the frost that savaged the Loire vineyards in April 1991. The frost damaged other French vineyards too, but the Loire, as France's most northerly vineyard region, was hit with particular harshness. And that was only the beginning. A cold June hampered flowering, there were scattered shellings of hail in August, and although the summer was warm and dry, heavy rain in late September could not have come at a worse time. Rot was widespread. Those grapes that survived this meteorological assault course made quite good wine, but it was essential for growers to select their crop very carefully.

The Loire was saved from total disaster by its lack of uniformity. We think of the Loire as a single zone, but it is far more dispersed than the other great French wine regions. The weather and growing conditions in the West, around Muscadet, often bear no relation to the conditions in the eastern Loire where the great Sauvignons are grown. And whereas in Bordeaux you can find dry reds, dry whites and sweet whites, the Loire offers all of these and a good deal of sparkling wine too. In vintages when the grapes ripen inadequately, it's possible to use them for delicious *crémant*s and other sparkling wines.

In 1991 the problem was not so much a lack of ripeness as a shortage of grapes. A few growers even managed to produce heady botrytized wines in Quarts de Chaume, and overall quality is probably slightly above average.

### Pre-freeze trio

Fortunately the Loire, like other parts of France, enjoyed three excellent vintages before the year of the frost. There are magnificent red wines from the Cabernet Franc appellations of Bourgeuil, Chinon and Saumur-Champigny in 1989, and the 1988 and 1990 vintages are not far behind in quality. But the real glory of the Loire during these years was in Vouvray and the sweet wine appellations of Coteaux du Layon and Bonnezeaux. In 1989 and again in 1990 botrytis swooped on the Chenin Blanc, resulting in wines of a richness and succulence matched only by the legendary 1947 vintage. I raved about these wines in these pages last year, but make no apology for mentioning them again, both because of their amazing quality and because they are still available in the shops. For £8-£12 it is still possible to buy top *cuvées* of botrytized Vouvray that will develop for a century. Delicious now, they will close up for a decade or so, and then improve well into the next millennium. That's what I call a bargain.

More commonly encountered white wines such as Sancerre and Pouilly-Fumé are of reasonable quality in 1991, although quantities are severely reduced. As for the western Loire, some growers didn't even attempt to produce Muscadet in 1991, so ravaged were the vines, and wine-lovers in search of inexpensive whites for everyday drinking should probably look elsewhere for a year or so. British wine merchants with long-standing loyalties in the region, such as Robin Yapp, did manage to secure allocations of the best of the 1991s, so if you insist in buying 1991 Muscadet or Anjou, it will be still be available from some specialist merchants. **STEPHEN BROOK**

# WHITE GRAPES & FLAVOURS

**CHARDONNAY** Increasingly widespread in the Loire and producing lean, light but tangy results in Haut-Poitou, in Anjou as Vin de Pays du Jardin de la France and in Orléans as Vin de l'Orléanais (where it's called Auvernat: *Clos St-Fiacre* is absolutely delicious). It also occurs in Muscadet (*Le Chouan* and *Domaine Couillaud* are found in the UK) and adds character and softness to Anjou Blanc.

**CHASSELAS** Makes adequate but dull wine at Pouilly-sur-Loire; it's actually best as a table grape, in a fruit salad.

**CHENIN BLANC** A grape that cries out for sun and ripens (if that's the word) well after the other varieties. Experiments with allowing the skins to steep in the juice before fermentation, and the quiet addition of a bit of Chardonnay, are beginning to produce outstanding peachy whites which make brilliant summer drinking.

It also performs superbly on the Loire in a few warm and misty microclimates (especially Quarts de Chaume and Bonnezeaux), where noble rot strikes the Chenin with enough frequency to make it worthwhile going through all the pain and passion of producing great sweet wine,

with steely acidity and honeyed, ripe-apple fruit. These wines can seem curiously disappointing when young, but fine sweet Chenin manages to put on weight and become sweeter for perhaps 20 years before bursting out into a richness as exciting as all but the very best from Germany or Bordeaux. And then it lasts and lasts...

**MELON DE BOURGOGNE** The grape of Muscadet, light and neutral. It's good at producing fresh, surprisingly soft, slightly peppery, dry white wine with a salty tang, generally for drinking young, though a good domaine-bottled *sur lie* can mature surprisingly well.

**SAUVIGNON BLANC** The grape of Sancerre, and the main white grape of Pouilly and Touraine, with a whole range of fresh, green, tangy flavours that might remind you of anything from gooseberries to nettles and fresh-cut grass, and there's sometimes even a whiff of newly roasted coffee. The wines are usually quite tart – but thirst-quenching rather than gum-searing – and have loadsafruit. Sauvignon can age interestingly in bottle, but the odds are against it, except for the high-priced oak-aged *cuvées*.

# WHITE WINES & WINE REGIONS

**ANJOU BLANC SEC, AC** France's cheapest AC dry white made from the hard-to-ripen Chenin Blanc, grown anywhere in the Anjou area upriver from the Muscadet region, often tart, sulphured and sour. But it *can* be good, steely and honeyed, especially from Savennières with its two tiny special ACs, Coulée-de-Serrant and La Roche aux Moines, and from names such as *Domaine Richou* who are beginning to mix Chardonnay with their Chenin, for extra flavour, fruit and body. They are allowed up to 20 per cent Chardonnay or Sauvignon Blanc. Some have planted a little bit more on the side, and it's no bad

thing. Other good producers are *Baranger, Château de Valliennes, Jaudeau*.

**BONNEZEAUX, AC** One of the most unfairly forgotten great sweet wines of France. After a long period of decline, this small AC centred round Thouarcé, inside the Coteaux du Layon, is on the up again. The vineyard area has grown from 42 hectares in 1975 to 157 hectares in 1985 and prices for the lovely noble-rot-affected wines are rising fast. So much the better; they were far too cheap before, and if you don't make it profitable for the growers to indulge themselves in the passion and commitment necessary for great sweet wine, they'll give up and plant apples. Look out for the outstanding Bonnezeaux of *Jacques Boivin* of *Château de Fesles* as well as *Goizil, Renou* and *Denéchère*.

**CHEVERNY, VDQS** An up-and-coming Touraine region, of interest as the home of the white Romorantin grape. Attractive Sauvignon (and Gamay) too. *Domaine des Huards* makes fine, delicate wines.

**COTEAUX DE L'AUBANCE, AC** A rambling *appellation* south of Anjou giving pleasant semi-sweet whites, quite cheaply. Good producers: *Domaine des Rochettes, Jean-Yves Lebreton* and *Domaine Richou*.

**COTEAUX DU LAYON, AC** A large *appellation* along the steep banks of the Layon river producing varying qualities of sweet white wine, at its best rich and tasty with a taut, cutting acidity that allows the wine to age for a long time. *Château de la Guimonière, Château de la Roulerie, Domaine Ambinois, Domaine du Petit Val, Domaine des Quarres, Domaine de la Soucherie* and *Ogereau* are worth seeking out and reasonably priced. There are also six Coteaux du Layon-Villages ACs that usually offer higher quality.

**CRÉMANT DE LOIRE, AC** Sparkling wine AC intended to denote higher quality but not used to any great extent. Compared with Saumur AC fizz, the yield must be lower (50 rather than 60 hectolitres per hectare), the juice extract less (150kg of grapes as against 130kg for one hectolitre of juice), and the wine must lie on its lees for 12 months rather than 9 after its second fermentation. The product is usually softer and more enjoyable than the frequently harsh products of Saumur, but the merchants have built up their brands on the name Saumur and don't seem inclined to put much effort into Crémant de Loire. Laudable exceptions are the first-rate house of *Gratien & Meyer*, St-Cyr-en-Bourg co-op, and the small *Cave des Liards*.

**GROS PLANT, VDQS** Gros Plant rejoices in being one of the rawest wines in France, and the prosperity of dentists in the Nantes area is thanks in no small measure to the local inhabitants' predilection for the stuff. That said, it *does* go amazingly well with seafood and is one of the wines that seems to suit oysters. *Bossard* manages to produce an example with a soft honeyed flavour. The dentists must be furious.

**HAUT-POITOU, AC** Produced in an isolated area south of the main Loire vineyards. Chardonnay and Sauvignon from the *Cave Co-opérative du Haut-Poitou* are good but tending to the lean side.

**MENETOU-SALON, AC** Small, growing AC to the west of Sancerre making pretty good Sauvignons (and some fair reds and rosés). The *Vignerons Jacques Coeur* co-op group, which spends most of its time organizing cereal farmers, produces about half the Sauvignon. *Henry Pellé* makes the best in Menetou, followed by *Jean-Max Roger* and *Domaine de Chatenoy*. Prices are lower than for Sancerre, and a top Menetou is always tastier than a mediocre Sancerre.

**MONTLOUIS, AC** Chenin area to the south of Vouvray. Makes similar wines, but frequently more robust – which, when it comes to the Chenin grape, isn't always a good idea. *Dominique Moyer, Domaine des Liards* and *Jean-Pierre Trouvé* are good, but lots are short on fruit, long on sulphur.

**MUSCADET, AC** Simple, light and neutral wine from the Nantes area of southern Brittany, near the Atlantic. Straight Muscadet, without any further regional title, is usually flat and boring. But at least it's light – the Muscadet ACs are the only ones in France to impose a *maximum* alcohol level (12.3 per cent).

*The price guides for this section begin on page 314.*

**MUSCADET DE SÈVRE-ET-MAINE, AC** The biggest Muscadet area, around the Sèvre and Maine rivers, making the most but also the best wine. A good one may taste slightly nutty, peppery or salty, even honeyed, sometimes with a creaminess from being left on the lees, sometimes a chewy apricot-skin taste and sometimes with a slight prickle. It should always have a lemony acidity, and should feel light. Buy domaine-bottled wine only, and check the address, looking out for *St-Fiacre* and *Le Pallet*, two of the best villages.

**MUSCADET DES COTEAUX DE LA LOIRE, AC** A small area along the banks of the Loire east of Nantes. In quality, it's somewhere between Muscadet and Muscadet de Sèvre-et-Maine.

**MUSCADET SUR LIE** This is the most important thing to look for on a Muscadet label – even though not all producers use the term honestly. The 'lie' is the lees or yeast sediment left after fermentation. The Muscadet tradition is to leave the new wine on the lees until bottling, instead of moving it to a clean vat. The wine then picks up yeasty, salty flavours, and keeps its fresh, prickly character. Because of the abuse to which the term may be subjected, it's best to buy only *sur lie* Muscadet labelled *mise en bouteille à la propriété / château / domaine*. Some merchants, such as *Sauvion*, have portable bottling lines, and bottle properly *sur lie* at the grower's cellar. Their *Château du Cléray* and the *Découvertes* range of single domaines are particularly good. *Guy Bossard* makes good organic Muscadet de Sèvre-et-Maine *sur lie*; also notable are *Domaine de Coursay-Villages, Domaine du Grand Mouton, Domaine de la Montaine, Château de Chasseloir, Clos de la Sénaigerie, Domaine du 'Perd-son-pain', Chéreau-Carré*, both *Michel* and *Donatien Bahuaud*'s single domaine wines, *Bonhomme* and *Guilbaud*.

**POUILLY-FUMÉ, AC** Just over the river from Sancerre and very similar. The wines

are said to smell of gunflint because of their smokiness. They can be more full-bodied than Sancerre, and the presence of flint in the soil does give the best wines a mineral complexity. Top growers include *J C Châtelain, Didier Dagueneau* (Pouilly's most brilliant wine-maker), *Serge Dagueneau, Château Favray, Masson-Blondelet, André Figeat* and the too-expensive *de Ladoucette*.

**POUILLY-SUR-LOIRE, AC** Made from the dull Chasselas grape which makes good eating but not memorable drinking. *Serge Dagueneau* makes a good example.

**QUARTS DE CHAUME, AC** A tiny 40-hectare AC in the Layon valley with a perfect microclimate for nobly-rotten sweet wines. They are rare and expensive, not quite as sweet as top Sauternes, but they can be even more intense, with high acid stalking the rich apricot and honey fruit. *Jean Baumard* is superb; also *Château de Bellerive* and *Château de l'Echarderie*.

**QUINCY, AC** Fairly pungent Sauvignon Blanc wines grown west of Sancerre. *Domaine de Maison Blanche, Pierre Mardon, Jacques Rouzé* and the co-op *Jacques Coeur* make good examples.

**REUILLY, AC** Light, fragrant Sauvignon Blanc wines from near Quincy, west of Sancerre. *Gérard Cordier* and *Claude Lafond* are the important growers. (There is also some tasty red and rosé.)

**SANCERRE, AC** Green, smoky, tangy wine from the Sauvignon Blanc grape grown at the eastern end of the Loire. Drunk young when it's at its best, it should be super-fresh and fruity, with a flavour and fragrance like gooseberries or fresh-cut grass, and a brilliant balance between sharpness and ripe, round body. But all too often it smells sulphurous or meaty, and tastes simply flabby. Look for single-domaine wines – especially those of *Pierre Archambault, Joseph Balland-Chapuis,*

*Henri Bourgeois, Francis & Paul Cotat, Lucien Crochet, Pierre & Alain Dézat, Domaine Laporte, Alphonse Mellot, Paul Millérioux, Bernard Noël-Reverdy, Jean-Max Roger, Pierre Riffault, Domaine Vacheron* and *André Vatan*.

**SAUMUR, AC** Champagne-method wine made from Chenin grapes, sometimes with the welcome addition of Chardonnay, Sauvignon or even Cabernet Franc, any of which can give a bit more roundness to the acid Chenin. Well-made sparkling Saumur (including a little rosé) is lively and appley but too many are just too rough to revel with. Best producers: *Ackerman Laurance, Bouvet-Ladubay, Gratien & Meyer* and *Langlois-Château*.

**SAUMUR BLANC, AC** White, usually ultra-dry, though it can occasionally be sweet, similar to Anjou Blanc.

**SAVENNIÈRES, AC** Some of the steeliest, longest-living, diamond-dry white wines in the world come from this tiny Anjou *appellation* just west of Angers. One vineyard, Savennières Coulée-de-Serrant, has its own AC within Savennières, and *Madame Joly*'s wines from the *Clos de la Coulée-de-Serrant* are extremely fine. Look out also for *Yves Soulez* from the *Château de Chamboreau, Clos du Papillon, Domaine de la Bizolière* and the *Domaine aux Moines*.

**TOURAINE, AC** Everybody sees Touraine Sauvignon, with some justification, as a Sancerre substitute. The *Confrérie des Vignerons de Oisly-et-Thésée* sell to half the British wine trade, and their wines are good, as are *Paul Buisse, Château de l'Aulée, Domaine de la Charmoise (Marionnet), Domaine des Corbillières, Domaine Joël Delaunay* and *Domaine Octavie*.

**VIN DE PAYS DU JARDIN DE LA FRANCE** The general title for *vin de pays* throughout the Loire valley. Usually light and unmemorable, though pleasant, but the results can be impressive, especially when based on Sauvignon and Chardonnay. *Biotteau's Château d'Avrille Chardonnay* and *Domaine des Hauts de Saulière's Chardonnay* have lovely fruit.

**VOUVRAY, AC** Sparkling wine and still whites ranging from the tangily dry to the liquorously sweet, though usually caught in the middle. In fact Vouvray is best at producing the off-dry *demi-sec* style, and from a good producer this Chenin wine, initially all searing acidity and rasping dryness, over a number of years develops a deep, nutty, honey-and-cream flavour. Most commercial Vouvray is poor. Good producers are: *Daniel Allias, Brédif, Bourillon Dorléans, Bernard Fouquet, Château Moncontour, Foreau, Huet* and *Prince Poniatowski*.

## RED GRAPES & FLAVOURS

**CABERNET SAUVIGNON** This doesn't always ripen too well in the Loire, but even so it is planted a fair bit to add some firm backbone to the wines. It is really at its best in the ripest years.

**CABERNET FRANC** The great quality grape of Anjou and Touraine. All the best reds are based on Cabernet Franc, and the styles go from the palest, most fleeting of reds to deep, strong, proud wines of great character and considerable longevity.

**GAMAY** This rarely achieves the lovely, juicy glugginess of Beaujolais, but when it is made by a careful modern wine-maker it can have a fair amount of fruit, though it always has a tough edge.

**PINOT NOIR** In Sancerre and the neighbouring villages this can, in warm years, produce a lovely, light, cherry-fragrant wine that will be either a rosé or a light red. But really interesting examples are rare in the Loire.

# RED WINES & WINE REGIONS

**ANJOU ROUGE CABERNET, AC** Until a few years ago Anjou Rouge was a byword for raw, rasping red fit to drive a chap to Liebfraumilch. But an increasing amount of excellent red is now made, light and dry from the co-ops, up to spicy, strong and capable of ageing from the best domaines. The top wines can rival Bourgueil. Best producers: *Château d'Avrille, Château de Chamboureau (Soulez), Clos de Coulaine, Domaine de la Petite Croix, Domaine du Petit Val, Domaine des Rochettes (Chauvin), Logis de la Giraudière (Baumard), Richou, Roussier.*

**ANJOU ROUGE GAMAY, AC** Rarely more than adequate, but in the hands of someone like *Richou*, the 'rooty' character is replaced by a fresh, creamy fruit that is sharp and soft all at once, and *very* good. *Domaine des Quarres* is also worth a try.

**ANJOU-VILLAGES, AC** A newish AC for red wine from the 46 best villages in Anjou, declared in October 1987. Only Cabernet Franc and Cabernet Sauvignon may be used, and the basic permitted yields are the same as for Anjou Rouge. Some will be labelled 'Anjou-Villages Val-de-Loire' – an optional extra. 1987 wasn't the greatest year to begin, but the signs are hopeful.

**BOURGUEIL, AC** Some of the best reds of the Loire come from this AC in Touraine. When they are young they can taste a bit harsh and edgy, but give them a few years and they will have a piercing blackcurrant fruitiness, sharp and thirst-quenching. They can age remarkably well, developing complex leathery, meaty flavours. Good producers: *Audebert* (estate wines), *Pierre Breton, Caslot-Galbrun, Domaine des Forges, Domaine des Ouches, Pierre-Jacques Druet, Lamé-Delille-Boucard.*

**CABERNET D'ANJOU, AC** (Rosé) There is a reasonable chance of a pleasant drink here, because the Cabernets – mostly Cabernet Franc, but often with some Cabernet Sauvignon in there too – do give pretty tasty wine, and it is usually made a good deal less sweet than simple Rosé d'Anjou. Various estates make it well – *Domaine Baranger, Domaine de Richou, Domaine de Hardières, Château de Valliennes.*

**CHINON, AC** From a good producer in a ripe year (1982, '83, '85, '88, '89, '90), Chinon, an AC within the Touraine AC, is the most delicious of all Loire reds, exhibiting from the start a great gush of blackcurrant and raspberry with the acid strongly evident just as it would be in fresh-picked fruit. There's an earthiness too, but it is soft and strangely cooling in its effect, and after a few years it seems to dissolve into the clear, mouthwatering fruit of the vine. Domaine wines are *far* better than *négociant* wines, which can be rather thin. Best producers: *Bernard Baudry, Jean Baudry, Couly-Dutheil, Domaine du Colombier, Domaine du Roncée, Domaine de la Tour, Druet, Gatien Ferrand, René Gouron, Charles Joguet, Pierre Manzagol, Jean François Olek, Jean-Maurice Raffault, Raymond Raffault.*

**HAUT-POITOU, AC** Fairly 'green' but reasonably enjoyable reds from the Loire hinterland, usually made from the Gamay grape.

**ROSÉ D'ANJOU, AC** The omnipresent and frequently omnihorrid French rosé. It is based on a pretty feeble grape, the Groslot, and suffers in the main from lack of fruit and excess of sulphur. A few producers like the co-op at *Brissac* can make it fresh and bright.

**ROSÉ DE LOIRE, AC** A rosé from Anjou or Touraine. It was intended to cater for the move in public taste to drier wines. However, the public decided it was tired of rosé in general and switched to dry white!

**SANCERRE ROUGE, AC** Pinot Noir, and in general much overrated, but occasionally you can find a fleeting cherry fragrance and lingering sweetness of strawberries that can even survive a year or two in bottle. If it weren't for the silly price it would be good for a whimsical mood. *Henri Bourgeois, Domaine Vacheron, Pierre and André Dezat,* and *Domaine de Chatenoy* at the nearby AC of Menetou-Salon are good.

**SAUMUR ROUGE, AC** Usually very light and dry Cabernet Franc from 38 villages round Saumur. Light, but the fruit is often marked and attractively blackcurranty. The co-op at *St-Cyr-en-Bourg* is good.

**SAUMUR-CHAMPIGNY, AC** Cabernet red from the best villages in the Saumur region. Deeper and more exciting than straight Saumur, the fruit is a marvellous reeking blackcurrant, appetizing and satisfying at the same time. *Domaine Filliatreau* makes an outstanding 'old vines' wine. Other good names: *Château de Chaintres, Château du Hureau, Château de Targé, Domaine Dubois, Domaine Lavigne, Domaine Sauzay-Legrand, Denis Duveau.*

**ST-NICOLAS DE BOURGUEIL, AC** These Cabernet reds from an AC within Touraine AC are grown on gravelly soil, so they tend to be lighter and more forward than nearby Bourgueils. They can be good, but I'd stick to warm years if I were you. The wines of *Claude Ammeux, Jean-Paul Mabileau* and *Joël Taluau* seem best for consistency and style.

**TOURAINE, AC** The reds aren't usually very exciting, being rather green and stalky on the whole. They are often Gamay-based but may be made from a variety of grapes, including Cabernet. The *Domaine de la Charmoise (Marionnet)*, and the co-op of *Oisly-et-Thésée* produce quite good Gamays.

**VIN DE PAYS DES MARCHES DE BRETAGNE** These wines from the mouth of the Loire are usually fairly flimsy numbers, but a good grower can use the denomination to produce something unusual and exciting. *Guy Bossard*, for instance, a leading Muscadet producer, makes an amazingly fragrant and fruity red from Cabernet Franc.

---

### LOIRE VINTAGES

Loire vintages are very important, and can be radically different along the river length. In poor vintages, Muscadet is most likely to be OK, while in hot vintages Sauvignon goes dull, but the Chenin finally ripens. The red grapes need the warm years.

**1991** Devastating April frosts and late September rains are the story here, as in other parts of France. In some areas, notably Muscadet, no wine was made at all. The East fared better, but even so Sancerre and Pouilly-Fumé were down by half. Quality is average. Reds were also badly affected, and cannot compete with the preceding years. Beware of overpricing, as growers attempt to make up for wretchedly small quantities.

**1990** Another *annus mirabilis*, to the astonishment and delight of all. The sweet white Chenins, again luscious and built to last, may sometimes even exceeed the great 1989s; Great reds too. Sancerre and Pouilly can be low in acidity, but the best producers had few problems, and once again late-harvest Sauvignon has given an encore.

**1989** An exceptional year, particularly for sweet Chenin Blancs, which are gorgeous, and comparable with the legendary 1947s. The reds were ripe, but some dry whites some lack acidity. Oddity of the year: sweet, botrytis-affected Sancerre in new oak.

**1988** Delicious Sancerres and Pouilly-Fumés, more classic in style than the richer 1989s and 1990s. Muscadet was first class and still enjoyable, especially the *sur lie*.

**1987** Some excellent Muscadet (still drinking well), and a surprising amount of good red.

# ALSACE

The winegrowers of Alsace are the brainy over-achievers of the French wine scene: you can tell by their low boredom threshold. Why, enquiring visitors ask, do you need to produce 35 different wines every year? The growers smile at each other before parrying this question with indulgent patience. 'We've got to keep ourselves amused somehow,' they say. 'Varietals are a doddle. We need a challenge.'

Well, let's hope consumers can keep up. It's not enough to know your grape varieties any more. You need to master the *grand cru* system, a very different animal to its Burgundian counterpart; you need to be able to handle a *lieu-dit* or a *cuvée particulière* if it comes flying your way; you need to learn how to meet the Baroque late-harvest wines in correct sensorial mode. (Lying on a couch, I'd suggest, with a particularly rich piece of Wagner in the background; the lack of acidity in most of these wines, and their rich, perfumed, deliquescent fruit, make them the natural choice for indolent sipping.) It helps if you have sugar-divining powers, too, especially when 1989 is on the neck label. Zind-Humbrecht's straight 1989 Gewürztraminer is a dessert wine; so is Lucien Albrecht's 1989 Gewürztraminer Grand Cru Pfingstberg. You'll find many a *vendange tardive* from other years and other growers with less residual sugar in it than either of these two.

In general, the degree to which fermentation is pursued for *vendange tardive*, and even some *grand cru* and varietal wines, varies greatly, and you often need to open the bottle to try a little before placing it with any confidence in the progress of a meal. A super-sunny year like 1989 intensified the problem, and many consumers must wish that the Alsaciens would follow Loire practice in announcing whether a wine is *sec, demi-sec, moelleux* or *doux*. Even an approximation would help. Minimum must sugar levels are all very well, but the residual sugar level is just as important in governing the taste of the end product.

As the *grand cru* system swings into action, too, its own weaknesses begin to become apparent. There are 50 *grand cru* sites, now, though the second batch of 25 are still awaiting the ministerial signature. Few would disagree with the assertion that such a system is worthwhile: Alsace is geologically complex, the perfect place for testing the great French belief that *terroir* (not just soil, but aspect and microclimate as well) governs wine quality.

## From *grand* to grandiose

The trouble is that everyone wants to be able to upgrade their best varietal *cuvées* to *grand cru* status. Yes, there has been a lot of hard bargaining, and compromises have been hammered out: out of the 100 or so sites (*lieux-dits*) which originally went on to the table, half have been rejected. (You can, however, still use a *lieu-dit* name with the ordinary Alsace AC.)

But was that level of rejection enough? And have the vineyard delimitations been strict enough? No-one ever picks up a pen to write about Burgundy without cautioning readers on Clos de Vougeot and its inconsistency as a *grand cru*. It's so big, we all write: 50 hectares, too many land-holders. Yet the *grand cru* of Eichberg is 58 hectares, Hengst 76 hectares, Brand 57 hectares and Schlossberg no less than 80 hectares. Among those sites not yet officially delimited, Frankstein, Mambourg, Pfersigberg, Vorbourg and Zinnkoepflé are all expected to surge past the 50-hectare mark. So, too, will Kaefferkopf, if and when it becomes a *grand cru*. Land-holdings in Alsace may not be quite as fragmented as in Burgundy, but sites of this size will still have many, many owners, each with his or her level of achievement. One dedicated grower's ordinary varietals will inevitably be better than another's *grand cru* wines. On present showing, the Alsace *grand cru* is decidedly a step down from Burgundy's *grand cru*. Perhaps *premier cru* would have been the better term, leaving the possibility of truly distinguished *grand cru* sites to emerge later – but the political difficulties of instituting a two-tier system would have been enormous.

### Alsace – we try harder

There are drawbacks, then, to all this restless Alsace creativity. Yet overall, unquestionably, progress is being made, and the levels of excellence attained in this long, thin, enchanting ribbon of hillside between Strasbourg and Mulhouse continue to win it devoted drinking friends. If nothing else, the reduction in yield that is implied by a grower's declaring a *grand cru* wine this year in place of last year's ordinary AC varietal should ensure a step or two up in quality.

Plantings of the more rewarding grape varieties continue to increase. Riesling is now the most widespread variety, with 22.3 per cent of the 13,487 hectares of planted vineyard land, while Sylvaner (which held this position up until 1983) is retreating – its 17.5 per cent has now been exceeded by Gewürztraminer (18.6 per cent) and Pinot Blanc/Auxerrois (20 per cent).

But, more than anything, it's energy and endeavour that counts. To make 35 different wines every year is not an easy option. Alsace at present is France's leading try-harder region; if they keep it up, Johnny Hugel's extravagant prediction that 'in the 21st century, as was the case from the 11th-16th centuries, Alsace wines will again become the finest white wines of Europe' may begin to look rather more credible. **ANDREW JEFFORD**

## GRAPES & FLAVOURS

In Alsace wines are generally labelled according to their grape type. Only the cheaper wines (labelled Edelzwicker or Vin d'Alsace) are blends of several grapes. For this reason, recommended producers are listed here under the name of the appropriate grape, for ease of reference.

**CHASSELAS** Pleasant enough when fresh from the last vintage, but Pinot Blanc and Sylvaner have taken over its role as the backbone of basic blends.

**EDELZWICKER** or **VIN D'ALSACE**
A blend of the less interesting grape varieties, in particular Chasselas, Pinot Blanc and Sylvaner. Usually it is fresh and nothing more. Just occasionally, it is spicy, and then much more enjoyable. Look for *Dopff & Irion, Rolly Gassmann, Klipfel, Maurice Schoech*. Some of the supermarket own-label Vin d'Alsace wines can be good.

**GEWÜRZTRAMINER** It can be hard to believe that these wines are dry, because they can be so fat, perfumed and spicy. But, with a few exceptions, (especially in 1989) dry they are, yet big, very ripe, and with all kinds of exotic fruit tastes – lychees, mangos, peaches – and if you're lucky, finishing off with black pepper. They smell of everything from musk rose to

*The price guides for this section begin on page 321.*

spice, though poor examples can smell like cheap soap. Best producers: *Becker, Beyer, Blanck, Caves de Turckheim, Dopff au Moulin, Domaine Ostertag, Théo Faller, Gisselbrecht, Heywang, Klipfel, Kreydenweiss, Kuentz-Bas, Muré, Rolly Gassmann, Schlumberger, Trimbach, Zind-Humbrecht.*

**MUSCAT** Light, fragrant, wonderfully grapy. Imagine crushing a fistful of green grapes and gulping the juice as it runs through your fingers. That's how fresh and grapy a good Muscat should be. Sadly much of what is sold in Britain is already too old. Best producers: *Théo Cattin, Dirler, Dopff & Irion, Gisselbrecht, Hugel, Trimbach, Zind-Humbrecht.*

**PINOT BLANC** This is taking over from Sylvaner as the basis for Alsace's bright and breezy young whites. It's a much better grape, giving light, appley wine, acidic and sometimes creamy. For some reason, Auxerrois is regarded in Alsace as being synonymous with Pinot Blanc (which it isn't) and wines labelled 'Pinot Blanc' may contain both. Mature Auxerrois can take on a lovely strawberry or white chocolate character. Best producers include: *Becker, Blanck, Gisselbrecht, Heim, Hugel, Humbrecht, Kreydenweiss, Rieffel, Rolly Gassmann (*Pinot Blanc and Auxerrois*), Scherer, Sparr, Trimbach, Zind-Humbrecht.*

**PINOT GRIS** Still called Tokay locally, though the EC title is Tokay-Pinot Gris. These are fat, musky and honeyed at best, though can run to flab if badly handled. Even the lighter ones are luscious behind their basically dry fruit. The best can age well. Best producers: *Becker, Caves de Turckheim, Éguisheim co-op, Théo Faller, Gisselbrecht, Hugel, Klipfel, Kreydenweiss, Kuentz-Bas, Trimbach, Zind-Humbrecht.*

**PINOT NOIR** The Burgundy grape makes light reds and rosés with attractive perfume and strawberryish flavour, worth seeking out. Some producers – *Muré, Hugel, Caves de Turckheim, Deiss* – are oak-ageing it, and the wines can be delicious. Also good: *Cattin, Éguisheim* co-op and *Zind-Humbrecht.*

**RIESLING** This is the grape of the great sweet wines of Germany. In Alsace, it is as steely; as it ages, it goes deliciously 'petrolly'. This is Alsace at its most serious. Best names: *Becker, Blanck, Deiss, Domaine Ostertag, Dopff & Irion, Théo Faller, Louis Gisselbrecht, Hugel, Klipfel, Kreydenweiss, Kuentz-Bas, Schaller, Trimbach, Zind-Humbrecht.*

**SYLVANER** Light, tart, slightly earthy and usually one-dimensional. With age it tastes of tomatoes, for some reason. Best producers: *Beyer, Gisselbrecht, Schlumberger, Seltz, Zind-Humbrecht.*

## CLASSIFICATIONS

**ALSACE, AC** This is the simple *appellation* for the whole region, normally used with a grape name. Thus: 'Riesling – Appellation Alsace Contrôlée'.

**CRÉMANT D'ALSACE, AC** White fizz, made in the same way as Champagne, but mainly from Pinot Blanc. The few who use a touch of Riesling make more interesting, flowery-fragrant versions and there are one or two good 100 per cent Rieslings worth trying. Look for wines from *Baron de Hoen,*

*Dopff & Irion, Gisselbrecht, Kreydenweiss, Schaller, Wolfberger.*

**GRAND CRU** Twenty-five historically excellent vineyards were classified as *grand cru* in 1983, and must meet stricter regulations than ordinary Alsace: they can only be planted with Riesling, Tokay-Pinot Gris, Gewürztraminer or Muscat, and notably lower (but still high) yields apply. They are recognized by the words *Appellation Alsace Grand Cru Contrôlée* on the label. A further 25 vineyards have been given permission to add the words *grand cru* to the name of the vineyard on the label, and their AC is, confusingly, *Appellation Alsace Contrôlée, Grand Cru*. They are due to receive official endorsement in 1993. In theory, any of the *grands crus* should be better than ordinary Alsace, and first signs are that the *grand cru* classification is inspiring growers to strive for quality. Delimitations are generous, however, and varieties such as Sylvaner are excluded from sites where they traditionally did well. In difficult years like 1986 or 1988, the better siting of the *grand cru* vineyards was crucial.

**RÉSERVE** 'Réserve', 'Réserve Personnelle' and 'Réserve Exceptionnelle' have long been used for a producer's best wines.

**SÉLECTION DE GRAINS NOBLES**
The higher of the two 'super-ripe' legal descriptions based on the very high sugar content in the grapes. It only applies to wines from Riesling, Tokay-Pinot Gris, Muscat (very rare) and Gewürztraminer and corresponds to a Beerenauslese. Don't expect German acidity levels, especially not from Pinot Gris or Gewürztraminer.

**SIGILLÉ** A 'Sigillé' label – a band with a red paper seal – means that blind tasting by a jury has confirmed the wine as a fine example of its type.

**SPÉCIAL** 'Cuvée Spéciale' or 'Sélection Spéciale' usually apply to a producer's best wines. The terms have no legal weight.

**VENDANGE TARDIVE** The first of the 'super-ripe' categories, made from late-picked grapes with more sugar and therefore more potential alcohol. Only applies to Riesling, Tokay-Pinot Gris, Muscat (rare) and Gewürztraminer. They are very full, fairly alcoholic and vary in sweetness from richly dry to dessert-sweet.

---

### ALSACE VINTAGES

**1991** After three years of euphoria, it was back to earth with a bump. Alsace was still lucky in the French context, however: unscathed by frost, the main problem, after a splendid summer, was late September and October rains. Careful vinification will have produced fresh, clean wines, but it is not a late-harvest year.

**1990** Some of the older growers say 1990 is the best they have ever vinified. With healthy grapes and no noble rot, 1990 will be a Vendange Tardive year. The early harvest was already too hot for Muscat. *Coulure* and over-ripening reduced the Gewürztraminer yield by up to half; Rieslings are powerful and will age well, while the Pinots look majestic.

**1989** Exceptional weather produced an abundant harvest of very good quality, though not as superb as first reported. Unusually hot weather meant fermentation problems in some cellars. Wines are already showing lively fruit, though some are low in acidity, and there will be some exceptional wines; look for *grand cru* sites and better producers.

**1988** Rain at harvest-time made for pleasant, but hardly inspiring wine. Those who waited did better, with Tokay-Pinot Gris and Riesling the most successful.

**1987** Not great, but better than first thought. Good single vineyard wines.

**1986** Better than was at first thought, and the best are at their peak. Good Vendange Tardive and even Sélection de Grains Nobles, enriched by some late, late botrytis.

**1985** An absolute corker – wonderful wines to drink now but they will keep.

**1983** A great year, but only at the top level. These top quality wines are brilliant – rich, ripe and bursting with character, and they will still keep for several years yet.

**1976** Brilliant, deep, late-picked wines bursting with flavour and richness, but still dry.

# SOUTH-EAST FRANCE

The wines of the French south coast deserved a break: for years the western side of the Littoral had been an embarrassment, and in the East, rooking tourists had always provided an easier living than tending vines.

Competition from the rest of the world seems to have done the trick: the wines have now improved beyond measure. In Languedoc-Roussillon the less suitable flat lands with their heavy yielding Aramon and Alicante Bouschet grapes have been largely grubbed up. Now the hillsides are the source of increasingly experimental wines at keen prices. There has been a revival of interest in the fortified *vins doux naturels*; not just the sweet Muscats but also the Grenache-based reds from Banyuls, Maury and Rivesaltes.

On the other side of the Rhône delta in Provence, the wines have always received a better press. Bandol has now become the most interesting wine of the coast, especially now that more and more growers have gone over to virtually pure Mourvèdre. Indeed, Mourvèdre has been seen as the saviour throughout the South-East, with some pretty impressive examples now coming from Collioure hard by the Spanish frontier. Besides Bandol, the other region to watch is Les Baux, where Cabernet has injected some character into the wines.

The rest of Provence still lacks cohesion, with the best wines coming from a handful of conscientious growers rather than any particular area. This is a disappointment. Provence is now less interesting for wine than the formerly execrable Languedoc.                    GILES MACDONOGH

# RED & ROSÉ WINES

**BANDOL, AC** Expensive, but without doubt one of the best Provence reds. These terraced vineyards west of Toulon are the heartland of the Mourvèdre, along with Grenache, Cinsaut and Syrah, and make gorgeous, dark, spicy, soft wine, with sweet fruit and a herby, tobacco edge. Most need five years' ageing. Rosé is also excellent, showing soft spice. Best estates: *Château Ste-Anne, Château Vannières, Domaine de la Bastide Blanche, Domaine Terrebrune, Domaine de Pibarnon, Domaine Ray-Jane, Domaine Tempier, Domaine du Cagueloup, Mas de la Rouvière, Moulin des Costes*.

**BELLET, AC** The reds from vineyards behind Nice can be pretty dire, but there are a few good ones, deeply coloured with blackberry-like fruit. *Château de Crémat* can be delicious and *Château de Bellet* isn't bad, though the population of Nice deny the existence of the AC altogether.

**CASSIS, AC** A gorgeous mini-region between Bandol and Marseille, making good but expensive whites, surprisingly fresh and fruity for so far south, and stylish rosés. Don't try the reds; they'll bring you back to earth with a bump.

**COLLIOURE, AC** Startling, intense reds from the ancient vineyards cramped in between the Pyrenees and the Med, just north of Spain. You can get *Domaine de la Rectorie* and *Domaine du Mas Blanc* in the UK – if you like that sort of thing.

**CORBIÈRES, AC** Coarsely fruity, peppery red based on Carignan, Grenache, Cinsaut and others from the welter of mountains stretching from Narbonne towards Spain. The region is wild, untamed and exciting – and it looks as though the wines are beginning to match the scenery. Good wines are emerging from

*Château des Colombes, Château de Montrabech* and *Château des Ollieux.* There is increasing use of *macération carbonique (à la Beaujolaise)* and the results, particularly from some of the co-ops like *Mont Tauch* and *Embrès et Castelmaure*, are very encouraging – the peppery bite is still there, but the fruit is enhanced to a really juicy level. New oak is popping up, too. Other names: *St Auréol, La Baronne, Fontsainte, Villemajou, La Voulte-Gasparets.*

**COSTIÈRES DE NÎMES, AC** Quite good rosés, and meaty, smoky reds from a large area between Nîmes and Montpellier. I find the meatiness dominates the fruit, and I'd rather it were the other way round. Called Costières du Gard until 1989.

**COTEAUX D'AIX-EN-PROVENCE, AC** Mostly reds and rosés grown to the south and east of Aix, upgraded from VDQS. An increase in Cabernet and Syrah, more careful selection and some new oak are rushing some into the top class. They range from very light, strawberry-fruited wines, to drink at a great rate and without fuss, to such thought-provoking properties as *Château Vignelaure*, a remarkable Cabernet-based wine that achieves a Provençal-Bordeaux style.Other producers 'worth a detour': *Château de Beaulieu, Domaine de la Crémade, Domaine de Paradis, Domaine du Château Bas, Château de Fonscolombe.*

**COTEAUX DES BAUX-EN-PROVENCE, AC** For some obscure local political reason Coteaux des Baux-en-Provence only enjoys its own AC as a subregion of Coteaux d'Aix-en-Provence, though its wines are different – and better. This is a wild, rock-cluttered moonscape of a region, with many of the vineyards literally blasted from the rock. The results are a sensation; as well as producing some very good, soft, fruity whites and some delicious rosés, the reds are the best in the whole of the Mediterranean region. Based on Syrah, Mourvèdre and Grenache they have an absurdly drinkable deep, ripe, raspberry juicy fruit. The finest property, *Domaine de Trévallon*, can make reds as exciting as almost any in France. In the lunatic way of French officialdom, this is now relegated to *vin de pays* because of the lack of Grenache in the vineyard, but you may still see some wines as AC on the UK market. Perhaps Trévallon should plant some Grenache – and make rosé out of it. Best wines: *Domaine de Trévallon, Mas du Cellier, Mas de la Dame, Mas de Gourgonnier, Terres Blanches.*

**COTEAUX DU LANGUEDOC, AC** Usually a pretty solid red. A whole series of former VDQS regions have been re-defined as Coteaux du Languedoc *crus*: Cabrières, La Clape, La Méjanelle, Montpeyroux, Picpoul-de-Pinet, Pic-St-Loup, Quatourze, St-Christol, St-Drézéry, St-Georges-d'Orques, St-Saturnin, Vérargues. ACs Faugères and St-Chinian now come under the Coteaux du Languedoc AC umbrella too. There is a sense of excitement in quite a few spots, like the *St-Georges-d'Orques co-op* where they're starting to use new wood, and at the *Prieuré de St-Jean de Bébian* where the owner says he has the same soil as Châteauneuf-du-Pape and so he's planted all 13 of the Châteauneuf grape varieties! Look forward to a flood of fresh, fruity wines at affordable prices as better grapes are planted and all the bad vineyards gradually disappear.

**COTEAUX VAROIS, VDQS** Large region recently upgraded. Slightly better than basic reds and rosés, particularly where Syrah and Cabernet are used. A few good estates, like *St-Jean de Villecroze.*

**CÔTES DE PROVENCE, AC** Sprawling, catch-all AC and a lot of mediocre wine. However, when a grower decides he can do better than provide swill for the sunseekers at St Trop, these scented southern hills can provide excellent rosé, good, fruity red and fair white. Only a few single domaines are worth seeking: *Château de Pampelonne, Château St-Maurs, Domaine Gavoty, Commanderie de la Peyrassol, Domaine de la Bernarde, Domaine des Féraud* and *Domaine de Rimauresq. Domaine Ott* is good, though expensive. The wines of *Les Vignerons de la Presqu'Île de St-Tropez* are widely available and good.

**CÔTES DU ROUSSILLON, AC** Good, fruity reds, just touched by the hot dust of the South. The Carignan is the dominant grape, mixed with Cinsaut, Grenache and Syrah. Carbonic maceration is being used, as in Beaujolais, to draw out the juicy fruit. Mostly good value, as are the rosés.

**CÔTES DU ROUSSILLON-VILLAGES, AC** Usually better than the basic AC, from higher up in the foothills of the Pyrenees. That juicy fruit and dust cocktail can be delicious in the best from *Vignerons Catalans* from villages like Caramany, Cassagnes and Rassiguères. Other names: *Cazes Frères, Château Corneilla* and *Château de Jau*. The best two villages have their own separate ACs, Côtes du Roussillon-Villages Caramany and Côtes du Roussillon-Villages Latour de France.

**FAUGÈRES** Big, beefy wine, but soft with it. A fad in France, so prices have risen, but the quality is there. A few bottles with Faugères AC are still around but it is now sold as a *cru* of Coteaux du Languedoc. Try *Gilbert Alquier, Château de Grézan, Ch Haut-Fabrègues, Domaine de Fraisse*.

**FITOU, AC** Traditionally a fine, rich, old-style red based on at least 70 per cent Carignan, from between Corbières and the plain running south. Sainsbury's began Fitou's phenomenal rise in the UK, after which it became so widely available that quality couldn't hold up. Fitou's importer at one point had orders for twice as much as the AC could produce! It's off the boil now, but as things calm down, quality should return. To check on progress, try the single domaine *Château des Nouvelles*.

**MINERVOIS, AC** The most forward-looking red of the Aude. Usually lighter than Corbières, with lots of raspberry fruit and pepper, mainly from the Carignan grape. Some juicy, carbonic maceration wines at the co-ops and deeper, wood-aged styles from *Château Fabas, Château de Gourgazaud, Château de Paraza, Château Villerambert-Julien, Domaine Maris* and *Domaine de Ste-Eulalie*.

**PALETTE, AC** Tiny, and hidden in the pine forests near Aix, this makes usually pretty hard and resiny reds that need time to develop. *Château Simone* is virtually the only producer.

**ST-CHINIAN, AC** A *cru* of AC Coteaux du Languedoc, making spicy, sturdy reds that are becoming fruitier. *Cave de Berlou, Caves de Roquebrun, Château Cazals-Vieil* and *Château Coujan* look good. *Domaine Guiraud-Boyer* is good for rosé.

**VIN DE CORSE, AC** The overall AC for the island. Figari, Sartène, Porto-Vecchio, Coteaux du Cap Corse and Calvi. Ajaccio and Patrimonio can use their own ACs. Grenache, Cinsaut, Carignan and other southern grapes are common, but it is the indigenous Nielluccio and Sciacarello which give Corsican wines a distinctive character. The best are warm, spicy, perfumed and rustic. White wines from the local Vermentino grape can be good when picked early. Try *Cantone, Clos d'Alzetto, Clos Capitoro, Domaine Martini, Domaine Peraldi, Domaine du Petit Fournil* and *Domaine de Torraccia*.

**VIN DE PAYS DE L'HÉRAULT** All the good guys are experimenting furiously with grape varieties and wine-making styles. Very good 'ordinary' *vins de pays* include *Domaine du Chapître*, made at the institute of oenology at Montpellier, *Domaine de St-Macaire*, and the innovative wines of Pierre Besinet, marketed here as *Domaine du Bosc* and *Domaine Cante-Cigale*. (Some of the better *vin de pays* –

like Coteaux de Bessilles – carry their own appellation.) *Mas de Daumas Gassac* is a weird and wonderful one-off using a variety of grapes, but primarily Cabernet Sauvignon, to produce concentrated reds.

**VIN DE PAYS DE MONTCAUME** Good reds from around Bandol. The *Bunan* family make a good Cabernet Sauvignon.

**VIN DE PAYS DES BOUCHES DU RHÔNE** Torrents of reasonable reds and rosés from this departmental zone.

**VIN DE PAYS DES SABLES DU GOLFE DU LION** Sandy coastal region to the west of the Rhône delta, and the only *vin de pays* to be delineated by its soil, not by administrative boundary. Mostly fairly light wines of all colours. However, the *Listel* operation, based out in the foggy sands of the wild Camargue, produces an astonishing range of every sort, shape and persuasion. It is one of France's foremost experimental wineries, and suggestions that they should upgrade to VDQS status are dismissed, since this would hinder their at present untrammelled experimentation, such as growing grapes in a salty swamp!

**VIN DE PAYS DU GARD** Produces interesting reds and whites from classic 'northern' grapes. It is the smallest of the 'big three' departmental *vins de pays* in the Midi, producing about 30 million bottles. The reds and the rosés are often supposed to have something of a Rhône quality. Most are light and spicy with a gamey earthiness. The rosés are often better.

# WHITE WINES

**BELLET, AC** One of the few pockets of 'special' wines in Provence, just behind Nice. It is a highly unusual, nutty white, expensive and popular with the Nice glitterati. On present experience, they can keep most of them. But the characterful *Château de Crémat* and *Château de Bellet* can be worth seeking out, and the latter improves with bottle age.

**BANDOL, AC** White Bandol can be the best white of Provence, with a remarkable aniseed-and-apples freshness. Best properties include *Château Vannières, Domaine de la Bastide Blanche* and *Domaine de la Laidière*.

**CASSIS, AC** No, not the blackcurrant liqueur, though Cassis (AC) and Cassis (Crème de) would mix to a good summer drink. This one is a very good but expensive white from a small, dauntingly beautiful vineyard tucked into the bluffs by the Mediterranean between Marseille and Toulon. The grapes are a blend of Clairette, Ugni Blanc and Marsanne (rare this far south), sometimes with a little Sauvignon Blanc. Its cool freshness and fruit is a rare find on this coast, though it has low acidity and needs to be drunk young. Look out for *Domaine du Paternel* and *Clos Ste-Magdeleine*.

**CLAIRETTE DE BELLEGARDE, AC** Small AC between Arles and Nîmes making dry, still white wine from 100 per cent Clairette grapes. Unmemorable, a dull old workhorse.

**CLAIRETTE DU LANGUEDOC, AC** Heavy, alcoholic whites, dry or semi-sweet, mercifully used, for the most part, as a base for French vermouth. Signs of improvement are visible from the likes of *Domaine de la Condemine Bertrand* and *Domaine St-André*.

The price guides for this section begin on page 326.

# FORTIFIED WINES

**BANYULS, AC** (*Vin doux naturel*) Based on at least 50 per cent Grenache, these are red or tawny, sweet or dryish, but always hefty and slightly grapy. Try *Domaine de la Rectorie* or *Domaine du Mas Blanc*.

**MAURY, AC** (*Vin doux naturel*) 100 per cent Grenache AC for red or rosé wines, quite light and fresh when young but often purposely oxidized to a rather sweet-sour, burnt caramel flavour. This style is called *rancio* and is done in other ACs too. *Mas Amiel* is the one estate (and the 15-year-old is worth looking out for).

**MUSCAT DE FRONTIGNAN, AC** (*Vin doux naturel*) The best-known of the fortified Muscats. Rich and raisiny but lacks, surprisingly, any great aroma. The fresher, more fragrant style of *Château de la Peyrade* is a step in the right direction.

**MUSCAT DE RIVESALTES, AC** (*Vin doux naturel*) Similar to Frontignan, but headier, fatter. With age a rather pungent sweetness not unlike cooked marmalade can develop. It's not the trendiest of styles, so some Muscat is being made as a dry white – which is rather good.

# SOUTH-WEST FRANCE

The South-West follows the line of the Garonne river, skirting the great Landes forest before fanning out along the foothills of the Pyrenees. There is a temptation to write the region off as just an extension of Bordeaux; lookalikes with less body. This is a mistake. There are some Bordeaux-styles , but most rely on their own highly individual grapes and produce very exciting flavours indeed.

In the past decade a new spirit of pride has has worked wonders in the South-West. After years of being tough and dull, the Malbec wines (here called Auxerrois) are increasingly supple and fruity. In the Armagnac region, white Côtes de Gascognes made from the Colombard grape has become a good value alternative to over-priced Muscadet. In the Frontonnais near Toulouse it is the Negrette which lends its character to the top wines, while Madiran has shown that the Tannat can produce superb brews. Down in the Pays Basque the tongue-twisting appellation of Irouléguy is looking increasingly convincing. Finally top Jurançon growers are achieving prices on a par with Sauternes for their best, sweet Petit Manseng; and they deserve it. GILES MacDONOGH

# RED & ROSÉ WINES

**BÉARN** Red and rosé from the far South-West. The reds are predominantly from Tannat, but with other local varieties and both Cabernets thrown in. They are basically undistinguished but the Jurançon star *Domaine Cauhapé* makes quite a good red, and you could also try the wines of the *Vinicole de Bellocq* co-op, or the co-op at *Crouseilles*.

**BERGERAC, AC** An eastward extension of the St-Émilion vineyards, Bergerac is a kind of Bordeaux understudy, but with more mixed results. The rosés are often extremely good, deep in colour, dry and full of fruit, but the reds are more exciting, with the fruit and bite of a good, simple Bordeaux without the rough edges. Like St-Émilion, it relies on the Merlot grape, with help from both Cabernets and Malbec, but the Bergerac reds are less substantial than St-Émilions. Sadly, most British merchants cut the prices too much for the potential of the area to be seen, so that what we get here is frequently tough, meaty, medicinal and charmless. Bergerac Rouge is usually at its best at between one and four years old, depending on vintage and style. The wines of *Château la Jaubertie* are very good and they've also produced a wood-aged 'Reserve' which looks promising. *Château le Barradis* is also very good, and *Château Court-les-Mûts* makes a delicious rosé and a good red. Most of the wines in the UK originate at the large central co-op, and quality depends on whether someone was prepared to pay a few extra centimes for a better vat.

**BUZET, AC** Used to be labelled Côtes de Buzet. The most exciting of the claret look-alikes from a region that was historically considered part of Bordeaux, a little way to the south-east. Made from Bordeaux grapes with Cabernet predominant, they can combine a rich blackcurrant sweetness with an arresting grassy greenness. They are for drinking at between one and five years old, depending on vintage and style. Look out for the wines of *Château Sauvagnères*, as well as those of the co-op, which dominates the area and produces a wood-aged *Cuvée Napoléon* and a *Château de Gueyze* that is pretty special. The co-op has a real rarity – its own cooper. Almost all the wine spends at least a couple of months in wood, and this contributes massively to Buzet's serious-but-soft appeal.

**CAHORS, AC** Of all the south-western country wines, Cahors is the most exciting. It's grown on both banks of the River Lot in the region of Quercy, practically due east of Bordeaux (though hotter, because it's well away from the influence of the sea). It's at least 70 per cent Auxerrois (Bordeaux's Malbec), the rest being made up of varying proportions of Merlot and Tannat.

Two hundred years ago, it was one of France's most famous wines, and the 'Black Wine of Cahors' is still held up as an example of how it used to be done. The wine was made black by the simple trick of giving the grapes a quick crushing and then, literally, boiling the must. Just as boiling gets the stain out of a shirt, so it gets the tannin and colour out of a grape skin. Fruit? Er, no, but strength (it was sometimes even fortified) and stability and massive ageing potential – yes. Without fruit, it's difficult to know what age was expected to do.

Adopting modern wine-making methods has added some lovely sweet fruit to the still dark, but now less aggressively tannic wines. There's a clear whiff of fine wine about some of the big, firm products of private growers. With age, they are often almost honeyed and raisiny, with plummy fruit that gets deeper, spicier and darker, often resembling tobacco and prunes. But another sort of Cahors has sprung up, too, lighter and less inspired, for drinking young. It can sometimes be very good. The raw materials for these are quite different: the best, traditional land of Cahors is up in the hills, but most grapes are now grown in easier vineyards on the valley slopes. One third of the wine comes from the co-op, *Côtes d'Olt*, which, after a pusillanimous, fruitless start, is beginning to produce some very good, lightish but proper-tasting wine with real style. Best are: *Château de Cayrou, Château de Chambert, Château de Haute-Serre, Clos de Gamot, Château St-Didier, Château de Treilles, Domaine du Cèdre,Clos la Coutale, Clos Triguedina, Domaine Eugénie, Domaine de Gaudou, Domaine de Paillas* and *Domaine de Quattre*.

**CÔTES DE BERGERAC, AC** This is to Bergerac what Bordeaux Supérieur is to Bordeaux: from the same region, but with slightly higher minimum alcohol. It should be better, and often is. Many are still basic Bergerac, although the excellent Château Court-les-Mûts now uses the AC.

**CÔTES DE DURAS, AC** Light, grassy claret look-alikes. *Château de Pilar* and *Le Seigneuret* from the co-op are quite good and cheap, as is a Beaujolais-type *cuvée* which is good quaffing stuff.

**CÔTES DU FRONTONNAIS, AC** This small area north of Toulouse and south-west of Gaillac makes reds largely from the local Négrette grape, along with both Cabernets, Malbec, Syrah, Cinsaut, Fer-Servadou and Gamay. At their best they are silky, plummy and unbelievably soft for red, sometimes with a touch of raspberry and liquorice. The distinctive Négrette grape is wonderfully juicy and tasty and there are now some 100 per cent Négrette *cuvées* from Bellevue-la-Forêt and Flotis. Great value. Best are *Domaine de Baudare, Château Bellevue-la-Forêt, Château Flotis, Château Montauriol, Château la Palme.*

**CÔTES DU MARMANDAIS, VDQS** Simple, soft, fruity wines for drinking young, made from the two Cabernets, Merlot, Fer and Abouriou. A few are for more serious ageing, but it doesn't suit them.

**GAILLAC, AC** One of the best known of the south-west wines. There are two styles: Duras plus Fer-Servadou and Syrah, or Duras plus Merlot and Cabernet. Mostly, this is co-op land, but the growers who care can make remarkable red. *Domaine Jean Cros* is especially delicious one. Others are *Lastours, Mas Pignou, Labarthe, Larroze.*

**IROULÉGUY, AC** A small AC in the Basque country on the border with Spain. The co-op dominates production which is mostly roughish, Tannat-based red. though Cabernet is increasing in the vineyards.

**MADIRAN, AC** Grown near Armagnac, midway between Bordeaux and the Spanish border, Madiran is often likened to claret, but only rarely shows anything approaching that finesse and excitement. It is generally about half Tannat, along with the two Cabernets and occasionally Fer, with 20 months minimum in wood. It is often rather astringent, and can be toughly tannic. Experts say you have to age it – and I'm having a go with a few. Good ones include *Château d'Arricau-Bordes, Château Aydie, Château Montus* (aged in new wood, and the only Madirans I find I really like), *Château Boucassé, Château Peyros, Domaine du Crampilh, Domaine Laplace* and *Domaine Meinjarre.*

**PÉCHARMANT, AC** The best red wine of Bergerac from the best slope of the region, east of Bordeaux, this is very good dry red that can take considerable ageing, but is deliciously full of quick-drinking blackcurrant fruit when young. Unlike Bergerac, Pécharmant doesn't cut its prices, and shows what could be achieved in other nearby regions if we paid a proper price. *Château de Tiregand* is very good indeed, but *Domaine du Haut-Pécharmant* is even better, resembling a top-line Médoc.

# WHITE WINES

**BERGERAC SEC, AC** A Bordeaux look-alike from east of Bordeaux, planted largely with Sémillon and Sauvignon. *Château Court-les-Mûts* and *Château de Panisseau* are good but the star is *Château la Jaubertie* where tremendous flavour and panache are extracted from Sauvignon, Sémillon and Muscadelle; this last grape is now being made into a 100 per cent varietal.

**BLANQUETTE DE LIMOUX, AC** This fizz from near Carcassonne claims to pre-date even Champagne. It's mostly made from Mauzac, with a green-apple bite often softened and improved by Chardonnay and Chenin Blanc. *Domaine de Martinolles* is good. A new AC, Crémant de Limoux, allows nearly 25 per cent of Chardonnay and Chenin in the blend – and is well worth looking out for.

**CÔTES DE DURAS, AC** Fairly good Sauvignon-based white that can be as fresh as good Bordeaux Blanc, but just a little chubbier. *Château de Conti* is good, as is *Le Seigneuret* from the co-operative.

**GAILLAC, AC** North-east of Toulouse and south of Cahors, Gaillac makes more white wine than red. It can be *moelleux* (medium sweet), *perlé* (very faintly bubbly) or dry; the dry is usually a little terse, though it can have a quite big apple-and-liquorice fruit if you're lucky. The sparkling wines can sometimes be superb: peppery, honeyed, apricotty and appley all at the same time. From producers like *Boissel-Rhodes, Cros* or *Robert Plageoles*, they are very good value. Other still wine producers to look out for are *Château Larroze, Domaine du Bosc Long* and *Domaine de Labarthe*. The co-op at *Labastide de Lévis* is the main, and improving, force in the area. One to watch.

**JURANÇON, AC** Sweet, medium or dry (though never *very* sweet or *totally* dry) wine from the Pyrenean foothills. Based on the Petit Manseng, Gros Manseng and Courbu, the dry wines are usually rather nutty and dull, but the sweet wines are not too sweet, honeyed, raisiny and peachy, yet with a lick of acidity. New oak is appearing in some cellars. Most wine is from the local co-op, and there are signs of improvement, but I'd plump for a grower's wine. The best are *Château Jolys, Clos de la Vierge* (dry), *Cancaillaü* (sweet), sweet *Cru Lamouroux*, *Clos Uroulat* (sweet), *Domaine de Cauhapé*.

**MONBAZILLAC, AC** From east of Bordeaux, south of Bergerac, this is one of the most famous names in the sweet wine world, but the general standard has been debased to an over-sulphured, artificially sweetened mediocrity. The occasional true Monbazillac is fine, rich and honeyed, even unctuous, yet never as good as a top Sauternes – more like a good Loupiac or Ste-Croix-du-Mont. Unlike in Sauternes, there are very few quality-conscious single properties prepared to make the real thing.

Ones worth seeking out include *Château du Treuil de Nailhac* and *Clos Fontindoule*; and the *Château de Monbazillac* and *Château Septy* of the co-op can be good.

**MONTRAVEL, AC** Dry to sweet white wine from the Dordogne. The wine is frequently sold as Côtes de Bergerac.

**PACHERENC DU VIC-BILH, AC** One of France's most esoteric whites, at its best dry and pear-skin-perfumed, sometimes rich and sweet, grown in the Madiran area near Armagnac. Look out for *Château d'Aydie, Château Boucassé* and *Domaine du Crampilh*.

**VIN DE PAYS CHARENTAIS** As Cognac production declines, table wine production increases, and the Charente produces some good, grassy-fresh whites with fairly sharp acidity, although sometimes the acidity gets the better of the fruit.

**VIN DE PAYS DES CÔTES DE GASCOGNE** The table wine of Armagnac, and the rising star of this corner of France. The Ugni Blanc is the major grape, in more abundant supply since the drop in Armagnac sales, and the Colombard adds a definite touch of class. They're trying out the Gros Manseng and Chardonnay too – which should be interesting. The co-operative of *Plaimont* supplies most of those on sale in Britain at very reasonable prices, but variable quality. However, the mood of change sweeping the south-western co-ops is evident here too. There are several labels available from the *Grassa* family estates – notably *Domaine de Planterieu* and *Domaine de Tariquet*, which are very good, full, dry and acid even. Usually an A1 bargain buy. Also good are the following producers: *Domaine St-Lannes, Domaine les Puts, San Guilhem*.

The price guides for this section begin on page 330.

# JURA

The Jura deserves to have a preservation order slapped on it. Few parts of France are now so remote: few can boast such individual grapes and wine-making. The whites are made from the Melon d'Arbois (alias Chardonnay) and the Savagnin (probably the yellow Traminer of Germany and Alsace). The reds come from the thin-skinned Poulsard or Ploussard, the earthy Trousseau (which can smell like Provençal drains) and the Gros Noirien or Pinot Noir.

Then there are the styles: the almost extinct *vin de paille,* made from grapes dried on straw mats, or hung up in draughty rooms. In the Jura it is the red Poulsard which is used to make these luscious sweet wines. *Vin jaune* is made from the Savagnin grape racked into barrels and left for over six years in warm, dry cellars until a sherry-style *flor* develops. The famous old rosé wines of Arbois are made by mixing all five local grapes. A typical version may be had from the Laguiche family of Château d'Arlay.

In the last few years, besides these splendid museum pieces, a number of growers have begun using modern techniques to produce straight Chardonnays and Pinot Noirs aged (and even fermented) in oak *barriques*. The name to remember here is Rolet.                                             **GILES MACDONOGH**

## WINES & WINE REGIONS

**ARBOIS, AC** The general *appellation* for wines of all types from the northern part of the Jura around the town of Arbois. Reds are mostly Trousseau and thuddingly full of flavour. Savagnin weaves its demonic spells on the whites, though Chardonnay is sometimes used to soften it. Interestingly there are some attractive light reds and rosés from Pinot Noir or Poulsard which seem positively out of place, they are so delicate. *Henri Maire* is the biggest producer, but the best wines come rom the village of Pupillin, where the *co-op* produces delicious Chardonnay and a fizz.

**CÔTES DE JURA, AC** These are the wines, of all colours, from the centre and south of the Jura. They are virtually indistinguishable from Arbois wines, though they are sometimes a little less disturbing in their weirdness.

**L'ÉTOILE, AC** Small area in the south producing whites from Savagnin and Chardonnay and, occasionally, from the red Poulsard, vinified without the colour-giving skins. Also Savagnin *vins jaunes.*

**VIN JAUNE** The kind of wine of which more than a small glass makes you grateful it is as rare as it is. It grows the same yeasty *flor* as dry sherry, and its startlingly, painfully intense flavours just get more and more evident as it matures. It seems virtually indestructible, as long as the cork is healthy.

*Château-Chalon* AC – the 'Montrachet' of *vin jaune*! Well, that's what they think, anyway. This is the most prized – and pricy – of the *vins jaunes*, and is difficult to find even in the region. *Vins jaunes* are sold in small 62cl *clavelin* bottles, which of course the EC tried to ban. That left me in two minds. I felt that 75cl of *vin jaune* would be just too much for anyone to handle, and indeed 37.5cl might be more like it. But I was blowed if the EC was going to destroy yet another great original in the stultifying name of conformity. The EC backed down and the 62cl *clavelin* lives. Actually there *is* a reason for the 62cl size, in that 100 litres of wine, kept in barrels for six years without being topped up, reduces to 62 litres, or 100 bottles. So they can order in nice round numbers.

# SAVOY AND THE BUGEY

As most people who have ski'd in the French Alps will know, the wines of Savoy and the Bugey are light and crisp and best drunk after a strenuous session on the *piste*. Names such as Apremont, Abysmes and Crépy conjure up good holiday memories, but they've rarely been shipped over here, since they're not cheap and their crisp, lean intensity isn't always seen as a virtue by the Brits back home.

This is only half the story. In fact the wines which fall either side of the upper reaches of the French Rhône can be both weighty and interesting. As far as white wines go, the wine most valued in Savoy is Chignin-Bergeron. This is made from the Bergeron grape: none other than the Roussanne of the Rhône, so recently revived by the Perrins at the Château de Beaucastel in Châteauneuf-du-Pape. In the Bugey the best whites are Chardonnays from the villages of Vongnes and Culoz, while the best reds are made from the Pinot Noir. Although Gamay was introduced to both sides of the Rhône after phylloxera, undoubtedly the most interesting black grape grown is the Mondeuse. In Australia Brown Brothers of Milawa have shown us how good Mondeuse can be: in a good year in Savoy (and there have been several recently) it can have all the delicious pungency of the best Syrah.                                   **GILES MACDONOGH**

## WINES & WINE REGIONS

**BUGEY, VDQS** This little VDQS half-way between Savoie and Beaujolais is a rising star for its deliciously crisp Chardonnays, although it also uses the other Savoyard grapes for whites and reds. It is one of the most refreshing, zippy Chardonnays in France, and, not surprisingly, has become a 'fad' wine with some of the local Michelin-starred restaurants. At least that means the growers will keep producing it.

**CRÉPY, AC** The least interesting Savoie region to the south of Lake Geneva, where the Chasselas produces an even flimsier version of the Swiss Fendant, if that's possible. Drink it very young, very fast, or not at all.

**ROUSSETTE DE SAVOIE, AC** This can be the fullest and softest of the Savoie whites. It can come from a blend of Altesse and Chardonnay or 100 per cent Altesse (also called Roussette) when it comes from one of the better villages like Frangy or Monterminod. Even at its basic level, it's good, crisp, strong-tasting white.

**SEYSSEL, AC** and **SEYSSEL MOUSSEUX, AC** The Roussette (sometimes blended with Molette) makes quite full, flower-scented but sharp-edged whites in this zone of the Haute-Savoie and the Ain. Sparkling Seyssel is also good, light but pepper-pungent and available in the UK from *Varichon et Clerc*.

**VIN DE SAVOIE, AC** Vin de Savoie covers the whole Savoie area, but produces the most interesting results in the South. These alpine vineyards are some of the most beautiful in France and produce fresh, snappy wines. The white, from the Jacquère or the Chardonnay, can be excellent, dry, biting, but with lots of tasty fruit. Avoid ageing them for too long. The reds from Pinot Noir are subtly delicious, while the Mondeuse produces some real beefy beauties when the vintage is hot enough. A *cru* name is often tacked on to the best wines. Ones to look out for are Abymes, Apremont, Chignin, Cruet and Montmélian, with Chautagne and Arbin quite important for reds.

# VINS DE PAYS

Even the name has all the right connotations. Translated into English, as 'country wines' there is something honest and simple and salt-of-the-earth about it: they are made, one imagines, by weatherbeaten peasants dressed in *bleu de travail* and reeking of garlic, who tend their few vines with loving care and wave happily at tourists .

Well, *vins de pays* may well be grown by such people. They are more likely to be made, however, in the stainless steel vats of the local co-operative – and what they taste like depends not only on the amount of loving care expended by the grower, but also the degree of cleanliness of those vats, and how interested the director of the co-operative is in lifting his wines above the wine lake level.

An increasing number are very interested indeed. French co-ops are only too aware that to survive they have to compete: the world is not crying out for plonk, and even the most fervent native consumers of three-star red are drinking less of it than they were. Growing and making *vins de pays* rather than *vins de table* is the first step towards quality.

They were so named in 1973, as a way of encouraging better grape varieties, better wine-making and lower yields and, not surprisingly, most of the *vins de pays* we see in Britain come from the south of France. There are plenty of them: the 1991 *vin de pays* harvest was some 11m hectolitres, or around a quarter of the total French wine harvest. They may be made from a single grape, which may be named on the label, or they may contain a traditional regional mix; either way, they are inexpensive. This is not the field in which to search for experimental designer wines – growers do not opt for making a chic, expensive *vin de pays* because the AC regulations do not suit their ideas. As a result, you can expect rusticity and typicality of the region; you can hope for bags of fruit and excellent wine-making. You might well get all four. *Vins de pays* come in three categories:

**VINS DE PAYS RÉGIONAUX** There are four of these, which between them cover a major portion of France's vineyards. Vin de Pays du Jardin de la France covers the whole Loire basin across almost to Chablis and down to the Charente. Vin de Pays du Comté Tolosan is for the South-West, starting just below Bordeaux, and covering Bergerac, Cahors, the Tarn and down to the Pyrenees, but not including the Aude and Pyrénées Orientales. Vin de Pays des Comtés Rhodaniens includes the Rhône and Savoy; Vin de Pays d'Oc covers Provence and the Midi right down to the Spanish border.

**VINS DE PAYS DÉPARTEMENTAUX** These are also large groupings, and each one is defined by the boundaries of the département. So, for instance, any wine of *vin de pays* quality grown in the département of Vaucluse will qualify for the title 'Vin de Pays du Vaucluse'.

**VINS DE PAYS DE ZONE** These are the tightest-controlled of the categories, and can apply to actual communes or at least carefully defined localities. The allowed yield is lower and there may be more control on things like grape varieties. So, for example, we could have a Vin de Pays de la Vallée du Paradis which is in the Aude, and could also be sold as Vin de Pays de l'Aude, or under the widest, least demanding description, Vin de Pays d'Oc.

# GERMANY

Two years ago I wandered into a local wine shop to see how my bottle of 1979 Scharzhofberger was coming along. A wonderfully elegant Saar Riesling from a great vineyard and a great producer, Egon Müller, it had been sitting on a bottom shelf for over two years. On this occasion I took pity on it and bought it. I have since drunk it, with enormous pleasure.

In another local wine shop, bottles from a top Rheingau estate, Langwerth von Simmern, remain unsold after three years and more on the shelves. And then there are restaurants: I recently studied the wine lists of some 30 top establishments. Only one, the White Horse at Chilgrove, offered a serious and well-chosen selection of German wines.

All this is depressing, but hardly unexpected. Fine German wines do not sell, which means that those who appreciate them can occasionally find splendid bargains. And yet there are signs, slight signs, of increasing interest. Germany has enjoyed three outstanding vintages, 1988, 1989 and 1990. Merchants such as Adnams, Lay & Wheeler, Oddbins and The Wine Society have located superb wines from superb estates. They are even managing to sell some of them.

All kinds of reasons are given for the overall failure of some of the finest white wines in the world to make the impression they deserve here. They include incomprehensible labelling, the difficulty of matching them with food, the indifference of restaurateurs and sommeliers and so forth. There is also the sorry example set by Liebfraumilch and its cousins, which have given people the immovable notion that German wine is sweet and insipid and £2.50 a bottle.

All these reasons are valid, but the French and Italians also make mediocre wines in vast quantities, and the oceans of Piat d'Or and Lambrusco have not prevented anybody from appreciating the finest wines of Bordeaux, Burgundy and Tuscany. Why, then, have the Germans failed to make the same impression?

## Reflected glory

The answer is simple. The French and the Italians lead from the top, the Germans from the bottom. The former insist that their fine wines are the finest in the world, with prices to match, but remind those of us with more modest resources that even their lesser wines, the distant relatives of the mighty clarets and ethereal Burgundies, can be good value and good drinking. The Germans, however, chose to swamp our market with their worst and most anonymous wines at rock-bottom prices, and then, as an afterthought, whispered that they also produced a few estate-bottled wines that just happened to be the finest Rieslings in the world. No wonder hardly anybody paid attention.

Nonetheless, there has never been a better time to buy German wines in Britain. Many wine merchants – still too few – offer an excellent selection, and recent vintages have been outstanding. In brief, 1988 is a classic vintage for Riesling, giving wines that are exceedingly well-balanced and only just beginning to open out. The most opulent is 1989, with gorgeous ripeness levels and thus an abundance of *Spätlesen* and *Auslesen* with hints of honeyed botrytis: some of the *Beerenauslesen* and *Trockenbeerenauslesen* from 1989 are perfect examples of their kind, but priced at levels that only Japanese stockbrokers can afford. 1990 is probably the best of the lot, since yields were halved, giving wines with all the structure of 1988 and ripeness of 1989, with a bonus of sheer concentration that few wines of the preceding vintages can match.

However, the most important piece of information on the label is the name of the estate. A wine from a 'lesser' vineyard but produced by Schloss Schönborn in the Rheingau or J J Prüm in the Mosel is likely to be far more rewarding than one from a famous site – Erbacher Marcobrunn or Wehlener Sonnenuhr, for example – produced by a mediocre *négociant*. The top estates have not been slow to capitalize on this, and most of them market a good basic Riesling. Some of the best value German wines are these estate Rieslings from the likes of Dr Loosen or Dr Dirk Richter. Other producers, such as Rainer Lingenfelder, give prominence on the label to the style of the wine – for example, Riesling Spätlese – and consign the unwieldy vineyard name to small print at the foot of the label.

These top producers are finding markets for their wines these days, but even so they argue that wine industry regulations in Germany are still too slack. The best growers may voluntarily restrict yields and maintain other standards that will improve quality, but as long as less conscientious producers can continue to wring yields four times higher, the great bulk of German wine will continue to be insipid and to depress the market as a whole. Growers' associations such as VDP, the Grosser Ring in the Mosel, and the Rheingau Charta group have worked hard

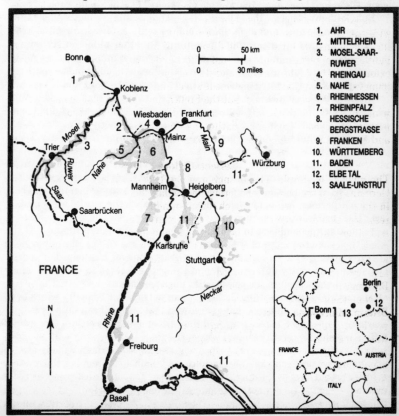

1. AHR
2. MITTELRHEIN
3. MOSEL-SAAR-RUWER
4. RHEINGAU
5. NAHE
6. RHEINHESSEN
7. RHEINPFALZ
8. HESSISCHE BERGSTRASSE
9. FRANKEN
10. WÜRTTEMBERG
11. BADEN
12. ELBE TAL
13. SAALE-UNSTRUT

to maintain higher standards than the law demands, but I suspect that they have been preaching to the converted. The Charta growers, whose wines are in the Halbtrocken style and thus well suited to accompany a variety of foods, have spent large sums on gastronomic events that attempt to prove their case, but whether they have had much effect on the tastes of consumers in Britain is doubtful. How many Chablis drinkers, one wonders, now switch, even on an occasional basis, to an equally racy and refreshing Charta wine?

## Style wars

The failure, at least until very recently, of top growers to make much impact with classic Riesling wines has persuaded some of them to seek new styles, but the results are a mixed bag. Germany came late to *barrique*-ageing, and it shows. *Barriques* can make a powerful contribution to broadly flavoured white grape varieties such as Chardonnay, Sémillon or Sauvignon Blanc, but the more finely tuned flavours of German varieties are less receptive. I have yet to taste a *barrique*-aged Riesling I have enjoyed, but Rülander (Pinot Gris), with its richer, spicier flavours responds well to discreet oak-ageing, as, of course, does Spätburgunder (Pinot Noir). German reds go on getting better – the Dornfelder grape, in particular, can be hedonistically juicy – but are they serious competition for their counterparts from elsewhere? On the whole, probably not.

But Germany is not all the Mosel or Nahe, and not all Riesling. Müller-Catoir in the altogether warmer Rheinpfalz makes truly astonishing wines from Rieslaner, Scheurebe and Grauer Burgunder (another name for Rülander), powerfully flavoured and alarmingly high in alcohol, reminiscent of an Alsace *vendange tardive* vinified to dryness. Similar wines are found in the southerly wine region of Baden; here too Joachim Heger's *barrique*-aged Pinot Noirs show promise. Weissburgunder (Pinot Blanc) works well in these regions, and it won't be long before German Chardonnays tiptoe on to the market to challenge all those other Chardonnays, from France, Australia, or northern Italy.

I wish we could find more from Franken (Franconia) in this country. Using grapes such as Müller-Thurgau, Silvaner, Rieslaner and Riesling, Franken makes delicious dry wines full of extract and character – but no many of them. The locals are aware of how good they are and there is not much left over.

So good German wine-makers are proceeding along two parallel tracks. There is much experimentation, and even though, inevitably, the results are mixed, at least they are working hard at finding out what grape varieties and styles of wine-making respond best to their particular soils and microclimates. At the same time the production of traditional Riesling in the classic Riesling regions goes from strength to strength. A string of great vintages has helped, of course, but so has the gritty determination of the great estates to persist in their traditional ways despite the commercial uncertainties of the past. The vogue, always much stronger within Germany than outside, for bone-dry wines even from regions and in vintages that guaranteed that such wines would be mouth-searingly unpleasant, is receding. And the best wine-makers ensure that even if a Riesling should retain residual sugar, the overall impression will be one of refreshing fruitiness, never of overbearing sweetness. German wine is always about balance, between sweetness, acidity, and alcohol. Therein lies the mystery of how a great German Riesling, with a mere 7 per cent of alcohol, can pack twice as much flavour into a bottle than can the most imperious fat, oak-aged Chardonnay with twice the power. **STEPHEN BROOK**

# CLASSIFICATIONS

The German classification system is based on sugar levels, and therefore potential alcohol, of the grapes when they are picked. The main categories are as follows:

**DEUTSCHER TAFELWEIN** Ordinary German table wine of supposedly tolerable quality; low natural strength, sugared at fermentation to increase alcohol, no specific vineyard origin. Deutscher Tafelwein must be 100 per cent German. From a good source, like the major supermarkets, it can be better than many QbAs. The most commonly available are labelled Rhein (or Hock) or Mosel and bear some resemblance to QbAs from the Rhine or Mosel areas. Cheaper wines labelled EC Tafelwein are not worth the price saving – they are usually bottled in Germany from very cheap imported wine. However, at the other end of the price spectrum are expensive 'designer table wines', red and white Deutscher Tafelweine from adventurous producers who may age them in oak *barriques*.

**LANDWEIN** German *vin de pays*, slightly up-market and drier table wine from one of 20 designated areas. It can be *Trocken* (dry) or *Halbtrocken* (half-dry).

**QbA** (Qualitätswein bestimmter Anbaugebiete) Literally 'quality wine from designated regions' – the specific areas being Ahr, Hessische Bergstrasse, Mittelrhein, Nahe, Rheingau, Rheinhessen, Rheinpfalz, Franken, Württemberg, Baden, Mosel-Saar-Ruwer, plus two regions in what was East Germany: Saale-Unstrut and Elbe Tal. QbAs can be mediocre, but are not necessarily so. In modest vintages such as 1987 and 1991 they can be very good indeed, as QbAs may be chaptalized, giving wines of better body and balance than minor Kabinetts. They may also include the products of of prestigious single vineyards, where growers set standards far above those required by the law. These wines can be brimming with class and outstanding value for money.

**QmP** (Qualitätswein mit Prädikat) Quality wine with special attributes, classified in ascending order according to the ripeness of the grapes: Kabinett, Spätlese, Auslese, Beerenauslese, Eiswein, Trockenbeerenauslese. Chaptalization is not allowed for QmP wines, and in each category, up to and including Auslese, the sugar content of the wine may range from virtually non-existent to positively luscious. Drier wines may be either Trocken (dry) or Halbtrocken (half-dry). Depending on the vintage conditions, some or all of the following QmP categories will be made.

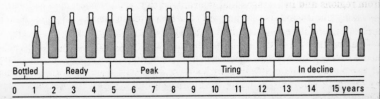

**MATURITY CHART**
1989 Mosel Riesling Kabinett
Keep back a few bottles from this superb vintage to watch their development

| Bottled | Ready | Peak | Tiring | In decline |
|---|---|---|---|---|

0   1   2   3   4   5   6   7   8   9   10   11   12   13   14   15 years

**KABINETT** Made from ripe grapes from a normal harvest. Usually lighter in alcohol than ordinary QbA, and often delicious.

**SPÄTLESE** From late-picked (therefore riper) grapes. Often moderately sweet, though there are now dry versions.

**AUSLESE** From selected bunches of very ripe, sometimes late-picked grapes. Often sweet and occasionally with noble rot richness, but many are now fermented dry, giving full wines packed with flavour.

**BEERENAUSLESE** (BA) From selected single grapes. Not so overripe as TBA, but almost always affected by 'noble rot', a fungus that concentrates the sugar and acidity in the grapes. BA from new, non-Riesling grapes can be dull: Huxelrebe takes to noble rot so easily that you can make a BA before you've even picked Riesling. But Riesling BA, and many a Scheurebe or Silvaner, will be astonishing.

**EISWEIN** Just that – 'ice wine' – often picked before dawn in the depths of winter when the grapes are actually frozen. They are dashed to the winery by the frost-bitten pickers; once there, quick and careful pressing removes just the slimy-sweet concentrate; the water, in its icy state, stays separate. Eiswein always has a high level of acidity and needs to be matured for at least seven years in bottle.

**TROCKENBEERENAUSLESE** (TBA) 'Shrivelled berries gathered late.' That's a pedestrian translation of one of the world's great tastes. To be TBA, juice has to reach about 22 degrees potential alcohol, and some of the greatest reach a remarkable 30 or more. Anything much over 15 degrees potential strength begins to stifle the yeasts – so much so that fermentation may hardly get going, and a year later the liquid may have five to six degrees alcohol but 15 to 20 degrees of unfermented sugar. A top Sauternes might be picked with 22 degrees potential alcohol, but end up with about 13 degrees or more, so that TBAs are usually among the sweetest wines in the world. But the tendency is to produce a slightly drier, more alcoholic style. Few growers try to make TBAs because of the risk and the cost. Remember that the vines are making a glass of wine each instead of a bottle, and picking is slow and labour-intensive – and the weather can easily ruin it all anyway. That's why TBAs are expensive – usually starting at £20 a half-bottle ex-cellars. But, even then, a grower won't make money; it's his pride that makes him do it. And the wines can age for as long as most of us.

## GRAPES & FLAVOURS

**RIESLING** About 90 per cent of the most exciting wines in Germany are made from Riesling. It generally grows on the best slopes in the best villages, and its slow ripening and reasonably restrained yield produce a spectrum of flavours: from steely, slaty, and dry as sun-bleached bones through apples, peaches, apricots, even lychees – more or less sweet according to the ripeness of the grapes and the intentions of the wine-maker, and finally arriving at the great sweet wines, which can be blinding in their rich, honeyed concentration of peaches, pineapples, mangoes, even raisins, with an acidity like a streak of fresh lime that makes them the most appetizing of great sweet wines.

**MÜLLER-THURGAU** The most widely planted German grape, this cross was propagated in 1882 to get Riesling style plus big yields and early ripening. Well, that's like saying, 'Hey, I've just found a way to turn this plastic bowl into a gold chalice'. You can't do it. Müller is now the workhorse, producing soft, flowery, grapy wines when ripe – and grassy, sharp ones when not. Maybe to disguise it, the name Rivaner can be used, but by keeping yields down a few growers make good wines.

**SILVANER** This was the German workhorse before Müller-Thurgau. At its worst it's a broad, earthy wine – dull, fat and vegetal. But on some sites in the Rheinhessen, Nahe and especially Franken, it is impressive – broad, yes, but powerful too, developing honeyed weight.

**WEISSBURGUNDER** or **WEISSER BURGUNDER** The Pinot Blanc is increasingly grown in Nahe, Rheinhessen, Rheinpfalz and Baden to make full dry whites, often as a Chardonnay substitute. It ripens more easily than Chardonnay though and in the right hands can produce soft, creamy wines with a touch of Alsace-like spice.

**KERNER** Another competitor in the 'Riesling-without-the-heartache' stakes. This was recently hailed as 'Riesling in type, but with bigger yields, and earlier ripening.' Is it? Of course not. It does ripen quickly, but the wine ages quickly, too, though with some peachy style.

**RULÄNDER** The French Pinot Gris. It produces two styles of wine in Germany. The first is strong, rather broad-shouldered, with a bite of kasbah spice and a big splash of honey. The second, sold as Grauburgunder, and increasingly aged in small oak *barriques*, is firm and dry and can make exciting drinking.

**SCHEUREBE** A tricky grape. When it's unripe, it can pucker your mouth with a combination of raw grapefruit and cat's pee. But properly ripe, it is transformed. The grapefruit is still there, but now it's a fresh-cut pink one from Florida sprinkled with caster sugar. There's honey too, lashings of it, and a crackling, peppery fire which, in the Rheinhessen, Rheinpfalz and even in the Rheingau, produces dry wines as well as sweeter, sometimes outstanding Auslese and Beerenauslese.

**SPÄTBURGUNDER** The Pinot Noir produces a more thrilling display further south in Burgundy. In Germany they have tended in the past to make gently fruity, slightly sweet, vaguely red wines. Now growers like *Becker* (Rheingau), *Lingenfelder* (Pfalz), *Karl-Heinz Johner* (ex Lamberhurst) in Baden and *Meyer-Näke* (Ahr) are doing more exciting things. Their wines have good colour and tannin, are dry and often have a spell in oak.

**DORNFELDER** A red variety grown mainly in the Rheinhessen and Rheinpfalz which at its best produces deep-coloured reds with great fruit concentration combined with firm structure. Made in two styles, either for early drinking (try *Lingenfelder's*) or aged in *barriques* for longer keeping. If you can find it, *Siegrist* produces one of the best around.

## WINES & WINE REGIONS

**AHR** This small area contrives to be famous for red wines, though the flavour and the colour are pretty light, and its Rieslings are in fact more interesting. The *Staatliche Weinbaudomäne* is the best producer of old-style Spätburgunder. *Meyer-Näkel* represents the new school.

**BADEN** In the distant, balmy south of the country, Baden makes some red and a lovely rosé in the hills near Freiburg, where they mix white Ruländer (the Pinot Gris or Tokay of Alsace) with red Pinot

Noir. Ruländer by itself, as a white wine, can be really special – often as good as the fine examples from Alsace, only an hour's drive away. In Baden, it produces absurdly good, honeyed wine. Gewürztraminer is often dense and spicy, and even grapes like Müller-Thurgau and Silvaner can get quite interesting. There's only a little Riesling, but it's good; Spätburgunder is definitely on top. Some good value comes from small co-ops, while the area is dominated by the vast *Badische Winzerkeller*. Top producers: *Karl-Heinz Johner, Dr Heger* and *Salwey*.

**DEUTSCHER SEKT** Often a sure route to intestinal distress and sulphur-led hangover, though Deinhard manages to express the lovely, lean grapiness of the Riesling; *Lila* is especially good. *Georg Breuer*'s Sekt is outstanding, but expensive. Avoid at all costs the stuff made from imported wines, labelled Sekt (not Deutscher Sekt), or worse, Schaumwein.

**ELBE TAL** Germany's easternmost region in the former GDR. The vineyards are near the banks of the river Elbe, close to the cities of Dresden and Meissen, and are dominated by Müller-Thurgau.

**FRANKEN** (Franconia) This eastern region, actually part of Bavaria, is dry wine country. The slightly earthy, slightly vegetal, big and beefy Franken wines in their flagon-shaped 'Bocksbeutel' bottles are usually based on solid Silvaner or Müller-Thurgau. The quality is, happily, good, but you can often get something much more interesting from elsewhere in Europe for a good deal less money. The best producers are Church and State – the *Juliusspital* and *Bürgerspital* charities and the *Staatlicher Hofkeller* – all in Würzburg, though *Johann Ruck* and *Hans Wirsching* at Iphofen are also good. The *Castell'sches Domänenamt* merits a detour.

**HALBTROCKEN** Half-dry. The general run of German wines used to go from slightly sweet to very sweet, and this 'half-dry' classification was created primarily to satisfy the Germans' own desire for dry wines to drink with food. First efforts were mean and unbalanced but three ripe vintages have shown that producers are learning how to preserve the fruit without oversweetening. At Kabinett and Spätlese level there are some quite good wines – but they're *not* cheap. Riesling Halbtrockens need at least three years to soften.

**HESSISCHE BERGSTRASSE** A tiny Rhine side-valley running down to Heidelberg, where, presumably, most of its wine is drunk – because it never gets over here. The central town of Bensheim has one of the highest average temperatures of any wine region in Germany, so the wine is worth seeking out. In general the Rieslings are of good quality. The *Staatsweingut Bergstrasse* is the best producer.

**LIEBFRAUMILCH** Liebfraumilch is a brilliant invention, an innocuous, grapy liquid, usually from the Rheinhessen or Rheinpfalz, that has dramatically fulfilled a need in the UK and US: as the perfect 'beginner's wine', it has broken through the class barriers and mystique of wine. In a way, the rest of German wine has let Liebfraumilch down, since if Liebfraumilch is the base, you should be able to move on to other things – yet many supposedly superior QbAs and even some Kabinetts, for all their high-falutin' names, are *less* satisfying than a good young Liebfraumilch.

**MITTELRHEIN** The Rhine at its most beautiful, providing all the label ideas for castles clinging to cliffs high above the boats and river-front cafés. It really is like that, and tourists sensibly flock there and just as sensibly drink most of its wine. One grower whose wines have got away is *Toni Jost* – his racy Rieslings are worth trying.

**MOSEL-SAAR-RUWER** When they are based on Riesling and come from one of the many steep, slaty, south-facing sites in the folds of the river, or strung out, mile upon mile, along the soaring, broad-shouldered valley sides, these northerly wines are unlike any others in the world. They can achieve a thrilling, orchard-fresh, spring flowers flavour, allied to an alcohol level so low that it leaves your head clear enough to revel in the flavour. Most Mosel comes from the river valley itself, but two small tributaries have been incorporated in the

The price guides for this section begin on page 334.

designation: the Saar and the Ruwer, with even lighter, perhaps sharper, perhaps more ethereal wines. Some of the best come from *Bischöfliches Konvikt, Bischöfliches Priesterseminar, Wegeler-Deinhard, Dr Loosen, Friedrich-Wilhelm-Gymnasium, Hohe Domkirche, Zilliken, Fritz Haag, von Hövel, von Kesselstatt, Karthäuserhof, Egon Müller-Scharzhof, J.J. Prüm, Mönchhof, S.A. Prüm, M.F. Richter, Schloss Saarstein, von Schubert, Selbach-Oster, Bert Simon, Studert Prüm, Thanisch, Vereinigte Hospitien, Weins-Prüm* and the *Staatliche Weinbaudomänen* based in Trier.

**NAHE** Important side-valley off the Rhine, snaking south from Bingen. Many of the best Kabinetts and Spätlesen come from its middle slopes, wines with a grapy taste, quite high acidity and something slightly mineral too. Away from this hub of quality, the wines are less reliable. Top names: *August Anheuser, Paul Anheuser, Crusius, Hermann Dönnhoff, Schloss Plettenberg, Prinz zu Salm Dalberg, Schlossgut Diel* and, a long mouthful to build up a thirst, *Verwaltung der Staatlichen Weinbaudomänen Niederhausen-Schlossböckelheim.*

**RHEINGAU** This fine wine area spreads north and east of Bingen. It is here, in the best sites, that the Riesling is at its most remarkable – given a long ripening period and a caring wine-maker. The Rheingau contains more world-famous villages than any other German vineyard area, and even its lesser villages are well aware of their prestige. It seems a shame to grow lesser grapes here, because the Riesling picks up the minerally dryness, the tangy acidity and a delicious, grapy fruitiness, varying from apple-fresh in a good Kabinett to almost unbearably honeyed in a great TBA. Even Kabinetts have body and ripeness. Around 45 good Rheingau producers have formed the *Charta Association*. The wines, off-dry Rieslings, need four years in bottle, and are recognisable by the embossed arches on the bottle. Top names: *Balthasar Ress, J.B. Becker* (also very good red), *G.*

*Breuer, Deinhard, Knyphausen, von Mumm, Nägler, Schloss Groenesteyn, Schloss Johannisberg, Schloss Reinhartshausen, Schloss Schönborn, Schloss Vollrads, Langwerth von Simmern, Sohlbach, Staatsweingut Eltville, Dr Weil.*

**RHEINHESSEN** The Rhine turns south at Wiesbaden and flows down the side of the Rheinhessen, which, despite having one village as famous as any in the world – Nierstein – is packed with unknown names. Wines from steep river-facing vineyards at Nierstein and its unsung neighbours Nackenheim, Oppenheim and Bodenheim can be superb, softer than Rheingaus, still beautifully balanced, flowery and grapy. Otherwise, we're in Liebfraumilch and Bereich Nierstein land, and a great deal of Rheinhessen ends up in one of these two. The village, rightly, feels aggrieved, since its own reputation – traditionally sky-high – is compromised by the mouthwash that oozes out under the Bereich name. Even this is a distortion of Rheinhessen's old reputation, which was built on light, flowery Silvaner. A recent revival of this has seen the emergence of some well-made drier styles from the steep sites on the so-called Rhine Terrace. Top names: *Balbach, Carl Koch Erben, Gunderloch-Usinger, Heyl zu Herrnsheim, Rappenhof, Senfter, Gustav Adolf Schmidt, Villa Sachsen, Guntrum.*

**RHEINPFALZ** Sometimes known in English as the Palatinate, this has two distinct halves. The northern half clusters round some extremely good villages like Forst, Wachenheim, Deidesheim and Ruppertsberg. There's lots of Riesling, and it has a big, spicy, fiery fruit, rather exotic in a tropical-fruit-salad way, but with the lovely, clear Riesling bite. Scheurebe is also fierily excellent. The best wines (white and red) come from sloping vineyards at Pinot grapes, making up to nearly 16 per cent alcohol – naturally – can be found. Look for: *Basserman-Jordan, von Buhl, Bürklin-Wolf, Wegeler-Deinhard, Koehler-Ruprecht, Müller-Catoir, Pfeffingen,*

*Rebholz, Georg Siben Erben, Siegrist* and *Lingenfelder*. There are some good, true-to-type wines from co-operatives.

**SAALE-UNSTRUT** Three large producers dominate the largest of the wine regions in what we used to call East Germany. The climate is similar to Franken, the grapes are mainly Müller-Thurgau and Silvaner.

**SEKT bA** (Sekt bestimmter Anbaugebiete). Deutscher Sekt increasingly comes from private estates, and is sometimes made by the traditional Champagne method. If the wine comes from one specific quality region it can be labelled accordingly – Rheinhessen Sekt for instance – and is generally a step above Deutscher Sekt. Riesling Sekt bA is especially worth looking out for. (Try *Schloss Wachenheim* or *Winzersekt*.)

**TROCKEN** Dry. The driest German wines. Back in the early 1970s these were painfully, searingly horrid creatures, but things have been improving with a series of warm vintages, and at Spätlese level in particular there are some positively attractive (though pricy) wines.

**WÜRTTEMBERG** We haven't seen much Württemberg wine here because most has been drunk on the spot. Württemberg's claim to fame – if fame is the right word – is for red, which accounts for half of the production. The most exciting grape is Lemberger, which makes dark, spicy wines suited to oak ageing. They're worth trying, especially from *Graf Adelmann* or the state-owned research centre, the snappily-titled *Staatliche Lehr- und Versuchsanstalt für Wein- und Obstbau*.

---

### REGIONAL DEFINITIONS

German wine is classified according to ripeness of grapes and provenance. The country is divided into wine regions (alphabetically listed on these pages – Rheingau, Rheinhessen, etc, and two in the former East); inside these there are three groupings.

**Bereich** This is a collection of villages and vineyard sites, supposedly of similar style, and grouped under a single name – generally that of the most famous village. So 'Bereich Nierstein' means 'a wine from the general region of Nierstein'. It could come from any one of 50 or more villages, regardless of quality.

**Grosslage** A group of vineyards supposedly all of similar type, and based on one or more villages. The objective was to try and make some sense of thousands of obscure vineyard names. But it doesn't work. Among the 152 designated names, there are a few good Grosslagen – like Honigberg, which groups the vineyards of Winkel in the Rheingau, or Badstube which covers the best sites in Bernkastel. In these Grosslagen, a blend of several different vineyard sites will produce a wine of good quality and identifiable local character. However, most Grosslagen debase the whole idea of a 'vineyard' identity. Taken to absurd limits, Germany's most famous Grosslage is Niersteiner Gutes Domtal. Gutes Domtal was originally a vineyard of 34 hectares in Nierstein – and not terribly special at that. The Niersteiner Gutes Domtal Grosslage covers 1300 hectares, spread over 15 villages, almost all of which share no quality traits with Nierstein whatsoever!

**Einzellage** This is a real single vineyard wine, corresponding to a 'cru' in Burgundy or Alsace. There are about 2600 of these, ranging from a mere half hectare to 250 hectares. All the best wines in Germany are from Einzellagen, though only a distressingly small proportion have real individuality. Some growers are using Einzellage names less, and emphasizing their estate and grape names more. To avoid some of the confusion between Grosslage and Einzellage designations, some producers have started naming QbA and QmP wines simply with the village name, such as Nierstein or Deidesheim, with no reference to vineyard. These wines may be made from grapes harvested within the village boundary, so are likely to be better than many from a Grosslage.

# WINERY PROFILES

**FRIEDRICH-WILHELM-GYMNASIUM**
★★★(★) (Mosel-Saar-Ruwer) Large Trier estate. The best wines are textbook Mosel, but can be inconsistent.

**FÜRSTLICH CASTELL'SCHES DOMÄNENAMT** ★★★★ (Franconia)
Princely estate in the Steigerwald hills which produces excellent Müller-Thurgau, Silvaner, Riesling and as a speciality in top years, wonderfully concentrated Rieslaner.

**SCHLOSSGUT DIEL** ★★★★(★) (Nahe)
One of the Nahe's top estates. Production is mainly of beautifully balanced dry wines, though sweeter styles from the warm concentrated vintage of 1990 will be well worth waiting for. Impeccably made, *barrique*-aged dry Grauburgunder.

**SCHLOSS VOLLRADS** ★★★ (Rheingau)
The Rheingau's most beautiful private estate. Very clean, steely, rather austere wines which can be overdone in less ripe vintages. Vollrads Beeren- and Trocken-beerenauslesen of top vintages are some of the world's most stunning dessert wines.

**STAATLICHE WEINBAUDOMÄNE**
★★★★(★) (Nahe) The State Domaine at Niederhausen is one of the great white wine estates of the world, producing Rieslings which combine Mosel-like flowery fragrance with a special mineral intensity. Prices are very reasonable, considering the very good quality.

**VON SCHUBERT** ★★★★★ (Mosel-Saar-Ruwer) Exquisitely delicate, fragrant Rieslings are grown on the slopes above the Maximin-Grünhaus, a former monastic property on the tiny Ruwer. The best vineyard at the top of the hill is called Abtsberg, because the wine was reserved for the abbot: the scarcely less good middle slope is called Bruderberg. Superlative at every level of quality.

**WEGELER-DEINHARD** ★★★★(★)
(Mosel-Saar-Ruwer) Koblenz-based shipper with substantial holdings in Rheingau and Rheinpfalz as well as Ruwer and Mosel, where it shares the famous Bernkasteler Doctor vineyard. Wines from all three estates are impeccably made, and Beeren- and Trockenbeerenauslesen can be delicious. Reliable, simply-labelled village wines.

**WEINGUT BALTHASAR RESS** ★★★★
(Rheingau) Stefan Ress's beautifully fresh, clean Riesling wines have performed consistently well in blind tastings. Highly successful at both traditional-style Spätlesen and Auslesen and off-dry wines under the Charta group label.

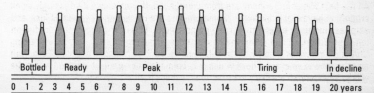

**MATURITY CHART**
1988 Rheingau Riesling Spätlese
Riesling Spätlese develops a more refined character after three years in bottle

| Bottled | Ready | | Peak | | | Tiring | | In decline |
|---|---|---|---|---|---|---|---|---|
| 0 1 2 | 3 4 5 6 | 7 8 9 | 10 11 12 | 13 | 14 15 | 16 17 18 | 19 | 20 years |

## WEINGUT DR BÜRKLIN-WOLF ★★★★

(Rheinpfalz) Bürklin's wines have an aristocratic elegance which sometimes suggests the Rheingau rather than the Pfalz. Its top Wachenheim wines, from flat vineyards, disprove the theory that great German wines must necessarily come from steep slopes.

## WEINGUT LOUIS GUNTRUM ★★★(★)

(Rheinhessen) Louis Guntrum wines are always reliable: the top Rieslings and Silvaners from the Oppenheimer Sackträger vineyard are impressively powerful, with a touch of earthiness to their fruit.

## WEINGUT HEYL ZU HERRNSHEIM

★★★★(★) (Rheinhessen) An estate that is scandalously underrated in Britain, producing magnificent, traditional-style Riesling Spätlese, ripe yet beautifully balanced, from the red slate vineyards of Nierstein.

## WEINGUT LINGENFELDER ★★★(★)

(Rheinpfalz) Dynamic small estate in northern Pfalz, producing excellent Riesling and Scheurebe, both dry and 'traditional' in style, as well as remarkably deep-coloured, full-bodied red Spätburgunder (alias Pinot Noir) and deliciously juicy red Dornfelder.

## WEINGUT J.J. PRÜM ★★★★★ (Mosel-

Saar-Ruwer) Legendary estate with large holding in the great Wehlener Sonnenuhr vineyard. These are wines for the long haul: often prickly with carbon dioxide when young, and high in acidity, they develop a marvellous peachy richness with time. Wonderful stuff.

---

### VINTAGES

**1991** A wet and sometimes frosty spring caused late flowering, but yields were low, thanks to frost, and gave very good wines in the Saar and Ruwer, and drought led to a preponderance of QbA wines in the Mosel and Rhine. Few wines will reach the heights of the preceding three vintages, but 1991 is not a vintage to write off. It will offer good, well-balanced Rieslings that should give ample pleasure while waiting for the mega-vintages to mature.

**1990** The third great vintage in a row and some say the best of all. A heatwave and drought conditions in the summer months led growers to think that acidity levels would plummet. They didn't, and producers were left with very low yields of highly concentrated sugars and acids. Some producers committed to dry wine production made their first sweet wines for a decade, saying the acidity was too high to get the balance right for dry wines. A great year for Spätlesen and Auslesen, though with little noble rot. In youth the wines have wonderful ripe fruit flavours but they will need several years for all that acidity to soften.

**1989** The vintage to prove the exception – that big can still be beautiful. Drier styles will be ready soon and have lovely balance. From Auslese upwards the wines are luscious, needing time for the flavours of noble rot to develop.

**1988** Wonderful, wonderful wines. Lovely fresh acidity, a beautiful clear, thrilling fruit and remarkable array of *personalities* – you really can see the differences between vineyard sites.

**1987** A lovely, dry, not entirely ripe vintage; lots of delicious QbAs from top vineyards. Rieslings are lasting well.

**1986** Not very ripe, not very clean, not very exciting. Buy only from top producers.

**1985** Very attractive, fresh-fruited wines overall, without the sheer zinging class of '88, but still drinking well.

# ITALY

Only three decades ago, Italy produced the blueprint for its wine industry; now, just when we've all begun to master the subtleties of DOC (Denominazione di Orgine Controllata) and Vino de Tavola, it's all going to change again. After only 30 years? I hear you shriek. Did they get it so hopelessly wrong? Well, they did and they didn't. It was a solid achievement, that law of 30 years ago. It assembled from dozens of wine traditions (remember that only 150 years ago Italy was still an aggregation of city-states) what was most worth preserving and put a workable structure to it. But no, it wasn't right.

One of the most confusing aspects of Italy's DOC/DOCG (Denominazione di Origine Controllata e Garantita) set-up was the extent to which gifted wine-makers aspired to produce their masterpieces outside the official system. Who could have foreseen that the description 'vino da tavola' might become a badge of merit, thereby leaving consumers to divine which were the great and inspired bottles, and which the crude and coarse? The new law has addressed this problem and moved on a number of others. It has acknowledged the importance of *terroir* in the quality and style of wine, whereas before it put emphasis on the grape varieties and on traditional vineyard and cellar practices, which are as often based on expediency as they are on the drive for quality.

The wine world has changed, of course, since the legislation of the 1960s. Cabernet Sauvignon and Chardonnay have invaded the vineyards in a way that was never envisaged then. If typicality of style was to be protected, this question had to be addressed. As did the matter of individual vineyard sites and their particular *terroirs*: again, wine-makers had moved ahead of the law in acknowledging their importance. The new wine law has a detailed pyramid of nine levels of geographic delimitation from Vino da Tavola at the bottom to the top categories of DOC and DOCG.

## Site testing

It aims to encompass every possible individual site. Communes may be divided into four ever-smaller units, namely localities, microzones, estates and finally individual vineyards. Producers in the more minutely-controlled and therefore (one assumes) better sites will be able to decide, at the time of the vintage and according to the quality of the year, whether to release the eventual wine under the smaller denomination or further down the quality scale. All those 'super-table wines' that lay outside the system — the Sassicaias, the Tignanellos — will now fall within DOC or DOCG territory and will qualify for one denomination or another. This should leave 'vino da tavola' on a label meaning what it was always supposed to mean — a modest, anonymous wine at the bottom of the quality chain. DOC and DOCG wines will carry full information about location and grapes on the labels.

Below DOC and DOCG level are IGT (Indicazione Geografica Tipica) wines, the new Italian version of *vin de pays* and *landwein*. These will carry the zone and grape variety on the label, and the latter has to be sanctioned for use in each region. After its heady days of glamour, Vino da Tavola will henceforth be permitted only to indicate colour on its labels. Each denomination will have its own maximum yield, with the yields going down as the denomination goes up.

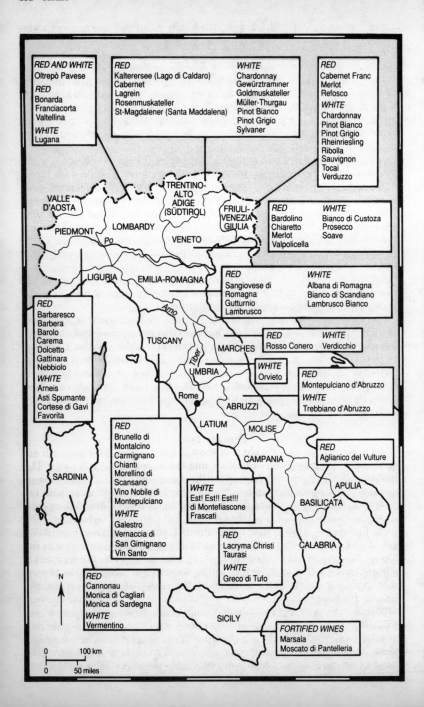

**RED AND WHITE**
Oltrepò Pavese

**RED**
Bonarda
Franciacorta
Valtellina

**WHITE**
Lugana

**RED**
Kalterersee (Lago di Caldaro)
Cabernet
Lagrein
Rosenmuskateller
St-Magdalener (Santa Maddalena)

**WHITE**
Chardonnay
Gewürztraminer
Goldmuskateller
Müller-Thurgau
Pinot Bianco
Pinot Grigio
Sylvaner

**RED**
Cabernet Franc
Merlot
Refosco

**WHITE**
Chardonnay
Pinot Bianco
Pinot Grigio
Rheinriesling
Ribolla
Sauvignon
Tocai
Verduzzo

VALLE D'AOSTA

TRENTINO-ALTO ADIGE (SÜDTIROL)

FRIULI-VENEZIA GIULIA

PIEDMONT

LOMBARDY

VENETO

Po

**RED**
Bardolino
Chiaretto
Merlot
Valpolicella

**WHITE**
Bianco di Custoza
Prosecco
Soave

LIGURIA

EMILIA-ROMAGNA

**RED**
Sangiovese di Romagna
Gutturnio
Lambrusco

**WHITE**
Albana di Romagna
Bianco di Scandiano
Lambrusco Bianco

Arno

**RED**
Barbaresco
Barbera
Barolo
Carema
Dolcetto
Gattinara
Nebbiolo

**WHITE**
Arneis
Asti Spumante
Cortese di Gavi
Favorita

TUSCANY

Tiber

MARCHES

**RED** Rosso Conero    **WHITE** Verdicchio

UMBRIA

**WHITE**
Orvieto

**RED**
Montepulciano d'Abruzzo

**WHITE**
Trebbiano d'Abruzzo

Rome

ABRUZZI

**RED**
Brunello di Montalcino
Carmignano
Chianti
Morellino di Scansano
Vino Nobile di Montepulciano

**WHITE**
Galestro
Vernaccia di San Gimignano
Vin Santo

LATIUM

MOLISE

CAMPANIA

**RED**
Aglianico del Vulture

SARDINIA

**WHITE**
Est! Est!! Est!!! di Montefiascone
Frascati

**RED**
Lacryma Christi
Taurasi

**WHITE**
Greco di Tufo

BASILICATA

APULIA

CALABRIA

N

**RED**
Cannonau
Monica di Cagliari
Monica di Sardegna

**WHITE**
Vermentino

SICILY

**FORTIFIED WINES**
Marsala
Moscato di Pantelleria

| 0 | 100 km |
| 0 | 50 miles |

That old chestnut, 'Superiore', almost universally misunderstood to mean a wine of higher quality rather than merely higher alcoholic strength, has been dropped (France take note!) and 'Novello' (for Nouveau-style wines) has been formally sanctioned. About 50 moribund DOCs will be dismantled.

There are to be tighter controls on wines for export and on bottling companies, particularly timely considering the batches of Veneto wines that had to be taken off the shelves in 1992. They had been found to contain high concentrations of pesticide because a bottler's biologist had suddenly decided it would be a great idea to use the substance in the bottling line as a cheaper means of sterilising the bottles...

The legislation has come at the right time, for the good both of the whole Italian wine industry and of the individual consumer. The *vino da tavola* situation, for example, had got completely out of hand. Names proliferated, each, we were to believe, the key to a wonderful wine, but how could we tell? Were we really expected to pay the high asking price every time just to find out? A survey in Italy counted 416 *vini da tavola* in just eight shops, and half of them were stocked in just one choice-laden outlet. One wine cost £15.65 in Milan and £29.13 in Naples; and when even the poor sales staff got confused between names, what chance did the rest of us stand?

Not that we, or they, will be let off the hook just yet. It will be a year or two before the wines start to shift into their new categories, and it will be the end of the decade before everything is finally in position.

There has been good news and bad for Chianti. The bad was that, incredibly, the Consorzio Chianti Classico have lost the right to continue with the words 'Gallo Nero', so long associated with them and their Black Rooster logo. They have lost it, believe it or not, to the Gallo brothers, American purveyors of large volumes of unexciting wines. The Gallos, in cock-of-the-walk fashion, brought in the lawyers; despite the fact that the Consorzio's Gallo Nero logo has been around for half the time the Gallos have been in business, the American firm won the day.

## Century duty

On the positive side, the first phase of the 'Chianti Classico 2000' research and replanting programme is now complete, and the second stage under way. This nine-year plan is to prepare the way for the replanting of the Chianti Classico vineyards, due to take place in time for the year 2000. In conjunction with two universities and 14 top wine estates, the Consorzio is researching, among other subjects, clones, rootstocks, planting densities, and cultivation techniques.

The first phase – the planting of experimental plots – took place from 1988 to 1991, and the second phase, of initial monitoring, completed its first year as this edition of *Webster's* went to press. Everything from sugar-levels to colour will be registered and every batch of grapes will be harvested separately so as to carry out individual analyses. Thirteen different vine clones, 18 different rootstocks, planting densities of 2,500 to 10,000 plants per hectare, traditional and non-traditional training systems – nothing is being left to chance.

But wine law – especially Italian wine law – makes cynics of us all. Will the replanting really be aimed at the highest possible quality? Will the new wine law, indeed, ensure the best possible quality? Or will politics, which always seem geared to lower quality and higher quantity, gain the upper hand? Let us hope not. Italian wine deserves better than that.                    **GORDON BROWN**

# RED WINES

Whereas France has been – and is – the model for all the New World exploits, and although grapes like Cabernet Sauvignon and Pinot Noir are important in Italy, the true glories of Italy are unimitated anywhere else. Red wines from Nebbiolo, Dolcetto, Montepulciano, Lagrein, Sangiovese, Aglianico, Sagrantino and many others are unique expressions of a wine culture which has been too inward-looking for too long. But the jewels are coming out of the woodwork – a mixed metaphor which is entirely apt for the strange delights I'm now lapping up.

## GRAPES & FLAVOURS

**AGLIANICO** A very late-ripening grape of Greek origin, grown in the South. At its most impressive in Aglianico del Vulture (Basilicata) and Taurasi (Campania).

**BARBERA** The most prolific grape of Piedmont and the North-West. The wines traditionally have high acidity, a slightly resiny edge and yet a sweet-sour, raisiny taste or even a brown-sugar sweetness. But they don't have to be like this: witness some of the lighter but intensely fruity Barberas from the Asti and Monferrato hills. The grape reaches its peak in the Langhe hills around Alba where growers like *Altare, Conterno Fantino* and *Gaja* have used low yields to great effect. Experiments with *barrique*-ageing are also encouraging, and wines like *Bertini's Alto Mango* are outstandingly richly flavoured. *Alfredo Prunotto's 1988 Pian Romualdo Barbera d'Alba* is oaky and rather special.

**BONARDA** Low acid, rich, plummy reds, often with a liquoricy, chocolaty streak and sometimes a slight spritz. Most common in the Colli Piacentini of Emilia Romagna where it is blended with Barbera as Gutturnio; also in the Oltrepò Pavese.

**CABERNET SAUVIGNON** A contentious grape in Italy, because of *tipicità* – local character. Many traditionalists are upset at how this world-class grape is usurping the place of indigenous varieties in the vineyard and also dominating any grape with which it is blended. In fact there has been Cabernet Sauvignon in Italy for well over a century, but, following the surge in popularity – and price – of top clarets as well as the new Australian and US classics, many Italians have succumbed to Cabernet fever. This is most evident in Tuscany, where Cabernet has added greatly to the fruit of many wines and, aged in small oak barrels, is producing potential world class. *Sassicaia* has spawned a host of imitators. There is Chianti with a dollop of Cabernet too, though the trend may have peaked.

**CABERNET FRANC** Fairly widely grown in the north-east of Italy, especially in Alto Adige, Trentino, Veneto and Friuli. It can make gorgeous grassy, yet juicy-fruited reds – unnervingly easy to drink young but also capable of a good few years' ageing.

**DOLCETTO** Makes good, brash, fruity, purple wine of the same name in Piedmont, ideally full yet soft, slightly chocolaty and spicy, and wonderfully refreshing when young. Try and find the exciting 1989s.

**LAGREIN** Local grape of the Alto Adige (Südtirol) and Trentino, making delicious, dark reds, strongly plum-sweet when they're young, ageing slowly to a smoky, creamy softness. It also makes one of Italy's best rosés, called Lagrein Kretzer.

**MERLOT** Widely planted in the North-East. Often good in Friuli; provides lots of jug wine in the Veneto but when blended with Cabernet Sauvignon by *Loredan*

*Gasparini* (Venegazzù) or *Fausto Maculan* (Brentino) achieves greater stature. Other Cabernet/Merlot blends are produced by *Mecvini* in the Marche and Trentino's *Bossi Fedrigotti* (Foianeghe). *Avignonesi* and *Castello di Ama* in Tuscany are getting promising results.

**MONTEPULCIANO** A much underrated grape. Yes, it has toughness, but it also has lots of plummy, herby fruit. *Banfi* in Montalcino has high hopes for it. It grows mostly on the Adriatic Coast, from the Marches down to to Puglia.

**NEBBIOLO** The big, tough grape of the North-West, making – unblended – the famous Barolos and Barbarescos as well as the less famous Gattinara, Ghemme, Carema, Spanna and plain Nebbiolo. This is a surly, fierce grape, producing wines that can be dark, chewy, unyielding and harsh behind a shield of cold-tea-tannin and acidity for the first few years; but which then blossom out into a remarkable richness full of chocolate, raisins, prunes, and an austere perfume of tobacco, pine and herbs. In the past, sloppy wine-making has been all too evident in the wines on sale here but shops are now more willing to fork out for the best. In 1985 modern wine-making allied to a beautiful vintage gave some stunning wines, but prices are pretty high, and anyway there's little left. 1986 and '87 were good, too. A few growers (*Elio Altare, Clerico, Conterno Fantino* and *Voerzio*) are producing some superb *vini da tavola* by ageing their wines in *barrique*, or blending it with Barbera, or both, as in *Sebaste's Briccoviole* (Tesco).

**SANGIOVESE** Too much is often asked of this Chianti mainstay. It is extremely good at providing purple-fresh, slightly rasping, herby wines, full of thirst-quenching, acid fruit, to be drunk young. It's not always so successful at providing the weight and personality needed for more 'serious' wines. This is mainly because the clones widely planted in the 1970s were high-yielding ones, rather than the native Tuscan variety. You can make decent quaffing wines from the high-yielders, but wines of real class and substance come only from the Tuscan clone. This makes deeper, plummier wine more suited to ageing and is contributing hugely to the improved quality of Tuscan reds.

**SCHIAVA** Quaffable, light reds with almost no tannin and a unique taste that veers between smoked ham and strawberry yoghurt. An Alto Adige (Südtirol) grape, Schiava is at its best in Kalterersee (Lago di Caldaro Scelto) and Santa Maddalena. The local population, which mostly speaks German, calls it by its German name, Vernatsch.

## WINES & WINE REGIONS

**AGLIANICO DEL VULTURE, DOC** (Basilicata) High up the side of gaunt Monte Vulture, in the wilds of Basilicata (Italy's 'instep'), the Aglianico grape finds sufficiently cool conditions to make a superb, thick-flavoured red wine. The colour isn't particularly deep, but the tremendous almond paste and chocolate fruit are matched by a tough, dusty feel and quite high acidity. What's more, it's *not* very expensive. Two good producers are *Paternoster, Fratelli d'Angelo*. D'Angelo's new *barrique*'d *Canneto d'Angelo* is good.

**ALTO ADIGE** Also called Südtirol as the majority of the population is German-speaking. Although the UK drinks mostly the whites, the attractive light reds made of the Vernatsch/Schiava grape – especially Kalterersee and St Magdalener – have until recently been the most famous offerings, because the Swiss, Austrians and Germans were keen on them. However, Cabernet, Pinot Nero, Lagrein and the tea-rose-scented Rosenmuskateller all make Alto Adige reds – and rosés – with a lot more stuffing to them.

**BARBARESCO, DOCG** (Piedmont)
Toughness and tannin are the hallmarks of
the Nebbiolo, Barbaresco's only grape, and
they can often overshadow its finer points:
a delicious soft, strawberryish maturity,
edged with smoke, herbs and pine. The
*riserva* category (four years' ageing) still
exists, but most producers these days stick
to the minimum two years' ageing (one in
wood) the law requires and preserve the
fruit by storing the wine in stainless steel
or bottle. When it works, the Nebbiolo can
show more nuances and glints of brilliance
than any other Italian grape. Best: *Luigi
Bianco, Castello di Neive, Cigliuti, Glicine,
Giuseppe Cortese, Gaja, Bruno Giacosa,
Marchesi di Gresy, Moresco, Pasquero,
Pelissero, Pertinace, Pio Cesare, Produttori
del Barbaresco, Roagna, Vietti* and *Scarpa*.

**BARBERA, DOC** (Piedmont and others)
Barbera is Italy's most widely planted red
vine, and makes a good, gutsy wine, usually
with a resiny, herby bite, insistent acidity
and fairly forthright, dry raisin sort of
fruit. It is best in Piedmont, where it has
four DOCs, Barbera d'Alba, d'Asti, del
Monferrato and Rubino di Cantavenna,
and in Lombardy under the Oltrepò Pavese
DOC; also found in Puglia, Campania,
Emilia-Romagna, Liguria, Sicily, Sardinia.

**BARDOLINO, DOC** (Veneto) A growing
number of pale pinky reds with a frail
wispy cherry fruit and a slight bitter snap
to the finish are appearing from the banks
of Lake Garda, along with some lovely
Chiaretto rosés and some excellent, *very*
fresh-fruited Novello wines. There are also
a few fuller, rounder wines like *Boscaini's
Le Canne* which can take some ageing. As
quality has risen, so have the prices. Also
*Arvedi d'Emilei, Guerrieri-Rizzardi,
Lenotti, Masi* (*Fresco* and *La Vegrona*),
*Portalupi* and *Le Vigne di San Pietro*.

**BAROLO, DOCG** (Piedmont) Praise be;
I'm slowly becoming a Barolo fan! Yet only
five years ago I wouldn't have found *any* I
liked. The raw material is still the Nebbiolo

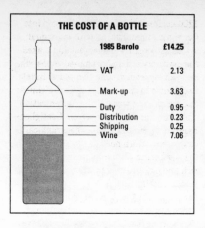

**THE COST OF A BOTTLE**

| 1985 Barolo | £14.25 |
| --- | --- |
| VAT | 2.13 |
| Mark-up | 3.63 |
| Duty | 0.95 |
| Distribution | 0.23 |
| Shipping | 0.25 |
| Wine | 7.06 |

grape, a monstrously difficult character
that has had to be dragged squealing and
roaring into the latter half of the twentieth
century. But many growers are trying to
stress fruit rather than raw, rough tannins
and not only will these wines be enjoyable
younger – in five years rather than 20 –
they will (according to the basic tenet of the
modern school) actually *age better* because
you can't age a wine without balance, and
balance is also what makes a wine
enjoyable reasonably young.

It would be easy to say only expensive
Barolo is any good, but the efforts of Asda,
Tesco, Sainsbury and Oddbins show that
good buyers *can* find bargains. Because the
Nebbiolo does have a remarkable, deep,
sweet, plum and woodsmoke richness,
even blackcurrants and raspberry pips,
often a dark, wild maelstrom of chocolate
and prunes and tobacco. By shortening
fermentation to extract less tannin, or by
bending the laws and ageing in stainless
steel, or bottling early, there are some
magical experiences to be had. The 1984s
from producers who ruthlessly cut out poor
grapes are dry, but delicious. I'm sticking
with '84 and '86 (brilliant but in short
supply) for the moment until the hefty '85s
come round. Some are already displaying
delicious perfume, and in the wines from
the best sites there's masses of sweet,
supple fruit to stand up to the tannin.

The area of production is small, around

1200 hectares in total, and is divided into five main communes, all with individual styles. La Morra is the largest and makes the most forward and perfumed wines, ripe and velvety from around five years. Barolo itself tends to make wines of more richness and weight, but without the concentration and structure of the wines from Castiglione Falletto, right on the zone's geographical centre, and which need ageing. Monforte, the southernmost commune, is known for rich and powerful wines often needing ten years in bottle. To the east, Serralunga is famous for the tough, jaw-locking style which ages more slowly than the others.

Over the last 20 years, producers have been fighting for official classification of the top sites: the new law should do this. Many growers are already citing vineyard names on the label, and, for the moment, the ones to look out for are: Arborina, Monfalletto, Marcenasco Conca, Rocche, Rocchette, Brunate, La Serra and Cerequio (La Morra), Cannubi, Sarmassa, and Brunate and Cerequio (again) which straddle the two communes (Barolo), Bricco Boschis, Rocche, Villero, Bric del Fiasc (Castiglione Falletto), Bussia Soprana, Santo Stefano and Ginestra (Monforte), Marenca-Rivette, Lazzarito, La Delizia, Vigna Rionda, Prapo, Baudana and Francia (Serralunga). The best wines come from producers like *Altare, Azelia, Borgogno, Bovio, Brovia, Cavallotto, Ceretto, Clerico, Aldo* and *Giacomo Conterno,* *Conterno Fantino, Cordero di Montezemolo, Fontanafredda* (only its *cru* wines), *Bruno Giacosa, Marcarini, Bartolo Mascarello, Giuseppe Mascarello, Migliorini, Pio Cesare, Pira, Prunotto, Ratti, Sandrone, Scarpa, Scavino, Sebaste, Vajra, Vietti* and *Voerzio*.

**BONARDA** (Lombardy) Delicious, young, plummy, fruity red with a dark chocolate bitter twist from Lombardy and Emilia in the central north. *Castello di Luzzano* is particularly good, with great tannic length, the right fruit impact and gently peppery push. Better than most. The 1987 is excellent.

**BREGANZE, DOC** (Veneto) Little-known but excellent claret-like red from near Vicenza. There's Pinot Nero, Merlot and Cabernet (Sauvignon and Franc) and these Bordeaux grapes produce a most attractive grassy, blackcurrant red, with a touch of cedar. Very good. *Maculan* age theirs in new wood, which is even more exciting.

**BRUNELLO DI MONTALCINO, DOCG** (Tuscany) A big, strong neighbour of Chianti traditionally better known for its ridiculous prices than for exciting flavours, but slowly coming to terms with a world in which people will pay high prices, but demand excellence to go with them. The reason why the wine can be disappointing is that it can lose its fruit during the three and a half years' wood ageing required by the regulations. But in the right hands, in a good, clean cellar, the fruit can hold out, and then the wine can achieve an amazing combination of flavours: blackberries, raisins, pepper, acidity, tannin with, hopefully, a haunting sandalwood perfume, all bound together by an austere richness resembling liquorice and fierce black chocolate. As such, I'll admit it can be great wine. But though such wines are a growing minority, scary prices are still the norm. The best wines come from *Altesino, Campogiovanni, Caparzo, Casanova, Case Basse, Il Casello, Col d'Orcia, Costanti, Pertimali, Il Poggione, Talenti* and *Val di Suga. Biondi Santi* is the most famous and the most expensive producer. I haven't yet had a bottle that justified the cost.

**CAREMA, DOC** (Piedmont) The most refined in bouquet and taste of the Nebbiolo wines from a tiny mountainous zone close to Val d'Aosta. *Luigi Ferrando* is the best producer, especially his 'black label', but almost all are good – and need five to six years to be at their best.

The price guides for this section begin on page 342.

**CARMIGNANO, DOCG** (Tuscany)
Although the advent of Cabernet
Sauvignon in Tuscany is often talked of as
being entirely recent, Carmignano – a
small enclave inside the Chianti zone to
the west of Florence – has been adding in
10 to 15 per cent Cabernet Sauvignon to its
wine since the nineteenth century. The
soft, clear blackcurrant fruit of the
Cabernet makes a delicious blend with the
stark flavours of the Sangiovese – the
majority grape. There is also some good
rosé and some *vin santo*. The zone rose to
DOCG status in 1990. *Capezzana* is the
original estate and the only one regularly
seen over here. Its '83 and '85 *riserva* wines
are special.

**CHIANTI, DOCG** (Tuscany) The first few
times I had real Chianti, fizzy-fresh,
purple-proud, with an invigorating,
rasping fruit, I thought it was the most
perfect jug wine I'd ever had. It still can be.
But following DOC in 1963, vineyards
expanded all over the place to meet a
buoyant demand. Chianti and Chianti
Classico especially suffered more than
their fair share of investors who cared only
about profit and knew nothing whatever
about wine.

But Chianti might have stood more
chance if the chief grape, the Sangiovese,
had not been debased, first by the planting
of inferior, high-yielding clones, and second
by the traditional admixture of an
excessive quantity of white juice from
Trebbiano and Malvasia grapes with the
red. Growers could at one time legally mix
in almost one-third white grapes in their
Chianti – and the inevitable result was
wines that simply faded before they even
made it into bottle.

Thankfully DOCG regulations limit the
proportion of white grapes to two to five per
cent. This seems to have stemmed the flow
of thin Chianti, and own-label examples
from companies like Asda can be very good.

Another development in the Chianti
region has been the emergence of Cabernet
Sauvignon as a component of the red

wines. Although not really permissible for
more than ten per cent of the total, a
number of growers use it to delicious effect,
though as clonal selection of better
Sangiovese develops, there may come a day
when this is no longer necessary. The
Chianti Classico Consorzio has set in train
an operation called 'Chianti Classico 2000'
which is intended to ensure that as
replanting takes place only top clones of
Sangiovese and Canaiolo are used. By 2000
we may well be classing Chianti Classico,
at least, as one of the world's great red
wines.

The Chianti region is divided into seven
regions as follows: Classico, Colli Aretini,
Colli Fiorentini, Colli Senesi, Colline
Pisane, Montalbano and Rufina. Classico
and Rufina are almost always marked on
the label, where appropriate, but most
wines from the other zones are simply
labelled 'Chianti'.

**CHIANTI STYLES** There are two basic
styles. The first is the sharp young red that
used to come in wicker flasks and just
occasionally still does. This starts out quite
purple-red, but quickly takes on a slightly
orange tinge and is sometimes slightly
prickly, with a rather attractive taste,
almost a tiny bit sour, but backed up by
good, raisiny-sweet fruit, a rather stark,
peppery bite and tobacco-like spice. This
style is traditionally made by the 'governo'
method, which involves adding – just after
fermentation – a small quantity of grapes
dried on racks, or concentrated must,
together with a dried yeast culture, so that
the wine re-ferments. Apart from the
prickle, this leaves the wine softer, rounder
and more instantly appealing, but makes it
age more quickly. So this is wine for
drinking young.

The second type is usually several
years old and, in the bad old days before
the advent of DOCG, had all the acidity
and tannin it needed, but the only fruit on
show was a fistful of old raisins and a
curious, unwelcome whiff of tomatoes.
Nowadays there are enough exceptions

around to reckon that they are becoming the rule. The Chiantis of top estates, especially in fine vintages such as 1985, 1986 and 1988 are gaining a range of slightly raw strawberry, raspberry and blackcurrant flavours backed up by a herby, tobaccoey spice and a grapeskinsy roughness that makes the wine demanding but exciting. Top estates include *Badia a Coltibuono, Castellare, Castello di Ama, Castello dei Rampolla, Castello di San Polo in Rosso, Castello di Volpaia, Felsina Berardenga, Fontodi, Montesodi* and *Nipozzano (Frescobaldi), Isole e Olena, Pagliarese, Peppoli (Antinori), Riecine, San Felice, Selvapiana, Vecchie Terre di Montefili* and *Villa di Vetrice*.

**DOLCETTO,** some **DOC** (Piedmont) At its best, delicious, full but soft, fresh, and dramatically fruity red, usually for gulping down fast and young, though some will age a few years. Wonderful ones come from *Altare, Castello di Neive, Clerico, Aldo Conterno, Giacomo Conterno, Marcarini, Mascarello, Oddero, Pasquero, Prunotto, Ratti, Sandrone, Scavino, Vajra, Vietti, Viticoltori dell'Acquese* and *Voerzio*.

**FRANCIACORTA ROSSO, DOC** (Lombardy) Raw but tasty blackcurranty wine from east of Milan. *Contessa Maggi, Bellavista, Ca' del Bosco* and *Longhi De' Carli* are all good.

**FRIULI** Six different zones (of which Grave del Friuli DOC is by far the most important quantitatively) stretching from the flatlands just north of Venice to the Yugoslav borders. The wines are characterized by vibrant fruit. In particular, the 'international' grapes, Cabernet Franc and Merlot, have an absolutely delicious, juicy stab of flavour; and Refosco has a memorable flavour in the tar-and-plums mould – sharpened up with a grassy acidity. Good Cabernet from *Ca' Ronesca* and *Russiz Superiore*. *La Fattoria* and *Collavini* make excellent Cabernet and Merlot too and *Pintar* in the Collio area makes good Cabernet Franc. *Borgo Conventi*'s reds are very good and worth looking out for.

**GATTINARA, DOC** (Piedmont) Good Nebbiolo-based red from the Vercelli hills in Piedmont, softer and quicker to mature than Barbaresco or Barolo, but also less potentially thrilling. *Brugo, Dessilani* and *Travaglini* are important producers.

**KALTERERSEE/LAGO DI CALDARO, DOC** (Alto Adige) Good, light, soft red with an unbelievable flavour of home-made strawberry jam and woodsmoke, made from the Schiava (alias Vernatsch) grape in the Alto Adige. It is best as a young gulper. Best producers include: *Gries* co-op, *Lageder, Muri-Gries, Hans Rottensteiner, St Michael-Eppan* co-op, *Tiefenbrunner* and *Walch*.

**LAGREIN DUNKEL,** some **DOC** (Alto Adige) Dark, chewy red from the Alto Adige (Südtirol) with a remarkable depth of flavour for the product of a high mountain valley. These intense wines have a tarry roughness jostling with chocolate-smooth ripe fruit, the flavour being a very successful mix between the strong, chunky style of many Italian reds and the fresher, brighter tastes of France. *Gries* co-op, *Lageder, Muri-Gries, Niedermayr* and *Tiefenbrunner* are particularly good. *Tiefenbrunner* also makes an outstanding pink Lagrein Kretzer.

**LAMBRUSCO,** some **DOC** (Emilia-Romagna) Good Lambrusco – lightly fizzy, low in alcohol, red or white, dry to vaguely sweet – should *always* have a sharp, almost rasping acid bite to it. Real Lambrusco with a DOC, from Sorbara, Santa Croce or Castelvetro, is anything but feeble and is an exciting palate-tingling accompaniment to rough-and-ready Italian food. But most Lambrusco is not DOC and is softened for fear of offending consumers. *Cavicchioli* is one of the few 'proper' ones that braves the UK shelves.

## MONTEPULCIANO D'ABRUZZO, DOC

(Abruzzi) Made on the east coast opposite Rome from the gutsy Montepulciano grape, a good one manages to be citrus-fresh and plummily rich, juicy yet tannic, ripe yet with a tantalizing sour bite. Fine wines are made by producers such as *Mezzanotte* and *Pepe*, while the standard of co-ops such as *Casal Thaulero* and *Tollo* is high. Other good names include *Colle Secc* (from Tollo), *Illuminati Invecchiato* and *Valentini*.

## MORELLINO DI SCANSANO, DOC

Tuscan backwater DOC that occasionally comes up with something interesting, like *Le Sentinelle Riserva* from *Mantellassi*. Similar grape-mix to Chianti gives fine, dry austerity with earthy tannins, deep, ripe fruit, and remarkable tarry spice.

## OLTREPÒ PAVESE, some DOC

(Lombardy) This covers reds, rosés, dry whites, sweet whites, fizz – just about anything. Almost the only wine we see is non-DOC fizz, usually Champagne-method, and based on Pinot Grigio/Nero/Bianco. Most Oltrepò Pavese is drunk in nearby Milan, where regularity of supply is more prized than DOC on the label. We see a little red – ideally based on Barbera and Bonarda, which is good, substantial stuff, soft and fruity – though if you drink it in Milan, don't be surprised to find it's fizzy.

## POMINO, DOC

(Tuscany) A DOC for red, white and the dessert wine *vin santo* in the Rufina area of Chianti. The red, based on Sangiovese with Canaiolo, Cabernet and Merlot, is rich, soft,velvety and spicy with age. Only producer: *Frescobaldi*.

## ROSSO CONERO, DOC

(Marches) A very good, sturdy red from the east coast opposite Florence and Siena. Combining the tasty Montepulciano grape and up to 15 per cent Sangiovese, Rosso Conero blends herb and fruit flavours; sometimes with some oak for richness. Look for *Bianchi*, *Garofoli* and *Mecvini*. *Marchetti*, who uses no Sangiovese in the blend, is best.

## ROSSO DI MONTALCINO, DOC

(Tuscany) DOC introduced in 1984 as an alternative for producers of Brunello who didn't want to age all that wine for Brunello's statutory four years, or who, like the top châteaux of Bordeaux, wanted to make a 'second wine'. Softer, more approachable and cheaper than Brunello di Montalcino.

## ROSSO DI MONTEPULCIANO, DOC

(Tuscany) New DOC, starting from the 1989 vintage. This is to Vino Nobile what Rosso di Montalcino is to Brunello di Montalcino, for the 'second wines' of Montepulciano.

## SPANNA

(Piedmont) A Nebbiolo-based wine with a lovely raisin and chocolate flavour in the old style. Even cheap 'trattoria' Spannas are usually a pretty good bet.

## TAURASI, DOC

(Campania) Remarkable, plummy yet bitingly austere red grown inland from Naples. To be honest, I'm *not* totally convinced, and am still waiting for a really exciting follow-up to the remarkable 1968. Recent releases just haven't had the fruit or, as with the 1983, are impossibly tannic. *Mastroberardino* is the chief name here.

## TORGIANO, DOC and DOCG

(Umbria) A region south-east of Perugia whose fame has been entirely created by *Lungarotti*. The reds are strong, plummy, sometimes overbearing, usually carrying the trade name *Rubesco*. Single vineyard *Monticchio* and *San Giorgio* Cabernet Sauvignon are exciting. In 1990 Torgiano Rosso Riserva became DOCG. White wines here are also clean and good. Lungarotti also makes a good *flor*-affected sherry-type wine called *Solleone*.

## TRENTINO, DOC

Just south of the Alto Adige (Südtirol), making reds either from local varieties such as Lagrein, Teroldego and Marzemino or from international grapes like Cabernet, Merlot and Pinot Noir. Too often their attractive fruit is hopelessly diluted by overcropping; a pity, because lovely Cabernet and Teroldego in particular has come from good producers, such as *Conti Martini Foradori, Istituto di San Michele, Gonzaga, Guerrieri, Pojer e Sandri, de Tarczal* and *Zeni*.

**VALPOLICELLA, DOC** (Veneto) Uses a variety of local grapes, especially Corvina, Rondinella and Molinara. Valpolicella *should* have delicious, light, cherry-fruit and a bitter almond twist to the finish – just a bit fuller and deeper than nearby Bardolino with a hint more sourness. But it's virtually a forlorn quest searching for these flavours, unless you can find *Masi's Fresco* or *Tedeschi's Capitel Lucchine*. It's worth going for a *classico* or a single-vineyard wine. The *superiore* has higher natural alcohol, but these are wines you really must drink young! Producers who can oblige with good flavours are *Allegrini, Boscaini, Guerrieri-Rizzardi, Quintarelli, Le Ragose, Santi, Tedeschi, Masi, Zenato*.

There are now a few single-vineyard wines appearing, like *Masi's Serègo Alighieri*, which are a street ahead of the 'generic' stuff. The wines cost more, but *Allegrini's La Grola* or *Tedeschi's Ca' Nicalo* may show you what once made Valpolicella great. You might also try wine made by the traditional *ripasso* method. New wine is pumped over the skins and lees of Recioto or Amarone, starting a small re-fermentation and adding an exciting sweet-sour dimension to the wine. *Masi, Quintarelli* and *Tedeschi* do this well.

But the wine which can really show you greatness is the weird and wonderful Recioto Amarone della Valpolicella. *Amaro* means bitter, and this huge wine, made from half-shrivelled Valpolicella grapes, *is* bitter, but it also has a brilliant array of flavours – sweet grape skins, chocolate, plums and woodsmoke – which all sound sweet and exotic and, up to a point, they are, but the stroke of genius comes with a penetrating bruised sourness which pervades the wine and shocks you with its forthrightness. The good stuff is usually

---

## CLASSIFICATIONS

Only 10 to 12 per cent of the massive Italian wine harvest is regulated in any way at present, and the regulations that do exist are treated in a fairly cavalier manner by many growers. At the same time producers, rebelling against the constraints imposed on their originality and initiative, have often chosen to operate outside the regulations and classify their – frequently exceptional – wine simply as vino da tavola, the lowest grade. This situation looks set to change, with up to 60 per cent of Italy's wines becoming subject to the law, and wines like Sassicaia in line for their own appellation, but for the time being the following are the main categories:

**Vino da Tavola** This is currently applied to absolutely basic stuff but also to 'maverick' wines of the highest class such as Sassicaia or Gaja's Piedmontese Chardonnay.

**Vino Tipico** This will apply to table wines with some reference to place, and maybe grape type, but which do not qualify for DOC.

**Denominazione di Origine Controllata (DOC)** This applies to wines from specified grape varieties, grown in delimited zones and aged by prescribed methods. Nearly all of Italy's traditionally well-known wines are DOC, but more get added every year. In future, the wines will also undergo a tasting test (as DOCG wines do now).

**Denominazione di Origine Controllata e Garantita (DOCG)** The top tier – a tighter form of DOC with more stringent restrictions on grape types, yields and a tasting panel. First efforts were feeble, but a run of good vintages in 1982, '83, '85, '86 and '88 gave the producers lots of fine material to work with. The revised DOCG should give due recognition to particularly good vineyard sites in future.

three times the price of simple Valpolicella, but it's still good value for a remarkable wine. If the label simply says 'Recioto della Valpolicella', the wine will be sweeter and may still be excellent but, to my mind, a little less strangely special. Fine examples from *Allegrini, Bertani, Masi, Quintarelli, Le Ragose, Tedeschi* and *Tramanal*.

**VALTELLINA, DOC** (Lombardy)
Nebbiolo wine from along the Swiss border, north-east of Milan. I find it a little stringy, but someone must drink it because it has the largest output of Nebbiolo of any DOC, including all those in Piedmont.

**VINO NOBILE DI MONTEPULCIANO, DOCG** (Tuscany) A neighbour of Chianti, with the same characteristics, but more so. Usually, this means more pepper, acid and tannin at a higher price; but increasingly fine Vino Nobile is surfacing, wines with a marvellously dry fragrance reminiscent almost of sandalwood, backed up by good Sangiovese spice, and a strong plum-skins-and-cherries fruit. Time was when you wouldn't go out of your way to find it, but not any more. The following producers are reliable: *Avignonesi, Boscarelli, La Calonica, di Casale, Fassati, Fattoria del Cerro, Fognano, Poliziano* and *Trerose*.

---

### NORTH-WEST ITALY VINTAGES

North-west vintages are difficult to generalize about because it isn't always easy to catch them at their best, and a good year for Nebbiolo may not have been a good one for Dolcetto. And vice versa. Also, styles of wine-making may vary from one producer to the next. In general, Dolcetto needs drinking in its youth, Barbera can last but is often at its best young, when the fruit is most vibrant, and although there are Barolo and Barbaresco wines which you can drink after five years or so, the best last for 20 years or more. Whites should be drunk as young as possible.

**1991** A very fragmented year. Good wines from grapes picked before the rains that fell during the vintage in Piedmont; Barolo excellent, Gattinara and Gavi good. difficult in Lombardy but good Valtellina and some exceptional whites. Fair to good overall so far.

**1990** A fabulous vintage: summer and early autumn were hot but with just the right amount of rain, producing grapes with very high sugar levels but good acidity too. Wines of tremendous colour, richness and perfume, Barolo and Barbaresco for long ageing and delicious Barbera. Wonderful Dolcetto again.

**1989** Unlike the rest of Italy, Piedmont basked in glorious sunshine in 1989. Dolcetto looks even better than in the last five (excellent) vintages, very good Barbera. Nebbiolo came in early at remarkable levels of ripeness.

**1988** Dolcetto and Barbera look really good, a little tough to start with perhaps, but the concentration and fruit are there. Nebbiolo got caught by the rain, but the good growers left the vineyards to dry out and picked healthy ripe grapes.

**1987** Very good for early varieties like Dolcetto and the whites, but the rains came at the wrong moment for Nebbiolo so Barolo and Barbaresco will be patchy.

**1986** Barbaresco and Barolo are overshadowed by '85's greatness but quality is good.

**1985** An exciting vintage when more and more growers decided to emphasize fruit and perfume in their wines. We will see some truly great '85s eventually.

**1983** All but the best are starting to fade.

**1982** Excellent, big ripe reds – which do have the fruit to age – when the wine-makers and the regulations let them.

**1978** Loads of concentrated fruit this year: a traditionalists' delight for those who are prepared to wait.

# WHITE WINES

It is only a few years since I used to write in my tasting notes, 'dull, sulphured, oxidized, dead – typical Italian'. An entire nation's wines dismissed in the irritated flourish of my pen. Thank goodness it would be impossible to make such a generalization today. The revolution in white-wine-making has been far-reaching. New, refrigerated, high-tech methods of wine-making with precise temperature control are now commonplace. In a warm climate like Italy's they are fundamentally important if the fruit character of the grape is to be preserved – although they can lead to an over-emphasis on neutrality and cleanness. However, the currently favoured practice of cold maceration of juice and skins, and fermentation at slightly warmer temperatures to emphasize fruit and perfume, seem to be overcoming the problem.

A welcome resurgence of interest in traditional Italian varieties has seen exciting grapes like Arneis in Piedmont, Grechetto in Umbria, Tocai and Ribolla in Friuli and Catarratto Lucido in Sicily being given the praise and attention they deserve.

The onward march of Chardonnay and Sauvignon – often in combination with barrel-fermentation and ageing in new oak – has already created wines of world-class potential. In Friuli especially, supposedly 'lesser' varieties like Pinot Bianco and Pinot Grigio, made in a rich but clear and precise unoaked style, have risen to new heights and give a lead for the rest to follow.

## GRAPES & FLAVOURS

**CHARDONNAY** Italy is still denying Chardonnay DOC status in some places, though the new law should change that. The typical Italian style is unoaked: lean, rather floral and sharply-balanced from the Alto Adige and usually more neutral, Mâconnais-style from elsewhere. There is exciting, creamy, spicy, *barrique*-aged wine being made by the likes of *Gaja, Marchesi di Gresy* and *Pio Cesare* in Piedmont, *Zanella* in Lombardy, *Maculan* in the Veneto and both *Caparzo (Le Grance)* and *Avignonesi (Il Marzocco)* in Tuscany. However the best of the 'oak-free' lobby are producing some ravishing stuff by focusing on low yields and picking at the optimum sugar-acid balance. *Zeni* (Trentino) and *Gradnik* (Friuli) make prime examples.

**GARGANEGA** The principal grape of Soave. Well, it *should* be the major grape, because it is supposed to make up the majority of the blend, and when well made it is particularly refreshing, soft, yet green-apple fresh. However, it has to compete with Trebbiano Toscano in cheaper blends, and often loses. Good producers use Trebbiano di Soave, which is much better.

**GEWÜRZTRAMINER** Although this is supposed to have originated in the Alto Adige (Südtirol) village of Tramin, most of the plantings there now are of the red Traminer, rather than the spicier, more memorable Gewürztraminer of Alsace. Gewürztraminer can be lovely, needing some time in bottle to develop perfume.

**GRECO/GRECHETTO** An ancient variety introduced to southern Italy by the Greeks, it makes crisp, pale and refreshing wines with lightly spicy overtones in Calabria and Campania and, as Grecanico, in Sicily. Grechetto is part of the same family and its delicious, nutty, aniseed character adds dramatically to Trebbiano-dominated blends in central Italy (Orvieto benefits significantly) as well as sometimes surfacing under its own colours in Umbria where *Adanti* makes a splendid version.

**MALVASIA** This name and the related Malvoisie seems to apply to a range of grapes, some not related. Malvasia is most consistently found in Tuscany, Umbria and Latium, where it gives a full, creamy nuttiness to dry whites like Frascati. It also produces brilliant, rich dessert wines with the density of thick brown-sugar syrup and the sweetness of raisins, in Sardinia and the island of Lipari north of Sicily.

**MOSCATO** The Alto Adige (Südtirol) grows various kinds of Muscat, including the delicious Rosenmuskateller and Goldmuskateller, making dry wines to equal the Muscats of Alsace and sweet wines of unrivalled fragrance. But it is at its best in Piedmont, where Asti Spumante is a delicious, grapy, sweetish fizz and Moscato Naturale is a heartily-perfumed sweet wine, full of the fragrance of grapes, honey, apples and unsmoked cigars. Best drunk young, though *Ivaldi*'s Passito from Strevi can age beautifully. Also fine dessert wines on Pantelleria, south of Sicily.

**MÜLLER-THURGAU** A soft, perfumy workhorse grape in Germany, but on the high, steep Alpine vineyards of the Alto Adige it produces glacier-fresh flavours; not bad in Trentino and Friuli either.

**PINOT BIANCO** Produces some of its purest, honeyed flavours in the Alto Adige (Südtirol), and can do very well in Friuli where the best are buttery and full.

**RHEINRIESLING/RIESLING RENANO** The true German Riesling is grown in the Alto Adige (Südtirol), making sharp, green, refreshing, steely dry wines – as good as most Mosel or Rhine Kabinett in Germany. It can be OK, and slightly fatter, in Friuli and Lombardy. Riesling Italico, nothing to do with real Riesling, is the dreaded Olasz/ Laski/Welsch Rizling, which so despoils Riesling's name across Eastern Europe.

**SAUVIGNON BLANC** Quite common in the North, and gives some acid bite to far-southern blends like Sicily's Regaleali. It can be spicy, grassy and refreshing from the Alto Adige and Friuli, though the style is usually more subtle than New World Sauvignon. *Volpaia* and *Castellare* have started making it in Chianti land as have *Banfi* in Montalcino; others will follow.

**SYLVANER** Grown very high in the northern valleys of the Alto Adige, at its best this can be chillingly dry, lemon-crisp and quite delicious. But there are still quite a few fat, muddy examples around.

**TREBBIANO** The widely-planted Trebbiano Toscano is a wretched thing, easy to grow, producing vast quantities of grapes with frightening efficiency. It is responsible for an awful lot of fruitless, oxidized, sulphured blaagh-ness. However, attempts to pick it early and vinify it sharp and fresh are having some effect, and at least its use in red, yes *red* Chianti is now severely restricted. Trebbiano di Soave, the Veneto clone, is much better. Lugana is a Trebbiano DOC of character (*Zenato's* is widely available and good). Abruzzi has a different strain again which *can* be tasty from producers like *Tenuta del Priore, Pepe* and *Valentini*.

**VERNACCIA** There are several types of Vernaccia – including some red – but we mostly just see two. Vernaccia di Oristano in Sardinia is a sort of Italian version of sherry, best dry – when it has a marvellous mix of floral scents, nutty weight and taunting sourness – but also medium and sweet. Vernaccia di San Gimignano *can* be Tuscany's best traditional white – full, golden, peppery but with a softness of hazelnuts and angelica. *Fagiuoli, Teruzzi & Puthod*, and *Sainsbury's* own-label show what can be done. Some producers have tried putting it in *barrique*, but so far *Teruzzi e Puthod is* the only one to understand that you need an abundance of fruit in order to balance the oak.

# WINES & WINE REGIONS

## ALBANA DI ROMAGNA, DOCG
(Emilia-Romagna) I resent putting DOCG against this uninspiring white, which some not particularly cynical people say was awarded DOCG *a* because they were the first to apply, *b* because they *had* to have a white DOCG and all the others were too frightful to contemplate and *c* because the local politicos in Bologna have a lot of clout. What's the wine like? Well, it's dry or sweet; still or slightly fizzy, or very fizzy; you see what I mean. At least these days it's less likely to be oxidized and, at its best, the dry version can be delicately scented with an almondy finish. The only really decent producer is *Fattoria Paradiso*.

## ALTO ADIGE, various DOC
The locals up here by the Austrian border answer more warmly to *grüss Gott* than to *buon giorno* so this area is often referred to as Südtirol. Wines from these dizzily steep slopes are much more Germanic than Italian. Most are red, but this is one of Italy's most successful white regions, making a higher percentage of DOCs than any other. The wines are light, dry and intensely fresh, with spice and plenty of fruit – qualities that become progressively rarer as you head south into the heart of Italy. The best come from *Tiefenbrunner* who specializes in an uplifting, aromatic German style and *Lageder* who makes fuller, rounder wines. Both are now experimenting with barrel maturation – to good effect. Also *Hofstätter*, *Schloss Schwanburg*, *Walch* and *Terlan*, *Schreckbichl* and *St Michael-Eppan* co-ops.

## ARNEIS
(Piedmont) Potentially stunning, apples-pears-and-liquorice-flavoured wines from an ancient white grape of the same name, with high prices to match – but since there's a feel of ripe white Burgundy about the best of them, that's not such a turn-off.

---

### CENTRAL ITALY VINTAGES

**1991** In Tuscany, early frosts and rain caused problems; small but heathy grapes were harvested and outstanding wines seem likely, including excellent Brunello. There will be few *riserva*, however. Drought reduced the yield in some places. Red and white Torgiano from Lungarotti should be very good, from elevated sites that escaped the frost. The Marches overall look good.

**1990** Already being hailed as one of the greatest vintages in living memory in Tuscany. Following a warm and dry summer, the early harvest yielded deeply-coloured wine of tremendous perfume. The wines will be rich, strong and built to last.

**1989** The spring was good, but in the summer the sun stopped shining, the rains came and the maturation of the grapes slowed to a snail's pace. The sun returned in the first week of October. Producers who had the courage to interrupt the harvest and wait for another week will have made the best wines.

**1988** 'Condition of grapes absolutely bloody marvellous ... Wow! Anyone who can't make good wines this year ought to give up wine-making completely!' Better than '85? Many think so. Reds in particular looking exciting, though some are disappointing at this stage.

**1987** Reasonable reds such as Carmignano and nice young Chiantis.

**1986** Some people are now rating 1986 Chianti Riserva more highly than the 1985s. Those who broke the law in Montalcino and bottled early will have produced the best wines.

**1985** Hardly a drop of rain from the Lords Test to the end of the season in September, so some of the wines are positively rich, but this vintage shows what DOCG is made of.

**1983** In Chianti, the best '83s have aged well and are better balanced than the '82s.

Unfortunately it is trendy so some may bear the name and not much more. *Arneis di Montebertotto, Castello di Neive* is intense yet subtle. *Bruno Giacosa's* softer, sweeter one has a taste of hops. *Deltetto, Malvirà, Negro, Vietti, Voerzio* are good.

**ASTI SPUMANTE, DOC** (Piedmont) It's difficult to believe that this frothy, crunchy, fruit-bursting sweet fizzy wine is made next door to beetle-browed Nebbiolo giants like Barolo and Barbaresco. Indeed, some producers make both! It's snobbery that defeats this wine, because it is absurdly delicious, with a magical, grapy freshness, and it's ultra-reliable – a poor Asti is difficult to find. It should be drunk very young. *Fontanafredda, Gancia, Martini* and *Riccadonna* are good, as are *Vignaioli di Santo Stefano* and *Duca d'Asti*.

**BIANCO DI CUSTOZA, DOC** (Veneto) Thought of as a Soave look-alike, but recent improvements in Soave make me wonder if Soave isn't a Bianco di Custoza look-alike. It contains Tocai, Cortese and Garganega, as well as Trebbiano, which helps. But the lack of pressure to produce any old liquid at the lowest possible price must be as important. *Gorgo, Portalupi, Santa Sofia, Tedeschi, Le Tende, Le Vigne di San Pietro* and *Zenato* are good.

**CORTESE DI GAVI, DOC** (Piedmont) Cortese is the grape, Gavi is the area in south-east Piedmont. The wine is dry and sharp, like a Sauvignon without the tang, and fairly full, like a Chardonnay without the class. So it should be a refreshing, straight-up gulper at a pocket-easy price. But restaurant chic in Italy coos over it. The only ones I've enjoyed at a reasonable price have been the fresh *Deltetto* and *Arione*, and the atypical but exciting oaked *Gavi Fior di Rovere* from *Chiarlo*.

**ERBALUCE DI CALUSO, DOC** (Piedmont) Half the price of Gavi, with a soft, creamy flavour. Clean-living, plumped-out, affordable white. *Boratto, Ferrando*

and *Marbelli* are good; *Boratto* also makes a rich but refreshing *Caluso Passito*.

**FIANO DI AVELLINO, DOC** (Campania) After numerous attempts to stomach this inexplicably famous wine from near Naples I got hold of a bottle of Mastroberardino's single-vineyard *Fiano di Avellino Vignadora* and found a brilliant spring flowers scent and honey, peaches and pear skins taste. But it may have been a flash in the pan.

**FRASCATI, DOC** (Latium) True Frascati remains a mirage: most relies on bland Trebbiano or is spoilt by mass production. But with enough Malvasia to swamp the Trebbiano and careful wine-making, it has a lovely, fresh, nutty feel with an unusual, attractive tang of slightly sour cream. Antonio Pulcini is way ahead with *Colli di Catone, Villa Catone* and *Villa Romana;* his *cru Colle Gaio* is very special. *Fontana Candida's* limited releases are also good.

**FRIULI, some DOC** Some very good fruity and fresh whites from up by the Yugoslav border in the North-East. There's above-average Pinot Bianco, good Pinot Grigio, Chardonnay, better Gewürz, Müller-Thurgau, Riesling Renano, Ribolla and Sauvignon, and the brilliantly nutty and aromatic white Tocai, all capturing the fresh fruit of the varietal for quick, happy-faced drinking. Prices are generally in the mid- to upper range, but they are good value, especially from names like *Abbazia di Rosazzo, Attems, Borgo Conventi, Villa Russiz, Collavini, Dri, EnoFriulia,Volpe, Gravner, Jermann, Livio Felluga, Puiatti, Ronchi di Cialla, Schioppetto, Pasini*. Of the big names *Collavini* is best, but getting pricy. The almost mythical Picolit sweet wine is beautifully made by *Al Rusignul* – the *only* producer I've ever found who took this difficult grape variety seriously.

**GALESTRO, DOC** (Tuscany) Created to mop up the Trebbiano and Malvasia no longer used in red Chianti. Low alcohol, lemony, greengage taste, high-tech style.

**GAVI, DOC** (Piedmont) (See *Cortese di Gavi*.) Grossly overpriced, clean, appley white from Piedmont. If it's labelled Gavi dei Gavi, double the number you thought of and add the price of your train fare home: Waterloo-to-Woking for some of the more sensible wine shops, King's Cross-to-Edinburgh for the more poncy restaurants.

**LACRYMA CHRISTI DEL VESUVIO, DOC** (Campania) The most famous wine of Campania and Naples. It can be red or white, dry or sweet: *Mastroberardino's* is good, I'm told, but otherwise, if you find a half-decent one, let me know.

**MOSCATO D'ASTI, DOC** (Piedmont) Celestial mouthwash! Sweet, slightly fizzy wine that captures all the crunchy green freshness of a fistful of ripe table-grapes, with spiciness and richness, too. Heavenly ones from *Ascheri, Dogliotti, Gatti, Bruno Giacosa, I Vignaioli di Santo Stefano, Michele Chiarlo, Rivetti* and *Vietti. Gallo d'Oro* is the most widely available here.

**ORVIETO, DOC** (Umbria) Umbria's most famous wine, grown bang in the centre of Italy, has shaken off its old, semi-sweet, yellow-gold image and emerged less dowdy and rather slick and anonymous – but just right to benefit from the boom in light whites. It used to be slightly sweet, rich, smoky and honeyed from the Grechetto and Malvasia grapes. Its modern, pale, very dry style owes more to the feckless Trebbiano. I must say I'm looking forward to Orvieto getting back to its golden days and there are signs that good producers are starting to make this happen. *Scambia* is lovely, peach-perfumed wine and *Barberani* and *Palazzone* are even better. *Decugnano dei Barbi* is good, while exciting wines, full, fragrant, soft and honeyed, come from *Bigi*, whose *Cru Torricella Secco* and *Cru Orzalume Amabile* (medium-sweet) are exceptional and not expensive. *Antinori's* is a typical over-modern, under-flavoured dry, though its medium is delicious, and a new Chardonnay, Grechetto, Malvasia and Trebbiano *vino da tavola* called *Cervaro della Sala* is outstanding. Sweet, unctuous, noble-rot affected wines (*Antinori's Muffato della Sala* and *Barberani's Calcaia*) are rarely seen but delicious.

**PROSECCO,** some **DOC** (Veneto) Either still or sparkling, a lovely fresh, bouncy, light white, often off-dry, at its best from the neighbourhoods of Conegliano and Valdobbiadene. *Sainsbury's* does a typical easy-going crowd-pleaser; also *Canevel, Le Case Bianche, Carpené Malvolti, Collavini.*

**SOAVE, DOC** (Veneto) At last turning from the tasteless, fruitless, profitless mass-market bargain basement to show as an attractive, soft, fairly-priced white. The turn-around in the last few years has been quite amazing. More often than not now an own-label Soave from a good shop will be pleasant, soft, slightly nutty, even creamy. Drink it as young as possible. *Tadiello, Pasqua, Bertani* and *Zenato* are supplying a lot of the decent basic stuff. On a higher level *Anselmi* is outstanding (try *Capitel Foscarino*) and *Pieropan*, especially single-vineyard wines *La Rocca* and *Calvarino*, is very good, if expensive. Other good ones are *Boscaini, Zenato, Costalunga, Bolla's Castellaro, Santi's Monte Carbonare, Tedeschi's Monte Tenda* and the local co-op's *Costalta. Anselmi* also makes a *Recioto di Soave dei Capitelli* which is shockingly good in its sweet-sour way, and *Pieropan's* unoaked *Recioto* is redolent of apricots.

**TOCAI, DOC** (Friuli) Full, aromatic, sometimes copper-tinged, sometimes clear as water, this grape makes lovely, mildly-floral and softly nutty, honeyed wines in Friuli, as well as increasingly good wines in the Veneto. Best: *Abbazia di Rosazzo, Borgo Conventi, Cà Bolani, Livio Felluga,*

> *Webster's* is an annual publication. We welcome your suggestions for next year's edition.

*Caccese, Collavini, Lazzarini, Maculan, Schiopetto, Villa Russiz, Volpe Pasini.*

**TRENTINO, DOC** This northern region, below Alto Adige, can make some of Italy's best Pinot Bianco and Chardonnay, as well as some interesting whites from Riesling, Müller-Thurgau and excellent dry Muscat. But until they stop grossly over-producing we're never going to see the full potential. The tastiest come from the mountainous bit north of the town of Trento. Look especially for *Conti Martini, Gaierhof, Istituto di San Michele, Mandelli, Pojer e Sandri, Spagnolli* and *Zeni.* Trentino also makes fizz from Chardonnay and Pinot Bianco ( *Ferrari* and *Equipe 5),* and fair Vino Santo (equivalent to Tuscan dessert wines) comes from *Pisoni* and *Simoncelli.*

**VERDICCHIO, DOC** (Marches) Of Italy's numerous whites, only Soave makes more than Verdicchio. It comes from the grape of the same name (with a little Trebbiano and Malvasia) on the east coast opposite Florence and Siena. The wines are reliable rather than exciting – usually extremely dry, lean, clean, nutty with a streak of dry honey, sharpened by slightly green acidity.

Occasionally you find fatter styles, and *Fazi-Battaglia's* single vineyard *vino da tavola Le Moie* shows the the area's potential. There is also a Verdicchio fizz. The two leading areas are Verdicchio dei Castelli di Jesi and Verdicchio di Matelica. The rarer Matelica wines often have more flavour. Good producers: *Brunori, Bucci, Fabrini, Fazi-Battaglia, Garofoli, Mecvini, Monte Schiavo, Umani Ronchi, Zaccagnini.*

**VERDUZZO, DOC** (Friuli and Veneto) Usually a soft, nutty, low acid yet refreshing light white. It also makes a lovely, gentle fizz, and in Friuli Colli Orientali some of Italy's best sweet wines, in particular *Dri's Verduzzo di Ramandolo* and *Abbazia di Rosazzo's Amabile.*

**VERNACCIA DI SAN GIMIGNANO, DOC** (Tuscany) This can be full, nutty, honeyed wine, slightly lanoliny in the mouth and perhaps with a hint of pepper. These are the good versions. Too much Vernaccia has had all the guts stripped out of it in the headlong pursuit of bland neutrality. *Frigeni, Fagiuoli, Falchini, San Quirico, Teruzzi & Puthod* and *La Torre* show what can be done.

---

### NORTH-EAST ITALY VINTAGES

**1991** Rain came at the right time in Veneto, so it is blessing its good fortune: good quality and yields up by 20 per cent were the happy result. It was a more difficult year in Trentino-Alto-Adige, though, but there were some fine whites and scattered good, if less imposing reds. Some excellent reds and elegant whites were made in Friuli, but these were down in quantity.

**1990** This vintage is already being compared with the legendary 1964. Crop levels were down in quantity, but a hot, dry summer was followed by an early harvest of superb quality. Friuli too fared extremely well. The best wines show impressive balance and concentration.

**1989** Cool weather was good for the whites, and meant more aromatic wines; the reds, though, were less concentrated.

**1988** The quantity was reduced this year, but the quality was tremendous, in particular for reds. There was some hail, however – which won't affect the good producers who made careful selections.

**1986** The year provided a good, balanced vintage, but there was too much overproduction for it to be exciting. The good news was that it was superb for Amarone and not bad for Ripasso Valpolicella.

# FORTIFIED WINES

The best known Italian fortified wine is Marsala from Sicily. The good examples may be sweet or dryish and have a nutty, smoky character which can be delicious. The off-shore island of Pantelleria produces Moscato which can be even better. Sardinia is strong on fortified wines, particularly from the Cannonau (or Grenache) grape. In general, however, the rich, dessert wines of Italy are made from overripe or even raisined grapes, without fortification.

**MARSALA** This Sicilian wine has, at its best, a delicious, deep brown-sugar sweetness allied to a cutting, lip-tingling acidity that makes it surprisingly refreshing for a fortified dessert wine. The rare Marsala Vergine is also good – very dry, lacking the tremendous concentration of deep, brown texture that makes an old *oloroso seco* sherry or a Sercial Madeira so exciting, but definitely going along the same track. But a once great name is now also seen on bottles of 'egg marsala' and the like. A few good producers keep the flag flying; *De Bartoli* outclasses all the rest, and even makes an intense, beautifully aged, but *unfortified* non-DOC range called *Vecchio Samperi*. His *Josephine Dore* is in the style of *fino* sherry.

**MOSCATO PASSITO DI PANTELLERIA** From an island closer to Tunisia than Sicily, a big, heavy wine with a great wodge of rich Muscat fruit and a good slap of alcoholic strength.

**VIN SANTO** Holy Wine? Well, I wouldn't be too pleased with these if I were the Almighty because too much *vin santo* is vaguely raisiny and very dull. It *should* have all kinds of splendid, rich fruit flavours – apricots, apples, the richness of ripe grape skins, the chewiness of toffee, smoke and liquorice. But it's sadly rare and only *Isole e Olena* has provided me with this thrill so far. If you can't get a bottle of that try *La Calonica* or *Avignonesi* in Tuscany or *Adanti* in Umbria.

# VINI DA TAVOLA

If I want to find out how exciting the wines can be from the Tuscan hills, I might buy a bottle of Sammarco, or Tignanello, Balifico or Vinattieri. Barolo is the famous name of Piedmont, but I can still learn about the region's capabilities if I get a bottle of Il Favot or Vigna Arborina. I'm tired of feeble Valpolicella, but if I get a bottle of Campo Fiorin or Capitel San Rocco, they might show me why the region used once to be famous.

All these wines have one thing in common – they are not sold with the DOC or DOCG of the area concerned. That none of these wines – and numerous other exciting taste experiences – like Spanna, Moscato di Strevi, Torcolato, Anghelu Ruju, Cuccanea – is produced according to the DOC is a heavy indictment of the present Italian wine regulations. The new law has arrived none too soon. No-one doubts that when the laws were drawn up in 1963 there was a desperate need for them, since Italian wine was rapidly sliding into an abyss. There weren't many wine-makers left who clung to quality and when it came to formulating the rules, they were outnumbered by those who neither cared about nor understood the true potential of their wines. Local politics and laziness triumphed

One option for a small but determined band of wine-makers who cared passionately about quality, was to confront the DOC regulations head-on and say, 'If you force mediocrity on us with your wretched laws then we shall operate outside the law'. Cabernet, Chardonnay and French oak barrels were soon all the rage. But the dust is now settling and the 'me too' philosophy appears to have run its course. In Piedmont, only Chardonnay seems to have a certain future, though *barriques* may have arrived to stay. Angelo Gaja, who led the revolt there, is the first to concede that his world-class Cabernet Sauvignon Darmagi serves mainly to focus attention back on his Barbaresco. The Piedmontese have an unflinching belief in their own red grape varieties and the other wine-makers who took the *vino da tavola* route did so to demonstrate their dissatisfaction with what they saw as the excessive minimum barrel ageing required by the law.

The major complaint for many Tuscans however focused on the grape varieties required by law. At first they saw Cabernet as their salvation. Antinori's Tignanello showed that careful techniques can make great wine out of Cabernet/Sangiovese blends and several top 'super' *vini da tavola* are still made from these. In turn this has given rise to a determination to make great wines solely from Sangiovese. Both styles are usually far more exciting than traditional Chianti. For some reason in England we call them the Super-Tuscans.

The new wine law, which will be coming into effect over the next few years, should build these 'Super-Tuscans' into the system. At the same time, high production figures are likely to become more and more unusual as the new EC viticultural programme for uprooting vines in undesirable areas takes effect. What's more, producers in DOC zones have been warned that future requests to raise yields are likely to be refused. If these plans come to fruition, there could be a serious danger that Italy, at long last, might be about to get it right.

## SANGIOVESE AND CABERNET SAUVIGNON

**ALTE D'ALTESI** A 30 per cent Cabernet Sauvignon, 70 per cent Sangiovese blend from Altesino, aged for about a year in new *barrique;* first made in 1985. The '86 has good colour, fruit, firmness and elegance.

**BALIFICO** Volpaia's 'special', two-thirds Sangiovese, one-third Cabernet Sauvignon aged for 16 months in French oak. Exciting, exotic, oaky-rich wine, rather French in its youth, more Tuscan as it ages.

**CABREO IL BORGO** From Ruffino in Tuscany, vervy wines with variegated flavours: blackcurrants one moment, raspberries and brambles the next.

**CA' DEL PAZZO** Brunello and Cabernet from Caparzo in Montalcino. Powerful wine behind juicy blackcurrant and vanilla oak.

**GRIFI** Avignonesi's Sangiovese/Cabernet Franc blend. It's cedary and spicily rich but lacks the class of Grifi's Vino Nobile di Montepulciano. The '85 is the best yet.

**SAMMARCO** Castello dei Rampolla's blend of 75 per cent Cabernet Sauvignon, 25 per cent Sangiovese. Magnificently blackcurranty, Sammarco is built to last.

**TIGNANELLO** The original super-Tuscan. First made in 1971 by Antinori, when it was Canaiolo, Sangiovese and Malvasia, it is now about 80 per cent Sangiovese and 20 per cent Cabernet Sauvignon. In the late 1970s it set standards that the others could only aspire to. 1982 is rather dull, '85 seems back on form, at a fiendish price.

## CABERNET SAUVIGNON

**CARANTAN** Merlot with both Cabernets , this, from Marco Felluga in Friuli, is big, savoury and tannic. The 1988 still has to come together, but shows terrific promise.

**GHIAIE DELLA FURBA** Made at Villa di Capezzana from roughly equal parts of both

Cabernets and Merlot, and more convincing each vintage. 1981 is at its blackcurrant peak now. The '83 is even better; the '85 is one of the best of this excellent vintage.

**MAURIZIO ZANELLA** Both Cabernets and Merlot, from Ca' del Bosco in Lombardy. Expensive but impressive, with roasted, smoky fruit. The '88 is potentially the best, with '89 and '87 not far behind.

**SASSICAIA** Cabernet (Sauvignon and Franc) from Bolgheri, south-east of Livorno, it has an intense Cabernet character but a higher acidity and slightly leaner profile than most New World Cabernets. It needs about eight to ten years to begin to show at its best; '68 was the first vintage, and remains, with '72 and '82, one of the best, but '85 is also supremely good.

**SOLAIA** Piero Antinori's attempt to match Sassicaia. A blend of 80 per cent Cabernet Sauvignon and 20 per cent Sangiovese. Sassicaia beats it for beauty of flavour but Solaia does have tremendous rich fruit and a truly Tuscan bitterness to balance.

**TAVERNELLE** Villa Banfi's 100 per cent Cabernet from young vines at Montalcino. It has good style and varietal character.

### SANGIOVESE

**CEPPARELLO** Very fruity rich wine from Isole e Olena, the oak beautifully blended: one of the leaders of the super-Sangioveses.

**COLTASSALA** Castello di Volpaia's Sangiovese/Mammolo blend, leaner and less rich than most; lovely, austere wine, needing time to soften and blossom.

**FLACCIANELLO DELLA PIEVE**
Fontodi's Sangiovese, aged in *barrique* and with a little *governo* used. Cedary, tightly grained fruit, oak and elegance.

**FONTALLORO** 100 per cent Sangiovese from Felsina Berardenga, fatter and richer

than the Flaccianello, with a spicy rather than a cedary oak character, which takes a long time to come out of its tannic shell.

**IL SODACCIO** 85 per cent Sangiovese, 15 per cent Canaiolo from Monte Vertine. It could have been a Chianti, but was too oaky when young. Elegant; drink young.

**I SODI DI SAN NICCOLÒ** One of the most distinctive of the new-wave wines first made in the late seventies. A little rare Malvasia Nera alongside Sangiovese adds a wonderfully sweet and floral perfume.

**LE PERGOLE TORTE** From Monte Vertine, the first of the 100 per cent Sangiovese, *barrique*-aged wines. Its success paved the way for others. It is intensely tannic and oaky when young, and needs at least five years to open up.

**PALAZZO ALTESI** 100 per cent Brunello, aged for about 14 months in new *barrique* at Altesino in Montalcino, packed with a delicious fruit and oakiness, and though it needs five years to develop and display its full splendour, its brilliant blackberry fruit makes it drinkable much younger.

**SANGIOVETO** Made from carefully selected old vines (about 40 years old) at Badia a Coltibuono in Chianti Classico. Yields are minute (15 to 20 hectolitres per hectare) giving tremendous concentration.

**VINATTIERI ROSSO** *Barrique*-aged blend of Sangiovese from Chianti Classico and Brunello, getting better each vintage, with the 1985 showing the superb rich Sangiovese fruit and sweet oak of the best of the 'New Classics' in Tuscany.

### WHITES
**CHARDONNAY** In Umbria, Antinori's *Cervaro della Sala* combines Chardonnay with Grechetto for extra-rich fruit and oak. Felsina Berardenga's *I Sistri* is fresh, zingy and grapy with an ice-cream core; Ruffino's *Cabreo La Pietra* is succulent and oaky.

# TUSCAN WINERY PROFILES

## MONTALCINO

**ALTESINO** Resurrected by Milanese money in the 1970s and now making excellent Brunello di Montalcino, Palazzo Altesi, a Sangiovese partially vinified by carbonic maceration, and Alte d'Altesi, 70 per cent Cabernet Sauvignon and 30 per cent Sangiovese.

**BANFI** Oenologist Ezio Rivella's space-age winery in the hills of Montalcino, created with the money of the Mariani brothers, who brought Lambrusco to the USA. Wines include: Brunello di Montalcino, Pinot Grigio, Fontanelle Chardonnay, Sauvignon, Tavernelle Cabernet Sauvignon; Castello Banfi, a blend of Pinot Noir, Cabernet Sauvignon and Sangiovese, and Moscadello Liquoroso. New versions of Pinot Noir and Syrah are due to be released in the near future. The Banfi Spumante is one of Italy's best.

**BIONDI SANTI** A legendary family making a fabulously priced, but not necessarily legendary wine; however there are indications that quality is improving again, with some modernization in the cellars of its Il Greppo estate. 1988 saw its celebration of the centenary of Brunello di Montalcino.

**CAPARZO** is one of the new wave of Montalcino estates; investment from Milan has turned it into a serious wine producer of not only Brunello and Rosso di Montalcino, but also oak-fermented Chardonnay called Le Grance, and Ca' del Pazzo, a barrel-aged blend of Cabernet Sauvignon and Sangiovese.

**FATTORIA DEI BARBI** is owned by one of the old Montalcinese families, the Colombinis. Traditional methods produce serious Brunello and Rosso di Montalcino, as well as Brusco dei Barbi, and a single-vineyard wine, Vigna Fiore.

## MONTEPULCIANO

**AVIGNONESI** An old Montepulciano family, but a relative newcomer to the ranks of serious producers of Vino Nobile, also two excellent Chardonnays: Terre di Cortona, without oak, and Il Marzocco, oak-fermented and aged wine of considerable depth. I Grifi is a barrel-aged blend of Prugnolo and Cabernet Franc.

**FATTORIA DEL CERRO** Traditional producers of Vino Nobile now experimenting with *barriques*. Its best wine remains the DOCG Vino Nobile: both 1985 and '86 were excellent and '88 will be even better.

## VERNACCIA DI SAN GIMIGNANO

**TERUZZI & PUTHOD** Commonly acknowledged to be the best producers of Vernaccia di San Gimignano. Most expensive is the oak-aged Terre di Tufo. Also Chianti Colli Senesi and Galestro.

## CHIANTI

**ANTINORI** is indisputably one of the great names of Chianti, boasting 600 years of wine-making. Not only does it make excellent Chianti Classico from its estates Peppoli and Badia a Passignano, but it initiated the moves towards modern wine-making in Tuscany, with the development of wines like Tignanello, which is the archetypal *barrique*-aged Sangiovese, Cabernet blend. Its Orvieto estate, Castello della Sala, is the source of exciting experiments with white grapes.

**BADIA A COLTIBUONO** A twelfth-century abbey that now belongs to the Stucchi family, and with the help of expert oenologist, Maurizio Castelli, it makes excellent Chianti, as well as a pure Sangiovese, called Sangioveto.

**CASTELLO DI AMA** Excellent single-vineyard Chianti Classico: San Lorenzo, La

Casuccia, Bellavista; also a Merlot that had critics raving in 1990. Promising Chardonnay and Pinot Grigio.

**FELSINA BERARDENGA** Winery very much on the up. Vigneto Rancia is a single-vineyard Chianti, I Sistri a *barrique*-aged Chardonnay. Fontalloro is a Sangiovese, aged in *barrique* for 12 months.

**FRESCOBALDI** The best Frescobaldi estate is Castello di Nipozzano, with a special selection Montesodi, from Chianti Rufina. It is also the producer of some excellent Pomino, including an oak-aged white, Il Benefizio. It also manages the Castelgiocondo estate further south near Montalcino, where it makes Brunello and a good white wine under the new Predicato label. Mormoreto is a fine, Cabernet-style red.

**ISOLE E OLENA** is rapidly increasing a reputation for fine Chianti Classico. Also Cepparello, a rich pure Sangiovese wine, made from the oldest vines of the estate; outstanding *vin santo* and a superb varietal Syrah.

**RICASOLI** As well as sound Chianti, Brolio makes a host of other Tuscan wines.

**RUFFINO** One of the largest producers of Chianti. Riserva Ducale is its best wine.

# PIEDMONT WINERY PROFILES

**ABBAZIA DELL'ANNUNZIATA** (Barolo, La Morra) One of the greats. Wines made by nephew Massimo Martinelli and his son Pietro since Ratti's death in 1988. All the wines are full of excitement, strongly perfumed and develop wonderfully.

**ELIO ALTARE** (Barolo, La Morra) New wave producer – wines of firm structure and tannin behind perfumed fruit. Highly successful 1984 Barolo. Very good Barbera and Dolcetto and *barrique*-aged Barbera Vigna Larigi and Nebbiolo Vigna Arborina.

**BRAIDA DI GIACOMO BOLOGNA** (Rochetta Tanaro) Saw early the potential of Barbera in *barrique*: *cru* Bricco dell' Uccellone continues to impress with depth, balance and richness. An equally good Bricco della Bigotta. Unoaked, youthful Barbera, La Monella. Good Moscato d'Asti and sweetish Brachetto d'Acqui.

**CASTELLO DI NEIVE** (Barbaresco, Neive) Impeccable, finely crafted, austerely elegant Barbaresco from Santo Stefano. *Barriqued* Barbera from *cru* Mattarello and firm, classic Dolcetto from three sites topped by Basarin. Revelatory Arneis.

**CERETTO** Known for both Barolo and Barbaresco. Barolo Bricco Rocche Bricco Rocche (yes) and Barbaresco Bricco Asili are legendary with prices to match. Also Barolos Brunate, Prapo, Zonchera, and Faset in Barbaresco. Light Barbera and Dolcetto. Arneis is disappointing.

**CLERICO** (Barolo, Monforte) Top-notch producer using *barrique* to fine effect in Nebbiolo/Barbera blend Arte. Barolo from two *crus* (Bricotto Bussia, Ciabot Mentin Ginestra) are among the best moderns.

**ALDO CONTERNO** (Barolo, Monforte) Great Barolo, traditionally made, slow to mature but worth the wait. Bussia Soprana is very special, Cicala and Colonello quite remarkable. Gran Bussia is made from selected grapes in the best years only. Il Favot (*barrique*-aged Nebbiolo), powerful Barbera, Dolcetto and Freisa also good.

**CONTERNO FANTINO** (Barolo Monforte) Although they only began bottling wine in 1982, Guido Fantino and Diego Conterno have already earned a reputation for fine Barolo from the Ginestra hillside. Rich but forward, perfumed wines, should age well.

**CARLO DELTETTO** (Roero, Canale) Good understated, intriguing whites from Arneis and Favorita. Reliable Roero and Gavi.

**ANGELO GAJA** (Barbaresco, Barbaresco) Uses *barriques* for most wines, including all Barbarescos: Costa Russi, Sori San Lorenzo, Sori Tildin. In vanguard of Piedmontese Cabernet (Darmagi) and Chardonnay (Gaia and Rey) production. Two Barberas (straight and *cru* Vignarey), two Dolcettos (straight and *cru* Vignabajla), Freisa and Nebbiolo also produced.

**BRUNO GIACOSA** (Barbaresco, Neive) Traditional wines of, at their best, mind-blowing quality, especially Barbaresco *cru* Santo Stefano and, best of all, Barolo from Serralunga's Vigna Rionda. Outstanding wines: rich, concentrated not overbearing yet elegant. Also a white Arneis and a highly rated fizz.

**MARCHESI DI GRESY** (Barbaresco, Barbaresco) The leading site, Martinenga, produces Barbaresco, two *crus* – Camp Gros and Gaiun, and a non-wood aged Nebbiolo called Martinenga. Elegant wines; fine '85s.

**GIUSEPPE MASCARELLO** (Barolo, Castiglione Falletto) Outstanding *cru* Monprivato at Castiglione Falletto. Also Villero from the same commune and other *crus* from bought-in grapes. Barbera d'Alba Ginestra and Dolcetto d'Alba Gagliassi are notable. Good '84 Barolo in a difficult year.

**PAOLO CORDERO DI MONTEZEMOLO** (Barolo, La Morra) Wines with the accent on fruit. Standard-bearer is *cru* Monfalletto from La Morra; for some the holy of holies. *Cru* Enrico VI is from Castiglione Falletto, refined, elegant scented. Barbera, Dolcetto etc also made.

**FRATELLI ODDERO** (Barolo, La Morra) Barolo, Barbera, Dolcetto etc from own vineyards in prime sites in the area and Barbaresco from bought-in grapes. Wines of good roundness, balance, style, value.

**PIO CESARE** (Barolo, Alba) Full spread of Barolo, Barbaresco, Nebbiolo d'Alba, Dolcetto, Barbera, Grignolino and Gavi. Wines are gaining elegance, losing a bit of punch but gaining harmony and balance. Experiments with *barriques*; also Nebbio (young-drinking Nebbiolo), Piodilei (*barriqued* Chardonnay).

**GIUSEPPE RIVETTI** (Asti, Castagnole Lanze) Smallish quantities of magical Moscato d'Asti which sell out in a flash.

**LUCIANO SANDRONE** (Barolo, Barolo) A small producer making tiny quantities of perfumed Barolo with lovely raspberry and black cherry flavours from the Cannubi-Boschis vineyard. Also excellent Dolcetto.

**PAOLO SCAVINO** (Barolo, Castiglione Falletto) Hailed locally as one of the emerging masters of Barolo, Enrico Scavino (the current owner) makes superb wines which combine purity of fruit with the depth and structure of low vineyard yields. Barolo Bric' del Fiasc' is his top wine; Cannubi and straight Barolo are not far behind. Delicious Dolcetto and Barbera.

**VIETTI** (Barolo, Castiglione Falletto) Goes from strength to strength. Classically perfect wines of their type, with a punch of acidity and tannin, plus elegance and class. Barolo (straight plus *crus* Rocche, Villero and Brunate) and Barbaresco (*normale* plus *crus* Masseria, Rabajà) are intensely complex wines. Dolcetto and Barbera also very good. Also one of the top Moscato d'Astis. Highly enjoyable Arneis.

**ROBERTO VOERZIO** (Barolo, La Morra) Ultra-modern approach. Attractive and fine wines, full of fruit and perfume, made with great skill, giving Roberto (not to be confused with brother Gianni) the reputation as an up and coming great. Produces Barolo, Dolcetto d'Alba, Barbera d'Alba, Freisa, and delicious *barrique*-aged Barbera/Nebbiolo blend Vignaserra, as well as fine Arneis.

# SPAIN

'I went to Spain just before Christmas,' said a buyer for a high street chain, 'expecting the same old thing.' By which he meant that not much would be happening outside Rioja. Producers all over Spain, selling their wines easily in the restaurants and bars of Madrid and Barcelona, would not give a monkey's about a foreigner complaining about oxidation and prattling on about terrific wines he had tasted from some place called Australia. 'If you don't like the wine,' they might grunt, 'why bother to poke your nose round the door?'

'But this time,' he said, 'I got a surprise.' He reeled off a list of crisp dry whites and fruity young reds, scarcely able to believe it. Spain, he had found, is changing.

Not before time, perhaps. From a distance, it has always been easy to see what was wrong: the climate, for a start. How Australia manages in similar conditions is a complete mystery, to the Spanish at any rate, but the rule of thumb for buyers in Spain has generally been: if you want fruit, freshness, and above all, quality, go north. Too often they simply carried on going, over the Pyrenees and into the arms of a grateful French Languedoc.

The grape varieties are a problem, too: acres of Airén, gallons of Garnacha, mile after mile of Monastrell, vatloads of Viura. Do all these make inherently boring wine, or are they just waiting for the right fairy wine-maker to come along and wave a magic stainless steel wand? Considering the successful rabbits that flying antipodean wine-makers have pulled out of the most unlikely hats, anything is possible. The trick might even work on Airén.

Recessions focus people's minds. As this one began to bite hard in Spain, domestic demand slowed to a trickle. As the doors of Europe creaked open, those Spaniards who could still afford to drink were looking outwards to new tastes. It finally dawned on producers that there really were people in the world who preferred the flavours of fresh fruit. Crikey. All that stainless steel will come in jolly handy, then.

They were helped too by France's disastrous 1991 harvest. It was not a brilliant year in Spain, but it was a darn sight better than most other places in Europe. Any country with enough drinkable wine was almost bound to clean up. But the real test will come with the next abundant harvest of high quality in France. Will Spain be able to hang on to its gains?

Spanish producers also worked out that, instead of sending grapes or must to France to be made into Euro-wine, they could get a better price by making it all themselves, now that they had the right equipment. Improvements had been going on for some time, and technology at its present level has been in place for four or five years. But only now is everything coming together.

Consumers are showing their appreciation in the usual way. While the total UK wine market was down by about 27 per cent in 1991, Spanish imports were up 17 per cent, with Navarra, Valencia and La Mancha showing the biggest regional increases. Straight *vino da mesa* was up a staggering 78 per cent, give or take. Some statistical quirks were cleaned out of the system, so the increases may not be quite as dramatic as they appear, but even so.

Prices have helped enormously. Spain's recession has put paid to any arrogance on price, and our own recession has sharpened buyers' determination to come away with a bargain. As a result it is now possible for buyers to do deals. Mature stock that has been languishing in the *bodega* desperately needs to be turned into cash, so quite a few *reserva* and *gran reserva* Riojas have become much more affordable of late. The basic asking price for young wine, especially *vino da mesa*, is also down, so a bottle can appear on the retail shelf at £2.69.

These less expensive wines – whether DO or *vino da mesa* – are largely coming from outside the familiar classic regions. Valencia and Utiel Requena are going from strength to strength; both are sources of mid-priced wines which, increasingly, have more of the classy Tempranillo grape in the blend, and sometimes a varietal label.

Jumilla is also coming up with new young wines, and turning them round fast. Stainless steel may not be the answer to everything, but nobody has broken the news to them in Jumilla, where this strange material has only just been discovered; it looks set to keep everybody busy for years to come.

La Mancha is still considered a sleeping giant. Its huge potential for making basic drinkable wines is barely being tapped, partly because good white wine-making needs a good bottling line to back it up, and good bottling lines in La Mancha have been as scarce as bullfights in Esher. The law hitherto insisted on bottling being carried out in the region of production, but 1992 saw the end of that restriction, for better or worse, and in La Mancha's case it will be very much for the better. Those with spare capacity elsewhere – perhaps in nearby Valencia – will bottle it for them. Freshness will become the norm. Airén has severe limitations, but cold fermentation, plus enough residual sweetness to take the rough edges off, can render it highly palatable, especially if the price is right.

The opposite case to La Mancha – small volumes of high quality wine – obtains in the Duero and Galicia. Ribera del Duero reds are recognized as world class, and generally sell for commensurate prices. The market is small, but new wines are appearing on the back of successes like Vega Sicilia and Pesquera, and some of these new boys, like Waitrose's, are not much more than a fiver.

Galicia's white Albariño is extremely impressive too, although the best, by common consent, stays on the home market. It is exceptionally trendy – Spain's answer to Italy's Gavi – but UK retailers find that at £10 it simply does not shift fast enough. 'At £4.99 it would sell like hot cakes,' reckons one high street chain buyer. But Galicia is a difficult place to make wine, as wet as Manchester, albeit somewhat warmer in the summer, so Albariño is unlikely to break through that price barrier.

New equipment has taken much of the credit for improving Spanish wines, but it could not have done that unless someone had considered it a worthwhile investment. In Spanish terms that required an attitude shift of Copernican proportions. While oenology students around the world were cutting their teeth on centrifuges and micropore filters, slotting in a gas chromatography or spectroscopic analysis during their coffee break, many Spanish winemakers were still covering their *tinajas*, those huge clay pots used for making wine since ancient times, with bits of old plastic held in place with a couple of bricks.

But a generation of young wine-makers is surfacing, from places like the oenological station at Navarra, and doing what young wine-makers do everywhere: turfing out old credos, re-writing the books and keeping an eye on what the rest of the world is up to. Go to Navarra, and you will find that the students have come across such trendy oddballs as Randall Grahm's Catalyst. 'If that is what somebody can do with Garnacha in California,' you can hear them thinking, 'we might be sitting on a goldmine after all.' To rise to this bait is

automatically to lift Spain up the quality ladder by several vital notches.

So far, Cabernet-Tempranillo blends and *barrique*-fermented Viura (such as Agramont from Navarra, £3.99 from Oddbins) show what can be done when the industry is energized by a generation with its eyes and ears open. But Rioja is engaging in some soul-searching about Cabernet Sauvignon. The old school predictably maintains that Rioja is no longer Rioja if it is adulterated with Cabernet Sauvignon. The new school believes that Tempranillo, good as it is, can benefit from an injection of it. This view maintains that the first object is to make a good wine, by whatever means, because if you don't it simply won't sell. 'Tradition is the king of mediocrity,' is how one prominent *bodega* baron summed up the new perspective. How refreshing to hear it uttered in a Spanish accent.

It is difficult to avoid comparisons with Tuscany in the 1970s and 1980s, when Cabernet crept in to improve the Sangiovese-based wines of Chianti. If that episode is anything to go by, Rioja producers may well find that Cabernet acts as a catalyst: those who believe in the inherent quality of Tempranillo will be forced to make better wines from it to prove their point. As it is, wherever a Rioja *bodega* instals a young wine-maker, you can virtually guarantee that the wine will be attractively ripe, supple, fresh and richly fruity, whatever the varieties used, and furthermore that it will be aged appropriately.

Too much Rioja has in the past been aged to a formula, ignoring its intrinsic characteristics. Thus a plain and simple, rather light *crianza* might have been left in American oak long enough to become a *reserva*. It would officially qualify for the *reserva* description, while having died long ago. If sales were particularly slow, it would have been kept imprisoned for another few years, eventually being allowed to take the name of *gran reserva* in vain. Absolutely correct by law, but oxidized, overpowered by oak, and next to undrinkable.

The simple expedient of designating a lighter wine as *crianza*, and sticking to it, while reserving the beefier wines for longer oak ageing, makes a huge difference. The practice is not as widespread as it should be, but the situation is improving, and Rioja is regaining a sense of identity lost during the 1980s.

It is also having to cope with increasing pressure from within. The 63 bodegas of the mid-1980s had increased to 125 by 1990 and 140 in 1991, while the cake they are all competing to share is not getting any bigger. Growth in the Rioja market was zero in 1991. This goes some way towards explaining the good deals that are around: enjoy them while they are still there.          **JIM AINSWORTH**

---

### CLASSIFICATIONS

Spain has the largest acreage of vineyards in the world, but a relatively small number of demarcated regions. The main category is Denominación de Origen, DO for short. The DO is based, like the French system of appellation contrôlée, on suitable terrain, permitted grape varieties, restricted yields and approved methods of vinification but, because the areas covered are so vast, the regulations are somewhat general and not too demanding, with the exception of a fairly comprehensive ban on irrigation which, especially in the arid central regions, naturally keeps yields extraordinarily low. A higher category, the Denominación de Origen Calificada (DOC) is being introduced; so far Rioja is the only official claimant. However, no changes have been made to the permitted yields, and so on.

Spain now has its own official equivalent of vins de pays, a category which has proliferated since the country joined the EC, but few of the vinos de la tierra would make the grade in France.

# RED & ROSÉ WINES

It would be too neat to conclude that 1992, the year of Expo, the Olympics and the 500th anniversary of Columbus's trans-Atlantic trip, was also the year when Spain's wines finally catapulted themselves *en masse* into the same league as those from Australia and California. Indeed this patently is not the case. But it may well come to be remembered as the beginning of the end of the old regime, a time when the groundwork, laid over the past decade and more, began to pay off.

When UK sales of La Mancha reds increase by over one third in a 12 month period (admittedly from a much lower base than whites) clearly there is something significant afoot. Shops, and their customers, have been quick to respond to lower prices and abundant harvests.

At this level we are likely to see more of Spain's traditional red grape varieties – Garnacha, Monastrell, Tempranillo – winning a share of the market. Variety, and a true sense of Spanish identity, are what is needed.

## GRAPES & FLAVOURS

**BOBAL** Good for deep-coloured, fruity red and stylish rosado wines in Utiel-Requena and Valencia. Reasonable acidity and relatively low alcohol keep the wines comparatively fresh and appetizing.

**CARIÑENA** A high-yielding grape (the Carignan of Southern France) producing extremely dark and prodigiously tannic wine. It has its own DO, Cariñena, south of Zaragoza, where it is thought the variety was first propagated, but the zone is now dominated by Garnacha and Bobal. Most Cariñena is grown in Catalonia, primarily as a beefy blender. It is also a minority grape in Rioja under the name Mazuelo. With its high tannin and acidity, and its aroma of ripe fruit, plums and cherries, it complements the Tempranillo so well – adding to its ageing potential – that, each vintage, the Rioja *bodegas* fight over the small quantities available from growers.

**GARNACHA** This is Spain's – and the world's – most planted red grape variety. It grows everywhere, except Andalucía, and makes big, broad, alcoholic, sometimes peppery or spicy wines. The French, who know it as Grenache, moan about its lack of colour; but here in Spain, where burning heat and drought naturally restrict its yield, there's more dark skin in proportion to pale juice, and the wines turn out darker. They don't last well, but they can be delicious drunk young, whether as red, or fresh, spicy rosé. In Navarra the presence of Garnacha is gradually giving way to Tempranillo and Cabernet.

**GRACIANO** This high quality red grape of Rioja and Navarra has all but died out because its yields are so low. Some *bodegas* still use it for its fresh, grassy, savoury aroma and good colour.

**MONASTRELL** Spain's second most planted red variety, used to add body and guts to many Catalonian Tempranillo blends. Produces good crops of dark, tasty, alcoholic reds and rosés right down the eastern seaboard in Alicante, Jumilla, Almansa, Yecla and Valencia – usually dry and stolid but sometimes made sweet.

**TEMPRANILLO** The fine red grape of Rioja and Navarra crops up all over Spain except in the hot South, but with a different name in practically every region (sometimes it's a slightly different strain too). It's called the Cencibel up on the plains of La Mancha and Valdepeñas, Ull de Llebre (hare's eye) in Penedés, Tinto

Fino in the Ribera del Duero, while elsewhere it may be Tinto de Madrid, Tinto de Toro, Tinto del País ... It is so highly thought of that it is being introduced into new areas (Cariñena, Somontano, the Rioja Baja ...) and its plantations are being extended elsewhere. The wines have a spicy, herby, tobacco-like character, along with plenty of sweet strawberry or sour cherry fruit, good, firm acidity and a bit of tannin. Tempranillo makes very good, vibrantly fruity wines for gulping down young, as well as more robust wines for longer ageing – and its flavours harmonize brilliantly with oak. It's often blended with other grapes, especially Garnacha.

## WINES & WINE REGIONS

**ALICANTE, DO** Heavy, rather earthy reds made in south-east Spain from the Monastrell grape; mostly useful blending wines.

**ALMANSA, DO** Falling between the high La Mancha plain and the near coastal plains of Alicante and Valencia, up-and-coming Almansa produces strong spicy reds from Monastrell and Garnacha, and even better reds from Tempranillo. *Bodegas Piqueras* make very good wines under the *Castillo de Almansa* and *Marius* labels.

**AMPURDÁN-COSTA BRAVA, DO** This part of Catalonia, right up in the North East, is a major supplier to the Costa Brava beaches. Seventy per cent is rosé, catering to the sun-freaks, but it also produces some so-called 'Vi Novell', supposedly modelled on the fresh, fruity style of Beaujolais Nouveau.

**CALATAYUD, DO** A newish DO south-east of Zaragoza. Reds are made from Garnacha, Mazuelo, Tempranillo and Monastrell, and must reach 12 degrees to get their DO. General quality benefits from the presence of the Calatayud Viticultural Station.

**CAMPO DE BORJA, DO** A newish DO in the heart of Aragón between Navarra and Cariñena. Hefty alcoholic reds made from Cariñena and Garnacha, now making way for lighter reds and very good rosés. *Bodegas Bordejé, the Borja co-op* and the *Santo Cristo* co-op look promising.

**CARIÑENA, DO** A lot of basic red from Cariñena, south-east of Rioja, finds its way as common *tinto* into Spain's bars, but the best co-ops (they make most of it) produce pleasant, full, soft reds. The main grape is the fat, jammy Garnacha, though a certain amount of Tempranillo firms up the better reds. Whites and rosés can be pleasant, but are mostly dull. The reds of the *Bodegas San Valero* co-operative are well made, sold here as *Don Mendo* and *Monte Ducay*.

**COSTERS DEL SEGRE, DO** A virtual one-producer DO (Raimat) in the Catalan province of Lérida. It's desert, but has been irrigated to grow cereals, fruit and vines, despite the fact that irrigation is officially banned both in Spain and the EC. But EC wine producers use two let-out clauses: if your vineyard is 'experimental', or if you can claim unusual local conditions, you can turn on the tap. Well, thank goodness the owners of the fine Lérida estate of *Raimat* knew how to get round the rules, because their whites and reds are some of Spain's most attractive. *Raimat Abadia*, based on Cabernet Sauvignon, Tempranillo and Garnacha and aged in oak, is consistently good, as is *Raimat Pinot Noir*. The *Raimat Cabernet Sauvignon* is also very good; ripe but light, blackcurranty-oaky wine. The *Raimat Tempranillo* isn't so different either, for that matter. *Raimat Merlot*, latest on the scene, is plummy and rich.

The price guides for this section begin on page 356.

**BIERZO, DO** A new DO in the cool mountains around Ponferrada, making rasping reds from the Mencia grape.

**JUMILLA, DO** Usually a palate-buster of a red from super-ripe Monastrell grapes grown in the dust bowls of Murcia. Much of it is sold in bulk for beefing up blends elsewhere. However, French investment is now creating a new fresh-flavoured red style. The *Condestable* brands, *Castillo de Jumilla* and *Con Sello*, are quite good and gentle as is the ripe, plummy *Taja* from French merchants Mahler-Besse. The *San Isidro* co-op is the biggest in Spain.

**LA MANCHA** Vast area south of Madrid. Only ten per cent red and most of this is pale semi-red plonk for the bars of Madrid. The wines *can* be highly enjoyable easy-going reds, yet so far only *Vinicola de Castilla, Cueva del Granero* and *Bodegas Rodriguez & Berger* are proving this with any regularity. *Arboles de Castillejo* from *Bodegas Torres Filoso* is a 100 per cent Tempranillo well worth a try.

**MENTRIDA, DO** Strong, sturdy reds produced bang in the middle of Spain.

**NAVARRA, DO** This large region just north of Rioja grows the same grapes, though with more Garnacha. The officially-funded experimental winery here, EVENA, is one of the most impressive in Europe, and their influence is already noticeable in the wines. As Garnacha gives way to plantings of Tempranillo and Cabernet, we can look forward to some sounder drinking.

Much Navarra wine is made in co-ops, then generally sold to *bodegas* for blending, and it's cheering to see how fast things are improving. The best wine is the single estate *Magaña*, which includes Cabernet and Merlot, not really DO-permitted varieties. Other potentially good names are *Chivite* and *Bodegas Cenalsa,* who also use the label *Agramont. Monte Ory* and *Bodegas Ochoa* wines are now much fresher, especially the new varietals. *Vinicola Navarra* make old-fashioned, oaky reds – look for *Castillo de Tiebas* – and the modernized *Bodegas Irache* are producing both fruity and oak-aged styles.

**PENEDÉS, DO** Catalonia's leading wine region. There is more *will* here to make good wines in commercial quantities to sell at a profitable but not silly margin than anywhere else in Spain due to that good old Catalan industriousness – and the investment the wealth of the region makes possible. Mostly, however, the usual Spanish problem of indifferent grape varieties causes most of the reds to be rather solid and unrefreshingly overripe. But there are high spots. *Jean León's Cabernet Sauvignon* is one – a superbly weighty, impressively long-lasting red, though sadly lighter since 1980. *Torres* is another, from the rich, rather sweetly oaky basic reds, right up to the exciting

**MATURITY CHART**
1986 Rioja Reserva
In general, Reservas are ready to drink when they are released, though they may stay at their peak for some years

| Bottled | | | | Ready | | Peak | | | | Tiring | | In decline |
|---|---|---|---|---|---|---|---|---|---|---|---|---|
| 0 | 1 | 2 | 3 | 4 | 5 | 6 | 7 | 8 | 9 | 10 | 11 | 12 | 13 years |

Cabernet-Sauvignon-based *Gran Coronas Black Label*, now called *Mas La Plana*. Other names to look out for are *Cavas Hill, Ferret i Mateu, Masia Bach, Mont Marçal, Vallformosa, René Barbier, Jaume Serra*.

**PRIORATO, DO** You need 13.5 degrees of alcohol here to get your DO! Cool, mountainous region, abutting the west of Tarragona. The reds from Garnacha and Cariñena are renowned – rich and full-bodied in style, and *Masia Barril, Scala Dei* and *de Muller* are worth trying.

**RIBERA DEL DUERO, DO** 'Ribera' means river bank, and this fine red wine region spreads out over the broad valley of the Duero (Portugal's Douro) and the smaller pine-clad valleys behind. The Tinto Fino grape (alias Tempranillo) is by far the main one, sometimes mixed with Garnacha for drinking young, but used alone for the bigger reds. There's interest in Cabernet for blending into the better wines, too. The wines we see most of are from the *Bodegas Ribera del Duero* co-op at Peñafiel, where a new wine-maker has meant improvements. The *joven* (young) reds show the soft fruit of the region.

*Vega Sicilia* is the famous name, an estate that has grown Cabernet, Merlot and Malbec to blend in with its Tinto Fino since early this century. These wines, which can be horribly expensive, taste like a mix of top Rioja and grand old-style Piedmont, with great concentration. Actually the second wine, *Valbuena*, is often more enjoyable: rich, but with less wood ageing – and less of an assault on the wallet. Two other *bodegas* offer lovely rich, oaked reds at rapidly sky-rocketing prices – a disease that seems to be afflicting this DO. Look out for the unctuous, ripe, but over-oaky *Tinto Pesquera* from *Bodegas Alejandro Fernandez*, whose 1986 is the best recent year, and the delicious *Viña Pedrosa* from *Bodegas Perez Pascuas*; *Bodegas Victor Balbas*; the *Ribera Duero* co-op (the young reds, not the more dubious *reservas*). *Bodegas Monte-Vannos reservas*.

---

### RIOJA CLASSIFICATIONS

Rioja is divided into three geographical sub-regions: Rioja Alta, Rioja Alavesa and Rioja Baja: most wines will be a blend from all three. The wine's age, indicated on the label, falls into one of four categories.

**Sin crianza** Without ageing, or with less than a year in wood; wine sold in its first or second year. (The words 'sin crianza' are not seen on the label.)

**Crianza** With a minimum of 12 months in wood and some months in bottle; cannot be sold before its third year. Whites will have had a minimum of six months in cask before bottling.

**Reserva** Selected wine from a good harvest with a minimum of 36 months' ageing, in cask and bottle, of which 12 months minimum in cask. It cannot leave the *bodega* until the fifth year after the vintage. Whites have at least six months in cask, and 24 months' ageing in total.

**Gran Reserva** Wine from an excellent vintage (supposedly) that will stand up to ageing: 24 months minimum in cask and 36 months in bottle, or vice-versa. Cannot leave the *bodega* until the sixth year after the vintage. White wines have six months in cask and 48 months' ageing in total.

---

**RIOJA, DOC** Classic reds from this newly upgraded region (from DO to DOC) taste of oak and vanilla sweetness. Oak – and in particular American oak, the type liked in Rioja – is full of vanilla, and wine leaches it out, taking up its buttery-vanilla-toffee aromas and flavours. The actual fruit in Rioja is usually rather light, sometimes peppery, with a strawberry jam sweetness.

Practically all the Rioja on sale here comes from firms who make or buy in wine from three distinct parts of the region and different grape varieties, blending and ageing them to a 'house style'. Some use more of the more elegant Tempranillo, some more of the fatter, riper Garnacha, perhaps adding a little of the two minority grapes, Graciano and Mazuelo. The Rioja Alavesa region makes more delicate, perfumed wines; Rioja Alta produces wines that are firmer, leaner, slower to show their character but slower to lose it, too, and the lower, hotter Rioja Baja grows mostly Garnacha, which gets super-ripe and rather lumpish. The tendency to use less and less oak, resulting in boring wines which are not cheap, is mercifully slowing. Best bets are *Bodegas Riojanas, Campo Viejo, El Coto, Cune, Faustino, Lopez de Heredia, Marqués de Cáceres, Marqués de Murrieta, Martínez Bujanda, Montecillo, Muga, Olarra, La Rioja Alta Palacio, Campillo, Amerzola de la Mora,* and an improving *Marqués de Riscal*.

There is little credence given, as yet, to the 'estate' mentality, but it will come, as expectations rise and the over-achievers of the area determine to set an individual stamp on their wines. It's already worth trying to search out the wines from *Barón de Ley, Contino* and *Remelluri*.

**SOMONTANO, DO** The most exciting of Spain's newly demarcated regions in the cool foothills of the Pyrenees, north of Zaragoza. It uses a clutch of grape varieties to make lightly perfumed, attractive reds, whites and rosés, and I've even tasted some pretty good fizz. The *Co-operativa de Sobrarbe* under the Camporocal label is encouraging. *Covisa* have been doing well with both Spanish and foreign grapes.

**TARRAGONA, DO** The largest DO in Catalonia, to the south of Penedés. Originally known for high-strength dessert wines; now making undistinguished and unimpressive reds, whites and rosés.

**TERRA ALTA, DO** Hefty, sometimes coarse red from west of Tarragona. Rather better at producing altar wine – *de Muller* is the world's biggest supplier.

**TORO, DO** Newish DO region to the west of Ribera del Duero and Rueda, capable of making excellent, inexpensive, beefy,

tannic but richly fruity reds from the Tinto de Toro – yet another alias for the Tempranillo. So far, the only really good wines are being made by *Bodegas Fariña*, whose *Gran Colegiata*, aged French-style in small oak barrels, is making waves here.

**UTIEL-REQUENA, DO** An extension of the central plateau to the west of Valencia. The reds, from the Bobal grape, are robust and rather hot and southern in style. The rosés *can* be better – delicate and fragrant.

**VALDEPEÑAS, DO** Until recently the home of soft, unmemorable reds, this DO, down in the south of the central plateau, has latterly much improved its wine-making and equipment. Many of these potentially rich, fruity wines are sadly emasculated by a generous dollop of white Airén wine; they are then unable to stand up to the ageing that's inflicted upon them. However, the best firms selling wine for export tend to make their top reds purely from Cencibel (alias Tempranillo), so that they can turn out deep and herby with good strawberry fruit – and excellent value at very low prices, even for *gran reservas* with a decade's ageing. One or two *bodegas* age their best growths in oak but this is rare. Look for for the succulently soft reds, aged in new oak, of *Señorio de los Llanos*; *Viña Albalí* from *Bodegas Felix Solis* and the young, fruity reds of *Marqués de Castañega* and *Casa de la Viña*.

**VALENCIA, DO** Large quantities of red, white and rosé wines of no great distinction are made on this coastal plain by a handful of producers. It's easy drinking, the sort of thing that's fine for the beach. Some low-priced reds from *Schenk* and *Gandia Pla* can be good and the sweet Moscatels can be tasty and good value. *Castillo de Liria*, from *Gandia*, is an attractive red.

**YECLA, DO** Sandwiched between Jumilla and Alicante, this dry region makes fairly full-bodied reds and more dubious whites. *La Purisima* co-op is the chief label we see.

# WHITE WINES

White wines respond quickly and easily to hygiene and care in the cellar, to stainless steel and cool fermentation. Buyers who ignored the wine last year will form an orderly queue this time round if the gadgetry has worked its magic. The result may not be particularly exciting, but it will be clean and sound. And in many parts of Spain that still constitutes a revolutionary change.

A more intractable problem concerns the uninspiring raw material. Airén in the centre, Viura (Macabeo) in Rioja, Garnacha Blanca, and Parellada and Xarello in Catalonia, are hardly suited to current international tastes. The New World has shown that powerful flavours attract powerfully. Anything else can seem insipid by comparison. Is it enough simply to be clean and sound, or must growers throw in their lot with Chardonnay?

Before they do, it is to be hoped that they will try to get more out of their native varieties. Those that show most promise — Albariño, Loureiro and Treixadura — are planted mainly in the damp North-West, in and around Galicia. How would they fare in La Mancha? Nobody knows. Torres has managed to make Parellada sing (in Viña Sol), and there is no reason why, with sufficient care, other varieties should not produce some hitherto unsuspected gems.

## GRAPES & FLAVOURS

**AIRÉN** This plain and simple white grape hardly deserves its prominence, but it covers far, far more land than any other grape on earth. It holds sway over Spain's central plateau, where the summers are baking hot, irrigation is banned, and the vines are widely spaced to survive. As a result, the Airén must be a front-runner for another record: the *smallest* producer per hectare. Traditionally, these grapes have yielded tired, alcoholic, yellow plonk to service the bars of Madrid. But new, cool wine-making methods can transform it into some of the most refreshing basic white yet produced in Spain, with a delicious light apple, lemon and liquorice flavour. Most, though, is still the same dull old hooch.

**GARNACHA BLANCA** A relation of the red Garnacha, and widely grown in the North-East. Like the red, it makes wines high in alcohol, low in acidity and with a tendency to oxidize, so they are usually blended in with wines of higher acidity, like Viura. Good growers are grubbing it up, but its high yields keep it popular, especially in Navarra.

**MALVASÍA** This interesting, aromatic, flavourful grape is difficult to grow in Spain, as it tends to produce wines of low acidity that turn yellow and oxidize rapidly unless extreme care is taken. It is also low-yielding and prone to rot, so many growers in its traditional homelands of Rioja and Navarra have been ousting it in favour of the less interesting Viura. Only five per cent of Rioja is now planted with Malvasia, although there are hints of new interest from *bodegas* like *Marqués de Cáceres*. When well made, Malvasía wine is full-bodied, fairly strongly scented, spicy or musky, often with a hint of apricots, and sometimes slightly nutty. It blends well with Viura, which ups its acidity, but more and more wooded white Riojas are now based solely on Viura, which can't meld in oaky softness as successfully as Malvasía. Ten years ago, good white Rioja *reservas* really *did* taste like white Burgundy – because of the high proportion of Malvasía in the blend. Still flying the flag for this style are the excellent *Marqués de Murrieta* and *Cune,* with their *Monopole* and their *reserva.*

**MESEGUERA** Valencia's mainstay white grape, also grown in Alicante and Tarragona, produces light, delicately aromatic and characterful wines.

**MOSCATEL** The Muscat of Alexandria (Moscatel) is mostly grown in the South, where it overripens, shrivels and makes big, rich fortifieds. Valencia can make some extremely good, grapy, sweet white from it and *Torres* makes a good, off-dry, aromatic version mixed with Gewürztraminer in Penedés, as does *de Muller* in Tarragona.

**PARELLADA** Touted as the provider of all the perfume and finesse in Catalonia's whites and in *cava* fizz, but Parellada doesn't honestly have much to say for itself, except in the hands of the best producers. *Torres Viña Sol* is refreshing and lemony; *Ferret i Mateu* and *Miret* are also good.

**VERDEJO** This native of Rueda on the River Duero is one of Spain's more interesting white grapes. Nowadays it's used more for table wines than for Rueda's traditional fortifieds, and makes a soft, creamy, slightly nutty white, sometimes a touch honeyed, with good, green acidity

and less alcohol than Viura. It isn't a world-beater, but it can make good fizz.

**VIURA** The main white grape of Rioja, made nowadays apple-fresh and clean and, at best, rather neutral-flavoured, at worst, sharp and grapefruity. It achieves similarly mixed results, under the name Macabeo, in Catalonia (where it also forms part of the *cava* fizz blend). Made in this light, modern style, it's a wine for gulping down young, in its first year. But blended with Malvasía, topped up with a slug of acidity and left to age in oak barrels, the Viura is capable of making some wonderful, rich, almost Burgundy-like white Riojas.

**XAREL-LO** One of the three main white grapes of Catalonia, heavier, more alcoholic and even less aromatic than the barely aromatic Parellada and Macabeo, with which it is generally blended. Some producers of *cava* and still wines like to use it to give extra body and alcohol to their wines, while others scorn it as coarse. It accounts for a third of all white plantings in Penedés. In Alella, it's known as the Pansá Blanca.

## WINES & WINE REGIONS

**ALELLA, DO** Catalonian wine region north of Barcelona, gradually disappearing under the suburban sprawl, whose best wine is from the impressive firm of *Marqués de Alella*. The vines are found on granitic slopes somewhat sheltered from the prevailing easterly wind. Its best-known wine is the off-dry, very fruity Marqués de Alella. Also look out for the light, pineapple-fresh *Chardonnay* and appley *Marqués de Alella Seco*, as well as the sparkling *Parxet*, which beats most of the famous *cavas* hands down with its fresh, greengagey flavour.

**CAVA, DO** The Spanish name for Champagne-method wine. Around 95 per cent of it comes from Catalonia in the East,

not far from Barcelona, and indeed the authorities there have been given the task of supervising the *cava Denominación de Origen* for the whole of Spain. Various other small vineyard enclaves have been granted the DO, odd little patches of Rioja and Aragon for instance. The DO was granted to regions or villages that already had a tradition of making *cava*, and one or two more recently introduced sparklers now have to take the term *cava* off their labels.

An absolutely delicious, fresh, fruity and nutty one in just such a position comes from *Bodegas Castilla la Vieja* in Rueda, worth looking out for in Spain though not available here. The *cava* authorities admit it's one of Spain's best, but it doesn't fit their rules! Raimat makes a very good 100 per cent Chardonnay, as does its sister company *Codorníu,* under its own name and bearing the *cava* DO.

Rioja *cava* suffers from the same ills as that of Catalonia – the Riojan base wines from Viura, like the Catalan from Parellada, Xarel-lo and Macabeo (Viura), are not long-keepers, and their fruit often fails to stand up to a year's ageing in bottle (let alone the three years to which many *cava* wines are treated). The famous sparklers of Catalonia generally end up with a rather dull, earthy, peppery taste, often aggravated by the use of extra-matured wine in the final topping-up liqueur after the bottles have been disgorged.

Some Catalan companies are now starting to turn out fresher, less earthy *cavas* by better wine-making and less excessive ageing, and where available by including some Chardonnay in the blends. *Cavas Hill, Codorníu, Juve y Camps, Mont Marçal* and *Rovellats* look hopeful, though there's a distressing trend to raise prices with the use of Chardonnay. But most producers are stuck with their grape varieties, none of which will ever be renowned for its perfume or fruit. Most appetizing of the Catalan brands are *Cavas Hill Reserva Oro Brut Natur, Codorníu Première Cuvée Brut, Mont Marçal Cava Nature* and *Chardonnay, Parxet, Raimat, Segura Viudas* and *Rovellats, Freixenet* and its subsidiary company *Condé de Caralt*.

**CONCA DE BARBERÁ, DO** A region next to Penedés making fairly ordinary whites and rosés.

**CONDADO DE HUELVA, DO** Faces Jerez across the Guadalquivir river in Andalucia and has broadly similar climate and soils. Wines resembling Montilla are made and have been mostly drunk locally, though some now reaches these shores. Tesco's *Tio Cani* will give you an idea of the sort of thing.

**COSTERS DEL SEGRE, DO** Raimat, virtually the only vineyard in the area, makes light, lemony, gently oaked *Raimat Chardonnay,* as well as a good sparkler, *Raimat Chardonnay Blanc de Blancs,* which is Spain's best fizz when demand isn't outstripping supply, though the price has gone up and it's no longer the bargain it once was.

**LA MANCHA, DO** Long dismissed as the most mediocre kind of base-wine producer, Spain's enormous central plateau of La Mancha – producing 40 per cent of all Spain's wine – is now bringing in cool fermentation methods for the whites and sterile, cool fermentation for the reds, and is already drawing out quite unexpected fresh flavours from both – and still at a pretty rock-bottom price. The traditional, typical wines were light yellow in colour, thanks to creeping oxidation, but this has changed. Some of the ones we see here now are the new style, either bland, but fresh and fruity, or else quite surprisingly young and bright-eyed. But you have to catch them *very* young. Best are *Casa la Teja, Castillo de Alhambra, Lazarillo, Señorio de Guadianeja, Viña Santa Elena, Yuntero, Zagarron.*

**NAVARRA, DO** Most Navarra white is a dull reflection of mediocre white Rioja, hardly helped by the fact that vintages on sale in this country are rarely the latest. However, a few are fresh, zippy, fairly neutral-flavoured, but adequate light summer gulpers. The most recent vintage from *Chivite* and *Bodegas Cenalsa* (Agramont and Campo Nuevo) or *Ochoa* might inspire you momentarily. Successful experiments with growing Chardonnay could promise more exciting wines in the future.

**PENEDÉS, DO** The general run of Penedés whites is either flabby and fruitless or lemony, spare and characterless. This uninspiring state of affairs arises because the three main grapes – Macabeo, Xarel-lo and Parellada – *all* lack personality. There are exceptions to the rule, especially *Miguel Torres*, who manages to extract a lean, lemony, sharply refreshing flavour from his Parellada. Other good whites from local varieties come from *Cavas Hill, Ferret i Mateu* and *Mont Marçal*. As well as these Torres and *Masia Bach* have Riesling, Chenin, Chardonnay, Sauvignon, and what have you; and *Jean León* makes a delicious oaky, pineappley Chardonnay. Of the new varieties Chardonnay is the only one officially permitted in wines labelled 'Penedés'.

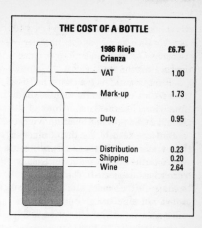

| THE COST OF A BOTTLE | |
| --- | --- |
| 1986 Rioja Crianza | £6.75 |
| VAT | 1.00 |
| Mark-up | 1.73 |
| Duty | 0.95 |
| Distribution | 0.23 |
| Shipping | 0.20 |
| Wine | 2.64 |

**RIAS BAIXAS, DO** Three separate districts make up this DO on the Galician coast north of Portugal. The Val de Salnes zone around Cambados makes whites almost purely from Albariño grapes – fresh and fragrant when well made. *Martin Codax* is good. Further south, *Condado de Tea* and *O Rosal* make Albariño-dominated wines, sometimes with a dash of Loureiro and Treixadura. As the wines become more fashionable in Spain, the prices are rising. *Bodegas Morgadio, Santiago Ruiz, Granja Fillaboa* and *Lagar de Cervera* are all good.

**RIBEIRO, DO** Since this Galician area was granted DO status, a zone once known for flabby dry whites has been benefitting from investment in vineyard and *bodega*. Fresh white wines from Treixadura and Torrontes are a distinct improvement on the old regime, though as in nearby Rias Baixas, demand is causing prices to rise.

**RIOJA, DOC** The first DO to be upgraded to DOC, though the rules stay the same. Styles vary. White Rioja *can* be buttery and rich, slightly Burgundian in style. It used to be made from a blend of Viura and the richer, more interesting Malvasía, aged for several years in oak. Some were awful, tired and flat; some were wonderful. The style is now starting to make a comeback. *Marqués de Murrieta* still makes a very good example, and so, with rather less oak,

does *Cune* with its *Monopole* and *reserva*, and *Bodegas Riojanas* with its *Monte Reál*. *Lopez de Heredia* makes an old-fashioned style, while *Navajas, Viña Soledad* from *Franco Españolas* and *Siglo Gold* from *AGE* are all in the oak-aged mould.The best new-wave white Riojas are full of fresh, breath-catching raw fruit, with the acid attack of unsugared grapefruit.

**RUEDA, DO** This predominantly white wine region lies north-west of Madrid, by the river Duero. Rueda used to be famous, or notorious rather, for its heavy, oxidized, sherry-type wines made from the Palomino grape of Jerez – high on alcohol, low on fruit and freshness. But production of these *vinos generosos* is now really limited to a couple of *bodegas*, and the rest of the region has switched over to light table wines, picked early and fresh and fermented in cool, modern style. They have a natural advantage here in their local grape, the Verdejo, which makes soft, full, nutty wines, sometimes padded out with the dull Palomino, or sharpened up with a little of the more acid Viura. Most are for drinking young, but there are oaked versions, too. The most interesting Rueda is *Marqués de Griñon*, made by *Bodegas Castilla La Vieja*. Others include *Alvarez y Diez*, who use no sulphur, *Martinsancho* and *Vinos Sanz*. The *La Seca* co-op makes good, clean dry whites.

# FORTIFIED WINES

If proof were ever needed that much of what is written about wine is totally ignored by drinkers, we would have only to turn to sherry. I can think of no single wine writer who is enthusiastic about 'British sherry'. Every single one, so far as I am aware, slams it in favour of the real thing: Spanish sherry, made in and around Jerez and Sanlúcar da Barrameda in Andalucía.

And the result? We drink more 'British sherry' (2.95 million cases in 1991) than we do real sherry (2.28 million cases). Daft, isn't it? Why do we bother?

We bother, I suppose, because things might be even worse if we didn't. We bother because we know there is a huge disparity in what they are made of, and in the resulting taste and value for money. On all counts, real sherry is streets ahead. On all counts, that is, except sales. Real sherry has dropped by over 1.1 million cases in the UK since 1984, while 'British sherry' has slipped a mere 184,000 cases. The total fortified wine market collapsed by over 2 million cases, down to 6 million in 1991, over the same period.

The trouble is that the sherry game is not conducted on a level playing field. First, it remains curious that grape juice concentrate from some other country (Cyprus is a common source) can be diluted with British water, and then take the name of a wine from Spain. Could you imagine the same thing happening with a concocted 'British Champagne' made from imported Algerian base wine and Welsh bubbles? The Champenois would be down on it like a ton of bricks.

Jerez has to suffer the indignity because other 'sherries' were traded in the EC before Spain's entry. It knew, in other words, what the position was before it joined. Consequently other 'sherries' can use the term legally until it comes up for renegotiation in 1995.

But the other 'sherries' selling now are not exactly the same as when Spain joined the EC. Their alcohol level has dropped slightly, to enable them to dip under the 15 per cent duty band (£1.26 per litre). Real sherry, on the other hand, remains at the higher level of £2.17 per litre, or in the case of wines over 18 per cent alcohol, as some *olorosos* are, £2.50 per litre. If the disparity were swept away, real sherry would probably come down about £1 a bottle.

On top of all this, shippers Matthew Clark & Co devised a clever little wheeze, tailor-made to get up the noses of the Jerezanos. They produced Stone's Original Pale Cream, a blend of 80 per cent 'British sherry' and 20 per cent 'fortified wines from Spain' (aka *fino*), selling in Tesco for £3.75 per 70cl bottle, and thus slotting neatly into the price gap between real sherry and other 'British sherries.'

At the same time, sherry producers (perhaps with one eye on the DOC, scheduled for 1993) continue to put their own house in order. After the boom and bust of the 1970s and 1980s it is recognized that production must be kept under control. Stability is the aim when limiting the vineyard area, the stocks of maturing wine and the sales. A plan, a sort of voluntary charter, has been drawn up and hailed as a landmark: the plan is to reduce the vineyard area to 13,000 hectares (from nearly 18,000 hectares in 1990); to reduce the amount of sherry passing through *soleras* by a quarter, down to the equivalent of 550 million bottles, by 1995; and to stabilize production at around the 1990 level of 140 million bottles a year. If all this maintains quality, and keeps prices on an even keel, it may yet succeed where wine writers have signally failed, and help to beat the living daylights out of imposters.

**JIM AINSWORTH**

## GRAPES & FLAVOURS

**MOSCATEL** Almost all Spanish Moscatel is the second-line Muscat of Alexandria rather than the top-quality Muscat à Petits Grains. Even so, it makes a lot of good wine – mostly rich and brown in Málaga, or fresh and grapy in Valencia. The Muscat de Chipiona from *Burdon* is wonderfully rich and peachy, and is usefully sold here in half bottles. Moscatel is also planted in Jerez to provide sweetening for cream sherries.

**PALOMINO** This is the dominant grape of the sherry region, making up 100 per cent of the dry sherries, and an increasing proportion of the others. Although it produces a great style of fortified wine it is not considered to be a great grape, though

it thrives in Jerez. It plays a minor role in Montilla-Moriles. As a table wine grape, it produces dull, fat stuff, but reacts brilliantly to the *flor* yeast which imparts to sherry that characteristic bone-dry, stark-sour perfume.

**PEDRO XIMÉNEZ** In decline in Jerez, where it used to be the chief component of sweet sherries, and still makes a startlingly rich wine essence for flavouring called 'PX'. It is sometimes made into dessert wine, deeply coloured and thick. It constitutes 95 per cent of the nearby Montilla-Moriles vineyards, as well as providing richness in Málaga; otherwise used extensively for rather dull dry white wines in the south of the country.

## WINES & WINE REGIONS

**MÁLAGA, DO** We don't see much Málaga here – in fact no-one sees much anywhere because Malaga's wine industry is beset by encroaching tourism. However, in the last century, Málaga was very popular and the wines are still worth a peep. Stirrings of revival have been noted. Málaga is generally full, brown and sweet in a raisiny, but not gooey, way and slightly smoky too. There is some dry Málaga, but you'll have to take a long weekend on the Costa del Sol to see much of that. Solera 1885 from *Scholtz Hermanos* is intense and raisiny while *Lagrima 10 Años* is very good sweet wine – and neither are expensive. *Bodega Lopez Hermanos is* also good.

**MONTILLA-MORILES, DO** Montilla wines are usually thought of as lower-priced – and lower-strength – sherry look-alikes but there is a great deal of fine wine made in Montilla-Moriles; the problem is getting any UK retailer to ship it. In general the dry wines, from Pedro Ximénez grapes, do not quite have the bite of really good sherry, but many of the mediums and sweets can outshine all but the best. I only

wish we saw these instead of the cheap dross that saturates our market. *Alvear* is a good name. *Tesco's Moriles* isn't bad and well worth trying as an alternative.

**SHERRY (JEREZ-XÉRÈS-SHERRY, DO)** There are two basic sherry styles, *fino* and *oloroso*, each with sub-divisions. *Fino*, from Jerez or Puerto de Santa Maria, should be pale and dry, with an unnerving dry austerity. The tang comes from a layer of natural yeast, called *flor*, that forms on the surface of the wine in the barrels. The lightest, freshest wines are selected for *fino*, and they are less fortified than the heavier *oloroso* wines. *Fino* is usually drunk cool and fresh, often as an aperitif.

*Manzanilla* is a form of *fino* matured by the sea at Sanlúcar de Barrameda. It can be almost savoury dry, and you might even imagine a definite whiff of sea salt – if you're lucky to catch it young enough. Best are *Barbadillo, Caballero, Diez-Merito, Don Zoilo, Garvey, La Guita, Hidalgo, La Ina, Inocente, Lustau, La Riva, Sanchez Romate, Tio Pepe*. Good Puerto *fino* comes from *Burdon* and *Osborne*.

On the UK market there is a desperate problem with freshness, and even good brands can suffer from tired-out tastes. Lesser brands and most own-labels are usually a disgrace (*Sainsbury's* half-bottles are an exception), softened and sweetened so that they certainly don't resemble real *fino*, and whatever it is they *do* resemble, I don't want it down my throat. Most dry sherry strengths have now been reduced from 17.5 per cent to 16.5 or even 15.5 per cent. The argument goes that this produces finer wine, and these days the extra strength isn't needed to preserve it. I'm not so sure; it seems to dilute it instead.

Real *amontillado* also started life as *fino*. It's a *fino* aged in cask until the *flor* dies and the wine deepens and darkens to a tantalizing, nutty dryness. In the natural state, as drunk in Spain, it is *completely* dry, and a proper *amontillado* will usually say *seco*, dry, on the label. But we've adulterated the word in English to mean a downmarket, bland, vaguely medium drink of no style or interest. Most sold here may have little or no real *amontillado* in it. But look out for sherries labelled *almacenista*, unblended wine from small stockholders, because these can be wonderful.

Look for *Principe* and *Solear* (a *manzanilla pasada*) from *Barbadillo*, *La Goya Manzanilla Pasada* and *Amontillado Fino Zuleta* (*Delgado Zuleta*), *Amontillado del Duque* (*Gonzalez Byass*), *Hidalgo Manzanilla Pasada*, *Sandeman Bone Dry Old Amontillado*, *Valdespino's Amontillado Coliseo* and *Don Tomás*. (*Manzanilla pasada* is an old *manzanilla* beginning to take on *amontillado* characteristics.)

Real *olorosos*, made from richer, fatter wines without any *flor*, are deep and dark, packed with violent burnt flavours – and usually dry, though you may find *oloroso dulce* (sweet) in Spain. In Britain most are sweetened with wine from Pedro Ximénez or Moscatel grapes. They usually come as 'Milk', 'Cream', or 'Brown'. Pale Creams are sweetened (inferior) *fino*, and are some of the dullest drinks around. For the real, dry thing, once again, look for *almacenista olorosos* from *Lustau*. There are a few good, concentrated sweetened *olorosos* on the market, including the fairly sweet *Matúsalem* from *Gonzalez Byass*, *Solera 1842* (*Valdespino*), *Apostoles Oloroso Viejo* from *González Byass*. Dry: *Barbadillo*, *Don Zoilo*, *Sandeman*, *Valdespino Don Gonzalo*, *Williams & Humbert Dos Cortados*. *Oddbins* seem to be the people taking most interest in top sherries – and most are under a tenner, making these intense old wines one of today's great bargains.

# WINERY PROFILES

**ANTONIO BARBADILLO** (Sanlúcar de Barrameda) ★★★★(★) Best *manzanilla bodega*. Principe is tangy, nutty, well-aged.

**CAMPO VIEJO** ★★★(★) Decent Riojas and soft, traditional *reservas*.

**VINICOLA DE CASTILLA** (La Mancha) ★★★ Up-to-date producer turning out 14 million litres a year, including white and oaky red Señorio de Guadianeja. Soft red Castillo de Alhambra is good value.

**CODORNÍU** (Penedés) ★★★ Giant *cava* company, owned by the Raventos family, making some of the most likeably reliable fizzes. Good soft and honeyed Anna de Codorníu fizz, and a very good, creamy Chardonnay *cava*.

**CONTINO (SOCIEDAD VINICOLA LASERNA)** (Rioja) ★★★★(★) Excellent, single-vineyard wine made from an estate half-owned by Cune, half by private investors. Vines are predominantly Tempranillo, planted in one 45-hectare vineyard in prime Rioja Alta land. Big, plummy and spicily complex, Contino is made only as *reserva* and *gran reserva*. If you see any '82, snap it up.

**CVNE** (Rioja) ★★★★ Old-established, traditionally-inclined; the initials stand for Compañía Vinícola del Norte de España. Blanco Viura is one of the best modern white Riojas, and Monopole has nice oak. Best of the reds are the rare Imperial range (especially the '81). Try the *reserva* white for a taste of good traditional Rioja.

**DOMECQ** (Jerez)★★★★★One of the oldest and most respected sherry houses, with top *fino* La Ina. Also impressive are Botaina *amontillado* and Rio Viejo *oloroso*. Also makes Rioja.

**FAUSTINO MARTÍNEZ** (Rioja) ★★★ Huge, family-owned *bodega* making good reds. Look also for the new Campillo *bodega*.

**FREIXENET** (Penedés)★★★High-tech *cava* firm best known for Cordon Negro, but also making good value Carta Nevada, Vintage Brut Nature which includes some Chardonnay, and upmarket Brut Barroco.

**GONZÁLEZ BYASS** (Jerez)★★★★★Huge, family-owned company, producers of the best-selling *fino* Tio Pepe. GB also makes an impressive top range of wines, and a Rioja, Bodegas Beronia.

**CAVAS HILL** (Penedés) ★★(★) Table wines as well as fresh, clean Cava Reserva Oro Brut Natur. Look out for Blanc Cru and Oro Penedés Blanco Suave whites, and Rioja-style reds, Gran Civet and Gran Toc.

**JEAN LEÓN** (Penedés) ★★★★ Jean León makes some of Spain's most 'Californian' wines, super-oaky, pineapple and honey Chardonnay, and soft, blackcurranty Cabernet Sauvignon.

**JULIAN CHIVITE** (Navarra)★★★ One of the most export-minded and state-of-the-art *bodegas* in Navarra, making a clean white from Viura, attractive *rosado* from Garnacha, and a good Tempranillo-based red, all under the Gran Feudo label.

**LOS LLANOS** (Valdepeñas) ★★★ The brightest spot here: wonderfully soft, oaky reds. 1978 Gran Reserva is especially good.

**LÓPEZ DE HEREDIA** (Rioja) ★★★★ Rich, complex whites, Viña Tondonia and Viña Gravonia, and delicate, ethereal reds, Viña Cubillo and Viña Tondonia.

**LUSTAU** (Jerez) ★★★ 'Reviving Traditional Sherry Values' with their wonderful range of *almacenista* wines.

**MARQUÉS DE CÁCERES** (Rioja) ★★★(★) Enrique Forner, who started this *bodega* in the mid-70s, trained in Bordeaux. Whites are cool-fermented and fresh, and reds have less wood ageing than usual, but still keep an attractive style.

**MARQUÉS DE GRIÑON** (Toledo) ★★★★ Carlos Falco, the Marqués de Griñon, makes very good Cabernet Sauvignons in his irrigated, wire-trained vineyard, aided by advice from Professor Emile Peynaud from Bordeaux.

**MARQUÉS DE MURRIETA** (Rioja) ★★★★ A remarkable, ultra-traditional winery built into a hill outside Logroño. Red, rosés and whites are oak-aged far longer than in any other Rioja *bodega*; the Etiqueta Blanca wines, the youngest sold, spend at least two years in barrel, and are richly oaky, pungent and lemony. The red is soft and fruity-oaky, while the *reservas* are deep and complex. The best wines of the very top years are sold as Castillo Ygay, and may sit in barrel for 40 years.

**MARTÍNEZ BUJANDA** (Rioja) ★★★(★) Wine is produced only from the family's own vineyards, and is very well made, from the super-fresh and lively Valdemar white to the strongly oaky Reserva and Gran Reserva Condé de Valdemar.

**MONTECILLO** (Rioja) ★★★★ Since 1973, this has belonged to Osborne, the sherry company, who built a new winery to turn out an exciting, aromatic white Viña Cumbrero, a raspberry and oak red, Viña Cumbrero *crianza*, and a classic *reserva*, Viña Monty.

**MUGA** (Rioja) ★★★(★) This has a sternly traditional image, which naturally extends to rather old-fashioned methods of wine-making. For reds, it does nothing but good, and the *crianza* is fragrant and delicate, while the Prado Enea *reserva* or *gran reserva* is more complex, but still subtle and elegant. It's not cheap, though.

**VIÑA PESQUERA** (Ribera del Duero) ★★★★ Prices have shot up since American wine writer Robert Parker likened this to Château Pétrus. Made from Tinto Fino and Garnacha, it's good but not *that* good, oaky and aromatic, with rich savoury fruit.

**RAIMAT** (Costers del Segre) ★★★★(★) The Raimat Chardonnay *cava* is honeyed, with grassy acidity. Abadía is an oak-enhanced blend of Cabernet, Tempranillo and Garnacha. Good varietals: Cabernet Sauvignon, Pinot Noir and Merlot.

**LA GRANJA REMÉLLURI** (Rioja) ★★★★ Single-estate wine; the Rodriguez family have completely rebuilt the winery, installing stainless steel fermentation tanks instead of the old wooden vats, and now make a fine, meaty *reserva*, aged in barrel for two to three years.

**LA RIOJA ALTA** (Rioja) ★★★★(★) A traditional *bodega*, firm believer in long barrel-ageing: over half the wines qualify as *reserva* or *gran reserva*. Even the Viña Alberdi *crianza* has a delightfully oaky flavour. They make two styles of *reserva*, the elegant Viña Arana and the rich Viña Ardanza. In the best years, they make exceptional *gran reservas*.

**RIOJANAS** (Rioja) ★★★(★) One of the few still using the open *lagar* method of semi-carbonic maceration. Best reds are the *reservas*: the light, elegant, plummy Viña

Albina and the richer, more concentrated Monte Reál. White Monte Reál *crianza* is soft and peachy, with just enough oak.

**MIGUEL TORRES** (Penedés) ★★★★(★) The best range of table wines in Spain. Viña Sol is a super-fresh modern white, fairly fizzing with fruit. Gran Viña Sol is half and half Parellada and Chardonnay, fresh and pineappley, enriched with hints of vanilla oak. Gran Viña Sol Green Label pairs the Parellada with the Sauvignon Blanc, like a richer, oakier Sancerre. The superstar white is Milmanda Chardonnay, with all the excitement you expect to find in expensive white Burgundy. Recent red additions are a Pinot Noir, Mas Borras, and a Merlot, Las Torres. Viña Esmeralda combines Gewürztraminer and Muscat d'Alsace. Gran Coronas Black Label is Torres' top red, pure Cabernet Sauvignon, packed with blackcurrant power, nicely tamed by oak-ageing. It now has the vineyard name, Mas La Plana, added to the label. Viña Magdala is equal parts of Pinot Noir and Tempranillo, Gran Sangredetoro is mainly Garnacha, and Coronas is the least exciting; savoury Tempranillo.

**VALDESPINO** (Jerez) ★★★★★ Another family-owned *bodega* making a range of top-class, dry sherries. Inocente is one of the last traditional *finos* at 17.5 degrees. Their Pedro Ximénez Solera Superior is one of the few examples of sherry's great sweetening wine bottled by itself.

**BODEGAS VEGA SICILIA** (Ribera del Duero) ★★★★(★) Makers of Spain's most famous and expensive red wine. Vega Sicilia Unico, the top wine, is sometimes kept in barrel for as long as ten years. Younger wines, called Valbuena, offer a cheaper glimpse of Vega Sicilia's glories.

**VINCENTE GANDIA**(Valencia) ★★★ Perhaps this DO's most go-ahead producer. Fresh white Castillo de Liria is made from Meseguera grapes, the juicy red and rosado from Bobal.

# PORTUGAL

'Lifestyle' defies translation into Portuguese. It exists, of course, but it hasn't been defined by a label-hungry media; Portugal, perched on Europe's westernmost prow, still seems less consumption-mad than the rest of us.

But as Lisbon's news-stands fill with home-grown glossies like *Olá!*, *Casa e Jardim* and *Elle Portuguesa*, so national habits are changing. The very first edition of *Webster's* (published all of seven years ago) blamed our lack of knowledge of Portuguese wine on the fact that the thirsty natives drank most of it themselves. At a time when 'Italy and France are finding their consumption dropping,' it said, 'Portugal is the leading wine country which is actually gulping down more.' How quickly the mood seems to have changed. Like so many other wine-producing countries, Portugal's per capita consumption, which peaked at over 100 litres per year, is now plummeting. As a brand new breed of Lisbon yuppie emerges from the shiny plate glass office blocks, 'less but better' seems to be the motto among the swelling ranks of the middle class.

The Portuguese still delight in the occasional *festa* or *feira do vinho* (wine festival) but they have little to do with the colourful sink-or-swim jamborees of yesteryear. Today, supermarkets with names like Pingo Doce (sweet drop) or Pão de Acucar (sugar loaf) hold their own wine *festas* to promote their expanding range of wines and, as the introduction to an impressively glossy Pingo Doce list explains, quality is the key. Back on the news-stands, specialist magazines like *Revista dos Vinhos* (Review of Wines) and *Escanção* (Wine Service) are rubbing shoulders with the glossies. At home, wine clubs appeal to a new type of wine drinker interested in taste rather than intoxication. But flicking through the pages of the new wine mags, or glancing at the shelves in any Lisbon supermarket, there is one thing that you can't fail to notice. All the wines come from Portugal. The Portuguese have always enjoyed waving their own flag, and rather than filling the shelves with international brands, Portugal's accession to the EC has wrought a steady transformation in the wine industry at home. Community money has been poured into down-at-heel wineries and is now being matched by private investors, always on the lookout for a bright prospect.

## The smell of change

Portugal's wine industry was certainly in need of a fillip. Vast co-operative wineries built in the 1950s and 1960s were (and a number still are) in desperate need of an overhaul. Just a walk past the grimy cement vats would tell even the most insensitive nose that something was badly wrong. They reeked of inefficiency. But over the last three years a metamorphosis has been taking place. Wines that used to be senile before they left the cellar door have, from one vintage to the next, become fresh and fruity. The results of stainless steel equipment, temperature controlled fermentation and a new generation of forward-thinking wine-makers are beginning to become apparent.

Against this spirit of innovation, it is heartening to find that tradition is not being completely cast aside. At a time when the Cabernet/Chardonnay bandwagon seems to be virtually unstoppable, one of Portugal's greatest assets is her treasure trove of native grapes, few of which have strayed abroad. Despite their international upbringing, wine-makers like the Australian Peter Bright at

J P Vinhos and the Californian-trained Domingos Soares Franco of José Maria da Fonseca are eager to do all they can with indigenous varieties – vines like Fernão Pires, Castelão Frances and Alfrocheiro. And wines such as José Maria da Fonseca's Periquita and Catarina or Tinto da Anfora combine Portugal's distinctly Old World flavours with New World skill.

So far, progress in Portugal's wine regions is still patchy. But, somewhat surprisingly, the Alentejo in the traditionally sleepy deep South has made some of the greatest headway. Wineries that once produced dismal hooch to quench the thirst of the parched but undemanding locals are suddenly gaining international renown. The co-op at Borba is worth singling out for its vibrant, sappy reds packed with dark cherry fruit, while the Portalegre co-op seems to be catching up. It is also worth keeping an eye on some of the Alentejo's single estates. The Rothschild family have bought a 50 per cent stake in Quinta do Carmo, already the source of an impressive red, and Herdade da Cartuxa, José da Sousa Rosado Fernandes, Morgado de Reguengo, Horta do Rocio and Roqueval complete the lengthening shortlist.

### Dão on an up

Dão is another region that has taken a giant step forward. For at least three decades, growers in these remote granite mountains lived with the delusion that they were making some of Portugal's best reds when in reality this was a long way from the truth. The archaic local regulations that kept private investment out of the region have finally been swept away. Sogrape, Portugal's largest wine-maker and producers of the leading brand of Dão, Grão Vasco, has seized the initiative, investing over £6 million in a new winery in the heart of the region. Its first wines certainly justify the expenditure. With peppery, all-spice flavours akin to a good southern French Syrah, they are worlds away from the lean, charmless demeanour of old-fashioned Dão.

All over Portugal, prices have settled as three good and plentiful vintages have made up for the near-catastrophic harvest in 1988. Vinho Verde has returned to the shelves offering reasonable value. Gazela and Aveleda are reliably crisp and crackling although single estate wines, especially those made from either the aromatic Loureiro or Alvarinho grape, have more flavour.

The recent decline in sales of port (see page 199) should leave a surplus of high quality grapes for the production of table wine in the Douro. Once again, Sogrape is in a good position to benefit from the others' misfortunes. The port house Ferreira (a Sogrape subsidiary since 1986) has produced Barca Velha, Portugal's most sought-after (and therefore most expensive) red wine. The savoury, smoky depth of Reserva Especial and the damson-like flavour of Esteva are much more affordable. Quinta do Côtto is a single estate worth singling out.

For new flavours (along with some old-fashioned prices) look to Bairrada, particularly the young red and white wines of Caves Alianca. Caves São João and Luis Pato make wonderfully solid, concentrated reds from the doughty Baga grape, but be prepared to tough it out with tannin.

For the best armchair insight into Portugal's emerging 'lifestyle' look out for the minimalist labels of Sogrape's superb *reservas*. The tropical, peach-like flavours of the oak-aged whites from Bairrada and the Douro are an epoch ahead of the flat, lifeless wines that used to appeal to the Portuguese but no one else. But beware of a future Pandora's Box. As demand gathers pace in the home market, prices will undoubtedly rise: buy now.                    RICHARD MAYSON

# WHITE WINES

Portuguese white wines are still dominated in our perception by Vinho Verde, despite the shortage after a duff 1988 vintage and subsequent price rises. Real Vinho Verde, made dry, and very slightly spritzy from good grapes – in particular Loureiro or Alvarinho – can be a magnificent, refreshing summer drink.

Portugal hasn't done so well with its other white wines so far, despite the fact that there are a number of perfectly good native white grapes. But standards are getting better, as recent releases from Sogrape, José Maria da Fonseca and JP Vinhos show. Most promising grape varieties: Loureiro, Malvasia, Viosinho, Maria Gomes/Fernão Pires. A dollop of Chardonnay can help to enliven some.

## WINES & WINE REGIONS

**BAIRRADA, DOC** Some increasingly good dry white wines from the Maria Gomes grape. Sogrape, makers of Mateus Rosé, have a winery at Anadia and have done the most to freshen up flavours. They produce the crisp, floral *Quinta de Pedralvites* here. Also very good: *Sogrape's Bairrada Reserva*, a ripe, peachy style, fermented and aged in new Portuguese oak.

**BUCELAS, DOC** Popular in Wellington's day, this dry white wine from a village close to the capital had almost been driven to extinction, with Caves Velhas left as the sole producer. However, two new wine-makers seem to be set on reviving the flagging fortune and reputation of Bucelas. Of the trio, Quinta da Romeira seems to be making the most of the ferociously acidic Arinto and Esgana Cão (Dog Strangler) grapes.

**DÃO, DOC** White Dão was traditionally (and mostly still is) yellow, tired and heavy. But a few companies are now making a lighter, fresher, fruitier style, and now that the co-ops are losing the upper hand with production, others look set to follow suit. White *Grão Vasco*, now made in Sogrape's shiny new winery at Quinta dos Carvalhais is a significant departure from tradition with its crisp lemon-zest appeal. Sadly, local regulations insist that the wine should be at least six months old before bottling, so it pays to catch the wine young. Look out for oak-aged *reservas* in future.

**DOURO, DOC** Nearly all the best table wines are red, though the *Planalto* white from *Sogrape*, the Mateus-makers, is full and honeyed and good, as is its oaked *Douro Reserva*, and *Esteva* from *Ferreira* is clean and crisp. *Quinta do Valprado* Chardonnay, made by the Seagram-owned *Raposeira* fizz company near Lamego, is honeyed and mouth-filling.

**SETÚBAL PENINSULA** This sub-divides into the IPR (Indicaçao de Proveniência Regulamentada, similar to France's VDQS) regions of Palmela and Arrábida. The best wines are produced on the limestone soils of the Arrábida hills where Peter Bright makes a rich, oak-aged Chardonnay, *Cova da Ursa*. The whole peninsula is about to become Portugal's first Vinho Regional, probably with the name of Entre Tejo e Sado. The *João Pires Muscat* is also good. *José Maria da Fonseca* prefers local grapes, though Chardonnay gives a lemony lift to the white *Pasmados*, and *Quinta da Camarate* boasts Riesling, Gewürztraminer and Muscat.

**VINHO VERDE, DOC** Verde here means youthful-green, immature-green, un-aged, not the colour of a croquet lawn. Ideally, these wines are extremely dry, positively tart, and brilliantly suited to the heavy, oily Portuguese cuisine. But we almost always get them slightly sweetened and softened, which is a pity, although it is in its peculiar way a classic wine style.

Most wines come from co-ops or are sold under merchants' brand names, but there is an increasing tendency for the larger, grander private producers to bottle their own. And some of the big firms are beginning to make characterful single-quinta Vinhos Verdes alongside their big brands. *Palacio da Brejoeira*, made from the Alvarinho grape, is much more alcoholic and full bodied, and expensive, for that matter, than the general run of Vinho Verde. *Casa de Cabanelas, Casa de Compostela, Casa de Sezim, Paço d'Anha, Paço de Cardido, Paço de Teixeiro, Quinta da Aveleda* (its *Grinalda* is one of the best),

*Quinta do Tamariz, Solar das Bouças, Quinta do Azevedo* and the pure Loureiro wines from the *Ponte do Lima* co-op are good too.

Vinho Verde can be made from a variety of grapes, but there's often a higher proportion of Loureiro in the single-property wines. Indeed, there's quite rightly a lot of interest in Loureiro, with its dry, apricotty, Muscatty aroma and flavour. It is more attractive than the much-praised Alvarinho, and it gives the wines a much more tangy but fruity character. *Peter Bright*'s new Vinho Verde, for example, is almost entirely Loureiro, as are the excellent *Solar das Bouças, Quinta do Tamariz* and *Casa dos Cunhas*. And *Sogrape* has planted predominantly Loureiro at Quinta de Azevedo.

# RED WINES

Portuguese red wines can be some of the most exciting in Europe. The country is a treasure-house of unique, indigenous grape types with flavours totally unrelated to the mainstream of the French or German classics. But most wines are vinified in a heavy-handed manner and aged too long in unsuitable concrete or old wooden vats. Paradoxically, it's in the established wine regions that ageing requirements are most heavy-handed. In areas like Ribatejo, Oeste or Alentejo, because there are no rules (except for grape variety recommendations), it's easier to bottle wine at its optimum age. The flavours of the young reds flowing out of these regions can be startling, and the price is never high. Now that various areas are getting demarcated status we're keeping our fingers crossed they won't be too restrictive, but we can't be sure, because trying to persuade a Portuguese wine-maker that his red is better as young as possible and bottled without any ageing requirement, is one of life's more thankless tasks. However, the new category of Vinhos Regionais is likely to be less restrictive than DOCs and IPRs.

## WINES & WINE REGIONS

**ALENTEJO** An area of great potential, where some producers are still very primitive, but more and more are well-equipped and capable of producing good wines. It's an enormous area, covering much of the southern part of the country, and there is no doubt it can produce exceptional grapes. The large *José Maria da Fonseca* company, which is the leading innovator in commercial red wine

production, has invested a lot of time and energy in the region. Apart from Fonseca's blends, and the *Tinto Velho* from the *JS Rosado Fernandes* estate, which Fonseca now owns, the best wines are from various co-ops. The reds from the *Redondo* co-op, with their big, brash grapy fruit show the potential waiting to be tapped. The upfront rich damson and raspberry fruit of the *Paço dos Infantes* from Almodovar, south of

Lisbon, shows the same marvellously untamed excitement. The *Borba* co-op, *Cartuxa, Esporão* and *Reguengos de Monsaraz* are producing reds with wonderful fruit. The Alentejo is attracting more interest than any other region in Portugal. The Rothschilds have bought a share of a property, *Quinta do Carmo,* near Estremoz, and they're not the only ones: other foreign investors are also looking seriously at the region.

**ALGARVE** The south coastal strip of the country, making undistinguished wines – mostly alcoholic reds. Once an *Região Demarcada* in its own right, it has now been split into four *Denominações de Origem Controlada,* Lagos, Portimão, Lagoa and Tavira. All deserve demotion from DOC status. Among producers, the *Lagoa* co-op is the best bet.

**BAIRRADA, DOC** In the flat land down towards the sea from the hilly Dão region, vineyards mingle with wheatfields, olive trees and meadows, and the wines frequently overshadow the more famous Dão reds. The wines are apt to be tannic, often the result of fermenting the wine with the grape stalks, but the Baga grape, the chief one in the blend, gives a sturdy, pepper, plum-and-blackcurrant fruit to the wine which can often survive the over-ageing, and at ten years old, although the resiny bite and peppery edge are apparent, a delicious, dry fruit is more in command. The best Bairrada wines age quite extraordinarily well. Some growers, like *Luis Pato,* are now experimenting with blending in a dollop of softening Cabernet Sauvignon.

Some Portuguese merchants will tell you that their own 'Garrafeira' wines are based on Bairrada, though the label won't say so. That's probably true, because of the traditional Portuguese approach to high quality reds – buy where the grapes are best, blend and age at your company's cellars, and sell the 'brew' under your own name. Since 1979, however, the Bairrada

region has been demarcated and bulk sales have been banned, and the challenging, rather angular, black fruit flavours of the wines now sport a Bairrada label. *São João* produces wine of world class. *Alianca* and *Sogrape* (one of the two big Mateus plants is in Bairrada) are good. The best co-op is *Vilharino do Bairro*, and *Cantanhede* and *Mealhada* aren't bad. Encouragingly, single-estate wines are emerging, with *Luis Pato* the leader so far. He must be good because he's already had some of his wine turned down by the Bairrada Região as untypical because he'd used new oak instead of old!

**COLARES, DOC** Grown in the sand dunes on the coast near Lisbon from the doughty but scented Ramisco grape. Almost all the wine is vinified at the local Adega Regional, stalks and all, aged in concrete tanks for two to three years, then sold to merchants for further maturation and sale. The young wine has fabulous cherry perfume but is *numbingly* tannic. As it ages it gets an exciting rich pepper and bruised plums flavour, but the 1974s are only just ready. The Adega no longer has a monopoly on Colares, but for the time being only *Carvalho, Ribeiro & Ferreira* show interest in exploiting the new freedom.

**DÃO, DOC** This upland eyrie, ringed by mountains, reached by steep, exotic, forest-choked river gorges, makes Portugal's most famous, if not always her most appetizing reds. They are reputed to become velvet-smooth with age. My experience is that they rarely achieve this and could do with less ageing in wood and more in bottle. They are made from a mixture of six grapes, of which the Touriga Nacional is the best, and they develop a strong, dry, herby taste, almost with a pine resin bite.

The protectionist rules that allowed companies to buy only finished wine, not grapes, from growers, and that forbade firms from outside the region to set up wineries there, have been abolished and *Sogrape*, with its own winery in the region, is making the most of its new-found freedom. Among the others, *Caves São João* deserves an honourable mention along with *Caves Alianca* and *José Maria da Fonseca* for its brand, *Terras Altas*. Other firms are persuading their co-op suppliers to leave the grape stalks out of the fermentation vats and make cleaner, more modern wines, but there's still a long way to go.

**DOURO, DOC** The Douro valley is famous for the production of port. But only a proportion of the crop – usually about 40 per cent – is made into port, the rest being

*The price guides for this section begin on page 366.*

sold as table wine. Traditionally, all the best grapes have gone into the region's most famous product, but a number of private producers and now quite a few of the port houses themselves have started making high quality table wines, based on Touriga Francesa, Touriga Nacional and Tinta Roriz, and one producer is working with Cabernet Sauvignon. The flavour can be delicious – soft and glyceriny, with a rich raspberry and peach fruit, and a dry perfume somewhere between liquorice, smoky bacon and cigar tobacco. Quality is still patchy, but then it's early days yet. Look out for *Quinta da Cismeira, Quinta do Côtto, Sogrape; Barca Velha, Reserva Especial* and *Esteva* from Ferreira.

**OESTE** Portugal's largest wine area north of Lisbon (and largest wine area, full stop, in terms of volume) is dominated by enormous co-operative wineries, some of which are just beginning to do something about quality. *Arruda* makes strong, gutsy reds, *Alenquer* makes softer, more glyceriny wine, while the *Obidos* reds are drier, more acid, but good in a cedary way. *Torres Vedras'* reds are lighter than Arruda, with a climate more influenced by cooling Atlantic air. Single-estate *Quinta de Abrigada* makes light, creamy whites and stylish damson and cherry reds, and *Quinta das Pancas* has some Chardonnay and some Cabernet. These two are the only private estates doing much so far, though *Paulo da Silva's Beira Mar and Casal de Azenha* are both good Oeste blends. The region sub-divides into six IPR regions: Arruda, Alenquer, Óbidos, Torres Vedras, Alcobaça and Encostas d'Aire.

**RIBATEJO** Portugal's second largest region, in the flat lands alongside the Tagus, provides the base wine for some important brands and some of Portugal's best 'garrafeira' wines – in particular the *Romeira* of *Caves Velhas. Carvalho Ribeiro* and *Ferreira,* recently bought by Costa Pina, a subsidiary of Allied Lyons, also bottle some good garrafeiras, and with multi-national backing their wines are likely to improve. The co-op at *Almeirim* markets good wine under its own name, and the *Torre Velha* brand isn't bad. The *Margaride* estate is the Ribatejo's leading estate. The wines are sold as *Dom Hermano, Margarides* and under the names of their properties, *Casal do Monteiro* and *Convento da Serra.* The wines are patchy, but can be very good. The region is being split up into six IPRs (Indicação de Proveniencia Regulamentada) the six being Almeirim, Cartaxo, Chamusca, Santarém, Tomar and Coruche.

**SETÚBAL PENINSULA** *JP Vinhos* and *José Maria da Fonseca* are the leading lights here, for reds and whites. Imports like Cabernet Sauvignon and Merlot are made as varietals in their own right as well as used in blends with local grapes like Periquita.

**VINHO VERDE, DOC** Sixty per cent of all Vinho Verde produced is, surprisingly, red, made from four different native grapes, of which the Vinhão is best. The wine is wonderfully sharp, harsh even, is hardly ever seen outside the country and goes a treat with traditional Portuguese dishes like *bacalhau,* or salt cod. Red Vinho Verde is losing its popularity even in Portugal. I think I am virtually alone in the entire English-speaking world in regretting this.

# FORTIFIED WINES

Rather like Britain's post-war economy, the port industry goes through cycles of boom and bust. At the end of the 1960s and early 1970s, the industry was very nearly bust. Then came a period of spectacular growth as port bucked the downward trend of other fortified wines. Worldwide sales peaked at 9.2 million cases, an all-time record, in 1988. But since then traditionally loyal markets like our own have not only stop drinking more port, but have actually begun to drink less of it.

The downturn could not happen at a more inopportune time for the port trade, both growers and shippers. With 2500 hectares of new vineyard, planted and subsidized under the 1980s World Bank Scheme and intended to bring greater prosperity to the area, now coming on stream, the Douro faces an increasing crisis of overproduction. These new vineyards, too, are all due to produce top-quality wine: some of the conditions attached to obtaining the World Bank subsidies were that the sites to be planted had to be grade A (see page 204) and had to be planted with just a handful of grape varieties deemed after long research, to be the best. In these circumstances, the usual EC solutions to overproduction – distillation and compulsory uprooting – would hardly be appropriate.

No longer does the trade trust the authorities to handle the problem. The Casa do Douro, the quasi-official body purporting to represent the interests of the growers, and controlling the production of port, has laid itself open to accusations of a conflict of interests by acquiring 40 per cent of Royal Oporto, one of port's largest shippers. The Instituto do Vinho do Porto, the trade's overall regulatory body, could take a lead but so far has not done so. It may be that decisive action will only come from Brussels; in the meantime, expect increasing quantities of good Douro table wine on the market, at agreeable prices. **RICHARD MAYSON**

## GRAPES & FLAVOURS

Eighteen different grape varieties are used to make red and white ports, and of these the most important in terms of quality and flavour are the Roriz, Barroca, Touriga Francesa and Touriga Nacional among the reds, and the Malvasia Dorada and Malvasia Fina in the whites. The Moscatel is chiefly grown in Setúbal just south of Lisbon, where it makes a famous, but not thrilling, sweet fortified wine.

## WINES & WINE REGIONS

**CARCAVELOS, RD** Just when Carcavelos looked as if it was about to disappear for ever, along comes a new vineyard. *Quinta dos Pesos* is making a good, nutty, fortified wine rather like an aged Tawny port.

**MADEIRA, RD** Each Madeira style is supposedly based on one of four grapes, Malmsey (Malvasia), Bual, Verdelho and Sercial, though at the moment only the more expensive Madeiras really live up to their labels – the cheaper ones, up to 'five-years-old', are almost all made from the inferior Tinta Negra Mole. The EC is enforcing a rule that 85 per cent of a wine labelled with a grape variety should be made from it, so the cheaper Madeiras are likely to start calling themselves, more honestly, 'Pale Dry', 'Dark Rich', and so on.

The Malmsey grape makes the sweetest Madeira, reeking sometimes of Muscovado sugar, dark, rich and brown, but with a smoky bite and surprisingly high acidity that makes it positively refreshing after a long meal. The Bual grape is also rich and strong, less concentrated, sometimes with a faintly rubbery whiff and higher acidity. Verdelho makes pungent, smoky, medium-sweet wine with more obvious, gentle fruit, and the Sercial makes dramatic dry wine, savoury, spirity, tangy, with a steely, piercing acidity. To taste what Madeira is all about you need a ten-year-old, and, frankly, really good Madeira should be two or three times that age.

The move into Madeira by the Symington family (of port fame) should herald new investment – and better wines.

**SETÚBAL, DOC** Good, but always a little spirity and never quite as perfume-sweet as one would like, perhaps because they don't use the best Muscat. It comes in a six-year-old and a 25-year-old version, and the wines do gain in concentration with age – the 25-year-old does have a lot more character and less overbearing spiritiness – but the sweetness veers towards the cooked marmalade of southern French Muscats rather than the honeyed, raisined richness of the Australian versions. You can still occasionally find older wines like *José Maria da Fonseca*'s 1934, or its intense, pre-phylloxera *Torna Viagem*, with a powerful treacle toffee character balanced by a sharp acidic tang.

**PORT (DOURO, DOC)** The simplest and cheapest port wines available in Britain are labelled simply 'Ruby' and 'Tawny'. Ruby is usually blended from the unexceptional grapes of unexceptional vineyards to create a tangy, tough, but warmingly sweet wine to knock back uncritically. It should have a spirity rasp along with the sweetness. Cheap Tawny at around the same price as Ruby is simply a mindless mixture of light Ruby and White ports, and is almost never as good as the Ruby would have been, left to itself.

Calling these inferior concoctions 'Tawnies' is very misleading because there's a genuine 'Tawny', too. Proper Tawnies are kept in wooden barrels for at least five, but preferably ten or more years to let the colour leach out and a gentle fragrance and delicate flavour of nuts, brown sugar and raisins develop. Most of these more expensive Tawnies carry an age on the label, which must be a multiple of 10: 10, 20, 30 or even 40 years old, but the figure indicates a style rather than a true date: a 10-year-old Tawny might contain some 6-year-old and some 14-year-old wine. Lack of age on a Tawny label – however often it says 'Fine', 'Old', and so on – is a bad sign and usually implies a cheap, Ruby-based blend, though there are some good brands like *Harvey's Director's Bin Very Superior Old Tawny* or *Delaforce His Eminence's Choice*. Most Tawnies reach their peak at somewhere between ten and 15 years, and few ports improve with more than 20 years in barrel, so don't bother to pay inflated prices for 30- and 40-year-old wine. Try *Cockburn 10-year-old*, *Ferreira 10* and *20-year-old*, *Fonseca 10-year-old* and *20-year-old*, *Harvey's Director's Bin*, *Sainsbury's 10-year-old*. *Colheita* ports – single vintage Tawnies – are increasingly available, usually from Portuguese houses, and can be really delicious. *Calem* and *Niepoort* are good.

**VINTAGE PORTS** are the opposite to the Tawnies, since the objective here is to make a big, impressive, concentrated mouthful, rather than anything too delicate. Vintage years are 'declared' by port shippers when the quality seems particularly good – usually about three times a decade although we managed five in the 1980s. They are matured in wooden casks for two years or so, then bottled and left to mature for a decade or two.

The final effect should have far more weight and richness than a Tawny of similar age, since the maturation has taken place in the almost airless and neutral confines of the glass bottle, which ages the wines far more slowly. There should also be a much more exciting, complex tangle of flavours; blackcurrant, plums, minty liquorice, pepper and herbs, cough mixture and a lot more besides. Vintage port you get animated and opinionated about, whereas Tawny is more a wine for quiet reflection.

If you want a peek at what Vintage port

can be like, buy Single-Quinta wine. Single Quintas (Portuguese for 'farms') are usually from the best vineyards in the less brilliant years, but instead of being bottled and shipped after only two years or so, they are bottled after two years, stored for up to ten years, and shipped ready to drink. They cost less than similarly mature Vintage port and are usually extremely good. Look for *Taylor's Quinta da Vargellas, Dow's Quinta do Bonfim, Warre's Quinta da Cavadinha, Fonseca's Quinta do Panascal* and *Quinta de la Rosa*.

Another good-value Vintage port look-alike is Crusted port. These are a British speciality, blends of wines from two or three different vintages, shipped in cask, then bottled slightly later than Vintage, say on average at three years old, so they retain the peppery attack of the top wines and also keep a good deal of the rich, exotic perfumed sweetness of real 'Vintage'. They are called Crusted because of the sediment that will form after three or four years in bottle. More and more houses are producing Crusted ports and they are often the best quality/price ratio on the market.

Two other types of port like to think of themselves as vintage style. Vintage Character and Late Bottled Vintage are bottled four to six years after the harvest. Ideally, this extra time maturing in wood should bring about an effect similar to a dozen years of bottle-ageing. Bottled at four years, and not too heavily filtered to remove all the sediment, it still can, but most Vintage Character and Late-Bottled ports are, sadly, too browbeaten into early decline and have about as much personality as a panful of potatoes. The best, labelled with the year of bottling, are from *Fonseca, Niepoort, Smith-Woodhouse, Ramos-Pinto* and *Warre*. They are delicious, high-quality products, can throw a sediment in the bottle, and may need decanting.

There are two styles of White port, dry and sweet. In general, the flavour is a bit thick and alcoholic, the sweet ones even tasting slightly of rough grape skins. But there are a few good dry ones, though I've never felt any great urge to drink them anywhere except in the blinding mid-summer heat of the Douro valley when they're refreshing with a few ice-cubes and a big splash of lemonade or tonic.

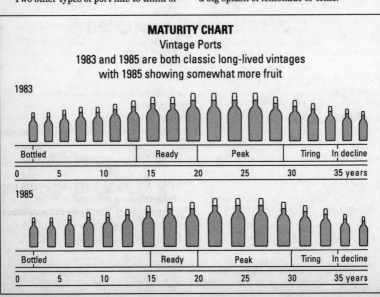

**MATURITY CHART**
Vintage Ports
1983 and 1985 are both classic long-lived vintages
with 1985 showing somewhat more fruit

1983

| Bottled | | Ready | Peak | Tiring | In decline |
|---|---|---|---|---|---|

0    5    10    15    20    25    30    35 years

1985

| Bottled | | Ready | Peak | Tiring | In decline |
|---|---|---|---|---|---|

0    5    10    15    20    25    30    35 years

# PORT SHIPPER PROFILES

**CÁLEM** ★★★★ Important Portuguese shipper founded in the last century and still family owned. Cálem produce excellent 10, 20, 30 and 40-year old Tawnies, good Colheitas, and good Vintage port from the spectacular Quinta da Foz at Pinhão.

**CHURCHILL GRAHAM** ★★★(★) Established as recently as 1981, the first independent port shipper to be founded in more than 50 years. John Graham is establishing a reputation for intense, concentrated wines made to last.

**COCKBURN** ★★★★ Shippers of the best-selling 'Fine Old Ruby' and 'Special Reserve'. At the forefront of research into viticulture in the Upper Douro. Recent Vintage ports have been stunning.

**CROFT** ★★(★) Quinta da Roeda near Pinhão forms the backbone of its Vintage wines, but many wines are over-delicate.

**DELAFORCE** ★★(★) The Tawny, His Eminence's Choice, is its best-known wine.

**DOW** ★★★★★ Quinta do Bomfim at Pinhão produces the backbone of Dow's firm-flavoured, long-living Vintage ports and has also been launched as a Single Quinta.

**FERREIRA** ★★★★ One of the best Portuguese-owned shippers, making elegant, early-maturing Vintages and two superb Tawnies; 10-year-old Quinta do Porto and 20-year-old Duque de Bragança. Bought by Sogrape in 1988.

**FONSECA GUIMARAENS** ★★★★★ Family-run shippers belonging to the Yeatman side of Taylor, Fladgate and Yeatman. Fonseca's wines are sweeter and less austere than Taylor's. The Vintage ports are often outstanding, but the quality of its commercial releases is reassuring.

**GOULD CAMPBELL** ★★★★ The name is used mainly for Vintage ports which tend to be ripe and relatively quick to mature.

**GRAHAM** ★★★★★ Graham's ports tend to be rich and sweet in style. Quinta dos Malvedos is its best-known property and is released as a Single-Quinta wine in lesser vintages. Fine Vintage styles.

**NIEPOORT** ★★★★★ Tiny firm run by the fourth and fifth generations of a Dutch family who share a total commitment to quality. Aged Tawnies, Colheitas, traditional LBVs and long-lasting Vintage wines.

**OFFLEY FORRESTER** ★★★(★) Famous for 'Boa Vista' Vintage and LBV ports. Vintage is mostly based on its own Quinta da Boa Vista and can be insubstantial. Excellent Baron de Forrester Tawnies.

**QUINTA DO NOVAL** ★★★★ A beautiful quinta high above Pinhão as well as a shipper. Noval's Nacional wines, produced from of pre-phylloxera, ungrafted vines, are legendary and fetch a stratospheric price at auction. Other Noval wines don't attempt such heights, but are usually good, if light. Noval LB is widely sold, but isn't actually that special; the Tawnies are much better.

**RAMOS-PINTO** ★★★★ Delicious Tawnies from two quintas – Ervamoira and Bom Retiro. Elegant, nutty and delicate.

**REAL VINICOLA** ★★(★) The largest port producer selling ports under seven different names. The wines can sometimes be good. Vintage ports are generally early maturing.

**SANDEMAN** ★★★ Best at making good, aged Tawnies and, recently, improved, quite concentrated vintage wines.

**SMITH WOODHOUSE** ★★★★ Some delicious Vintage and LBVs. Concentrated Vintage wines which tend to mature early. Full-flavoured Crusted.

**TAYLOR, FLADGATE AND YEATMAN** ★★★★★ Very high quality range, some would say of 'first growth' level. Even so, some recent commercial releases have seen standards slip a little, and their Vintage port is no longer ahead of the field. Quinta de Vargellas produces some of the best single-quinta wines, worth the hunt.

**WARRE** ★★★★★ The first port company in which the entrepreneurial Symington dynasty became involved. Warre produces serious wines: good LBVs and Vintage, fine 'Nimrod' Tawny. Quinta da Cavadinha has recently been launched as a Single Quinta.

## PORT CLASSIFICATION

If you think that Burgundy and Bordeaux make a meal out of classifying their vineyards, just look at how rigidly port is controlled. Nothing is left to chance. The age of the vines is classified on a scale from 0 to 60 points. The level of upkeep of the vines is ruthlessly marked from –500 to +100 points. The objective is to score as many points as possible. The highest possible score would be +1680 points, while the bottom score possible would be a massively embarrassing –3430. The classification, based on points scored, is from A to F, and controls how many litres of juice per 1000 vines can be turned into port. The rest has to be made into table wine, which gives a smaller return.

### The Vineyard Calculation

**Productivity** (Ranging from about 500 litres per 1000 vines to about 2000 litres; the lower the yield the higher the points scored.)
Worst: 0 points          Best: +80 points
**Altitude** (Ranging from a highest allowable altitude of 650 metres to a lowest of 150 metres.)
Worst: –900 points          Best: +150 points
**Soil** (Scored according to type. Schist scores best, granite worst.)
Worst: –350 points          Best: +100 points
**Geographical position** (Predetermined locations score different marks.)
Worst: –50 points          Best: +600 points
**Upkeep of vineyard** (Good housekeeping awards for various factors.)
Worst: –500 points          Best: +100 points
**Variety and quality of grapes**
Worst: –300 points          Best: +150 points
**Gradient** (From 1-in-6 to 1-in-30 – the steeper the better.)
Worst: –100 points          Best: +100 points
**Shelter**
Worst: 0          Best: +70 points

**Age of vines** (With 5-year-olds scoring 30; up to 25-year-olds scoring 60.)
Worst: 0          Best: +60 points
**Distance root to root** (The distance from the end of one vine's root to the start of the next root – too close is frowned upon.)
Worst: –50 points          Best: +50 points
**Nature of land**
Worst: –600 points          Best: +100 points
**Aspect**
Worst: –30 points          Best: +100 points

### THE TOTAL
The experts then add up all these points and classify the vineyards according to score, allowing each group to make a certain number of litres of wine per 1000 vines, as follows:

| | |
|---|---|
| A (1201 points or more) | 600 litres |
| B (1001–1200 points) | 600 litres |
| C (801–1000 points) | 590 litres |
| D (601–800 points) | 580 litres |
| E (401–600 points) | 580 litres |
| F (400 points or less) | 260 litres |

## PORT VINTAGES

Not every year produces a crop of fine enough quality for vintage-dated wine to be made, and a few houses may not make Vintage port even in a generally good year. All depends on the quality the individual house has produced, although it is extremely rare for a house to declare two consecutive years. Announcing the intention to bottle Vintage port is known as 'declaring'. Only five vintages were good enough in the 1980s, and there has been no general declaration since 1985.

**1987** Four shippers, Ferreira, Martinez, Niepoort and Offley, chose to declare this small but good vintage. Coming so hard on the heels of the nearly universal 1985 declaration, most shippers opted instead for Single Quinta wines for medium term drinking.

**1985** A tremendously ripe and healthy crop of grapes – along with the rest of Europe. A unanimous 'declaration' of a vintage is not that common, but 1985 was declared a 'vintage' year by every important shipper. The prices were high but are coming down, and the quality is exceptionally good. The wines don't quite have the solidity of the 1983s but they make up for this with a juicy ripeness of fruit and unusually precocious signs of fragrant perfumes to come. Although *Taylor* isn't as outstanding as usual, several perennial under-achievers like *Croft* and *Offley* are very good, *Cockburn* is very attractive, and *Fonseca* is rich and lush. However, my favourites are *Graham, Warre, Dow, Gould Campbell* and *Churchill Graham*. The price makes me nervous; but the wine's seductive in the extreme.

**1983** Marvellous wine, strong and aggressive to taste at the moment, but with a deep, brooding sweetness which is all ripe, clean fruit. This won't be one of the most fragrant vintages, but it will be a sturdy classic in a dozen years' time.

**1982** Perfectly nice but lacking the brilliance of a great year. The wines have a slightly concocted sweetness about them, and lack the hidden depth which great Vintage port needs to reveal as it matures. Good, not great.

**1980** A good vintage, though excessively expensive when first offered. Although they were consequently unpopular, the wines are developing a delicious, drier than usual style. It should be starting to soften now, and will peak about 1995.

**1977** Brilliant wine which has hardly begun to mature. The flavour is a marvellous mixture of great fruit sweetness and intense spice and herb fragrance. Still extremely youthful, these wines need years yet. They will rock you back on your heels if you drink them now, but maybe you like that sort of thing.

**1975** These in general don't have the stuffing that a true vintage style demands, but some are surprisingly gaining weight and richness and are excellent for drinking now. *Noval, Taylor, Dow, Warre* and *Graham* need no apologies. Most of the others do.

**1970** Lovely stuff, but, curiously, only cautiously praised. Fainthearts, take up your corkscrews! This is exceptional, balanced port, already good to drink, very sweet, and ripe with a fascinating citrus flash of freshness. It'll last for ages but it's delicious already. All the top houses are really special – lead by *Fonseca, Taylor, Warre, Graham* and Dow, but lesser houses like *Calem* and *Santos Junior* are also excellent.

**1966** They didn't rate this at first, but they do now. It's gained body and oomph and is now approaching its best. Doesn't *quite* have the super-ripe balance of the '70 or the startling, memorable character of the '63, but a very good year just the same. *Fonseca* is the star at the moment.

**1963** They call it the 'classic' year, and one can see why. It's big, deep, and spicy, with a remarkable concentration of flavours based on any really ripe red or black fruit you can think of washed in an essence of liquorice, mint and herbs. One or two have lost a surprising amount of colour recently, but in the main it's so good that if you decide to see in the millennium with a bottle of *Fonseca, Taylor, Graham, Dow* or *Cockburn* ... get my address from *Webster's!*

# UNITED STATES

Discussion about California wines is focussing more and more on price. We know that the state can produce world class wines: Chardonnays, Cabernets and, increasingly, Pinot Noirs (Saintsbury and Etude for example) to rival many French. There is a wealth of flavour, the oaky monsters have dwindled, the reds are beginning to avoid excessive tannin, and relative subtlety rules. If you had only California wines for the rest of your life, you could die reasonably happy.

That is, if you could afford them. The argument from California typically goes like this: if I can sell my wine for US$30 at home, why should I offer it for US$15 to the UK? There is no reason at all, or hardly any, if the wine sells. But, as US consumption has fallen, as recession and a virulent neo-fascist Prohibitionist movement has gained the public ear, so the little 'if' has grown into a bigger IF.

Prices were set purposely high. They were felt to reflect of the worth of the wine (and perhaps the ego of the maker); aim lower than your neighbour, and you were admitting his wine was better. Land prices, especially in Napa, are horrendous: US$50-60,000 per planted acre of vineyard; it doesn't take a hot-shot accountant to point out that you need to make a stack of money to recoup that. Yet we in the UK can buy good wines from all over the world for less. Why should we pay US$30 for California?

That was roughly the stand-off position until the beginning of 1992. Then something happened, a combination perhaps of sluggish sales and a realization that they (the Californians) had measured the UK all wrong. We obviously weren't going to budge, so they had to. Suddenly, wines that had been sitting on shelves at £10 and over were shifting at £8.99, £7.99, even £6.99. Suddenly there was a whole shoal of wines under £5, where previously Gallo and a couple of undistinguished others had fished alone. A prime example was Randall Grahm's Catalyst, on sale at Oddbins for £4.99; some bottles stayed on the shelf for up to half an hour. Perhaps they should have called it Dyno-Rod, because it helped to unblock the whole system.

Not all producers are equally keen on this approach, however. At the time of writing, of the 144 California wineries that export to the UK, only about 20 compete at all under £6.

### Wine the Henry Ford way

Mention of Randall Grahm recalls another problem. His Catalyst was made from Grenache, and he has been through most of the Rhône varieties like a child let loose in a sweet shop. Italian varieties are his current fad: next year, who knows, it may be Portuguese. Grahm, because of his iconoclastic reputation, can sell these curiosities, but many other growers seem rooted to the spot. Echoing Henry Ford, they offer us any grape variety we like, providing it is either Chardonnay or Cabernet Sauvignon. There is not much Pinot Gris, Malvasia or Marsanne about. They claim that land prices are at the root of this too: if they can't balance the books with $30 Chardonnay, who on earth is going to pay that for a Marsanne? They are prisoners of real estate, and can grow nothing else.

But how much Chardonnay and Cabernet can we all tolerate? Perhaps, now that everybody is having to grub up vines infected with phylloxera they will turn to more adventurous alternatives. Some estimate that 80-90 per cent of Napa

Valley is affected, so the scope is enormous. Watch out, though, for the canny marketing of 'pre-phylloxera' wines.

Sadly, Pinot Noir is hard to sell, because the California style is increasingly, gloriously different to that of Burgundy. If there were a prize for code-cracking head-banging I'm-going-to-do-this-if-it-kills-me cussedness, Tim Mondavi would undoubtedly win: his Reserves are some of the finest examples anywhere. Several others in Carneros and South of the Bay are making similarly exciting wines – but it's been a helluva sweat.

It's Oregon that has the Pinot Noir reputation, but the proof is not yet conclusive. The Burgundian skills of the Drouhin family are now producing top quality wines there, so obviously there are good grapes. They might also like to give some of the local growers some viticulture lessons, and give some of the more disarmingly chaotic wine-makers a few wine-making lessons, too. But no lessons in Napa-style self-promotion, please: Oregon has a charm and sincerity, and indeed a pioneering spirit that has long since disappeared from Napa.

Although it is difficult to generalize about an Oregon Pinot Noir style, the best have a lightness and freshness allied to clean, ripe, and sometimes powerful fruit: as if made from raspberries instead of grapes. The poorest are heavy and jammy, as if made from concentrate; chaptalization is not unusual. Standards of wine-making vary widely and not all wines are as clean as they might be; but then Burgundy suffers from that too, if you call high prices suffering.

Good acidity benefits most varieties, so Chardonnays can be racy and elegant, although they are competing against a better bunch from around the world. Other odd surprises pop up: Pinot Blanc, Pinot Gris, Sauvignon Blanc, Chenin Blanc, Gewürztraminer. 'Everybody writes about Pinot Noir,' said one producer, 'but Riesling pays the bills.' So, presumably, does a wine called Cache Phloe Red.

We are still waiting for the full force of America's sleeping giant, Washington. Some of the cheap wines over here have been poor, but Chateau Ste Michelle and Columbia Crest make big volumes of tasty wine, and prices must be negotiable in the current US slump. Smaller wineries, too, make delicious, original flavours at by no means silly prices. JIM AINSWORTH

## RED GRAPES & FLAVOURS

**BARBERA** There have always been a few good Barberas – *Louis M Martini* in Napa and *Sebastiani* in Sonoma were always true to the variety – but the new wave is coming from Amador County in the Sierra foothills, led by *Monteviña* with an intense, blackberry and black cherry wine; *Preston Vineyards* (Sonoma County) is also good.

**CABERNET SAUVIGNON** There was not a single 'bad' vintage in the 1980s. The best vintages of the late 1980s are the '85, '86 and '88, but any of them are good; the '87s are proving very elegant, with subtle, well-balanced flavours and marvellous ripe fruit that often seems to leap out of the

glass, which is, of course, the great strength of California Cabernet. A little further north in Washington, there are some increasingly good Cabernets, a bit more restrained than California. For serious cellaring, good producers are: *Beringer Reserve, Buena Vista, Burgess, Cain, Carmenet Reserve, Caymus, Chimney Rock, Clos du Bois, Clos du Val, Conn Creek, Cuvaison, Diamond Creek, Dunn, Franciscan, Grgich Hills, Groth, Heitz Bella Oaks, William Hill, Inglenook Reserve Cask, Kenwood Artist Series, La Jota, Laurel Glen, Louis M Martini, Robert Mondavi Reserve* and *Opus One, Chateau Montelena, Newton, Raymond Reserve,*

*Ridge Monte Bello, Sequoia Grove, Shafer Hillside Select, Stag's Leap Cask 23, Sterling Vineyards Diamond Mountain Ranch,* (California); *Ste Chapelle* (Idaho); *Fall Creek Vineyards, Llano Estacado, Messina Hof, Oberhellmann, Pheasant Ridge* (Texas); *Arbor Crest, Hogue Cellars, Chateau Ste Michelle, Staton Hills* (Washington). For a lighter Cabernet quaff, the list is practically endless. Try *Beringer Napa Valley, Caymus Liberty School, Chateau Souverain, Christian Brothers, Clos du Bois, Cosentino, Fetzer, Estancia, Foppiano, Glen Ellen, Kendall-Jackson* (California); *Columbia Crest* (Washington).

**MERLOT** A lot is blended with Cabernet Sauvignon, and often Cabernet Franc as well. Such Bordeaux blends are christened Meritage (rhymes with heritage) as a sales ploy. Still, there is lots of good varietal Merlot, with that lovely, soft, perfumed fruit. Best are *Cuvaison, Dehlinger, Louis M Martini, Duckhorn, Robert Keenan, Gundlach-Bundschu, Matanzas Creek, Newton, Shafer, Sterling* (California); *Arbor Crest, Leonetti, Hogue, Columbia, Haviland, Paul Thomas* (Washington).

**PETITE SIRAH** Not the same as the great red Syrah grape of the Rhône or the Shiraz of Australia. It produces big, stark, dry, almost tarry wines – impressive, but usually lacking real style. *Ridge Vineyards* is the exception. In good years Ridge Petite Sirah is capable of making real Rhône Syrah blush. The story goes that Gérard Jaboulet of Hermitage carries Ridge Petite Sirah to show people the competition!

**PINOT NOIR** Burgundy's great red grape has not yet made the sea change to the New World with total success. But there are brief flashes of excitement in California and an occasional gleam in Oregon. Good if not great California Pinot Noir comes from the lower cooler reaches of the Russian River Valley in Sonoma County and from Carneros in Napa-Sonoma. But the best is probably in the chalky, dry cliffs of San Benito County (east of Monterey) where *Calera* is located. Other good ones are *Au Bon Climat, Acacia, Bay Cellars* (made from Oregon grapes), *Bonny Doon, Chalone, Carneros Creek, Dehlinger, Iron Horse, Mondavi* (getting better with each vintage), *Rasmussen, Saintsbury, ZD* (California); *Adelsheim, Amity, Chateau Benoit, Eyrie, Forgeron, Knudsen-Erath, Rex Hill, Scott Henry, Sokol-Blosser* (Oregon).

**SYRAH/RHÔNE VARIETALS** There has been an explosion of interest in the wines of the Rhône in California; they seem in many ways more suited to California's Mediterranean climate than the Bordeaux or Burgundian grapes. Most eyes are on Syrah, but there are also plantings of Mourvèdre, Cinsaut, Grenache and Carignan, the last two of which were used in the past in Central Valley jug wines. First results are encouraging, both in public acceptance and in the quality of the wine. Best producers are *Bonny Doon, Duxoup, Kendall-Jackson, La Jota, McDowell Valley, Joseph Phelps Mistral* series, *Qupé, Santino* (California).

**ZINFANDEL** Its friends keep predicting a surge of interest in red Zinfandel because of the success of the light, sweet white or blush Zins, but so far it hasn't happened. Still, the wine can be good, either in the hearty, almost overpowering style or the lighter 'claret' style. Best of the big Zins are *Cline Cellars, Deer Park, Kendall-Jackson Ciapusci Vineyard, Preston Vineyards Estate, La Jota, A Rafanelli, Ravenswood, Rosenblum, Shenandoah, Joseph Swan.* For a lighter elbow-bender, try *Buehler, Buena Vista, Burgess, Clos duVal, Fetzer, Haywood, Kendall-Jackson Mariah Vineyard, Kenwood, Louis M Martini, Nalle, Quivira, Ridge.* Best for blush are *Amador Foothill, Beringer, Buehler, Ivan Tamas.*

The price guides for this section begin on page 373.

# WHITE GRAPES & FLAVOURS

**CHARDONNAY** Wine-makers are learning how to blend different areas for more balanced, rounded wines: offsetting the austerity of Napa Carneros, for example, with the tropical intensity of Sonoma County Russian River (*Louis M Martini*).

American Chardonnay will age, but look for the controlled, balanced fruit of *Acacia, Arrowood, Buena Vista, Beringer, Chalone, Flora Springs, Cuvaison, Dehlinger, Kistler, Mondavi Reserve, Raymond Reserve, Simi, Chateau St Jean* and *Sonoma-Cutrer* (California); *Bridgehampton* (NY); *Prince Michel* (Virginia); *Hogue* (Washington). For more instant gratification, try *Callaway, Clos du Bois, Franciscan, Estancia, Glen Ellen, Matanzas Creek, Kendall Jackson, Morgan, Mirassou, Mondavi* non-reserve, *Phelps, Monterey, Parducci, Signorello* (yummy); *Wente Bros* (California); *Fall Creek* (Texas); *Chateau Ste Michelle* (Washington).

**GEWÜRZTRAMINER** Looking up, but California still falls short of Alsace. The problem is that the grape ripens too fast, too soon. A few people are beginning to get it right, making wines with that spiciness that keeps you reaching for another glass. Look for *Adler Fels* (the best New World Gewürz?), *Lazy Creek, Handley Cellars, Rutherford Hill, Obester* (California); *Llano Estacado* (Texas); *Columbia, Ch Ste Michelle* (Washington).

**RIESLING** Like Gewürz, most Riesling in California has been planted in the wrong (warm) place. Riesling (in the US called Johannisberg or White) makes a dull wine then; it is the cooler areas of California, Oregon, New York and Washington that are beginning to show what it can do. Best are *Alexander Valley Vineyards, Konocti, Navarro* (California); *Wagner Vineyards* (NY); *Amity* (Oregon); *Chateau Morrisette, Prince Michel* (Virginia); *Hogue Cellars, Columbia Cellars, Chateau Ste Michelle* (Washington).

**SAUVIGNON BLANC/FUMÉ BLANC** Now being tamed; its tendency to extreme herbal/ grassy tastes is now often moulded into complex spicy/appley fruit. If you are a fan of the big, grassy wines, those that smell like a field of new-mown hay, you'll like *Dry Creek Vineyards* Reserve, which carries that about as far as it can go. For more restraint look for *Ferrari-Carano, Hanna, Simi, Robert Mondavi, Newton, Sterling, Chateau St Jean, William Wheeler* (California); *Hargrave* (New York State); *Arbor Crest, Columbia* (Washington).

**SÉMILLON** Can add complexity to Sauvignon Blanc (*Clos du Val* and *Vichon*, California). For stand-alone Sémillon try *Alderbrook, R H Phillips, Ahlgren, Congress Springs* (California); *Ch Ste Michelle* (Washington).

## MATURITY CHART
### 1990 Carneros Chardonnay
The best are elegant, and recent vintages have been made to age well

| Bottled | Ready | Peak | Tiring | In decline |
|---|---|---|---|---|

| 0 | 1 | 2 | 3 | 4 | 5 | 6 | 7 | 8 | 9 | 10 years |

# WINE REGIONS

**CARNEROS** (California) Right at the southern end of the Napa and Sonoma Valleys, snuggled against San Francisco Bay. Breezes from the Bay hold the temperature down and create an ideal climate for Chardonnay and Pinot Noir.

**CENTRAL VALLEY** (California) Once a vast inland sea, the Central Valley runs from the San Joaquin/ Sacramento River Delta in the North to the unappealing flatlands of Bakersfield in the South, from the foothills of the Sierra range in the East to the coastal ranges in the West. It can be 110°F during the day, and hardly cooler at night. It's a brutal life, but with modern techniques there are some decent quaffs.

**IDAHO** Minor vineyard acreage so far but interesting, promising quality, especially Gewürztraminer, Riesling and Chardonnay. The best hope is for fizz.

**LAKE COUNTY** (California) Grapes were grown in Lake County (north of Napa County and east of Mendocino County) in the last century; recently there has been a revival of interest with major plantings by *Louis M Martini, Konocti* and *Guenoc*. It's good Cabernet Sauvignon and Sauvignon Blanc territory, with warm days and cool nights, and a very long growing season.

**LIVERMORE VALLEY** (California) One of California's oldest vine-growing regions, this largely suburban valley, just over the first lap of the Coastal range from San Francisco Bay, has been enjoying a bit of a comeback. It was the first in California to grow Sauvignon Blanc and the century-plus old Wente Bros winery in Livermore is increasingly good for that. The region is also proving good for Cabernet. Several small wineries have recently sprung up or been revived; early bottlings are promising.

**MENDOCINO COUNTY** (California) Mendocino is a rugged, coastal county with one major inland valley opening up north of the Russian River, and several cool east-west valleys running from the interior to the dramatic, rocky coastline. This range of pocket climates makes it possible to grow a range of grapes, with Cabernet Sauvignon at its best in Round Valley in the interior but excellent Riesling, Gewürztraminer, Chardonnay and Pinot Noir doing well in the cool Anderson Valley, where Pacific fog and winds follow the Anderson River inland. This valley is also becoming a leading sparkling wine district, with *Roederer US* making some outstanding bubbly and the tiny *Handley Cellars Brut* one of the best California can offer.

**MONTEREY COUNTY** (California) Monterey came late to grape growing: only in the early 1970s did pioneering plantings by *Mirassou* and *Wente Bros* begin to bear fruit. Early Cabernet efforts had a distinct taste of green peppers and other less appealing vegetal smells. Now growers have found more suitable grapes, especially Riesling, Chenin Blanc and Pinot Noir. Even Cabernet has made a comeback, on hillsides in the cool Carmel Valley.

**NAPA COUNTY** (California) There are several important subregions within Napa: Calistoga, Carneros, Chiles Valley, Howell Mountain, Mount Veeder, Oakville, Pope Valley, Rutherford, Spring Mountain and Stag's Leap. Some of these are formally designated viticultural regions. This is California's classic wine country. Napa's strong suit is red – Cabernet Sauvignon and Merlot – with Pinot Noir in Carneros.

**NEW MEXICO** Northern New Mexico grows mostly hybrid grape varieties but some interesting wines are coming from irrigated vineyards in the southern part of the state. Good producers are *Anderson Valley*, especially for Chardonnay and a sparkling wine from *Devalmont Vineyards* on the Gruet label.

**NEW YORK STATE** The big news in New York continues to be Long Island, with outstanding Chardonnay and Pinot Noir. The Chardonnay is very different from those of California, with more austere flavours, a bit like ripe Chablis. There's also decent Chardonnay from the Finger Lakes and the Hudson River Valley. The Lake Erie-Niagara region is lagging behind the other three, with more native grapes. Try *Bridgehampton, Pindar, Brotherhood, Hargrave, Lenz, Le Reve* and *Wagner*.

**OREGON** Despite all the press attention, Oregon Pinot Noir has never really lived up to its advance notices. The 1987s seemed to be getting on track, but there's still a long way to go. Probably the most successful 'Oregon' Pinots were made by California wineries from Oregon grapes – *Bay Cellars* and *Bonny Doon*. The Chardonnay shows occasional flashes but is, on the whole, a little hard. Oregon's best and most consistent wines so far have been Riesling and Pinot Gris. Good producers for Pinot Gris are *Adelsheim, Eyrie, Knudsen Erath* and *Forgeron*; for Riesling the best are *Amity, Forgeron* and *Oak Knoll*.

**SAN LUIS OBISPO COUNTY** (California) A Central Coast growing area with the best wines coming from cool regions in canyons opening in from the coast. There are good sites here for Pinot Noir, Chardonnay and a few surprising old Zinfandel vineyards. Edna Valley is the chief subregion with a deserved reputation for Chardonnay.

**SANTA BARBARA COUNTY** (California) This growing region just to the north of Los Angeles is divided into two major subregions, the Santa Maria and Santa Ynez valleys. Both are coastal valleys with openings to the Pacific which means that both day and night are fairly cool. There are some outstanding Pinot Noirs from both regions with some good Sauvignon Blanc and Merlot from the Santa Ynez Valley.

**SANTA CRUZ MOUNTAINS** (California) Just south of San Francisco, this has lured several people who believe it to be Pinot Noir heaven. Despite some occasional successes, the track record is spotty, but progress is being made. *Bonny Doon, David Bruce, Congress Springs, McHenry* and *Santa Cruz Mountain Winery* have all made Pinot with various degrees of success. Surprisingly, for a cool climate region, some very good Cabernet has been made – notably from *Mount Eden* winery.

**SIERRA FOOTHILLS** (California) California's gold country was one of the busiest wine zones in the state in the last century but only a few Zinfandel vineyards survived Prohibition. These are the basis of the area's reputation today, plus good Sauvignon Blanc and Barbera. Subregions include Amador County, El Dorado County and Calaveras County. Best are *Amador Foothill Winery, Boeger Winery, Monteviña, Santino* and *Shenandoah Vineyards*.

**SONOMA COUNTY** (California) On the West Coast, people are beginning to realize that Sonoma's Chardonnay, long in the shade of Napa, need take a back seat to no-one. The Sonoma Valley, running down to the Bay, is the great historic subregion, but many exceptional vineyards are in the Russian River area, in particular Alexander Valley, Chalk Hill, Dry Creek, Knight's Valley, and the Russian River Valley itself (including its subregion Green Valley). In general, Cabernet and Chardonnay yield the best wines, usually a little fruitier and softer than in Napa.

**TEXAS** Texas wines continue to amaze. Major regions are the Austin Hills and the Staked Plains region of west Texas, centred around Lubbock. Cabernets from Texas have a drink-me-now rich fruitiness and the Chardonnays and Sauvignon Blancs are looking better every year. In short, it's goodbye Chateau Redneck. Best currently are *Fall Creek, Llano Estacado, Messina Hof, Oberhellmann* and *Pheasant Ridge*.

**VIRGINIA** Growing good wine grapes in Virginia's hot, humid climate is certainly a man-over-nature drama. Besides the heat and the humidity, there is also the occasional hurricane. Nevertheless, there are some good Rieslings and Chardonnays coming from the state. Top producers are *Chateau Morrisette, Ingleside Plantation* and *Prince Michel*.

**WASHINGTON STATE** There are those who believe that in the long run, the finest wines from North America may come from Washington State. There is an incredible intensity of fruit right across the board in all varietals that is simply astonishing. When the first serious wines started appearing only about 15 years ago, the best were Riesling and Chardonnay; but most recently, the Cabernets and Merlots can be outstanding, as can the Sauvignon Blanc and Sémillon, varieties which are taken very seriously in Washington. Good wineries: *Arbor Crest, Chateau Ste Michelle, Columbia Cellars, Columbia Crest, Hogue Cellars, Staton Hills*.

# WINERY PROFILES

**ACACIA** ★★★★ (Carneros/Napa) Acacia continues to produce attractive Pinot Noir and delightfully understated Chardonnay.

**ADLER FELS** ★★★ (Sonoma) A quirky winery, taking chances that sometimes miss. Outstanding Gewürztraminer and an unusual Riesling fizz that is a treat.

**ARROWOOD** ★★★★★ (Sonoma) Richard Arrowood was responsible for the great Chateau St Jean Chardonnays of the late 1970s and early 1980s. At his own winery, Cabernet is the best of the range.

**AU BON CLIMAT** ★★★★ (Santa Barbara) A growing reputation for Pinot Noir. The best is soft and approachable, with intense black cherry fruit. Chardonnay can also be impressive.

**BEAULIEU VINEYARDS** ★★★★(★) (Napa) Beautour label takes up the bulk of production; easy-drinking, stylish 1989 Cabernet Sauvignon is a steal. Top of the range is George de Latour Private Reserve Cabernet, rich, supple and able to age.

**BERINGER** ★★★★★ (Napa) This always outstanding performer gets better and better. A fantastic 1986 Cabernet Reserve and 1988 Chardonnay Reserve, but also the low-priced, very drinkable Napa Ridge.

**BETHEL HEIGHTS** ★★★(★) (Oregon) Impressive, intense Pinot Noirs. The Reserves can be among Oregon's finest.

**BONNY DOON** ★★★ (Santa Cruz) Some of the liveliest wines in California. Randall Grahm doesn't make them often enough to polish the edges, but that is part of their appeal. Sometimes he will only make one seat-of-the-pants vintage, and then move on. Buy anything of his, just for fun.

**BRIDGEHAMPTON** ★★★(★) (New York) A first-class Chardonnay from Long Island vineyards as well as a fresh, light quaffable Pinot Noir and a fruity, forward Merlot.

**BUENA VISTA** ★★★ (Sonoma/Carneros) Wine-maker Jill Davis has worked wonders with a winery that was in the doldrums a decade ago. Well-balanced, elegant wines. Cabernet Sauvignon, Pinot Noir and Riesling can be excellent.

**CAKEBREAD CELLARS** ★★★ (Napa) Always sound, sometimes outstanding; One of the best Sauvignon Blancs.

**CALERA** ★★★★(★) (San Benito) The best Pinot Noir in California, according to a lot of critics. It's rich, intense wine. The Jensen Vineyard – named after the family of winemaker Josh Jensen – is the best.

**CAYMUS** ★★★★ (Napa) The Caymus Cabernets of the early '80s are benchmark California Cab, and later ones show no sign of faltering. Also a good Zinfandel and good value wines under the Liberty School label.

**CHALONE** ★★★★(★) (Monterey) A reputation for individualistic Pinot Noir and big, buttery Chardonnay. Also some nice Pinot Blanc and Chenin Blanc.

**DOMAINE CHANDON** ★★★ (Napa) A producer of consistently good fizz, with the best being Chandon Reserve in magnum. Over-production in the mid-1980s may have hurt, but it seems back on track.

**CHATEAU POTELLE** ★★★(★) (Napa) A new winery operated by two transplanted French wine buffs, Jean Noel and Marketta Fourmeaux. Promising Sauvignon Blanc and Cabernet Sauvignon.

**CHATEAU ST JEAN** ★★★(★) (Sonoma) A Chardonnay specialist (look for Belle Terre and Robert Young vineyards), with interesting Gewürztraminer, Riesling, Sauvignon Blanc and Cabernet; toying with Mourvèdre, Nebbiolo and Sangiovese.

**CHATEAU STE MICHELLE** ★★★(★) (Washington) The biggest winery in the North-West makes about half a million cases each of Ch Ste Michelle and second label Columbia Crest; also owns Snoqualmie winery. Good for Cabernet, Merlot, Chardonnay and Sauvignon Blanc.

**CLOS DU BOIS** ★★★ (Sonoma) Now owned by Hiram Walker-Allied Vintners, Clos du Bois makes consistently good Merlots, Chardonnays and claret-style Marlstone.

**CLOS DU VAL** ★★★★ (Napa) Bordeaux-trained owner and winemaker Bernard Portet makes silky, elegant, well-balanced reds, with an emphasis on delicious fruit. Best wines from this underrated winery are Cabernet Sauvignon and Zinfandel.

**COLUMBIA** ★★★(★) (Washington) David Lake's pioneering winery, founded in 1962 by a group of university professors, makes a basketful of varietals including Sémillon, Gewürztraminer, Chardonnay and Riesling (especially Wyckoff vineyard); plus Syrah, soft, peppery Pinot Noir, seductive Merlot (Red Willow vineyard), and surprisingly ripe Cabernet Sauvignon (Otis vineyard).

**CUVAISON** ★★★★ (Napa) Gifted wine-maker John Thacher turns first class fruit into elegant, well defined, incisive and balanced wines. The 1990 Chardonnay is a beaut; also tops for Merlot, Cabernet Sauvignon, Pinot and (now sadly discontinued) Zinfandel.

**DEHLINGER** ★★★★ (Sonoma) Makes one of the best Pinots in North America from cool vineyards along the Russian River Valley County, just a few miles from the Pacific. Also good Cabernets including a good value Young Vine Cabernet.

**DOMAINE MUMM** ★★★★ (Napa) Early releases of fizz have been outstanding. If quality remains consistent, Domaine Mumm could become one of the best two or three sparkling wines in North America.

**DROUHIN** ★★(★) (Oregon) The first few Pinot Noirs have been made with bought-n grapes and are good, but the Drouhin potential will only be seen when its own vines come on stream. The paint isn't even dry at the winery yet.

**DUCKHORN** ★★★(★) (Napa) Intensely flavoured, deep and rich Merlot, blended with a little of both Cabernets.

**DRY CREEK VINEYARDS** ★★★ (Sonoma) Big, herbal Fumé Blanc loaded with fruit. The reserve bottling ages nicely.

**ELK COVE VINEYARDS** ★★★(★) (Oregon) Perhaps the best Pinot Noir in Oregon, with the '86 Estate top of the list.

**EYRIE** ★★★ (Oregon) David Lett is Oregon's Pinot pioneer. His obsession has spawned a whole industry, and his wines are still some of the best: generally supple, light but flavoursome, exceptionally good in 1988. Pinot Gris, though, forms the bulk of production.

**FALL CREEK VINEYARDS** ★★★ (Texas) These wines can hold their heads up anywhere: a delicious Proprietor's Red (Cabernet, Ruby Cabernet, Merlot and Carnelian), a charming Sémillon and a first-rate Cabernet Sauvignon.

**FETZER** ★★★ (Mendocino) Great value from this large Mendocino producer. Look for Cabernet from Lake County and several different Zinfandels (especially the Ricetti Vineyard). Sundial Chardonnay is tasty.

**FLORA SPRINGS** ★★★★ (Napa) Excellent Chardonnay (especially 1990) and a three-way blend of both Cabernets and Merlot called Trilogy. Soliloquy is a creamy, rich, floral white that belies its Sauvignon Blanc base.

**FOPPIANO** ★★★ (Sonoma) Has been around since the end of Prohibition. In the last ten years it has made outstanding Cabernet Sauvignon and a good if low-key Pinot Noir. Really good Cabernets from Fox Mountain Vineyard.

**FRANCISCAN** ★★★★ (Napa) Has had a complete turnaround in recent years. Best wines are the rich, lush Cabernets with delicious, forward fruit flavours and complex, barrel-fermented Chardonnay. Estancia is a good value second label.

**HANDLEY CELLARS** ★★★★ (Mendocino) Very good Chardonnay from family-owned vineyards in Sonoma's Dry Creek Valley and a terrific *brut* sparkler that some say is one of the best in the West.

**HEITZ** ★★★ (Napa) The Martha's Vineyard Cabernet Sauvignon has a devoted following and fetches high prices, but it seems a bit of a dinosaur compared with the elegant, sleek Cabernets of today.

**IRON HORSE** ★★★★ (Sonoma) Terrific racy, incisive fizz, and now engaged in a joint venture with Laurent-Perrier of Champagne. Very good Pinot Noir and Chardonnay. A Sangiovese/ Merlot blend (Mergiovese) is on the drawing board and looking terrific. Second label: Tin Pony.

**JORDAN** ★★★★ (Sonoma) The wine makes up for the architecture. A rich, ripe Cabernet Sauvignon that ages quite well and a 'wannabe Meursault' Chardonnay from this French lookalike winery in northern Sonoma. A sparkling wine called J was released in the spring of 1991.

**KENDALL-JACKSON** ★★★(★) (Lake) Owns what is probably the biggest Chardonnay vineyard in the world (1200 acres) in Santa Barbara. Chardonnay is smooth, rich, sometimes spicy, invariably seamless; Proprietor's Grand Reserve intense and buttery. Juicy Sauvignon Blanc and rather dense Pinot Noir.

**KENWOOD** ★★★(★) (Sonoma) A consistent producer of well above-average quality. The Jack London and Artist series Cabernets are outstanding, as is the Zinfandel and Sauvignon Blanc.

**LAUREL GLEN** ★★★★(Sonoma) Big, fruit-packed Cabernet for long keeping. But Patrick Campbell is no meek follower of Bordeaux orthodoxy, and is contemplating the addition of Syrah, Sangiovese or Mourvèdre for a unique Californian style.

**LOUIS MARTINI** ★★★★★ (Napa) A delightful range, from simple varietals to single vineyards. Sensationally drinkable Gamay Beaujolais; lively, fruity Barbera; very good Merlot; some glorious Cabernet Sauvignons (1985 Monte Rosso) that age well; excellent Petite Sirah; complex Pinot Noir and a rich, ripe Gewürz.

**MAYACAMAS** ★★★ (Napa) A reputation in the past for big, hard Cabernets that would take decades to come around. There are signs that the reputation is justified, but a lot of people are still waiting.

**ROBERT MONDAVI** ★★★★★ (Napa) A California 'first growth'. Mondavi's major strength is in reds: both the straight and Reserve Cabernets are among the best in the world, though Opus One reds seem to lack the Reserve's intensity. Wine-maker Tim Mondavi has made Pinot Noir his pet project. Pleasant, fruity Fumé Blanc.

**NEWTON** ★★★★ (Napa) Excellent, reasonably priced Chardonnay; cedary, cinnamon-spiced Cabernet and increasingly good Merlot.

**PHELPS** ★★★(★) (Napa) Best here is the Insignia Vineyard Cabernet Sauvignon but exciting things are happening with Rhône grapes, particularly Syrah, released under the Mistral label. Also a nice light touch with that most civilized of wines, Riesling.

**PHEASANT RIDGE** ★★(★) (Texas) Quite good Chardonnay and Sémillon; promising Cabernet Sauvignon in recent vintages.

**RIDGE** ★★★★(★) (Santa Clara) California benchmark Zinfandel. The Monte Bello Cabernets are also remarkable, with great balance and long-lasting, perfumed fruit. Petite Sirah from York Creek is brilliant, under-valued and under-appreciated.

**SAINTSBURY** ★★★★ (Napa) A young Carneros winery with a growing reputation for Pinot Noir and Chardonnay. Garnet, from young Pinot Noir vines, is delicious.

**SANFORD WINERY** ★★★ (Santa Barbara) At its best, Sanford Pinot Noir can be a real treat, with spicy, lush, intense fruit. An occasional and pleasant Vin Gris.

**SCHRAMSBERG** ★★★★ (Napa) The best fizz in California can still come from here,

but the challengers are rapidly gaining ground. The vintage sparklers age beautifully into lush, rich wines.

**SHAFER** ★★★★ (Napa) Very good, long-lived Cabernet Sauvignon and Merlot from hillside vineyards.

**SIMI** ★★★★(★) (Sonoma) Rich, sometimes voluptuous, always reliable Chardonnay; a light dusting of botrytis (as in 1989) intensifies the style. Concentrated Cabernets are made to be drinkable young, but really need time. Reserves are excellent, as is Sauvignon Blanc.

**SONOMA-CUTRER** ★★★★ (Sonoma) A reputation for Chardonnay from three different Russian River vineyards. The Les Pierres is a restrained classic away from the California mainstream, made to age. Russian River Ranches is more forward and fruity for immediate fun and games while the Cutrer is rich, full and more in the California tradition.

**STAG'S LEAP WINE CELLARS** ★★★(★) (Napa) Fine, elegant Chardonnay with lean, appley fruit. The Cabernets, with which this winery made its reputation, seemed to be missing a beat for a few years, but the straight 1987 bottling may be a welcome turn for the better.

**ROD STRONG VINEYARDS** ★★★(★) (Sonoma) At this much underrated winery on the Russian River, Rod Strong makes some very fine Cabernet Sauvignon and Pinot Noir from river-terrace vineyards.

**TREFETHEN** ★★★ (Napa) A consistent producer of good middle-of-the road Cabernet Sauvignon and Chardonnay. Best is a dry Riesling, one of the state's finest. Best value are the Eshcol reds and whites.

**ZD WINES** ★★★(★) (Napa) Cabernet Sauvignon, Pinot Noir and Chardonnay of great intensity and depth. The Pinot Noir, especially, seems to improve each vintage.

# AUSTRALIA

So Australia was just a flash in the pan, was it? Some flash, some pan. If the Jonahs of the wine trade who predicted that Australia was last year's flavour of the month had been talking about cricket, they might have had a point. But far from losing popularity, the sheer exuberant fruitiness of Strine wine, coupled with realistic prices, has continued to prove an unbeatable formula. Australia is now a permanent feature, both on the wine map and on the dinner table.

'Everyone will be able to make hay while the sun shines,' predicted Huon Hooke writing in this space last year. How right he was. The figures speak for themselves. In 1991, the UK imported 24.28 million bottles of Australian wine. By March 1992, Australia was showing an increase of 79 per cent over the same period the year before. And while table wines, both red and white, have improved their ratings, the performance of fizz, with 2.4 million bottles imported, has been sparkling. Someone must have been reading Oz Clarke in last year's *Webster's*. Australian fizz accounts for a substantial six per cent share of the sparkling wine market – a figure to cause a sleepless night or two in Champagne.

Australian wines continue to do well in comparative tastings. Once again they netted an impressive haul of medals at the International Wine Challenge in May. Yet the importance of beating a *grand cru* Burgundy here, a *cru classé* Bordeaux there, is no longer the be all and end all. As James Halliday points out in his illuminating *Wine Atlas of Australia and New Zealand*, 'cultural cringe is an unnecessary and debilitating disease'.

Instead of being held up as mirror images of their European counterparts, Australian wines can be enjoyed for their differences rather than for their similarities. Traditionalists might argue that their ability to age is as yet untried. But Australian wine is no shrinking violet; its appeal lies in the bold, uncomplicated pleasure of lusciously seductive fruit flavour, often with the added smoke, spice or sweetness of oak. In any event, the litany of golden oldies is testimony, if it were needed, to the ageing capacity of great Australian Cabernets, Shiraz, Sémillons and Rieslings.

## Passion versus recession

With consumption at home declining, Australia's wine producers are on a mission to increase their exports. The Big Four – Penfolds, Orlando/Wyndham, Mildara/Blass and Thomas Hardy – between them account for some 75 per cent of the Australian market. Competition is fierce. With mechanization, irrigation and optimization of yields, production costs can be pared to the bone. According to James Halliday, the big companies can produce grapes even in premium areas such as Coonawarra and Padthaway for as little as A$200 per tonne. Add to this spirit of competition the recession and a weak Australian dollar, and Australian wine looks particularly good value on export markets – the most important of which to Australia, both in volume and in value, is now the UK.

Competition and recession have also made life tough for the 550 or so smaller wineries, many of which are family-owned. Early in 1992, I went to see Denis Power of Rothbury Estate in the Hunter Valley. Spread on the table in front of him were the particulars of numerous wineries up for sale. Recession had hit Australia even worse than the UK, and the predators were circling to snap up the victims as cheaply as possible. Yet with the odds stacked against them, Australia's small wineries continue to set examples of fine quality that the rest of the industry seeks to emulate. Consumed by pride and a passion for their work, they still manage to make a noise out of proportion to their size – and provide relief from the sometimes monotonous brand culture of the Big Four.

In March 1992, more than a hundred members of the British wine trade and press visited Australia on what was christened the Wine Flight of a Lifetime. If they had been less than convinced before they went, I know of no-one who did not return converted and anxious to do their bit to spread the word to their own customers. 'There's a whole buzz about it,' said Hazel Murphy of the Australian Wine Bureau six weeks after returning. 'The little guys are all holding tastings of Australian wines.' Within weeks of their return, I was tasting a host of fine wines snapped up by wine merchants. New names appeared: Rockford's Basket Press Shiraz, Charles Melton's Nine Popes, St Hallett's Shiraz and Chardonnay, Jim Barry's The Armagh and Parker Estate Coonawarra Cabernet.

After a winter of cool weather and unseasonal rains in most regions, there was something of a scare over the 1992 vintage. At the time of writing, a question mark still hangs over the white wines, although, according to John Duval, chief wine-maker of Penfolds, 'it will be a fantastic year for sparkling wines'. Most wine-makers over here for the London Wine Trade Fair in May 1992 were confident that 1992 will turn out to be a good year for reds too. As the competition from new wine-making countries hots up, Australia is better placed than ever to take on all-comers.                                                                    **ANTHONY ROSE**

## WHITE GRAPES & FLAVOURS

**CHARDONNAY** Several leading wine-makers admit they haven't yet mastered the variety – but that merely whets the taste-buds because already some are world-class. Oak barrel ageing – and, increasingly, fermentation in the barrel – is the rule for all but the cheapest.

Often the wine is a shockingly bright gold-yellow colour, and the fruit generally rich but not too lush; a suggestion of ripe apples, melons, figs or pineapples, but with a savoury toastiness from the wood. The one major criticism is that acidity levels need to be adjusted upwards in some of the very warm regions and this is not always done subtly enough, leaving a slight lemon-peel citric flavour. The wines mature quickly – two years is often enough – but they don't fade too fast. Leading names include: *Bannockburn* (Geelong), *Basedow* (SA), *Capel Vale* (Capel Vale, WA), *Coldstream Hills* (Yarra), *Dalwhinnie* (Victoria), *Dromana* (Mornington), *Evans Family* (Hunter Valley), *Hardy's*

(Padthaway), *Krondorf Show Chardonnay* (Barossa), *Lake's Folly* (Hunter Valley), *Leeuwin Estate* (Margaret River), *Lillydale* (Yarra), *Lindemans* (Padthaway), *Moss Wood* (Margaret River), *Mountadam* (Adelaide Hills), *Nicholson River* (Gippsland), *Penfolds* (Clare Valley), *Penley Estate* (Coonawarra), *Petaluma* (Adelaide Hills), *Peterson* (Hunter Valley), *Pierro* (Margaret River), *Piper's Brook* (Tasmania), *Rosemount Show Reserve* and *Roxburgh* (Hunter Valley), *Rouge Homme* (SA), *Orlando St Hilary* (Barossa), *St Huberts* (Yarra), *St Leonards* (NE Victoria), Stoniers Merricks (Mornington), *Tyrrell* (Hunter Valley), *Geoff Weaver* (SA), *Simon Whitlam* (Hunter Valley), *Wolf Blass* (SA), Wynns (Coonawarra), *Yalumba* (Coonawarra), *Yarra Yering* (Yarra Valley).

**CHENIN BLANC** This ripens to a much fuller, fruitier and blander style than its steelier Loire counterpart. A good example is from *Moondah Brook* (Swan Valley).

**GEWÜRZTRAMINER** Called Traminer, this is planted mostly in South Australia and New South Wales. Blowsy and spicy, it is often added to Riesling for a tasty, commercial blend. In cool parts of Victoria, it can be sublimely scented and delicate. *Delatite* and *Lillydale* are excellent, but the best yet is from *Brown Bros'* new high altitude vineyard at Whitlands. In South Australia *Orlando* does well in the Eden Valley, as does *Tolley* in the Barossa.

**MARSANNE** In Central Victoria, both *Chateau Tahbilk* and *Mitchelton* have made big, broad, ripe Marsanne.

**MUSCAT** There are two types of Australian Muscat: first, the 'bladder pack' Fruity Gordo, which translated into English becomes bag-in-box Muscat of Alexandria – fruity, sweetish, swigging wine, from a heavy-cropping lowish-quality grape grown in irrigated vineyards along the Murray River; second, Liqueur Muscat, made from the Brown Muscat, a strain of the top quality Muscat à Petits Grains, grown in north-east Victoria. It is a sensation: dark, treacly even, with a perfume of strawberry and honeyed raisins. Best producers: *All Saints, Bailey's, Bullers, Campbells, Chambers, Morris* and *Stanton & Killeen*.

**RIESLING** The true German Riesling is always called Rhine Riesling in Australia, where it is the most widely planted noble white grape. In the Barossa Valley of South Australia it usually makes off-dry wine, with appley fruit and a decent lick of lemony acidity. But Australia also makes some of the world's greatest dry Riesling – a steely, slaty wine, full, but flecked with limey acidity, which after a few years develops strong, petrolly aromas. This comes from the hills above Adelaide and the Barossa – at Springton, Eden Valley, Clare (especially good) and Pewsey Vale. The Coonawarra, Western Australia and cool-climate areas of Victoria make equally exciting dry Riesling. There are also some

sweet, botrytis-affected Rieslings from the Barossa and Adelaide Hills. Top names: *Leo Buring, Orlando, Yalumba/Hill-Smith* (Barossa), *Leconfield, Wynns* (Coonawarra), *Petaluma* (with Clare fruit), *Jim Barry, Tim Knappstein, Mitchell, Pike* (Clare), *Brown Bros (Whitlands), Delatite, Diamond Valley, Lillydale* (Victoria), *Moorilla Estate, Pipers Brook* (Tasmania).

**SAUVIGNON BLANC** Sauvignon Blanc has caught on in a big way – mostly in South Australia, with one or two bright spots in Victoria. It overripens quickly, though, becoming oily, flat and fruitless. Nonetheless, there is some good stuff from *Jim Barry* (Clare), *Fleurieu* (McLaren Vale), *Saltram* (Barossa Valley), *Hardy's Collection, Lindemans* (Padthaway), *Hill-Smith* (Adelaide Hills), *Primo Estate* and *Wirra Wirra* (McLaren Vale), and *Geoff Weaver Stafford Ridge*, all in South Australia; *Taltarni* and *Tisdall* in Victoria and *Alkoomi, Cullens* and *Goundrey* in Western Australia. Sometimes Sauvignon Blanc wine is called Fumé Blanc.

**SÉMILLON** At its finest in Australia. An excellent blender – fattening up the rather lean flavours of Sauvignon, and broadening a less than top-line Chardonnay. By itself, the greatest examples are from the Hunter Valley and Western Australia, where it starts slowly, building up gradually into a magnificent strong white full of mineral, toasted nut, herb and honey flavours. South Australia makes a less majestic, more modern style. Top producers: *Lindemans, McWilliams, Peterson, Rothbury, Sutherland, Tyrrell* (NSW), *Tim Adams, Basedow, Jeffrey Grosset, Hamilton, Hardy's, Hill-Smith, Mount Horrocks, Penfolds, Yalumba* (SA), *Brown Bros, Morris, Yarra Ridge* (Victoria), *Cape Mentelle, Chateau Xanadu, Moss Wood, Sandstone* (WA). It also makes a sweet, noble-rot-affected wine: *De Bortoli, Rosemount* (NSW), *Basedow, Wolf Blass, Peter Lehmann,* (SA) and *Rumbalara* (Granite Belt).

# RED GRAPES & FLAVOURS

**CABERNET SAUVIGNON** A top quality variety here, but can be grown superbly well even at the most basic level in the irrigated riverlands where high yields produce an attractive, gently blackcurranty wine. Blackcurrant is the key to Australian Cabernet, and it is at its most splendid in Western Australia, SA's Southern Vales and cooler parts of Victoria, and at its most delicately balanced in South Australia's Coonawarra. Top producers: *Bailey's, Bowen Estate* (Coonawarra), *Brown Bros Koombahla, Capel Vale* (Capel Vale, WA), *Chateau Le Amon, Chateau Tahbilk, Coldstream Hills, Dromana Estate, Delatite, Hollick*), *Freycinet* (Tasmania), *Mildara Alexanders* (Coonawarra), *Mount Langi-Ghiran, Parker Estate, Penley Estate* (Coonawarra), *Plantagenet* (Margaret River), *Seppelt's Drumborg, Seville Estate, St Huberts, Tisdall Mount Helen, Yarra Yering* (Victoria), *Cape Mentelle, Leeuwin Estate, Moss Wood, Vasse Felix* (WA), *Bowen, Chateau Reynella, Elderton, Jeffrey Grosset, Katnook, Leconfield, Lindeman's St George, Geoff Merrill, Orlando, Penfolds, Petaluma, Pike, Pirramimma, Rosemount, Shottesbrooke, Wirra Wirra Estate, Wolf Blass, Wynns Coonawarra, Brokenwood, Lake's Folly, Peterson, Saxonvale* (NSW) *Moorilla Estate, Pipers Brook* (Tasmania), *Robinson Family* (Queensland).

**PINOT NOIR** As in the rest of the world, a thoroughly troublesome variety. However, there are signs that a distinctly Australian flavour is starting to emerge which is quite different from the overworked Burgundian model. At its best, it is remarkably perfumed, and has big, soft, rather glyceriny flavours of plum and cherry, mint and even honey. We may not see *many* great Australian Pinot Noirs, but those that we do see will be among the finest in the world. Top producers: *Moss Wood* (WA), *Leeuwin* (WA), *Bannockburn, Coldstream Hills, Delatite, Dromana Estate, Giaconda, Mount Mary, St Huberts,* *Yarra Burn, Yarra Yering* (Victoria), *Rothbury, Tyrrells* (NSW), *Moorilla Estate, Pipers Brook* (Tasmania), *Heemskerk* (Tasmania) and *Wignalls* (Mount Barker).

**SHIRAZ** This marvellous grape (the Syrah of France) can make sensational wine in Australia, and yet is generally used as a bulk-producing makeweight. Yet even at its most basic level, it will produce juicy, chunky reds in enormous quantities. Often blended with Cabernet Sauvignon for richness of texture. *Penfolds' Grange Hermitage* shows just how successful this blend can be. Other good examples are *Drayton* and *Lindemans' Coonawarra Limestone Ridge*. By itself, Shiraz has a brilliant array of flavours from leathery, deep wines, full of dark chocolate, liquorice and prunes intensity to a rich, spicy, plums and coconut, blackcurrant lusciousness that is most unusual in a dry red wine – and delicious! Top producers: *Bailey's, Best's, Cathcart Ridge, Chateau Le Amon, Chateau Tahbilk, Dalwhinnie, Hanging Rock, Heathcote, Montara, Mount Langi-Ghiran, Redbank Mountain Creek, St Leonards Wahgunyah, Wynns Ovens Valley, Yarra Yering* (Victoria), *Cape Mentelle, Evans & Tate Gnangara, Plantagenet* (WA), *Tim Adams, Basedow, Bowen, Coriole, Penfolds, Orlando* (SA), *Drayton, Lindemans, Montrose, Rosemount, Rothbury, Tyrrell* (NSW), *Bannockburn* (Victoria), *Cape Mentelle* (Margaret River), *Capel Vale* (Capel Vale, WA), *Jasper Hill* (Bendigo), *Charles Melton* (Barossa), *Coriole* (Southern Vales). *Jim Barry's The Armagh* (Clare Valley), *St Hallett Old Block* (Barossa Valley), *Penley Estate* (Coonawarra) and the *Rockford Basket Press* from the Barossa Valley.

> *The price guides for this section begin on page 378.*

# WINES & WINE REGIONS

**ADELAIDE HILLS** (South Australia) An ill-defined, but top quality, high altitude zone east of Adelaide. First-class vineyards for cool-climate whites include *Orlando's Steingarten*, *Mountadam* and *Yalumba's Heggies*, *Pewsey Vale* and *Petaluma*, whose '*Croser*' fizz is one of Australia's best.

**BAROSSA VALLEY** (South Australia) A large, well-known zone north of Adelaide. Various of the greatest Australian wine companies are established here – *Basedow*, *Leo Buring*, *Hill-Smith*, *Orlando*, *Penfolds*, *Seppelt*, *Tollana*, *Wolf Blass* and *Yalumba*. They process a huge amount of fruit, but 75 per cent of it comes from outside the Barossa. In Australia trucking grapes, juice or wine hundreds of miles for blending is fine – so long as you tell people.

**BENDIGO** (Victoria) This great 19th-century wine region, totally destroyed by phylloxera, has been re-planted since 1969 and now produces much excellent Cabernet Sauvignon, good Shiraz and even some Pinot Noir. *Balgownie* is the leading estate, with *Chateau Le Amon*, *Craiglee*, *Harcourt Valley*, *Heathcote*, *Mount Ida*, *Passing Clouds* and *Yellowglen* also important.

**CANBERRA DISTRICT** (ACT) Within the Australian Capital Territory, Canberra boasts a number of modest wineries producing wines to match.

**CENTRAL VICTORIA** Goulburn Valley is the most important vineyard area, with *Chateau Tahbilk* producing big old-style Shiraz and Cabernet, and some interesting white Marsanne. *Tisdall* makes superbly fruity Cabernet Sauvignon, Chardonnay and Sauvignon Blanc; *Mitchelton* is also good. The *Delatite* vineyards at Mansfield produce delicate whites and remarkably intense reds in cool-climate conditions.

**CLARE VALLEY** (South Australia) A warm area north of Adelaide, first planted to red grapes, but now making more fine white, in particular a deftly fragrant style of Rhine Riesling and soft, attractively grassy Sauvignon; Chardonnay is gentle and good. Best exponents: *Jim Barry*, *Tim Knappstein*, *Horrocks*, *Mitchells* and *Pike* but many Barossa wineries use Clare fruit, and *Petaluma* and *Wolf Blass* have vines there. *Tim Adams*, *Jeffrey Grosset*, *Tim Knappstein*, *Leasingham* and *Wendouree* produce the best reds.

**COONAWARRA** (South Australia) One of the most carefully defined wine zones in Australia, and perhaps the most famous. Incredibly fertile and planted to the hilt, this streak of red soil is about 14.5km long and between 1.5km and 200 metres wide. Cabernet Sauvignon is the main variety, characterized by a soft, blackcurranty fruit turning cedary with age. Shiraz is good, as are Merlot and Malbec. There are also some beautifully stylish Rhine Rieslings and Chardonnays. Best names: *Bowen Estate*, *Brand's Laira*, *Hardy*/*Chateau Reynella*, *Hollick*, *Katnook*, *Leconfield*, *Lindemans Limestone Ridge* and *St George*, *Mildara*, *Orlando*, *Petaluma*, *Penfolds*, *Rosemount*, *Seppelt* and *Wynns*.

**GEELONG** (Victoria) The best wines are dark, intensely-flavoured Cabernets from vineyards like *Idyll* and *Bannockburn*, Pinot Noir from *Prince Albert* and *Bannockburn* and whites from *Idyll*.

**GLENROWAN** (Victoria) Famous for the *Ovens Valley Shiraz* which *Wynns* (of SA) make into a good commercial red, and for the great wines produced by *Bailey's* – torrid, palate-blasting reds from Cabernet Sauvignon and Shiraz ( called Hermitage here) and, more importantly, Liqueur Muscats. These are intensely sweet, seeming to distil the very essence of the overripe brown Muscat grape, as well as adding an exotic tangle of orange and honey. At Milawa, *Brown Brothers* makes a wide range of good table wines and fortifieds, but its best wines are from the Koombahla vineyard in King Valley, and the high altitude Whitlands site.

**GRANITE BELT** (Queensland): The Granite Belt sits on a plateau about 1000 metres up: altitude and southern latitude allow grapes to be grown in a banana, pineapple and mango belt. Most wines serve the captive local markets and some (*Ballandean, Koninos Wines, Rumbalara, Robinsons Family* and *Stone Ridge*) are good. *Ironbark Ridge* is one to watch.

**GREAT WESTERN** (Victoria) Historic area round Ararat, best known as the original source of base wine for Australia's celebrated sparkler – *Seppelt's Great Western* – but more exciting for the quality of its reds. Great Western Shiraz is outstanding, full of chocolate, coconut and cream flavours as at *Cathcart Ridge*, or dry, liquoricy and with an impressive pepperiness as at *Mount Langi-Ghiran*. *Best's, Montara* and *Seppelt* are other top producers. There is also excellent Chardonnay from *Best's* and *Seppelt,* and good Cabernet Sauvignon from *Mount Langi-Ghiran* and 'Vintage port' from *Montara*.

**HUNTER VALLEY** (New South Wales) Leading NSW wine region, making great wines. Hunter reds are traditionally based on Shiraz (Hermitage) and whites on Sémillon. Both can age better than almost any other Australian wines. The Shiraz used to be notorious for a 'sweaty saddle' sulphurous flavour when young which disappeared with time to give a gentle, buttery, smoky flavour. The Sémillon often ages even better, starting out rather tart and lifeless but over 10 to 15 years developing a luscious, honeyed nuttiness, tempered by a vaguely old-Riesling, oily, herby character. Nowadays riper Sémillon grapes are giving a more immediately attractive style. Cabernet and Chardonnay are both successful here. Pinot Noir, especially from *Rothbury* and *Tyrrell* can be very fine, and there's even some good Traminer and sweet, botrytis-affected Sémillon.

The valley is in two halves. Upper Hunter is a recent, irrigated development, dominated by *Rosemount*, but *Arrowfield* can also be good. The region is basically a white wine producer, but on the whole Cabernet Sauvignon has fared much better than Shiraz. Lower Hunter is the traditional quality area. Best producers: *Allandale, Brokenwood, Evans Family, Hungerford Hill, Lake's Folly, Lindeman, McWilliams, Peterson, Rothbury Estate, Saxonvale, Sutherland, Tyrrell, Simon Whitlam*.

**LOWER GREAT SOUTHERN** (Western Australia) A vast, rambling area dotted with vineyards of considerable promise, especially in the zone round Mount Barker.

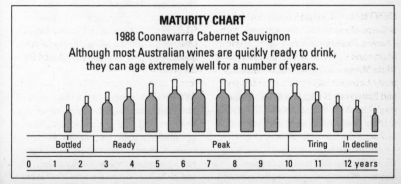

**MATURITY CHART**

1988 Coonawarra Cabernet Sauvignon

Although most Australian wines are quickly ready to drink, they can age extremely well for a number of years.

| Bottled | Ready | Peak | Tiring | In decline |
|---|---|---|---|---|

0  1  2  3  4  5  6  7  8  9  10  11  12 years

*Alkoomi, Forest Hill, Goundrey, Howard Park* and *Plantagenet* are good. The whites are fragrant and appetizing, with Riesling and Sauvignon Blanc showing great zestiness, but the reds are even more exciting, with particularly spicy, tobaccoey Cabernet Sauvignons.

**MARGARET RIVER** (Western Australia) There has been an astonishing number of superb wines from this area. Foremost among them are *Cape Mentelle, Cullens, Leeuwin Estate, Moss Wood, Sandalford, Redgate* and *Vasse Felix*. At their best, the Margaret River Cabernets exhibit magnificent fruit with a streak of grassy acidity and are as good as top-line Classed Growths in Bordeaux. Pinot Noir also does well sometimes. Chardonnay is increasingly barrel-fermented and shows enormously rich flavours, balanced by acidity and toasty oak. Sémillon is frequently now made in an apple-fresh, but weighty style – though old-style Sémillons age superbly. There is also some port-style wine and *Happ's* have planted traditional Portuguese varieties which are looking interesting.

**MCLAREN VALE** (South Australia) Important area just south of Adelaide. Originally known for thick, heavy reds, it has recently begun to make beautifully balanced reds and whites of positively cool-climate style. Great Cabernet, Shiraz and Chardonnay have already been produced, and much fine Sauvignon Blanc and Sémillon, too. Good producers: *Blewitt Springs, Chateau Reynella, Coriole, Hardy's, Richard Hamilton, Geoff Merrill, Middlebrook, Pirramimma, Reynella, Shottesbrooke, Wirra Wirra, Woodstock*.

**MORNINGTON PENINSULA** (Victoria) One of the coolest wine zones of Australia, this is a weekend playground for the rich of Melbourne. It has a patchwork of 80 vineyards and relatively small wineries, among the best of which are *Dromana, Stoniers Merricks* and *Moorooduc Estate*.

**MUDGEE** (New South Wales) Capable of producing good table wines owing to a late spring and cold nights. Though established on Shiraz (*Montrose* is outstanding) the best reds have been deep, tarry, plummy Cabernets. But Chardonnay is even more successful, usually made rich, soft and full of fruit-salad flavours. Look for *Montrose, Craigmoor, Huntington, Miramar*.

**MURRUMBIDGEE IRRIGATION AREA** (New South Wales) Known as the MIA, this vast irrigated area centred round Griffith provides between 15 and 20 per cent of the total Australian crop. Most of it is bulk wine blended by various companies in various states, but *McWilliams* makes some attractive wines, as does *de Bortoli*, including a Sauternes-style Sémillon.

**PADTHAWAY** (South Australia) An increasingly important high-quality area, especially for whites, notably Chardonnay, Rhine Riesling and Sauvignon Blanc. Established in the 1960s when pressure on land in Coonawarra forced major wineries to look elsewhere. Padthaway was chosen because it also had some of the 'terra rossa' soil which makes Coonawarra so special. Grapes are grown here for sparkling wine, and there is some exceedingly good sweet Riesling. Best producers: *Hardy's, Lindemans, Seppelt*; other major producers such as *Orlando* also use the grapes.

**'PORT'** Shiraz and other Rhône-type grapes are often used to make exceptionally high-quality 'port'. The 'Vintage ports' are wonderful. Top names include: *Lindemans, Montara, Penfolds, Saltram, Seppelt, Stanton & Killeen, Yalumba*.

**PYRENEES** (Victoria) Area north-west of Melbourne, producing very dry Shiraz and Cabernet reds, and primarily Sauvignon whites. Top names: *Dalwhinnie, Mount Avoca, Redbank, Taltarni, Warrenmang*, and for sparkling wines, *Chateau Remy* and *Taltarni*.

**RIVERLAND** (South Australia) The grape basket of Australia – a vast irrigation project on the river Murray providing 38 per cent of the national crop. Dominated by the highly efficient co-ops of *Berri Renmano* as well as the *Angoves* company, it produces enormous quantities of bag-in-box wines of a consistently good quality. But it also yields fresh, fruity Rhine Riesling, Chardonnay, Sauvignon, Colombard, Chenin, Cabernet Sauvignon and Shiraz.

**RUTHERGLEN** (Victoria) The centre of the great fortified wine tradition. The white table wines are generally dull, except for some consistently fine wines from *St Leonards*. The reds are rich and robust. The fortified wines, either as *solera*-method 'sherries', as 'Vintage ports', or as intense, brown sugar-sweet Tokays, are all memorable. The true heights are achieved by the Liqueur Muscats, unbearably rich but irresistible with it. Good producers: *Bullers, Campbells, Chambers, Morris, Stanton & Killeen*.

**SPARKLING WINES** Along with Pinot Noir, quality sparkling wine is a Holy Grail in Australia. Leading the pack are *Croser, Domaine Chandon, Yalumba D* and *Ian Wilson*. Cheaper are *Seaview, Angas Brut, Orlando Carrington*; going upmarket, look for *Seppelt's Chardonnay, Vintage Brut* and *Salinger, Yellowglen* and *Andrew Garrett 'Randall'*.

**SWAN VALLEY** (Western Australia) One of the hottest wine regions in the world, the Swan Valley made its reputation on big, rich reds and whites, but even the famous *Houghton's Supreme* is now much lighter and fresher. Good names: *Bassendean, Evans and Tate, Houghton, Moondah Brook, Sandalford*.

**TASMANIA** Only tiny amounts so far, but there is some remarkable Cabernet from *Pipers Brook, Heemskerk, Moorilla Estate*. Pinot Noir from here can be better than mainland versions.

**YARRA VALLEY** (Victoria) There is a distinct possibility that the Yarra Valley is about to emerge as Victoria's table wine superstar. It is cooler than any other mainland Australian area, with a variety of soil types suitable for different grapes' needs. Successes are equally divided between red and white wines, but most excitement has been generated by the traditional 'Bordeaux blend' of Cabernet Sauvignon, Cabernet Franc and Merlot. Pinot Noir is arguably the best in Australia. Whites, too; the scented flavours of Gewürztraminer, Rhine Riesling and Chardonnay are a revelation. Good producers include the following: *Coldstream Hills, De Bortoli, Diamond Valley, Lillydale, Mount Mary, Seville Estate* (who also make great sweet wine), *St Huberts, Yarra Burn, Yarra Yering, Yeringberg*.

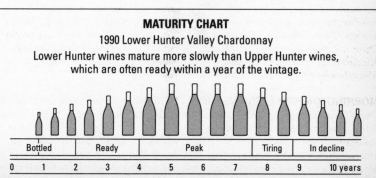

**MATURITY CHART**
1990 Lower Hunter Valley Chardonnay
Lower Hunter wines mature more slowly than Upper Hunter wines, which are often ready within a year of the vintage.

| Bottled | Ready | Peak | Tiring | In decline |

| 0 | 1 | 2 | 3 | 4 | 5 | 6 | 7 | 8 | 9 | 10 years |

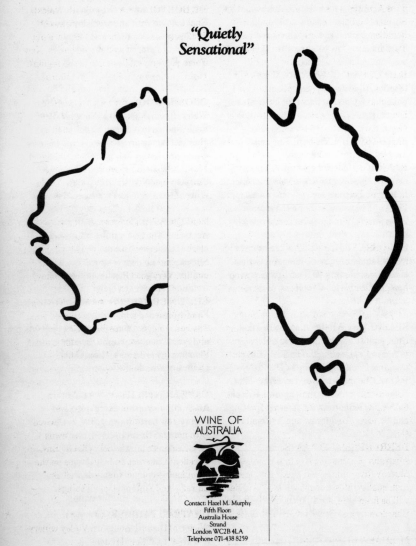

# WINERY PROFILES

**TIM ADAMS** ★★★★ (South Australia)
Spectacular early results: spellbinding
Sémillon and a dense, full-flavoured Shiraz.
Tiny amounts but building a cult following.

**BAILEY'S OF GLENROWAN** ★★★★(★)
(Victoria) Greatest of Australia's fortified
wine-makers, its 'Founder' Liqueur Muscat
is an unbearably delicious concentration of
sweet, dark flavours. Also splendidly
impenetrable Cabernet and Shiraz.

**BANNOCKBURN** ★★★★(★) (Victoria)
Gary Farr, wine-maker at Domaine Dujac
in Burgundy, produces some of cool-climate
Geelong's best wines: a rich Pinot Noir,
full-bodied Chardonnay and Shiraz.

**BAROSSA VALLEY ESTATES** ★★★(★)
(South Australia) Berri-Renmano-owned,
this specializes in high quality cheap wine
and provides much of Oddbins' basic range.

**JIM BARRY** ★★★★ (South Australia)
Clare Valley winery producing outstanding
Chardonnay, Rhine Riesling, Sauvignon
Blanc and a splendid Shiraz, The Armagh.

**BASEDOW** ★★★ (South Australia) Old
Barossa winery now surging ahead with big,
oaky Chardonnay, fine Watervale Riesling,
hearty, chocolaty Shiraz and Cabernet.

**BERRI-RENMANO** ★★★ (South
Australia) Enormous co-op in the irrigated
Murray River hinterland making pretty
high quality. Most cheap own-label Aussies
will be from here, but Chairman's Selection
Chardonnay and Cabernet are high class.

**MILDARA BLASS** ★★★(★) (South
Australia) Now owned by Mildara, with a
knack of producing what people like: wines
of tremendous fruit and well-judged oak.
Good Riesling; voluptuous Chardonnay;
five styles of red: in rising price order, red,
yellow, grey, brown and black label.

**DE BORTOLI** ★★★ (New South Wales)
Shot to fame with an astonishing sweet
1982 botrytis Sémillon, and has since put
together a string of well-priced basics. New
Yarra property makes some of the region's
best Chardonnay, Cabernet and Shiraz.

**BROKENWOOD** ★★★★(★) (New South
Wales) Small, high-class Hunter Valley
winery noted for eclectic blends such as
Hunter/Coonawarra Cabernet and latterly
Hunter/McLaren Vale Sémillon/Sauvignon
Blanc. Low-yielding Graveyard vineyard
produces one of Australia's best Shiraz:
concentrated, profound and long-living.

**BOWEN ESTATE** ★★★★ (South
Australia) The best value in Coonawarra:
elegant Cabernet/Merlot and razor-fine
Shiraz renowned for consistency and
quality. Very good Riesling, Chardonnay.

**BROWN BROTHERS** ★★★(★) (Victoria)
Family firm, and a huge range of good wine.
The best vineyards are the cool Koombahla
and even cooler Whitlands; look for Muscat,
Sémillon, Chardonnay, Koombahla
Cabernet, Whitlands Gewürz and Riesling.

**CAPE MENTELLE** ★★★★ (Western
Australia) Important Margaret River
winery now part-owned by Veuve Clicquot
with founder David Hohnen; also owns
New Zealand's buzz winery Cloudy Bay.
Excellent Cabernet and variations on the
Sémillon/Sauvignon theme as well as
Shiraz – and Zinfandel, of all things.

**CHATEAU TAHBILK** ★★★★(★)
(Victoria) Historic Goulburn Valley winery
and great traditional reds.

**COLDSTREAM HILLS** ★★★★(★)
(Victoria) Aussie wine writer James
Halliday opted for practising what he
preached. World class Pinot Noir in the
offing, exciting Chardonnay and Cabernet.

**DELATITE** ★★★★(★) (Victoria) 'A magic piece of dirt, it could grow anything' is how the owners describe the Delatite vineyard. The wines have an individuality of fruit plus superb wine-making which puts them in the top class. Dry Riesling is delicious, the sweet superb, while Pinot Noir, Gewürz, Cabernet and Shiraz are brilliant.

**DOMAINE CHANDON** ★★★★ (South Australia) Moët & Chandon's Green Point Estate in the Yarra Valley released its first Champagne method sparkler in the UK in 1992, after massive investment.

**DROMANA** ★★★★(★) (Victoria) Excellent Chardonnay, promising Pinot Noir and Cabernet/Merlot in the Mornington Peninsula, as well as the good-value Schinus Molle label.

**HARDY** ★★★★(★) (South Australia) Impressive quality level across the entire range. Particularly good Padthaway Chardonnay and Fumé Blanc, and delicious McLaren Vale Cabernet. Also controls Chateau Reynella, a high quality producer of Cabernet and Chardonnay.

**HENSCHKE** ★★★★★ (South Australia) Old red vines, some of them 100 years old, yield deep, dark, curranty wines of top class. Whites equally stunning – Riesling, Sémillon and Chardonnay.

**HILL-SMITH/YALUMBA** ★★★(★) (South Australia) A large Barossa company producing good wines under the Yalumba and Hill Smith labels, and exceptional ones under the Signature, Heggies and Pewsey Vale Vineyard labels, where dry and sweet Rieslings are some of the finest in Australia. Yalumba D is very good fizz.

**HOLLICK** ★★★★ (South Australia) With vineyards on the best soils of Coonawarra, Ian Hollick and wine-maker Pat Tocaciu harvest some of the region's suavest reds; a soft and tobaccoey Cabernet/Merlot and an outstanding Cabernet *cuvée*, Ravenswood.

They make fine Pinot and Chardonnay fizz and regularly confound the sceptics with this red district's most successful Riesling.

**HOWARD PARK** ★★★★ (Western Australia) Expensive but superb, long-living wines. The Riesling is intense, perfumed and austere; the Cabernet deep and structured. Both need cellaring.

**LAKE'S FOLLY** ★★★★ (New South Wales) Tiny Hunter Valley winery making highly idiosyncratic Chardonnay and Cabernet, very exciting with age.

**LEEUWIN ESTATE** ★★★★ (Western Australia) Ultra-high profile, ultra-high prices for exciting Chardonnay and Pinot Noir, blackcurrant-and-leather Cabernet Sauvignon, good Riesling and Sauvignon.

**LINDEMANS** ★★★★(★) (Victoria) Remarkable company now part of Penfolds. Based at Karadoc, with holdings in the Hunter, Padthaway, Coonawarra and Barossa. Exceptionally good basic varietals, while the old-style Hunters, plus Padthaways and Coonawarras, are some of Australia's finest. Coonawarra reds Limestone Ridge and St George are tiptop, as is the Bordeaux blend, Pyrus.

**MCWILLIAMS** ★★(★) (New South Wales) Old-fashioned giant now rapidly improving its quality. Though traditionally a Hunter company, much McWilliams wine now comes from Griffith in the MIA. Blends like the Hillside Colombard/Chardonnay show what can be done with fairly basic fruit.

**CHARLES MELTON** ★★★★ (South Australia) A 1000-case winery in the Barossa, with a Grenache-based Nine Popes and a Shiraz of exceptional concentration and character.

**GEOFF MERRILL** ★★★(★) (South Australia) The walrus-moustached, charismatic and irreverent Merrill combines an instinctive feel for wine with marketing ability. His McLaren Vale base, Mount Hurtle, makes worthy Cabernet, full Chardonnay, crisp Sauvignon/Sémillon and thirst-quenching Grenache rosé.

**MILDARA** ★★★(★) (South Australia) Based in the irrigated Murray River hinterland, but with large holdings in Coonawarra. Quality is erratic, though price is fair. It also owns Yellowglen and Balgownie in Victoria, Krondorf in SA and Morton Estate in New Zealand.

**MITCHELTON** ★★★(★) (Victoria) Wide range of styles in the Goulburn Valley, notably fine, full-flavoured Rieslings, good Chardonnay under the Preece label and the speciality of the house, Marsanne.

**MOORILLA ESTATE** ★★★★ (Tasmania) The first of the new-wave Tasmanian wineries, producing a polished range of crisp cool-climate wines. Pinot Noir is a speciality; aromatic Riesling, Chardonnay and Gewürztraminer are also excellent.

**MOSS WOOD** ★★★★★ (Western Australia) Superbly original wines from Margaret River. Sémillon, with and without wood-ageing, is some of the best in Australia. Pinot Noir is daring and delicious, Chardonnay less daring but just as delicious, Cabernet rich and structured.

**MOUNTADAM** ★★★★ (South Australia) David Wynn established this Adelaide Hills vineyard after selling Wynns in Coonawarra. His son Adam makes complex, Burgundian Chardonnay, substantial Pinot Noir, idiosyncratic Riesling, lean Cabernet.

**MOUNT LANGI-GHIRAN** ★★★★ (Victoria) New Great Western district winery already making dry, intense, Shiraz and long-lasting Cabernet.

**MOUNT MARY** ★★★★ (Victoria) Finely structured Cabernet-based Bordeaux blend and a Pinot Noir improving with age. Tiny production, much sought-after.

**ORLANDO** ★★★(★) (South Australia) Barossa winery with fine quality at every level. Its boxed wine is outstanding, its RF Cabernet, Riesling and Chardonnay are usually the best in the price bracket, and St-Helga Riesling, St-Hilary Chardonnay and St-Hugo Cabernet are among the best.

**PENFOLDS** ★★★★★ (South Australia) The greatest red winemakers in Australia, and now good in whites too. Its basics are clean and tasty, its varietals packed with flavour, and its special selection reds, culminating in the deservedly legendary Grange Hermitage, are superlative, hugely structured wines of world class. If you can't afford Grange, try Bin 28, Bin 128, Bin 389 or Bin 707. Bin 820 is even better but they won't let us have any.

**PENLEY ESTATE** ★★★★ (South Australia) Kym Tolley is a scion of the Penfolds and Tolley families, hence Penley. He planted this Coonawarra estate in 1988, and is already producing award-winning Shiraz, Cabernet/Shiraz and Chardonnay.

**PETALUMA** ★★★(★) (South Australia) The baby of Brian Croser is slowly hitting its stride. Some of his Rieslings, sweet and dry, have been tip-top, his Chardonnays less so, and his Cabernet-based reds are improving each year. Also 'Croser' fizz.

**PIPERS BROOK** ★★★★ (Tasmania) Keenly-sought wines which combine classy design, clever marketing and skilful wine-making by Andrew Pirie. Steely aromatic Riesling, classically reserved Chardonnay, serious Pinot Noir and tasty, barrel-fermented Sauvignon Blanc are the best.

**PLANTAGENET** ★★★(★) (Western Australia) In an unglamorous apple packing shed in chilly Mount Barker, John Wade and Tony Smith make a fine range. Noted for peppery Shiraz, melony/nutty Chardonnay, fine limey Riesling and elegant Cabernet Sauvignon.

**ROCKFORD ★★★★** (South Australia)
The individuality of Rocky O'Callaghan's
wines, especially his Basket Press Shiraz,
has made him a Barossa cult.

**ROSEMOUNT ★★★★** (New South Wales)
The company which did more than any to
help Australia take the UK by storm with
Chardonnay, Fumé Blanc and Cabernet.
The last two are no longer so good, though
Chardonnay is on the way back and the
single vineyard Roxburgh Chardonnay is
impressive. Worldwide, the Chardonnays
have set new standards for affordable
quality. We are seeing surprising Pinot
Noir, excellent Sémillon and sweet wine,
and the gluggable Diamond Reserve range.

**ROTHBURY ★★★★** (New South Wales)
One of the leading Hunter companies
founded by the indomitable Len Evans. Its
wines went through a bad patch a few years
ago, but are now back on form with classic
flavours. The Chardonnay and Sémillon
are now some of the Hunter's best and
Pinot Noir and Shiraz increasingly good.

**ST HALLETT ★★★(★)** (South Australia)
Big Bob McLean (a small wine-maker only
in one sense), with Stuart Blackwell and
the Lindner family in the Barossa, makes
full, oaky Sémillon and Chardonnay and a
rich Shiraz, Old Block, from old vines.

**ST HUBERTS ★★★★** (Victoria) One of the
original Yarra Valley vineyards, now back
in the top class. Equally brilliant with
whites and reds; the Chardonnay and
Cabernet Sauvignon are exceptional.

**SEPPELT ★★★★** (Victoria) Leading
makers of quality fizz from Champagne
grapes, peaking with Salinger. Also fruity,
easy-drinking styles. Now part of Penfolds.

**SHAW & SMITH ★★★★** (South Australia)
Itinerant wine-maker Martin Shaw and his
cousin, Michael Hill-Smith MW, make fine
Sauvignon Blanc and Chardonnay in the
Southern Vales. A duo to watch.

**STONIERS MERRICKS ★★★★** (Victoria)
Fine Chardonnay and Cabernet from this
Mornington Peninsula winery.

**TALTARNI ★★★(★)** (Victoria) Remarkable
bone-dry, grassy-sharp Fumé Blanc and
fine Cabernet and Shiraz which soften
(after about a decade) into classy, if austere
reds. If that all sounds more French than
Australian – well, the wine-maker grew up
at Château Lafite in Bordeaux.

**TISDALL ★★★** (Victoria) Goulburn
winery making fresh, easy-to-drink reds
and whites and cool-climate, quality
classics from its Mount Helen grapes.

**TYRRELL ★★★(★)** (New South Wales)
Famous, eccentrically brilliant Hunter
winery which sells 'port' and 'blackberry
nip' to tourists through the front door while
making some great classic wines out the
back. There has never been a more exciting
Australian Chardonnay than the Vat 47 of
the early '80s, and for years Tyrrell was the
only Aussie who could make great Pinot
Noir. Vat 1 Sémillon is also excellent, as is
his 'plonk' – Long Flat Red and White.

**VASSE FELIX ★★★★(★)** (Western
Australia) One of the original Margaret
River wineries. Classic regional style of
rich, leafy/curranty Cabernet and spicy,
fleshy Shiraz.

**WYNNS ★★★★(★)** (South Australia) Spot-
on Riesling, big, oaky Chardonnay, perfect,
refined Cabernet and Shiraz from this
Coonawarra company. Wynn's Ovens
Valley Shiraz is a lot less refined, but good
value. Top-line John Riddoch Cabernet is
expensive but worth every penny.

**YARRA YERING ★★★★★** (Victoria)
Wonderful Yarra Valley winery, where
Bailey Carrodus labels his Cabernet-based
wine Dry Red No.1 and his Shiraz-based
wine Dry Red No.2: exceptional, powerful
and concentrated yet fragrant reds. Fine
Pinot Noir as well.

# NEW ZEALAND

New Zealand wine has been sharing flavour of the month in Britain awards with Australia for several years now, and we show no sign of kicking the Kiwi habit. Quite the reverse, in fact. We drank almost three times as much New Zealand wine in 1988 as the year before, virtually doubled-up again in 1991, and figures so far for 1992 are 50 per cent up again. All this in a recession, to boot.

Luckily for us, the wine industry there is in bullish mood. Even recession has not prevented the birth of new wineries. However, their domestic consumption is declining; they must export or die. And we are the chief beneficiaries.

In the range of wine styles and producers, New Zealand is the very antithesis of, for example, Chile. It produces only a tenth of the latter's total output, but from ten times as many producers, and with far greater diversity of styles, despite the preponderance of Sauvignon Blanc in the public's eye. Certainly, Chardonnay has proved to be at least as good as Sauvignon Blanc and, since 1989, several regions have been turning out stunning red wines. But Pinot Gris could be good as well, Riesling can be world class, some of the finest Chenin is produced here, as well as Gewürztraminer that is the equal of Alsace. The experimentation is continuing, but must be pursued aggressively, if only to withstand the inevitable onslaught of Sauvignon Blanc and Chardonnay.

## Youth training

Two recently established areas are already making waves with their quality. Waiheke Island is turning out to be one of the most underrated wine areas in New Zealand, and is home to one of the most ebullient of those new wineries: the irrepressible Terry Dunleavy, who used to run the New Zealand Wine Guild in unashamedly cavalier fashion, has just planted the island's largest vineyard with Bordeaux grapes and, much to the chagrin of the island's three established wineries, has registered the name Waiheke Vineyard. Martinborough's Pinot Noir is proving to be some of New Zealand's best, and its Chardonnay is some of the North Island's most intense. The vines in the region are young, though, and many wine-makers are short on experience — though they seem to learn fast.

Experience is in greater supply in the area of sparkling wine. Daniel le Brun of Marlborough has always been New Zealand's brightest hope for fizz, with a style very close to that of Champagne. Only his non-vintage is currently shipped to the UK, but with luck that will change, since his 1990 vintage and his *blanc de blancs* are even better than his '89.

Morton Estate, although not in the same class as Daniel le Brun, easily makes the second best range of sparkling wines in New Zealand. Third comes Deutz Marlborough Cuvée, but watch out for Australia's Domaine Chandon, which is launching a new *cuvée* from Marlborough (from Hunter's, in fact). The first release of a sparkling wine from Cloudy Bay called Pelorus will not have Veuve Clicquot quaking in its boots, but the first release from Roederer Estate in California did not shake the world either, and look at the goodies that came next.

At the time of writing the 1992 vintage is still in the fermentation vats, which makes it rather too young to assess. But 1991 was a winner; almost as successful as 1989 across the country, but particularly for Marlborough Sauvignon Blanc, which is nothing less than spectacular. **TOM STEVENSON**

## WHITE GRAPES & FLAVOURS

**CHARDONNAY** New Zealand's vineyards are only a dolphin's leap from the South Pole, and the cool ripening period makes Chardonnay light, but with intense, high-acid flavours – a penetrating fruit bowl of apple, peach, pineapple and pear, softened by new oak barrels into some of the most original in the New World. Hawke's Bay makes classics, followed by Marlborough, Nelson and Wairarapa. Gisborne's are softer, less intense. Top wines: *Babich, Cloudy Bay, Collards* (*Tolaga, Rothesay*), *Cooks* (Hawke's Bay and Gisborne), *Coopers Creek, Delegat's, Kumeu River, Hunters, Morton Estate, Matawhero, Matua Valley,* (*Judd, Yates* and *Egan Estates*), *Nobilo* (*Dixon Estate, Te Karaka*), *de Redcliffe, Selaks, Te Mata, Vidals, Villa Maria.*

**CHENIN BLANC** This tricky Loire grape is at its most versatile here, ranging from stone-dry to rich. Best with some sweetness. It could make fine Vouvray styles, but is usually too overcropped. *Collards* is good; *Cooks* and *Matawhero* not bad.

**GEWÜRZTRAMINER** Can be world class: pungent, reeking of black pepper, mangoes, lychees, yet dry and refreshing. Gisborne is a good region and *Matawhero* can be great. Others: *Cooper's Creek, Morton Estate, Nobilo, Pacific Wines, Villa Maria.*

**MÜLLER-THURGAU** The dominant NZ grape. When well made, as by *Montana*, it has a flowering currant, green tang, or, from *Nobilo*, the grapiness of many German

Rheinhessens. Also good: *Collards, Cooks, Delegat's, Matawhero, Matua Valley, Totara.*

**RIESLING** A lot of Rhine Riesling (as NZ calls it) is made into bland blends, but there are outstanding wines, either in the bone-dry Alsace style, or occasionally big, rich and sweet. *Corbans Stoneleigh* is good, as are *Babich, Collards, Coopers Creek, Selaks Brigham Creek, Delegat's, Matua Valley, Millton, Seifried* (*Redwood Valley Vineyard*). *Montana* is lean but OK; *Giesen* may make the most classic dry Riesling yet. *Delegat's, Ngatarawa, St Helena, Corbans* and *Seifried* have made rich late-harvest wines. NZ could become a great sweet wine land.

**SAUVIGNON BLANC** A few top the world already. The best, such as *Montana Marlborough Sauvignon*, or *Selaks* from Hawke's Bay, bring nettly, asparagus and gooseberry fruit to fresh, sharp balance, rounded off with honey and spice. Recent attempts to modify the grassy style and introduce complexity seem successful. Also good: *Cloudy Bay, Babich, Brookfields, Coopers Creek, Corban's Stoneleigh, Selaks, Hunters, Delegat's, Montana's Brancott Estate, Morton Estate, Vidal, Villa Maria.*

**SÉMILLON** Steering away from the heavy, oily Aussie tradition to something fresher, like the grassy *Vidal* or the classic beeswax and sweet apples of *Villa Maria, Montana* and *Delegat's*. It is increasingly blended with Sauvignon or Chardonnay as at *Babich, Delegat's* and *Mission.*

## RED GRAPES & FLAVOURS

**CABERNET SAUVIGNON** The Cabernets, weedy and green in the early days, are certainly still dry, but the fruit has developed into a piercing, fresh, grassy, blackcurrant-and-nettles style about as pure as you can get. *Cooks* Hawke's Bay Cabernet is usually grassy, soft and delicious but there are also many single

estates producing outstanding wine. Each successive vintage shows improvements. Top wineries for Cabernet include the great *Te Mata, Cloudy Bay* (from 1987), *Cook's Fernhill, Goldwater, Kumeu River, Montana, Matua Valley, Neudorf, Ngatarawa, St Nesbit, Selaks, Vidal* and *Villa Maria.*

**MERLOT** Planted primarily for blending with Cabernet (the *Te Mata* Coleraine is classic), but also made into varietals. *Kumeu River* is full, peppery and plummy and *Esk Valley* is packed with fruit.

**PINOT NOIR** The record is less than uniform, but there have been shining examples, from wineries like *St-Helena* and *Martinborough,* and as the vines (and skills) mature, the wines improve in concentration and quality each vintage. Up-and-coming names to watch are *Waipara Springs* and *Omihi Hills.* Also makes excellent perfumed white – *Matua Valley's* is first-rate.

## WINES & WINE REGIONS

**GISBORNE** (North Island) They call Gisborne 'carafe' country, because it's a positive grape basket of a region, planted with one-third of the nation's vines. Above all, it is the home of Müller-Thurgau, which can yield 20 to 25 tons per hectare on the Poverty Bay alluvial flats. In general, the wine is light but good, but there are exceptions. Matawhero is a high-quality sub-area, as are Tolaga and Tikitiki further north. From these areas, Chenin and Gewürztraminer and, increasingly, award-winning Chardonnay, can be excellent. Reds on the whole are less exciting in Gisborne, although *Delegat's* have produced some good Cabernet.

**HAWKE'S BAY** (North Island) Potentially New Zealand's greatest wine region: it is becoming evident that, as well as fine whites, great reds could also be made here. Indeed, the deep gravel banks, allied to its being one of the country's sunniest areas, mean that there is enormous potential for Cabernet and Merlot to produce top quality claret-type reds. I believe that if *any* of the world's regions is ever going to produce the flavour equivalent of a Médoc Classed Growth it will be Hawke's Bay, but in the meantime the joyous originality of the fruit flavours is as shocking as it is delightful. Good producers: *Brookfield's, Cooks, Matua Valley, Ngatarawa, Vidal, Villa Maria* and, above all, *Te Mata.*

The price guides for this section begin on page 386.

**MARLBOROUGH** (South Island) Now one of the biggest vineyard regions in the country – and still growing. The strengths – thanks to a long, slow ripening period – have always been white wines: outstanding Rhine Riesling, Chardonnay and especially Sauvignon. Reds are improving dramatically.

**OTHER NORTH ISLAND** North of Auckland, at Waimauku (with *Matua Valley* and *Collards*), Huapai (*Nobilo*) and Kumeu (*Coopers Creek, Kumeu River* and *Selaks*) there are excellent reds and whites, though frequently vinified from grapes grown elsewhere on the island. West of Auckland at Henderson the top producers include *Babich, Collards, Delegat's* who produce award-winning white wines, and *Pacific.* South of Auckland is the impressive *Villa Maria* as well as *St Nesbit* and *de Redcliffe.* On Waiheke Island, *Goldwater Estate* and *Stonyridge Vineyard* are producing excellent wine. *Morton Estate* on Bay of Plenty is already established as one of New Zealand's best producers.

**OTHER SOUTH ISLAND** Nelson to the east of Marlborough is a minor area, but has good performers in *Neudorf* and *Seifried.* Canterbury is dominated by the excellent *St Helena* and *Giesen, Larcomb, Omihi Hills* and *Waipara Springs* look set to produce exciting wines. And at *Gibbston Valley* and *Rippon Vineyard,* good Chardonnay and Pinot Noir are showing what the world's most southerly vineyards can achieve.

# WINERY PROFILES

**BABICH** ★★★ Leading Henderson winery. Look for fresh Fumé Vert (Sémillon and Chardonnay), oaky Irongate Chardonnay, grassy Cabernet from Hawke's Bay grapes.

**DANIEL LE BRUN** ★★★★ New Zealand's finest sparkling wine producer found a new gear in 1989 and is now one of the three top producers outside the Champagne region.

**CLOUDY BAY** ★★★★★ Highest profile of the small South Island wineries. Excellent Sauvignon, fattened with a little Sémillon, sells out within days. Chardonnay and, eventually, Cabernet may be even better.

**CORBANS** ★★★(★) Includes Cooks and McWilliams. Some good special bottlings under the Stoneleigh label, as well as plain varietals. Cooks Fernhill is a rich Cabernet Sauvignon, Longridge a nice Chardonnay.

**DELEGAT'S** ★★★★ White specialist near Auckland, using mostly Hawke's Bay and Gisborne fruit. Fine Sauvignon, Chardonnay and sweet wine; promising Cabernet.

**KUMEU RIVER** ★★★★ Imaginative winery just north of Auckland experimenting with considerable success with growing, making and maturation methods. Merlot/Cabernet, and Chardonnay increasingly exciting.

**MARTINBOROUGH** ★★★★ New and exciting operation in the far south of the North Island, with lovely Riesling, Muller-Thurgau, Sauvignon, Chardonnay and outstanding Pinot Noir.

**MATUA VALLEY** ★★★★(★) High quality winery producing superb single-estate Chardonnays and exciting Cabernet reds. Also delicious Riesling, lovely Gewürztraminer and some of New Zealand's best Müller-Thurgau. It makes sensible use of the problematic Pinot Noir by turning it into a very decent rosé.

**MONTANA** ★★★(★) Marlborough Sauvignon Blanc from here is regularly one of New Zealand's best. Latest releases of Cabernet are also very much on the up. New fizzes, Lindauer and upmarket Deutz (made with French help) are great value.

**MORTON ESTATE** ★★★★ Exceptional winery east of Auckland, so far focussing on whites with award-winning Sauvignon, Chardonnay and Gewürz. Winemaker John Hancock has begun his assault on red wine territory and in the meantime makes top quality Champagne-method fizz.

**NGATARAWA** ★★★ Newish Hawke's Bay winery likely to make great red and sweet in the near future, and fine Chardonnay.

**NOBILO** ★★★(★) Family-run estate at Huapai making good Chardonnay (oak-aged and single vineyard), barrel-fermented Sauvignon and a Müller-Thurgau called White Cloud.

**ST HELENA** ★★★(★) Shot to prominence with its world-famous 1982 Pinot Noir. Perhaps inevitably, it's taken a while to match that peak again but (1989 excepted) the last few vintages have been superb.

**SELAKS** Excellent bone-dry wines from north of Auckland. Spot-on Sauvignon Blanc and Sauvignon/Sémillon, a 3:2 blend. Top of the range is Founder's Selection.

**TE MATA** ★★★★★ Te Mata Coleraine is the most consistently impressive and most sought-after of NZ reds. Te Mata Awatea is also a fine red and Elston Chardonnay, is rich, powerful and Burgundian in style.

**VILLA MARIA** ★★★★ Vidal, Esk Valley and Villa Maria Reserve Bin wines from Sauvignon to Merlot. Classic Cabernets and rich, juicy Chardonnays. Prices are very fair.

# UNITED KINGDOM

Forget Cabernet Sauvignon, forget Chardonnay. The grape that gives the best results in the vineyards of the United Kingdom is French, certainly, but not in the same hall of fame as those two (indeed many French viticulturalists have never heard of it) and the EC wants it eradicated from European vineyards by the year 2010. Combine that with the vagaries of the British climate and it becomes clear that running an English or Welsh vineyard is less akin to rustic tranquillity than it is to waging guerrilla war.

The grape in question is Seyval Blanc, a hybrid. Decades ago, Seyval produced poor, even bad wine, but technology has been kind to it and its wines have improved dramatically. The French, however, used it to overcrop hugely in the Midi. The intelligent EC answer was therefore to ban all hybrids for use in quality wine.

Quality wine in EC terms means the equivalent of *appellation contrôlée*, and the EC view of Seyval Blanc is only relevant to Britain because Britain is producing so much wine these days. Any country that makes over 25,000 hectolitres a year, says the EC, must have a quality wine system. Since the United Kingdom is getting close to this magic level, the English Vineyards Association has set up a pilot scheme. And from it, of course, Seyval, the hybrid, must be excluded.

The variety, though, is grown by fully half of the United Kingdom's winemakers. It produces reliable crops in our climate, and in addition keeps on winning the Gore-Browne Trophy, the top award for English wines, so the growers are not well pleased. For the first official appraisal for Quality Wine status in April 1992 there were only three applications from UK vineyards, and for the whole of 1992 there may well turn out to be fewer than 30. Since 1978 in fact the English Vineyards Association has run its own Certification Scheme whereby wines are analyzed, tasted and awarded, where merited, a licence to display a Gold Seal.

Geoffrey Bond of the Association regards the Certification examination as being even more stringent than the requirements for Quality Wine status and, since Seyval (as well as all other vines grown in the United Kingdom) is eligible for it, many producers are expected to stay with the established local scheme rather than move to the EC one.

### Siberia in Sussex

Alternative thinking on vines appropriate to the British weather could push our viticulture even further from the European fold if it is followed up. The late Professor Becker of the viticultural research station at Geisenheim in Germany suggested that the future for English and Welsh wine may lie in *Vitis amarensis*, a totally different species of vine to *Vitis vinifera*, the basis of virtually all wine as we consumers know it. Amarensis is to Siberia what vinifera is to Europe, and Becker had canes from it in his experimental plots at Geisenheim. Gillian Pearkes at Yearlstone in Devon and Kenneth McAlpine at Lamberhurst are continuing these experiments.

Recent vintages in Britain have been very good – 1989 was the best for a long while – and 1992 got off to an excellent start with some early fine weather, no late frost, good bud-burst and healthy vines. 1991 shared late-May frosts and bad autumn weather with other regions, and in addition had a wet spell during flowering, so the quantity was down – 2 tonnes per acre on average – but the quality ended up generally good. The 1990 harvest was also of high quality but a little short on quantity.

1989, however, was outstanding with a long, warm autumn that meant that many grapes could be picked in late November. This enabled some growers to make wines they had never been able to contemplate before, such as the botrytized Late Harvest produced at St George's in East Sussex. Some vineyards were claiming yields of 10 tonnes per acre – the kind of volume that leaves vines clapped out in quite a short time – but the quality-conscious properties tended to be happy with four or five.

In 1992, the English Vineyards Association celebrated its silver jubilee. The last 25 years have seen great changes in the vineyards of England and Wales; what the next 25 years will hold is anybody's guess. It is probably fair to say, though that unless the greenhouse effect gives Britain a climate akin to that of at least the Loire or Rhine, then the wine-growers of England and Wales are unlikely to be able to rely on the sort of non-hybrid vines for their production. That is, if they are to have any chance of developing the style and quality of English and Welsh wine. The battle of Seyval Blanc looks set to continue for many, many years yet.

**GORDON BROWN**

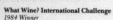

# WHITE WINES

**BACCHUS** In Germany, this new crossing usually produces fat, blowsy, marmalade-Muscatty flavours. In England it is more likely to produce a sharp wine, with strong flavours of gooseberry and elderflower as well as something of orange rind. *Barkham, Patridge Vineyard, Three Choirs, Coddington and Shawsgate* are good; *Chiltern Valley's 1989 Noble Bacchus* showed that a warm English summer can produce lusciously rich wines too.

**FABER** A crossing of Pinot Blanc and Müller-Thurgau, making fragrant wines with good acidity. One of the few varieties where you can actually taste Riesling characteristics.

**HUXELREBE** A cross (of Gutedel, alias Chasselas, with Courtillier Musqué) that in Germany beetles to overripeness in no time at all. The wine there is usually rich, flat and grapy. In England it's generally the exact opposite, renowned for a grapefruit pith taste and a greenish bite. For this reason it is often softened up by blending. *Headcorn's* version is almost as delicate as a German Mosel; *Lamberhurst* and *Biddenden* are fuller; *Staple St James* and *Pilton Manor* more grapefruity and smoky. *Nutbourne Manor's* is concentrated, *Astley* mixes it with Müller-Thurgau for Huxelvaner while *Three Choirs* late-picks it and tries to make a sweetie.

**KERNER** A bright, new German crossing of Riesling and Trollinger that is producing good results. *Astley's* is light and *Oatley* mixes it with Kernling for gingery, apple-sweet wine in best Cox's Orange Pippin style.

**MADELEINE ANGEVINE** Basically this is a table grape, but it performs quite well in England, where its somewhat 'fruit-juicy' character is matched by good acidity, either in the green but refreshing elderflower perfumed style of *Astley* 1985 and '86, or the more honeyed but appley style of *Hooksway* 1984. *Sharpham* mixes it with Huxelrebe to produce a flinty Loire lookalike.

**MÜLLER-THURGAU** One of the original German crosses – from Riesling and Silvaner in 1882 – and the English work-horse, taking up over one-third of the acreage. Consequently, there is a fair bit of dull Müller (sometimes called Rivaner) about, needing beefing up with something more aromatic. *Wootton, Bruisyard St Peter, Breaky Bottom, St Nicholas of Ash, Staple St James, Tenterden, St George's* are good. And it can make very attractive, slightly sweet wine (through the addition of *Süssreserve,* or unfermented grape juice, just before bottling), as at *Pulham, Lamberhurst* and *Rowney.*

**ORTEGA** German cross making fat, rich, grapy wine mostly in the Mosel, of all places, but better suited to England. *Hidden Spring* is concentrated,and *Biddenden,* in particular, makes a delicious, slightly sweet but tremendously fruity elderflower and apricot-tasting example. It is usually blended and rarely seen on its own.

**REICHENSTEINER** A real 'EC' grape, since it is a crossing of French Madeleine Angevine, German Müller-Thurgau and Italian Calabrese. Does this multi-coloured background make it an exciting, tempestuous grape? Sadly, it's rather more of a Brussels bureaucrat clone. It's usually pretty dull made dry but made slightly sweet, it can develop a pleasant, smoky, quince and peaches taste which ages well.

*The price guides for this section begin on page 389.*

*Carr Taylor* and *Rock Lodge* use it for Champagne-method fizz, *Three Choirs '90 'New Release'* was 50/50 Huxelrebe and Reichensteiner and *Nutbourne Manor*'s version is also good.

**SCHEUREBE** Silvaner crossed with Riesling, capable of producing good grapefruity, curranty wines in good years. *Thames Valley's* late-harvest version is seductively good.

**SCHÖNBURGER** A *good,* pink grape. It makes a fat wine by English standards, with a pears and lychees flavour and good acidity. Dry versions like *Saxon Valley's* need ripe fruit to balance the acidity, and it needs expert wine-making, or it can end up tasting like bathroom detergent. The best are made by *Lamberhurst, Wootton, Carr Taylor, Coxley* and *Three Choirs*.

**SEYVAL BLANC** A French hybrid with around 15 per cent of UK acreage. *Breaky Bottom* is the most successful – dry and Sauvignon-like when young, honeyed like Burgundy after four to five years – but it is generally best blended with something more exotic like Schönburger or Huxelrebe, or made sweetish. *Hambledon* blends it with Pinot Meunier and Chardonnay, *Three Choirs* with Reichensteiner and *Adgestone* with Reichensteiner and Müller, while *Tenterden* makes a very good oaked Reserve. *Thames Valley*, too hits it with oak for its *Fumé; Hidden Spring* and *Headcorn* are also good.

**OTHER WHITES** Numerous other varieties are being tried. The most interesting are Gewürztraminer at *Barton Manor* on the Isle of Wight where it was planted in plastic tunnels in 1984 and Ehrenfelser, aged in a 4000-litre oak barrel, at *Penshurst*; *Wootton's* Auxerrois is a pungent, salty-sappy wine, while *Tenterden* also achieves lean and nervy results with this variety. *Carr Taylor* has achieved good results with Pinot Blanc for its concentrated *Kemsley Dry*. There are also some efforts with Chardonnay, at, for example, the new, 250-acre *Denbies Estate* at Dorking in Surrey, England's most ambitious vineyard project yet.

# RED & ROSÉ WINES

**CABERNET SAUVIGNON** *Beenleigh* in Devon has been growing Cabernet Sauvignon in plastic tunnels, along with Merlot, and the 1989 version is clean and fresh, if light.

**PINOT NOIR** There are now over 20 hectares of the great Burgundy grape planted! So far, full reds have been difficult to achieve, but Kent has several patches making very good rosé – *Chiddingstone* blends it with Pinot Meunier to make a delicious wine redolent of eucalyptus; *Bodiam Castle* makes a tasty rosé blended with Blauburger, as well as a dry, honeyed Blanc de Pinot Noir white; *Biddenden* mixes it with Dornfelder and Gamay to produce a light, cherryish red; and *Tenterden's* blend with Dunkelfelder makes a gently honeyed, smoky mango-flavoured pink. *Three Choirs* rosé from Pinot Noir has earthy raspberry and Morello cherry fruit; *Conghurst* rosé is also good, with grapy, herbaceous flavours. Some estates are now planting Pinot Noir for sparkling wine.

**TRIOMPHE D'ALSACE** This hybrid, one of whose parents is the Alsace Knipperlé, is proving a popular variety in England's trying climate. The best examples have a fresh, raspberry-and-spice character like *Meon Valley's Meonwara* or *Thames Valley's* balanced *Dry Red*. The trick, as with all reds in England, is to settle for a light, graceful wine and not to over-extract flavour – the deepest English reds tend to taste of vegetation rather than fruit.

# EASTERN EUROPE

There's no such thing as an Eastern European wine, of course. There's probably no such thing as a Yugoslavian wine either, though the labels on the vintages over here don't yet reflect Yugoslavia's disastrous recent history. And what of the other countries? At the time of writing Czechoslovakia seems about to split and the USSR has been defunct for some while. Open a bottle of some of these wines and you're tasting history.

But then national boundaries in this part of the world have long reflected political divisions rather than geographical ones. And while the geography of Eastern Europe certainly affects the wines – the four distinct climates, for example, that it boasts – it is political and economic realities that will be putting perhaps a pound on a bottle as state subsidies are phased out, and it is the shortage of equipment, expertise and cash that will determine how quickly these countries bring their wines up to world standards.

## BULGARIA

Bulgarian Cabernet Sauvignon has an image akin to that of Marks & Spencer: cheap, cheerful and dead reliable. To some extent it's justified; and yet, and yet. Does having a range of a dozen different basic Cabernet Sauvignons really help the consumer? Yes, of course they're all from different areas and as good Europeans we know that geographical origin is terrifically important, but when there are 27 Controliran regions and 43 viticultural regions and most of them seem to grow pretty similar styles of Cabernet...

Yields are low – 25-40 hectolitres per hectare – partly due to unsophisticated vineyard methods, there's a fair bit of *barrique*-ageing about, and as well as the familiar western varietals there are indigenous grapes like Gamza and Melnik to explore. And when Bulgaria learns to handle white grapes as well as it handles red, and produce Chardonnay and, even dodgier at the moment, Sauvignon Blanc, that is reliably clean, fresh and fruity, it will be a force to reckon with.

## CZECHOSLOVAKIA

After some intermittent export activity a decade ago, the wines slid off the retail shelves here in order to produce extremely basic plonk for what was then the guaranteed Russian market.

However, the days of 50 per cent state subsidies are gone, every winery that has a bottling line is now a separate business. From the morass of awful wines – some of them used to last only six weeks in bottle, and that must sometimes have seemed too long – new ventures are emerging. Angela Muir at Heart of Europe is one of the new Western brooms sweeping clean and has already conjured four fine, very fruity, dry varietals out of Slovakian vineyards near Bratislava.

## HUNGARY

Hungary's on its way: the Aussies are moving in. Several West European companies have set up in business there, and one of those, Hanwood, has brought in an Australian wine-maker; another, based in Budapest and overseeing a number of different vineyards, works with wine-maker Hugh Ryman, who has produced Sauvignon Blanc and Chardonnay from the Gyöngyös Estate. Where

Australian wine-makers lead, freshness and fruit invariably follow.

At the moment most Hungarian wines are still being exported in bulk for bottling outside the country; and at the same time, because of the loss of Hungary's Comecon markets, which used to drink half its production, many operations are at a standstill for lack of money. Even the producers of Bull's Blood have come a cropper, although others are likely to pick up the brand-name.

The withdrawal of state funding has meant that only the outfits which find investors will survive. The Tokaji vineyards are now run by a trust. Even there, changes may yet produce Tokaji that lives up to its old reputation.

## ROMANIA

Romania has had French and German vines in its vineyards for the past century. Since the December 1989 Revolution, much former State land has gone back to individual ownership. There are 37 official vineyards within eight viticultural regions, but the only names drinkers here really need to remember are Murfatlar, and Tamaioasa for dessert wines.

## RUSSIA

The quality of the Massandra wines made for the Czar a century ago shows that Russians can produce high-class wines when they absolutely have to. Under Communism, volume was all that mattered (since the party bosses drank French) but now some decent-to-excellent wines are appearing, including some exciting Cabernet Sauvignon and Merlot from the Krikova (Kodru 1988) and Kozhushny (Directors' Reserve 1987) wineries in Moldova.

## YUGOSLAVIA

Wines continued to be exported, at least until the summer of 1992, in spite of the civil war. Prices of Serbian wines are likely to rise because of the withdrawal (again) of their preferential EC supply quotas and the necessary re-routing around war-zones of Serbian wine consignments. In Croatia, no grapes could be picked in 1991, but other zones were unaffected. In Slovenia the taxes the new republic formerly handed over to Belgrade will henceforth be ploughed into the improvement of local wineries. That, and better sourcing, could mean a better outlook for what were tough, unfriendly reds and dull whites.

---

### EASTERN EUROPEAN CLASSIFICATIONS

**BULGARIA** In order of quality there are Country Wines (replacing the old Mehana, or bistro wines); Varietal Wines with Stated Geographic Origin (from 43 regions) and Controliran wines, from 27 zones. Special Reserves and Estate Selections are not official terms but indicate high quality.

**HUNGARY** 'Minosegi Bor' means 'Quality Wine', and is more or less equivalent to AC.

**ROMANIA** In order of quality there are VS (Vinul de Calitate Superioara, or Superior Quality); VSO (Vinul de Calitate Superioara & Denumire de Origine, or Superior Quality with Appellation of Origin); VSOC (Vinul Superioara de Origine Controlata) which includes Spätlese, Auslese and TBA lookalike categories.

**YUGOSLAVIA** All six republics had their own coloured seal quality coding system. Most seen here is Premium (Kvalitetno) Wine, from a specific region. Select Wine (Cuveno or Vrhunsko Vino) can be from a single vineyard.

**CZECHOSLOVAKIA, RUSSIA** No classifications.

# RED GRAPES & WINES

**CABERNET SAUVIGNON** Widely grown, and spans the quality scale. Bulgaria has the best; some oak-aged examples from Villanyi in Hungary, Kozhushny in Moldavia, and Dealul Mare and Murfatlar in Romania are rich, ripe and silky.

**FRANKOVKA** Native Czech grape yielding attractive grassy, peppery wines.

**GAMZA** Bulgarian grape, meaty, tarry, ripe wines. Often teamed with Merlot.

**KADARKA** Hungarian vine which yields spicy wine with good body and tannin.

**KEKFRANKOS** Thought to be the Gamay from Beaujolais. Also called Blaufrankisch.

**MAVRUD** Bulgarian; rich fruit, but can be rather tannic and unbalanced.

**MELNIK** Indigenous Bulgarian grape making concentrated, spicy reds.

**MERLOT** Widely grown. At its best it is full, oaky, soft and blackcurranty. Bulgaria's Stambolovo and Sakar are good for older, oakier ripe Reserves. Romanian Merlots from Murfatlar and Dealul Mare can need about eight years to mellow.

**PINOT NOIR** Decidedly variable. None of the Pinot Noirs in this year's *Webster's* tasting showed particularly well. It's a difficult grape, and Eastern Europe is not the only place not to have conquered it.

**ST LAURENT** Muscatty Austrian grape that could have potential in Czechoslovakia.

**VRANAC** Montenegran speciality, making robust reds.

# WHITE GRAPES & WINES

**ALIGOTÉ** Light, dry wines in Romania, Bulgaria and Russia. Sometimes blended with Ugni Blanc.

**CHARDONNAY** Everywhere in all guises from the matey to the seriously aristocratic. But the success rate is not great.

**EZERJO** Widely grown Hungarian: grassy, light wine, sometimes short on acidity.

**FURMINT** Hungarian; wines high in alcohol. Very susceptible to noble rot, and is the principal grape in Tokaji.

**GEWÜRZTRAMINER** Fair examples from Villanyi in Hungary, though balance is not always right.

**IRSAY OLIVER** Czech grape, gentle fruit and light, spice, needs more acidity.

**MUSCAT** Usually the Ottonel variety, grown for medium-sweet and dessert wines.

**PINOT BLANC** Elegant from Nagyréde and Dunavár in Hungary; also some from Czechoslovakia.

**PINOT GRIS** Full from Lake Balaton and smokier and rounder (under its Ruländer description) in Czechoslovakia.

**RIESLING** Seldom exciting, and why bother, when Germany, Alsace and others can do so much better?

**SAUVIGNON BLANC** Best are from Gyöngyös in Hungary: assertive, spicy and authentic.

**TRAMINER** Some attractive, zingy, aromatic Traminer from Moravenka in Czechoslovakia is starting to appear.

**WELSCHRIZLING** (Same as Laski-, Olasz- and Riesling Italico.) Produces medium-dry, sometimes fruity, sometimes dirty wines, often best avoided.

# OTHER WINE REGIONS

## ARGENTINA

Argentina is still the sort of place that makes people laugh when I mention it as a potential source of highly enjoyable wine – but it is, it is. But potential is the operative word. Nature has done her bit with the right climate, if winemakers choose properly, but until very recently man was doing his best to mess it up by making nothing but cheap and not very cheerful wines, in large quantities.

But things are looking up, slowly. There are now some producers making good quality everyday wines that are temptingly cheap, and that can offer a change from the everlasting Chardonnay and Cabernet Sauvignon.

Some of these, if they are red, are made from Malbec, a grape grown in southwest France but not much regarded elsewhere. In Argentina the quality can vary somewhat but wines from *Trapiche* are worth investigating.

The indigenous white grape to look out for is Torrontes, an aromatic, lime-and-orange scented number especially good from *Michel Torino* or *Etchart* (who labels it *Cafayate*; try also the *Cafayate* Cabernet Sauvignon). The French varieties are out in force in Argentina as well, of course; *Flichman* and *Trapiche* Cabernets are worth a look, as is *Flichman*'s Syrah.

## AUSTRIA

Austria is slowly getting its act together, but the aftermath of the 'anti-freeze' scandal is still with us. There have been worse wine scandals elsewhere since, but no country suffered the same devastation of its wine industry as Austria did. One long-term result has been a big, but not yet universal, improvement in wine-making standards. The other has been a swing to dry, often searingly dry, wines.

Personally, I preferred the older-style wines, the ones that made fewer demands on my tooth-enamel. In swinging to the extremes of dryness (for the Austrian wines that were exported pre-scandal were generally drier than their German equivalents) too many wines have lost individuality, and gained nothing except acidity and a fierce fashionability – on their home ground at least.

Yet it is only fair to point out that the Austrian wines we see over here are not always the most interesting. The structure of the industry there tends to mean that it is the larger companies who are most geared up to export, and they have not always been the quickest to acquire the smart new wine-making equipment they need, or the smart new wine-makers to go with it. Or if they have, they may still lack something – character, maybe.

Go to the Wachau region, however, and you will find serious, classic Rieslings; Lower Austria has lively, young Grüner Veltliners and southern Burgenland has some increasingly good reds.

The northern Burgenland, round the broad, shallow lake called the Neusiedlersee, is the home of Austria's sweet wines. Noble rot hits the grapes here every year without fail – and here, after the scandal, a fair number of growers decided that their only future lay in dry wines. A shame, but luckily enough have persevered for there to be some good sweet wines coming into Britain. Look out particularly for those of *Willi Opitz*, shipped by T&W Wines, or the *Robert Wenzel* Ausbruch imported by Barwell & Jones. Others to try are those of *Lenz Moser* or the international styles of *Georg Stiegelmar,* but the good news is that new ones are popping up here all the time.

## CANADA

The bulk of Canada's vineyards are planted with hybrid grapes, and the climate militates against *Vitis vinifera*. However, some Ontario producers are sufficiently undaunted by this to have formed a Vintners' Quality Alliance with minimum standards of grape varieties, origin and ripeness. The most widely planted vinifera grapes include Johannisberg Riesling and Chardonnay, but they are hardly set to take over the world.

## CHILE

The name Chile has made for itself so far has been largely because of its reds: soft, approachable Cabernet Sauvignons with plenty of rich blackcurranty fruit. The whites can be less exciting, partly because of staggeringly high yields, although where yields are controlled then Chile can produce the goods in white wine as well as reds.

The wine industry in Chile is dominated by large companies, but the good news is that the large companies are keen to export, and therefore keen to take on board international views on what wine should taste like. So the best of them control yields, ferment at low temperatures and invest in oak barrels instead of the traditional beech. Chile has also opened the doors to international investment in the wine industry, and Torres, Château Lafite Rothschild, Franciscan Cellars of California, William Fèvre from Chablis and Bruno Prats of Château Cos d'Estournel in Bordeaux have all been quick to spot opportunities.

The grape varieties seen on labels in Europe are mostly familiar, since Chile has no native vines. The red País, the most widely planted vine in the country, has no international potential. Among white wines, I have been impressed by *Caliterra*'s Chardonnay, toasty, vegetal and distinctly Burgundian, as opposed to Australian, in style, and *Torres*' 1987 Riesling, full of limy, nutty fruit. Of the reds, *Errázuriz Panquehue*'s Merlot is showing well, as is *Concha y Toro*'s Cabernet.

## CYPRUS

To describe many Cyprus wines as 'unexciting' is a compliment; all too often 'undrinkable' is the more appropriate term. There's Cyprus 'sherry' of course, but it's hardly fashionable and not terribly good. The table wines we see over here are frequently tired, flabby and oxidized; for some reason, though, they sell, though not, I'm sure, to anybody who reads *Webster's*.

There's nothing in the land or climate that dictates that Cyprus wines should be awful. Arid vineyards and hot climates have been tackled by Australian winemakers with spectacularly fresh and fruity results; in Cyprus, though, growers are generally paid by the sugar level in their grapes, which means too much alcohol and not enough acidity in the wines; and neither growers nor winemakers trouble themselves too much if the grapes take so long to arrive at the wineries that they are already fermenting away merrily.

Thankfully, a few bright spots are appearing in this otherwise depressing picture. The Xynisteri grape is one of them. When grown in the cooler, mountainous centre of the island it can produce fresh, lively whites – if it is handled properly. At present it accounts for some ten per cent of the vineyards, and is mostly not handled properly. *ETKO* makes a respectable version, called *Nefeli*, and *Keo* have a cool-fermented Xynisteri which is remarkably fragrant.

The other most widely planted native grape variety – in fact the most widely

planted of all – is the black Mavro, which so far makes better raisins than it does wine. There is a debate going on as to whether Cyprus should move whole-heartedly towards French varieties like Cabernet Sauvignon and Chardonnay, and the government's research station at Limassol grows these and more. If the pioneering work on grapes and wine-making being done here were taken up by the big producers, then Cyprus would at last begin to fulfil its potential.

## GREECE

Greece's wine-making history is rather more glorious than its present, but since the Greeks like their wines oxidized, there are only a handful of companies making wines that are likely to appeal to international tastes. There is a whole raft of appellations, of which the Côtes de Meliton is the best all-round bet; Muscats are also generally sound, and sometimes excellent if from Samos.

*Château Carras* is a pretty good shot at the classic Bordeaux blend, and is enthusiastically promoted and therefore quite expensive. *Tsantali* reds are also fairly reliable, and cheaper, and *Xinomavro Naoussis* is surprisingly good, with herby, slightly earthy fruit.

For Retsina addicts (yes, they do exist), *Tsantali* and *Metaxa* have the authentic taste, and Sainsbury's own-label is good, with a little more resin.

## INDIA

Money can buy you anything if you're a millionaire; even your very own Champagne lookalike. A perfectly good wine it is too, which is astonishing in a country that produces hardly any other wine. But when Bombay millionaire Sham Chougule decided he wanted to produce wine, he asked Piper Heidsieck to come and help; a state-of-the-art winery was built to process the grapes from high-altitude vineyards, and *Omar Khayyam* is the result. It's not cheap, though.

## ISRAEL

The Israeli wine industry was originally intended to produce kosher wines for a captive market at home and abroad. Founded in the late nineteenth century by Baron Edmond de Rothschild, its wines were generally sweetish, sticky and overripe, and modern wine-making techniques penetrated only relatively slowly.

Problems of terrain and climate could, however, both be overcome. In the late 1960s a professor from the University of California at Davis, visiting a kibbutz in the Golan Heights, concluded that the volcanic soil would be ideal for wine grapes, and that the lack of rain could be solved by the nearby reservoirs. The heat that made the wines from the coastal regions so overripe would be tempered by the altitude of the Golan Heights, which justify their name by being up to 3000 metres above sea level. The nights here are cool, and even the days are not that hot compared to the traditional wine-growing regions of Israel. Planting began in 1977, and in 1986 the first commercial wines, a Cabernet Sauvignon under the *Gamla* label and a Sauvignon Blanc under the name of *Yarden*, were released. Both are kosher, in other words made under the direct supervision of a rabbi. Both, too, are excellent, and Sémillon, Chenin Blanc, Colombard, Riesling, Chardonnay, Pinot Noir and Merlot also grow on the 160-hectare site.

The Golan Heights wines, however, are expensive, and so it is still more remarkable to find a dry Muscat from *Baron Wine Cellars* that is sherbetty-fresh, with lively lime juice and orange peel fruit – and being sold, by Corney & Barrow, for around a fiver.

## LEBANON

Lebanese wine is, to all intents and purposes for us in Britain, *Château Musar*. There are other vineyards, to be sure, but it is *Musar* that is sought-after and admired; it is also Musar that puts the worries of most other wine-makers firmly in the shade.

Frost and rot, the causes of most growers' sleepless nights, are not a problem for Serge Hochar of *Musar*. Civil war, on the other hand, is, and in 1984 he was not able to make a wine at all: the front line between Christian and Muslim zones ran between the vineyards and the winery, and the grape-laden lorries were not able to cross it.

In other years the chances of a successful vintage have looked thin, yet the wine has been made. In 1989 the winery, the office and Hochar's apartment were all hit by shelling, yet the wine was good; in 1990 the grapes narrowly missed being caught by the blockade which began on 28 September. In 1991, by contrast, the winery was regarded locally as one of the safest places to be, and many of the villagers took shelter in the cellars – and the wine, says Hochar, is 'massive. When I first tasted it it took me two hours to understand how big it was. My mouth seemed full of very ripe black cherries from the high mountains of Lebanon.'

This big, powerful style is typical of *Musar*. For a time in the late sixties Hochar turned to making lighter wines more reminiscent of Médoc, but now the wines are huge again, and age superbly – Hochar in fact reckons they should be drunk at 15 years, and will be even better at 30. The trouble is, they're often so wonderful at seven, when they are released, that keeping them that long requires an awful lot of willpower.

## LUXEMBOURG

Luxembourg's wines, from the banks of the Mosel, are of little other than local interest. They lack the body, the interest and the ageing potential of the best of their neighbours further down the river in Germany, but are perfectly acceptable, with light, delicate fruit. Most are made from Müller–Thurgau, here called Rivaner, which accounts for half the area under vine. Other grapes grown are Elbling, Riesling, Auxerrois, Gewürztraminer and Pinot Gris, with the last two making some of the most interesting wines.

## NORTH AFRICA

Forget all those jokes about Algerian Burgundy: the march of Islamic fundamentalism in North Africa means that the vineyard area is shrinking and output is falling. At this rate, any sort of Algerian wine could eventually be no more than a memory.

It wouldn't, it has to be said, be a particularly fond memory for most people. Algeria, Tunisia and Morocco did a great deal to beef up the weaker, weedier French wines in the years before such things became illegal; independence from France in the fifties and sixties followed by the tightening up of EC rules in the seventies dealt all three countries a double blow, and the loss of the French market has not been replaced by demand from other export markets, or at home.

The wines are still seen in Britain, however. Morocco makes some decent reds, like *Sidi Brahim*, made only from Cinsaut, and *Tarik*, a hot-climate blend of Cinsaut, Carignan and Grenache. Tunisia might have a name for its Muscats, if they were less generally oxidized, and Algeria, the biggest producer of the three in terms of quantity, can boast the Coteaux de Mascara, which makes heavy, rustic, rather coarse reds. All three countries have *appellation contrôlée* systems based on the French model. The term is *Appellation d'Origine Garantie* in Algeria and Morocco and *Appellation d'Origine Contrôlée* in Tunisia.

## SOUTH AFRICA

Isolation is not the best way of developing a country's wine industry. For years everyone knew that South Africa grew Pinotage, Chardonnay, Cabernet and a whole raft of other classic European varieties; but with very few exceptions the wines were not on sale here. Now they are, and it is becoming clear that while the wine-making is sound it's going to take a little more time before the wines match up to what, say, Australia is serving up. Make no mistake, South Africa will get there, but what's needed is foreign competition to bring those Chardonnays and Pinot Noirs up to top quality. At the moment names like *Hamilton-Russell*, *Neil Ellis*, *Rustenberg*, *Warwick Farm* and *Owergaauw* are all names to look for; and if anyone doubted that South African wine-makers are keen to compete, they need only look at the prices over here, which are very good good value indeed.

## SWITZERLAND

Swiss wines may be labelled in French, German or Italian, but little is seen in Britain in any language. The most popular grape, the Chasselas, changes its name to Dorin in the Vaud, Perlan in Geneva and Neuchatel and Fendant in the Valais. Pinot Noir can be good, but like all Swiss wines, it is light, clean, fruity and expensive.

## TURKEY

Turkey's history of viticulture is rather more impressive than  the wine itself. Although only three per cent of the total – huge – grape crop is made into wine, wine-making can be traced back some 4000 years – plenty of time in which to count the 1172 different grape varieties currently registered as being cultivated. The authorities are now desperately trying to modernize the industry, but it is uphill work. Agriculture in general is very backward and there is inevitably a distinct lack of commitment to wine in a Muslim population. Producers tend to blend in grapes from other regions and vintage dates are treated in a very cavalier fashion – bottles of so-called 1929 red still crop up regularly.

Four regions account for over 90 per cent of production with Thrace, in the North-West along the shores of the Sea of Marmara, the most important, followed by the Central North, Aegean, Central South and the rest of Marmara. It's hard positively to recommend Turkish wines or even any individual grape varieties, but *Buzbag* (red), *Villa Doluca* and *Doluca* (red and whites), *Hosbag* (red), *Villa Dona* (red and white) are brand names to consider.

## ZIMBABWE

An enterprising Leeds wine merchant, Vinceremos, imports a range of wines from Zimbabwe. You have to admire their temerity, which is not to say that the wines are bad, but they're a mixed bunch under the gloriously irrelevant brand name of *Flame Lily*. The grapes are grown over 4000 metres above sea level, and the wines are bottled at the Mukuy Winery for a négociant firm called Philips central Cellars of Harare. If you're feeling brave, try the Premium Dry White but just remember, when I had to blind taste it on TV I said it was Scottish.

# PRICE GUIDES

I suppose it could cross your mind that you don't need price guides – perish the thought, because if nobody wants a Price Guide I shall be back to doing pantomime at Northampton rep by next Christmas. But does that mean that you don't feel the need to know where you're likely to find the best price for your favourite wine? That you don't want to find out what alternatives you can expect for the amount of money you wish to spend? That you don't want to know if you're on to a super bargain? Surely not!

On expensive wines the price differences are often dramatic. On cheaper wines, the differences may be small but they're still worth knowing about. And our specially recommended wines may well be in limited distribution: it's of crucial importance to find out *where* the wines are stocked, as well as what the price differences are. By using these price guides judiciously, you should be able to drink *better* and more *cheaply* during the coming year.

● All prices are *per bottle inclusive of VAT*, unless otherwise stated. Remember that many merchants sell only by the case, and that price should be affected positively if you buy a case or more.

● Wines are listed in price bands and by vintage. Price bands run from the lowest to the highest. Vintages run from the most recent to the oldest. Within these categories the wines are listed in alphabetical order to help you find a particular wine more easily.

● Within the price bands, stockists are listed in brackets after each entry in ascending order of price. Occasionally, the same wine will fall into more than one price band, but before you get too agitated about variations in price, remember that wine warehouses, for example, often come out much cheaper because you have to buy by the case, they do not deliver, they do not have smart high street premises, and so on. Equally, there's no getting away from the fact that the price of a given wine sometimes varies wildly for no good reason.

● The claret prices are a special case. Specific prices are shown in ascending order by vintage. There *are* some dramatic price variations here – some are to do with keen pricing and the reverse; more often they will be because claret is now (for better or for worse) an investment medium and responsive to market pressures. A merchant buying wine *en primeur* in Bordeaux on Monday *afternoon* may pay 25 per cent more than the going rate that morning! Replacement stocks over the years will vary in cost and currency movements will also be a factor. So – for the sake of clarity – the prices we list were valid in the late spring/early summer of 1992.

● In the claret guide, all châteaux are listed alphabetically regardless of class. When a wine is quoted EC or IB, it means that the wine is offered on an *en primeur* basis (in Bordeaux or at the châteaux) or in bond (in the UK). All EC and IB prices are per dozen. The EC price simply includes the price of the wine in the bottle and excludes shipping, duties and taxes such as VAT. The EC price is usually payable when the wine is offered in the summer following the vintage. The other costs (including VAT on both invoices) become payable when the wine is shipped. The *crus classés* and better *bourgeois* are shipped two years later, and the *petits châteaux* and the lesser *bourgeois* after a year. You should check the exact terms of sale with your merchant who will give you a projection of the final 'duty paid delivered' price at current rates of shipping, duty and VAT.

● Where merchants sell only by the case we have divided by 12 the VAT-inclusive price of a single case.

● When clubs (e.g. Les Amis du Vin) have both member and non-member prices we have used the *non-member* prices.

● Stars (★) denote wines that the editors consider particularly good value for money *in their class*.

● To get the most out of the lists in the book, please remember that *Webster's* is a price GUIDE not a price LIST. An invaluable reference whenever you are ordering or buying wine, it is not meant to replace up-to-date merchants' lists. What it *does* do, however, is give you a unique opportunity to compare prices; to develop a sense of what you can reasonably expect to pay for any given wine; to spot a bargain; to work out exactly what you can afford – *and to find it*.

# MERCHANT CODES

The following list of abbreviations enables you to identify the merchants from whose lists the wines in the price guides were selected. For more detailed information on each merchant, see the Merchant Directory on page 398.

| | | | |
|---|---|---|---|
| AD | Adnams | BUT | Bute Wines |
| AMI | Les Amis du Vin (also Cullen's) | BY | Anthony Byrne |
| AN | André Simon Wines | BYR | D. Byrne & Co |
| AS | Ashley Scott | CAP | Cape Province Wines |
| ASD | ASDA | CB | Corney & Barrow |
| ASK | Askham Wines | CH | Chaplin & Son |
| AUG | Augustus Barnett | CHA | Châteaux Wines |
| AUS | Australian Wine Centre | CV | Celtic Vintner |
| AV | Averys | DAV | Davisons |
| BAR | Barnes Wine Shop | EL | Eldridge, Pope & Co |
| BE | Bedford Fine Wines | FA | Farr Vintners |
| BEK | Berkmann Wine Cellars | FIZ | Fine Wines of New Zealand |
| BER | Berry Bros & Rudd | GA | Gateway Food Markets |
| BIB | Bibendum | GE | Gelston Castle Fine Wines |
| BO | Booths Fine Wines | GRE | Peter Green |
| BOD | Bordeaux Direct | GRG | Grog Blossom |
| BOR | Borg Castel | HAL | Halves |
| BOT | Bottoms Up | HA | John Harvey & Sons |
| BR | Broad Street Wine Company | HAC | Harcourt Fine Wine |
| BU | The Butlers Wine Cellar | HAG | Gerard Harris Fine Wines |

| | | | |
|---|---|---|---|
| HAH | Haynes Hanson & Clark | REI | Reid Wines |
| HAU | Haughton Fine Wines | ROB | Roberson |
| HAW | Roger Harris Wines | SAF | Safeway |
| HAY | Richard Harvey Wines | SAI | Sainsbury |
| HE | Douglas Henn-Macrae | SOM | Sommelier Wine Company |
| HIC | Hicks & Don | TAN | Tanners |
| HIG | High Breck Vintages | TES | Tesco |
| HOG | J.E. Hogg | THR | Thresher |
| HUN | Hungerford Wine Company | TW | T. & W. Wines |
| IR | Irvine Robertson Wines | UN | Unwins |
| KA | J.C. Karn & Son Ltd | VA | Valvona & Crolla |
| LAY | Lay & Wheeler | VIC | Victoria Wine |
| LO | London Wine | VIG | La Vigneronne |
| LOE | O.W. Loeb | VIN | Vintage Wines |
| LOR | Lorne House Vintners | WAI | Waitrose |
| MAJ | Majestic Wine Warehouses | WCL | Winecellars |
| MAR | Marks & Spencer p.l.c. | WHI | Whitesides of Clitheroe |
| MOR | Moreno Wines | WIC | Sunday Times Wine Club |
| MV | Morris & Verdin | | |
| NA | The Nadder Wine Co Ltd | WIW | Wines of Westhorpe Ltd |
| NI | James Nicholson | WR | Wine Rack |
| OD | Oddbins | WRI | Wright Wine Company |
| PD | Peter Dominic | WS | Wine Society |
| PE | Thos. Peatling | WW | Windrush Wines |
| PEN | Penistone Court Wine Cellars | WY | Peter Wylie Fine Wines |
| PIP | Christopher Piper Wines | YAP | Yapp Brothers |
| RAE | Raeburn Fine Wines | YF | Yorkshire Fine Wines |

# RED BORDEAUX

**d'Agassac** *cru bourgeois Haut-Médoc*
**1986** £8.25 (WAI)
**1982** £11.85 (WHI)

**Amiral-de-Beychevelle** *St-Julien*
**1988** £13.66 (PIP)
**1986** £11.67 (PEN)

**Andron-Blanquet** *cru bourgeois St-Éstèphe*
**1983** £7.50 (SOM) £9.45 (PIP)
**1978** £12.58 (BUT)

**l'Angélus** *grand cru classé St-Émilion*
**1990 EC** £162.00 (BUT)
**1989 IB** £183.00 (BUT)
**1985** £15.47 (AV)
**1983** £19.75 (AD)
**1981** £19.50 (ROB)
**1961** £70.00 (BIB)
**1959** £49.94 (REI)

**d'Angludet** *cru bourgeois Margaux*
**1990 IB** £102.00 (NI)
**1990 EC** £75.00 (BE) £77.00 (HIC)
**1989** £10.45 (LAY) £10.45 (BE)
**1989 IB** £90.00 (BUT)
**1989 EC** £84.00 (HAG) £90.00 (HAY)
★ **1988** £8.80 (HAG) £10.70 (BE) £11.25 (DAV)
**1986** £9.20 (CV) £11.50 (BE) £12.40 (BEK)
    £12.95 (DAV) £14.60 (PIP)
★ **1985** £9.20 (CV) £12.20 (BE)
**1983** £13.28 (BUT)
**1982 magnum IB** £100.00 (FA)
**1978** £18.09 (BUT)

**l'Arrosée** *grand cru classé St-Émilion*
**1989 EC** £178.00 (BIB)
**1988** £17.50 (GE)
**1987** £12.15 (GE) £15.94 (BY)
**1983** £15.49 (BEK)

**Ausone** *1er grand cru classé St-Émilion*
**1989** £53.85 (MV)
**1989 IB** £618.00 (BUT)
**1987** £29.50 (MV)
**1986** £47.23 (AV) £49.00 (MV) £49.50 (AD)
**1985** £49.95 (AD) £73.10 (AN)
**1985 IB** £500.00 (FA)
**1983** £56.06 (BUT) £58.95 (AD)
**1982** £86.19 (UN) £105.00 (BIB)
**1970** £91.06 (BIB)

**Bahans-Haut-Brion** *Graves*
**1990 EC** £102.00 (BUT)
**1989** £13.95 (RAE)
**1989 IB** £126.00 (BUT)
**1985** £22.96 (CB) £23.81 (BO)

**Batailley** *5ème cru classé Pauillac*
**1990 EC** £70.00 (HIG)
**1989** £10.99 (OD)
**1989 IB** £96.00 (BUT)
**1989 EC** £108.00 (HIG)
**1988** £10.18 (HIG) £10.75 (BER)
**1987** £10.75 (WRI)
**1986** £13.59 (NA) £14.75 (DAV)
**1986 magnum** £24.89 (NA)
**1985** £14.55 (BYR) £16.75 (DAV)
**1983** £10.00 (WY) £13.25 (BIB) £16.39 (HA)
**1982** £16.20 (HA) £16.50 (BIB) £16.95 (DAV)
**1978** £25.75 (DAV)
**1970** £20.00 (BU) £24.00 (WY) £24.28 (BUT)
    £25.00 (BIB) £30.00 (VIG)
**1966** £23.50 (WY)
**1961** £57.50 (VIG) £65.80 (BIB)

**Beau-Site** *cru bourgeois St-Éstèphe*
**1990 EC** £46.00 (HIG)
**1989 IB** £60.00 (BUT)
**1986** £8.34 (HA) £8.45 (DAV) £8.70 (WRI)
**1985** £11.20 (WRI)

**Beaumont** *cru bourgeois Haut-Médoc*
**1989** £6.39 (NA) £8.80 (WRI)
**1989 IB** £55.00 (BUT)
**1989 EC** £48.00 (LOE)
**1986** £6.99 (BEK) £7.95 (DAV) £9.65 (GRE)
**1985** £10.49 (HA)

**Beauséjour** *1er grand cru classé St-Émilion*
**1990 EC** £156.65 (HAH)
**1987** £5.91 (BUT)
**1970** £12.50 (BU)

**Belair** *1er grand cru classé St-Émilion*
**1990** £5.25 (CH)
**1990 EC** £160.00 (LOE)
**1989** £4.49 (NA)
**1989 IB** £190.00 (BUT)
**1989 EC** £188.00 (LOE)
**1988** £9.55 (DAV) £16.65 (LOE)
**1985** £17.82 (LOE) £19.00 (MV) £19.78 (BUT)
    £19.90 (LAY) £19.95 (AD)

**1983** £18.50 (BUT)
**1982** £21.68 (BUT)
**1961** £39.50 (BU)

**Bel-Air-Marquis d'Aligre** *cru bourgeois Margaux*
**1981** £11.95 (MAJ)

**Beychevelle** *4ème cru classé St-Julien*
**1990 EC** £145.00 (HIG) £149.00 (LOE)
**1989 IB** £165.00 (WY) £180.00 (BUT)
**1988** £14.35 (NI) £17.05 (BYR) £18.41 (LOE)
**1986** £19.21 (BO) £19.69 (NA) £20.55 (HA)
**1985** £18.99 (AUG) £27.59 (VIC) £28.32 (TAN)
**1983** £19.89 (WHI) £19.92 (TAN) £20.94 (YF)
**1983 magnum IB** £130.00 (FA)
**1982** £18.00 (WY) £20.10 (HAG) £21.50 (HAY)
£22.03 (BIB) £23.44 (BY) £24.00 (GE)
£24.09 (TAN) £26.45 (WHI) £28.35 (PE)

**1982 IB** £190.00 (WY) £195.00 (FA)
**1982 magnum** £49.50 (NA)
**1981** £15.00 (WY) £19.78 (CH) £22.60 (PIP)
£26.00 (ROB) £36.85 (HA)
**1981 IB** £165.00 (WY)
**1981 magnum** £36.22 (BIB)
**1979** £20.00 (WY) £33.00 (ROB)
**1978** £22.50 (BU) £22.72 (FA) £24.00 (WY)
**1978 magnum** £49.00 (WY)
**1970** £34.27 (FA) £35.50 (WY) £54.50 (ROB)
**1966** £37.50 (BU) £47.00 (WY) £53.85 (BIB)
£65.11 (YF) £85.00 (ROB)
**1966 IB** £465.00 (WY)
**1964** £40.00 (VIG)
**1964 IB** £250.00 (FA)
**1961** £88.00 (WY)
**1961 IB** £880.00 (FA)
**1961 magnum** £200.00 (WY)
**1955** £55.00 (WY)
**1945** £115.00 (WY) £170.00 (BIB)

**le Bon-Pasteur** *Pomerol*
**1989** £19.75 (HUN)
**1989 magnum** £41.50 (HUN)
★ **1985** £9.79 (FA) £15.58 (BUT)

**Bouscaut** *cru classé Pessac-Léognan*
**1990 EC** £73.00 (LOE) £75.00 (RAE)
**1989** £11.75 (RAE)
**1989 EC** £91.00 (LOE)
**1988** £10.50 (RAE)
**1985** £9.50 (RAE)

**Boyd-Cantenac** *3ème cru classé Margaux*
**1987** £8.70 (SOM)
**1979** £16.95 (MAJ)

**Branaire-Ducru** *4ème cru classé St-Julien*
**1989 IB** £131.00 (BUT)
**1986** £16.25 (LOR)
**1985** £14.88 (LOE) £15.08 (BUT) £15.26 (AV)
£15.99 (MAJ) £16.94 (AN) £18.50
(ROB) £19.21 (BO)
**1983 IB** £105.00 (FA)
**1982** £19.00 (WY) £21.00 (GRG) £22.50 (BAR)
**1982 IB** £195.00 (WY)
**1978** £17.50 (WY)
**1978 IB** £155.00 (FA) £180.00 (WY)
**1970** £26.00 (WY) £26.93 (BIB) £47.81 (TAN)

**Brane-Cantenac** *2ème cru classé Margaux*
**1990 EC** £115.00 (RAE)
**1989** £17.95 (RAE)
**1988 EC** £98.00 (BIB)
**1986** £17.50 (HAG) £19.69 (VIC)
**1986 magnum** £13.90 (LOE)
**1985** £21.39 (VIC)
**1983** £17.85 (WHI) £22.75 (VIC)
**1982** £16.00 (WY) £16.09 (UN) £19.09 (BIB)
**1979** £15.00 (WY)
**1978** £17.50 (WY) £29.13 (YF)
**1977** £12.95 (RAE)
**1970** £21.54 (FA) £22.58 (BUT) £25.00 (WY)
£25.05 (PE) £28.95 (NI)
**1970 IB** £260.00 (WY)
**1966** £28.75 (NI) £30.50 (WY)
**1962 IB** £300.00 (FA)
**1961** £59.00 (WY) £67.56 (REI) £87.60 (YF)
**1959** £110.00 (BIB)
**1949** £80.00 (WY) £120.00 (BIB)

**Cabannieux** *Graves*
**1989** £8.75 (HUN)
**1986** £7.65 (WHI)

**Calon-Ségur** *3ème cru classé St-Éstèphe*
**1990 EC** £160.00 (HUN)
**1989** £21.75 (HUN)
**1988** £15.78 (AV) £19.65 (BER)

**1987** £11.00 (LOR)
**1986** £17.25 (LOR)
**1985** £16.58 (BIB) £16.83 (BUT) £16.84 (AV)
**1985 IB** £121.00 (HAG) £130.00 (FA)
**1983** £22.35 (UN)
**1982** £24.89 (UN) £25.56 (EL)
**1982 IB** £210.00 (FA)
**1970** £25.70 (HAG) £28.89 (FA) £29.50 (WY)
    £35.74 (BIB) £42.90 (BE)
**1966** £38.68 (BIB)
**1961** £59.00 (WY) £75.00 (ROB) £96.03 (YF)
**1961 IB** £520.00 (FA)
**1949** £80.00 (WY)
**1945** £85.00 (WY)

**de Camensac** *5ème cru classé Haut-Médoc*
**1986** £10.00 (LOR)
**1985** £9.99 (TES)
**1985 magnum** £17.95 (ROB) £24.50 (BU)
**1983** £10.00 (LOR) £10.50 (ROB) £10.75 (BU)
    £11.04 (HA) £12.04 (YF)
**1982** £10.77 (BIB) £13.70 (NI)
**1979** £11.72 (HA)
**1970** £17.30 (HA) £18.00 (BU)

**Canon** *1er grand cru classé St-Émilion*
**1990 EC** £175.00 (LOE) £181.00 (BUT)
**1989** £29.00 (RAE)
**1989 IB** £265.00 (BUT)
**1989 EC** £259.00 (LOE)
**1987** £13.25 (NI) £14.60 (RAE)
**1986** £19.62 (AV) £20.80 (RAE)
**1985** £24.63 (BUT)
**1983** £19.09 (BIB) £29.09 (WHI)
**1982 IB** £300.00 (FA)
**1979** £28.75 (ROB)
**1970** £34.66 (REI)
**1966** £48.47 (BIB)
**1959** £35.00 (BU)

**Canon-la-Gaffelière** *grand cru classé St-Émilion*
**1989** £14.50 (RAE)
**1989 IB** £128.00 (BUT) £130.00 (WY)
**1987** £10.48 (BER)
**1982** £13.99 (BYR)
**1966** £28.88 (BIB)

**Cantemerle** *5ème cru classé Haut-Médoc*
**1989 IB** £143.00 (BUT)
**1988** £13.00 (GE)
**1987** £12.59 (TES)
**1985** £13.22 (BIB) £15.88 (BO) £16.55 (PE)
    £17.95 (BER) £18.50 (VIG) £18.75 (AS)
**1983** £16.95 (BAR)

**1982** £20.89 (HA)
**1981** £11.99 (GRG) £12.25 (HAY) £13.90
    (HOG) £14.25 (BYR) £19.05 (PE)
**1980** £14.95 (VIG)
**1979** £10.28 (FA) £13.00 (WY) £20.00 (VIG)
**1978** £16.50 (WY) £18.00 (BU)
**1970** £20.00 (BU) £25.00 (WY) £28.89 (BIB)
**1966** £29.50 (WY) £45.00 (BIB)

**Cantenac-Brown** *3ème cru classé Margaux*
**1989** £17.75 (HUN)
**1987** £10.69 (BY) £11.79 (YF)
**1982** £22.25 (WRI)
**1970** £20.58 (BUT) £33.49 (TW)
**1959** £29.50 (BU)

**Carbonnieux** *cru classé Pessac-Léognan*
**1988** £9.00 (LOE)
**1985** £14.85 (ROB)
**1982** £12.95 (BU)
**1978** £10.75 (BU)
**1959** £55.00 (WY)

**de Cardaillan** *Graves*
**1987** £6.25 (DAV)
**1985** £6.75 (BU)

**la Cardonne** *cru bourgeois Médoc*
**1987** £7.50 (ROB) £9.18 (PIP)
**1986** £6.95 (GRG)

**Caronne-Ste-Gemme** *cru bourgeois Haut-Médoc*
**1988** £7.64 (EL)
**1986** £8.95 (HAG)
**1985** £6.89 (BYR) £8.87 (EL) £9.09 (HA)
    £10.79 (BOR)
**1983** £6.89 (BYR) £8.15 (LOR) £9.30 (BIB)
    £10.10 (HAG)
**1982** £11.00 (GE)

**Certan-de-May** *Pomerol*
**1989 IB** £356.00 (BUT)
**1987** £18.95 (RAE)
**1985** £28.88 (BIB) £43.65 (BUT) £52.00 (HUN)
**1983** £29.90 (LAY)
**1983 IB** £275.00 (FA)

> *Stars (★) indicate wines selected by the editors as particularly good value in their class.*

**Certan-Giraud** *Pomerol*
**1990 EC** £130.00 (LOE)
**1989 IB** £154.00 (BUT)
**1986** £13.99 (MAR)

**Chasse-Spleen** *cru bourgeois Moulis*
**1990 EC** £83.00 (BIB) £84.00 (LOE) £89.00
    (BUT) £110.00 (HUN)
**1990 magnum EC** £97.00 (BUT) £125.00
    (HUN)
**1989** £12.75 (LAY) £13.85 (GRE)
**1989 IB** £124.00 (BUT)
**1988** £10.59 (BYR) £10.80 (BE) £10.99 (GRE)
    £12.50 (VIG) £12.95 (LAY)
**1988 magnum** £21.15 (BYR)
**1987** £9.05 (BYR) £9.85 (LAY) £10.56 (CHA)
    £10.94 (BY) £15.47 (TAN)
**1986** £11.95 (WW) £14.34 (TAN)
★ **1985** £11.25 (NI) £12.20 (BE)
**1983** £12.06 (BO) £12.65 (CV)
**1982** £14.08 (BUT) £21.65 (PE)

**Chauvin** *grand cru classé St-Émilion*
**1990 EC** £76.00 (LOE) £78.00 (RAE)
**1989 EC** £94.00 (LOE) £95.00 (BIB)
**1988** £9.30 (LOE) £10.95 (RAE)
**1987** £8.99 (RAE)
**1983** £10.95 (RAE)

**Cheval-Blanc** *1er grand cru classé St-Émilion*
**1990 EC** £395.00 (BIB) £400.00 (FA) £550.00
    (HUN)
**1989** £53.00·(RAE) £65.00 (ROB) £75.00 (HUN)
**1989 IB** £565.00 (BUT)
**1989 magnum** £152.50 (HUN)
**1987** £32.99 (BYR)
**1986** £40.15 (BIB) £52.75 (DAV)
**1986 magnum** £37.60 (LOE)
**1985** £41.52 (LOE) £48.18 (BUT) £55.69 (WHI)
    £56.75 (DAV) £64.99 (VIC)
**1985 IB** £385.00 (FA)
**1983** £40.54 (LOE) £55.00 (WS) £55.75 (DAV)
**1983 IB** £310.00 (HAG)
**1982** £67.00 (WY) £76.45 (UN) £82.00 (AD)
**1982 IB** £650.00 (WY) £680.00 (FA)
**1982 magnum** £133.00 (WY)
**1981** £46.00 (BER) £49.00 (NI) £54.71 (VIN)
**1979** £38.00 (WY) £74.75 (DAV)
**1979 IB** £445.00 (WY)
**1978** £66.00 (BER) £85.00 (ROB)
**1978 magnum** £100.00 (WY)
**1970** £70.00 (WY) £125.00 (DAV)
**1970 IB** £900.00 (FA)
**1966** £95.00 (WY)

**1962** £66.09 (FA) £82.25 (REI)
**1961** £165.00 (WY) £317.25 (FA)
**1959** £147.00 (WY)
**1955** £100.00 (WY) £129.25 (FA)
**1953** £185.00 (WY) £217.38 (REI)
**1953 magnum** £325.00 (WY)
**1949 magnum** £225.00 (WY)

**Cissac** *cru bourgeois Haut-Médoc*
**1990 IB** £94.80 (NI)
**1990 EC** £60.00 (HIC)
**1989** £12.50 (HUN)
**1989 IB** £77.00 (BUT)
**1989 EC** £70.00 (HAY)
**1988** £8.95 (HAY) £9.61 (AV) £10.80 (NI)
    £10.93 (EL) £11.59 (TAN)
**1987** £8.88 (TAN) £9.85 (YF)
**1986** £10.25 (CH) £10.95 (LAY) £13.28 (TAN)
**1985** £9.60 (NI) £9.99 (OD) £10.58 (EL)
    £10.70 (TAN) £10.80 (MV) £11.28
    (BUT) £11.40 (WRI) £11.95 (CH) £11.99
    (HIG) £12.33 (HA) £16.59 (VIC)
**1983** £10.76 (BUT) £11.10 (TAN) £11.14 (BEK)
    £11.85 (WRI) £12.50 (HIG) £12.50 (NI)
**1982** £12.38 (BUT) £12.92 (WW) £12.95 (PE)
    £13.00 (MV) £13.75 (GRG) £14.54 (ASK)
**1981** £12.08 (CV) £12.95 (NI)
**1979** £13.50 (WRI) £14.20 (BIB) £14.69 (YF)
**1979 magnum** £12.92 (FA)
**1961** £29.50 (BU)

**Citran** *cru bourgeois Haut-Médoc*
★ **1983** £6.85 (BYR)

**Clarke** *cru bourgeois Listrac*
**1986** £11.35 (NI)
**1985** £14.05 (PE)
**1983** £9.75 (BU)

**Clerc-Milon** *5ème cru classé Pauillac*
**1989** £15.49 (OD)
**1989 IB** £130.00 (BUT)
**1988** £13.43 (AV)
**1985** £13.51 (REI) £14.65 (AUG) £17.95 (BAR)
**1983** £13.50 (SOM) £14.75 (ROB) £15.45
    (AUG) £18.15 (UN) £20.95 (YF)
**1981** £14.60 (SOM) £19.00 (ROB)

**Clinet** *Pomerol*
**1990 IB** £230.00 (WY)
**1990 EC** £253.00 (BUT)
**1989 IB** £225.00 (BUT)
**1985** £20.56 (FA)
**1982** £19.00 (WY)
**1982 IB** £180.00 (WY)

**Clos des Jacobins** *grand cru classé St-Émilion*
**1989 IB** £169.00 (BUT)
**1986** £12.25 (HAY)
**1985** £14.69 (YF) £16.95 (ROB)
**1983** £18.85 (GRG)

**Clos du Marquis** *St-Julien*
**1990 EC** £72.00 (BUT) £76.00 (LOE)
**1989** £12.75 (RAE)
**1989 IB** £104.00 (BUT)
**1989 EC** £103.00 (LOE)
**1988** £9.99 (RAE) £10.45 (PIP) £12.95 (THR)
**1987** £9.03 (BUT) £13.50 (ROB)
**1986** £21.00 (VIC)
**1983 IB** £95.00 (FA)

**Clos l'Eglise** *Lalande-de-Pomerol*
**1990 EC** £102.00 (LOE)
**1989 IB** £131.00 (LOE)
**1988** £5.50 (PEN) £7.17 (EL)
**1985** £14.20 (LOE) £17.99 (BIB) £19.06 (BUT)
**1983** £17.45 (BUT)

**Clos Fourtet** *1er grand cru classé St-Émilion*
**1990 EC** £134.00 (LOE)
**1989 EC** £179.00 (LOE)
**1985** £22.79 (VIC) £24.77 (PIP)
**1949** £80.00 (WY)
**1945** £90.00 (WY)

**la Clotte** *grand cru classé St-Émilion*
**1989 IB** £170.00 (BUT)
**1988** £11.44 (CB)
**1987** £10.86 (CB)
**1986** £12.74 (CB)

**Connétable Talbot** *St-Julien*
**1987** £9.99 (AUG)
**1985** £11.35 (PE) £11.85 (DAV)
**1983** £9.95 (VIC) £11.45 (PE)

**la Conseillante** *Pomerol*
**1990 EC** £277.00 (LOE) £304.00 (BUT)
**1989 IB** £415.00 (BUT)
**1988** £24.09 (LOE) £35.46 (AV)

**1987** £20.65 (WHI)
**1986** £25.47 (AV) £27.63 (BO)
**1985** £27.76 (BUT) £29.09 (AV)
**1985 magnum** £35.15 (LOE)
**1983** £22.00 (GE)
**1981** £22.03 (BIB)
**1978** £21.54 (FA)

**Corbin-Michotte** *grand cru classé St-Émilion*
**1986** £5.95 (DAV)
**1970** £20.00 (BU)

**Cos d'Estournel** *2ème cru classé St-Éstèphe*
**1990 IB** £155.00 (WY)
**1990 EC** £175.00 (RAE) £180.00 (HIG) £225.00 (HUN)
**1989** £32.71 (CB)
**1989 IB** £258.00 (BUT)
**1989 EC** £240.00 (LOE)
**1987** £14.20 (NI) £15.29 (BYR)
**1986** £19.78 (BUT) £24.19 (AN) £25.26 (TAN)
**1985** £21.15 (NI) £23.58 (BUT)
**1983** £20.50 (HA) £20.78 (CH) £22.03 (BIB) £23.77 (BUT) £26.00 (BER) £28.25 (NI) £28.60 (CB) £29.59 (TAN)
**1983 magnum** £38.50 (LAY)
**1982** £27.83 (BUT) £35.25 (BIB) £39.00 (MV) £45.55 (UN) £49.95 (DAV)
**1982 imperial** £323.13 (FA)
**1979** £30.00 (HUN) £31.50 (BAR)
**1979 double magnum** £176.25 (BIB)
**1978** £45.00 (ROB)
**1970** £42.58 (BUT) £44.55 (BIB) £45.00 (BIB)
**1964 IB** £250.00 (FA)
**1962** £39.17 (FA) £53.00 (WY)
**1960** £14.68 (TW)
**1959** £39.50 (BU) £58.75 (FA)
**1955** £80.29 (FA)
**1945** £140.00 (WY) £210.00 (BIB)

**Cos Labory** *5ème cru classé St-Éstèphe*
**1987** £9.42 (HA) £9.44 (SAF)
**1985** £14.75 (PIP)
**1970** £19.58 (BIB)
**1966** £22.50 (BU)

**Coufran** *cru bourgeois Haut-Médoc*
**1988** £9.20 (ROB)
★ **1985** £8.84 (BEK) £10.19 (PIP)
**1981** £9.09 (HA) £10.14 (YF)
**1979** £10.75 (GRE)
**1978** £9.75 (BU) £12.58 (BUT)
**1964** £20.00 (VIG)

**Couvent-des-Jacobins** *grand cru classé St-Émilion*
**1985** £17.28 (PIP)
**1982** £20.32 (ASK)

**le Crock** *cru bourgeois St-Éstèphe*
**1988 EC** £50.00 (BIB)
**1986** £9.50 (RAE)
**1985** £9.35 (PE)

**la Croix** *Pomerol*
**1983** £16.23 (PEN)

**la Croix-de-Gay** *Pomerol*
**1990 EC** £104.00 (HAH)
**1989 IB** £138.00 (BUT)
**1986** £17.41 (YF)
**1985** £11.25 (BIB) £14.00 (LOE) £14.50 (BAR)
   £15.95 (ROB) £16.85 (BYR)
**1982** £17.41 (BO)
**1981** £12.60 (HOG)

**la Croix-du-Casse** *Pomerol*
**1986** £11.29 (BEK)
**1982** £16.88 (VIN)

**Croizet-Bages** *5ème cru classé Pauillac*
**1982** £15.75 (UN)

**Dassault** *grand cru classé St-Émilion*
**1975** £25.00 (VIG)

**Desmirail** *3ème cru classé Margaux*
**1990 EC** £81.00 (LOE) £82.50 (RAE) £90.00
   (HIG)
**1985** £19.10 (WRI)

**Domaine de Chevalier** *cru classé Pessac-Léognan*
**1990 EC** £168.00 (RAE)
**1989** £27.50 (RAE) £32.50 (HUN)
**1989 IB** £200.00 (FA) £249.00 (BUT)
**1989 EC** £259.00 (LOE)
**1987** £13.61 (LOE) £17.10 (BER) £18.96 (YF)
**1985** £22.21 (AV) £23.96 (BIB) £29.82 (BUT)
   £33.25 (WHI)
**1983** £19.84 (CV) £21.50 (BAR) £21.60 (HAG)
   £22.00 (GE) £23.43 (PIP) £25.58 (BO)
   £27.50 (AD)
**1983 IB** £165.00 (FA)
**1982** £24.44 (BIB) £25.97 (BUT) £32.00 (BE)
**1982 IB** £250.00 (FA)
**1978** £24.88 (BUT) £30.00 (GE)
**1966** £53.00 (BIB)
**1961** £87.64 (FA)

**Domaine de l'Eglise** *Pomerol*
**1990 EC** £85.00 (HIG)
**1989 IB** £149.00 (BUT)
**1989 EC** £124.00 (HIG)
**1988** £11.75 (HIG)
**1986** £15.75 (DAV)
**1983** £12.92 (HIG)

**Domaine la Grave** *Graves*
**1990 EC** £50.00 (HIG)
**1989** £11.05 (HAH)
**1989 EC** £50.00 (GE) £70.00 (HIG)
★ **1988** £6.50 (GE) £7.63 (HIG)
**1986** £6.50 (GE) £8.81 (HIG)

**la Dominique** *grand cru classé St-Émilion*
**1989 IB** £155.00 (BUT)
**1986** £16.50 (BER) £17.95 (ROB)
**1982** £19.09 (BIB) £25.76 (BUT)
**1955** £35.00 (VIG)

**Ducru-Beaucaillou** *2ème cru classé St-Julien*
**1990 EC** £172.00 (RAE) £178.00 (BUT)
**1990 magnum EC** £186.00 (BUT)
**1989** £27.42 (MV) £29.00 (RAE) £35.77 (CB)

**1989 IB** £268.00 (BUT)
**1989 EC** £259.00 (LOE)
**1989 magnum** £76.50 (HUN)
**1988** £20.80 (RAE) £21.25 (LOE)
**1988 EC** £210.00 (HAY)
**1986** £24.96 (CB) £25.46 (BIB) £33.89 (VIC)
**1985** £24.19 (LOE) £24.58 (BUT) £28.88 (BIB)
**1985 IB** £200.00 (FA)
**1983** £24.49 (VIC) £24.51 (BEK) £25.87 (CV)
   £25.96 (LAY) £28.36 (CB) £29.09 (WHI)
   £29.50 (AD) £31.42 (BUT) £32.00 (BER)
**1983 IB** £180.00 (FA)
**1983 magnum IB** £180.00 (FA)
**1982** £36.65 (UN) £40.00 (WY)
**1981** £28.14 (TAN) £28.95 (DAV)
**1981 magnum** £48.45 (HA) £73.00 (SOM)
**1979** £18.90 (HOG) £29.85 (PE) £30.95 (DAV)
**1978** £31.82 (HA) £35.00 (WY) £45.24 (REI)

**1970** £50.00 (WY) £50.92 (FA) £55.32 (BIB)
**1970 magnum** £50.92 (FA)
**1961** £117.50 (FA) £146.88 (REI)
**1959** £90.00 (WY)

**Duhart-Milon-Rothschild** *4ème cru classé Pauillac*
**1989** £19.75 (HUN)
**1989 IB** £142.00 (BUT)
**1986** £18.50 (HAG) £20.96 (PEN)
**1983** £14.00 (GE)

**Durfort-Vivens** *2ème cru classé Margaux*
**1985 IB** £129.00 (HAG)
**1970** £25.26 (LO) £34.50 (ROB)

**l'Église-Clinet** *Pomerol*
**1990 EC** £140.00 (RAE)
**1989 IB** £198.00 (BUT)
**1988** £18.00 (GE)

**l'Enclos** *Pomerol*
**1989** £12.63 (TAN)
**1988** £11.00 (LOR)
**1986** £14.10 (CV)
**1985** £13.77 (BUT)
**1980** £11.80 (PIP)
**1979** £15.12 (BO)

**l'Évangile** *Pomerol*
**1990 EC** £282.00 (LOE) £300.00 (BUT)
**1989 EC** £350.00 (LOE)
**1987** £19.95 (VIG) £20.74 (YF)
**1986** £29.08 (LOE) £29.49 (AV)
**1985** £35.05 (LOE) £39.18 (BUT)
**1982 IB** £395.00 (FA)

**Feytit-Clinet** *Pomerol*
**1985** £9.25 (CH) £16.20 (AD)
**1959** £40.00 (ROB)

**Les Fiefs-de-Lagrange** *St-Julien*
**1989 EC** £70.75 (HAH)
**1988 EC** £9.99 (THR)
**1986** £9.59 (WHI) £10.59 (HOG)
**1985** £17.05 (BUT)

**de Fieuzal** *cru classé Pessac-Léognan*
**1989** £15.99 (OD)
**1989 IB** £115.00 (WY) £142.00 (BUT)
**1985** £12.34 (REI) £14.05 (PE) £14.79 (AN)
      £15.63 (BO) £16.13 (BUT) £16.75 (AD)
**1984** £9.15 (PE) £9.50 (BO)
**1983** £15.95 (ROB) £17.86 (PIP)
**1982** £15.00 (SOM) £19.00 (HA) £21.65 (PE)

**Figeac** *1er grand cru classé St-Émilion*
**1990 EC** £168.00 (BUT) £169.00 (RAE)
      £172.00 (HIC) £175.00 (LOE)
**1989** £28.50 (RAE)
**1989 IB** £251.00 (BUT)
**1989 EC** £257.00 (LOE)
**1987** £14.25 (NI) £21.88 (YF)
**1986** £21.54 (AV) £22.03 (BIB)
**1985** £29.99 (VIC) £34.63 (BUT)
**1982** £28.89 (FA) £33.29 (BIB)
**1966 IB** £595.00 (FA)

**la Fleur-Pétrus** *Pomerol*
**1990 IB** £210.00 (FA)
**1990 EC** £247.00 (BUT)
**1985** £39.29 (BUT)
**1983** £28.95 (LAY)
**1947** £225.00 (ROB)

**Fombrauge** *grand cru St-Émilion*
**1988** £7.95 (CH)
**1987** £8.38 (BOR)
**1986** £9.25 (HA) £11.10 (BER)
**1985** £10.46 (HA) £10.95 (GRG) £11.95 (GRE)
      £12.80 (BUT) £12.90 (BE)
**1983** £9.89 (HA) £11.25 (WHI)

**Fonbadet** *cru bourgeois Pauillac*
**1985** £12.15 (BUT)
**1983** £11.56 (HOG)

**Fonréaud** *cru bourgeois Listrac*
**1982** £9.79 (AN)

**Fonroque** *grand cru classé St-Émilion*
**1990 EC** £78.00 (LOE)
**1989 EC** £103.00 (LOE)
**1986** £10.18 (LOE) £12.50 (CB) £16.95 (VIG)
**1983** £9.20 (CV)

**les Forts-de-Latour** *Pauillac*
**1990 EC** £135.00 (BUT) £138.00 (HIC)
**1985** £19.75 (WAI)
**1983** £13.80 (HA) £16.79 (SAI) £19.65 (WHI)
**1982** £26.40 (HA) £26.69 (TES)
**1982 IB** £270.00 (FA)
**1979** £17.77 (HA) £22.03 (YF)
**1978** £25.35 (HA) £27.50 (OD) £35.99 (VIC)
**1970** £29.37 (FA) £39.00 (WY) £41.52 (HA)

**Fourcas-Dupré** *cru bourgeois Listrac*
**1986** £6.95 (BO) £8.00 (GE) £9.69 (WCL)
**1985** £8.93 (CV) £9.28 (PIP)
**1983** £8.89 (PIP)
**1982** £12.55 (HA)

**Fourcas-Hosten** *cru bourgeois Listrac*
**1989** £8.99 (GRE)
**1988** £8.02 (HIG)
**1986** £9.40 (HIG)
**1985** £8.99 (BO) £9.40 (HIG) £12.50 (ROB)
**1949** £88.13 (REI)

**Franc-Mayne** *grand cru classé St-Émilion*
**1986** £9.22 (HOG) £11.37 (BY)

**de France** *Pessac-Léognan*
**1986** £6.59 (BYR)
**1985** £10.95 (BYR)

**la Gaffelière** *1er grand cru classé St-Émilion*
**1985** £17.64 (AV)

**la Garde** *Pessac-Léognan*
**1985** £6.68 (BO)

**le Gay** *Pomerol*
**1990 EC** £104.00 (LOE)
**1989 IB** £146.00 (BUT) £170.00 (WY)
**1985** £14.68 (BIB) £15.68 (BUT) £16.00 (WY)
**1982 IB** £195.00 (FA)
**1970** £35.25 (TW)

**Gazin** *Pomerol*
**1990 EC** £145.00 (LOE)
**1989** £23.75 (HUN)
**1989 IB** £135.00 (WY) £177.00 (BUT)
**1988** £13.02 (LOE) £15.60 (MV)
**1987** £14.97 (CB)
**1985 IB** £115.00 (HAG)
**1982 magnum IB** £150.00 (FA)
**1978** £19.09 (BIB)
**1961 magnum** £48.96 (FA)
**1947** £94.00 (REI)
**1945** £96.00 (WY)

**Giscours** *3ème cru classé Margaux*
**1989** £16.30 (BE)
**1986** £17.25 (CH) £18.40 (BE) £21.90 (PEN)
**1985** £19.50 (ROB)
**1983** £20.70 (HAU)
**1982** £19.09 (BIB) £24.60 (IR) £37.00 (ROB)
**1978** £19.58 (fa)
**1970** £33.00 (WY) £36.72 (FA) £38.68 (BIB)
   £42.90 (BE) £55.00 (ROB) £60.57 (TAN)
**1966** £29.00 (NI) £40.00 (WY)
**1966 IB** £350.00 (FA)
**1961** £73.00 (WY) £88.12 (REI)
**1961 magnum** £116.52 (BIB)

**du Glana** *cru bourgeois St-Julien*
**1982** £14.05 (YF)

**Gloria** *cru bourgeois St-Julien*
**1990 EC** £82.00 (BUT) £89.00 (LOE)
**1989** £14.69 (PEN)
**1989 IB** £105.00 (BUT)
**1988** £11.75 (EL)
**1986** £12.25 (HAY) £15.32 (CHA)
**1985** £12.53 (BIB) £12.90 (HAG) £13.95 (NI)
**1983** £14.50 (PIP) £18.55 (CHA) £19.58 (BUT)
**1979** £20.00 (VIG)

**Grand-Barrail-Lamarzelle-Figeac**
*grand cru classé St-Émilion*
**1985** £12.95 (ROB)

**Grand-Mayne** *grand cru classé St-Émilion*
**1990** £3.00 (SOM)
**1989 IB** £107.00 (BUT)
**1989 EC** £104.00 (BIB)

**Grand-Pontet** *grand cru classé St-Émilion*
**1988** £10.75 (LAY)

**Grand-Puy-Ducasse** *5ème cru classé Pauillac*
**1988** £9.79 (BYR) £11.45 (GRE)

**1985** £17.41 (BO) £17.50 (ROB)
**1983** £18.99 (VIC)
**1966** £38.18 (REI)

**Grand-Puy-Lacoste** *5ème cru classé Pauillac*
**1990 EC** £110.00 (BUT) £111.00 (LOE)
**1989** £15.47 (MV) £16.95 (RAE)
**1989 IB** £148.00 (BUT)
**1989 EC** £145.10 (HAH) £148.00 (LOE)
**1988** £14.88 (LOE) £14.95 (RAE) £17.75 (DAV)

**1986** £16.07 (BUT) £16.96 (LAY) £17.95 (DAV)
£19.25 (ROB)
**1983** £15.18 (WW) £17.45 (WHI) £18.62 (BUT)
**1982** £30.35 (WHI)
**1982 IB** £180.00 (FA)
**1978** £24.00 (GE) £26.97 (TAN)
**1978 IB** £200.00 (FA)
★ **1970** £23.50 (FA) £33.00 (GE) £38.18 (REI)
£45.00 (VIG)
**1949** £115.00 (WY)
**1949 magnum** £215.00 (WY)
**1945** £125.00 (WY) £185.00 (BIB)

**Grangeneuve de Figeac** *grand cru St-Émilion*
**1987** £10.39 (REI)

**la Grave-Trigant-de-Boisset** *Pomerol*
**1989 IB** £189.00 (BUT)
**1986** £16.25 (LOE)
**1985 IB** £110.00 (FA)
**1970** £26.00 (BIB)

**Gressier-Grand-Poujeaux** *cru bourgeois Moulis*
**1989** £10.00 (HUN)
**1983** £7.95 (ROB) £11.45 (WRI)
**1981** £7.50 (GE) £8.84 (BEK) £10.59 (PIP)
**1979** £12.80 (WRI) £12.80 (WRI) £13.50 (ROB)

**Greysac** *cru bourgeois Médoc*
**1987** £6.91 (BUT)
**1986** £6.05 (HOG) £6.99 (GRG)

**Gros-Caillou** *St-Éstèphe*
**1989 IB** £50.00 (BUT)

**Gruaud-Larose** *2ème cru classé St-Julien*
**1990 EC** £225.00 (HUN)
**1990 magnum EC** £179.00 (BUT)
**1989 IB** £224.00 (BUT)
**1988** £18.30 (BO)
**1987** £17.25 (SAI)
**1985** £16.29 (BIB) £17.58 (BUT) £20.00 (LOR)
**1985 double magnum** £79.90 (BIB)
**1983** £14.00 (WY) £19.10 (AN) £19.50 (GE)
£19.58 (BUT) £22.65 (PE)
**1983 ½ bottle** £10.80 (HAG)
**1982** £23.03 (BO) £24.97 (BIB) £26.44 (FA)
£27.75 (PE) £27.85 (WHI) £28.05 (HA)
**1982 magnum** £54.50 (BAR)
**1982 double magnum** £126.90 (BIB)
**1981** £17.97 (BIB) £18.25 (GRG) £20.65 (PE)
£22.10 (WHI)
**1981 magnum** £41.09 (PE)

**1979** £15.67 (FA) £22.00 (WY) £23.38 (TW)
£25.95 (GRG) £27.75 (PE)
**1979 jeroboam** £223.25 (BIB)
**1978** £20.00 (WY) £22.52 (BIB) £27.00 (HA)
**1973** £13.59 (BOR)
**1970** £31.33 (FA) £33.00 (WY) £38.68 (BIB)
**1970 IB** £325.00 (WY)
**1970 magnum** £62.00 (WY)
**1966** £31.33 (FA) £38.67 (BIB) £41.00 (WY)
£45.00 (VIG) £56.22 (TAN)
**1966 ½ bottle** £23.00 (WY)
**1961** £120.00 (WY) £122.40 (FA) £159.15 (YF)
**1955** £75.00 (WY)
**1949** £135.00 (WY)
**1945 magnum** £490.00 (WY)

**Guillot** *Pomerol*
**1989 EC** £95.00 (GE)
**1985** £11.25 (GE)

**la Gurgue** *cru bourgeois Margaux*
**1989 IB** £111.00 (BUT)
**1988** £9.50 (GE) £9.55 (BYR) £9.80 (BE)
**1987** £8.10 (BYR) £8.35 (BE) £8.63 (CV)

**Hanteillan** *cru bourgeois Haut-Médoc*
**1990 EC** £55.00 (HUN)
**1989** £9.00 (HUN)
**1989 EC** £42.70 (HAH)
**1987** £6.41 (CV) £6.73 (HA)
**1986** £6.17 (BO) £7.95 (HAY) £8.75 (WHI)

**Haut-Bages-Avérous** *cru bourgeois Pauillac*
**1990 EC** £110.00 (HUN)
**1989 IB** £102.00 (BUT)
**1988** £13.15 (THR) £13.70 (HAU)
**1987** £12.50 (ROB) £12.96 (BY)
**1985** £14.70 (HAU) £16.63 (BY) £17.04 (SAF)
**1983** £13.50 (ROB)

**Haut-Bages-Libéral** *5ème cru classé Pauillac*
★ **1988** £9.40 (HAG) £10.19 (BYR) £10.45
(BE) £10.95 (GRE) £13.50 (LOR)
**1986** £11.50 (GE)
**1985** £10.57 (LOE) £12.75 (BYR)
**1982** £14.00 (BE)

*Webster's is an annual publication. We welcome your suggestions for next year's edition.*

**Haut-Bailly** *cru classé Pessac-Léognan*
**1989** £15.95 (RAE) £18.50 (HUN)
**1989 EC** £133.00 (LOE)
**1989 magnum** £38.50 (HUN)
**1988** £11.06 (BIB) £11.75 (LOE) £12.50 (RAE)
    £14.29 (BYR) £14.50 (HAY)
**1988 EC** £98.00 (BIB)
**1986** £10.38 (HA) £15.00 (HAY)
**1986 magnum** £37.79 (NA)
**1985** £14.95 (BAR) £18.20 (BUT) £18.95 (ROB)
    £19.29 (EL)
**1985 IB** £104.00 (HAG)
**1981** £14.00 (GE) £21.50 (ROB)
**1979** £17.03 (REI)
**1975** £14.00 (WY)
**1964** £18.00 (BU)
**1953** £61.69 (REI)

**Haut-Batailley** *5ème cru classé Pauillac*
**1989** £12.34 (MV)
**1989 IB** £100.00 (WY) £115.00 (BUT)
**1989 EC** £103.00 (LOE)
**1986** £10.48 (LOE) £10.67 (HA) £12.05 (HOG)
    £14.60 (PIP) £15.19 (BYR) £17.95 (VIG)
**1985** £16.10 (BYR) £16.40 (TW)
**1985 IB** £127.00 (HAG)
**1983 IB** £80.00 (HAG)
**1982** £17.41 (BO) £19.99 (BUT) £23.50 (GRE)
**1981** £22.50 (ROB)
**1979 magnum** £26.00 (WY)
**1970** £20.56 (FA) £23.00 (WY)
**1970 magnum** £67.56 (REI)

**Haut-Brion** *1er cru classé Pessac-Léognan*
**1990 EC** £335.00 (FA) £375.00 (BUT)
    £375.00 (BIB) £377.00 (RAE)
**1990 magnum EC** £383.00 (BUT)
**1989 IB** £637.00 (BUT)
**1988** £85.00 (HUN)
**1988 imperial** £780.00 (HUN)
**1986** £36.62 (LOE) £43.13 (HA) £46.03 (BO)
**1985** £40.98 (HA) £49.35 (PIP) £52.88 (EL)
    £54.08 (BUT)
**1985 IB** £380.00 (FA)
**1983** £37.85 (BIB) £38.09 (LOE) £40.00 (HOG)
    £47.05 (PE)
**1983 IB** £295.00 (FA)
**1982** £51.88 (BUT) £54.00 (WY) £54.25 (LOE)
    £62.29 (BIB) £66.75 (UN) £75.00 (ROB)
**1981** £26.50 (NI) £42.15 (UN) £47.00 (BER)
**1979 imperial** £280.00 (WY)
**1978** £46.00 (BIB) £49.58 (BUT) £55.00 (HA)
    £58.65 (UN) £59.99 (PE) £62.00 (BER)
**1978 magnum** £92.00 (BIB)
**1978 magnum IB** £480.00 (FA)

**1970** £63.65 (FA) £65.00 (WY) £80.50 (BIB)
    £110.00 (ROB)
**1970 magnum** £142.25 (HA)
**1966** £70.50 (TW) £82.00 (WY) £107.70 (BIB)
**1966 IB** £900.00 (FA)
**1964** £79.22 (HA)
**1964 IB** £750.00 (FA)
**1960** £32.00 (WY) £41.12 (FA)
**1959** £137.08 (BIB) £140.00 (WY)
**1955** £117.50 (FA)
**1953** £146.88 (FA)
**1949** £188.00 (FA) £211.50 (WY)
**1949 magnum** £470.00 (FA) £500.00 (WY)
**1947** £145.00 (WY)
**1945** £353.00 (WY)

**Haut-Marbuzet** *cru bourgeois St-Éstèphe*
**1986** £13.20 (BYR) £13.50 (GRE) £14.65 (WRI)
**1985** £13.04 (BO) £14.89 (BYR) £14.95 (GRE)
    £15.85 (WHI) £16.35 (WRI)
**1985 magnum** £34.99 (BYR)
**1982** £16.15 (WRI)

**Haut-Sarpe** *grand cru classé St-Émilion*
**1985** £15.28 (CV)
**1978** £14.09 (PEN)

**Houissant** *cru bourgeois St-Éstèphe*
**1989** £9.79 (NA)
**1988** £6.46 (EL)

**d'Issan** *3ème cru classé Margaux*
**1989 IB** £134.00 (BUT)
**1989 EC** £128.00 (LOE)
**1988** £12.04 (LOE) £12.95 (RAE) £14.86 (CHA)
**1985** £13.95 (NI) £15.28 (BUT) £15.95 (BAR)
    £18.95 (HAU) £19.75 (VIG) £22.25
    (ROB)
**1983** £18.75 (ROB)
**1983 IB** £95.00 (FA)
**1955** £55.00 (VIG)

**Kirwan** *3ème cru classé Margaux*
**1989** £12.64 (BO)
**1987** £9.54 (SAF)
**1986** £13.95 (GRE)
**1983** £17.04 (TW)

**Labégorce** *cru bourgeois Margaux*
**1975** £10.75 (BU)

**Labégorce-Zédé** *cru bourgeois Margaux*
**1989** £11.00 (AD) £11.50 (TAN)
**1989 IB** £108.00 (BUT)
**1989 EC** £90.00 (HAY)

**1988** £ 8.33 (BIB) £11.25 (DAV)
**1988 EC** £70.00 (BIB)
**1985** £9.10 (BIB) £10.75 (GE) £11.42 (BUT)
**1985 IB** £95.00 (FA)
**1983** £5.15 (BIB) £12.00 (GE)

**Lacoste-Borie** *Pauillac*
**1990 IB** £59.40 (NI)
**1988** £8.81 (EL) £9.02 (AV)
**1986** £9.95 (DAV)
**1985** £11.35 (BUT)

**Lafite-Rothschild** *1er cru classé Pauillac*
**1990 EC** £550.00 (HUN)
**1989** £53.85 (MV) £65.45 (PEN)
**1989 IB** £540.00 (BUT)
**1986** £46.03 (BO) £64.00 (MV) £69.59 (VIC)
**1985 IB** £450.00 (FA)
**1983 IB** £350.00 (FA)
**1982** £72.00 (WY) £74.27 (BIB) £85.08 (BUT)
**1982 IB** £850.00 (FA)
**1982 magnum IB** £860.00 (WY)
**1981** £33.65 (BO) £55.00 (GE) £58.90 (HAG)
**1981 magnum** £80.00 (WY)
**1980** £43.14 (PE)
**1979 magnum IB** £480.00 (FA)
**1978** £71.30 (HAG) £96.91 (TAN)
**1970** £82.50 (WY) £87.64 (BIB) £130.00 (ROB)
    £145.58 (YF)
**1970 IB** £900.00 (FA)
**1970 ½ bottle** £40.00 (WY) £86.17 (FA)
**1970 magnum** £93.02 (FA) £150.00 (WY)
**1966** £106.00 (WY) £178.99 (PE)
**1966 magnum** £225.00 (WY)
**1964** £40.00 (WY)
**1964 IB** £450.00 (FA)
**1962** £60.00 (WY) £73.44 (FA)
**1961** £269.27 (FA)
**1961 ½ bottle** £100.00 (WY) £117.50 (FA)
**1961 magnum** £293.75 (FA) £585.00 (WY)
**1959** £160.00 (WY) £270.25 (FA)
**1959 ½ bottle** £85.00 (WY)
**1955** £115.00 (WY) £170.00 (BIB)
**1955 IB** £1,586.25 (FA)
**1955 magnum** £250.00 (WY)
**1953** £180.00 (WY) £230.00 (REI) £258.50
**1953 magnum** £445.00 (WY)
**1949** £269.27 (BIB) £282.00 (WY)
**1949 ½ bottle** £164.50 (EL)
**1949 magnum** £700.00 (WY)
**1947** £220.00 (WY)
**1947 ½ bottle** £70.00 (WY)
**1947 magnum IB** £2,500.00 (FA)
**1945** £425.00 (WY) £446.50 (FA)
**1945 magnum** £940.00 (FA)

**Laffitte-Carcasset** *cru bourgeois St-Éstèphe*
**1988** £7.29 (TES)
**1983** £9.00 (IR)

**Lafleur** *Pomerol*
**1989 IB** £885.00 (BUT)
**1984** £16.16 (LOE)

**Lafleur-Gazin** *Pomerol*
**1989** £14.50 (HUN)
**1985** £15.94 (LAY)
**1981** £18.25 (WS)

**Lafon-Rochet** *4ème cru classé St-Éstèphe*
**1987** £8.48 (BER) £9.39 (TES)
**1986** £9.89 (LOE) £11.38 (HOG)
**1985** £10.09 (LOE) £11.75 (LOR) £12.19 (BYR)
**1982** £14.00 (HOG) £22.02 (YF)

**Lagrange** *Pomerol*
**1989 IB** £121.00 (BUT)
**1985** £13.69 (BUT)
**1982 IB** £115.00 (FA)

**Lagrange** *3ème cru classé St-Julien*
**1990 EC** £100.00 (LOE)
**1989** £18.50 (HUN)
**1988** £15.50 (DAV)
**1985** £12.34 (REI) £16.36 (BUT)
**1982** £15.19 (UN)
**1981** £14.35 (BYR) £20.15 (PE)
**1978** £15.50 (WY)
**1970** £22.03 (WY)
**1964** £9.00 (WY)

**la Lagune** *3ème cru classé Haut-Médoc*
**1990 EC** £93.00 (BUT) £125.00 (HUN)
**1990 magnum EC** £101.00 (BUT)
**1989** £14.65 (RAE)
**1989 EC** £128.00 (LOE)
**1989 IB** £124.00 (BUT)
**1988** £11.75 (WW) £13.22 (ASK) £13.70 (HIG)
    £14.95 (LAY) £16.50 (DAV)
**1988 magnum** £39.50 (VIG)
**1987** £11.25 (LOR) £11.54 (SAF) £15.50 (ROB)

**1986** £9.95 (VIG) £12.92 (FA) £14.68 (HIG)
£15.18 (WW) £16.11 (HOG) £16.75
(DAV) £17.09 (ASK) £17.50 (BAR)
£18.95 (ROB) £19.28 (CHA)
**1985** £17.50 (NI) £17.51 (TAN) £18.98 (BUT)
£19.29 (EL)
**1983** £15.17 (BIB) £16.20 (HA) £16.97 (HOG)
£17.20 (BE) £17.50 (NI) £18.75 (DAV)
£19.50 (BAR) £21:96 (YF)
**1982** £19.29 (UN) £20.58 (BUT) £22.03 (BIB)
£24.99 (MAJ) £25.50 (GRE) £25.75
(DAV)
**1979** £23.95 (DAV)
**1978** £20.28 (BUT) £29.20 (BE) £29.95 (DAV)
**1970** £38.68 (BIB) £42.90 (BE)
**1970 IB** £320.00 (FA)
**1970 magnum** £29.37 (FA)
**1970 jeroboam** £299.63 (BIB)
**1962 IB** £350.00 (FA)

**Lalande-Borie** *cru bourgeois St-Julien*
**1990 EC** £63.00 (LOE) £85.00 (HUN)
**1989** £11.35 (HAU)
**1989 EC** £90.00 (LOE)
**1988** £8.81 (LOE) £10.40 (EL)
**1985** £9.30 (LOE) £9.48 (HA) £11.66 (BUT)

**de Lamarque** *cru bourgeois Haut-Médoc*
**1989** £9.33 (CB)
**1988** £9.21 (CB)
**1987** £7.33 (CB)

**Lamothe-Cissac** *cru bourgeois Haut-Médoc*
**1988** £6.75 (CH)
**1986** £6.75 (CH)
**1985** £8.05 (VIN)

**Lanessan** *cru bourgeois Haut-Médoc*
**1989 IB** £67.00 (BUT)
**1988** £8.52 (EL)
**1985** £8.75 (BIB) £9.48 (BUT) £15.93 (PIP)
**1983** £11.50 (NI) £12.95 (HAU)
**1982** £11.75 (BIB)
**1979** £17.50 (ROB)

**Langoa-Barton** *3ème cru classé St-Julien*
**1990 EC** £98.00 (BUT) £99.00 (BIB) £101.70
(HAH)
**1987** £11.35 (TAN) £11.60 (NI) £11.75 (TES)
£14.95 (VIG)
★ **1986** £11.50 (NI)
**1985** £19.75 (NA)
**1982** £27.95 (VIG)
**1981** £20.15 (PE)

**1981 magnum** £31.30 (HA)
**1980 magnum** £24.85 (HA)
**1978** £20.13 (BIB)
**1964** £30.00 (VIG)

**Larcis-Ducasse** *grand cru classé St-Émilion*
**1985** £10.25 (GE) £12.04 (REI)

**Larmande** *grand cru classé St-Émilion*
**1990 EC** £98.00 (LOE)
**1989** £13.61 (MV) £17.50 (HUN)
**1989 IB** £137.00 (BUT)
**1989 EC** £125.00 (LOE)
**1986** £20.00 (VIG)
**1962** £18.00 (BU)

**Larose-Trintaudon** *cru bourgeois Haut-Médoc*
**1985** £7.56 (BEK) £8.67 (PIP)
**1982** £11.08 (YF)

**Laroze** *grand cru classé St-Émilion*
**1986** £10.91 (SAF) £11.16 (HIG)
**1985** £11.75 (HIG)

**Larrivet-Haut-Brion** *Pessac-Léognan*
**1989 IB** £112.00 (BUT)
**1985** £9.69 (REI) £12.15 (BUT)

**Lartigue-de-Brochon** *cru bourgeois Haut-Médoc*
**1988 EC** £36.00 (BIB)
**1988** £6.56 (BIB) £6.60 (RAE)

**Lascombes** *2ème cru classé Pauillac*
**1987** £13.49 (AUG)
**1986** £15.49 (AUG)
**1985** £14.99 (AUG) £18.75 (ROB)
**1983** £18.95 (ROB)
**1982** £17.99 (AUG) £23.85 (GRE)
**1981** £14.49 (AUG) £19.55 (VIN)
**1970** £35.00 (ROB)
**1961** £59.00 (VIG) £65.00 (WY) £85.00 (HUN)
**1955** £55.00 (ROB)
**1949** £50.00 (WY)

**Latour** *1er cru classé Pauillac*
**1990 EC** £380.00 (RAE) £385.00 (BUT)
**1989** £47.00 (PEN) £53.85 (MV)
**1989 IB** £536.00 (BUT)
**1988** £38.00 (RAE)
**1986** £42.59 (BIB) £44.25 (HA) £46.03 (BO)
££49.00 (MV)
**1985 IB** £395.00 (FA)
**1983** £38.58 (LOE) £39.50 (NI) £39.50 (BU)
£40.08 (BUT) £44.75 (HA) £47.00
(HOG) £56.45 (PE) £59.29 (VIC)
**1983 magnum** £90.45 (HA) £120.00 (ROB)
**1983 magnum IB** £340.00 (FA)
**1982** £73.00 (WY) £80.59 (UN) £83.23 (FA)
£85.68 (BIB) £99.88 (PEN) £99.99 (VIC)
£100.05 (HA)
**1982 magnum** £145.00 (WY)
**1982 double magnum** £370.00 (WY)
**1980** £34.85 (HA) £49.00 (VIG)
**1979** £47.45 (HA) £64.50 (GRE)
**1979 double magnum** £176.00 (WY)
**1978** £65.55 (HAG) £75.45 (HA) £80.00 (HOG)
£89.75 (DAV)
**1978 magnum** £140.16 (BUT)
**1970** £94.00 (WY) £105.08 (BUT)
**1970 IB** £980.00 (FA)
**1966** £115.25 (PE) £117.50 (WY)
**1966 IB** £1,100.00 (FA)
**1962** £77.84 (BIB) £100.00 (WY) £117.21 (YF)
£128.00 (HUN)
**1961** £350.00 (PE) £395.00 (WY)
**1961 magnum** £881.25 (FA)
**1961 jeroboam** £4,230.00 (FA)
**1959** £164.50 (REI) £217.00 (WY)
**1955** £135.00 (WY)
**1953** £195.00 (ROB)
**1953 magnum** £295.00 (WY)
**1949** £250.00 (WY)
**1949 magnum** £580.00 (WY)
**1947** £165.00 (WY) £225.00 (BIB)
**1945** £525.00 (WY) £611.98 (FA) £763.75
(REI)

**Latour-à-Pomerol** *Pomerol*
**1990** £250.00 (CB)
**1990 EC** £190.00 (BUT)
**1988** £29.16 (BO)
**1987** £19.08 (CB)
**1986** £23.55 (CB) £25.46 (LOE)
**1986 IB** £170.00 (FA)
**1985 IB** £165.00 (FA)
**1982** £28.00 (WY) £52.92 (CB)
**1982 IB** £310.00 (WY)
**1981** £25.00 (WY)
**1970** £53.85 (FA)

**Laujac** *cru bourgeois Médoc*
**1988** £7.41 (AV)
**1986** £5.68 (AN)

**Léoville-Barton** *2ème cru classé St-Julien*
**1990 EC** £110.00 (BIB) £112.00 (BUT)
£122.88 (LAY) £125.00 (HIG) £134.20
(HA) £145.00 (HUN)
**1990 magnum EC** £165.00 (HUN)
**1989** £14.55 (LAY) £14.65 (AD) £16.50 (RAE)
**1989 IB** £136.00 (BUT)
**1988** £14.00 (GE) £14.25 (BE) £14.29 (BYR)
£14.99 (OD)
**1988 magnum** £28.99 (BYR)
**1987** £10.00 (HOG) £11.00 (WAI) £11.25
(LOR) £11.65 (BYR) £12.19 (SAI)
£12.54 (BY) £12.76 (TAN) £13.25 (NI)
**1987 magnum** £35.00 (VIG)
**1986** £14.35 (BYR) £15.99 (HOG) £16.00 (GE)
£16.95 (DAV)
**1985** £14.00 (WY) £17.40 (PE) £20.95 (DAV)
**1983** £14.50 (NI) £17.29 (WHI) £17.58 (BUT)
£18.75 (DAV)
**1982** £20.08 (BIB) £28.25 (DAV) £36.50 (VIG)
**1982 IB** £185.00 (FA)
**1979 IB** £135.00 (FA)
**1979 magnum** £32.00 (WY)
**1978** £23.48 (BIB) £24.82 (HA) £28.71 (BUT)
**1970** £30.50 (WY) £37.70 (BIB)
**1970 magnum** £62.00 (WY)
**1970 magnum IB** £360.00 (WY)
**1966** £33.54 (BIB) £38.00 (WY) £47.00 (REI)
**1962** £38.19 (REI) £40.00 (VIG)
**1961** £76.00 (WY)
**1961 magnum** £153.00 (WY)
**1949** £90.00 (WY)

**Léoville-Las-Cases** *2ème cru classé St-Julien*
**1990 EC** £180.00 (RAE) £195.00 (BUT)
**1989** £30.00 (RAE) £35.00 (ROB)
**1989 IB** £230.00 (WY) £325.00 (BUT)
**1988** £23.30 (LOE)
**1986** £25.46 (BIB) £27.55 (AV)
**1985** £26.83 (LOE) £27.25 (HA) £28.27 (BIB)
£28.55 (AV) £30.53 (BUT) £35.50 (VIC)
**1985 IB** £190.00 (FA)
**1985 double magnum** £141.00 (BIB)
**1985 jeroboam** £270.25 (BIB)
**1985 imperial** £311.38 (BIB)
**1983** £20.17 (LOE) £21.55 (HA) £23.99 (PIP)
£28.36 (CB) £29.09 (WHI) £29.50 (AD)
**1983 IB** £180.00 (FA)
**1983 ½ bottle** £14.04 (HAL)

**1982** £44.06 (FA) £45.00 (VIG) £46.49 (UN)
**1981** £22.03 (BIB) £24.95 (HAG) £28.14 (TAN)
**1979** £18.11 (FA) £28.00 (GE)
**1978** £31.15 (BIB) £31.62 (CV) £38.00 (MV)
 £45.00 (ROB)
**1970** £38.00 (WY) £38.68 (BIB) £39.17 (FA)
 £39.58 (BUT) £43.10 (HA) £50.00 (WS)
**1970 IB** £400.00 (WY)
**1970 ½ bottle** £39.17 (FA)
**1970 magnum** £60.81 (BIB)
**1970 jeroboam** £423.00 (BIB)
**1966** £75.50 (NI)
**1964** £41.12 (FA)
**1962** £29.50 (BU)
**1961** £107.71 (FA) £112.00 (WY) £115.00
 (REI)
**1955** £105.00 (ROB)

**Léoville-Poyferré** *2ème cru classé St-Julien*
**1989 EC** £154.00 (LOE)
**1988** £14.75 (RAE)
**1987** £11.50 (RAE) £14.76 (YF)
**1985** £14.10 (REI) £19.92 (EL)
**1983** £13.22 (BIB) £13.55 (HA) £15.90 (HOG)
 £17.00 (GE) £17.80 (BER) £19.50 (BAR)
**1982** £22.00 (MV) £24.00 (GE) £24.75 (LAY)
 £24.75 (GRE)
**1979 magnum** £9.79 (FA)
**1978** £25.58 (BO) £40.35 (VIC)
**1976** £22.91 (TW)
**1975 jeroboam** £176.25 (EL)
**1975 imperial** £217.38 (BL) £270.25 (BIB)
**1970** £23.00 (WY) £28.27 (BIB)
**1966** £25.00 (WY) £31.85 (HAG)
**1962** £32.50 (BIB)
**1955** £50.00 (VIG)
**1953** £38.18 (REI) £49.00 (VIG)
**1949** £50.00 (WY)

**Lestage** *cru bourgeois Listrac*
**1986** £7.00 (HA)
**1985** £7.94 (CV)
**1983** £7.94 (CV)
**1959** £27.50 (VIG)

**Liversan** *cru bourgeois Haut-Médoc*
**1989** £10.49 (OD)
**1988** £8.55 (NI) £9.02 (AV)
**1983** £8.65 (CH)
**1979** £10.49 (OD)

**Loudenne** *cru bourgeois Médoc*
**1988** £6.43 (HOG) £7.99 (NA)
**1986** £6.43 (HOG) £6.59 (BYR) £7.99 (NA)

**la Louvière** *Pessac-Léognan*
**1989** £12.50 (HUN)
**1989 IB** £96.00 (BUT)
**1989 EC** £93.20 (HAH)

**Lynch-Bages** *5ème cru classé Pauillac*
**1990 IB** £185.00 (WY)
**1990 EC** £163.00 (BUT)
**1989** £22.90 (LAY) £26.99 (OD)
**1989 IB** £180.00 (WY) £232.00 (BUT)
**1989 EC** £240.00 (LOE)
**1988** £18.25 (BYR) £18.50 (DAV)
**1987** £15.25 (LOR) £16.83 (BY) £17.43 (YF)
 £20.50 (ROB)
**1986** £19.90 (BIB)
**1986 IB** £150.00 (FA)
**1985** £21.50 (BIB) £23.21 (REI) £23.69 (WHI)
 £24.06 (YF) £24.75 (DAV) £24.99 (VIC)
 £25.85 (BUT) £26.81 (EL) £29.99 (PIP)
 £30.75 (THR)
**1983** £20.50 (HA) £21.00 (BER) £21.15 (PEN)
 £22.75 (DAV) £22.83 (YF)
**1982** £23.00 (WY) £25.46 (FA) £25.46 (BIB)
 £27.00 (MV) £28.91 (BO) £32.75 (DAV)
 £38.00 (ROB)
**1981** £19.09 (BIB) £23.50 (DAV) £25.07 (BO)
 £28.00 (ROB)
**1981 jeroboam** £213.85 (BIB)
**1979** £18.00 (WY) £21.56 (BIB) £24.31 (BO)
 £26.95 (DAV) £27.75 (PE)
**1978** £23.75 (HA) £24.00 (WY) £25.95 (BIB)
 £32.75 (DAV)
**1978 IB** £240.00 (FA) £265.00 (WY)
**1978 magnum** £50.00 (WY)
**1970** £45.00 (WY) £53.28 (BUT) £63.65
 (FA)
**1966** £51.41 (BIB)
**1961** £112.00 (WY)
**1945** £160.00 (WY)

**Lynch-Moussas** *5ème cru classé Pauillac*
**1988** £15.08 (BUT)
**1986** £13.39 (NA)

**Magdelaine** *1er grand cru classé St-Émilion*
**1989 IB** £263.00 (BUT)
**1987 IB** £110.00 (FA)
**1986** £19.08 (CB) £19.68 (LOE)
**1986 IB** £165.00 (FA)
**1985 IB** £150.00 (FA)
**1983 IB** £150.00 (FA)
**1982** £25.00 (WY)
**1981** £22.58 (BUT)
**1966** £45.00 (BU)

**Malartic-Lagravière** *cru classé Pessac-Léognan*
**1985** £14.41 (BUT)
**1978** £20.00 (VIG)

**Malescasse** *cru bourgeois Haut-Médoc*
**1989** £7.70 (HAU)
**1988** £6.46 (LOE)
**1986** £6.28 (BUT) £7.05 (HIG) £7.70 (BER)

**Malescot-St-Exupéry** *3ème cru classé Margaux*
**1986** £10.66 (HOG)
**1985** £11.93 (HOG) £16.14 (BO) £16.74 (IR)
**1982** £13.22 (BIB) £19.96 (BO) £20.00 (VIG)
**1978** £15.84 (BOR)
**1970** £31.33 (BIB)
**1966** £23.50 (BIB) £35.00 (VIG)

**Margaux** *1er cru classé Margaux*
**1990** £8.39 (THR)
**1989** £53.85 (MV)
**1989 IB** £536.00 (BUT)
**1988** £49.50 (LAY)
**1988 IB** £375.00 (FA)
**1987** £7.49 (THR)
**1986** £53.85 (BIB)
**1985** £41.12 (FA) £42.68 (BUT) £49.50 (BU)
  £54.50 (GRE) £60.00 (ROB)
**1985 magnum** £88.16 (BUT)
**1983** £43.47 (LOE) £47.00 (WY) £48.47 (BIB)
  £49.50 (BU) £55.75 (DAV) £55.98
  (BUT) £69.10 (WHI) £72.99 (VIC)
**1983 IB** £480.00 (WY)
**1983 magnum IB** £425.00 (FA)
**1982** £59.00 (WY) £64.69 (BIB) £80.60 (GRE)
**1982 IB** £685.00 (WY)
**1981 magnum** £97.10 (BER)
**1978** £68.52 (BIB) £77.44 (FA)
**1970** £71.88 (BIB) £93.98 (TAN) £105.05 (PE)
**1970 IB** £650.00 (FA)
**1966** £88.00 (WY) £95.96 (FA) £140.00 (ROB)
**1964** £45.00 (WY) £48.47 (BIB)
**1964 IB** £500.00 (FA)
**1962** £80.00 (BU)
**1962 IB** £650.00 (FA)
**1961 IB** £2,950.00 (FA)
**1960** £32.00 (WY) £37.60 (FA)
**1959** £186.04 (BIB)
**1955** £50.00 (WY) £99.88 (FA)
**1953** £188.00 (FA) £235.00 (WY)
**1953 magnum** £620.00 (WY)
**1949** £188.00 (FA) £282.00 (WY)
**1947** £147.00 (WY) £188.00 (FA)
**1945** £341.00 (WY)

**Marquis d'Alesme-Becker** *3ème cru classé Margaux*
**1982** £8.81 (FA) £11.26 (BIB)

**Marquis de Ségur** *St-Éstèphe*
**1985** £17.05 (BUT)

**Marquis-de-Terme** *4ème cru classé Margaux*
**1990 EC** £110.00 (HUN)
**1988** £10.80 (MV) £12.62 (PEN)
**1985** £15.14 (BUT) £17.19 (NA)
**1983** £13.50 (HOG)
**1962** £22.50 (BU)

**Martinet** *grand cru St-Émilion*
**1988** £6.50 (GE)
**1982** £10.00 (GE)

**Maucaillou** *cru bourgeois Moulis*
**1989** £12.89 (BEK)
**1988** £10.49 (SAI) £10.75 (NI)
**1985** £9.39 (WHI) £10.29 (VIC) £11.25 (NI)

**Meyney** *cru bourgeois St-Éstèphe*
**1989 IB** £99.00 (BUT)
**1988** £9.54 (BO)
**1986** £11.35 (WHI) £15.80 (GRE)
**1985** £11.15 (PE) £12.96 (BUT) £13.15 (LO)
**1983** £11.94 (HOG) £11.95 (GRG) £12.99
**1982** £14.38 (BIB) £14.55 (PE) £14.95 (BAR)
**1982 magnum** £10.77 (FA) £38.00 (VIG)
**1978 magnum** £34.95 (BAR)
**1970** £20.00 (BU)
**1966 magnum** £50.00 (WY)
**1961** £48.47 (BIB)

**la Mission-Haut-Brion** *cru classé Pessac-Léognan*
**1990 EC** £295.00 (RAE) £298.00 (BIB)
  £304.00 (LOE) £385.00 (HUN)
**1989 IB** £450.00 (FA) £530.00 (BUT)
**1986 magnum** £77.95 (BIB)
**1985** £35.55 (HA) £38.58 (LOE)
**1985 IB** £260.00 (FA)
**1985 magnum** £111.62 (BUT)
**1983** £29.67 (HA) £31.24 (LOE) £33.50 (GRE)
  £34.00 (HOG) £36.72 (BIB) £51.25 (PE)
**1983 IB** £275.00 (FA)
**1982** £49.00 (BIB) £52.00 (WY) £62.75 (DAV)
  £70.00 (ROB)
**1982 IB** £495.00 (FA)
**1981 magnum** £52.00 (WY)
**1981 magnum IB** £285.00 (WY)
**1980** £25.50 (ROB) £45.00 (VIG) £46.41 (TW)

**1978** £47.00 (WY) £49.50 (BER)
**1978 IB** £495.00 (FA)
**1970** £60.00 (WY) £63.65 (FA)
**1966** £100.00 (WY) £102.81 (FA)
**1964** £88.12 (FA)
**1962** £73.44 (FA) £117.50 (REI)
**1961** £269.27 (BIB) £288.85 (FA)
**1959** £182.13 (FA)
**1955** £211.50 (FA)
**1945** £335.00 (WY)
**1945 IB** £4,000.00 (FA)
**1945 magnum** £700.00 (WY)

**Monbousquet** *grand cru St-Émilion*
**1988** £9.95 (GRE) £10.25 (CH)

**Monbrison** *cru bourgeois Margaux*
**1990 EC** £145.00 (HUN)
**1989 IB** £150.00 (BUT)
**1987** £14.95 (VIG)
**1985** £11.22 (BUT)

**Monlot-Capet** *St-Émilion*
★ **1988** £8.25 (AD) £8.95 (LAY)
**1985** £10.20 (AD)

**Montbrun** *cru bourgeois Margaux*
**1985** £9.95 (DAV)
**1945** £40.00 (WY)

**Montrose** *2ème cru classé St-Éstèphe*
**1990 IB** £155.00 (WY)
**1990 EC** £145.00 (LOE) £175.00 (HUN)
**1989** £19.98 (PEN)
**1989 IB** £186.00 (BUT)
**1985 ½ bottle** £11.95 (ROB)
**1983** £19.60 (AV) £20.40 (WRI) £23.49 (VIC)
**1983 IB** £120.00 (FA)
**1982** £17.00 (WY) £18.50 (LOR) £19.09 (BIB)
      £21.75 (UN) £22.03 (BY)
**1982 IB** £170.00 (FA)
**1980** £16.58 (BUT)
**1979** £16.00 (WY)
**1978** £19.09 (BIB) £22.00 (WY)
**1978 IB** £220.00 (WY)
**1977** £19.58 (BUT)
**1970** £36.50 (BU) £38.68 (FA) £40.00 (WY)
**1966** £37.50 (BU) £40.00 (WY) £47.00 (PEN)
**1966 IB** £395.00 (FA)
**1966 ½ bottle** £22.00 (WY)
**1962** £29.50 (BU)
**1961** £38.00 (BIB) £55.00 (NI)
**1955** £59.00 (VIG)
**1949** £110.00 (WY)
**1947** £111.62 (REI)

**Moulin-des-Carruades** *Pauillac*
**1989 IB** £140.00 (BUT)
**1986** £17.45 (BUT)
**1985** £16.58 (BUT)
**1983** £16.50 (BU)
**1979 IB** £110.00 (FA)

**Moulin-du-Cadet** *grand cru classé St-Émilion*
**1985** £15.60 (AD)
**1962** £18.00 (BU)

**Moulinet** *Pomerol*
**1986** £14.99 (THR)

**Mouton-Baronne-Philippe** *5ème cru classé Pauillac*
**1990 EC** £90.00 (BUT) £92.00 (LOE)
**1989** £13.99 (RAE) £14.49 (OD) £16.25 (HUN)
**1989 IB** £115.00 (BUT)
**1988** £11.65 (BYR) £12.99 (OD)
**1987** £9.99 (OD)
**1986** £18.55 (UN)
**1985** £12.99 (OD) £13.22 (REI) £17.10 (EL)
**1983** £11.99 (AUG) £12.85 (GRE) £13.32 (BO)
      £14.99 (MAJ) £16.50 (BU) £19.68 (YF)
**1982** £15.90 (GRE)
**1979** £12.95 (BU)

**Mouton-Rothschild** *1er cru classé Pauillac*
**1990 EC** £370.00 (RAE) £385.00 (FA)
      £385.00 (BUT) £395.00 (BIB) £430.00
      (HIG) £550.00 (HUN)
**1990 imperial EC** £625.00 (HUN)
**1989** £55.00 (AD)
**1989 IB** £549.00 (BUT)
**1988** £53.00 (MAJ)
**1986** £46.03 (BO) £58.26 (BIB) £60.48 (BUT)
**1985** £39.36 (AN) £41.81 (LOE) £42.10 (BIB)
      £46.58 (BUT) £64.70 (VIC)
**1985 IB** £420.00 (FA)
**1984** £23.30 (LOE) £27.75 (PE) £27.99 (BYR)
      £32.50 (BU) £35.70 (HAH) £37.39 (BY)
      £37.50 (ROB) £39.00 (VIG) £43.00
      (BER)
**1983** £36.89 (AUG) £42.30 (PEN) £45.77 (BO)
      £47.00 (HOG) £47.08 (BUT) £52.88
      (AN) £55.75 (DAV) £56.29 (VIC)
**1983 magnum** £70.00 (WY)
**1983 magnum IB** £360.00 (FA)
**1983 jeroboam** £311.38 (FA)
**1983 imperial** £470.00 (FA)
**1982** £97.43 (BIB) £98.96 (FA) £99.00 (WY)
      £113.45 (UN) £129.00 (DAV)

**1982 magnum** £206.00 (NA)
**1982 jeroboam** £725.00 (WY) £763.75 (FA)
**1981** £38.26 (HOG) £40.15 (BIB) £46.25 (WHI)
£54.75 (DAV) £61.08 (YF) £61.55 (PE)
**1981 jeroboam** £305.50 (FA) £546.00 (HUN)
**1980 magnum** £65.00 (WY) £95.00 (VIG)
**1979** £49.99 (PE) £65.80 (NI) £74.75 (DAV)
**1979 double magnum** £315.00 (WY)
**1979 jeroboam** £334.88 (BIB) £352.50 (FA)
**1978** £53.85 (FA) £62.00 (BIB) £66.00 (HOG)
£68.50 (BER) £69.95 (UN)
**1978 magnum** £60.12 (LOE)
**1978 double magnum** £294.00 (WY)
**1970** £84.33 (BIB) £95.00 (BU) £99.99 (PE)
£100.00 (WY) £127.00 (DAV)

**1970 IB** £1,000.00 (FA)
**1970 magnum** £97.92 (FA)
**1966 IB** £1,300.00 (FA)
**1964 magnum IB** £720.00 (FA)
**1961** £430.00 (WY) £440.62 (FA)
**1961** ½ **bottle** £391.67 (FA)
**1961 magnum** £881.25 (FA)
**1961 double magnum** £2,585.00 (FA)
**1959** £258.00 (WY) £305.50 (FA)
**1955** £210.00 (WY)
**1955 magnum** £415.00 (WY)
**1953** £470.00 (WY)
**1947** £750.00 (WY)
**1945** £1,034.00 (FA)
**1945 magnum** £2,820.00 (FA)

**Nenin** *Pomerol*
**1989** £16.49 (OD)
**1985** £20.84 (YF)
**1949** £100.00 (WY)
**1945** £55.00 (WY)

**Notton** *Margaux*
**1988** £9.99 (MAR)
**1980** £7.95 (RAE)

**d'Olivier** *cru classé Pessac-Léognan*
**1989** £11.49 (OD)

**les Ormes-de-Pez** *cru bourgeois St-Éstèphe*
**1990 EC** £85.00 (BUT)
**1989 IB** £99.00 (BUT)
**1987** £10.96 (YF) £11.70 (HAU) £12.63 (BY)
**1985** £10.58 (BIB)
**1983** £12.40 (BEK) £14.30 (PIP) £14.45 (DAV)

**Palmer** *3ème cru classé Margaux*
**1990 IB** £258.00 (NI)
**1990 EC** £195.00 (BE) £198.00 (BUT)
£199.00 (BIB) £201.00 (LOE)
**1990 magnum EC** £206.00 (BUT)
**1989** £25.75 (BE)
**1989 IB** £245.00 (FA) £275.00 (BUT)
**1989 EC** £240.00 (HAG) £257.00 (LOE)
**1988** £21.35 (HAG) £23.74 (TAN) £25.95 (AMI)
£26.50 (DAV) £28.50 (BE)
**1988 EC** £200.00 (HAY)
**1987** £12.99 (NI) £17.30 (BE) £17.41 (BO)
£24.75 (ROB)
**1985** £21.54 (FA) £23.96 (BIB) £24.06 (YF)
£25.26 (LOE) £25.75 (AD) £25.88 (CV)
£27.50 (LOR) £29.00 (BE) £29.50
(HAG) £30.01 (BUT) £41.25 (WHI)
**1984** £14.95 (BU) £17.89 (WCL) £19.20 (BE)
£22.51 (EL) £24.00 (BER)
**1983 IB** £350.00 (FA)
**1982** £25.00 (WY) £28.89 (BIB) £39.00 (BE)
£39.50 (BER) £39.74 (BY) £43.50 (ROB)
£45.00 (VIG) £46.15 (PE)
**1982 magnum** £99.50 (AN)
**1979** £41.00 (BE) £52.87 (TW)
**1978** £47.50 (BE) £49.15 (HAG) £49.50 (WY)
£58.16 (REI)
**1978 magnum** £82.42 (BIB) £84.21 (BIB)
**1970** £73.00 (WY) £73.44 (BIB) £73.44 (FA)
£75.00 (WS) £79.74 (BO) £81.70 (BE)
**1970 IB** £750.00 (WY)
**1966** £112.60 (BIB) £195.00 (ROB)
**1961** £300.00 (WY) £334.87 (REI)
**1961 IB** £3,000.00 (FA)
**1960** £40.00 (VIG)
**1959** £210.00 (ROB)
**1955** £105.75 (FA)
**1953** £176.25 (EL)
**1953 magnum** £352.50 (EL)

**Pape-Clément** *cru classé Pessac-Léognan*
**1990 EC** £133.00 (BIB) £141.00 (LOE)
£170.00 (HUN)
**1989** £20.50 (RAE) £25.00 (HUN)

**1989 EC** £178.00 (BIB)
**1987** £14.69 (AN) £15.42 (YF)
**1985** £20.08 (BUT) £26.25 (BER)
**1970** £28.00 (WY) £28.89 (FA) £28.95 (NI)
    £32.50 (BU) £44.50 (ROB)
**1966** £35.00 (VIG)
**1966 IB** £360.00 (FA)
**1949** £85.00 (WY)


**Patache d'Aux** *cru bourgeois Médoc*
**1989** £6.99 (NA) £7.20 (HAU)
**1988** £7.21 (HAU) £7.39 (TES) £8.50 (PIP)
**1986** £5.99 (GRG) £6.85 (PE) £7.20 (HAU)
**1985** £6.25 (SOM) £7.34 (BIB) £8.75 (WHI)
**1982** £9.30 (FA) £10.08 (BUT) £14.95 (ROB)


**Paveil-de-Luze** *cru bourgeois Margaux*
**1988** £9.45 (CH)
**1986** £8.65 (CH)


**Pavie** *1er grand cru classé St-Émilion*
**1990 EC** £142.00 (RAE) £149.00 (LOE)
**1989 IB** £195.00 (BUT)
**1987** £13.22 (BIB)
**1985** £19.22 (BUT) £19.59 (VIC) £20.56 (REI)
**1982** £25.00 (HOG) £25.20 (BUT) £25.85 (UN)
    £30.85 (VIC) £32.00 (ROB)
**1981 magnum** £38.00 (ROB)
**1966** £77.48 (YF)
**1964 IB** £350.00 (FA)
**1962 IB** £320.00 (FA)


**Pavie-Decesse** *grand cru classé St-Émilion*
**1990 EC** £82.00 (LOE) £84.00 (RAE)
**1989 IB** £112.00 (BUT)
**1989 EC** £106.00 (LOE)
**1988** £11.50 (GE)


**Pavillon-Rouge-du-Château Margaux**
*Margaux*
**1990 EC** £111.00 (BUT) £114.00 (LOE)
**1989** £18.99 (OD)
**1989 EC** £157.00 (LOE)
**1988** £14.30 (LOE) £17.04 (TES) £17.89 (BYR)
**1987** £13.55 (BYR) £19.79 (PEN) £22.36 (BY)
**1986 IB** £185.00 (WY)
**1985** £19.05 (BUT) £24.75 (NI)
**1983** £24.25 (AD)


**Petit-Village** *Pomerol*
**1990 EC** £195.00 (BUT)
**1989** £31.25 (HUN)
**1989 IB** £253.00 (BUT)
**1983 IB** £175.00 (FA)

**1982** £34.76 (BIB)
**1982 IB** £220.00 (FA)
**1970** £33.49 (REI) £38.68 (BIB)

**Pétrus** *Pomerol*
**1990 IB** £282.05 (CB)
**1990 EC** £1650.00 (BIB)
**1989** £282.05 (CB)
**1988** £164.50 (FA)
**1987 IB** £1,100.00 (FA)
**1986 IB** £1,650.00 (FA)
**1985** £176.25 (FA)
**1983 IB** £1,680.00 (FA)
**1983 magnum IB** £1,600.00 (FA)
**1982** £387.80 (CB)
**1982 IB** £3,000.00 (FA)
**1981** £156.67 (FA) £164.54 (BO)
**1981 magnum IB** £1,600.00 (FA)
**1980 IB** £1,200.00 (FA)
**1978** £176.25 (FA)
**1978 magnum IB** £1,800.00 (FA)
**1976** £287.50 (BIB)
**1976 IB** £1,650.00 (FA)
**1976 magnum IB** £1,600.00 (FA)
**1975 IB** £2,850.00 (FA)
**1970** £275.00 (WY) £410.00 (ROB)
**1970 IB** £3,000.00 (FA)
**1966** £411.30 (CB)
**1964 magnum** £550.00 (WY)
**1961** £1,292.50 (FA)
**1961 magnum** £2,585.00 (FA)
**1947** £1,233.75 (FA) £1,468.80 (CB)


**de Pez** *cru bourgeois St-Éstèphe*
**1990 EC** £89.00 (HIC)
**1988** £13.50 (WRI)
**1986** £10.52 (HOG) £10.89 (BYR) £12.49
    (GRG) £13.30 (WRI)
**1985** £11.24 (BUT) £11.61 (HOG)
**1978** £27.42 (WRI)
**1966** £22.50 (BU)
**1959** £27.50 (BU)
**1945** £79.00 (VIG)

**Phélan-Ségur** *cru bourgeois St-Éstèphe*
**1990 EC** £90.00 (HUN)
**1989** £10.99 (OD)
**1982** £12.94 (BIB) £15.86 (HOG)
**1981** £11.89 (PEN)

**Pibran** *cru bourgeois Pauillac*
**1990 EC** £84.00 (BUT)
**1989 IB** £106.00 (BUT)
**1988** £10.50 (GE)
**1987** £11.87 (BY)

**Pichon-Longueville** *2ème cru classé*
*Pauillac*
**1990 IB** £222.00 (NI)
**1990 EC** £165.00 (BUT) £165.00 (RAE)
     £166.00 (BIB)
**1989** £23.21 (MV) £24.80 (RAE) £32.75 (HUN)
**1989 IB** £205.00 (WY) £225.00 (BUT)
**1989 EC** £200.00 (GE)
**1988** £17.23 (LOE) £17.99 (OD) £18.95 (NI)
**1987** £17.38 (BY)
**1986** £19.50 (GE) £24.60 (ROB)
**1985** £26.85 (UN)
**1985 IB** £115.00 (FA)
**1982** £14.20 (FA) £15.00 (WY) £23.72 (PIP)
**1981** £17.91 (PIP) £18.85 (ASK) £22.75 (ROB)
**1979** £23.50 (ROB)
**1970** £28.89 (BIB)
**1970 IB** £250.00 (FA)
**1966** £25.00 (WY)
**1962 IB** £300.00 (FA)
**1961** £60.71 (FA)
**1959** £60.00 (WY)
**1955 IB** £450.00 (FA)

**Pichon-Lalande** *2ème cru classé Pauillac*
**1990 EC** £165.00 (BUT) £166.00 (BIB)
     £175.00 (LOE) £185.00 (HIG)
**1990 magnum EC** £173.00 (BUT)
**1990 imperial EC** £245.00 (HUN)
**1989** £29.50 (RAE) £29.99 (OD) £40.00 (HUN)
**1989 IB** £225.00 (FA) £260.00 (WY)
**1989 EC** £259.00 (LOE)
**1989 magnum** £82.25 (HUN)
**1988 EC** £210.00 (HAY)
**1988 imperial** £375.00 (HUN)
**1987** £13.14 (AV) £15.99 (BYR) £17.49 (BUT)
**1987 magnum** £34.69 (BYR)
**1986** £25.08 (BUT) £33.99 (VIC) £38.11 (TAN)
**1985** £23.58 (BUT) £24.19 (LOE) £24.47 (AN)
     £26.92 (BIB) £28.41 (AV) £29.95 (AD)
**1985 jeroboam** £270.25 (BIB)
**1983** £24.00 (WY) £24.46 (BIB) £29.24 (BUT)
     £29.59 (BEK) £31.00 (ROB)

**1983 IB** £260.00 (WY)
**1983 magnum IB** £200.00 (FA)
**1983 jeroboam** £276.13 (BIB)
**1982** £38.68 (BIB) £40.00 (WY) £41.58 (BUT)
**1982 IB** £400.00 (FA)
**1981** £23.96 (BIB) £24.08 (BUT) £29.00 (BE)
**1979** £28.00 (WY)
**1979 IB** £270.00 (FA)
**1978 IB** £425.00 (FA)
**1975** £37.21 (BIB) £38.00 (WY) £39.50 (BU)
**1970** £66.00 (NI) £85.00 (ROB)
**1970 IB** £595.00 (FA)
**1970 jeroboam** £335.00 (WY)
**1957** £29.37 (FA)
**1955 IB** £650.00 (FA)
**1955 magnum IB** £650.00 (FA)
**1949 IB** £1,100.00 (FA)
**1947** £115.00 (WY) £170.00 (BIB)

**le Pin** *Pomerol*
**1990 EC** £895.00 (BIB)
**1988** £95.47 (FA)

**Pique-Caillou** *Graves*
**1988** £6.56 (BIB)
**1988 EC** £52.00 (BIB)
**1985** £7.98 (BIB)

**Plagnac** *cru bourgeois Médoc*
**1987** £7.69 (WHI)
**1985** £6.85 (PE) £9.19 (YF)

**la Pointe** *Pomerol*
**1983** £18.75 (ROB)
**1953** £85.00 (ROB)
**1945** £95.00 (WY)

**Pontet-Canet** *5ème cru classé Pauillac*
**1989 IB** £125.00 (BUT)
**1986** £12.73 (WW) £13.20 (BER) £13.44 (HOG)
**1985** £13.62 (HOG) £16.15 (WW) £19.50 (ROB)
**1983** £14.00 (HOG) £17.50 (ROB)
**1982** £14.38 (BIB)
**1945** £65.00 (WY)

**Potensac** *cru bourgeois Médoc*
**1990 EC** £51.00 (BUT) £55.00 (HIC) £55.00
     (HAH)
**1989** £8.65 (RAE)
**1989 IB** £63.00 (BUT)
**1989 EC** £60.00 (HAY)
**1988** £7.75 (AN) £7.95 (RAE) £7.95 (HAY)
**1988 EC** £45.00 (BIB)
**1987** £6.68 (BO) £7.69 (NA)
**1986** £9.74 (CHA) £9.88 (BUT)

**1985** £8.50 (BIB) £9.35 (PE) £9.75 (ROB)
£11.70 (NI) £11.75 (HA)
**1983** £10.50 (HAY) £10.74 (CHA) £11.75 (BU)
**1982** £12.53 (BIB) £20.75 (ROB)
**1982 IB** £115.00 (FA)

**Poujeaux** *cru bourgeois Moulis*
**1989** £9.50 (SOM) £13.00 (HUN)
**1989 IB** £93.00 (BUT)
**1989 EC** £89.00 (BIB)
**1988** £12.34 (EL)
**1986** £9.35 (NI) £10.79 (BUT)
**1985** £8.15 (BIB) £11.33 (PIP) £11.41 (BUT)
**1983** £10.14 (BEK) £11.99 (PIP) £14.67 (CHA)
**1982** £10.54 (BIB) £13.50 (GE)

**Prieur de Meyney** *St-Éstèphe*
**1988** £8.65 (WHI) £9.25 (ROB) £9.59 (UN)

**Prieuré-Lichine** *4ème cru classé*
*Margaux*
**1988** £14.47 (CHA)
**1986** £10.38 (HA)
**1983** £14.34 (BO) £15.87 (BEK)
**1982** £16.08 (BUT) £17.89 (BYR) £21.29 (PE)
**1975** £25.00 (ROB)
**1970** £35.00 (ROB)

**Rahoul** *Graves*
**1986** £11.85 (HUN)
★ **1985** £8.78 (BUT)

**Ramage-la-Bâtisse** *cru bourgeois Haut-Médoc*
**1988** £9.40 (CV)
**1987** £6.29 (THR) £7.00 (BOR)
**1986** £8.34 (HA)
**1985** £7.64 (BIB)

**Rausan-Ségla** *2ème cru classé Margaux*
**1989** £26.99 (OD) £28.50 (HUN)
**1985** £17.75 (GE) £17.90 (BE) £18.43 (BO)
**1982** £16.16 (BIB)
**1978** £18.00 (BU)
**1966** £24.48 (FA) £28.42 (BUT)
**1961** £50.00 (WY)
**1947** £70.00 (WY)

**Rauzan-Gassies** *2ème cru classé Margaux*
**1988** £14.75 (DAV)
**1985** £11.98 (BIB) £18.95 (DAV)
**1983** £12.92 (WW) £16.95 (DAV)
**1978** £14.95 (BU)
**1970** £39.50 (ROB)
**1945** £55.00 (WY)

**Réserve de la Comtesse** *Pauillac*
**1988** £12.89 (SAI) £13.72 (AV)
**1986** £11.95 (LAY)
**1985** £14.05 (PE)
**1983** £17.50 (WS)

**Respide** *Graves*
**1988** £4.99 (GRE)

**de Roquetaillade-la-Grange** *Graves*
**1988** £6.70 (BE) £7.50 (CH)
**1986** £6.95 (DAV) £7.50 (CH)
**1985** £6.25 (GE)

**Rouget** *Pomerol*
**1988** £11.26 (LOE)
**1985** £13.51 (REI) £15.32 (BUT)

**Rozier** *grand cru St-Émilion*
**1989** £8.39 (SAI)
**1983** £8.50 (HAY)

**St-Bonnet** *cru bourgeois Médoc*
**1985** £8.18 (BUT)
**1983** £6.50 (BE) £7.64 (IR)
**1982** £10.30 (WRI)

**St-Jacques** *Montagne-St-Émilion*
**1988** £4.95 (SOM) £7.95 (BAR)

**St-Pierre** *4ème cru classé St-Julien*
**1990 EC** £112.00 (LOE)
**1989 IB** £140.00 (BUT)
**1987** £12.07 (BY) £12.15 (YF)
**1982** £17.89 (BYR) £24.50 (AD)

**de Sales** *Pomerol*
**1985** £10.00 (WY) £13.50 (BUT) £15.76 (AN)
**1983** £14.60 (BEK) £15.75 (ROB) £17.31 (PIP)

**Sarget de Gruaud-Larose** *St-Julien*
**1986** £11.99 (WHI)
**1985** £12.45 (DAV)
**1983** £10.75 (GE) £10.77 (BO) £12.95 (LAY)
£13.75 (VIG) £13.95 (PE)
**1982** £14.55 (PE)

**Sénéjac** *cru bourgeois Haut-Médoc*
**1989** £7.50 (CH)
**1988** £8.55 (PIP)
**1987** £6.40 (MV) £6.76 (EL) £6.85 (WW)

**Sénilhac** *cru bourgeois Haut-Médoc*
**1989** £3.69 (WAI)
**1986** £5.32 (YF)

**la Serre** *grand cru classé St-Émilion*
**1990 EC** £85.00 (LOE) £91.50 (HIC)
**1989** £12.60 (RAE)
**1988** £8.33 (BIB)
**1988 EC** £70.00 (BIB)
**1987** £7.75 (GE)
**1985 IB** £87.00 (HAG)

**Sestignan** *Médoc*
**1988** £6.60 (WRI)
**1983** £7.45 (WRI)

**Siran** *cru bourgeois Margaux*
**1990 EC** £83.50 (HIC)
**1987** £8.70 (CV) £8.99 (PIP)
**1986** £11.60 (NI)
**1985** £15.50 (ROB)
**1985 IB** £89.00 (HAG)
**1982** £15.55 (SOM) £19.52 (PIP)
**1979** £18.50 (SOM) £19.00 (NI)

**Smith-Haut-Lafitte** *cru classé Pessac-Léognan*
**1985** £11.79 (BO) £11.95 (WHI)
**1982** £10.28 (FA) £12.24 (BIB) £18.90 (WRI)
**1978** £10.75 (BU)
**1959** £27.50 (BU)

**Sociando-Mallet** *cru bourgeois Haut-Médoc*
**1990 EC** £84.00 (RAE) £92.00 (BUT)
**1989** £12.75 (RAE) £16.25 (HUN)
**1989 IB** £128.00 (BUT)
**1988** £9.40 (LOE) £10.50 (RAE) £11.65 (BYR)
**1988 EC** £75.00 (BIB) £85.00 (HAY)
**1987** £8.95 (RAE) £9.53 (YF) £9.99 (WHI)

**Soutard** *grand cru classé St-Émilion*
**1988** £11.75 (WW) £13.22 (ASK)
**1983** £13.21 (BIB)
**1962** £22.50 (BU)

**Talbot** *4ème cru classé St-Julien*
**1989** £19.49 (OD)
**1989 IB** £135.00 (WY) £165.00 (BUT)
**1988** £18.50 (DAV)
**1986** £20.60 (WHI) £23.05 (TAN) £24.52 (BO)
**1985** £15.33 (BIB) £17.08 (BUT) £19.05 (WRI)
**1985 magnum** £30.67 (BIB)
**1983** £19.75 (DAV) £20.05 (PE) £21.08 (BUT)
**1983 magnum** £40.00 (VIG)
**1982** £19.39 (BIB) £20.00 (WY) £20.78 (BUT)
    £21.50 (BO) £23.75 (HA) £24.75 (PE)
**1981** £15.28 (BUT) £16.00 (BIB) £19.05 (PE)
    £19.50 (HAG) £23.50 (DAV)

**1980** £17.66 (BUT)
**1979** £19.08 (BUT) £19.09 (BIB) £22.65 (PE)
**1979 double magnum** £99.88 (BIB)
**1978** £19.58 (BIB) £20.00 (WY) £22.08 (BUT)
    £23.15 (HAG) £27.50 (GRG)
**1978 IB** £215.00 (WY)
**1978 double magnum** £105.00 (WY)
**1975** £18.00 (WY) £24.00 (GE) £33.95 (DAV)
**1975 magnum IB** £215.00 (WY)
**1975 double magnum** £135.13 (BIB)
**1970** £29.50 (WY) £35.75 (BIB) £52.05 (TAN)
**1970 magnum** £52.00 (WY)
**1966 double magnum** £159.00 (WY)

**1962 double magnum** £176.25 (FA)
**1961** £60.00 (WY)
**1959** £65.00 (WY)
**1955** £56.50 (BUT)
**1949** £90.00 (WY)
**1947** £140.00 (ROB)

**Terrey-Gros-Caillou** *St-Julien*
**1989** £11.00 (HUN)
**1988** £12.20 (PIP)
**1986** £9.12 (HOG)

**du Tertre** *5ème cru classé Margaux*
**1986** £13.50 (LOR)
**1983** £15.95 (ROB)

**le Tertre Rôteboeuf** *grand cru St-Émilion*
**1989** £15.86 (IR)
**1989 IB** £182.00 (BUT)
**1986** £15.68 (BUT)

**la Tour-de-By** *cru bourgeois Médoc*
**1990 EC** £50.00 (HIG)
**1989** £7.75 (BU)
**1989 EC** £70.00 (HIG)
★ **1988** £6.95 (GRE) £7.06 (BOR) £7.50 (ROB)
    £7.63 (HIG) £7.89 (BYR)

**1987** £6.88 (CV) £7.00 (HA) £7.06 (BOR)
**1986** £7.85 (PE) £8.59 (UN) £9.30 (PIP)
**1985** £6.29 (AUG) £8.03 (BUT) £9.55 (ASK)
**1983** £9.09 (WHI)
**1980** £8.62 (BIB)
**1978** £12.88 (BUT)

**la Tour-de-Grenet** *Lussac-St-Émilion*
**1988** £5.30 (SOM)

**la Tour-de-Mons** *cru bourgeois Margaux*
**1988** £9.80 (SAF)
★ **1983** £8.16 (HOG)
**1966** £25.00 (VIG)

**la Tour-Figeac** *grand cru classé St-Émilion*
**1985** £13.95 (ASD)
**1982** £18.58 (BUT)

**la Tour-Haut-Brion** *cru classé Pessac-Léognan*
**1985** £18.87 (AV)

**la Tour-Martillac** *cru classé Pessac-Léognan*
**1983** £12.50 (NI)

**la Tour-St-Bonnet** *cru bourgeois Médoc*
**1990 EC** £38.00 (BUT)
**1989** £5.89 (NA)
**1988** £5.39 (BYR) £6.17 (EL) £6.50 (RAE)
£6.70 (BER) £8.41 (YF)
**1986** £5.96 (HOG) £6.39 (NA) £6.75 (DAV)
£6.89 (CH) £6.89 (LO) £6.95 (GRE)
**1985** £7.95 (ROB) £7.99 (UN)
**1982** £10.50 (GE)

**Tour-du-Haut-Moulin** *cru bourgeois Haut-Médoc*
**1989** £9.75 (HUN)
**1986** £7.45 (LOR) £9.19 (BEK)
**1985** £7.75 (LOR) £8.82 (BUT)

**Tronquoy-Lalande** *cru bourgeois St-Éstèphe*
**1988** £8.52 (EL)
**1982** £10.80 (MV)

**Troplong-Mondot** *grand cru classé St-Émilion*
**1990 EC** £109.00 (BUT)
**1989 IB** £129.00 (BUT)
**1987** £10.40 (GE)
**1985** £13.95 (DAV)

**Trotanoy** *Pomerol*
**1989 IB** £443.00 (BUT)
**1988** £38.11 (BO)
**1988 IB** £320.00 (FA)
**1985 IB** £275.00 (FA)
**1983 IB** £215.00 (FA)
**1982** £78.77 (CB)
**1978** £85.00 (ROB)
**1978 IB** £425.00 (FA)
**1966 IB** £1,000.00 (FA)
**1962** £75.00 (BU)
**1959 IB** £1,600.00 (FA)
**1955** £95.00 (WY) £141.00 (FA)

**Trottevieille** *1er grand cru classé St-Émilion*
**1990 EC** £130.00 (HIG)
**1989 IB** £175.00 (BUT)
**1988** £17.62 (HIG) £18.45 (BER)
**1985** £14.68 (BIB)
**1983** £17.95 (DAV)
**1982** £15.75 (BIB) £22.50 (ROB)

**Verdignan** *cru bourgeois Médoc*
**1985** £8.59 (BEK) £9.89 (PIP)
**1982** £10.55 (YF)
**1978** £13.58 (BUT)

**Vieux-Château-Certan** *Pomerol*
**1990 EC** £220.00 (RAE) £222.00 (LOE)
£223.00 (BUT) £226.00 (BIB)
**1990 magnum EC** £231.00 (BUT)
**1989** £32.90 (RAE) £40.25 (HUN)
**1989 IB** £220.00 (FA) £283.00 (BUT)
**1988** £19.50 (NI) £24.95 (HAG) £28.50 (BER)
**1987** £18.11 (BIB) £18.95 (RAE)
**1985** £24.48 (BIB) £25.16 (LOE)
**1983** £20.39 (BYR) £26.65 (BER) £30.00 (ROB)
**1983 IB** £175.00 (FA)
**1982** £25.95 (FA) £33.90 (NI)
**1970 IB** £370.00 (FA)
**1962 IB** £480.00 (FA)

**Villegeorge** *cru bourgeois Haut-Médoc*
**1989 EC** £73.00 (RAE)
**1988** £7.83 (LOE)
**1988 EC** £63.50 (RAE)
**1986** £8.05 (PE) £8.95 (RAE)
**1985** £9.50 (RAE)
**1979** £10.50 (HAY)

**Villeneuve de Cantemerle** *Haut-Médoc*
**1986** £7.95 (HAY) £8.21 (BO) £8.73 (LO)
£8.79 (WHI) £9.95 (VIG) £10.99 (GRG)
**1985** £18.06 (BUT)

# PETITS CHÂTEAUX

**de Barbe** *Côtes de Bourg*
★ **1988** £4.99 (DAV) £5.05 (EL)

**Beau-Rivage** *1ères Côtes de Bordeaux*
**1989** £3.60 (EL) £4.35 (DAV)

**Bédats-Bois-Montet** *1ères Côtes de Bordeaux*
**1986** £4.20 (LOR)

**Belair** *1ères Côtes de Blaye*
**1988** £6.66 (LOE)

**de Belcier** *Côtes de Castillon*
**1988** £6.85 (ASK) £7.39 (WCL)
**1986** £5.99 (DAV) £6.59 (BYR)

**Bonnet** *Bordeaux supérieur*
**1989** £5.60 (NI) £5.65 (THR)

**du Bousquet** *Côtes de Bourg*
**1989** £4.89 (SAI)
**1962** £18.00 (BU)

**Calon** *Montagne-St-Émilion*
**1985** £6.95 (SOM)

**la Claverie** *Côtes de Francs*
**1987** £6.75 (WW)
**1986** £7.03 (BEK) £7.64 (WW) £8.06 (PIP)
£9.30 (ROB)

**la Croix-des-Moines** *Lalande-de-Pomerol*
**1985** £8.35 (AUG)

**de la Dauphine** *Fronsac*
**1989** £6.85 (MV) £7.50 (CH) £7.64 (ASK)
£7.95 (AD) £69.00 (WW)
**1988** £9.02 (AV)
**1985** £10.99 (NA)

**Domaine de l'Ile Margaux** *Bordeaux supérieur*
**1986** £5.11 (IR)

**le Gardera** *1ères Côtes de Bordeaux*
**1989** £4.75 (WAI)
**1986** £4.99 (AUG) £5.55 (PE)
**1984** £4.99 (GRG)

**du Gazin** *Canon-Fronsac*
**1985** £7.25 (PE)

**Grand-Mazerolles** *1ères Côtes de Blaye*
**1985** £6.05 (PE)

**Guionne** *Côtes de Bourg*
**1989** £4.00 (HOG)
**1988** £4.00 (HOG)

**Haut-Castenet** *Côtes de Bourg*
**1976** £6.50 (BU)

**Haut-Gillet** *Montagne-St-Émilion*
**1985** £5.64 (EL) £5.76 (IR) £6.09 (BYR)

**Jalousie-Beaulieu** *Bordeaux supérieur*
**1990 EC** £35.00 (HUN)
**1989** £6.00 (HUN)

**du Juge** *1ères Côtes de Bordeaux*
**1989** £4.35 (LOR)
**1988** £4.35 (AUG) £4.77 (BY) £5.84 (AV)

**du Lyonnat** *Lussac-St-Émilion*
**1988** £8.95 (ROB)
**1986** £6.89 (BYR) £7.29 (CV) £7.46 (HIC)
£9.25 (ROB)

**Macquin-St-Georges** *St-Georges-St-Émilion*
**1989** £5.95 (AD) £5.99 (TAN)
**1985** £5.65 (DAV)

**de Martouret** *Côtes de Castillon*
**1989** £4.30 (SOM)

**Mazeris** *Canon-Fronsac*
**1988** £6.85 (LOE) £8.00 (MV)
**1986** £9.09 (CB)
**1985** £9.60 (LOE) £10.95 (ROB) £11.56 (CB)

**de Méaume** *Bordeaux supérieur*
**1989** £4.99 (MAJ)
**1988** £5.59 (MAJ)
**1987** £5.40 (HA)
**1986** £5.67 (HA)

**le Menaudat** *1ères Côtes de Blaye*
**1989** £5.39 (AV)
**1986** £4.99 (LOE)

**Mendoce** *Côtes de Bourg*
**1989** £4.70 (SAF)
★ **1988** £4.99 (DAV)

**Moulin-de-Brion** *Médoc*
**1985** £6.93 (TAN)

**Péconnet** *Bordeaux supérieur*
**1986** £3.99 (SOM)
**1985** £5.65 (PE)

**les Petits Arnauds** *Côtes de Blaye*
**1983** £4.38 (CH)

**Peyrabon** *cru grand bourgeois Haut-Médoc*
**1985** £6.95 (PE)

**Pitray** *Bordeaux supérieur Côtes de Castillon*
**1990 EC** £28.00 (BIB)
**1989** £5.85 (PIP)
**1989 EC** £30.00 (BIB)
**1988** £5.75 (GRG)
**1986** £5.25 (PE) £5.98 (BIB)
**1982** £6.50 (BIB)

**Plaisance** *Montagne-St-Émilion*
**1989** £4.39 (ASD) £5.33 (PEN)
**1986** £5.64 (IR)
**1961** £22.50 (BU)

**de Prade** *Bordeaux supérieur*
**1990 EC** £34.00 (BIB)
**1989** £4.59 (WAI)

**la Prade** *Côtes de Francs*
**1990 EC** £50.00 (HUN)
**1989** £6.22 (WW)

**Puygueraud** *Côtes de Francs*
**1990 EC** £65.00 (HUN)
**1989** £9.00 (HUN)
**1988** £8.11 (TAN)
**1985** £9.57 (BUT)

**Richotey** *Fronsac*
**1989** £5.25 (AD)
★ **1985** £5.15 (RAE)

**la Rivière** *Fronsac*
**1990 EC** £56.00 (BE)
**1989** £8.20 (BE)
**1988** £8.70 (BE)
**1987** £7.95 (BE)
**1986** £4.54 (SAF) £8.75 (BE)
**1985** £9.95 (BE) £13.63 (TW)
**1983** £8.95 (BE)
**1982** £9.75 (BE)

**1981** £9.46 (IR)
**1979** £12.07 (YF)

**Rouet** *Fronsac*
**1986** £6.25 (HAY) £6.35 (PE)
**1985** £6.75 (HAY) £6.75 (ROB) £6.95 (RAE)
£7.55 (PE)

**St-André-Corbin** *Montagne-St-Émilion*
**1988** £6.17 (LOE) £7.26 (AV)

**Segonzac** *1ères Côtes de Blaye*
**1986** £4.52 (LO) £6.95 (ROB)

**Sirius** *Bordeaux*
**1988** £5.00 (GE) £5.45 (BYR) £5.95 (BE) £5.95
(CH) £5.99 (THR) £6.66 (HA)

**Tanesse** *1ères Côtes de Bordeaux*
**1988** £5.35 (WHI)
**1987** £5.49 (GRG)
**1985** £6.35 (PE)

**la Terrasse** *Bordeaux supérieur Côtes de Castillon*
**1989** £4.63 (PEN)
**1986** £4.81 (NA) £4.89 (LO) £5.40 (HA)

**Thieuley** *Bordeaux supérieur*
**1989** £5.60 (PIP)
**1983** £5.75 (WS)

**Timberlay** *Bordeaux supérieur*
**1989** £4.95 (DAV) £4.99 (HAH)
**1988** £4.95 (DAV)
**1987** £4.55 (AUG)

**Toumalin** *Canon-Fronsac*
**1988** £5.50 (GE)
**1986** £6.00 (GE)

**Tour de l'Espérance** *Bordeaux supérieur*
**1988** £4.37 (YF)

**Tour-Musset** *Montagne-St-Émilion*
**1988** £7.30 (PIP)

**de Toutigeac** *Bordeaux supérieur*
**1989** £3.79 (TES)

**Villars** *Fronsac*
**1989** £6.85 (MV)
**1988** £8.00 (MV)
**1986** £6.95 (LOR) £8.45 (DAV)
**1985** £8.45 (DAV)

# WHITE BORDEAUX

## DRY

### Under £5.00

**Non-vintage**
Asda Bordeaux Blanc (ASD)
**1991**
Carriole Barton Sauvignon (BIB)
Safeway Château Canet (SAF)
**1990**
Bonnet (NI, EL)
Moulin de Launay (TAN, AD)
la Rose St-Germain (AN)
★ Thieuley (AD)
Trois Mouline Sauvignon (PE)
de Vergnes (AN)
**1989**
Trois Mouline Sauvignon (YF)
la Tuilerie (GE, AUG, YF)
**1987**
Tertre de Launay (DAV)

### £5.00 to £6.99

**1992**
Thieuley (PIP)
**1991**
Maitre d'Estournel (AD)
Thieuley (HAH, WCL)
**1990**
Coucheroy (NI, THR)
de l'Étoile (TAN, AD)
★ de Landiras (GE)
Maitre d'Estournel (AUG)
Petit Mouta (AN)
Reynon (TAN)
Reynon Vieilles Vignes (OD)
★ de Sours (MAJ, CB, BAR, BUT)
Thieuley (OD)
**1989**
de l'Étoile (BYR)
de Landiras (GE)
de Ricaud (ROB)
Roquetaillade-la-Grange (BEK, DAV)
Sirius (BYR, THR)
Thieuley (HIC, YF)
**1988**
Cabannieux (WHI)
Roquetaillade-la-Grange (GE, TES, BE)
Sirius (GE, BYR, TES, BE)
**1987**
Cabannieux (WHI)
de l'Étoile (GRG)
Sirius (GE, BE)

### £7.00 to £8.99

**1991**
Bonnet (THR)
**1990**
Cruzeau (EL)
de Rochemorin (WAI)
Thieuley (CB)

**1989**
Cruzeau (EL)
la Grave (GE)
★ Reynon Vieilles Vignes (WS)
**1988**
Cabannieux (ROB)
Château Talbot Caillou Blanc (WHI)
**1987**
Montalivet (REI)
**1985**
la Tour Martillac (RAE)
**1983**
Guiraud 'G' (BU)
**1979**
de Rochemorin (RAE)

### £9.00 to £11.99

**1990**
de la Garde (BEK)
**1989**
Château Talbot Caillou Blanc (BYR, PE)
Grand Vin Sec du Château Doisy-Daëne
  (TAN)
Montalivet (AD, TAN)
Rahoul (HA)
**1988**
Bouscaut (RAE)
**1987**
Bouscaut (BER, BIB)
la Louvière (BER)
**1985**
Carbonnieux (PE)
Rieussec `R' (ROB)
**1982**
Carbonnieux (WY)

─────── £12.00 to £14.99 ───────

**1989**
Bouscaut (RAE)
Carbonnieux (GE)
Couhins-Lurton (RAE, TAN, AD, BIB)
la Tour Martillac (NI)
**1988**
Carbonnieux (HAH)
Couhins-Lurton (REI, WS)
Smith-Haut-Lafitte (GRG)
**1971**
Carbonnieux (FA)

─────── £15.00 to £19.99 ───────

**1989**
la Louvière (HUN)
Pavillon Blanc du Château Margaux (LAY)
la Tour Martillac (GRE)
**1988**
Pavillon Blanc du Château Margaux (WY, LOE, LAY)
la Tour Martillac (BUT)
**1987**
de Fieuzal (HA, BEK, BER)
'L' de la Louvière (RAE, AD)
**1981**
Couhins-Lurton (RAE)
Rieussec 'R' (DAV)
**1976**
Roumieu (WY)

─────── £20.00 to £29.99 ───────

**1990**
de Fieuzal (AD)
**1989**
de Fieuzal (PIP, TAN)
**1988**
Laville-Haut-Brion (LOE)
**1987**
Laville-Haut-Brion (BEK)
**1985**
Pavillon Blanc de Château Margaux (VIG)
**1967**
Laville-Haut-Brion (FA)

─────── £30.00 to £59.99 ───────

**1988**
Haut-Brion Blanc (RAE, BIB, LOE)
Domaine de Chevalier (HUN)
**1986**
Domaine de Chevalier (BUT, HA)
**1983**
Domaine de Chevalier (BER)
Haut-Brion Blanc (WY)
Laville-Haut-Brion (AN, BER)

─────── £65.00 to £75.00 ───────

**1983**
Haut-Brion Blanc (TW)
**1967**
Laville-Haut-Brion (VIG)
**1949**
Carbonnieux (WY)

─────── c. £95.00 ───────

**1947**
Laville-Haut-Brion (WY)

## SWEET

─────── Under £5.00 ───────

**Non-vintage**
Asda 1ères Côtes de Bordeaux (ASD)
Bastor-Lamontagne ¹/₂ bottle (CAP)
**1990**
Lamothe-Guignard (BO)
**1989**
Bastor-Lamontagne ¹/₂ bottle (SAF)
**1988**
★ Bastor-Lamontagne ¹/₂ bottle (SAF)
de Berbec (WAI)

─────── £5.00 to £5.99 ───────

**1989**
de Berbec (SAF, OD, THR)
**1988**
de Berbec (CV)
Loupiac Gaudiet (HOG)
**1986**
la Nère (CH)

─────── £6.00 to £6.99 ───────

**1990**
★ Clos St-Georges (SAI)
Fayau (MV)
**1989**
Bastor-Lamontagne (GA)
Cantegril (ROB)
★ Mayne des Carmes (OD)
du Tich (RAE)
**1988**
des Arroucats (HAH)
Domaine de Noble (BIB)
Grand Vignot (UN)
Laurette (YF)
la Nère (GE)
du Tich (PE)
**1987**
Rabaud-Promis ¹/₂ bottle (RAE)
**1986**
des Tours (HIC)

─────── £7.00 to £8.99 ───────

**1990**
Lousteau-Vieil (HAU)
**1989**
des Arroucats (CB)
Fayau (GRE)
Loupiac Gaudiet (HA)
Lousteau-Vieil (PIP)
des Tours (AD)
**1988**
Coutet ¹/2 bottle (WY)
Filhot (OD)
Liot (BIB)
Loupiac Gaudiet (YF)
la Nère (EL, TES, BE, PIP)
Rabaud-Promis ¹/2 bottle (RAE)
Rayne-Vigneau ¹/2 bottle (WY)
**1986**
Domaine de Noble (HIC)
Terfort (HAG)
**1985**
Bastor-Lamontagne (VIC)
Doisy-Dubroca ¹/2 bottle (WCL)
Doisy-Védrines ¹/2 bottle (BER)
Lamothe-Guignard (REI)
**1983**
Doisy-Dubroca ¹/2 bottle (HAL)

─────── £9.00 to £11.99 ───────

**1989**
Guiteronde du Hayot (AD)
Liot (TAN, AD)
**1988**
Bastor-Lamontagne (WHI)
★ Caillou (HAY)
Guiteronde du Hayot (HOG)
Lamothe-Guignard (LOE)
Liot (HAY)
Menota (SOM)
★ St-Amand (BYR)
la Tour Blanche (EL)
**1987**
Guiteronde du Hayot (BYR)
**1986**
Climens ¹/2 bottle (BUT)
Rieussec ¹/2 bottle (WY, BIB, REI)
Romer du Hayot (HOG, BYR)
Suduiraut ¹/2 bottle (CB)
de Veyres (EL)
**1985**
Climens ¹/2 bottle (REI)
Coutet ¹/2 bottle (DAV, VIG)
les Justices ¹/2 bottle (BAR)
de Malle (BU)
Nairac ¹/2 bottle (BYR, VIG)

**1983**
★ Coutet (GRG)
Rabaud-Promis ¹/2 bottle (HAG)
Suduiraut ¹/2 bottle (WY, BIB)
de Veyres (BUT)
**1980**
Guiraud ¹/2 bottle (HAG)
**1979**
Coutet ¹/2 bottle (WY)
Doisy-Védrines (WY)
Rayne-Vigneau (HAG)
**1975**
d'Arricaud (RAE)

─────── £12.00 to £14.99 ───────

**1989**
Lamothe-Guignard (WS)
Mayne des Carmes (SAI)
Romer du Hayot (AD)
**1988**
Broustet (BUT)
Cantegril (AD)
la Chartreuse (TAN)
Coutet (FA)
Guiraud (BYR, OD)
Rieussec (OD)
St-Amand (BE, TES)
**1987**
Rabaud-Promis (BIB)
Rieussec ¹/2 bottle (VIG)
**1986**
la Chartreuse (EL)
Rabaud-Promis (BUT)
Rayne-Vigneau (AD)
St-Amand (GE, HIC)
**1985**
Lamothe-Guignard (PIP, LAY)
Rayne-Vigneau (HA)
**1983**
Climens ¹/2 bottle (WY)
Rayne-Vigneau (WY)
Suduiraut ¹/2 bottle (HAL)
**1981**
la Tour Blanche (WY)
**1970**
★ Doisy-Védrines (WY)

─────── £15.00 to £19.99 ───────

**1989**
Coutet (TAN)
Doisy-Daëne (AD, TAN)
Rayne-Vigneau (AD)
**1988**
Broustet (LOE)
Climens (NI)

★ Coutet (HOG, PE, BYR, CB, BER)
Doisy-Daëne (HAH)
Filhot (CB)
Lafaurie-Peyraguey (BAR)
de Malle (PIP)
Rabaud-Promis (RAE)
**1986**
d'Arche (GE, TAN)
Broustet (PIP)
Climens (PE)
Coutet (BIB, GRE)
Doisy-Daëne (HA)
Lafaurie-Peyraguey (HAY)
de Malle (PIP)
Nairac (BAR)
Rieussec (WY)
**1985**
Climens (HAH)
Coutet (DAV)
Filhot (DAV)
Nairac (BYR, GRG)
Suduiraut (TAN, AD)
**1983**
Climens (CH)
Coutet (BIB, GRE, HAG)
Filhot (WY, AN, ROB, DAV)
Lamothe-Guignard (GE, BE, TES)
de Malle (DAV)
Rabaud-Promis (HOG)
Rieussec ½ bottle (WS, WY, DAV)
**1981**
Coutet (NI)
Rieussec (DAV)
**1980**
Lafaurie-Peyraguey (GRG)
**1979**
Rieussec (WY)
**1976**
Coutet ½ bottle (WY)
**1971**
★ Doisy-Védrines (WY)
**1970**
de Malle (HA)
**1966**
★ Doisy-Daëne (WY)

─────── £20.00 to £29.99 ───────
**1988**
Climens (BAR)
Guiraud (LOE, EL)
Suduiraut (EL, BER, CB)
la Tour Blanche (PIP)
**1986**
Coutet (AD)
Guiraud (HAG)

**1985**
Climens (BYR, VIC)
Lafaurie-Peyraguey (PE, BER)
Rieussec (BYR, DAV)
Suduiraut (PEN)
**1983**
d'Arche (YF)
Climens (WY, GRG, MV, GE)
Coutet (BE, TES, HAH, PIP, AD, ROB, HA, TAN)
Lafaurie-Peyraguey (FA, BAR)
Rieussec (FA, WY, BIB)
Rieussec ½ bottle (BUT)
Suduiraut (BUT, HAG, BIB, AN)
la Tour Blanche (AD)
**1981**
Rieussec (ROB)
**1980**
Guiraud (HAG)
**1975**
Filhot (FA)
Lafaurie-Peyraguey (REI)
Rieussec (BAR)
**1971**
Romer du Hayot (VIG)

─────── £30.00 to £39.99 ───────
**1989**
Suduiraut (TAN)
**1988**
Climens (BER)
**1986**
Climens (TAN)
**1983**
Climens ½ bottle (HA)
Raymond Lafon (WY, YF)
Rieussec (DAV)
**1979**
Climens (YF)
**1976**
Climens (WY)
**1975**
Coutet (WY)
Filhot (WY)
**1971**
Lafaurie-Peyraguey (REI)
Rieussec (BIB)

─────── £40.00 to £59.99 ───────
**1985**
de Fargues (LOE, BUT)
**1983**
de Fargues (WY, LOE)
Rieussec (BUT)
**1981**
d'Yquem ½ bottle (WY)

**1980**
de Fargues (VIG)
**1976**
Climens (NI)
**1970**
Coutet (VIG)
Rieussec (ROB)
**1966**
Climens (WY)
**1956**
Gilette (YF)
**1949**
d'Arche (WY)

─────── £60.00 to £99.99 ───────

**1986**
d'Yquem ½ bottle (WY, BIB)
**1985**
d'Yquem ½ bottle (AN, TW, ROB)
**1984**
d'Yquem (BIB, LOE, YF)
**1983**
d'Yquem ½ bottle (WY)
**1981**
d'Yquem (WY)
d'Yquem ½ bottle (UN, FA)
**1980**
d'Yquem (WY, BUT)
d'Yquem ½ bottle (FA)
**1979**
d'Yquem ½ bottle (EL, FA)
**1967**
Gilette (WY)
Gilette Crème de Tête (TW)
**1962**
Gilette (WY)
Rieussec (WY)
**1959**
Coutet (VIG)
Rieussec (WY)
la Tour Blanche (VIG)

─────── £100.00 to £149.99 ───────

**1986**
d'Yquem (WY, BUT, BIB, EL, TAN, AD)
**1985**
d'Yquem (LAY, BUT, AN)
**1983**
d'Yquem (WY, FA, BUT, AN, HA)
**1981**
d'Yquem (UN, HA)
**1976**
d'Yquem (WY)
**1971**
de Fargues (WY)

─────── £150.00 to 199.99 ───────

**1976**
d'Yquem (FA)
d'Yquem ½ bottle (FA)
**1971**
d'Yquem (WY)

─────── £200.00 to £299.99 ───────

**1965**
d'Yquem (BIB)
**1962**
d'Yquem (FA)
**1960**
d'Yquem (WY)
**1958**
d'Yquem (FA)
**1950**
d'Yquem (FA)
**1949**
Gilette Crème de Tête (TW)

─────── £300.00 to £399.99 ───────

**1967**
d'Yquem (WY, FA)
**1959**
d'Yquem (FA)
**1954**
d'Yquem (BIB)
**1953**
d'Yquem (WY)

─────── £400.00 to £499.99 ───────

**1955**
d'Yquem (BIB)
**1949**
d'Yquem (REI)
**1948**
d'Yquem (WY)

─────── c. £700.00 ───────

**1945**
d'Yquem (FA)

─────── c £960.00 ───────

**1900**
d'Yquem (FA)

> *Please remember that* **Webster's** *is a price GUIDE and not a price LIST. It is not meant to replace up-to-date merchant's lists.*

# BASIC BURGUNDY

## RED

### ———— Under £5.00 ————
**Non-vintage**
Asda Bourgogne Rouge (ASD)
Sainsbury's Burgundy Pinot Noir (SAI)
**1989**
★ Bourgogne Pinot Noir Cave de Buxy
  (OD, WAI)

### ———— £5.00 to £5.99 ————
**1990**
Bourgogne Passe-Tout-Grain, Rion (MV)
Bourgogne Rouge Tasteviné, Bichot (DAV)

### ———— £6.00 to £6.99 ————
**1988**
Bourgogne Pinot Noir Domaine de la
  Combe (BIB)
Bourgogne Rouge Boisson-Vadot (BEK)
**1987**
Bourgogne Passe-Tout-Grain, Lejeune
  (RAE)
**1986**
Bourgogne Passe-Tout-Grain, Vallet (BOR)
Bourgogne Rouge Tasteviné, Bichot (UN)
**1985**
Bourgogne Rouge Vaupaisseau, Delaloge
  (RAE)

### ———— £7.00 to £7.99 ————
**1989**
Bourgogne la Digoine Villaine (AD)
Bourgogne Pinot Noir Jadot (VIC)
**1988**
★ Bourgogne la Digoine Villaine (AD)
Bourgogne Passe-Tout-Grain, Jayer (RAE)
**1987**
Bourgogne Rouge Rossignol (BEK)

### ———— £10.00 to £16.99 ————
**1987**
Bourgogne Pinot Noir Jadot (THR)
Bourgogne Rouge Jayer (RAE)

## WHITE

### ———— Under £5.00 ————
**Non-vintage**
Sainsbury's Burgundy Chardonnay (SAI)
**1990**
★ Bourgogne Aligoté Brocard (WAI)

### ———— £5.00 to £5.99 ————
**1990**
Bourgogne Aligoté Larousse (AN)
Bourgogne Chardonnay Sorin (HOG)
**1989**
Bourgogne Aligoté Tabit (GRG)

### ———— £6.00 to £7.99 ————
**1990**
Bourgogne Aligoté Bichot (UN)
Bourgogne Aligoté Rollin (BIB)
**1989**
Bourgogne Aligoté de Bouzeron, Villaine
  (BUT, BY, TAN)
Bourgogne Aligoté Diconne (BEK)
Bourgogne Aligoté Vallet (ASK)
Bourgogne Blanc Brocard (WCL)
Bourgogne Blanc les Clous, Villaine (AD)
**1988**
Bourgogne Aligoté Sorin-Defrance (VIG)
Bourgogne Chardonnay Jadot (THR)

### ———— £8.00 to £9.99 ————
**1990**
Bourgogne Chardonnay Jadot (VIC)
**1988**
Bourgogne Blanc Jobard (RAE)

### ———— £10.00 to £15.00 ————
**1986**
Bourgogne Blanc Jobard (BUT)
Bourgogne Blanc Leflaive (BUT)

## SPARKLING

### ———— Under £7.00 ————
**Non-vintage**
★ Crémant de Bourgogne Cave de Lugny
  (WAI, GA)
Sainsbury's Crémant de Bourgogne (SAI)
**1990**
Crémant de Bourgogne Cave de Viré (CV)
**1988**
Crémant de Bourgogne Cave de Viré (MAJ)
**1987**
Crémant de Bourgogne Cave de Viré (THR,
  AUG)

### ———— £7.00 to £9.99 ————
**1987**
Crémant de Bourgogne Rosé, Cave de
  Bailly (HAU)

# CÔTE D'OR

## RED

### Under £6.00

**1989**
Hautes-Côtes de Beaune, Caves des
Hautes-Côtes (TES, WAI)
**1988**
Hautes-Côtes de Beaune, Caves des
Hautes-Côtes (EL, OD, WAI)
Hautes-Côtes de Nuits, Caves des Hautes-
Côtes (OD)

### £6.00 to £6.99

**1989**
Chorey-lès-Beaune Maillard (WAI)
**1987**
Côte de Beaune-Villages Viénot (IR)

### £7.00 to £7.99

**1989**
Monthélie Garnier (LOE)
**1988**
Hautes-Côtes de Beaune, Mazilly (MV)
★ St-Aubin Thomas Père et Fils (WCL)
**1987**
Chorey-lès-Beaune Tollot-Beaut (LOE)

### £8.00 to £8.99

**1989**
★ Chorey-lès-Beaune les Beaumonts,
Machard de Gramont (AD)
Côte de Beaune-Villages Drouhin (NI)
**1987**
Hautes-Côtes de Nuits, Verdet (HAU)
Savigny-lès-Beaune Latour (TAN)
**1986**
Auxey-Duresses Roulot (BUT)
Hautes-Côtes de Nuits, Michel Gros (BY,
WW)
Monthélie Garnier (LOE)
**1985**
Savigny-lès-Beaune Chauvenet (GRG)

### £9.00 to £9.99

**1990**
Chorey-lès-Beaune Tollot-Beaut (AD)
Savigny-lès-Beaune Faiveley (WAI)
★ St-Aubin les Frionnes, Prudhon (TAN,
HAY)
**1988**
★ Chassagne-Montrachet Albert Morey
(BEK)
Côte de Beaune-Villages Viénot (BER)
St-Aubin Sentier du Clou, Prudhon (BIB)
Santenay la Maladière, Jaffelin (OD)
Savigny-lès-Beaune les Serpentières,
Drouhin (OD)
Savigny-lès-Beaune Pavelot (DAV)
**1987**
Nuits-St-Georges Gouges (LOE)
Santenay la Maladière, Prieur (EL)
Savigny-lès-Beaune Henri de Villamont
(ROB)
Savigny-lès-Beaune les Lavières, Tollot-
Beaut (LOE)
**1986**
Chassagne-Montrachet Lamy (PE)
Monthélie Garnier (BYR)
Santenay Clos Tavannes, Domaine de la
Pousse d'Or (DAV)
Savigny-lès-Beaune les Lavières, Camus-
Bruchon (RAE)
**1983**
Pernand-Vergelesses Île de Vergelesses,
Chanson (BUT)

### £10.00 to £10.99

**1990**
Marsannay Charlopin (WCL)
**1989**
Chassagne-Montrachet Henri Germain
(AD, TAN)
Savigny-lès-Beaune les Guettes, Machard
de Gramont (AD)
**1988**
Monthélie Monthélie-Douhairet (MV)
St-Romain Domaine Gras (ROB)
**1987**
Santenay la Maladière, Girardin (BEK)
Savigny-lès-Beaune Capron-Manieux (MV)
**1986**
Chorey-lès-Beaune Tollot-Beaut (GRE, YF)
**1985**
Hautes-Côtes de Nuits, Michel Gros (BUT)
St-Aubin les Castets, Lamy (PE)

───────── £11.00 to £11.99 ─────────

**1989**
Chassagne-Montrachet Gagnard-
    Delagrange (AN)
**1988**
Santenay Drouhin (NI)
★ Nuits-St-Georges Gouges (LOE)
**1987**
Chassagne-Montrachet Clos de la
    Boudriotte, Ramonet-Prudhon (LOE)
Gevrey-Chambertin Chanson (PEN)
Meursault Latour-Giraud (REI)
Monthélie Drouhin (AN)
Pommard les Cras, Belland (LOR)
Savigny Peuillets, Capron-Manieux (MV)
Vosne-Romanée les Violettes, Georges
    Clerget (BY)
**1986**
Beaune Bressandes, Chanson (BYR)
Morey-St-Denis Regis Bouvier (BEK, DAV)
**1985**
Santenay Latour (WHI)
**1983**
Beaune 1er Cru, Domaine du Château de
    Meursault (BO)
**1982**
Beaune Teurons, Rossignol (CHA)

───────── £12.00 to £12.99 ─────────

**1990**
Savigny-lès-Beaune les Lavières, Chandon
    de Briailles (WW)
**1989**
Savigny-lès-Beaune Aux Grands Liards,
    Bize (AD)
Savigny-lès-Beaune Champs-Chevrey,
    Tollot-Beaut (LAY)
**1988**
★ Beaune Grèves, Albert Morey (BEK)
Nuits-St-Georges Caves des Hautes Côtes
    (WAI)
Santenay Grand Clos Rousseau, Albert
    Morey (BEK)
Savigny-lès-Beaune Latour (DAV)
★ Savigny Peuillets, Capron-Manieux (MV)
**1987**
Aloxe-Corton Tollot-Beaut (LOE)
Beaune Clos du Roi, Tollot-Beaut (LOE)
Beaune les Montrevenots, Boillot (BEK)
Chassagne-Montrachet Champs-Gains,
    Jean-Marc Morey (DAV)
Nuits-St-Georges les Pruliers, Gouges (LOE)
Savigny-lès-Beaune Girard-Vollot (WCL)
Savigny-lès-Beaune les Lavières, Chandon
    de Briailles (IR)

**1986**
Aloxe-Corton Tollot-Beaut (LOE)
Beaune Grèves, Moillard (WRI)
Beaune Teurons, Jadot (GRE)
Beaune Vignes Franches, Latour (HOG)
Gevrey-Chambertin Faiveley (BYR)
Morey-St-Denis Dujac (LOE)
Nuits-St-Georges Faiveley (BYR)
Volnay Boillot (ASD)
**1985**
Beaune Montée Rouge, Voarick (WRI)
Beaune Teurons, Chanson (BYR)
Chorey-lès-Beaune Tollot-Beaut (BUT)
Santenay Latour (YF)
**1983**
Aloxe-Corton les Chaillots, Latour (WHI)
Beaune Clos du Roi, Chanson (BUT)

───────── £13.00 to £13.99 ─────────

**1990**
Beaune Bressandes, Henri Germain (TAN)
**1989**
Aloxe-Corton les Morais, Machard de
    Gramont (AD)
Beaune Chouacheux, Machard de Gramont
    (AD)
Côte de Nuits-Villages Jayer-Gilles (AD)
**1988**
Beaune Vignes Franches, Mazilly (MV)
Gevrey-Chambertin Trapet (BY)
Nuits-St-Georges Labouré-Roi (PIP)
Pernand-Vergelesses Île de Vergelesses,
    Chandon de Briailles (BEK)
Savigny-lès-Beaune les Serpentières,
    Drouhin (BER)
Vosne-Romanée Mongeard-Mugneret (GE)
**1987**
Chambolle-Musigny Noëllat (BEK)
Gevrey-Chambertin Rossignol (BEK)
**1986**
Aloxe-Corton Rollin (RAE)
Chambolle-Musigny Faiveley (HOG)
Nuits-St-Georges Clos de la Maréchale,
    Faiveley (HOG)
**1985**
Chambolle-Musigny Chanson (BO)
Côte de Nuits-Villages Jayer-Gilles (PE)
**1983**
Beaune Blanches Fleurs, Tollot-Beaut
    (RAE)
Beaune Marconnets, Chanson (BYR)
Gevrey-Chambertin Chanson (BUT)
Nuits-St-Georges les Pruliers, Gouges (LOE)
**1982**
Savigny-lès-Beaune Ampeau (REI)

## £14.00 to £14.99

**1989**
Chambolle-Musigny Dujac (BUT)
Nuits-St-Georges en la Perrière Noblot,
    Machard de Gramont (AD)
**1988**
Beaune Clos du Roi, Chanson (TAN, BO)
Beaune Épenottes, Parent (CV)
★ Beaune Teurons, Rossignol-Trapet (BY)
Chambolle-Musigny Dujac (LOE)
Gevrey-Chambertin Bachelet (MV)
Gevrey-Chambertin Rodet (WHI)
Savigny-lès-Beaune Champs-Chevrey,
    Tollot-Beaut (VIG)
**1987**
Aloxe-Corton Voarick (YF)
Beaune Épenottes, Parent (HA)
Chambolle-Musigny Dujac (BY)
Vosne-Romanée Engel (ROB)
**1986**
Côte de Nuits-Villages Jayer-Gilles (AD)
★ Morey-St-Denis, Dujac (BYR)
Nuits-St-Georges les Porets St-Georges,
    Gouges (LOE)
Nuits-St-Georges Rion (MV)
**1985**
Beaune Marconnets, Bouchard Père (BO)
Nuits-St-Georges les Pruliers, Gouges (LOE)
Pommard la Platière, Coche (RAE)
**1983**
Beaune Clos des Fèves, Chanson (BYR)
Chambolle-Musigny Roumier (RAE)
Corton Viénot (HAG)
Volnay Chanson (BUT)
**1982**
Aloxe-Corton Latour (HAG)
Auxey-Duresses Ampeau (CHA)

## £15.00 to £15.99

**1989**
Nuits-St-Georges Rodet (WHI)
**1988**
Aloxe-Corton Machard de Gramont (TAN)
Chambolle-Musigny Chanson (TAN)
★ Gevrey-Chambertin Armand Rousseau
    (TAN, EL)
Morey-St-Denis Bruno Clair (BYR)
**1987**
Gevrey-Chambertin Cazetiers, Armand
    Rousseau (BYR)
Mazis-Chambertin Armand Rousseau (LOE)
Pommard les Saucille, Boillot (BEK)
Volnay Lafarge (BEK)
Vosne-Romanée les Suchots, Noëllat (BEK)
Vosne-Romanée Rion (MV)

**1986**
Beaune Grèves, Tollot-Beaut (HAY)
Chapelle-Chambertin Trapet (GRE)
Gevrey-Chambertin Clos de la Justice,
    Vallet (AS)
Volnay Santenots Lafon (MV)
**1985**
Beaune Grèves, Moillard (VIC)
Chambolle-Musigny Moillard (VIC)
Morey-St-Denis Clos des Ormes, Lignier
    (BUT)
Nuits-St-Georges les Vaucrains, Gouges
    (LOE)
**1983**
Corton Chandon de Briailles (BYR)

## £16.00 to £16.99

**1989**
Aloxe-Corton Tollot-Beaut (LAY)
Morey-St-Denis Dujac (AD)
Nuits-St-Georges les Damodes, Machard
    de Gramont (AD)
**1988**
Beaune 1er Cru, Domaine du Château de
    Meursault (LO)
Gevrey-Chambertin Chanson (TAN)
Morey-St-Denis 1er Cru, Faiveley (BYR)
Morey-St-Denis Clos de la Bussière,
    Roumier (TAN)
**1987**
Beaune Clos des Ursules, Jadot (GRE)
Corton-Bressandes Tollot-Beaut (LOE)
Corton Tollot-Beaut (LOE)

Gevrey-Chambertin Clos St-Jacques,
    Armand Rousseau (BYR)
Volnay 1er Cru Lafarge (BEK)
Volnay Santenots Matrot (CB)
**1986**
Beaune Bressandes, Henri Germain (AD)
Chambolle-Musigny la Combe d'Orvaux,
    Grivot (LAY)
Charmes-Chambertin Armand Rousseau
    (LOE)
Pommard les Épenots, Mme de Courcel
    (LOE)

**1985**
Beaune Grèves, Albert Morey (DAV)
Savigny-lès-Beaune les Vergelesses, Bize
(BUT)
**1983**
Beaune Teurons, Domaine du Château de
Beaune (PEN)
**1982**
Corton Bouchard Père (BO)

────────── £17.00 to £19.99 ──────────

**1989**
Gevrey-Chambertin Cazetiers, Armand
Rousseau (AD)
Nuits-St-Georges les Vignerondes,
Chartron & Trébuchet (AN)
Volnay Lafarge (WS)
Volnay Santenots Boillot (WW)
Vosne-Romanée Jean Gros (WW, THR)
**1988**
Chambolle-Musigny Beaux Bruns, Rion
(MV)
Chambolle-Musigny Faiveley (BYR)
★ Nuits-St-Georges les St-Georges,
Gouges (LOE)
Nuits-St-Georges Rion (MV)
Nuits-St-Georges Vignes Rondes, Rion
(WCL)
Pommard les Bertins, Lescure (PIP)
Savigny-lès-Beaune les Vergelesses, Bize
(HAH)
Volnay Champans, Gagnard-Delagrange
(BY)
Volnay Champans, Marquis d'Angerville
(LOE)
Volnay Lafarge (RAE)
Volnay les Caillerets, Marquis d'Angerville
(EL)
**1987**
Beaune Clos des Mouches, Drouhin (GRE)
Gevrey-Chambertin Drouhin (NI)
Morey-St-Denis Clos des Ormes, Faiveley
(BYR)
Morey-St-Denis Clos des Ormes, Lignier
(BIB)
Nuits-St-Georges les Cailles, Michelot (BEK)
Pommard Lejeune (RAE)
Pommard Rugiens Domaine Courcel (LOE)
Vosne-Romanée Mongeard-Mugneret (BYR)
**1986**
Clos de la Roche Armand Rousseau (EL,
LOE, BUT)
Échézeaux Mongeard-Mugneret (IR)
Gevrey-Chambertin Domaine des Varoilles
(HAU)

Latricières-Chambertin Trapet (BEK, BY)
Nuits-St-Georges Clos de Thorey, Moillard
(SAI)
Nuits-St-Georges Jadot (VIC)
Nuits-St-Georges les Pruliers, Grivot (LAY)
Pommard Parent (BYR)
Pommard Rugiens Domaine Courcel (LOE)
Volnay Caillerets Cuvée Carnot, Bouchard
Père (BYR)
Volnay Lafon (AD)
**1985**
Aloxe-Corton Voarick (BUT)
Gevrey-Chambertin Cazetiers, Armand
Rousseau (BUT)
Nuits-St-Georges Faiveley (HOG)
Nuits-St-Georges les Pruliers, Grivot (DAV)
Nuits-St-Georges Michelot (BEK)
Pommard Clerget (HA)
Volnay Santenots Rougeot (PE, PE)
Vosne-Romanée Jean Gros (BUT)
Vosne-Romanée les Violettes, Georges
Clerget (BUT)
**1983**
Beaune Clos des Ursules, Jadot (LAY)
Clos de la Roche Armand Rousseau (LOE,
ROB)
Clos de Vougeot Moillard (TES, BE)
Volnay les Caillerets, Domaine de la
Pousse d'Or (BYR)
**1982**
Beaune Clos du Roi, Ampeau (CHA)
Pommard Ampeau (CHA)
Volnay Santenots Ampeau (CHA)

────────── £20.00 to £24.99 ──────────

**1989**
Clos de la Roche Armand Rousseau (BUT)
Nuits-St-Georges Clos de Forets St-
Georges, Domaine de l'Arlot (BY)
Volnay les Caillerets, Clos des 60 Ouvrées,
Domaine de la Pousse d'Or (LAY)
**1988**
Chambolle-Musigny Dujac (VIG)
Charmes-Chambertin Armand Rousseau
(EL, LOE)
Clos de la Roche Armand Rousseau (BUT,
LOE)
Corton-Bressandes Tollot-Beaut (LOE)
Corton Tollot-Beaut (LOE)
Gevrey-Chambertin Clos des Varoilles,
Domaine des Varoilles (TAN)
Nuits-St-Georges les Vaucrains, Gouges
(YF)
Pommard les Épenots, Mme de Courcel
(LOE)

Pommard Rugiens Domaine Courcel (LOE, EL)
Volnay Clos des Chênes, Lafarge (BEK, PIP)
Volnay Clos des Ducs, Marquis d'Angerville (LOE, EL)
Volnay Santenots Lafon (MV)
Vosne-Romanée Beaux Monts, Thomas-Moillard (BER)
Vosne-Romanée les Beaumonts, Domaine Rion (OD)

**1987**
Corton-Bressandes Tollot-Beaut (BEK, BY)
Corton-Bressandes Voarick (YF)
Corton Languettes, Voarick (YF)
Échézeaux Mongeard-Mugneret (BYR)
Échézeaux Mugneret (BEK)
Gevrey-Chambertin Clos St-Jacques, Armand Rousseau (BUT)
Nuits-St-Georges Clos de Forets St-Georges, Domaine de l'Arlot (LAY)
Volnay Clos des Chênes, Lafarge (BEK)
Volnay les Caillerets, Domaine de la Pousse d'Or (YF)
Volnay Santenots-du-Millieu, Tête de Cuvée, Lafon (TAN)
Vosne-Romanée les Beaumonts, Domaine Rion (MV)
Vosne-Romanée les Chaumes, Rion (MV)

**1986**
Chambertin Clos-de-Bèze, Armand Rousseau (BUT)
Chambertin Trapet (BEK, BY)
Charmes-Chambertin Armand Rousseau (VIG)
Clos de Vougeot Grivot (PIP, BUT)
Clos de Vougeot Noëllat (BEK)
Clos St-Denis Dujac (LOE)
Clos St-Denis Lignier (HAU)
Gevrey-Chambertin Clos St-Jacques, Armand Rousseau (BUT, LOE, EL)
Gevrey-Chambertin Vieille Vigne, Domaine des Varoilles (HAU)
Latricières-Chambertin Trapet (PIP)
Mazis-Chambertin Armand Rousseau (VIG)
Pommard les Chaponniers, Parent (ROB)

**1985**
Chambolle-Musigny la Come d'Orvaux, Grivot (BUT)
Chapelle-Chambertin Trapet (BEK)
Gevrey-Chambertin Clos des Varoilles, Domaine des Varoilles (ROB)
Gevrey-Chambertin Leclerc (BYR)
Morey-St-Denis Dujac (FA)
Volnay Clos des Ducs, Marquis d'Angerville (GRE)

**1983**
Beaune Clos des Ursules, Jadot (BUT)
Clos St-Denis Lignier (BUT)
Corton-Grancey Latour (WY)
Latricières-Chambertin Trapet (BY)
Nuits-St-Georges Clos de Thorey, Moillard (PEN)
Pommard les Argillières, Lejeune (BUT)
Vosne-Romanée les Beaumonts, Prosper Maufoux (BER)

**1982**
Corton Bonneau du Martray (BO)
Corton Clos des Cortons, Faiveley (GRE)
Corton-Grancey Latour (HAG)
Mazis-Chambertin Armand Rousseau (FA)
Pommard Ampeau (LAY)
Volnay Santenots Ampeau (BUT)

——————— £25.00 to £29.99 ———————

**1989**
Charmes-Chambertin Dujac (BUT)
Corton Tollot-Beaut (AD)
Gevrey-Chambertin Combottes, Dujac (BUT)
Nuits-St-Georges Clos de Forets St-Georges, Domaine de l'Arlot (BOT, WR)
Volnay Clos de la Bousse d'Or, Domaine de la Pousse d'Or (BOT, WR)

**1988**
Corton-Bressandes Tollot-Beaut (AD)
Latricières-Chambertin Trapet (BY)
Nuits-St-Georges Clos de Forets St-Georges, Domaine de l'Arlot (BY, BUT, WR, BOT)
Pommard Pezerolles Domaine de Montille (HAH)
Ruchottes-Chambertin Armand Rousseau (LOE)

**1987**
Bonnes-Mares Dujac (LOE)
Bonnes-Mares Roumier (BUT, TAN)
Chambertin Clos-de-Bèze, Armand Rousseau (LOE)
Charmes-Chambertin Armand Rousseau (THR)
Charmes-Chambertin Bachelet (MV)
Charmes-Chambertin Dujac (BUT, BY)
Clos de Vougeot Grivot (LAY)
Corton Pougets, Jadot (VIC)
Échézeaux Dujac (LOE)
Échézeaux Henri Jayer (RAE)
Gevrey-Chambertin Combottes, Dujac (YF)
Volnay Clos de la Bousse d'Or, Domaine de la Pousse d'Or (THR)
Volnay Santenots Lafon (VIG)

**1986**

Bonnes-Mares Dujac (LOE)
Bonnes-Mares Roumier (BUT)
Chambertin Armand Rousseau (LOE)
Chambertin Clos-de-Bèze, Faiveley (GRE)
Charmes-Chambertin Dujac (BY)
Clos de la Roche Dujac (BUT)
Corton Pougets, Jadot (THR)
Échézeaux Dujac (LOE)
Échézeaux Henri Jayer (RAE)
Gevrey-Chambertin Combottes, Dujac (BY)
Pommard Clos Blanc, Machard de
 Gramont (VIG)

**1985**

Chambolle-Musigny les Charmes, Michel
 Clerget (BUT)
Corton-Bressandes Voarick (BUT)
Corton les Renardes, Voarick (BUT)

Échézeaux Mongeard-Mugneret (BUT)
Volnay Clos des Chênes, Lafarge (BUT)
Volnay les Caillerets, Domaine de la
 Pousse d'Or (WS)
Volnay Santenots Lafon (BUT)

**1983**

Beaune Dames Hospitalières, Hospices de
 Beaune (EL)
Clos de la Roche Dujac (CB)
Clos de la Roche Prosper Maufoux (BER)
Pommard Clos de la Commaraine,
 Jaboulet-Vercherre (WRI)

**1982**

Clos de la Roche Armand Rousseau (VIG)
Volnay Santenots-du-Millieu, Tête de
 Cuvée, Lafon (VIG)

────── **£30.00 to £39.99** ──────

**1989**

Chambertin Armand Rousseau (BUT, AD)
Chambolle-Musigny les Amoureuses,
 Roumier (TAN)
Clos de Vougeot Méo-Camuzet (HAH)
Clos de Vougeot Mongeard-Mugneret (AD)
Clos St-Denis Dujac (BUT)
Gevrey-Chambertin Clos St-Jacques,
 Armand Rousseau (BUT)

**1988**

Bonnes-Mares Dujac (LOE)
Chambertin Armand Rousseau (THR)
Chambertin Trapet (BY)
Charmes-Chambertin Dujac (BUT, AD)
Clos de la Roche Dujac (BUT)
Clos de Vougeot Grivot (BUT)
Clos St-Denis Dujac (TAN, BUT)
Échézeaux Dujac (LOE)
Échézeaux Faiveley (WS)
Gevrey-Chambertin Clos St-Jacques,
 Armand Rousseau (BUT, LOE)
Gevrey-Chambertin Combottes, Dujac
 (BUT, YF)
Musigny Prieur (EL)

**1987**

Chambertin Armand Rousseau (BUT)
Clos de Vougeot Arnoux (WHI)
Échézeaux Jacqueline Jayer (BUT)
Latricières-Chambertin Ponsot (MV)
Nuits-St-Georges les Boudots, Méo-
 Camuzet (BIB)

**1986**

Bonnes-Mares Bertheau (BEK)
Clos de la Roche Ponsot (MV)
Clos de Vougeot Grivot (DAV)
Clos de Vougeot Méo-Camuzet (PE)
Clos St-Denis Dujac (BY)
Échézeaux Henri Jayer (BUT)
Romanée-St-Vivant Voarick (YF)

**1985**

Beaune Dames Hospitalières, Hospices de
 Beaune (EL)
Charmes-Chambertin Dujac (BIB)
Clos de la Roche Armand Rousseau (BUT)
Clos de Vougeot Grivot (DAV)
Corton Clos des Cortons, Faiveley (BIB)
Corton-Grancey Latour (WY)
Échézeaux Georges Jayer (PE)
Gevrey-Chambertin Clos St-Jacques,
 Armand Rousseau (BUT)
Grands-Échézeaux Mongeard-Mugneret
 (BIB)

**1983**

Chambertin Clos-de-Bèze, Faiveley (AUG)
Clos de Vougeot Moillard (PEN)
Échézeaux Dujac (FA)
Griotte-Chambertin Drouhin (AD)
Romanée-St-Vivant Domaine de la
 Romanée-Conti (FA)

**1982**

Chambertin Trapet (BY)
Clos de Tart Mommessin (YF)
Romanée-St-Vivant Domaine de la
 Romanée-Conti (BIB)

─────── £40.00 to £49.99 ───────

**1989**
Chambertin Clos-de-Bèze, Armand
Rousseau (TAN)
**1988**
Chambertin Vieilles Vignes, Trapet (PIP)
Échézeaux Domaine de la Romanée-Conti
(FA)
**1987**
Musigny Vieilles Vignes, de Vogüé (AN)
**1986**
Chambertin Armand Rousseau (VIG)
Clos de la Roche Vieilles Vignes, Ponsot
(YF)
Échézeaux Domaine de la Romanée-Conti
(BUT)
**1985**
Chambertin Armand Rousseau (BUT)
Chambertin Clos-de-Bèze, Armand
Rousseau (PE)
**1983**
Échézeaux Domaine de la Romanée-Conti
(BIB, WY)
**1982**
Clos de la Roche Dujac (YF)
Échézeaux Domaine de la Romanée-Conti
(VIN)
Richebourg Domaine de la Romanée-Conti
(FA)
La Tâche Domaine de la Romanée-Conti
(WY)

─────── £50.00 to £59.99 ───────

**1988**
Richebourg Domaine Gros (AN)
**1987**
Échézeaux Domaine de la Romanée-Conti
(BUT)
**1985**
Chambertin Clos-de-Bèze, Faiveley (TW)
Échézeaux Domaine de la Romanée-Conti
(BUT, WY)
**1982**
Grands-Échézeaux Domaine de la
Romanée-Conti (ROB)
Richebourg Domaine de la Romanée-Conti
(HAG)
Romanée-St-Vivant Domaine de la
Romanée-Conti (ROB)

─────── £60.00 to £79.99 ───────

**1987**
Grands-Échézeaux Domaine de la
Romanée-Conti (BUT)
Richebourg Domaine Gros (BY)

**1986**
Romanée-St-Vivant Domaine de la
Romanée-Conti (BUT)
**1985**
Richebourg Domaine Gros (BUT)
Romanée-St-Vivant Domaine de la
Romanée-Conti (WY)
**1983**
Richebourg Domaine de la Romanée-Conti
(FA)
**1982**
Romanée-St-Vivant Domaine de la
Romanée-Conti (YF)
La Tâche Domaine de la Romanée-Conti
(BO, VIN)

─────── £80.00 to £99.99 ───────

**1988**
Richebourg Domaine de la Romanée-Conti
(FA)
**1986**
La Tâche Domaine de la Romanée-Conti
(WY)
**1985**
Chambertin Ponsot (BIB)
Clos de la Roche Vieilles Vignes, Ponsot
(FA)
Romanée-St-Vivant Cuvée Marey Monge,
Domaine de la Romanée-Conti (BUT)
**1983**
Échézeaux Henri Jayer (FA)
Grands-Échézeaux Domaine de la
Romanée-Conti (YF, TW)
La Tâche Domaine de la Romanée-Conti
(FA, WY)

─────── £100.00 to £139.99 ───────

**1987**
La Tâche Domaine de la Romanée-Conti
(BUT)
Richebourg Domaine de la Romanée-Conti
(BUT)
**1986**
Richebourg Domaine de la Romanée-Conti
(BUT)
**1985**
La Tâche Domaine de la Romanée-Conti
(BUT)
Richebourg Domaine de la Romanée-Conti
(BUT)

─────── £140.00 to £190.00 ───────

**1988**
La Tâche Domaine de la Romanée-Conti
(CB)

--- c. £350.00 ---

**1986**
Romanée-Conti Domaine de la Romanée-Conti (BUT)

--- c. £470.00 ---

**1983**
Romanée-Conti Domaine de la Romanée-Conti (FA)

--- c. £650.00 ---

**1988**
Romanée-Conti Domaine de la Romanée-Conti (TW)

## WHITE

--- Under £10.00 ---

**1990**
Pernand-Vergelesses Leflaive (AD)
★ St-Romain Leflaive (AD)
**1989**
St-Romain Labouré-Roi (PIP)
**1988**
Marsannay Jadot (THR)
**1987**
Pernand-Vergelesses Chanson (TAN)
Santenay Blanc Lequin-Roussot (RAE)

--- £10.00 to £11.99 ---

**1990**
Monthélie le Champ Fulliot, Garaudet (PIP)
St-Aubin Charmois, Leflaive (AD)
**1989**
Auxey-Duresses Labouré-Roi (PIP)
Pernand-Vergelesses Capron-Manieux (MV)
Pernand-Vergelesses Leflaive (WS)
St-Aubin Prudhon (HAY, BIB)
**1988**
Auxey-Duresses Diconne (BEK)
★ Savigny-lès-Beaune Capron-Manieux (MV)
**1987**
Meursault Clos du Château, Château de Meursault (BO)
**1986**
Pernand-Vergelesses Guyon (HOG)

--- £12.00 to £13.99 ---

**1990**
Meursault Chevalier Brunet (EL)
Meursault Jaffelin (GA)
**1989**
Chassagne-Montrachet Latour (WHI)
Meursault Latour (WHI)
St-Aubin 1er Cru, Leflaive (BUT)
St-Aubin Charmois, Jean-Marc Morey (BEK)
St-Aubin Charmois, Leflaive (BYR)
**1988**
Pernand-Vergelesses Dubreuil-Fontaine (BY)
Pernand-Vergelesses Rollin (RAE, BIB)
**1987**
★ Meursault Clos des Meix-Chavaux, Jean Germain (GE)
Meursault Ropiteau (HOG)
Pernand-Vergelesses Vallet (BOR)
**1983**
Pernand-Vergelesses Rollin (BUT)
★ St-Aubin Albert Morey (BUT)

--- £14.00 to £15.99 ---

**1990**
Meursault Clos du Cromin, Javillier (LAY)
Puligny-Montrachet Leflaive (LAY)
**1989**
Chassagne-Montrachet Niellon (BUT)
Meursault Boisson-Vadot (BEK)
St-Aubin Albert Morey (DAV)
St-Aubin Drouhin (NI)
**1988**
Chassagne-Montrachet Albert Morey (BEK)
Chassagne-Montrachet Niellon (LOE)
Meursault Boisson-Vadot (BYR)
Meursault Jaffelin (OD)
Meursault Latour (HOG)
Puligny-Montrachet Carillon (ASD)
**1987**
Chassagne-Montrachet la Boudriotte, Gagnard-Delagrange (LOE)
Meursault Chanson (PEN)
Meursault les Luchets, Roulot (BUT)
Meursault l'Ormeau, Coche (RAE)
Puligny-Montrachet Ropiteau (HOG)
**1986**
Meursault Labouré-Roi (CV)
Meursault les Meix Chavaux, Roulot (BUT)
**1982**
Puligny-Montrachet les Combettes, Prieur (WY)
**1981**
★ Meursault Perrières, Prieur (WY)

──────── £16.00 to £17.99 ────────

**1990**
Puligny-Montrachet Carillon (AD)
**1989**
Chassagne-Montrachet Fontaine-Gagnard (AN)
Chassagne-Montrachet la Boudriotte, Gagnard-Delagrange (HAH)
Meursault Charmes, Brunet (EL)
Meursault les Tillets, Chouet-Clivet (VIG)
Puligny-Montrachet Carillon (WW)
**1988**
Chassagne-Montrachet Drouhin (BR)
Chassagne-Montrachet Latour (HOG)
Chassagne-Montrachet Leflaive (AMI)
Chassagne-Montrachet les Champs Gains, Albert Morey (BEK)
Chassagne-Montrachet Sauzet (TAN)
Clos du Château de Meursault Bourgogne Chardonnay (VIN)
Meursault Blagny, Latour (WY)
Meursault Drouhin (OD)
Meursault Goutte d'Or, Garnier (LOE)
Meursault Henri Germain (TAN)
Meursault Jobard (MV)
Meursault l'Ormeau, Coche (BIB)
Meursault Matrot (CB)
Meursault Michelot-Buisson (HAG, BY)
Puligny-Montrachet Clerc (BY)
Puligny-Montrachet Latour (HOG)
Puligny-Montrachet Sauzet (LOE)
**1987**
Chassagne-Montrachet Albert Morey (DAV)
Meursault Jobard (RAE)
**1986**
Chassagne-Montrachet Javillier (IR, VIN)
Meursault Charmes, Abel Garnier (LOE)
Meursault Clos du Cromin, Moillard (VIC)
Puligny-Montrachet Carillon (GE)
Puligny-Montrachet Jean Germain (AUG)
Puligny-Montrachet Leflaive (PE)
**1985**
★ Puligny-Montrachet Jean Germain (GE)
**1982**
Meursault Clos du Cromin, Morey (BY)

──────── £18.00 to £19.99 ────────

**1990**
Meursault Charmes, Henri Germain (TAN)
**1989**
Chassagne-Montrachet la Maltroie, Fontaine-Gagnard (AN)
Chassagne-Montrachet Leflaive (BYR)
Chassagne-Montrachet les Caillerets, Albert Morey (BUT)

Chassagne-Montrachet les Embrazées, Albert Morey (BUT)
Chassagne-Montrachet Roux (HA)
Meursault Santenots, Monthélie-Douhairet (MV)
Puligny-Montrachet Drouhin (NI)
Puligny-Montrachet Leflaive (BYR)
Puligny-Montrachet les Folatières, Latour (WY)
Puligny-Montrachet Sauzet (LOE, TAN)
**1988**
Chassagne-Montrachet les Chaumes, Jean-Marc Morey (DAV)
Chassagne-Montrachet les Embrazées, Albert Morey (PIP)
Meursault Genevrières, Latour (HOG)
Meursault les Vireuils, Roulot (HAY)
Puligny-Montrachet Carillon (MV, LAY)
Puligny-Montrachet Leflaive (HA)
Puligny-Montrachet les Folatières, Boisson-Vadot (BYR)
Puligny-Montrachet Moillard (PEN)
**1987**
Puligny-Montrachet les Perrières, Leflaive (BYR)
Puligny-Montrachet Sauzet (PE)
**1986**
Meursault Genevrières, Latour (BUT)
Meursault Jadot (VIC)
Meursault Jobard (BUT)
Meursault Rougeots, Coche-Dury (HA)
**1985**
Chassagne-Montrachet Roux (PE)
Meursault Jaffelin (PEN)
Puligny-Montrachet Clos de la Mouchère, Boillot (DAV)
**1982**
Chassagne-Montrachet Bachelet-Ramonet (BIB)

──────── £20.00 to £24.99 ────────

**1989**
Chassagne-Montrachet Drouhin (HUN)
Chassagne-Montrachet les Caillerets, Bachelet-Ramonet (BIB)
Meursault Charmes, Boillot (WW)
Meursault Charmes, Henri Germain (AD)
Meursault Clos de Mazeray, Prieur (WHI)
Meursault Genevrières, Jobard (AD)
Meursault Jobard (HAH)
Meursault Michelot (YF)
Puligny-Montrachet Clos de la Garenne, Drouhin (WY)
Puligny-Montrachet les Combettes, Prieur (WHI)

**1988**

Chassagne-Montrachet la Romanée, Moillard (VIC)

Chassagne-Montrachet Marquis de Laguiche (BUT)

Meursault Poruzots, Jobard (MV, BIB)

Puligny-Montrachet la Garenne, Thomas (WCL)

Puligny-Montrachet Leflaive (TW, AD, BIB)

Puligny-Montrachet les Referts, Sauzet (LOE)

**1987**

Chassagne-Montrachet Jadot (THR)

Chassagne-Montrachet Niellon (VIG)

Corton-Charlemagne Drouhin (WY)

Meursault Genevrières, Jobard (RAE)

Meursault Poruzots, Jobard (RAE, MV)

Puligny-Montrachet Champs Canet, Sauzet (BEK)

Puligny-Montrachet les Folatières, Clerc (PE)

Puligny-Montrachet les Pucelles, Leflaive (LAY)

Puligny-Montrachet les Referts, Sauzet (BEK)

**1986**

Meursault Clos du Cromin, Leflaive (BUT)

Meursault Poruzots, Germain (AUG)

Puligny-Montrachet Clerc (PE)

Puligny-Montrachet Labouré-Roi (CV)

Puligny-Montrachet les Referts, Jadot (PE)

**1983**

Chassagne-Montrachet les Embrazées, Albert Morey (BUT)

Puligny-Montrachet les Folatières, Latour (BUT)

**1982**

Meursault Charmes, Matrot (FA)

Meursault Perrières, Matrot (FA)

─────── **£25.00 to £29.99** ───────

**1989**

Meursault Charmes, Leflaive (TW)

Puligny-Montrachet Clavoillon, Leflaive (AD)

Puligny-Montrachet la Truffière, Sauzet (LOE)

Puligny-Montrachet les Perrières, Sauzet (LOE)

**1988**

Beaune Clos des Mouches, Drouhin (RAE)

Puligny-Montrachet Clavoillon, Leflaive (AMI)

Puligny-Montrachet les Combettes, Sauzet (TAN, LOE)

**1986**

Meursault Genevrières, Jobard (BUT)

Puligny-Montrachet Clavoillon, Leflaive (PE, LAY)

Puligny-Montrachet les Folatières, Bouchard Père (PEN)

**1985**

Chassagne-Montrachet Morgeot, Henri Germain (AD)

Puligny-Montrachet les Folatières, Bouchard Père (HA)

**1983**

Meursault Ampeau (CHA)

─────── **£30.00 to £39.99** ───────

**1989**

Corton-Charlemagne Bonneau du Martray (LAY, BUT)

Corton-Charlemagne Leflaive (AD)

Puligny-Montrachet Champs Canet, Sauzet (AD, YF)

Puligny-Montrachet Clavoillon, Leflaive (CB, RAE, BIB)

Puligny-Montrachet les Pucelles, Leflaive (AD)

**1988**

Bâtard-Montrachet Albert Morey (BEK)

Corton-Charlemagne Bonneau du Martray (BUT, BEK)

Corton-Charlemagne Latour (WY, LOR)

Corton-Charlemagne Rollin (RAE, BIB)

Meursault Clos de la Barre, Lafon (VIG)

Puligny-Montrachet les Combettes, Leflaive (HAY, CB)

Puligny-Montrachet les Pucelles, Leflaive (MV)

**1987**

Bâtard-Montrachet Clerc (PIP)

Bienvenues-Bâtard-Montrachet Bachelet (RAE, BIB)

Bienvenues-Bâtard-Montrachet Leflaive (TAN)

**1986**

Chassagne-Montrachet Marquis de Laguiche (BER)

Corton-Charlemagne Bouchard Père (PEN)

Corton-Charlemagne Latour (FA)

Corton-Charlemagne Leflaive (HAH)

Corton-Charlemagne Thévenot (EL)

Puligny-Montrachet Clavoillon, Leflaive (BUT)

**1985**

Chassagne-Montrachet Marquis de Laguiche (WY)

Corton-Charlemagne Latour (FA)

Puligny-Montrachet les Pucelles, Leflaive
  (FA)
Puligny-Montrachet Sauzet (WS)
**1983**
Chassagne-Montrachet Drouhin (WY)
Corton-Charlemagne Tollot-Beaut (BUT)
Puligny-Montrachet Remoissenet (GRG)

——————— £40.00 to £49.99 ———————
**1989**
Bâtard-Montrachet Gagnard-Delagrange
  (LOE)
Bâtard-Montrachet Leflaive (AD)
Bâtard-Montrachet Sauzet (LOE)
Bienvenues-Bâtard-Montrachet Clerc (YF)
Corton-Charlemagne Latour (VIG)
**1988**
Bâtard-Montrachet Gagnard-Delagrange
  (LOE, BY)
Bienvenues-Bâtard-Montrachet Clerc (WHI)
Meursault Perrières, Lafon (FA)
**1987**
Chevalier-Montrachet Chartron (AN, ROB)
**1986**
Bâtard-Montrachet Latour (WY, BUT)
Bienvenues-Bâtard-Montrachet Leflaive
  (FA, BUT)
Corton-Charlemagne Bonneau du Martray
  (GE, BUT)
**1985**
Bâtard-Montrachet Leflaive (HA)
Corton-Charlemagne Bonneau du Martray
  (BUT, VIG)
**1983**
Beaune Clos des Mouches, Drouhin (WY)
Corton-Charlemagne Bonneau du Martray
  (BO)

——————— £50.00 to £69.99 ———————
**1988**
Bâtard-Montrachet Leflaive (CB)
Chevalier-Montrachet Leflaive (AD, HAY,
  CB, REI)
Corton-Charlemagne Tollot-Beaut (YF)
Puligny-Montrachet Leflaive (BO)
**1986**
Chevalier-Montrachet Bouchard Père (PEN)
Chevalier-Montrachet les Desmoiselles,
  Latour (FA)
Corton-Charlemagne Latour (AMI, VIC, BER)
le Montrachet Latour (WY)
le Montrachet Thénard (BUT)
**1985**
Bâtard-Montrachet Latour (WY)
Corton-Charlemagne Latour (WY)

**1983**
Corton-Charlemagne Latour (BUT, PE, WY)
le Montrachet Château Herbeux (BUT)
**1982**
Chevalier-Montrachet Leflaive (FA)

——————— £70.00 to £99.99 ———————
**1989**
Chevalier-Montrachet Leflaive (BIB)
le Montrachet Thénard (WS)
**1987**
le Montrachet Gagnard-Delagrange (HAH)
le Montrachet Marquis de Laguiche (BUT)
**1986**
Chevalier-Montrachet Leflaive (BUT)
le Montrachet Marquis de Laguiche (WY)
**1982**
Bâtard-Montrachet Leflaive (ROB)

——————— £100.00 to £130.00 ———————
**1985**
le Montrachet Marquis de Laguiche (WY)
**1982**
le Montrachet Marquis de Laguiche (WY)

——————— £145.00 to £175.00 ———————
**1988**
le Montrachet Marquis de Laguiche (ROB)
**1983**
le Montrachet Marquis de Laguiche (HUN)

——————— c. £290.00 ———————
**1983**
le Montrachet Domaine de la Romanée-
  Conti (WY)

——————— £325.00 to £390.00 ———————
**1987**
le Montrachet Domaine de la Romanée-
  Conti (BUT)
**1986**
le Montrachet Domaine de la Romanée-
  Conti (BUT)

——————— c. £590.00 ———————
**1969**
le Montrachet Domaine de la Romanée-
  Conti (FA)

> *In each price band wines
> are listed in vintage order.
> Within each vintage they
> are listed in A-Z order.*

# CÔTE CHALONNAISE

## RED

──────── **Under £9.00** ────────
**1989**
Rully Drouhin (OD)
**1988**
Givry Chanson (AS)
Givry Voarick (WRI)
Mercurey Domaine du Meix-Foulot (CV)
★ Rully Clos de Bellecroix, Domaine de la
    Folie (BUT)
**1987**
Mercurey Domaine du Meix-Foulot (ROB)
Rully Bouchard Père (PEN)

──────── **£9.00 to £10.99** ────────
**1989**
Mercurey Domaine de la Croix, Jacquelet-
    Faiveley (NA, WRI)
**1988**
★ Mercurey Château de Chamirey (EL, WHI)
Mercurey Domaine de la Croix, Jacquelet-
    Faiveley (BE, TES, GRG)
Mercurey Latour (PEN)
**1986**
Mercurey les Veleys, de Launay (GE, TAN)
**1985**
★ Mercurey Domaine de la Croix,
    Jacquelet-Faiveley (AUG)
**1983**
Mercurey Château de Chamirey (GRG)
Mercurey Clos l'Évêque, Juillot (RAE)
★ Rully Domaine de l'Hermitage, Chanzy
    (BUT)

──────── **£12.00 to £15.00** ────────
**1988**
Mercurey Château de Chamirey (BER)
**1985**
Mercurey Clos des Barraults, Juillot (BUT)
Mercurey Juillot (BUT)
**1976**
★ Givry Remoissenet (BUT)

## WHITE

──────── **Under £9.00** ────────
**1990**
Montagny 1er Cru Alain Roy, Cave des
    Vignerons de Mancey (BEK)
Montagny 1er Cru, Leflaive (AD, LAY)
Montagny les Loges, Sarjeant (TAN, DAV)

Montagny Château de Davenay, Moillard
    (SAI)
Rully Marissou, Dury (RAE)
**1989**
Montagny 1er Cru Alain Roy, Cave des
    Vignerons de Mancey (NA)
Montagny 1er Cru, Cave de Buxy (GA, BYR,
    LO, PIP)
★ Montagny 1er Cru, Leflaive (BYR)
Montagny Latour (LOR, BYR)
Montagny Picard, Château de Davenay (IR)
Rully Domaine de l'Hermitage, Chanzy
    (WHI)
Rully la Chaume, Dury (RAE, THR)
Rully Protheau (CH)
**1988**
★ Montagny 1er Cru, Cave de Buxy (CV)
Montagny Château de Davenay, Moillard
    (VIN)
Montagny Latour (HOG)
**1987**
★ Rully Clos St-Jacques, Domaine de la
    Folie (BUT)
Rully la Chaume, Dury (HAY)

──────── **£9.00 to £10.99** ────────
**1990**
Mercurey Chartron et Trébuchet (AN)
Mercurey Clos Rochette, Faiveley (GRE)
Montagny Latour (CH)
Rully la Chaume, Chartron et Trébuchet
    (AN)
**1989**
Givry Ragot (ROB)
Mercurey Voarick (WRI)
Montagny Latour (PEN, WHI)
Montagny Leflaive (BUT)
Rully Grésigny, Cogny (AD)
Rully la Bergerie, Dury (BO)
**1988**
Montagny Latour (YF)
Rully Cogny (AD)
**1986**
Montagny Latour (BUT)

──────── **£11.00 to £12.99** ────────
**1990**
Mercurey Château de Chamirey, Rodet (WHI)
Mercurey Clos Rochette, Faiveley (NA)
**1986**
Rully Clos St-Jacques, Domaine de la Folie
    (BUT)

# MÂCONNAIS

## RED

### ———— Under £5.00 ————
**1991**
Mâcon Rouge Loron (EL)
**1989**
Mâcon Rouge Loron (UN)
Mâcon Rouge Pasquier-Desvignes (AUG)

### ———— c. £5.50 ————
**1990**
Mâcon-Supérieur Rouge, Cave de Buxy
(BYR)
**1989**
Mâcon-Supérieur Rouge, Cave de Buxy (BYR)

## WHITE

### ———— Under £5.00 ————
**1991**
Mâcon-Villages Cave Co-op. de Viré (GA)
**1990**
Mâcon-Villages Rodet (MAR)
Tesco Mâcon Blanc-Villages (TES)
**1989**
★ Mâcon-Lugny les Genièvres, Latour
½ bottle (HAG)
Mâcon-Villages Château de Mirande,
Loron (BO)

### ———— £5.00 to £5.99 ————
**1991**
Mâcon-Villages Cave Co-op. de Viré (CV)
St-Véran Domaine de Vignemont (PEN)
**1990**
Mâcon Blanc Clos de Condemine, Luquet
(LOR)
Mâcon Chardonnay Talmard (LAY, AD)
Mâcon-Lugny Duboeuf (BEK)
Mâcon-Prissé Duboeuf (NI)
Mâcon-Solutré Depardon (BU)
Mâcon-Villages Cave Co-op. de Viré (SAF,
CV)
Mâcon-Villages Domaine de Rochebin (BIB)
Mâcon-Villages Loron (BO, TAN)
St-Véran Cave Co-op. Prissé (TES)
St-Véran Depardon (CHA)
**1989**
Mâcon-Lugny les Genièvres, Latour (HOG)
Mâcon-Prissé Duboeuf (BEK, NI)
Mâcon-Villages Duboeuf (NI)
Mâcon-Viré Domaine des Chazelles (ASD)

### ———— £6.00 to £6.99 ————
**1991**
Mâcon la Roche Vineuse, Merlin (BIB)
Mâcon-Prissé Duboeuf (DAV)
St-Véran Duboeuf (DAV)
**1990**
Mâcon Chardonnay Talmard (TAN)
Mâcon la Roche Vineuse, Merlin (MV)
Mâcon-Lugny Duboeuf (PIP)
Mâcon-Lugny les Genièvres, Latour (LOR,
WHI, BYR, CH)
Mâcon-Prissé Cave Co-op. Prissé (HAH)
Mâcon-Prissé Duboeuf (DAV)
St-Véran Depardon (WHI, VIN)
St-Véran Domaine St-Martin, Duboeuf
(PIP)
St-Véran Duboeuf (NI, DAV, THR)
**1989**
Mâcon-Clessé Guillemot (TAN)
Mâcon-Lugny les Genièvres, Latour (YF)
Mâcon-Peronne Domaine de Mortier,
Josserand (PE, BIB)
St-Véran Duboeuf (BEK)
St-Véran Latour (HOG)
St-Véran Prissé (HAH)
St-Véran Vincent (EL)
**1988**
Mâcon-Viré Cuvée Spéciale, Bonhomme (GE)
St-Véran Cave Co-op. Prissé (CV)
**1987**
Mâcon-Lugny les Genièvres, Latour (GE)

### ———— £7.00 to £7.99 ————
**1991**
Pouilly-Fuissé la Mure, Depardon (CH)
Pouilly-Vinzelles Mathias (PIP)
**1990**
Mâcon Blanc Clos de Condemine, Luquet
(ROB)
Mâcon-Lugny les Genièvres, Latour (HIG, DAV)
St-Véran Domaine Deux Roches (HAH,
HAU)
St-Véran Domaine les Colombiers (PIP)
**1989**
Mâcon-Clessé Signoret (HAW)
Mâcon-Lugny les Genièvres, Latour (HAG)
Mâcon-Villages Domaine d'Azenay (BR)
Mâcon-Villages Ferraud (YF)
Mâcon-Viré Clos du Chapitre, Dépagneux
(LOE)
★ Pouilly-Fuissé Domaine Bourdon (THR)
St-Véran Latour (BYR)

**1988**
Mâcon-Viré Clos du Chapitre, Dépagneux (ASK)
**1985**
Pouilly-Fuissé Cave Co-op. Prissé (TES)

——————— £8.00 to £9.99 ———————
**1991**
Pouilly-Fuissé Domaine de Pouilly, Duboeuf (DAV)
**1990**
Mâcon-Clessé Thévenet (WW)
Mâcon la Roche Vineuse, Merlin (WCL)
Mâcon-Lugny les Genièvres, Latour (VIN)
Mâcon Monbellet, Goyard (WS, BIB)
Mâcon-Villages Domaine de la Bon Gran, Thévenet (AD)
Mâcon-Viré Goyard (RAE)
Pouilly-Fuissé Dépagneux (BYR)
Pouilly-Fuissé Domaine Béranger, Duboeuf (NI)
Pouilly-Fuissé Domaine de Pouilly, Duboeuf (DAV)
Pouilly-Fuissé la Mure, Depardon (WHI)
Pouilly-Loché Cave des Crus Blancs (HAW)
St-Véran Corsin (AD)
St-Véran Vincent (AD)
**1989**
Mâcon-Clessé Domaine de la Bon Gran, Thévenet (TAN)
Mâcon Monbellet, Goyard (WS)
Pouilly-Fuissé Domaine Béranger, Duboeuf (BEK, NI)
Pouilly-Fuissé la Mure, Depardon (HIG)
Pouilly-Fuissé Latour (WHI, HOG)
Pouilly-Fuissé les Vieux Murs, Loron (WRI)
Pouilly-Fuissé Loron (BO)
**1988**
Mâcon-Viré Clos du Chapitre, Dépagneux (WS)
St-Véran Vincent (HAG)
**1986**
St-Véran Corsin (BUT)
St-Véran Latour (BUT)
St-Véran Vincent (BUT)

——————— £10.00 to £14.99 ———————
**1990**
Pouilly-Fuissé les Crays, Forest (NA)
**1989**
Mâcon-Villages Domaine de la Bon Gran, Thévenet (AD)
Pouilly-Fuissé Corsin (AD)
Pouilly-Fuissé Manciat-Poncet (HAW)
Pouilly-Fuissé Vincent (BYR)

**1988**
Mâcon-Villages Domaine de la Bon Gran, Thévenet (YF)
**1986**
Pouilly-Fuissé Domaine de l'Arillière (BUT)
Pouilly-Fuissé Latour (BUT)

——————— £15.00 to £19.99 ———————
**1990**
Pouilly-Fuissé Château Fuissé, Vincent (AD)
**1989**
Pouilly-Fuissé Château Fuissé, Vincent (TAN, AD)
Pouilly-Fuissé Château Fuissé Vieilles Vignes, Vincent (LOE, SOM, AD)
**1988**
Pouilly-Fuissé Château Fuissé, Vincent (RAE)
**1984**
Pouilly-Fuissé Château Fuissé, Vincent (ROB)

——————— £20.00 to £30.00 ———————
**1988**
Pouilly-Fuissé Château Fuissé Vieilles Vignes, Vincent (BYR)
**1986**
Mâcon-Clessé Thévenet (BR)
**1985**
Pouilly-Fuissé Château Fuissé Vieilles Vignes, Vincent (BUT)
**1982**
Pouilly-Fuissé Château Fuissé Vieilles Vignes, Vincent (BUT)

——————— £45.00 to £60.00 ———————
**1979**
Pouilly-Fuissé Château Fuissé, Vincent (VIG)
**1978**
Pouilly-Fuissé Château Fuissé, Vincent (VIG)
**1962**
Pouilly-Fuissé Château Fuissé, Vincent (VIG)

# CHABLIS

## WHITE

### Under £6.00

**1991**
★ Sauvignon de St-Bris, Brocard (CH)
Sauvignon de St-Bris, Sorin (WHI)
**1989**
Sauvignon de St-Bris, Brocard (HIC)
Sauvignon de St-Bris, Domaine des
    Remparts (HOG)
**1988**
Chablis Drouhin (BU)

### £6.00 to £6.99

**1990**
Chablis Domaine de Biéville, Moreau (HOG)
★ Chablis Domaine de Colombier, Mothe
    (WHI)
Chablis la Chablisienne (WAI, MAR, VIC)
Chablis Moreau (THR)
Chablis Mothe (WHI)
Chardonnay Domaine des Remparts, Sorin
    (HIG)
Sainsbury's Chablis (SAI)
**1989**
Chablis Labouré Roi (PIP)
Sauvignon de St-Bris, Defrance (HAU, VIG)
Sauvignon de St-Bris, Labouré Roi (NA)

### £7.00 to £7.99

**1990**
Bourgogne St-Bris Chardonnay, Felix (ROB,
    BAR)
★ Chablis Brocard (OD)
Chablis Château de Maligny (BY)
Chablis Christian Adine (AN)
Chablis Domaine des Manants, Brocard (AD)
Chablis Domaine Ste-Anne, Louis Petit
    (BEK)
Chablis Drouhin (NI)
Chablis Durup (IR, THR)
Chablis Grossot (LAY)
★ Chablis Légland (BIB)
★ Chablis Louis Michel (LOE)
Chablis Simmonet-Febvre (CHA)
Chablis Vocoret (HA, BUT)
**1989**
Chablis Domaine de l'Églantière (SOM)
Chablis Domaine Ste-Claire, Brocard (CV)
Sauvignon de St-Bris, Renard (WRI)
**1988**
★ Chablis Régnard (HOG)

### £8.00 to £9.99

**1990**
Chablis 1er Cru, Adine (AN)
Chablis Bernard Defaix (RAE, PE)
Chablis Brocard (HIC)
Chablis Château de Maligny, Durup (THR)
Chablis Domaine de Biéville, Moreau (WHI)
Chablis Domaine du Valéry, Durup (TAN)
Chablis Domaine Pico Race (AN)
Chablis Domaine Servin (WRI)
Chablis Droin (HAY)
Chablis Durup (HAH)
Chablis Fèvre (BAR)
Chablis Gautheron (UN)
Chablis Hamelin (THR)
Chablis la Chablisienne (HAG)
Chablis Moreau (DAV)
Chablis Pautré (HIG)
Chablis Vocoret (WCL, YF)
**1989**
Chablis Château de Maligny (BY)
Chablis Domaine Servin (WRI)
Chablis Droin (PIP)
Chablis Latour (PEN)
Chablis Montmains, Louis Michel (LOE)
Chablis Moreau (HA)
Chablis Pautré (HIG)
Chablis Séchet, Louis Michel (LOE)
Chablis Vaillons, Simmonet-Febvre (CHA)
Chablis Vau Ligneau, Hamelin (BEK)
**1988**
Chablis Laroche (AUG)
★ Chablis Montmains, Louis Michel (LOE)
Chablis Séchet, Louis Michel (LOE)
**1987**
★ Chablis la Forêt, René Dauvissat (BUT)
**1986**
★ Chablis Fourchaume, Domaine de
    Colombier (ASD)
Chablis Labouré Roi (BYR)

### £10.00 to £11.99

**1990**
Chablis 1er Cru, Pico Race (AN)
Chablis Domaine de Vauroux (VIG)
Chablis la Forêt, René Dauvissat (TAN)
Chablis Mont de Milieu, Grossot (LAY)
Chablis Montée de Tonnerre, Domaine de
    la Tour Vaubourg (LOR)
Chablis Montmains, Légland (BIB)
Chablis Vaillons, Raveneau (HAH)
Chablis Vaillons, Vocoret (WCL)

**1989**
Chablis Fourchaume, Durup (EL)
Chablis Fourchaume, Louis Michel (LOE)
Chablis Fûts de Chêne, Grossot (LAY)
Chablis Hamelin (BO)
Chablis la Forêt, René Dauvissat (BUT)
Chablis la Forêt, Vocoret (YF)
Chablis Laroche (BYR)
Chablis Montée de Tonnerre, Louis Michel
   (LOE, OD, WHI)
Chablis Montmains, Brocard (CV)
Chablis Montmains, Laroche (GRE)
Chablis Montmains, Louis Michel (OD)
Chablis Vaillons, Fèvre (IR)
Chablis Vaillons, Moreau (HOG)
★ Chablis Vaillons, René Dauvissat (TAN)
**1988**
Chablis Montée de Tonnerre, Durup (BY)
Chablis Montmains, Louis Michel (HOG, NI)
Chablis Vaillons, Fèvre (IR)
Chablis Vaillons, Robin (BR)
Chablis Vaillons, Servin (GRE)
★ Chablis Vaudésir, Fèvre (BYR)
**1987**
Chablis Defaix (ROB)
Chablis Laroche (BYR)
★ Chablis Montée de Tonnerre, Regnard
   (HOG, GRE)
**1986**
Chablis Régnard (BUT)
Chablis Séchet, Louis Michel (BUT)

─────── **£12.00 to £13.99** ───────
**1990**
Chablis 1er Cru, Drouhin (NI)
★ Chablis Vaillons, Droin (HAY)
**1989**
Chablis Fourchaume, Fèvre (BYR, PE)
Chablis Montée de Tonnerre, Domaine
   Servin (WRI)
Chablis Montmains, Domaine Pico Race
   (VIG)
Chablis Vaillons, Droin (PIP)
**1988**
Chablis la Forêt, Pinson (BIB)
Chablis Mont de Milieu, Pinson (BIB,
   HUN)
Chablis Vaillons, Servin (WRI)
**1987**
Chablis Mont de Milieu, Pinson (WCL)
Chablis Mont de Milieu, Rémon (BOR)
Chablis Vaillons, Laroche (AUG)
**1986**
★ Chablis Bougros, Domaine de Colombier
   (ASD)

─────── **£14.00 to £16.99** ───────
**1989**
Chablis Fourchaume, Laroche (GRE)
★ Chablis les Clos, Louis Michel (LOE)
Chablis Vaudésir, Louis Michel (LOE)
**1988**
Chablis les Clos, Louis Michel (LOE)
Chablis les Clos, Pinson (MV)
**1987**
Chablis les Lys, Daniel Defaix (VIG)
Chablis Vaudésir, Louis Michel (HOG)
**1986**
Chablis Valmur, Moreau (HOG, HA)
**1985**
Chablis Fourchaume, Pic (BER)
Chablis Mont de Milieu, Pic (BER)
Chablis Vaillons, Vocoret (BUT)

─────── **£17.00 to £19.99** ───────
**1990**
Chablis Blanchots, Servin (DAV)
Chablis les Clos, Droin (RAE, HAY)
Chablis Vaudésir, Droin (TAN)
**1989**
Chablis Valmur, Droin (RAE, TAN)
**1988**
Chablis les Clos, Pinson (BIB)
★ Chablis Vaudésir, Droin (PIP)
**1987**
Chablis les Clos, Pinson (WCL)
Chablis Vaudésir, Robin (BEK)
**1986**
Chablis Blanchots, Laroche (HA)
Chablis Grenouilles, Louis Michel (BUT)
Chablis Valmur, Moreau (WHI)

─────── **£20.00 to £24.99** ───────
**1989**
Chablis Grenouilles, Droin (YF)
Chablis Laroche (PEN)
**1988**
Chablis Blanchots, Laroche (BYR, GRE)
**1987**
Chablis Blanchots, Laroche (GRE)
Chablis les Preuses, Pic (BER)

## RED

─────── **£5.00 to £7.50** ───────
**1990**
Pinot Noir de St-Bris, Brocard (AD)
**1988**
★Bourgogne Irancy, Bienvenu (HAU)
Bourgogne Irancy, Domaine Ste-Claire,
   Brocard (BEK)

# BEAUJOLAIS

## RED

**Non-vintage**
Asda Beaujolais (ASD)
Sainsbury's Beaujolais (SAI)
**1990**
Beaujolais Duboeuf (MAR)
Beaujolais-Villages Château des Vergers
 (SAI)
Beaujolais-Villages Cellier des Samsons
 (WAI)
Waitrose Beaujolais (WAI)

**1991**
★ Beaujolais-Villages Domaine de la
 Ronze (ASD)
Beaujolais-Villages Jaffre (CH)
★ Juliénas Pelletier (EL)
Morgon le Clachet, Brun (EL)
**1990**
Beaujolais Duboeuf (BYR, NI, PIP)
Beaujolais-Villages Château du Basty (OD)
Beaujolais-Villages Duboeuf (LO)
Beaujolais-Villages Cellier des Samsons (BY)
**1989**
Beaujolais Duboeuf (NI)
Beaujolais-Villages Château de Néty (EL)
**1988**
Beaujolais-Villages Domaine Chizeaux,
 Fessy (ASK)

**1991**
Beaujolais Lantignié, Domaine Joubert
 (AD)
Beaujolais-Villages Château de la Roche,
 Loron (CH)
Beaujolais-Villages Château Lacarelle
 (ASK)
★ Beaujolais-Villages Depardon (HAH)
Juliénas les Envaux, Pelletier (CHA)
Morgon le Clachet, Brun (CH, CHA)
**1990**
Beaujolais-Villages Château de la Roche,
 Loron (CH)
Beaujolais-Villages Château des Vierres,
 Duboeuf (BYR)
Beaujolais-Villages Domaine des Dîmes
 (NA)
Beaujolais-Villages Duboeuf (NI)

Beaujolais-Villages Latour (HOG)
Regnié Duboeuf (LO)
**1989**
Beaujolais-Villages Château Lacarelle
 (BYR, CV)
Beaujolais-Villages Duboeuf (NI)
Chénas Domaine de la Combe Remont,
 Duboeuf (BEK)
Juliénas Pelletier (CH)
Morgon Loron (UN)
**1988**
Beaujolais-Villages Château de Néty (GRG)

**1991**
Beaujolais-Villages Depardon (VIG)
Beaujolais-Villages Rochette (HAY)
Chiroubles Domaine de la Grosse Pierre
 (CH, CHA)
Juliénas les Envaux, Pelletier (HAH)
Moulin-à-Vent le Vivier, Brugne (EL, CH)
Regnié Braillon (VIG)
**1990**
Beaujolais Cave Beaujolais de St-Verand
 (HAW)
Beaujolais Château de Tanay (HAW)
Beaujolais-Villages Cave des Producteurs
 Juliénas (HAW)
Beaujolais-Villages Château des Vierres,
 Duboeuf (DAV)

Beaujolais-Villages Château du Basty (TAN)
Beaujolais-Villages Duboeuf (THR)
Brouilly de Pierreux, Duboeuf (BYR)
Brouilly Duboeuf (MAR)
Brouilly Large (CHA)
★ Chénas Château de Chénas (WHI)
Chénas Duboeuf (LO, PIP)
Chiroubles Château de Javernand,
 Duboeuf (BYR)
Chiroubles Dépagneux (BYR)
Chiroubles Domaine de la Grosse Pierre
 (WHI)

Côte de Brouilly Duboeuf (NI)
Juliénas Domaine de Beauvernay, Piat (BO)
Juliénas Domaine des Mouilles, Duboeuf
  (PIP)
Juliénas les Envaux, Pelletier (CHA)
★ Morgon Domaine Jean Descombes,
  Duboeuf (BEK)
Regnié Château de la Pierre, Loron (WRI)
Regnié Château de la Tour Bourdon,
  Duboeuf (PIP)
**1989**
Brouilly Château de St-Lager, Dépagneux
  (AUG)
Brouilly Loron (UN)
Chénas Domaine de Chassignol,
  Dépagneux (LOE)
Juliénas Domaine de Berthets, Dépagneux
  (BYR)
Juliénas Loron (UN)
**1988**
Brouilly Château de la Chaize, Marquis de
  Roussy de Sales (BU)
Morgon les Versauds, Dépagneux (LOE)
**1987**
Brouilly Château de la Chaize, Marquis de
  Roussy de Sales (BU)
Morgon Côte de Py, Gaget (IR)
**1986**
Juliénas Domaine de Berthets, Dépagneux
  (LOE)
**1985**
Morgon Domaine des Vieux Cèdres, Loron
  (BU)

─────── **£6.00 to £6.49** ───────
**1991**
Beaujolais Blaise Carron (HAW)
Beaujolais Garlon (HAW)
Brouilly Château de Nevers, Duboeuf (DAV)
Chiroubles la Maison des Vignerons (AD)
Fleurie Sélection Éventail, Domaine de
  Montgénas (CHA, CH)
★ Juliénas Domaine Joubert (AD)
Juliénas Pelletier (WRI)
Regnié Rochette (HAY)
St-Amour Domaine des Pins, Echallier
  (SOM)
**1990**
Beaujolais-Villages Château du Grand
  Vernay (HAW)
Beaujolais-Villages Latour (AMI)
Brouilly Château de Nevers, Duboeuf (DAV)
Brouilly Château des Tours (SOM)
Brouilly Grand Clos de Briante, Loron
  (WRI)

Brouilly Latour (HOG)
Chénas Château de Chénas (HIG, HAW)
Chiroubles Duboeuf (PIP)
Chiroubles Méziat (OD)
Fleurie la Madone, Duboeuf (BEK)
Juliénas Domaine de la Vieille Église,
  Loron (WRI)
Juliénas Domaine du Grand Cuvage,
  Duboeuf (DAV)
Morgon Aucoeur (AD)
Morgon Côte de Py, Savoye (HIC)
Morgon Domaine des Versauds, Duboeuf
  (LO)
Morgon Domaine des Vieux Cèdres, Loron
  (WRI)
Morgon Domaine Jean Descombes,
  Duboeuf (NI)
Morgon Jambon (ASD)
Morgon Janodet (MV)
Moulin-à-Vent le Vivier, Brugne (EL)
Regnié Château de Basty (OD)
St-Amour Pierre Patissier (EL)
**1989**
Beaujolais-Villages Colonge (HIC)
Fleurie Château de Fleurie, Loron (EL)
Morgon Château Gaillard (BO)
Morgon Domaine des Versauds, Duboeuf
  (LO)
Morgon les Versauds, Dépagneux (LOE)
**1988**
Chénas Château Bonnet (HOG)
Juliénas Clos des Poulettes, Loron (GRE)
Juliénas Domaine de la Seigneurie (BYR)
Juliénas les Capitans, Louis Tête (HOG)

─────── **£6.50 to £6.99** ───────
**1991**
Brouilly Château des Tours (PIP)
Brouilly Château Thivin (AD)
Chiroubles Château de Raousset (HAU)
Chiroubles Passot (WW)
Juliénas Domaine de Berthets, Dépagneux
  (ROB)
Morgon le Clachet, Brun (VIG)
**1990**
Beaujolais Cuvée Centenaire, Charmet
  (HAW)
Brouilly Château des Tours (PIP)

┌─────────────────────────────┐
│ *In each price band wines*   │
│ *are listed in vintage order.* │
│ *Within each vintage they*   │
│ *are listed in A-Z order.*   │
└─────────────────────────────┘

Chiroubles Loron (TAN)
Fleurie la Madone, Duboeuf (NI, BYR)
Morgon Domaine Jean Descombes,
    Duboeuf (PIP)
Moulin-à-Vent Brugne (CHA)
Moulin-à-Vent Domaine des Rosiers,
    Duboeuf (BYR)
Regnié Château de Basty (TAN)
Regnié Noël (HAW)
Regnié Roux (HAW)
St-Amour Domaine du Paradis (BYR)
**1989**
Beaujolais-Villages Jadot (VIC)
Brouilly Château de la Chaize, Marquis de
    Roussy de Sales (BU)
Brouilly Grand Clos de Briante, Loron (HUN)
Chiroubles Château de Javernand,
    Duboeuf (BYR)
Côte de Brouilly Château Thivin (RAE)
Côte de Brouilly Domaine de Chavannes
    (OD)
Fleurie Domaine des Quatre Vents,
    Duboeuf (BEK)
Juliénas Aujas (GRG)
Juliénas les Envaux, Pelletier (BU)
Morgon Château Gaillard (RAE)
Morgon Côte de Py, Savoye (HA)
Morgon Domaine Jean Descombes,
    Duboeuf (NI)
Morgon Fontcraine, Loron (GRE)
Moulin-à-Vent Domaine des Héritiers
    Tagent, Duboeuf (BEK)
St-Amour Château St-Amour (IR)
St-Amour Domaine du Paradis (BEK)
**1988**
Chénas Duboeuf (ROB)
Moulin-à-Vent Loron (UN)
**1987**
Moulin-à-Vent Domaine de la Tour du
    Bief, Dépagneux (LOE)
**1985**
Beaujolais Villages Duboeuf (BUT)

─────────── £7.00 to £7.49 ───────────
**1991**
Brouilly Jean Lathuilière (WCL)
Chiroubles la Maison des Vignerons (HAW)
**1990**
Brouilly Geoffray (HAW)
Brouilly Jean Lathuilière (HAW)
Brouilly Michaud (MV)
Chénas Léspinasse (HAW)
Côte de Brouilly Château du Grand
    Vernay (HAW)
Côte de Brouilly Château Thivin (HAW)

Côte de Brouilly Joubert (TAN)
Fleurie Château de Fleurie, Loron (TAN)
Fleurie Château des Deduits, Duboeuf (PIP)
Fleurie Duboeuf (THR, LO)
Fleurie Sélection Éventail, Domaine de
    Montgénas (WHI)
Juliénas Aujas
Juliénas Domaine Joubert (TAN)
Juliénas Léspinasse (HAW)
Morgon Aucoeur (HAW)
Morgon Domaine Jean Descombes,
    Duboeuf (THR)
Moulin-à-Vent le Vivier, Brugne (HIG)

**1989**
Fleurie Collin-Bourisset (BOR)
Fleurie Loron (UN)
Morgon Château Gaillard (BIB)
★ Moulin-à-Vent Domaine de la Tour du
    Bief, Dépagneux (LOE)
Moulin-à-Vent le Vivier, Brugne (WRI)
Regnié Duboeuf (ROB)
**1988**
Moulin-à-Vent Domaine de la Teppe,
    Chanut (IR)
Moulin-à-Vent Domaine de la Tour du
    Bief, Duboeuf (DAV)
St-Amour Louis Tête (HOG)

─────────── £7.50 to £7.99 ───────────
**1991**
Chiroubles Loron (ROB)
Fleurie Verpoix (ASD)
Moulin-à-Vent le Vivier, Brugne (VIG)
**1990**
Chénas Benon (HAW)
Fleurie Château de Fleurie, Loron (CH,
    WRI)
Fleurie la Madone, Duboeuf (DAV)
Fleurie Sélection Éventail, Domaine de
    Montgénas (CHA)
Juliénas Benon (HAW)
Juliénas Condemine (HAW)
Moulin-à-Vent Domaine Bruyère (OD)
Moulin-à-Vent Duboeuf (LO)
Moulin-à-Vent Janin (HAY)

**1989**
Chiroubles Louis Tête (GRE)
Côte de Brouilly Château Thivin (GRE)
Fleurie Château de Fleurie, Loron (GRE)
Fleurie Domaine des Côtes de Fontabon,
   Boulon (HA)
Fleurie la Madone, Louis Tête (HOG)
Juliénas Aujas (LAY)
Moulin-à-Vent Domaine de la Tour du
   Bief, Duboeuf (NI)
Moulin-à-Vent Domaine Lemonon, Loron
   (WRI)
St-Amour Domaine des Billards, Loron
   (GRE)
St-Amour les Bonnets, Bernard Patissier
   (PE)
**1988**
Fleurie Cave Co-op. de Fleurie (CV)
Fleurie la Roilette, Vin Dessalle (ASK)
Moulin-à-Vent Château des Jacques (AS)
Moulin-à-Vent Domaine Bruyère (LAY)
Moulin-à-Vent Domaine de la Tour du
   Bief, Duboeuf (NI)
**1987**
Moulin-à-Vent Domaine de la Tour du
   Bief, Duboeuf (NI)

――――――― £8.00 to £8.99 ―――――――
**1991**
Fleurie Michel Chignard (MV)
**1990**
Brouilly Château des Tours (HAG, ROB)
Fleurie Cave Co-op. de Fleurie (HAW)
Fleurie Colonge (BIB)
**1989**
Brouilly Château des Tours (YF)
Brouilly Domaine de Saburin (PEN)

Fleurie Château de Fleurie, Loron (HUN)
Fleurie Château du Grand Pré (YF)
Fleurie Colonge (PE, HAG)
Moulin-à-Vent Ferraud (YF)
St-Amour Domaine des Pins, Duboeuf (PIP)
**1988**
Moulin-à-Vent Domaine de la Tour du
   Bief, Duboeuf (THR)

――――――― £9.00 to £10.99 ―――――――
**1990**
Fleurie Colonge (ROB, TAN)
Moulin-à-Vent Château du Moulin-à-Vent
   (HAW)
**1989**
Moulin-à-Vent Fût de Chêne, Berrod (YF)
**1988**
Fleurie la Madone, Louis Tête (BO)
Fleurie les Garans, Latour (WY)

## WHITE

――――――――― Under £6.00 ―――――――――
**1990**
Beaujolais Blanc Duboeuf (BEK)

――――――― £6.00 to £8.50 ―――――――
**1990**
Beaujolais Blanc Charmet (HAW)
Beaujolais Blanc Château des Tours (PIP)

## ROSÉ

――――――――― c. £6.00 ―――――――――
**1990**
Beaujolais Supérieur Rosé, Cave
   Beaujolais du Bois d'Oingt (HAW)

# CHAMPAGNE

## SPARKLING WHITE

──────── Under £9.99 ────────

**Non-vintage**
Moët & Chandon ¹/2 bottle (BYR, THR, WHI, AUG)

──────── £10.00 to £11.99 ────────
**Non-vintage**
Adnams Champagne (AD)
Alexandre Bonnet Prestige (LOR)
Alfred Gratien ¹/2 bottle (WCL)
Asda Champagne (ASD)
Boizel (AUG)
Bollinger ¹/2 bottle (BYR, BUT)
Ellner (LAY)
Moët & Chandon ¹/2 bottle (TAN, OD, AN, BO)
Sainsbury's Champagne (SAI)
Tanners Reserve (TAN)
de Telmont (MAJ)
Tesco Champagne (TES)
Veuve Clicquot ¹/2 bottle (BYR, GRG, BO, ROB)
Waitrose Champagne (WAI)

──────── £12.00 to £14.99 ────────
**Non-vintage**
Alexandre Bonnet Prestige (HAY, BAR)
Ayala (MAJ)
Beerens (BIB)
Blin (OD)
Boizel Rich (AUG)
Bricout Carte Noire (THR)
★ Bruno Paillard (LOR)
Camuset Réserve (YF)
Canard-Duchêne (HOG, MAJ, GRE)
Chiquet Blanc de Blancs (LOR)
Descombes (THR)
Deutz (AN)
Duchâtel (UN)
George Goulet (SOM)
Heidsieck Dry Monopole (LO, OD)
Jacquesson Perfection (YAP)
Joseph Perrier (LO)
Lanson (HOG)
Laurent-Perrier (BIB)
Massé (BAR)
Mercier (WHI, WAI, ASD, LAY, TES, VIC, SAF)
Michel Gonet (BU)
★ Pierre Vaudon 1er Cru (HAH)
Piper Heidsieck (TES, MAJ, HOG, GRG, GA, NI, AUG)
Pommery (HOG)

de Venoge Cordon Bleu (GRG)
Veuve Clicquot ¹/2 bottle (AN)
**1986**
Sainsbury's Champagne (SAI)
**1985**
Alexandre Bonnet Prestige (LOR)
de Telmont (MAJ)
**1983**
Veuve Clicquot ¹/2 bottle (GRG, EL)
Waitrose Champagne (WAI)

──────── £15.00 to £19.99 ────────
**Non-vintage**
★ Alfred Gratien (HAY, WCL)
Besserat de Bellefon Crémant (GRE)
Billecart-Salmon (IR, WW, ASK, BYR)
★ Bollinger (HOG, HAY, GRE)
Bricout d'Or (WCL)
Bruno Paillard (BYR, BUT, ROB)
Bruno Paillard Blanc de Blancs (BEK)
Canard-Duchêne (GE, ROB, BYR, MV)
Charles Heidsieck (WAI, BO)
Comte de Robart (VIG)
Henriot Blanc de Blancs (VIC, GRG)
Jacquesson Blanc de Blancs (YAP)
Joseph Perrier (GRG, HIC, PE, BYR, TAN)
Joseph Perrier Cuvée Royal (ROB, HA)
Lanson (HA, LAY, ASD, WHI, AUG, GA, THR, TES, WAI, SAF, VIC, PE, DAV, UN, CH, YF, WRI, BYR, EL)
Laurent-Perrier (LAY, AMI, MAJ, VIC, WHI, MV, THR, OD, AD, EL, BAR, PE, YF, PEN, CHA, HAH, AN, CB)
Laurent-Perrier Ultra Brut (ASD)
★ Le Mesnil Blanc de Blancs (HAY, BIB)
★ Louis Roederer (HOG, WAI, NI, MAJ, GRE)
Louis Roederer Rich (NI)
Mercier (UN, THR, ROB, PE)
Moët & Chandon (HOG, BO, LAY, GRE, WAI, ASD, SAF, AUG, DAV, THR, TES, WHI, SAI, VIC, UN, WRI, CH, EL, HA, PE, TAN, AN)
Mumm Cordon Rouge (LO, OD, SAF, TES, GA, ASD, THR, AUG, VIC, UN)
Mumm Crémant de Cramant Blanc de Blancs (GRG)
Perrier-Jouët (GRG, REI, OD, WAI, PIP, WHI, HA, WRI)
Piper Heidsieck (OD, GRE, ASD)
Pol Roger (REI, BYR)
Pol Roger White Foil (BOR, HUN, HOG, GRE, GE, PEN, CH, MAJ, TES, ASD, THR, WRI, UN, OD)

Pommery (NA, GRE)
The Society's Champagne (WS)
Taittinger (LAY, IR, BIB, OD)
Thienot (AMI)
Veuve Clicquot (WY, HOG, BO, GRE, HAY, LO,
   WHI, LAY, GRG, MAJ, TES, OD, GA)
**1986**
Duval Leroy Fleur de Champagne (TAN)
**1985**
Ayala (ASD)
Binet Blanc de Blancs (BER)
Bollinger ½ bottle (HAL)
Bruno Paillard (LOR, BEK)
Descombes (THR)
Deutz (AN, ROB)
Ellner (LAY, DAV)
Heidsieck Dry Monopole (OD)
Jacquesson Perfection (YAP)
Joseph Perrier (HIC)
Le Mesnil Blanc de Blancs (AD)
Perrier-Jouët (OD)
Piper Heidsieck (NI)
Thienot (AMI)
**1983**
Bauget-Jouette (HIG)
Canard-Duchêne (GE, ROB)
Duchâtel (UN)
de Venoge (WHI, GRG)
**1982**
★ Billecart-Salmon Cuvée N.F. Billecart
   (ASK)
Charles Heidsieck (BO)
Piper Heidsieck (GRG)
Pommery (ROB)

─────── **£20.00 to £24.99** ───────
**Non-vintage**
Bollinger (PIP, WHI, LAY, MAJ, WCL, MV, TAN,
   WRI, BE, AD, TES, EL, WAI, CH, BUT, ASD,
   DAV, TES, SAF, HA, GRG, AUG, CB, PE, UN,
   THR, VIC, AN, BER, HIG, HAH, YF)
Charles Heidsieck (UN, BYR)
Gosset Brut Reserve (AMI)
Henriot Blanc de Blancs (TES, BE)
Lanson Red Label (AUG)
Laurent-Perrier Ultra Brut (AD, ROB)
Louis Roederer (HAY, AD, LAY, WRI, MV, HA,
   WHI, CV, WCL, BIB, AMI, HIC, TAN, EL, TES,
   CB, PE, BER, DAV, UN, THR, AN, HAG, BAR,
   HAH, VIC, WS, YF)
Moët & Chandon (CB, YF, VIN, BUT)
Mumm Crémant de Cramant Blanc de
   Blancs (ROB, VIC, YF)
Pol Roger White Foil (TAN, HAH, YF, VIN, VIG)
Taittinger (WAI, WHI, GRG, WRI, AN, UN, YF)

Veuve Clicquot (WAI, THR, BIB, WCL, DAV,
   TAN, CH, AUG, MV, UN, PE, WRI, ROB, AN, CB,
   YF, HAH, VIN)
**1986**
Moët & Chandon (WHI, EL)
**1985**
Billecart-Salmon Cuvée N.F. Billecart (WW)
Deutz Blanc de Blancs (AN)
George Goulet (PIP)
George Goulet Crémant Blanc de Blancs
   (PIP)
Joseph Perrier (GRG)
Lanson Red Label (BYR)
Laurent-Perrier (BO, CHA, AD, YF, CB)
Laurent-Perrier Ultra Brut (BYR)
Moët & Chandon (WHI, THR, TAN, EL, OD, UN,
   DAV, AN, HAG, VIC)
Mumm Cordon Rouge (OD)
Perrier-Jouët (PIP, HA, GRG, AMI, HIC)

Pol Roger (PEN, HOG, REI, OD, GRE)
Taittinger (IR, BYR)
Veuve Clicquot Gold Label (BYR)
**1983**
Bruno Paillard (BYR, BEK)
Lanson (WHI, THR, WAI, GA, VIC, PE)
Lanson Red Label (BYR)
Laurent-Perrier (BYR)
Laurent-Perrier Ultra Brut (BYR)
Moët & Chandon (CH, WRI, AUG, PE)
Taittinger (BYR, GRG)
Veuve Clicquot (HIC, HOG, GRE, CH, WHI,
   GRG, WCL)
**1982**
Canard-Duchêne (BUT)
Georges Gardet (HIC)
Perrier-Jouët (PEN)
Piper Heidsieck Sauvage (GRG)
Pol Roger (GE)
**1979**
★ Bollinger RD (VIN)
Pol Roger (GE)

─────── **£25.00 to £29.99** ───────
**Non-vintage**
Louis Roederer (VIN)
Perrier-Jouët Blason de France (PIP, AMI)

**1986**
Louis Roederer (CV)
**1985**
Billecart-Salmon (OD, BAR)
Billecart-Salmon Blanc de Blancs (WW)
Bollinger (AD, HOG, MV, WCL, GRE, WHI, TAN, PIP, EL, CH, WRI, GRG, THR, PE)
Bollinger RD (PEN, BUT, ROB)
Laurent-Perrier (LO, AN)
Louis Roederer (MAJ, BIB, MV, CV, TAN, WCL, ROB)
Louis Roederer Blanc de Blancs (LAY, NI)
Pol Roger (TAN, BYR, YF, VIN)
Taittinger (WHI)
Veuve Clicquot (MV)
**1983**
Billecart-Salmon (BYR)
Billecart-Salmon Blanc de Blancs (IR)
Bollinger (AUG)
Jacquesson Signature Cuvée de Prestige (YAP)
Louis Roederer (BYR, PEN)
Louis Roederer Blanc de Blancs (GRE)
Pol Roger (BYR)
Taittinger (VIG)
Veuve Clicquot (CB, EL, WRI, AN, PIP, THR, UN, WS, PE, BIB, HAH)
**1982**
Alfred Gratien Crémant (HAY)
Billecart-Salmon Cuvée N.F. Billecart (IR)
Pol Roger Blanc de Chardonnay (GRE)
Veuve Clicquot (GE)
**1979**
Pol Roger (BIB)
**1976**
Veuve Clicquot (FA)
**1971**
Charles Heidsieck (BUT)
**1966**
Bollinger ½ bottle (BUT)

───────── £30.00 to £39.99 ─────────
**Non-vintage**
Lanson magnum (HA, LAY, AUG, WHI, WRI)
Laurent-Perrier magnum (YF, CHA)
Moët & Chandon magnum (LAY, WAI, WRI, THR, WHI, TAN, AUG)
Pol Roger White Foil magnum (PEN)
Veuve Clicquot magnum (GRG)
**1985**
Billecart-Salmon Blanc de Blancs (BYR)
Bollinger (CB, TES, BE, HAG, TW, AN, BAR, HAH, DAV, VIN)
Deutz Cuvée de William Deutz (AN)
Heidsieck Diamant Bleu (OD)

Louis Roederer (CB)
Perrier-Jouët Belle Époque (BY)
Pol Roger (BER)
Pol Roger Blanc de Chardonnay (REI, PEN, AMI, VIN)
**1983**
Alfred Gratien (WS, WCL)
Billecart-Salmon Blanc de Blancs (BYR)
Bollinger (VIC)
Dom Ruinart Blanc de Blancs (BAR)
Louis Roederer Blanc de Blancs (PEN)
Perrier-Jouët Belle Époque (HA, GRG)
Taittinger (YF)
**1982**
Dom Ruinart Blanc de Blancs (HAH)
Pol Roger Blanc de Chardonnay (GE, ROB)
**1981**
Dom Ruinart Blanc de Blancs (VIC)
Louis Roederer Cristal (BO)
**1979**
Bollinger RD (BO)
Bruno Paillard (BUT)
Lanson magnum (BO)
Pol Roger (BUT)
Pol Roger Cuvée Sir Winston Churchill (GRE)
**1976**
Bruno Paillard (BUT)
Krug (BUT)
Laurent-Perrier Millésime Rare (CHA)
Taittinger Comtes de Champagne Blanc de Blancs (BUT)
**1975**
Bruno Paillard (BUT)
**1969**
Bruno Paillard (BUT)

───────── £40.00 to £49.99 ─────────
**Non-vintage**
Bollinger magnum (LAY, GRG, TAN, CH, HA, BUT, AD)
Dom Pérignon (HOG)
Krug Grande Cuvée (BO, HUN)
Laurent-Perrier Cuvée Grande Siècle (HAG)
Moët & Chandon magnum (AUG)
Pol Roger White Foil magnum (WRI, ROB)
**1985**
Louis Roederer Cristal (MAJ)
Moët & Chandon magnum (UN)
Perrier-Jouët Belle Époque (PIP, WRI, WHI, EL, OD, HAG, GRE, TES, BE)
Pol Roger Cuvée Sir Winston Churchill (HIC)
Taittinger Comtes de Champagne Blanc de Blancs (LAY)

**1983**
Dom Pérignon (WY, CV)
Dom Ruinart (PE)
Louis Roederer Cristal magnum (FA)
Perrier-Jouët Belle Époque (WHI, EL, PEN, AD)
Taittinger Comtes de Champagne Blanc de Blancs (IR, BYR)
Veuve Clicquot la Grande Dame (VIC)
Veuve Clicquot magnum (GRG)

**1982**
Bollinger RD (WCL, PIP, GRE, GRG, ROB)
Dom Ruinart Blanc de Blancs (VIG)
Pol Roger Cuvée Sir Winston Churchill (PEN, GE)
Pol Roger Cuvée Sir Winston Churchill magnum (REI)
Taittinger Comtes de Champagne Blanc de Blancs (HAH)

**1981**
Bollinger RD (CH)
Taittinger Comtes de Champagne Blanc de Blancs (HAG)

**1979**
Bollinger Année Rare RD (BUT)
Bollinger RD (TAN, AD, HIG, YF)

**1976**
Bollinger RD (BUT)

**1971**
Piper Heidsieck (BUT)

--------- £50.00 to £59.99 ---------
**Non-vintage**
Krug Grande Cuvée (HA, MV, VIC, AMI, REI, BYR, BUT, CH, LAY, EL, WHI, BAR, AD)
Laurent-Perrier Cuvée Grande Siècle (AD, EL, CB, CHA, YF)

**1986**
Louis Roederer Cristal (LAY)

**1985**
Bollinger magnum (TAN)
Dom Pérignon (DAV)
Louis Roederer Cristal (WCL, MV, NI, BIB, EL, CV, PEN, WHI, THR, WRI)
Perrier-Jouët Belle Époque (VIN)
Taittinger Comtes de Champagne Blanc de Blancs (WHI)

**1983**
Dom Pérignon (HA, BIB, LAY, EL, TAN, LO, ROB, PE, WHI, THR, BY, HAG, OD, UN, CB, WRI, PEN, DAV, HAH, AMI, BYR, AN)
Louis Roederer Cristal (BO, BYR, GRE, TAN, AD)
Taittinger Comtes de Champagne Blanc de Blancs (WHI, ROB, AN)
Veuve Clicquot la Grande Dame (ROB)

**1982**
Bollinger Tradition RD (BIB)
Dom Pérignon (BUT, TES, WHI, AUG)
George Goulet Cuvée de Centenaire (PIP)
Krug (FA)
Pol Roger Cuvée Sir Winston Churchill (TAN, ROB)
Salon le Mesnil (CB)
Taittinger Collection Artist's Label (GE)
Taittinger Comtes de Champagne Blanc de Blancs (BUT, GRG)

**1979**
Bollinger RD (VIN)
Louis Roederer Cristal (WY)

**1975**
Bollinger (VIG)

**1973**
Dom Pérignon (WY)

--------- £60.00 to £74.99 ---------
**Non-vintage**
Krug Grande Cuvée (PE, PEN, TAN, CB, AUG, YF, BIB, HAH, AN, ROB, VIN)

**1985**
Louis Roederer Cristal (OD, CB, HA, ROB, GRG, LO, AN, PE, BAR)

**1983**
Dom Pérignon (VIC, YF, VIN, VIG)
Louis Roederer Cristal (AUG, HAH, AMI, YF, VIN)
Taittinger Comtes de Champagne Blanc de Blancs (YF)

**1982**
Krug (MV, CH, AUG, LAY, WHI, WS, OD, AD, TAN, CB, BER)
Taittinger Collection Artist's Label (VIG)

**1981**
Krug (TW)
Taittinger Collection Artist's Label (VIG)

**1980**
Krug Clos du Mesnil Blanc de Blancs (BO)

**1979**
Krug (REI, GRE)

**1978**
Dom Pérignon (WY)
**1975**
Bollinger Année Rare RD (TAN, BUT)
Bollinger RD (VIG)
**1973**
Bollinger Année Rare RD (AD)
**1970**
Bollinger magnum (BUT)
**1947**
Pommery (WY)

──────── £75.00 to £99.99 ────────

**Non-vintage**
Bollinger jeroboam (TAN, LAY)
Pol Roger White Foil jeroboam (WRI)
**1985**
Taittinger Collection Artist's Label (ROB)
**1982**
Bollinger Vieilles Vignes Françaises, Blanc de Noirs (GRE)
Krug (BIB, DAV, HAH, ROB, YF, VIN)
Taittinger Collection Artist's Label (ROB)
**1981**
Krug (BAR)
**1980**
Dom Pérignon magnum (WY)
**1976**
Krug (TW)
**1949**
Louis Roederer (WY)
**1978**
Dom Pérignon (BIB)
Taittinger Collection Artist's Label (GRG)
**1975**
Dom Pérignon (ROB)
Krug (TW)
**1971**
Dom Pérignon (WY, FA)
**1969**
Dom Pérignon (VIG)
**1966**
Krug (BIB)
**1929**
Mumm Cordon Rouge (BUT)

──────── £100.00 to £120.00 ────────

**Non-vintage**
Laurent-Perrier Cuvée Grande Siècle magnum (CHA)
Lanson jeroboam (WRI)
Krug magnum (BUT)
**1983**
Dom Pérignon magnum (ROB)

**1979**
Pol Roger Cuvée Sir Winston Churchill magnum (VIN)
**1964**
Dom Pérignon (WY)
**1961**
Krug (FA)
**1955**
Dom Pérignon (WY)
**1949**
Krug (WY)

──────── £130.00 to £165.00 ────────

**1982**
Krug Clos du Mesnil Blanc de Blancs (ROB)
Krug magnum (BUT, YF)
**1981**
Krug Clos du Mesnil Blanc de Blancs (YF)
**1980**
Krug Clos du Mesnil Blanc de Blancs (GRE)
**1979**
Krug Clos du Mesnil Blanc de Blancs (HUN)
**1955**
Dom Pérignon (BIB)

──────── £195.00 to £205.00 ────────

**Non-vintage**
Pol Roger White Foil methuselah (WRI, PEN)
**1973**
Krug Collection (ROB)

──────── c. £275.00 ────────

**Non-vintage**
Pol Roger White Foil salmanazar (PEN, WRI)

──────── c. £530.00 ────────

**1969**
Bollinger Tradition RD (FA)

## SPARKLING ROSÉ

──────── Under £14.99 ────────

**Non-vintage**
Alexandre Bonnet Prestige (LOR, HAY)
Sainsbury's Champagne Rosé (SAI)
de Telmont (MAJ)
Waitrose Champagne Rosé (WAI)

──────── £15.00 to £19.99 ────────

**Non-vintage**
Alexandre Bonnet Prestige (WCL)
Bauget-Jouette (HIG)
Billecart-Salmon (ASK)

Bruno Paillard (LOR, BYR)
★ Canard-Duchêne (GE, ROB, MAJ, WHI)
Charbaut (PEN)
Jacquart (MV)
Jacquesson (YAP)
Lanson (WHI, BYR)
Mercier (ROB, THR, UN, BYR)
Bruno Paillard (BEK)
Joseph Perrier Cuvée Royale (GRG)
Piper Heidsieck (NI)
Pommery (ROB)
Tanners Reserve (TAN)
**1985**
George Goulet (SOM)
**1982**
Piper Heidsieck (GRG)

──────── £20.00 to £29.99 ────────
**Non-vintage**
Billecart-Salmon (IR, OD, WW, BAR, BYR, ASK)
Bricout (WCL)
Canard Duchêne (BUT)
Lanson (LAY, HA, PE, VIC, THR, UN)
Laurent-Perrier (REI, AMI, MV, WHI, LAY,
   MAJ, UN, OD, CHA, THR, TAN, BO, CB, EL,
   PEN, AUG, ROB, BIB, GRE, WRI, AN, LO, YF)
Louis Roederer (BO, BAR, NI, BIB)
Veuve Clicquot (VIC)
**1986**
Louis Roederer (WHI)
**1985**
Bollinger (TAN)
Deutz (AN, ROB)
George Goulet (PIP)
Moët & Chandon (WHI, UN)
Pol Roger (WRI, ROB)
Veuve Clicquot (BYR)
**1983**
Moët & Chandon (WHI)
Veuve Clicquot (GE, BYR, GRE, GRG, BO)
**1982**
Pol Roger (GE, OD, PEN)

──────── £30.00 to £39.99 ────────
**1985**
Bollinger (GRG)
Perrier-Jouët Belle Époque (GRG)
**1983**
Bollinger (TES, BE)
Veuve Cliquot (ROB)
**1982**
Perrier-Jouët Belle Époque (PIP)
Pol Roger (YF)
**1981**
Taittinger Comtes de Champagne (FA)

──────── £40.00 to £49.99 ────────
**Non-vintage**
Krug (BO)
Laurent-Perrier magnum (CHA, YF)
**1985**
Taittinger Comtes de Champagne (IR)
**1982**
Perrier-Jouët Belle Époque (PEN)
Taittinger Comtes de Champagne (IR)
**1981**
Dom Ruinart (GE)

──────── £50.00 to £65.00 ────────
**1985**
Taittinger Comtes de Champagne (WHI)
**1983**
Taittinger Comtes de Champagne (WHI,
   BIB, YF)

──────── £120.00 to £150.00 ────────
**Non-vintage**
Dom Pérignon (LO)
Krug Grande Cuvée (WHI)
**1982**
Dom Pérignon (HA, FA, BIB)
**1980**
Dom Pérignon (FA)

──────── c. £340.00 ────────
**1982**
Dom Pérignon magnum (ROB)

## STILL WHITE

──────── £15.00 to £17.99 ────────
**Non-vintage**
Laurent-Perrier Blanc de Chardonnay
   Coteaux Champenois (CHA, YF)
Ruinart Coteaux Champenois Chardonnay
   (VIC)

──────── c. £21.00 ────────
**Non-vintage**
Moët & Chandon Saran Nature Coteaux
   Champenois (AN)

## STILL RED

──────── £15.00 to £17.00 ────────
**Non-vintage**
Laurent-Perrier Pinot Franc, Cuvée de
   Pinot Noir, Coteaux Champenois (CHA)
**1982**
Bollinger Ay Rouge la Côte aux Enfants
   Coteaux Champenois (GRE)

# NORTHERN RHÔNE

## RED

──────── **Under £5.00** ────────

**Non-vintage**
Sainsbury's Crozes-Hermitage (SAI)
**1989**
Crozes-Hermitage Cave des Clairmonts
(WAI)
Crozes-Hermitage Jaboulet (OD)
**1988**
★ Crozes-Hermitage Cave des Clairmonts
(WAI)

──────── **£5.00 to £6.99** ────────
**1989**
Crozes-Hermitage Chapoutier (TAN)
Crozes-Hermitage Delas (AN)
Crozes-Hermitage Domaine de Thalabert,
Jaboulet (HOG)
Crozes-Hermitage Domaine des Entrefaux
(PIP, ASK, BY)
Crozes-Hermitage Domaine des
Remizières, Desmeure (DAV, RAE)
**1988**
Crozes-Hermitage Delas (AUG, CV, PEN)
★ Crozes-Hermitage Domaine de
Thalabert, Jaboulet (LOE, VIC)
Crozes-Hermitage Jaboulet (HOG, LOE, BYR)
Crozes-Hermitage Pascal (LO)
St-Joseph Cave Co-op. Agricole de St
Désirat-Champagne (WAI)
**1986**
Crozes-Hermitage Chapoutier (GRG)
Crozes-Hermitage Domaine de Thalabert,
Jaboulet (HOG, ASK, HAY)
St-Joseph Cave Co-op. Agricole de St
Désirat-Champagne (YAP)
★ St-Joseph le Grand Pompée, Jaboulet
(LOE, HOG)
**1985**
Crozes-Hermitage Jaboulet (VIC)
Crozes-Hermitage Pascal (CH)

──────── **£7.00 to £8.99** ────────
**1990**
Crozes-Hermitage Graillot (OD, YAP, BY)
St-Joseph Coursodon (WR, BOT)
**1989**
Cornas Delas (BO)
Crozes-Hermitage les Meysonniers,
Chapoutier (HAU)
St-Joseph Courbis (BUT)

**1988**
Crozes-Hermitage Domaine des
Remizières, Desmeure (WCL)
Crozes-Hermitage les Meysonniers,
Chapoutier (AD)
St-Joseph Delas (PEN)
★ St-Joseph Grippat (YAP)
St-Joseph Larmes du Père, Paret (ROB)
St-Joseph le Grand Pompée, Jaboulet (LOE,
SAI, VIC, BYR)
**1987**
Cornas Delas (PEN, AN)
Cornas Jaboulet (LOE)
Crozes-Hermitage Domaine des
Remizières, Desmeure (PE)
**1986**
Cornas Jaboulet (HOG)
St-Joseph Deschants, Chapoutier (BYR)
**1985**
Cornas Jaboulet (ASK)
Crozes-Hermitage Domaine de Thalabert,
Jaboulet (HOG)
St-Joseph Deschants, Chapoutier (BUT)
St-Joseph le Grand Pompée, Jaboulet (HOG)
**1983**
Crozes-Hermitage Domaine des
Remizières, Desmeure (BUT)
★ St-Joseph Clos de l'Arbalestrier,
Florentin (WCL)
**1982**
St-Joseph Clos de l'Arbalestrier, Florentin
(BAR)

──────── **£9.00 to £11.99** ────────
**1990**
St-Joseph Deschants, Chapoutier (HAU)
St-Joseph Grippat (YAP)
**1989**
Cornas Verset (BUT)
Côte-Rôtie Delas (BO)
St-Joseph Grippat (BYR)
**1988**
★ Cornas de Barjac (TAN)
Cornas Michel (YAP)
**1987**
Cornas Clape (YAP)
Cornas Verset (WCL, RAE)
Côte-Rôtie Champet (YAP)
Côte-Rôtie Delas (AN, PEN, SAI)
Hermitage la Chapelle, Jaboulet (LOE)
St-Joseph Clos de l'Arbalestrier, Florentin
(DAV, RAE)

**1986**
Cornas Clape (BUT)
Cornas de Barjac (BUT, LAY, HA)
Cornas Verset (HAY, BUT, BIB)
Côte-Rôtie Delas (AUG)
Hermitage la Sizeranne, Chapoutier (BYR)
**1985**
Cornas de Barjac (BUT)
Hermitage Sorrel (BIB, BUT)
St-Joseph Réserve Personnelle, Jaboulet
   (LOE)
**1984**
Côte-Rôtie Delas (HAG)
Hermitage la Chapelle, Jaboulet (LAY)
**1983**
Côte-Rôtie Gérin (CV)
Crozes-Hermitage Domaine de Thalabert,
   Jaboulet (BUT, HOG, LOE)
Hermitage Domaine des Remizières (BUT)
Hermitage Jaboulet (LOE)
Hermitage la Sizeranne, Chapoutier (HOG)

——————— **£12.00 to £14.99** ———————
**1989**
Côte-Rôtie Burgaud (BUT)
Côte-Rôtie Champet (YAP)
Hermitage Sorrel (BIB)
**1988**
Cornas Clape (BUT, YAP, OD)
Côte-Rôtie Delas (CV)
★ Côte-Rôtie Jamet (BYR)
**1987**
Côte-Rôtie Barge (GE)
Côte-Rôtie Brune et Blonde, Guigal (OD)
Côte-Rôtie les Jumelles, Jaboulet (LOE)
Hermitage Chave (YAP, ROB)
**1986**
Côte-Rôtie Barge (MV, RAE)
Côte-Rôtie Champet (OD, WAI)
Côte-Rôtie Côte Blonde la Garde,
   Dervieux-Thaize (WCL)
Côte-Rôtie Jamet (BIB)
★ Hermitage Chave (OD)
Hermitage Domaine des Remizières (RAE,
   BUT, WCL)
Hermitage Marquise de la Tourette, Delas
   (BYR)
**1985**
Cornas Michel (LAY)
Côte-Rôtie Brune et Blonde, Guigal (YF, BO,
   FA)
Côte-Rôtie Chapoutier (LAY, BUT)
Hermitage Desmeure (BIB)
Hermitage Guigal (FA)
St-Joseph Grippat (AD)

**1983**
Côte-Rôtie Chapoutier (HOG, BO, BUT)
Côte-Rôtie les Jumelles, Jaboulet (BYR)
Hermitage de Vallouit (LAY)
**1982**
Côte-Rôtie les Jumelles, Jaboulet (HOG)

——————— **£15.00 to £19.99** ———————
**1990**
Cornas Clape (YAP)
Côte-Rôtie Burgaud (YAP)
Côte-Rôtie Champet (YAP)
Côte-Rôtie Jasmin (YAP)
Hermitage Grippat (YAP)
**1989**
Côte-Rôtie Chapoutier (AD, HAU)
Hermitage Grippat (YAP)
Hermitage la Chapelle, Jaboulet (HOG, OD)
**1988**
Côte-Rôtie Barge (MV)
Côte-Rôtie Brune et Blonde, Guigal (AD, NI)
Côte-Rôtie les Jumelles, Jaboulet (HOG, AD)
Hermitage Guigal (BY, AD)
Hermitage la Chapelle, Jaboulet (LOE, HOG,
   MV, VIC)
Hermitage la Sizeranne, Chapoutier (AD)
Hermitage Sorrel (BY)
**1987**
Côte-Rôtie Brune et Blonde, Vidal-Fleury
   (GRG)

Côte-Rôtie Côte Brune, Gentaz-Dervieux
   (RAE)
Côte-Rôtie Guigal (BE, TES, TAN)
**1986**
Côte-Rôtie Côte Brune, Gentaz-Dervieux
   (BUT, RAE)
Hermitage Guigal (OD, TES, BE)
Hermitage la Chapelle, Jaboulet (HOG, LOE,
   MV, HAY, BYR, VIC, WHI, AUG, AD)
**1985**
Cornas Clape (BUT)
Cornas de Barjac (ROB)
Côte-Rôtie Jamet (BUT)
Côte-Rôtie les Jumelles, Jaboulet (RAE,
   HAG)

**1983**

Côte-Rôtie Brune et Blonde, Guigal (FA, HAG, GE, HA)

Côte-Rôtie les Jumelles, Jaboulet (BUT, VIG, WS)

Hermitage Guigal (PE, AD, NI)

**1982**

Côte-Rôtie Champet (VIG)

Côte-Rôtie Jasmin (GE)

Hermitage Guigal (BAR)

**1980**

Côte-Rôtie Chapoutier (GRG)

Côte-Rôtie les Jumelles, Jaboulet (WHI)

─────── **£20.00 to £29.99** ───────

**1990**

Hermitage Chave (YAP)

Hermitage la Chapelle, Jaboulet (AD, CB)

**1989**

Côte-Rôtie les Jumelles, Jaboulet (CB)

Hermitage Chave (AD)

Hermitage Grippat (BO)

**1988**

Côte-Rôtie Chapoutier (VIG)

Hermitage Grippat (BYR)

**1985**

Côte-Rôtie Burgaud (BUT)

Hermitage Chave (BUT)

Hermitage la Chapelle, Jaboulet (HAY, LAY, PIP, BUT, AD, LOE, ROB)

**1982**

Hermitage Chave (BIB, GE)

Hermitage la Chapelle, Jaboulet (HOG, WW, BAR)

**1981**

Hermitage Chave (REI)

Hermitage Guigal (BUT)

**1979**

Hermitage Guigal (BUT)

Hermitage la Chapelle, Jaboulet (GRG)

**1976**

Hermitage la Chapelle, Jaboulet (FA)

─────── **£30.00 to £39.99** ───────

**1987**

Côte-Rôtie la Landonne Côte Brune, Guigal (BE, TES)

Côte-Rôtie la Mouline Côte Blonde, Guigal (BE, TES)

**1983**

Hermitage la Chapelle, Jaboulet (BUT)

**1979**

Côte-Rôtie Brune et Blonde, Guigal (VIG)

**1978**

Côte-Rôtie les Jumelles, Jaboulet (VIG)

─────── **£40.00 to £60.00** ───────

**1986**

Côte-Rôtie la Landonne Côte Brune, Guigal (TES, BE)

**1983**

Hermitage la Chapelle, Jaboulet (GRG, LOE, AD)

**1978**

Côte-Rôtie Brune et Blonde, Guigal (VIG)

Côte-Rôtie Jasmin (REI)

Côte-Rôtie la Chevalière d'Ampuis, Jasmin (BUT)

**1971**

Côte-Rôtie les Jumelles, Jaboulet (VIG)

**1964**

Cornas Jaboulet (WS)

**1962**

Côte-Rôtie les Jumelles, Jaboulet (REI)

─────── **£65.00 to £80.00** ───────

**1978**

Hermitage Chave (BUT)

Hermitage la Chapelle, Jaboulet (MV, FA)

**1972**

Hermitage la Chapelle, Jaboulet (BIB)

─────── **c. £93.50** ───────

**1969**

Hermitage la Chapelle, Jaboulet (FA)

─────── **c. £176.50** ───────

**1976**

Côte-Rôtie la Mouline Côte Blonde, Guigal (FA)

## WHITE

─────── **Under £7.00** ───────

**1990**

Crozes-Hermitage Domaine des Entrefaux (PIP)

Crozes-Hermitage la Mule Blanche, Jaboulet (LOE)

**1989**

Crozes-Hermitage Domaine des Clairmonts (YAP)

Crozes-Hermitage Domaine des Entrefaux (BY)

Crozes-Hermitage la Mule Blanche, Jaboulet (HOG)

**1986**

Crozes-Hermitage la Mule Blanche, Jaboulet (LAY)

**1985**

St-Joseph Chapoutier (BER)

─────── **£7.00 to £8.99** ───────

**1990**
St-Joseph Courbis (BUT)
**1989**
St-Joseph Grippat (YAP)
**1988**
Crozes-Hermitage Domaine des Remizières
  (RAE)
St-Joseph Courbis (PIP)
St-Joseph le Grand Pompée, Jaboulet (HA)


─────── **£9.00 to £11.99** ───────

**1989**
Côtes du Rhône Viognier, Dumazet (BIB)
Hermitage la Tourette Delas (PEN)
**1988**
Hermitage Chante-Alouette, Chapoutier
  (TAN, BER)
**1986**
St-Joseph Clos de l'Arbalestrier, Florentin
  (RAE)
**1984**
Hermitage Domaine des Remizières (PE)


─────── **£12.00 to £15.99** ───────

**1990**
Hermitage Grippat (YAP)
**1988**
Hermitage Chevalier de Stérimberg,
  Jaboulet (LOE)
Hermitage Guigal (BE)
Hermitage les Rocoules, Sorrel (BY)
**1987**
Condrieu Delas (AN)
Hermitage Chevalier de Stérimberg,
  Jaboulet (WHI, VIG)
Hermitage les Rocoules, Sorrel (BIB)
**1986**
Hermitage Chante-Alouette, Chapoutier
  (GRG)
Hermitage Guigal (BO, TES, BE)
**1985**
Hermitage Chevalier de Stérimberg,
  Jaboulet (LOE, TAN, HAG)
**1983**
Hermitage Domaine des Remizières (RAE)


─────── **£16.00 to £19.99** ───────

**1990**
Condrieu Château du Rozay Cuvée
  Ordinaire (YAP)
Condrieu Guigal (AD, MV)
Condrieu Vernay (YAP)
Hermitage Chevalier de Stérimberg,
  Jaboulet (VIG)


**1989**
Condrieu Barge (MV, RAE)
Condrieu Delas (BO, PEN)
Condrieu Guigal (MV, BE, TES)
Hermitage Chave (YAP)
Hermitage Grippat (BYR)
**1988**
Condrieu Barge (MV)
Condrieu Guigal (BUT)
Condrieu Pinchon (MV)
Hermitage Chave (YAP, ROB)
**1985**
Condrieu Dumazet (BUT)
Hermitage les Rocoules, Sorrel (BUT)
St-Joseph Clos de l'Arbalestrier, Florentin
  (BUT)


─────── **£20.00 to £24.99** ───────

**1990**
Condrieu Vernay (BYR, HAG)
**1989**
Condrieu Château du Rozay (BYR)
Condrieu Jurie des Camiers (REI)
Condrieu Vernay (EL, BYR)
**1985**
Hermitage Chave (BUT)
**1983**
Hermitage Guigal (VIG)


─────── **£25.00 to £29.99** ───────

**1990**
Condrieu Coteau de Vernon, Vernay (YAP)
**1974**
Condrieu Delas (VIG)


─────── **£30.00 to £45.00** ───────

**1990**
Château Grillet (YAP)
**1989**
Château Grillet (YAP)
**1988**
Condrieu Vernay (YF)
**1987**
Condrieu Coteau de Vernon, Vernay (ROB)
**1982**
Château Grillet (VIG)
**1980**
Château Grillet (YF)
**1979**
Hermitage Chante-Alouette, Chapoutier
  (VIG)


─────── **c. £68.00** ───────

**1976**
Château Grillet (REI)

# SOUTHERN RHÔNE

## RED

─────── Under £3.00 ───────

**Non-vintage**
Asda Coteaux du Tricastin (ASD)
Asda Côtes du Rhône (ASD)
Sainsbury's Vin de Pays de l'Ardèche (SAI)
Tesco Côtes du Rhône (TES)
**1990**
Côtes du Ventoux la Falaise (BYR)
Waitrose Côtes du Rhône (WAI)

─────── £3.00 to £3.99 ───────

**Non-vintage**
Sainsbury's Côtes du Rhône-Villages (SAI)
**1990**
Côtes du Rhône Domaine de la Renjardière
  (EL)
Vin de Pays des Coteaux de l'Ardèche,
  Duboeuf (BEK)
**1989**
Côtes du Rhône Château du Bois de la
  Garde, Mousset (ASD)
Côtes du Ventoux la Vieille Ferme (WHI, MV)
Côtes du Ventoux Pascal (LO)
Sainsbury's Côtes du Ventoux (SAI)
Vin de Pays de Vaucluse, Domaine de
  l'Ameillaud (AUG)
**1988**
Côtes du Rhône Valréas, Bouchard (GRG)
★ Côtes du Ventoux Jaboulet (HOG, OD)
Côtes du Ventoux la Falaise (GRG)
Côtes du Ventoux Pascal (LO)

─────── £4.00 to £4.99 ───────

**1991**
Côtes du Rhône Domaine Apollinaire (SAI)
Vin de Pays des Coteaux de l'Ardèche,
  Duboeuf (DAV)
**1990**
Coteaux du Tricastin Domaine de
  Grangeneuve (ASD)
Côtes du Rhône Caves des Vignerons de
  Vacqueyras (TAN)
★ Côtes du Rhône Château du Grand
  Moulas (LAY, TAN, CV)
Côtes du Rhône Domaine St-Gayan (YAP)
★ Côtes du Rhône Parallèle 45, Jaboulet
  (NI)
Côtes du Rhône-Villages Château du
  Grand Moulas (LAY)
Côtes du Rhône-Villages Rasteau (CV)

**1989**
Côtes du Rhône Parallèle 45, Jaboulet
  (HOG, LOE)
Côtes du Rhône Puyméras (YAP)
Côtes du Rhône Valréas, Bouchard (WS)
Côtes du Rhône-Villages Cairanne,
  Thompson (AN)
Côtes du Rhône-Villages Rasteau (BYR, CV)
**1988**
★ Côtes du Rhône Cuvée Personnelle,
  Pascal (LO)
★ Côtes du Rhône Guigal (BO, HAY, OD)
Côtes du Rhône-Villages Rasteau (OD)
Côtes du Ventoux la Vieille Ferme (YF)
Lirac la Fermade, Domaine Maby (LOR)
Vacqueyras Jaboulet (HOG, AUG)
**1987**
Lirac la Fermade, Domaine Maby (LO)
**1986**
Côtes du Rhône Cuvée Personnelle, Pascal
  (ASK)
Côtes du Rhône Jaume (WS)
Côtes du Rhône Parallèle 45, Jaboulet
  (LOE)
Lirac les Queyrades, Mejan (AUG)
**1985**
Côtes du Rhône Cuvée Personnelle, Pascal
  (LOR, WW, LO)
**1980**
Côtes du Rhône Parallèle 45, Jaboulet
  (LOE)

─────── £5.00 to £6.99 ───────
**1990**
Côtes du Rhône-Villages Cuvée de l'Ecu,
  Château du Grand Moulas (AD)
**1989**
Châteauneuf-du-Pape les Arnévels (TES)
Châteauneuf-du-Pape Quiot (MAR)
Côtes du Rhône Guigal (AD)
Côtes du Rhône-Villages Domaine Ste-
  Anne (TAN)
Côtes du Rhône-Villages Jaboulet (LOE)
Côtes du Rhône-Villages Rasteau Domaine
  la Soumade (WHI, PIP)
Lirac Sabon (PIP)
Vacqueyras Caves Bessac (EL)
Vacqueyras Domaine le Clos des Cazeaux
  (HAU)
Vacqueyras Domaine le Sang des Cailloux
  (PIP)
Vacqueyras Pascal (DAV)

**1988**

Côtes du Rhône Château Redortier (PE)

Côtes du Rhône Domaine la Garrigue (HIC)

Côtes du Rhône Guigal (TES, BE, TES, BUT, NI, MV, BAR, LAY, BY, YF)

Côtes du Rhône-Villages Jaboulet (LOE)

Gigondas Domaine du Grand Montmirail (YAP, DAV)

Lirac Domaine de Castel Oualou (GRE)

Lirac les Queyrades, Mejan (AD, TAN)

Vacqueyras Cuvée Spéciale, Pascal (VIN)

Vacqueyras Domaine de la Couroulu (PE)

Vacqueyras Domaine la Garrigue (HIC)

**1987**

Côtes du Rhône-Villages Domaine Ste-Anne (HA)

**1986**

Côtes du Rhône-Villages Château la Couranconne (BIB)

Côtes du Rhône-Villages Jaboulet (LOE)

**1985**

Côtes du Rhône-Villages Jaboulet (LOE)

Côtes du Rhône-Villages Rasteau Domaine la Soumade (HAG)

Gigondas Domaine du Grand Montmirail (WW, ASK)

Lirac la Fermade, Domaine Maby (YAP)

Vacqueyras Pascal (YAP)

Vacqueyras Sélection Maître de Chais, Combe (ASK)

**1983**

Vacqueyras Jaboulet (LOE)

───── **£7.00 to £8.99** ─────

**1990**

Châteauneuf-du-Pape Domaine de la Solitude (BYR)

Châteauneuf-du-Pape Domaine Font de Michelle (THR)

Châteauneuf-du-Pape Domaine la Roquette (PIP)

Côtes du Rhône Coudelet de Beaucastel (MV, ROB, WCL)

Gigondas Jaboulet (VIG)

Vacqueyras Jaboulet (CB, VIG)

**1989**

★ Châteauneuf-du-Pape Château des Fines Roches (ASD)

Châteauneuf-du-Pape Delas (BO)

Châteauneuf-du-Pape Domaine Brunel (SAI)

Châteauneuf-du-Pape Domaine de la Solitude (GA)

Châteauneuf-du-Pape Domaine de Mont-Redon (EL)

★ Châteauneuf-du-Pape Domaine du Vieux Télégraphe (LAY)

Châteauneuf-du-Pape Vieux Donjon (YAP)

Côtes du Rhône Coudelet de Beaucastel (ROB)

Côtes du Rhône-Villages Cuvée St-Gervais, Domaine Ste-Anne (AD)

Gigondas Domaine du Cayron (BUT, AD)

Gigondas Jaboulet (LOE, WHI)

Vacqueyras Domaine la Fourmone, Combe (TAN)

**1988**

Cairanne Rabasse-Charavin (PIP)

Châteauneuf-du-Pape Chante-Cigale (YAP)

Châteauneuf-du-Pape Delas (AUG, ROB)

Châteauneuf-du-Pape Domaine de la Solitude (WAI, BYR)

Châteauneuf-du-Pape Domaine de Nalys (WW, IR)

Châteauneuf-du-Pape Domaine du Père Caboche (YAP)

Châteauneuf-du-Pape Domaine la Roquette (BEK)

Châteauneuf-du-Pape les Cailloux, Brunel (BYR)

Châteauneuf-du-Pape Vieux Donjon (YAP)

Côtes du Rhône Coudelet de Beaucastel (YF)

Gigondas Côtes de la Tour, Sarrazine (HAH)

Gigondas Domaine du Cayron (BUT)

Gigondas Domaine Raspail (LAY, BYR)

Gigondas Guigal (TES, BE, TES)

Gigondas Jaboulet (HOG)

Gigondas Perrin (GRE)

**1987**

Châteauneuf-du-Pape Chante-Cigale (BYR)

Gigondas Domaine Raspail (ROB)

Gigondas Domaine St-Gayan, Roger Meffre (YAP)

**1986**

Châteauneuf-du-Pape Delas (AUG, PEN)

Châteauneuf-du-Pape Domaine de Nalys (HOG)

Châteauneuf-du-Pape Domaine Font de Michelle (DAV)

Châteauneuf-du-Pape les Cailloux, Brunel (BYR)

Châteauneuf-du-Pape Réserve, Sabon (HIC)

Châteauneuf-du-Pape Vieux Donjon (GE, YAP)

Côtes du Rhône Château de Fonsalette (LOE)

Gigondas Domaine St-Gayan, Roger Meffre (YAP, BYR)

Gigondas Jaboulet (LOE, BYR)

**1985**

★ Châteauneuf-du-Pape Domaine de
Mont-Redon (BR)

Châteauneuf-du-Pape les Cèdres, Jaboulet
(LOE)

Gigondas Guigal (NI)

**1983**

★ Gigondas Jaboulet (BUT)

──────── £9.00 to £11.99 ────────

**1989**

Châteauneuf-du-Pape Clos Mont Olivet
(FA)

Châteauneuf-du-Pape Domaine du Vieux
Télégraphe (TAN, AD, AN, CV, PIP)

Châteauneuf-du-Pape les Cailloux, Brunel
(FA)

**1988**

Châteauneuf-du-Pape Chante-Perdrix
(BYR)

★ Châteauneuf-du-Pape Château de
Beaucastel (MV, TAN, AD)

Châteauneuf-du-Pape Château Fortia (BYR)

Châteauneuf-du-Pape Clos des Papes,
Avril (BUT, RAE)

Châteauneuf-du-Pape Clos Pignan,
Reynaud (LOE)

Châteauneuf-du-Pape Domaine du Vieux
Télégraphe (TAN, AD, BYR, CV)

Châteauneuf-du-Pape Réserve, Sabon
(WHI)

Gigondas Domaine les Pallières (WHI, BYR,
PIP, BIB)

**1987**

Châteauneuf-du-Pape Château de
Beaucastel (MV, WCL, YF, BYR, ROB)

Châteauneuf-du-Pape Clos des Papes,
Avril (BIB, RAE, HAY)

**1986**

Châteauneuf-du-Pape Chante-Cigale (ASK)

Châteauneuf-du-Pape Clos des Papes,
Avril (ROB)

Châteauneuf-du-Pape Clos Mont Olivet
(BYR)

Gigondas Domaine les Pallières (HIC)

**1985**

Châteauneuf-du-Pape Château de la Font
du Loup (HOG)

Châteauneuf-du-Pape Clos Pignan,
Reynaud (BUT)

Châteauneuf-du-Pape Domaine du Père
Caboche (YAP)

Châteauneuf-du-Pape Domaine du Vieux
Télégraphe (BUT)

Châteauneuf-du-Pape Vieux Donjon (GE,
BUT)

Côtes du Rhône Château de Fonsalette (BUT)

**1983**

Châteauneuf-du-Pape les Cèdres, Jaboulet
(LOE, BUT)

──────── £12.00 to £14.99 ────────

**1985**

Châteauneuf-du-Pape Clos des Papes,
Avril (BUT)

Châteauneuf-du-Pape la Bernardine,
Chapoutier (MAJ)

**1980**

Châteauneuf-du-Pape les Cèdres, Jaboulet
(HUN)

──────── £15.00 to £19.99 ────────

**1988**

Châteauneuf-du-Pape Château Rayas (LOE)

**1986**

Châteauneuf-du-Pape Château Rayas (LOE,
HOG, BYR)

**1985**

Châteauneuf-du-Pape Château de
Beaucastel (BUT, ROB)

──────── £20.00 to £30.00 ────────

**1989**

Châteauneuf-du-Pape Château Rayas (AD)

**1985**

Châteauneuf-du-Pape Château Rayas (BUT)

**1978**

Châteauneuf-du-Pape Château de
Beaucastel (BUT)

Châteauneuf-du-Pape les Cèdres, Jaboulet
(WS)

──────── £35.00 to £45.00 ────────

**1962**

Châteauneuf-du-Pape Clos de l'Oratoire
des Papes (REI)

Châteauneuf-du-Pape la Grappe des
Papes, Jaboulet (FA)

Châteauneuf-du-Pape les Cèdres, Jaboulet
(FA, VIG)

## WHITE

──────── Under £5.00 ────────
**1990**
Côtes du Rhône Domaine Pelaquié (BUT)
Côtes du Rhône Puyméras (YAP)
Vin de Pays des Coteaux de l'Ardèche
   Chardonnay, Latour (HOG)
**1989**
Lirac la Fermade, Domaine Maby (LOR)
**1988**
Côtes du Rhône Parallèle 45, Jaboulet
   (HOG)

──────── £5.00 to £6.99 ────────
**1991**
Côtes du Rhône Domaine Pelaquié (BIB)
**1990**
Côtes du Rhône Domaine St-Gayan (YAP)
Côtes du Rhône Guigal (AD)
Lirac la Fermade, Domaine Maby (YAP)
Vin de Pays des Coteaux de l'Ardèche
   Chardonnay, Latour (TAN, BUT, REI)
**1989**
Château St-Estève d'Uchaux (PE)
Côtes du Rhône Domaine Pelaquié (BUT)
Côtes du Rhône Guigal (BE, TES, NI, YF)
Vin de Pays des Coteaux de l'Ardèche
   Chardonnay, Latour (HAG)
**1988**
Lirac la Fermade, Domaine Maby (IR)

──────── £7.00 to £9.99 ────────
**1990**
Châteauneuf-du-Pape Domaine de Mont-
   Redon (EL)
Châteauneuf-du-Pape Domaine de Nalys
   (IR)
Châteauneuf-du-Pape Domaine du Père
   Caboche (YAP)
Châteauneuf-du-Pape les Cailloux (BYR)
**1989**
Châteauneuf-du-Pape Domaine de Mont-
   Redon (EL)
Châteauneuf-du-Pape Domaine de Nalys
   (WW, HOG)
Châteauneuf-du-Pape les Cèdres, Jaboulet
   (LOE)

> *In each price band wines*
> *are listed in vintage order.*
> *Within each vintage they*
> *are listed in A-Z order.*

**1988**
Côtes du Rhône Château de Fonsalette
   (LOE)
**1987**
Châteauneuf-du-Pape Domaine du Père
   Caboche (BO)
Côtes du Rhône Château de Fonsalette
   (LOE)
**1986**
Châteauneuf-du-Pape Clos Pignan (LOE)
Châteauneuf-du-Pape les Cèdres, Jaboulet
   (LOE)
Côtes du Rhône Château de Fonsalette
   (LOE)

──────── £10.00 to £12.99 ────────
**1991**
Châteauneuf-du-Pape Domaine du Vieux
   Télégraphe (AD)
**1990**
Châteauneuf-du-Pape Domaine du Vieux
   Télégraphe (SOM, LAY)
Châteauneuf-du-Pape Domaine Font de
   Michelle (DAV, THR)
Viognier Domaine Ste-Anne (AD, TAN)
**1989**
Châteauneuf-du-Pape Domaine de Nalys
   (GRE)
**1988**
Châteauneuf-du-Pape Domaine de Mont-
   Redon (WS)
**1986**
Châteauneuf-du-Pape Domaine du Père
   Caboche (BU)

──────── £13.00 to £15.99 ────────
**1989**
Châteauneuf-du-Pape Domaine du Vieux
   Télégraphe (YF)
**1985**
Châteauneuf-du-Pape Château Rayas (LOE)
**1982**
Châteauneuf-du-Pape les Cèdres, Jaboulet
   (BUT)

──────── £16.00 to £19.99 ────────
**1990**
Châteauneuf-du-Pape Château de
   Beaucastel (AD)
**1989**
Châteauneuf-du-Pape Château de
   Beaucastel (TAN)
**1988**
Châteauneuf-du-Pape Roussanne Vieilles
   Vignes, Château de Beaucastel (GRE)

**1987**
Châteauneuf-du-Pape Château de
  Beaucastel (HAU)
Châteauneuf-du-Pape Château Rayas (LOE)
**1986**
Châteauneuf-du-Pape Château Rayas (LOE)
Châteauneuf-du-Pape Liquoreux, Château
  Rayas (HOG)

─────── **£20.00 to £24.99** ───────
**1989**
Châteauneuf-du-Pape Château de
  Beaucastel (VIG)
**1988**
Châteauneuf-du-Pape Château Rayas (VIG)
Châteauneuf-du-Pape Roussanne Vieilles
  Vignes, Château de Beaucastel (WCL,
  HAU, AD)
**1985**
Chateauneuf-du-Pape, Chateau Rayas (AD)

─────── **£25.00 to £30.00** ───────
**1989**
Châteauneuf-du-Pape Roussanne Vieilles
  Vignes, Château de Beaucastel (VIG)
**1982**
Châteauneuf-du-Pape Château de
  Beaucastel (VIG)

## ROSÉ

─────── **Under £7.99** ───────
**1990**
Lirac Rosé la Fermade, Domaine Maby (YAP)
Tavel Château de Trinquevedel (EL)
Tavel Domaine de la Genestière (PIP)
Tavel la Forcadière, Domaine Maby (LOR,
  YAP, PE)
Tavel l'Espiègle, Jaboulet (LOE)
**1989**
Lirac Domaine des Causses, Assémat (TAN)
Tavel Château de Trinquevedel (HOG)
Tavel Domaine de la Genestière (WHI)
Tavel la Forcadière, Domaine Maby (AN,
  BYR)
**1988**
Tavel l'Espiègle, Jaboulet (HOG)

## SPARKLING

─────── **£7.00 to £8.00** ───────
**Non-vintage**
Clairette de Die Brut Archard-Vincent (YAP)
Clairette de Die Tradition Demi-sec
  Archard-Vincent (YAP)

## FORTIFIED

─────── **Under £7.00** ───────
**1988**
Muscat de Beaumes-de-Venise Domaine de
  Coyeux 1/2 bottle (AD, THR)
Muscat de Beaumes-de-Venise Jaboulet 1/2
  bottle (HAL, OD)
**1987**
Muscat de Beaumes-de-Venise Cave Co-op.
  de Beaumes-de-Venise (BUT)

─────── **£7.00 to £9.99** ───────
**Non-vintage**
Muscat de Beaumes-de-Venise Cave Co-op.
  de Beaumes-de-Venise (OD, IR, NA, LAY,
  AD, CV, WHI, YF)
Muscat de Beaumes-de-Venise Cuvée des
  Papes (BYR)
Muscat de Beaumes-de-Venise Cuvée
  Pontificale, Pascal (YAP, DAV, LO)
Rasteau Vin Doux Naturel, Domaine la
  Soumade (PIP)
**1990**
Muscat de Beaumes-de-Venise Domaine de
  Durban (BUT, EL, SOM, YAP)
**1989**
Muscat de Beaumes-de-Venise Jaboulet
  (LOE, GRE, MV)
**1988**
Muscat de Beaumes-de-Venise Domaine de
  Coyeux (HAY, LAY)
Muscat de Beaumes-de-Venise Jaboulet
  (HOG)
**1986**
Muscat de Beaumes-de-Venise Perrin (PE)

─────── **£10.00 to £12.99** ───────
**1990**
Muscat de Beaumes-de-Venise Domaine de
  Durban (PIP)
Muscat de Beaumes-de-Venise Domaine
  des Bernardins (PIP)
**1989**
Muscat de Beaumes-de-Venise Domaine de
  Coyeux (YF)
Muscat de Beaumes-de-Venise Jaboulet
  (VIG)

> *In each price band wines
> are listed in vintage
> order. Within each vintage
> they are listed in A-Z order.*

# LOIRE

### DRY WHITE

#### —————— Under £4.00 ——————
**Non-vintage**
Asda Muscadet de Sèvre-et-Maine (ASD)
Sainsbury's Blanc de Blancs du Val de
Loire Saumur (SAI)
Sainsbury's Muscadet de Sèvre-et-Maine
(SAI)
Sainsbury's Sauvignon de Touraine (SAI)
**1990**
★ Chardonnay du Haut Poitou Cave Co-op
(WAI)
Muscadet les Ormeaux, Sauvion (NI)
Saumur Blanc Cave de St Cyr-en-Bourg
(SOM)
Saumur Cave des Vignerons de Saumur
(MAJ)
Sauvignon de Touraine Comte d'Ormont,
Saget (MAJ)
Sauvignon de Touraine Langlois-Château
(HOG)
★ Sauvignon du Haut Poitou, Cave Co-op
(WAI, CH, MAJ)
Waitrose Muscadet (WAI)
**1989**
Muscadet les Ormeaux, Sauvion (NI)
Saumur Cave des Vignerons de Saumur
(TES)

#### —————— £4.00 to £4.99 ——————
**1991**
Chardonnay du Haut Poitou Cave Co-op
(LO, HAY)
★ Muscadet sur lie Chéreau, Domaine de
la Mortaine (YAP)
★ St-Pourçain Cuvée Printanière, Union
des Vignerons (PIP)
Sauvignon de Touraine Comte d'Ormont,
Saget (MAR)
Sauvignon de Touraine Domaine de la
Charmoise, Marionnet (WHI, BIB)

Sauvignon de Touraine Domaine de la
Renaudie (KA)
Sauvignon de Touraine Plouzeau (KA)
Sauvignon du Haut Poitou, Cave Co-op
(HAY, LO)
Vin de Pays du Jardin de la France Cépage
Chardonnay (ASK)
Vin de Thouarsais, Gigon (YAP)
**1990**
Chardonnay du Haut Poitou Cave Co-op
(DAV)
Muscadet de Sèvre-et-Maine sur lie Carte
d'Or, Sauvion (BEK)
★ Muscadet de Sèvre-et-Maine sur lie
Château de Cléray (ROB)
Muscadet de Sèvre-et-Maine sur lie
Château de la Ferronière (EL)
Muscadet de Sèvre-et-Maine sur lie
Château de la Jannière (BU, DAV)
Muscadet de Sèvre-et-Maine sur lie
Thuaud (CHA)
Muscadet des Coteaux de la Loire Guindon
(BIB)
Pineau de la Loire, Confrérie d'Oisly et
Thésée (WS)
★ Quincy Domaine de la Maison Blanche
(ASD, SAI)
Saumur Cave des Vignerons de Saumur
(YAP)
★ Sauvignon de Touraine Confrérie
d'Oisly et Thésée (WW)
Sauvignon de Touraine Domaine de la
Garrelière (KA)
Sauvignon de Touraine Domaine de la
Presle (NI)
Sauvignon de Touraine Domaine Guy
Mardon (VIC)
Sauvignon de Touraine Domaine Octavie,
Barbeillon (MAJ)
**1989**
Muscadet de Sèvre-et-Maine Grand
Mouton (SOM)
Sauvignon de Touraine Confrérie d'Oisly
et Thésée (OD)
Sauvignon de Touraine Domaine Octavie,
Barbeillon (YF)
**1988**
Saumur Blanc Domaine Langlois (HOG)
Sauvignon du Haut Poitou, Cave Co-op
(AUG)
Vin de Pays du Jardin de la France Cépage
Sauvignon (RAE)

─────── **£5.00 to £5.99** ───────
**1991**
Azay-le-Rideau la Basse Chevrière (YAP)
Gros Plant sur lie, Château du Cleray (PIP)
Muscadet de Sèvre-et-Maine Fief de la
 Brie, Bonhomme (AD)
Muscadet de Sèvre-et-Maine sur lie
 Château de Cléray (PIP)
**1990**
Cheverny Cépage Sauvignon, Cazin (PIP)
Menetou-Salon Domaine de Chatenoy (WAI,
 NI)
★ Menetou-Salon Morogues, Pellé (CH)
★ Muscadet de Sèvre-et-Maine sur lie les
 Découvertes, Sauvion (BYR)
Muscadet de Sèvre-et-Maine Fief de la
 Brie, Bonhomme (TAN)
Muscadet de Sèvre-et-Maine sur lie
 Château de Chasseloir (HUN, IR)
Muscadet de Sèvre-et-Maine sur lie
 Château de Cléray (NI)
Muscadet de Sèvre-et-Maine sur lie Clos
 des Bourguignons (HAH)
Muscadet de Sèvre-et-Maine sur lie
 Domaine des Dorices (GRE, NA)
Muscadet de Sèvre-et-Maine sur lie Moulin
 de la Gravelle (LOR)
Muscadet sur lie Château l'Oiselinière,
 Carré (WS)
★ Pouilly-Fumé Saget (GRE)
Quincy Clos des Victoires, Duc de Berri
 (TAN)
Sauvignon de Touraine Confrérie d'Oisly
 et Thésée (HAH, ASK)
Sauvignon de Touraine Domaine du Clos
 St-Georges, Oisly et Thésée (CB)
Vouvray Château Moncontour (OD)
**1989**
Muscadet de Sèvre-et-Maine sur lie les
 Découvertes, Sauvion (BEK)
Muscadet de Sèvre-et-Maine sur lie
 Château de Cléray (NI)
Muscadet de Sèvre-et-Maine sur lie
 Domaine de Maretière (SOM)
Muscadet sur lie Domaine de Chasseloir
 (LOR)
Reuilly Beurdin (HA)
Saumur Blanc Domaine Langlois (GRG)
Vouvray Domaine de l'Épinay (ASD)
**1988**
Muscadet de Sèvre-et-Maine sur lie
 Château de la Ragotière Black Label
 (AUG)
Muscadet de Sèvre-et-Maine sur lie Cuvée
 de Millénaire, Marquis de Goulaine (BYR)

**1986**
Montlouis Demi-sec Deletang (RAE)
Montlouis Sec Deletang (RAE)
**1985**
★ Montlouis Sec Deletang (RAE)

─────── **£6.00 to £6.99** ───────
**1991**
Menetou-Salon Domaine de Chatenoy (GA)
Menetou-Salon Morogues, Pellé (CH, WCL)
Menetou-Salon Pellé (LOR)
★ Pouilly-Fumé les Chantalouettes,
 Gitton (SAI)
Reuilly Robert & Gérard Cordier (YAP)
**1990**
Cheverny Cépage Sauvignon, Cazin (BEK)
Menetou-Salon les Thureaux, Mellot (HOG)
Menetou-Salon Domaine de Chatenoy
 (WRI)
Menetou-Salon Fournier (PIP)
Menetou-Salon Sauvignon, Rat (PE)
Menetou-Salon Teiller (YAP)
Pouilly-Fumé Bailly (WS)
Pouilly-Fumé les Loges, Saget (MAJ)
Quincy Jaumier (YAP, BYR)
Quincy Pierre Mardon (AD, AN)
Reuilly Beurdin (AD, WCL)
Sancerre Château de Thauvenay (ASD)
★ Sancerre Clos du Chêne Marchand,
 Crochet (BO)
Sancerre Domaine du P'tit Roy (SOM)
★ Savennières Clos du Papillon, Baumard
 (HOG, EL)
Savennières Domaine de la Bizolière (YAP)
Savennières Domaine du Closel, Mme de
 Jessey (YAP, HAU)
**1989**
Montlouis Domaine des Liards, Berger
 (YAP)
Muscadet de Sèvre-et-Maine sur lie
 Château de la Ragotière Black Label
 (VIG)
Vouvray Château Moncontour (NI, UN)
**1988**
Menetou-Salon Roger (WHI)
★ Savennières Château de Chamboureau,
 Soulez (YAP)
Vouvray Château de Monfort (GRG)
Vouvray Domaine de l'Épinay (CV)
**1987**
Vouvray Clos Naudin, Foreau (HOG)
Vouvray Jarry (BYR)
**1986**
Jasnières Caves aux Tuffières, Pinon (YAP)
Vouvray Jarry (BYR)

**1984**
Vouvray le Haut Lieu, Huet (RAE)
**1982**
★ Vouvray Clos Naudin, Foreau (LOE)
**1980**
Vouvray Clos Naudin, Foreau (LOE, AD)

─────── **£7.00 to £7.99** ───────
**1991**
Menetou-Salon Domaine de Chatenoy (VIG)
Menetou-Salon Morogues, Pellé (CV)
Menetou-Salon Pellé (AD, HAH)
Menetou-Salon Roger (HAU)
Sancerre Delaporte (GRE)
Sancerre Dézat (CV)
Sancerre Domaine de Montigny, Natter
   (BIB)
Sancerre la Reine Blanche (WS)
Sancerre les Perriers, Vatan (YAP)
Sancerre Riffault (HAU)
**1990**
Menetou-Salon les Thureaux, Mellot (GRE)
Menetou-Salon Montaloise (ROB)
Menetou-Salon Morogues, Pellé (ASK, CV)
Menetou-Salon Roger (TAN)
★ Pouilly-Fumé Dageneau (BR)
Pouilly-Fumé Domaine de Petit Soumard
   (ROB)
Pouilly-Fumé Domaine des Berthiers,
   Dagueneau (IR)
Pouilly-Fumé Domaine des Chailloux,
   Chatelain (WAI, BEK)
Pouilly-Fumé Domaine des Rabichattes
   (RAE)
Pouilly-Fumé les Champs de la Croix (AN)
Pouilly-Fumé les Loges, Jean-Claude
   Guyot (YAP)
Pouilly-Fumé Saget (MAR)
Pouilly-Fumé Seguin Père et Fils (HAY,
   RAE)
Quincy Pierre Mardon (ROB)
Sancerre Clos du Roy, Millérioux (HOG)
Sancerre André Dézat (WHI, CV)
Sancerre Domaine du Nozay, de Benoist
   (CB)
Sancerre Laporte (PIP)
Sancerre les Crilles, Gitton (BYR)
Sancerre les Tuileries, Redde (EL)
★ Sancerre Vacheron (CH, MAJ)
Savennières Clos de Coulaine (RAE, BIB)
Savennières Clos du Papillon, Baumard
   (GRE, BEK)
**1989**
Muscadet de Sèvre-et-Maine sur lie Cuvée
   de Millénaire, Marquis de Goulaine (AV)

Pouilly-Fumé Domaine des Berthiers,
   Dagueneau (BU)
Pouilly-Fumé les Folatières, Gitton (BYR)
Pouilly-Fumé les Griottes, Bailly (CH)
Pouilly-Fumé Redde (HOG)
Sancerre le Croupon, Balland-Chapuis
   (GRG)
Sancerre les Tuileries, Redde (EL)
Sancerre Paul Prieur (HA)
Savennières Baumard (BYR)
Savennières Château d'Epiré (YAP)
Savennières Clos du Papillon, Baumard
   (BYR)
Vouvray Domaine Peu de la Moriette (PIP)
**1988**
Muscadet sur lie Château de Chasseloir de
   St-Fiacre Fût de Chêne Neuf (LOR)
Pouilly-Fumé Domaine de Petit Soumard
   (AUG)
Pouilly-Fumé Domaine des Berthiers,
   Dagueneau (BU)
Pouilly-Fumé Jean Pabiot (GRG)
Savennières Clos de Coulaine (RAE)
Vouvray Clos Naudin, Foreau (LOE)
Vouvray le Haut Lieu, Huet (RAE)

─────── **£8.00 to £9.99** ───────
**1991**
Pouilly-Fumé Domaine des Berthiers,
   Dagueneau (BR)
Sancerre Clos du Roy, Millérioux (CB)
Sancerre Daulny (HAH)
Sancerre Vacheron (AD)
**1990**
Menetou-Salon Domaine de Chatenoy
   (BAR)
Menetou-Salon Pellé (MV)
Pouilly-Fumé Château de Tracy (LOR, AD,
   LAY, TAN)
Pouilly-Fumé Château Fauray (NA, BAR)
Pouilly-Fumé Domaine des Berthiers,
   Dagueneau (WRI)
Pouilly-Fumé Domaine des Rabichattes
   (PE)
Pouilly-Fumé Domaine Thibault (TAN, LAY,
   HIC)
Pouilly-Fumé Jean Pabiot (BE)
Pouilly-Fumé la Charnoie, Renaud (HAH)
Pouilly-Fumé la Loge aux Moines, Moreux
   (CB)
Pouilly-Fumé les Folatières, Gitton (ASK)
Pouilly-Fumé les Pechignolles (HIG)
Pouilly-Fumé Redde (EL)
Pouilly-Fumé Seguin Père et Fils (ROB)
Sancerre André Dézat (TAN, BER)

Sancerre Clos des Roches, Vacheron (WHI, ROB)

Sancerre Clos du Chaudenay Vieilles Vignes, Daulny (HAH)

Sancerre Clos du Roy, Millérioux (HAG)

Sancerre Domaine du P'tit Roy (NI)

Sancerre Laporte (HUN)

Sancerre le Chêne Marchand, Roger (TAN)

Sancerre le Grand Chemarin, Balland (HIC, PE)

★ Sancerre les Romains, Gitton (HIG)

Sancerre Roger (MV)

Savennières Clos de Coulaine (BER)

Vouvray Clos Naudin, Foreau (LOE)

Vouvray le Haut Lieu, Huet (AD)

**1989**

Pouilly-Fumé Château de Tracy (CV, BYR)

Pouilly-Fumé de Ladoucette, Château du Nozet (HOG)

Pouilly-Fumé Domaine des Chailloux, Chatelain (BYR)

Pouilly-Fumé Domaine Thibault (BER)

Pouilly-Fumé les Champs de la Croix (HA)

Pouilly-Fumé les Loges, Saget (VIN)

Sancerre Chavignol les Monts Damnés, Cotat (AN)

Sancerre Clos de la Crêle, Lucien Thomas (BYR)

Sancerre Comte Lafond, Château du Nozet (HOG)

Sancerre Domaine du P'tit Roy (NI)

Sancerre les Galinots, Gitton (HIG)

Sancerre les Romains, Gitton (HIG)

Vouvray le Haut Lieu, Huet (RAE)

**1988**

Muscadet Vieilles Vignes, Château de Chasseloir (HAG)

Pouilly-Fumé Domaine Thibault (BER)

Pouilly-Fumé les Pechignolles (HIG)

Savennières Clos St-Yves (AV)

**1987**

Muscadet de Sèvre-et-Maine sur lie Château de Chasseloir (GRG)

Savennières Roche-aux-Moines, Soulez (YAP)

**1985**

Savennières Roche-aux-Moines, Domaine Aux Moines (BO)

Vouvray Aigle Blanc, Poniatowski (VIG)

**1984**

Sancerre Clos des Roches, Vacheron (BUT)

Vouvray le Haut Lieu, Huet (BIB)

**1983**

Vouvray le Haut Lieu, Huet (AV)

Vouvray le Mont, Huet (AD)

**1976**

★ Vouvray Château de Vaudenuits (UN)

——————— **£10.00 to £14.99** ———————

**1990**

Pouilly-Fumé Dageneau (TAN)

Pouilly-Fumé de Ladoucette, Château du Nozet (GRE, ROB)

Pouilly-Fumé du Buisson Menard, Dagueneau (BOT, WR)

Pouilly-Fumé Vieilles Vignes, Dagueneau (BR)

Sancerre Chavignol la Grande Côte, Cotat (AD)

Sancerre Clos des Roches, Vacheron (AV)

Savennières Roche-aux-Moines, Soulez (WS)

**1989**

Pouilly-Fumé Cuvée Prestige, Châtelain (MV)

Pouilly-Fumé de Ladoucette, Château du Nozet (VIC, AN, BER)

Savennières Clos du Papillon, Baumard (VIG)

**1988**

Pouilly-Fumé Cuvée Prestige, Châtelain (BEK)

**1987**

Pouilly-Fumé de Ladoucette, Château du Nozet (WHI)

**1986**

Pouilly-Fumé de Ladoucette, Château du Nozet (BUT)

**1984**

Pouilly-Fumé Domaine de l'Abbaye, Chatelain (BUT)

——————— **£15.00 to £25.00** ———————

**1989**

Pouilly-Fumé Dageneau (BUT)

**1986**

Pouilly-Fumé Baron de L Château du Nozet (WHI)

Savennières Coulée-de-Serrant Château de la Roche-aux-Moines, Nicolas Joly (BO)

──────── c. £27.00 ────────
**1988**
Pouilly-Fumé Baron de L Château du
　Nozet (AN, ROB)
**1986**
Pouilly-Fumé Baron de L Château du
　Nozet (WRI)

──────── c. £50.00 ────────
**1959**
Vovray Brédif (ROB)

## SPARKLING

──────── Under £6.00 ────────
**Non-vintage**
Saumur Ackerman 1811 Brut (AUG)
Saumur Brut Gratien & Meyer (GE)
Saumur Rosé Gratien & Meyer (GE)
Vouvray Tête de Cuvée Méthode
　Champenoise Château de Vaudenuits
　(SAF)

──────── £6.00 to £7.99 ────────
**Non-vintage**
Anjou Rosé Gratien & Meyer (HAY)
Cadre Noir Saumur (WHI, CH)
Château Langlois Crémant de Loire (HOG)
★ Crémant de Loire Brut Gratien &
　Meyer (WS)
Diane de Poitiers Chardonnay du Haut
　Poitou Brut (AD)
Montlouis Mousseux Brut Berger (YAP)
Saumur Ackerman 1811 Brut (BYR, CH, DAV)
Saumur Ackerman 1811 Rosé (BYR, DAV)
Saumur Brut Bouvet-Ladubay (BYR)
Saumur Brut Gratien & Meyer (HOG, HAY)
Saumur Langlois-Château (GRG)
Saumur Rosé Langlois-Château (GRG)
Vouvray Brut Jarry (YAP)
Vouvray Foreau (AD)
★ Vouvray Pétillant Brédif (BYR)
**1989**
Bouvet Saphir (NI)
Saumur Brut Bouvet-Ladubay (MAR)
**1985**
Crémant de Loire Brut Gratien & Meyer
　(THR)

┌─────────────────────────────┐
│ *Stars (★) indicate wines* │
│ *selected by the editors as* │
│ *particularly good value* │
│ *in their class.* │
└─────────────────────────────┘

──────── £8.00 to £9.99 ────────
**Non-vintage**
Saumur Langlois-Château (HAG)
Vouvray Brut Brédif (AUG, ROB)
Vouvray Méthode Champenoise, Huet
　(THR, RAE)

## SWEET WHITE

──────── Under £7.00 ────────
**1990**
Coteaux du Layon Château de la Roulerie
　(YAP)
Coteaux du Layon Leblanc (HAY)
Malvoisie Guindon (YAP)
**1989**
Coteaux du Layon Domaine des Saulaies
　(TAN)
Vouvray Château de Vaudenuits (GRE)
**1988**
★ Coteaux du Layon Clos de Ste-
　Catherine, Baumard (HOG)
Coteaux du Layon Domaine Sauveroy (OD)
**1987**
Vouvray Brédif (GRE)
**1985**
Montlouis Moelleux Domaine des Liards,
　Jean & Michel Berger (YAP)
**1982**
Coteaux du Layon Beaulieu, Chéné (MV)
★ Vouvray Clos du Bourg, Huet (BOR)

──────── £7.00 to £8.99 ────────
**1989**
Coteaux du Layon Leblanc (RAE)
Vouvray Domaine Peu de la Moriette (TAN)
Vouvray Moelleux Jarry (YAP)
**1988**
Coteaux du Layon Clos de Ste-Catherine,
　Baumard (BYR)
Vouvray le Haut Lieu, Huet (RAE)
**1985**
Montlouis Moelleux Deletang (RAE)
Vouvray Moelleux Bourillon Dorléans (MV)
**1978**
Coteaux du Layon Beaulieu, Chéné (MV)

──────── £9.00 to £12.99 ────────
**1989**
Coteaux du Layon Clos de Ste-Catherine,
　Baumard (HOG, EL, GRE)
**1988**
Quarts-de-Chaume Baumard (GRE, BYR)
Vouvray Clos du Bourg, Huet (AD)
Vouvray Moelleux Huet (LAY)

**1987**
Quarts-de-Chaume Château de Bellerive
(ws)
**1986**
Quarts-de-Chaume Baumard (HOG)
Vouvray Brédif (GRG)
**1982**
Quarts-de-Chaume Baumard (HOG)
**1981**
Anjou Moulin Touchais (EL, ROB)
**1980**
Bonnezeaux Château de Fesles (HAG)
**1976**
Anjou Moulin Touchais (BYR)
Coteaux du Layon Beaulieu, Chéné (MV)
**1975**
★ Anjou Moulin Touchais (EL)
**1970**
Coteaux du Layon Ravouin-Gesbron (RAE)

——— **£13.00 to £15.99** ———
**1990**
Coteaux du Layon Clos de Ste-Catherine,
  Baumard (EL)
Vouvray le Haut Lieu, Huet (AD)
**1989**
Bonnezeaux Château de Fesles (MV)
Coteaux de l'Aubance Domaine de Bablut
  (AD)
Quarts-de-Chaume Baumard (HOG, EL)
Vouvray Moelleux Bourillon Dorléans (MV)
**1982**
Coteaux du Layon Clos de Ste-Catherine,
  Baumard (EL)
**1971**
Anjou Moulin Touchais (GRG)
Coteaux du Layon Ravouin-Gesbron (AD)

——— **£16.00 to £19.99** ———
**1990**
Bonnezeaux Château de Fesles (TAN)
**1989**
Coteaux du Layon Clos de Ste-Catherine,
  Baumard (VIG)
Quarts-de-Chaume Baumard (GRE)
Quarts-de-Chaume Château de
  l'Echarderie (YAP)
Vouvray Clos du Bourg, Huet (LAY)
Vouvray Moelleux Bourillon Dorléans (VIG)
Vouvray Moelleux Huet (RAE)
**1988**
Bonnezeaux la Chapelle, Château de
  Fesles (MV)
**1979**
Anjou Moulin Touchais (WRI)

——— **£20.00 to £29.99** ———
**1990**
Vouvray Moelleux Bourillon Dorléans (VIG)
**1964**
Vouvray Moelleux Bourillon Dorléans (MV)

——— **£30.00 to £45.00** ———
**1989**
Vouvray Cuvée Constance, Huet (BIB)
**1969**
Vouvray Clos du Bourg, Huet (AD)
**1959**
Vouvray Brédif (HAG)

## ROSÉ

——— **Under £5.00** ———
**Non-vintage**
Tesco Rosé d'Anjou (TES)
**1990**
Anjou Rosé Cellier de la Loire (IR)
Cabernet d'Anjou Château Perray-
  Jouannet (YAP)
Coteaux d'Ancenis Guidon (YAP)
Rosé d'Anjou Sauvion (NI)
Rosé de Cabernet du Haut Poitou Cave Co-
  op (WAI)
Waitrose Rosé d'Anjou (WAI)
**1989**
Rosé d'Anjou Sauvion (NI)
Vin de Thouarsais, Gigon (YAP)

——— **£5.00 to £7.99** ———
**1990**
Reuilly Pinot Gris Cordier (YAP)
Reuilly Pinot Noir, Beurdin (AD)
Sancerre Rosé Dezat (LAY)
**1989**
Azay-le-Rideau la Basse Chevrière, Pavy
  (YAP)
Cabernet d'Anjou Domaine de Bellevue
  (HIG)

——— **£8.00 to £9.99** ———
**1990**
Sancerre Rosé les Romains, Vacheron
  (WHI)
**1989**
Sancerre Rosé Domaine de la Pousse,
  Cordier (PE)

——— **c. £22.00** ———
**1961**
Cabernet d'Anjou Domaine de Bablut
  Demi-Sec (AD)

## RED

──────── **Under £4.00** ────────
**1991**
Gamay du Haut Poitou Cave Co-op (LO)
**1990**
Gamay du Haut Poitou Cave Co-op (WAI)
Saumur Cave des Vignerons de Saumur
(SOM)

──────── **£4.00 to £4.99** ────────
**1991**
Cabernet de Touraine Domaine de la
Renaudie (KA)
Gamay de Touraine Domaine de la
Charmoise, Marionnet (BIB, RAE)
**1990**
Bourgueil Clos de la Henry, Morin (BYR)
Gamay de Touraine Domaine de la
Charmoise, Marionnet (WHI, HAY, RAE)
Saumur-Champigny Caves des Vignerons
de Saumur (SOM)
Vin de Thouarsais Gigon (YAP)
**1989**
Bourgueil Clos de la Henry, Morin (BYR)
Bourgueil Domaine de Raguenières (CV)
★ Chinon Domaine Morin (BYR)
Chinon Langlois-Château (HOG)
St-Pourçain Union des Vignerons (YAP)

──────── **£5.00 to £6.99** ────────
**1990**
Bourgueil Clos de la Henry, Morin (AV)
Bourgueil Domaine des Ouches (PIP)
Chinon Château de Ligre (HAY)
Chinon l'Arpenty Desbourdes (YAP)
Menetou-Salon Rouge, Pellé (BYR)
St-Nicolas de Bourgueil Clos du Vigneau
(HAY)
St-Nicolas-de-Bourgueil Domaine du
Fondis (TAN)
Saumur-Champigny Domaine des Nerleux
(BEK)
★ Saumur-Champigny Filliatreau (YAP)
St-Nicolas-de-Bourgueil Taluau (HAU)
**1989**
Anjou Rouge Tijou (HIG)
★ Bourgueil la Hurolaie Caslot-Galbrun
(TES)
Chinon Cuvée Prestige, Gouron (KA)
Chinon Domaine Dozon (BYR)
Chinon Domaine Morin (AV)
Chinon les Gravières (LAY)
Chinon Vieilles Vignes, Angelliaume (SOM,
PIP)

**1988**
Anjou Cabernet Clos de Coulaine (BIB)
Bourgueil Domaine des Ouches (WHI)
Chinon Domaine Morin (GRG)
★ Chinon les Grezeaux, Baudry (MV)
Menetou-Salon Rouge, Pellé (MV)
**1987**
Anjou Cabernet Clos de Coulaine (RAE)
Bourgueil Domaine de Raguenières (LOE)
**1986**
Chinon Domaine de la Chapellerie, Olek
(RAE)
Chinon Domaine de Turpenay, Couly (EL,
BYR)
Saumur-Champigny Caves des Vignerons
de Saumur (TES)
**1983**
Anjou Cabernet Clos de Coulaine (LAY)
Bourgueil Domaine de Raguenières (LOE,
BYR)

──────── **£7.00 to £9.99** ────────
**1990**
Menetou-Salon Domaine de Chateney,
Clement (BAR)
Menetou-Salon Rouge, Pellé (WCL)
Sancerre André Dezat (PIP)
Sancerre Reverdy (HAY)
**1989**
Bourgueil Vieilles Vignes, Lamé-Delille-
Boucard (VIG)
Reuilly Pinot Noir, Beurdin (BAR)
Saumur-Champigny Lavigne (TAN)
Sancerre André Dezat (LAY)
Saumur-Champigny Château des
Chaintres (KA)
Saumur-Champigny Vieilles Vignes,
Filliatreau (YAP)
**1988**
Bourgeuil Cuvée Vaumoreau, Druet (BYR)
Bourgueil Beauvais, Druet (AD)
★ Chinon Clos de la Dioterie, Joguet (LOE)
Sancerre Clos du Roi, Crochet (BYR)
Sancerre Clos du Roy, Millerioux (HOG)
Sancerre Domaine du P'tit Roy (NI)
**1987**
Bourgueil Beauvais, Druet (BY)
Bourgueil Grand Mont, Druet (BY, YAP)
Sancerre Domaine de Montigny, Natter
(BIB)
**1986**
Bourgueil Domaine du Grand Clos,
Audebert (BER)
Bourgueil Grand Mont, Druet (BY)
Chinon Domaine de Turpenay, Couly (TAN)

# ALSACE

## WHITE

──────── **Under £4.00** ────────

**Non-vintage**
Sainsbury's Pinot Blanc (SAI)
**1990**
★ Pinot Blanc Cave Co-op. Turckheim
(THR, NI)
**1988**
Tokay-Pinot Gris Cave Co-op. Turckheim
(GRG)

──────── **£4.00 to £4.49** ────────

**Non-vintage**
Sainsbury's Riesling (SAI)
**1990**
Pinot Blanc Cave Co-op. Turckheim (BYR,
LO, VIC, OD)
**1989**
Pinot Blanc Cave Co-op. de Ribeauvillé
(AUG)
Pinot Blanc Dopff & Irion (HOG, EL)
Sylvaner Dopff & Irion (EL)
**1987**
Tokay-Pinot Gris Tradition, Cave Co-op.
Turckheim (ASK)

──────── **£4.50 to £4.99** ────────

**1991**
Pinot Blanc Cave Co-op. Turckheim (CH)
**1990**
Muscat Cave Co-op. Turckheim (BYR)
Pinot Blanc Ingersheim (DAV)
Pinot Blanc Tradition, Cave Co-op.
Turckheim (CV, PEN, BR)
Riesling Cave Co-op. Turckheim (BYR)
Sylvaner Hugel (LOE)
Sylvaner Louis Gisselbrecht (PIP)
Tokay-Pinot Gris Cave Co-op. Turckheim
(BYR, BAR)
Waitrose Gewürztraminer (WAI)
**1989**
Gewürztraminer Turckheim, Dopff (GRG)
Muscat Cave Co-op. Turckheim (AS)
Pinot Blanc Louis Gisselbrecht (NI)
Pinot Blanc Schlumberger (HOG)
Riesling Haut Rhin Réserve (CHA)
Riesling Louis Gisselbrecht (NI)
★ Riesling Turckheim, Zind-Humbrecht
(VIC)
Tokay-Pinot Gris Cave Co-op. Turckheim
(AS)

**1988**
Edelzwicker Rolly Gassmann (BIB)
Gewürztraminer Louis Gisselbrecht (SOM)
Riesling Cave Co-op. de Ribeauvillé (AUG)
Riesling Louis Gisselbrecht (SOM)
Sylvaner Dopff & Irion (GRE)
**1987**
Gewürztraminer Réserve Prestige, Cave
Co-op. Turckheim (ASK)

──────── **£5.00 to £5.99** ────────

**Non-vintage**
Sainsbury's Gewürztraminer (SAI)
Tesco Gewürztraminer (TES)
**1991**
Gewürztraminer Turckheim, Dopff (CH)
Pinot Blanc Ostertag (MV)
Pinot Blanc Trimbach (GRG)
Tokay-Pinot Gris Cave Co-op. Turckheim
(WCL)
**1990**
Gewürztraminer Cave Co-op. Turckheim
(BYR, VIC, LO)
Muscat Louis Gisselbrecht (PIP)
Muscat Réserve, Cave Co-op. Turckheim
(OD)
Muscat Tradition, Cave Co-op. Turckheim
(PEN)
Pinot Blanc Clos de Stangenberg, Heim (IR)
Pinot Blanc Louis Gisselbrecht (PIP, HIC)
Pinot Blanc Muré (BEK, ROB)
Tokay-Pinot Gris Cave Co-op. Turckheim
(BR)
Riesling Louis Gisselbrecht (HIC)
★ Sylvaner Vieilles Vignes, Ostertag (MV)
Sylvaner Zind-Humbrecht (THR, BY)
Tokay-Pinot Gris Louis Gisselbrecht (PIP)
Tokay-Pinot Gris Tradition, Cave Co-op.
Turckheim (PEN)
**1989**
Gewürztraminer Cave Co-op. Turckheim
(THR, AS)
Gewürztraminer Caves de Bennwihr (PE)
Gewürztraminer Dopff & Irion (HOG)
Gewürztraminer Haut Rhin Réserve (CHA)
Gewürztraminer Réserve Prestige, Cave
Co-op. Turckheim (NI)
Gewürztraminer Réserve Speciale,
Gisselbrecht (NI)
Gewürztraminer Tradition, Cave Co-op.
Turckheim (YF)
Pinot Blanc Cave Co-op. Turckheim (HA)

Pinot Blanc Hugel (LOE, HOG, HAG)
Pinot Blanc Trimbach (HOG, BYR)
★ Riesling Blanck (AV)
Riesling Caves de Bennwihr (PE)
Riesling Seigneur d'Alsace, Dopff & Irion (EL)

**1988**
Gewürztraminer Cave Co-op. de Ribeauvillé (AUG)
Muscat Froehn, Beck (BEK)
Pinot Blanc Trimbach (BUT)
Riesling Dopff & Irion (GRE)
Riesling Hugel (LOE)
Riesling les Faitières (CHA)
Riesling Sipp (WHI)
Sylvaner Schleret (YAP)
Sylvaner Trimbach (HOG)

**1987**
Muscat Tradition, Hugel (LOE)
Riesling Hugel (HOG)
Tokay-Pinot Gris Tradition, Kuentz-Bas (HOG)

**1986**
Riesling Muré (BU)

─────── £6.00 to £6.99 ───────

**1991**
Gewürztraminer Tradition, Cave Co-op. Turckheim (ASK)

**1990**
Gewürztraminer Ingersheim (DAV)
Gewürztraminer Louis Gisselbrecht (HIC)
Gewürztraminer Muré (BEK)
Gewürztraminer Sipp (WHI)
Gewürztraminer Trimbach (GRG)
Pinot Blanc Schleret (YAP)
Riesling les Murailles, Dopff & Irion (EL)

**1989**
Gewürztraminer Hugel (LOE)
Gewürztraminer Louis Gisselbrecht (NI)
Gewürztraminer Schmidt (AN)
Muscat Schleret (YAP)
Pinot Blanc Tradition, Kuentz-Bas (BER)
Riesling Réserve, Dopff & Irion (BYR)
Tokay-Pinot Gris Réserve, Cave Co-op. Turckheim (VIN)

> *Please remember that*
> **Webster's** *is a price
> GUIDE and not a price
> LIST. It is not meant to
> replace up-to-date
> merchant's lists.*

**1988**
Gewürztraminer Hugel (BO)
Gewürztraminer Réserve, Cave Co-op. Turckheim (BYR)
Gewürztraminer Schléret (YAP)
★ Gewürztraminer Trimbach (BYR)
Gewürztraminer Wiederhirn (HIG)
Muscat les Amandiers, Dopff & Irion (HOG)
Pinot Blanc les Amours, Hugel (VIN, BUT)
Tokay-Pinot Gris les Maquisards, Dopff & Irion (HOG)
★ Riesling Herrenweg, Zind-Humbrecht (THR)
Riesling Réserve, Dopff & Irion (GRG)
Riesling Trimbach (HOG, CH)
Sporen Hugel (LOE)
Tokay-Pinot Gris Dopff & Irion (BYR)

**1987**
Riesling Rolly Gassmann (HAY)
Riesling Zind-Humbrecht (BY)

**1986**
Gewürztraminer Trimbach (HOG)

**1985**
Riesling les Murailles, Dopff & Irion (HOG)
Tokay-Pinot Gris Tradition, Hugel (LOE)

**1983**
Riesling Kirchberg, Sipp (GRG)

─────── £7.00 to £8.99 ───────

**1991**
Gewürztraminer Blanck (AN)
Muscat Blanck (AD)

**1990**
Gewürztraminer les Faitières (CHA)
Gewürztraminer Réserve, Cave Co-op. Turckheim (WCL)
Gewürztraminer Schléret (LAY)
Muscat Réserve, Trimbach (WS)
Muscat Schlumberger (HIC)
Muscat Wiederhirn (HIG)
Riesling Réserve, Dopff & Irion (ROB)
Tokay-Pinot Gris les Maquisards, Dopff & Irion (EL)
Tokay-Pinot Gris Schleret (YAP)

**1989**
Auxerrois Rolly Gassmann (PE)
Gewürztraminer Beyer (HAG)
Gewürztraminer Bollenberg, Cattin (CB)
Gewürztraminer Herrenweg, Zind-Humbrecht (THR)
Gewürztraminer Rolly Gassmann (RAE, HAY, BIB)
Muscat les Amandiers, Dopff & Irion (GRE, BYR)
Muscat Réserve, Trimbach (ROB)

Tokay-Pinot Gris Schlumberger (TAN, HIC)
Riesling Grand Cru Frankstein (PIP)
Riesling Heimbourg Cave Co-op.
  Turckheim (WCL)
Riesling Princes Abbés, Schlumberger (BO)
★ Riesling Reserve Particulière, Faller (LOE)
Tokay-Pinot Gris Hatschbourg, Cattin (CB)
Tokay-Pinot Gris Réserve, Trimbach (BYR)
Tokay-Pinot Gris Wiederhirn (HIG)

**1988**
Auxerrois Rolly Gassmann (RAE, BIB)
Gewürztraminer des Princes Abbés,
  Schlumberger (TAN)
Gewürztraminer Schlumberger (NI)
Gewürztraminer Tradition, Hugel (LOE)
Gewürztraminer Tradition, Kuentz-Bas
  (BER)
Gewürztraminer Zind-Humbrecht (BY)
Muscat Réserve, Heydt (CB)
Muscat Schlumberger (YF)
Muscat Zind-Humbrecht (BY)
Tokay-Pinot Gris les Maquisards, Dopff &
  Irion (GRE, BYR)
Riesling Clos Haüserer, Zind-Humbrecht
  (THR)
Riesling Réserve, Trimbach (VIG)
Riesling Schoenenberg, René Schmidt (BER)
Riesling Tradition, Hugel (LOE)

**1987**
Gewürztraminer Réserve Rolly Gassmann
  (BIB)
Muscat Moench Reben, Rolly Gassmann
  (BIB, RAE)
Tokay-Pinot Gris Hugel (HAG)

**1986**
Muscat Réserve, Trimbach (GRG)
Riesling Saering, Schlumberger (HOG)
Riesling Tradition, Hugel (HAG)

**1985**
Gewürztraminer Trimbach (BUT)
Pinot Gris Réserve Spéciale, Schlumberger
  (BO)
★ Tokay-Pinot Gris Réserve Spéciale,
  Schlumberger (BO)
Riesling Tradition, Hugel (BUT)
Tokay-Pinot Gris Réserve, Trimbach (GRG)

**1983**
★ Gewürztraminer Vendange Tardive,
  Muré (BU)
Pinot Blanc Hugel (BUT)
Tokay-Pinot Gris Hugel (BUT)
Tokay-Pinot Gris Vendange Tardive, Willy
  Gisselbrecht (ASK)

**1979**
★ Riesling Frédéric Emile, Trimbach (FA)

───────── **£9.00 to £11.99** ─────────

**1990**
Gewürztraminer Herrenweg, Zind-
  Humbrecht (BR)
Riesling Herrenweg, Zind-Humbrecht (BY)

**1989**
Gewürztraminer Réserve Particulière,
  Faller (LOE, BUT, BYR)
Gewürztraminer Tradition, Kuentz-Bas
  (AV)
Muscat Faller (LOE, HA)
Riesling Herrenweg, Zind-Humbrecht (FA,
  BUT)
Riesling Schlossberg, Blanck (AD)
Riesling Schlossberg, Faller (LOE, BUT, BYR,
  LAY)
Riesling Tradition, Hugel (AD)
Tokay-Pinot Gris Cave Co-op. Turckheim
  (ASK)
Tokay-Pinot Gris Réserve, Faller (LAY)

**1988**
Gewürztraminer Brand Grand Cru de
  Turckheim (BYR)
★ Gewürztraminer Clos Windsbuhl, Zind-
  Humbrecht (FA)
Gewürztraminer Jubilee, Hugel (LOE, HOG)
Riesling Fronholz Ostertag (MV)
Riesling Heissenberg Ostertag (MV)
Tokay-Pinot Gris Grand Cru Brand, Cave
  Co-op. Turckheim (BYR)

**1987**
Tokay-Pinot Gris Rolly Gassmann (TAN,
  BIB)

**1986**
Gewürztraminer Kessler, Schlumberger
  (BYR)
Gewürztraminer Seigneurs de
  Ribeaupierre, Trimbach (HOG, CH, BYR)
Riesling Frédéric Emile, Trimbach (HOG,
  BYR, GRE)
Riesling Kitterlé, Schlumberger (HOG, BYR)

**1985**
Gewürztraminer Brand Grand Cru de
  Turckheim (OD, PEN)
Gewürztraminer Clos Gaensbroennel, A.
  Willm (AMI)
Gewürztraminer Kessler, Schlumberger
  (GRE)
Gewürztraminer Osterberg, Sipp (WHI)
Gewürztraminer Seigneurs de
  Ribeaupierre, Trimbach (BUT)
Muscat Clos St-Landelin, Muré (BU)
Riesling Frédéric Emile, Trimbach (BUT)
Riesling Jubilee, Hugel (LOE)
Riesling Kitterlé, Schlumberger (BO)

Tokay-Pinot Gris Cave Co-op. Turckheim
(BYR)
**1983**
Gewürztraminer Hugel (BUT)
★ Tokay-Pinot Gris Réserve Spéciale,
Schlumberger (BUT)

─────── **£12.00 to £14.99** ───────
**1989**
Tokay-Pinot Gris Kitterlé, Schlumberger
(BYR)
Tokay-Pinot Gris Cuvée Exceptionnelle,
Schleret (YAP)
Tokay-Pinot Gris Faller (LOE)
**1988**
Gewürztraminer Goldert, Zind-Humbrecht
(BY)
Gewürztraminer Réserve, Trimbach (BUT)
Muscat Goldert, Zind-Humbrecht (THR)
Riesling Brand, Zind-Humbrecht (BY)
Riesling Ste-Cathérine, Faller (LOE)
**1987**
Gewürztraminer Rangen, Zind-Humbrecht
(BY)
**1986**
Gewürztraminer Kitterlé, Schlumberger
(NI)
Tokay-Pinot Gris Schlumberger (DAV)
**1985**
Riesling Réserve Personnelle, Hugel (TAN,
DAV, AV, BUT)
**1983**
Gewürztraminer Eichberg, Dopff au
Moulin (BUT)
Gewürztraminer Réserve Personnelle,
Hugel (BUT, WRI)
Tokay-Pinot Gris Réserve, Rolly Gassmann
(RAE)

─────── **£15.00 to £19.99** ───────
**1990**
Tokay-Pinot Gris Rangen Vendange
Tardive, Zind-Humbrecht (WR, BOT)
**1989**
Gewürztraminer Cuvée Exceptionelle,
Schléret (YAP)
Gewürztraminer Herrenweg Vendange
Tardive, Zind-Humbrecht (BY, FA)
Gewürztraminer Vendange Tardive,
Wiederhirn (HIG)
Riesling Altenberg de Bergheim, Koehly
(BUT)
Riesling Clos St-Urbain, Zind-Humbrecht
(FA)
Tokay-Pinot Gris Schlumberger (BER)

**1988**
Gewürztraminer Sélection de Grains
Nobles, Cave Co-op. de Turckheim (CV)
Gewürztraminer Vendange Tardive, Heim
(IR)
**1985**
Gewürztraminer Fronholz Vendange
Tardive, Ostertag (MV)
Gewürztraminer Kitterlé, Schlumberger
(HOG, GRE)
Gewürztraminer Vendange Tardive, Cave
Co-op. de Turckheim (PEN)
Gewürztraminer Vendange Tardive, Hugel
(HAG)
**1983**
Gewürztraminer Eichberg Vendange
Tardive, Dopff au Moulin (BE, TES)

Gewürztraminer Vendange Tardive,
Ostertag (MV)
Tokay-Pinot Gris Vendange Tardive, Dopff
& Irion (HOG, EL)
Riesling Bergheim Burg Vendange
Tardive, Deiss (REI)
Riesling Vendange Tardive, Dopff & Irion
(HOG, EL)
Tokay-Pinot Gris Réserve Personnelle,
Trimbach (BYR)
**1976**
★ Gewürztraminer Seigneurs de
Ribeaupierre, Trimbach (RAE)

─────── **£20.00 to £24.99** ───────
**1985**
Riesling Clos Ste-Hune, Trimbach (AD)
Riesling Vendange Tardive, Faller (LOE)
**1983**
Gewürztraminer Vendange Tardive, Dopff
& Irion (HOG, EL, GRE)
Gewürztraminer Vendange Tardive, Hugel
(HOG)
Gewürztraminer Vendange Tardive
Sélection Personnelle, Hugel (GRE)
Riesling Sélection de Grains Nobles, Dopff
& Irion (HOG, EL)

──────── £25.00 to £29.99 ────────

**1988**

Gewürztraminer Vendange Tardive, Faller (LOE)

Tokay-Pinot Gris Vendange Tardive, Faller (LOE)

**1986**

Gewürztraminer Cuvée Christine, Schlumberger (GRE, NI, LAY)

Gewürztraminer Hengst Vendange Tardive, Zind-Humbrecht (BY)

Gewürztraminer Sélection de Grains Nobles, Dopff & Irion (EL)

**1985**

Gewürztraminer Cuvée Anne Vendange Tardive, Rolly Gassmann (RAE)

Gewürztraminer Cuvée Christine, Schlumberger (REI)

Gewürztraminer Vendange Tardive, Faller (BUT)

Gewürztraminer Vendange Tardive, Christine Schlumberger (BO)

**1983**

Gewürztraminer Cuvée Christine, Schlumberger (BUT)

Gewürztraminer Vendange Tardive, Trimbach (BUT)

Riesling Vendange Tardive, Hugel (LOE)

Tokay-Pinot Gris Vendange Tardive, Hugel (LOE)

──────── £30.00 to £39.99 ────────

**1989**

Gewürztraminer Anne Schlumberger (GRE, AMI)

Gewürztraminer Clos Windsbuhl, Zind-Humbrecht (FA)

Gewürztraminer Vendange Tardive, Anne Schlumberger (REI)

**1976**

Gewürztraminer Vendange Tardive, Hugel (FA)

Tokay-Pinot Gris Réserve Personnelle, Trimbach (VIG)

──────── £40.00 to £49.99 ────────

**1983**

Gewürztraminer Sélection de Grains Nobles, Hugel (LOE)

**1976**

Gewürztraminer Cuvée Christine, Schlumberger (VIG)

Riesling Frédéric Emile Vendange Tardive, Trimbach (VIG)

Riesling Vendange Tardive, Hugel (VIG)

──────── £50.00 to £59.99 ────────

**1988**

Tokay-Pinot Gris Sélection de Grains Nobles, Dopff au Moulin (BER, VIG)

**1983**

Gewürztraminer Sélection de Grains Nobles, Heydt (CB)

**1976**

Gewürztraminer Sélection de Grains Nobles, Hugel (FA)

──────── c. £88.50 ────────

**1976**

Tokay-Pinot Gris Sélection de Grains Nobles, Hugel (REI)

## RED

──────── Under £7.00 ────────

**1990**

Pinot Noir Louis Gisselbrecht (PIP)

**1989**

Pinot Noir Herrenweg, Zind-Humbrecht (BOT, WR)

**1988**

Pinot Noir Hugel (BO)

──────── £7.00 to £9.99 ────────

**1990**

Pinot Noir Schleret (YAP)

Pinot Noir Rolly Gassmann (RAE, BIB)

**1986**

Pinot Noir Hugel (WRI)

**1985**

Pinot Noir Réserve, Rolly Gassmann (RAE)

──────── £11.00 to £13.00 ────────

**1989**

Pinot Noir l'Ancienne, Cave Co-op. Turckheim (ROB)

**1988**

Pinot Noir Réserve Personelle, Hugel (DAV)

## SPARKLING

──────── Under £8.99 ────────

**Non-vintage**

Crémant d'Alsace Cuvée Julien, Dopff au Moulin (GRG, GRE, HOG, WHI)

Crémant d'Alsace Dopff & Irion (EL)

──────── £9.00 to £11.99 ────────

**Non-vintage**

Crémant d'Alsace Cuvée Julien, Dopff au Moulin (ROB, VIG)

# SOUTH-EAST FRANCE

## RED

─────── Under £3.00 ───────

**Non-vintage**
Asda Côtes de Roussillon (ASD)
Asda Minervois (ASD)
Côtes du Roussillon-Villages, Latour de France (GA)
Sainsbury's Corbières (SAI)
Sainsbury's Côtes du Roussillon (SAI)
St-Chinian Rouanet (WAI)
Tesco Corbières (TES)
Tesco Vin de Pays Catalan (TES)
Vin de Pays de l'Hérault, Domaine de la Garrigue (GRG)
Vin de Pays d'Oc Cabernet Sauvignon, Listel (GA)

**1990**
★ Costières de Nîmes Château de Nages (WAI)
Vin de Pays de l'Aude Cabernet Sauvignon, Foncalieu (WAI)

**1988**
Coteaux de Murviel Domaine de Grézan (ASK)
★ Côtes de la Malpère Château Malviès (AUG)

─────── £3.00 to £3.49 ───────

**1990**
★ Cabardès Château Ventenac (MAJ)
Côtes du Lubéron Cellier de Marrenon (LOR)
Faugères l'Estagnon (THR)
Minervois Château Millegrand (EL)
★ Safeway Vin de Pays d'Oc Cépage Merlot, Domaine Anthea (SAF)
Sainsbury's Vin de Pays de la Cité de Carcassonne, Domaine Sautès le Bas (SAI)

**1989**
Corbières Château de Jonquières (TES, BE)
Côtes de Thongue, Clos Ferdinand (BYR)
Minervois Domaine de l'Abbaye de Tholomies (SAF)
St-Chinian Gaston (BYR)

**1988**
Corbières Château les Ollieux (BO)
★ Corbières Chatellerie de Lastours (ASK)
Côtes du Roussillon-Villages, Vignerons Catalans (GE)
★ Fitou Caves du Mont Tauch (HOG, AUG)

─────── £3.50 to £3.99 ───────

**Non-vintage**
Corbières Château de Montrabech (LAY)
Coteaux d'Aix-en-Provence Château la Coste (WHI)
Fitou Mme Claude Parmentier (VIC)

**1991**
Côtes de Thongue Domaine Comte de Margon (AD)

**1990**
Corbières Château de Mandourelle (TAN)
Côtes de Thongue, Clos Ferdinand (WCL)
Côtes du Vivarais Domaine de Belvezet (MV, LAY)
Fitou Caves du Mont Tauch (NI)
Minervois Château de Paraza (OD)
★ Minervois Domaine de Ste-Eulalie (DAV)
Vin de Pays des Maures, Domaine d'Astros (BIB)
Vin de Pays du Gard Domaine de Valescure (BIB)

**1989**
★ Corbières Château de Cabriac (EL, NI, AN, DAV)
Coteaux d'Aix-en-Provence Château de Fonscolombe (LAY)

★ Safeway Corbières, Château de Caraguilhes (SAF)
Sainsbury's Minervois, Château de Gourgazaud (SAI)
St-Chinian Rouanet (HIG)
Vin de Pays de l'Aude Domaine du Puget (PEN, CV)
Vin de Pays de Mont Caume Cabernet Sauvignon, Bunan (ASD)

**1988**
★ La Clape Domaine de Pech Celeyran (AD)
★ Faugères Château de Grézan (PEN)
Fitou Resplandy (BO)
St-Chinian Domaine des Soulié (AUG)

**1986**

Corbières Château de Mandourelle (BU)

──────── **£4.00 to £4.99** ────────

**1991**

Côtes du Vivarais Domaine de Belvezet (AD)

Coteaux de Murviel, Domaine de Limbardie (AD)

Vin de Pays d'Oc Domaine d'Ormesson (PIP)

**1990**

★ Corbières Château St-Auriol (THR)

Coteaux d'Aix-en-Provence Château de la Gaude (YAP)

★ Coteaux des Baux-en-Provence Mas de Gourgonnier (HAU)

Coteaux du Lyonnais, Duboeuf (PIP)

Côtes du Lubéron Château Val Joanis (ASD, ASK)

**1989**

Corbières Château de Lastours (CV, THR)

Corbières Château les Ollieux (PE, RAE, WCL)

Corbières Chatellerie de Lastours (CV)

Coteaux du Languedoc Domaine de l'Abbaye de Valmagne (EL, GRE)

Côtes de Provence les Maîtres Vignerons de St-Tropez (BEK)

Minervois Château de Gourgazaud (REI)

Minervois Château de Paraza (NA)

Minervois Château Villerambert, Julien (TAN)

Minervois Maris (HAU)

**1988**

Coteaux d'Aix-en-Provence Château de la Gaude (BYR)

Coteaux d'Aix-en-Provence Domaine de Paradis (YF)

Coteaux du Languedoc Château Pech-Celeyran (TAN, BER)

Faugères Domaine de Fraisse (WHI)

Minervois Château de Paraza (MV)

Sainsbury's Corbières, Château St-Auriol (SAI)

**1987**

★ Coteaux d'Aix-en-Provence Mas de la Dame (AUG)

Vin de Pays de Mont Caume, Bunan (YAP)

Vin de Pays des Sables du Golfe du Lion, Domaine du Bosquet (PEN, HAG)

**1986**

Côtes de Provence Domaine de Rimauresq (BYR)

**1983**

Corbières Château de Mandourelle (BU)

──────── **£5.00 to £6.99** ────────

**1990**

Costières de Nîmes Château de la Tuilerie (AV)

Côtes de Provence les Maîtres Vignerons de St-Tropez (PIP)

Côtes du Lubéron Château de Canorgue (YAP)

Faugères Château de Grézan (ASK)

Minervois Daniel Domergue (CB)

**1989**

Côtes de Provence Château Rimauresq (ASK)

Côtes du Roussillon Black Label, Domaine Sarda Malet (BIB)

**1988**

Corbières Château de Lastours (PEN, ROB)

Coteaux Varois Domaine St-Estève (BYR)

Côtes de Provence Château de Pampelonne, les Maîtres Vignerons de St-Tropez (BEK)

Côtes du Lubéron Château de l'Isolette (PIP)

**1987**

★ Bandol Mas de la Rouvière, Bunan (NI)

Coteaux d'Aix-en-Provence les Baux Terres Blanches (HAG)

Coteaux Varois Cuvée Speciale, Domaine de St-Jean de Villecroze (BYR)

Côtes de Provence les Maîtres Vignerons de St-Tropez (WHI)

**1986**

Corbières Domaine de Fontsainte (YF)

**1985**

Bandol Domaine de Cagueloup (BYR)

Coteaux de Murviel, Domaine de Ravanes (HIC)

**1983**

★ Bandol Château Vannières (BUT)

──────── **£7.00 to £8.99** ────────

**1989**

★ Bandol Domaine Tempier (WW)

Coteaux Varois Cépage Syrah, Domaine de St-Jean de Villecroze (BYR)

Côtes de Provence Domaine Richeaume (SAF)

**1988**

Bandol Domaine Tempier (WS)

Bandol Mas de la Rouvière, Bunan (YAP, BYR)

Coteaux d'Aix-en-Provence Domaine les Bastides Cuvée Speciale (WW)

**1984**

Bandol Domaine Tempier (GE)

─────── **£9.00 to £10.99** ───────

**1990**
Vin de Pays de l'Hérault, Mas de Daumas
  Gassac (AD, HAU)
**1989**
Bandol Cuvée Migoua (WW, BYR)
Bandol Cuvée Tourtine (WW, BYR)
Vin de Pays de l'Hérault, Mas de Daumas
  Gassac (SOM, OD, GRE)
**1988**
Coteaux d'Aix-en-Provence Domaine de
  Trévallon (SOM, YAP)
**1987**
Bandol Château de la Rouvière, Bunan
  (YAP)
Bandol Domaine de Pibarnon (BEK, PIP)
**1986**
Bandol Château Vannières (REI)

─────── **£11.00 to £14.99** ───────

**1990**
Bellet Château de Crémat, Jean Bagnis
  (YAP)
Coteaux d'Aix-en-Provence, Domaine de
  Trévallon (YAP)
**1988**
Vin de Pays de l'Hérault, Mas de Daumas
  Gassac (BO, AMI, BUT)
**1986**
Vin de Pays de l'Hérault, Mas de Daumas
  Gassac (VIG)
**1985**
Vin de Pays de l'Hérault, Mas de Daumas
  Gassac (BO)

─────── **£15.00 to £20.00** ───────

**1989**
Côtes de Provence Domaines Ott (PEN)
**1983**
Vin de Pays de l'Hérault, Mas de Daumas
  Gassac (VIG)

## WHITE

─────── **Under £4.00** ───────

**Non-vintage**
Tesco Vin de Pays de l'Aude (TES)
**1991**
Côtes du Lubéron la Vieille Ferme (MV)
**1990**
Coteaux d'Aix-en-Provence Château de
  Fonscolombe (LAY)
**1989**
Corbières les Producteurs du Mont Tauch
  (AUG)

─────── **£4.00 to £4.99** ───────

**Non-vintage**
Vin de Pays des Sables du Golfe du Lion,
  Listel Blanc (PE)
**1991**
Côtes de Provence Mas de Cadenet (WW)
Côtes du Lubéron Château Val Joanis (ASK)
★ Vin de Pays d'Oc Cépage Chardonnay,
  Ryman (SAI)
**1990**
Coteaux d'Aix-en-Provence Domaine de
  Paradis (YF)
Côtes du Lubéron la Vieille Ferme (GRE)
Vin de Pays de l'Hérault, Cante-Cigale
  (TAN)
Vin de Pays de l'Hérault Marsanne, du
  Bosc (TAN, AD)
**1989**
Côtes du Lubéron Château Val Joanis
  (WHI)

─────── **£5.00 to £6.99** ───────

**Non-vintage**
Côtes de Provence l'Estandon Blanc de
  Blancs, Bagnis (YAP)
**1989**
Bandol Mas de la Rouvière, Bunan (YAP)

─────── **£7.00 to £8.99** ───────

**1991**
Coteaux des Baux-en-Provence Terres
  Blanches (VIG)
**1990**
Cassis Clos Ste-Magdeleine, Sack (YAP)
**1987**
Bandol Château de la Rouvière, Bunan
  (YAP)

─────── **£10.00 to £12.99** ───────

**1990**
Bellet Château de Crémat, Jean Bagnis
  (YAP)
Vin de Pays de l'Hérault Mas de Daumas
  Gassac (SOM)
**1988**
Palette Château Simone (YAP)

─────── **£14.00 to £17.99** ───────

**1991**
Vin de Pays de l'Hérault Mas de Daumas
  Gassac (HAU)
**1989**
Côtes de Provence Domaines Ott (PEN)
Vin de Pays de l'Hérault Mas de Daumas
  Gassac (BUT, BO, AMI)

---------------- c. £21.00 ----------------
**1987**
Vin de Pays de l'Hérault Mas de Daumas
  Gassac (BUT)

## ROSÉ

---------------- Under £4.00 ----------------
**Non-vintage**
Gris de Gris Listel (BYR, AUG, HAG)
Vin de Pays des Sables du Golfe du Lion
  Gris de Gris, Domaine de Jarras (CH)

---------------- £4.00 to £4.99 ----------------
**1991**
Coteaux d'Aix-en-Provence Château de
  Fonscolombe (AD)
Côtes du Lubéron Château Val Joanis
  (ASK)
**1990**
Coteaux d'Aix-en-Provence Château de la
  Gaude, Baron de Vitrolles (YAP)
Vin de Pays de l'Hérault, Mas de Daumas
  Gassac (SOM)

---------------- £5.00 to £6.99 ----------------
**1991**
Vin de Pays de l'Hérault, Mas de Daumas
  Gassac (HAU)
**1990**
Costières de Nîmes Château de la Tuilerie
  (AV)

---------------- £7.00 to £9.99 ----------------
**1991**
Coteaux des Baux-en-Provence Terres
  Blanches (VIG)
**1990**
Bandol Mas de la Rouvière (YAP)
**1989**
Vin de Pays de l'Hérault, Mas de Daumas
  Gassac (BUT)
**1986**
Vin de Pays de l'Hérault, Mas de Daumas
  Gassac (BUT)

---------------- £11.00 to £13.99 ----------------
**1990**
Côtes de Provence Château de Selle Coeur
  de Grain, Domaines Ott (BYR)
Côtes de Provence Château de Selle,
  Domaines Ott (AN)
**1989**
Côtes de Provence Château de Selle,
  Domaines Ott (HAG, GRG)

## SPARKLING

---------------- Under £7.00 ----------------
**Non-vintage**
Blanquette de Limoux Brut Delmas (THR)
★ Blanquette de Limoux Philippe Vergnes
  (HAG)
**1985**
Blanquette de Limoux Aimery (HOG, AN)
Blanquette de Limoux Brut Producteurs de
  Blanquette (BO)

---------------- c. £9.00 ----------------
**1983**
Blanquette de Limoux Sieur d'Arques (BER)

## FORTIFIED

---------------- Under £3.00 ----------------
**Non-vintage**
★ Sainsbury's Muscat de St-Jean de
  Minervois ½ bottle (SAI)

---------------- £6.00 to £7.99 ----------------
**Non-vintage**
★ Muscat de Frontignan, Château de la
  Peyrade (HAU)
**1989**
Muscat de Rivesaltes Domaine Cazes (WW)
**1986**
★ Vintage Rivesaltes Domaine Cazes (BAR)

---------------- £8.00 to £9.99 ----------------
**1990**
Muscat de Rivesaltes Domaine Cazes (ROB,
  BAR)
**1987**
Muscat de Rivesaltes Château de Jau (BO)
**1978**
Muscat de Rivesaultes Vieux, Domaine
  Cazes (WW)

---------------- c. £23.00 ----------------
**1969**
Maury Mas Amiel (VIG)

# SOUTH-WEST FRANCE

## RED

### ———— Under £3.00 ————

**Non-vintage**
Asda Cahors (ASD)
Sainsbury's Bergerac (SAI)
**1990**
Côtes du Marmandais Château Marseau
(WAI)
**1989**
Côtes de Duras Seigneuret (WAI)
Côtes de St-Mont, Producteurs Plaimont
(SOM)
Côtes du Marmandais Château Marseau
(WAI)
**1988**
Côtes de Duras Seigneuret (WAI)

### ———— £3.00 to £3.99 ————

**Non-vintage**
Asda Fronton (ASD)
**1990**
Côtes de Gascogne Domaine le Puts (BO)
Côtes de St-Mont Les Hauts de Bergelle
(TAN)
Côtes de St-Mont, Producteurs Plaimont
(PIP, AD)
Côtes du Frontonnais Carte Blanche
Château Montauriol (OD)
★ Côtes du Frontonnais Château
Bellevue-la-Forêt (SAI, OD)
Côtes du Marmandais Cave de Cocumont
(GA)
Gaillac Domaine de Labarthe (SOM)
**1989**
Cahors Carte Noire, Rigal (HAY)
Cahors Château St-Didier-Parnac, Rigal
(OD)
Côtes de St-Mont, Producteurs Plaimont
(TAN, MAR)
Côtes du Frontonnais Château Ferran
(BYR)
**1987**
Cabardès Domaine de Cannettes Hautes
(HAY)
Côtes de Duras les Producteurs Réunis
(AUG)

### ———— £4.00 to £4.99 ————

**1991**
Gaillac Cépage Gamay Domaine Jean Cros
(CH)

**1990**
★ Cahors Château de Gaudou (WCL)
Cahors Domaine Pierre Sèche (CV)
Côtes du Frontonnais Château Bellevue-
la-Forêt (NI)
Côtes du Frontonnais Château Ferran (CV,
WCL)
Gaillac Cépage Gamay Domaine Jean Cros
(BO)
★ Gaillac Château Clement Termes (THR,
ASK, BAR)
Madiran Domaine Damiens (BIB)
**1989**
★ Bergerac Château la Jaubertie (NI)
Côtes de St-Mont Les Hauts de Bergelle
(ROB)
Côtes de St-Mont, Producteurs Plaimont
(HAU)
Côtes du Frontonnais Château Baudare
(CV)
Côtes du Frontonnais Château Flotis (HAU)
Gaillac Château Larroze (BE, TES)
**1988**
Côtes de Bergerac Château le Tour des
Gendres (NI)
Côtes de St-Mont Les Hauts de Bergelle
(ROB)
Côtes du Frontonnais Château Baudare
(CV)
Côtes du Frontonnais Château Bellevue-
la-Forêt (AUG)
Gaillac Domaine Jean Cros (TES, BE)
**1987**
Buzet Tradition les Vignerons de Buzet
(PE)
Cahors Domaine Pierre Sèche (CV)

### ———— £5.00 to £5.99 ————

**1990**
Marcillac Domaine du Cros, Teulier (AD)
**1989**
Bergerac Château la Jaubertie (WHI, LAY)
Cahors Clos la Coutale (WW)
Cahors Domaine de la Pineraie (CV)
Côtes de Duras Domaine de Laulan (HUN)

---

*Stars (★) indicate wines
selected by the editors as
particularly good value
in their class.*

**1988**
Bergerac Château la Jaubertie (CH)
★ Cahors Château d'Eugénie (PIP)
Cahors Château St-Didier-Parnac, Rigal
  (LAY)
Cahors Domaine de la Pineraie (BYR, CV)
Côtes de Bergerac Château Court-les-Mûts
  (BIB)
Côtes du Frontonnais Château Flotis (HAU)
Marcillac Domaine du Cros, Teulier (VIG)
**1987**
Cahors Château de Grezels, Rigal (AUG)
**1986**
Cahors Domaine de la Pineraie (BYR)
Madiran Château de Peyros (REI)

─────── **£6.00 to £7.99** ───────
**1989**
Pécharmant Château de Tiregand (TAN)
**1988**
Bergerac Reserve Château la Jaubertie
  (VIC)
Cahors Château Lagrezette (BEK, ROB)
Madiran Château d'Aydie (PIP)
Madiran Domaine Boucassé, Alain
  Brumont (HAU)
**1986**
Cahors Prieuré de Senac (THR)
**1985**
Bergerac Reserve Château la Jaubertie
  (NI)

─────── **£8.00 to £9.99** ───────
**1989**
Madiran Château Montus (HAU)
**1985**
Cahors Château du Cayrou, Jouffreau
  (TAN)

─────── **£12.00 to £13.99** ───────
**Non-vintage**
Côtes du Marmandais Château Sarazière
  (MAR)
**1989**
Bergerac Reserve Château la Jaubertie
  (REI)

## DRY WHITE

─────── **Under £3.00** ───────
**Non-vintage**
Asda Vin de Pays des Côtes de Gascogne
  (ASD)
Sainsbury's Bergerac (SAI)
**1991**
Côtes de Gascogne Producteurs Plaimont
  (SOM)
**1990**
Côtes de Duras Croix du Beurrier (WAI)

─────── **£3.00 to £3.99** ───────
**Non-vintage**
Asda Côtes de Duras (ASD)
**1991**
Bergerac Sauvignon Foncaussade (SAF)
Côtes de Gascogne Domaine de Planterieu
  (WAI)
Côtes de Gascogne Domaine de Rieux (PE,
  REI, NA, TAN, AD)
★ Côtes de Gascogne Domaine de San de
  Guilhem (HOG, MV)
Côtes de Gascogne Domaine de Tariquet
  (BAR, THR, BU)
Côtes de Gascogne Domaine le Puts (MAJ,
  CV)
Côtes de Gascogne Producteurs Plaimont
  (TAN, HAU)
Côtes de St-Mont Producteurs Plaimont
  (AD)
Vin de Pays Charentais Cave St-André
  (ROB)
**1990**
Côtes de Gascogne Cépage Colombard
  (LOR, LAY, EL, IR, ROB)
Côtes de Gascogne Domaine de Rieux (CH)
Côtes de Gascogne Domaine de Tariquet
  (BYR, BU)
Côtes de Gascogne Producteurs Plaimont
  (MAR)
Côtes de St-Mont Producteurs Plaimont
  (LAY, TAN)
Vin de Pays des Landes, Domaine du
  Comte (GE)
★ Vin de Pays des Terroirs Landais,
  Domaine de Laballe (BER)

┌─────────────────────────┐
│ *In each price band wines* │
│ *are listed in vintage order.* │
│ *Within each vintage they* │
│ *are listed in A-Z order.* │
└─────────────────────────┘

--------- **£4.00 to £4.99** ---------

**Non-vintage**
Côtes de Gascogne Domaine de Tariquet
(BO)
**1991**
Côtes de Gascogne Domaine de Rieux (BER)
Pacherenc du Vic-Bilh Domaine Damiens
(BIB)
**1990**
Bergerac Château la Jaubertie (NI, MAJ,
VIC)
Bergerac Château le Fagé (BER, NA)
Bergerac Sec Château de Tiregand (TAN)
Chardonnay Ryman (MAJ)
Côtes de Duras Sauvignon, les Vignerons
des Coteaux de Duras (BEK)
Côtes de Gascogne Domaine des
Cassagnoles (BOD)
Côtes de St-Mont Les Hauts de Bergelle
(TAN, ROB, BER)
**1989**
★ Bergerac Château la Jaubertie (NI)
**1988**
Bergerac Domaine de Grandchamp (GE)

--------- **£5.00 to £5.99** ---------

**1991**
Côtes de Gascogne Cuvée Bois Domaine de
Tariquet (THR)
**1990**
Bergerac Château la Jaubertie (HIG)
Bergerac Château la Jaubertie Cépage
Sauvignon (NI)
Bergerac Domaine de Grandchamp (WHI)
Côtes de Gascogne Domaine de Tariquet
(MAJ)
Côtes de Saussignac Château Court-les-
Mûts (BIB)
**1989**
Bergerac Château la Jaubertie (LAY)
**1988**
Cahors Clos de Lagarde, Perez (CB)

--------- **£6.00 to £6.99** ---------

**1991**
Pacherenc du Vic-Bilh Domaine Boucassé
(HAU)
**1990**
Bergerac Château la Jaubertie Cépage
Sauvignon (HIG)
**1989**
Bergerac Château la Jaubertie Cépage
Sauvignon (WHI)
**1988**
★ Jurançon Sec Domaine Cauhapé (NI)

--------- **£7.00 to £8.99** ---------

**1990**
Jurançon Château Jolys (TAN)
Jurançon Sec Domaine Cauhapé (MV, AD,
TAN)

**1989**
Jurançon Sec Domaine Cauhapé (ROB)

--------- **£9.00 to £12.99** ---------

**1991**
Jurançon Sec Domaine Cauhapé (WCL)
**1990**
Jurançon Sec Domaine Cauhapé (VIG)
**1988**
Jurançon Sec Domaine Cauhapé (WCL)

### SWEET WHITE

--------- **Under £7.00** ---------

**1989**
Jurançon Moelleux Château Jolys (WHI)
Monbazillac Château Theulet (BAR, ROB)
**1986**
Monbazillac Château la Brie (AUG)

--------- **£7.00 to £7.99** ---------

**1989**
Jurançon Clos Guirouilh (ROB)
Monbazillac Château Theulet (VIG)
**1986**
Jurançon Cru Lamouroux (HAY)

--------- **£12.00 to £14.99** ---------

**1990**
Jurançon Moelleux Domaine Cauhapé (AD)
**1989**
Jurançon Grains Nobles, Cave de Gan (REI)
Jurançon Moelleux Domaine Cauhapé (AD)
**1980**
Monbazillac Clos Fontindoule (VIG)

### ROSÉ

--------- **£4.00 to £5.99** ---------

**1990**
Bergerac Château la Jaubertie (NI)

# JURA

## RED

### £5.00 to £6.99

**1988**
★ Côtes de Jura Pinot Noir/Trousseau,
  Boilley (CV, WCL)
**1985**
Côtes de Jura Pinot Noir/Trousseau,
  Boilley (GRG)

## WHITE

### Under £5.00

**1988**
Côtes du Jura Chardonnay, Germain (YF)

### £5.00 to £6.99

**1987**
Côtes de Jura Cépage Chardonnay, Boilley
  (CV, GRG)
**1986**
Côtes de Jura Cépage Savagnin, Boilley
  (ASK)

### The Hugh Johnson Collection

Hugh Johnson's shop is a treasure
house of beautiful and functional
things for the wine connoisseur. Wine
glasses, decanters, claret jugs, wine
funnels, corkscrews, port tongs, cellar
books, decanting cradles, wine
coolers, decanter labels, bottle
carriers, coasters, pictures, maps and
everything collectable is to be found
here, either as antiques or craftsman-
made to Hugh Johnson's own design.

**68 St. James's Street
London SW1A 1PH.
Tel: 071-491 4912 Fax: 071-493 0602**
Monday to Friday 9.30 to 5.30

### £7.00 to £8.99

**1989**
Côtes de Jura Cépage Savagnin, Boilley
  (WCL)
**1987**
Côtes du Jura Vin Jaune Château d'Arlay
  (VIG)

### c. £17.00

**1964**
Vin Jaune de Gard, d'Arlay (ASK)

### £22.00 to £28.99

**1982**
Côtes du Jura Vin Jaune Château d'Arlay
  (REI)
Vin Jaune d'Arbois, d'Arlay (TAN)
**1979**
Château-Chalon Vin Jaune, Maire
  (ROB)

### c. £32.00

**1979**
Château-Chalon Vin Jaune, Bourdy (WS)

## ROSÉ

### c. £4.00

**Non-vintage**
Cendre Vin Gris, Maire (HAG)

## SAVOIE

## WHITE

### £4.00 to £5.99

**1991**
★ Apremont Pierre Boniface (TAN)
Vin de Savoie Abymes, Perrier (EL)

## OTHER FRENCH SPARKLING

### Under £5.00

**Non-vintage**
Cavalier Cuvée Close (MAJ, AUG, CV)

### £5.00 to £6.99

**Non-vintage**
Comte de Neufchâtel Brut (BAR, WRI)
Flutelle (BAR, ROB)
Kriter Brut (UN)
Veuve du Vernay (SAI, BO, AUG, UN, EL)

# RHINE

| | | |
|---|---|---|
| Kab. | = | Kabinett |
| Spät. | = | Spätlese |
| Aus. | = | Auslese |
| BA | = | Beerenauslese |
| TBA | = | Trockenbeerenauslese |

## WHITE

--------------- Under £3.00 ---------------

**Non-vintage**
Asda Liebfraumilch (ASD)
Asda Niersteiner Spiegelberg Kab. (ASD)
Liebfraumilch Rudolf Müller (LAY)
★ Rheingau Riesling, Schloss
  Reinhartshausen (GA)
Sainsbury's Liebfraumilch (SAI)
Sainsbury's Trocken QbA, Rheinhessen
  (SAI)
Tesco Hock (TES)
Tesco Niersteiner Gutes Domtal (TES)
Victoria Wine Liebfraumilch (VIC)
Waitrose Liebfraumilch (WAI)

--------------- £3.00 to £3.99 ---------------

**Non-vintage**
Liebfraumilch Black Tower (ASD, GA, SAF,
  WHI, THR)
**1991**
Liebfraumilch Blue Nun (BO, GA, SAF, THR,
  WHI, UN)
Liebfraumilch Crown of Crowns (PE, WHI)
Tesco St-Johanner Abtei Kab. (TES)
**1990**
Liebfraumilch Blue Nun (WAI, DAV)
Niersteiner Gutes Domtal, Rudolf Müller
  (HAH, CB)
★ Niersteiner Spiegelberg Riesling Kab.,
  Rudolf Müller (TAN)
Sainsbury's Oppenheimer Krötenbrunnen
  Kab. (SAI)
**1988**
Erben Kab., Langguth (AUG)
Niersteiner Gutes Domtal, Deinhard (HOG)

--------------- £4.00 to £4.99 ---------------

**1990**
Binger Scharlachberg Riesling Kab., Villa
  Sachsen (TES)
Mainzer Domherr Bacchus Kab., Guntrum
  (PIP)

**1989**
Mainzer Domherr Bacchus Kab., Guntrum
  (WRI)
Niersteiner Spiegelberg Kab., Guntrum
  (PIP)
**1983**
★ Oestricher Doosberg Riesling Kab.,
  Schönborn (GA)

--------------- £5.00 to £5.99 ---------------

**1991**
Niersteiner Spiegelberg Kab., Guntrum
  (DAV)
**1990**
Niersteiner Spiegelberg Kab., Guntrum
  (DAV)
**1989**
Kreuznacher St-Martin Riesling Kab.,
  Anheuser (BYR)
Niersteiner Auflangen Riesling Kab.,
  Gessert (LOE)
Niersteiner Rosenberg Riesling Kab.,
  Rappenhof (BER)
Oppenheimer Schloss Müller-Thurgau
  Trocken, Guntrum (WRI)
**1988**
Dexheimer Doktor Spät., Guntrum (AS)
★ Schloss Böckelheimer Kupfergrube
  Riesling Aus., Staatsdomäne (GE)
★ Wachenheimer Rechbächel Riesling
  Kab., Bürklin-Wolf (ASD)
**1986**
Wallhäuser Muehlenberg Riesling
  Trocken, Prinz zu Salm-Dalberg'sches
  Weingut (HAC)
**1985**
Eltviller Sonnenberg Riesling Kab.,
  Simmern (RAE)
**1983**
Kiedricher Sandgrub Riesling Kab.,
  Fischer (LOE)
★ Niederhäuser Hermannsberg Riesling
  Kab., Staatliche Weinbaudomäne (LOE)
**1982**
Hochheimer Domdechaney Riesling Kab.,
  Aschrott (BU)

--------------- £6.00 to £6.99 ---------------

**1990**
Niersteiner Klostergarten Riesling Kab.,
  Balbach (AD)
Niersteiner Oelberg Spät., Gessert (NI)

**1989**
Schloss Vollrads Grün-Gold, Matuschka-
Greiffenclau (EL)
**1988**
Deidesheimer Kieselberg Riesling Kab.,
Basserman-Jordan (WCL)
Hochheimer Hölle Riesling Kab., Aschrott
(WHI)
Johannisberger Erntebringer Riesling
Kab., Hessisches Weingut (WCL)
Kreuznacher Kahlenberg Riesling Spät.,
Paul Anheuser (CV)
Niederhauser Felsensteyer Riesling Spät.,
Anheuser (HA)
Niersteiner Oelberg Spät., Gessert (LOE)
Schloss Böckelheimer Kupfergrube
Riesling Kab., Staatliche
Weinbaudomäne (GE, LAY)
Winzenheimer Rosenheck Riesling Spät.,
Plettenberg (MAJ)

**1987**
Wallhäuser Johannisberg Riesling Aus.,
Prinz zu Salm-Dalberg'sches Weingut
(WCL)
**1986**
Eltviller Sonnenberg Riesling Kab.,
Fischer (LOE)
Forster Jesuitengarten Riesling Kab.,
Bürklin-Wolf (PIP)
Rauenthaler Baiken Riesling Kab.,
Simmern (BYR)
**1985**
Deidesheimer Hohenmorgen Riesling Kab.,
Basser-Jordan (LAY)
★ Niersteiner Pettenthal Riesling Spät.,
Balbach (TES)
Schloss Böckelheimer Kupfergrube
Riesling Kab., Staatliche
Weinbaudomäne (LOE)
**1983**
★ Kreuznacher Kapellenpfad Riesling
Spät., Plettenberg (LOE, BYR)
Norheimer Dellchen Riesling Spät.,
August Anheuser (HOG)

Oestricher Doosberg Spät., Schönborn (EL)
**1975**
★ Forster Freundstück Riesling Spät.,
Buhl (LOE)

——————— £7.00 to £7.99 ———————
**1990**
Kiedricher Sandgrub Riesling Kab.,
Schloss Groenesteyn (HOG)
Kreuznacher Kahlenberg Riesling Spät.,
Plettenberg (WR, BOT)
Schloss Böckelheimer Kupfergrube
Riesling Kab., Staatliche
Weinbaudomäne (TAN)
**1989**
Deidesheimer Herrgottsacker Riesling
Kab., Bürklin-Wolf (BYR)
Eltviller Sonnenberg Riesling Kab.,
Simmern (AD)
Forster Kirchenstuck Riesling Kab.,
Bassermann-Jordan (BIB)
★ Forster Mariengarten Riesling Kab.,
Bürklin-Wolf (ROB)
Oppenheimer Herrenberg Scheurebe Spät.,
Guntrum (WRI)
Oppenheimer Kreuz Riesling Spät.
Trocken, Guntrum (PIP)
**1988**
Hochheimer Hölle Riesling Kab., Aschrott
(AV)
Johannisberg Deinhard Heritage Selection
(DAV, THR)
★ Kreuznacher Kahlenberg Riesling Spät.,
Paul Anheuser (ROB)
Niersteiner Oelberg Riesling Kab.,
Herrnsheim (HAC)
Winkeler Hasensprung Riesling Spät.,
Eser (LOE)
**1987**
Grosskarlbacher Burgweg Scheurebe Kab.,
Lingenfelder (HAC)
**1986**
Erbacher Marcobrunnen Riesling Kab.,
Simmern (LAY)
Freinsheimer Goldberg Riesling Spät.,
Lingenfelder (HAC)
Winkeler Hasensprung Riesling Kab.,
Deinhard (ROB)
**1985**
Kreuznacher Brückes Riesling Spät.,
August Anheuser (LOE)
Kreuznacher Kahlenberg Riesling Spät.,
Plettenberg (LOE, PE)
Niederhauser Hermannshöhle Riesling
Spät., Staatliche Weinbaudomäne (LOE)

★ Schloss Böckelheimer Kupfergrube
  Riesling Spät., Staatliche
  Weinbaudomäne (RAE)
**1983**
★ Hochheimer Hölle Riesling Spät.,
  Aschrott (LOE)
Traisener Rotenfels Riesling Spät.,
  Crusius (HOG)
**1982**
Deidesheimer Herrgottsacker Riesling
  Spät., Deinhard (HAG)

──────── **£8.00 to £9.99** ────────
**1990**
Schloss Vollrads Blau-Silber, Matuschka-
  Greiffenclau (EL)
**1989**
Johannisberger Erntebringer Riesling
  Kab., Deinhard (BER)
Riesling Spät. Trocken, Weingut
  Lingenfelder (NI, AD)
★ Steinberger Riesling Kab.,
  Staatsweingüter Eltville (HOG)
**1988**
Deidesheimer Hohenmorgen Riesling
  Spät., Basser-Jordan (RAE)
Forster Jesuitengarten Riesling Kab.,
  Bassermann-Jordan (VIC)
Forster Kirkenstuck Aus., Bassermann-
  Jordan (HAY)
Forster Mariengarten Riesling Kab.,
  Bürklin-Wolf (HAC)
Forster Ungeheuer Riesling Spät.,
  Deinhard (PEN)
★ Freinsheimer Goldberg Scheurebe
  Spät., Lingenfelder (HAC)
Johannisberg Deinhard Heritage Selection
  (AV)
Kreuznacher St-Martin Riesling Kab.,
  Anheuser (PE)
Niederhauser Hermannsberg Riesling
  Kab., Staatliche Weinbaudomäne (AD)
Niederhauser Steinberg Riesling Spät.,
  Staatliche Weinbaudomäne (GE)
Schloss Vollrads Blau-Gold, Matuschka-
  Greiffenclau (BYR)
Schloss Vollrads Blau-Silber, Matuschka-
  Greiffenclau (BYR)
Winkeler Hasensprung Riesling Spät.,
  Eser (BYR)
**1987**
Hochheimer Königin Victoria Berg
  Riesling Kab., Deinhard (WHI)
Rüdesheimer Berg Roseneck Riesling Kab.,
  Deinhard (PEN)

**1986**
Niersteiner Oelberg Riesling Spät., Senfter
  (HOG)
Rauenthaler Baiken Riesling QbA Charta,
  Verwaltung der Staatsweingüter Eltville
  (HAC)
Wachenheimer Goldbachel Riesling Spät.,
  Bürklin-Wolf (LOE)
**1985**
Erbacher Siegelsberg Riesling Kab.,
  Schloss Reinhartshausen (AN, HAC, ROB)
Forster Jesuitengarten Riesling Spät.,
  Buhl (LOE)
Hochheimer Domdechaney Riesling Kab.,
  Aschrott (BYR)
Kiedricher Sandgrub Riesling Kab.,
  Schloss Groenesteyn (BER)
Kreuznacher Brückes Riesling Aus.,
  Plettenburg (LOE)
Schloss Böckelheimer Kupfergrube
  Riesling Kab., Staatliche
  Weinbaudomäne (BYR)
★ Winkeler Hasensprung Riesling Spät.,
  Deinhard (BER)
**1983**
Deidesheimer Herrgottsacker Riesling
  Aus., Deinhard (HOG)
Hochheimer Hölle Riesling Spät., Aschrott
  (BER)
★ Wachenheimer Gerümpel Riesling
  Spät., Bürklin-Wolf (BYR, GRE)
**1976**
★ Schloss Böckelheimer Burgweg Riesling
  Aus., Pleitz (HE)
**1975**
Forster Freundstück Riesling Spät., Buhl
  (BYR)

──────── **£10.00 to £11.99** ────────
**1990**
Scheurebe Spät. Trocken, Lingenfelder
  (WCL)
**1989**
Freinsheimer Goldberg Riesling Spät.,
  Lingenfelder (WCL, ROB)
Schloss Böckelheimer Felsenberg Riesling
  Aus., Crusius (HA)
**1988**
Hochheimer Königin Victoria Berg
  Riesling Spät., Deinhard (PEN)
Scheurebe Spät. Trocken, Lingenfelder
  (AD)
**1986**
Ruppertsberger Hoheburg Riesling Aus.,
  Bürklin-Wolf (GE)

**1985**

Hochheimer Hölle Riesling Spät., Aschrott
(BER)

Kreuznacher Brückes Riesling Aus.,
Plettenburg (BYR)

Niersteiner Rehbach Riesling Spät.,
Herrnsheim (HAC)

Winkeler Hasensprung Riesling Spät.,
Deinhard (TAN)

**1983**

★ Erbacher Marcobrunnen Riesling Spät.,
Staatsweingüter Eltville (HOG)

Freinsheimer Goldberg Riesling Spät.,
Lingenfelder (HAC)

Hochheimer Königin Victoria Berg
Riesling Spät., Deinhard (PEN)

Niersteiner Oelberg Riesling Aus., Senfter
(WHI)

★ Rauenthaler Baiken Riesling Spät.,
Staatsweingüter Eltville (HOG)

Wachenheimer Gerümpel Riesling Spät.,
Bürklin-Wolf (HAC)

**1976**

Kreuznacher Narrenkappe Riesling Aus.,
Anheuser (TES)

─────── **£12.00 to £14.99** ───────

**1985**

Hochheimer Hölle Riesling Aus., Aschrott
(LOE)

**1983**

Hattenheimer Wisselbrunnen Riesling
Aus., Schloss Reinhartshausen
(HAG)

Oestricher Lenchen Riesling Aus.,
Deinhard (HAG)

Wachenheimer Mandelgarten Scheurebe
Aus., Bürklin-Wolf (PE)

**1976**

★ Erbacher Siegelsberg Riesling Spät.,
Schloss Reinhartshausen (BER)

Kiedricher Sandgrub Riesling Aus.,
Fischer (LOE)

─────── **£15.00 to £19.99** ───────

**1985**

Wachenheimer Rechbächel Riesling Aus.,
Bürklin-Wolf (AD)

**1983**

Wachenheimer Böhlig Riesling Aus.,
Bürklin-Wolf (BER)

**1979**

Erbacher Marcobrunnen Riesling Spät.,
Staatsweingüter Eltville (HAC)

**1976**

Bechtheimer Stein BA, Wissmann (HAG)

Johannisberger Hölle Riesling Aus.,
Deinhard (BER)

Kiedricher Sandgrub Riesling Aus.,
Fischer (BYR)

Oestricher Lenchen Riesling Aus.,
Deinhard (YF)

─────── **£20.00 to £29.99** ───────

**1976**

Niersteiner Kranzberg Riesling BA,
Senfter (WRI)

Niersteiner Oelberg Riesling BA,
Herrnsheim (HAC)

Niersteiner Oelberg Riesling & Ruländer
TBA, Senfter (GRE)

─────── **£30.00 to £40.00** ───────

**1971**

Hattenheimer Wisselbrunnen Riesling
Aus., Schloss Reinhartshausen (HAC)

**1985**

Grosskarlbacher Burgweg Scheurebe TBA
½ Bottle, Lingenfelder (HAC)

─────── **c. £44.00** ───────

**1976**

Binger Scharlachberg Riesling BA,
Staatliche Weinbaudomänen (AD)

─────── **c. £92.00** ───────

**1971**

Oestricher Lenchen Riesling TBA,
Deinhard (TAN)

### RED

─────── **£8.00 to £12.00** ───────

**1989**

Spätburgunder QbA, Lingenfelder (ROB)

**1987**

Spätburgunder QbA, Lingenfelder (HAC)

**1986**

Spätburgunder QbA, Lingenfelder (VIG)

# MOSEL/FRANKEN/BADEN

| Kab. | = | Kabinett |
|------|---|----------|
| Spät. | = | Spätlese |
| Aus. | = | Auslese |
| BA | = | Beerenauslese |
| TBA | = | Trockenbeerenauslese |

## MOSEL WHITE

### Under £3.00

**Non-vintage**
Sainsbury's Mosel (SAI)
Sainsbury's Piesporter Michelsberg (SAI)
Zeller Schwarze Katz Zentralkellerei (TES)
**1990**
Waitrose Bereich Bernkastel (WAI)
Waitrose Piesporter Michelsberg (WAI)

### £3.00 to £3.99

**1991**
Bereich Bernkastel Riesling, Schneider
(WHI)
Piesporter Michelsberg Schneider (WHI)
**1990**
Bereich Bernkastel Riesling, Schneider
(EL, WHI)
Piesporter Michelsberg Schneider (WHI, EL)
Wiltinger Scharzberg Riesling Kab.,
Zentralkellerei (TES)
**1989**
Bereich Bernkastel Riesling, Schneider
(EL)
Piesporter Michelsberg Kessler (YF)
Piesporter Michelsberg Schneider (EL)

### £4.00 to £4.99

**1990**
Deinhard Green Label (WHI)
Falkensteiner Hofberg Riesling Kab., F-W-
Gymnasium (WS)
Piesporter Michelsberg Rudolf Müller (CB)
**1989**
Bereich Bernkastel, Rudolf Müller (CB)
Piesporter Michelsberg Rudolf Müller
(HAH)
Waldracher Krone Riesling Kab., Scherf
(BYR)
**1988**
★ Brauneberger Juffer Riesling Spät.,
Deinhard (AUG)
Deinhard Green Label (HOG)

### £5.00 to £5.99

**1990**
Reiler Mullay Hofberg Riesling Kab.,
Rudolf Müller (TAN)
Waldracher Krone Riesling Spät., Scherf
(BYR)
**1989**
Brauneberger Juffer Riesling Kab.,
Kesselstatt (BY)
Falkensteiner Hofberg Riesling Kab., F-W-
Gymnasium (LOE)
★ Graacher Himmelreich Riesling Kab., F-
W-Gymnasium (LOR, LOE)
Graacher Himmelreich Riesling Kab.,
Kesselstatt (EL)
Trittenheimer Apotheke Riesling Kab.,
Clusserath-Weiler (HOG)
Waldracher Krone Riesling Spät., Scherf
(BYR)
**1988**
★ Bernkasteler Badstube Riesling,
Lauerberg (WAI)
Deinhard Green Label (AUG)
Scharzhofberger Riesling Kab., Kesselstatt
(EL)
**1987**
Neefer Frauenberg Riesling Kab. (BOR)
**1986**
Piesporter Goldtröpfchen Riesling Kab.,
Kesselstatt (LOE)
**1983**
Kanzemer Sonnenberg Riesling Kab.,
Zentralkellerei (ASK)
**1981**
★ Scharzhofberger Riesling Kab., Hövel
(THR)

### £6.00 to £6.99

**1990**
Ayler Kupp Riesling Spät., Bischöfliches
Konvikt (AD)
**1989**
Brauneberger Juffer Riesling Kab., Richter
(BIB)
Falkensteiner Hofberg Riesling Kab., F-W-
Gymnasium (BYR)
Graacher Himmelreich Riesling Kab., F-
W-Gymnasium (WHI, AD)
Piesporter Goldtröpfchen Riesling Kab.,
Kesselstatt (LOE)
Waldracher Krone Riesling Kab., Scherf
(BER)

**1988**

Bernkasteler Badstube Riesling Kab.,
Deinhard (BYR)

Falkensteiner Hofberg Riesling Kab., F-W-
Gymnasium (BYR)

Graacher Himmelreich Riesling Spät., F-
W-Gymnasium (LOR)

★ Ockfener Bockstein Riesling Spät., Dr
Fischer (ASD)

Scharzhofberger Riesling Kab., Kesselstatt
(NI)

Serriger Antoniusberg Riesling Kab.,
Simon (HOG)

**1987**

Neefer Frauenberg Riesling Kab. (PEN)

Wehlener Sonnenuhr Riesling Kab.,
Loosen (ASK)

**1985**

Scharzhofberger Riesling Kab., Kesselstatt
(BY)

★ Zeltinger Sonnenuhr Riesling Spät.,
Kesselstatt (BU)

––––––––– £7.00 to £7.99 –––––––––

**1990**

Graacher Himmelreich Riesling Spät., F-
W-Gymnasium (CV)

★ Scharzhofberger Riesling Spät., Hohe
Domkirche (AD)

Scharzhofberger Riesling Spät., Hövel
(WW)

**1989**

Bernkasteler Badstube Riesling Kab., J.J.
Prüm (LOE)

Graacher Himmelreich Riesling Kab., F-
W-Gymnasium (BYR)

Graacher Himmelreich Riesling Spät., F-
W-Gymnasium (BYR)

Josephshof Riesling Spät., Kesselstatt
(LOE, NI)

Oberemmeler Hutte Riesling Spät., Hövel
(LOE)

Ockfener Bockstein Riesling Spät.,
Staatlichen Weinbaudomänen (HOG)

Scharzhofberger Riesling Kab., Kesselstatt
(BER)

**1988**

Bernkasteler Badstube Riesling Kab., J.J.
Prüm (LOE)

Brauneberger Juffer Riesling Kab., Richter
(BER)

Graacher Himmelreich Riesling Spät., F-
W-Gymnasium (BYR, CV)

Kaseler Nies'chen Riesling Kab., Deinhard
(PEN)

Serriger Antoniusberg Riesling Kab.,
Simon (WCL, ROB)

**1986**

Graacher Himmelreich Riesling Kab.,
Deinhard (TAN)

**1983**

Bernkasteler Badstube Riesling Spät.,
Heidemanns-Bergweiler (HOG)

★ Eitelsbacher Marienholz Riesling Spät.,
Bischöfliches Konvikt (HOG)

Ockfener Bockstein Riesling Spät.,
Rheinart (GRE)

––––––––– £8.00 to £9.99 –––––––––

**1990**

Bernkasteler Bratenhöfchen Riesling
Spät., Lauerburg (BE, TES)

★ Serriger Schloss Saarsteiner Riesling
Spät., Schloss Saarstein (BAR)

Wehlener Sonnenuhr Riesling Kab.,
Loosen (AD)

**1989**

Eitelsbacher Marienholz Riesling Spät.,
Bischöfliches Konvikt (PE)

Graacher Himmelreich Riesling Aus., F-W-
Gymnasium (TES)

Graacher Himmelreich Riesling Spät., F-
W-Gymnasium (TAN)

Maximin-Grünhäuser Abtsberg Riesling
Kab., Schubert (LOE)

Maximin-Grünhäuser Herrenberg Riesling
Kab., Schubert (BYR)

Scharzhofberger Riesling Spät., Hohe
Domkirche (TAN, HOG)

★ Wehlener Sonnenuhr Riesling Kab., J.J.
Prüm (LOE, NI, HOG)

Wehlener Sonnenuhr Riesling Spät.,
Weins Prüm (THR)

**1988**

Bernkasteler Badstube Riesling Spät.,
Heidemanns-Bergweiler (GRE)

Graacher Himmelreich Riesling Aus., F-W-
Gymnasium (WHI)

Graacher Himmelreich Riesling Spät., F-
W-Gymnasium (ROB)
Oberemmeler Hutte Riesling Aus., Hövel
(LOE)
Ockfener Bockstein Riesling Spät.,
Staatlichen Weinbaudomänen (YF)
**1986**
Josephshof Riesling Spät., Kesselstatt
(BYR)
Maximin-Grünhäuser Abtsberg Riesling
Kab., Schubert (BYR)
Scharzhofberger Riesling Kab., Egon
Müller (BYR)
**1985**
Josephshof Riesling Aus., Kesselstatt (LOE)
Maximin-Grünhäuser Abtsberg Riesling
Kab., Schubert (GRE)
**1983**
Bernkasteler Graben Riesling Aus.,
Heidemanns-Bergweiler (HOG)
Falkensteiner Hofberg Riesling Spät., F-
W-Gymnasium (GRE)
Graacher Domprobst Riesling Aus.,
Richter (GRG)
★ Graacher Himmelreich Riesling Aus., F-
W-Gymnasium (LOR)
**1982**
Oberemmeler Hutte Riesling Kab., Hövel
(VIG)
**1981**
Kaseler Nies'chen Riesling Spät.,
Bischöfliches Priesterseminar (PE)
**1976**
Wehlener Munzlay BA, Schneider ½ bottle
(WHI)

─────── **£10.00 to £11.99** ───────
**1990**
Oberemmeler Hutte Riesling Aus., Hövel
(WW)
Trittenheimer Apotheke Riesling Aus., F-
W-Gymnasium (TAN)
**1989**
Trittenheimer Apotheke Riesling Aus., F-
W-Gymnasium (WHI)
Urziger Würzgarten Riesling Spät.,
Richter (VIG)
Wehlener Sonnenuhr Riesling Kab.,
Deinhard (TAN)
**1988**
Josephshof Riesling Aus., Kesselstatt (NI)
**1985**
Josephshof Riesling Aus., Kesselstatt (BYR)
Wehlener Sonnenuhr Riesling Spät.,
Weins Prüm (YF)

**1983**
Bernkasteler Schlossberg Riesling Aus.,
P.J. Hauth (HAC)
Dhroner Hofberger Riesling Aus.,
Bischöfliches Priesterseminar (PE)
★ Kaseler Nies'chen Riesling Aus.,
Bischöfliches Priesterseminar (GRE, PE)
Serriger Vogelsang Riesling Aus.,
Staatlichen Weinbaudomänen (HAC,
WCL)
Wehlener Sonnenuhr Aus., J.J. Prüm
(HOG)

─────── **£12.00 to £14.99** ───────
**1989**
Maximin-Grünhäuser Herrenberg Riesling
Spät., Schubert (LOE)
Wehlener Sonnenuhr Aus., J.J. Prüm (LOE)
**1988**
Graacher Himmelreich Riesling Aus., F-W-
Gymnasium (BAR)

Maximin-Grünhäuser Abtsberg Riesling
Spät., Schubert (LOE)
Wehlener Sonnenuhr Aus., J.J. Prüm (LOE)
**1983**
Bernkasteler Bratenhöfchen Riesling Aus.,
Deinhard (PEN)
Bernkasteler Graben Riesling Spät.,
Deinhard (AD)
Graacher Himmelreich Riesling Spät.,
Prüm (WS)
Maximin-Grünhäuser Herrenberg Riesling
Aus., Schubert (GRE)
Oberemmeler Hutte Riesling Aus., Hövel
(WS)
Wehlener Sonnenuhr Riesling Aus., F.W.
Prüm (PE)

─────── **£15.00 to £19.99** ───────
**1990**
Graacher Himmelreich Riesling Aus., J.J.
Prüm (NI)
Maximin-Grünhäuser Abtsberg Riesling
Aus., Schubert (LAY)

**1983**
Bernkasteler Bratenhöfchen Riesling Aus.,
Deinhard (AD)
Wehlener Abtei Eiswein, Schneider 1/2
bottle (WHI)

───── **£25.00 to £29.99** ─────
**1989**
Mulheimer Helenkloster Riesling Eiswein,
Richter 1/2 bottle (BIB)
**1985**
Bernkasteler Doctor Riesling Spät.,
Deinhard (PEN)

───── **£30.00 to £39.99** ─────
**1989**
Maximin-Grünhäuser Abtsberg Riesling
Aus., Schubert (LOE)
**1986**
Mulheimer Helenkloster Riesling Eiswein,
Richter 1/2 bottle (BIB)
**1983**
Bernkasteler Doctor Riesling Aus.,
Deinhard (BER)

───── **£45.00 to £55.00** ─────
**1983**
Bernkasteler Graben Riesling Eiswein,
Deinhard 1/2 bottle (AD)
**1975**
Bernkasteler Bratenhöfchen Riesling BA
Eiswein, Deinhard (WRI)

───── **£75.00 to £90.00** ─────
**1976**
Serriger Würzberg TBA, Simon (BOR)
**1983**
Bernkasteler Graben Riesling Eiswein,
Deinhard (TAN)

## FRANKEN WHITE

───── **£8.00 to £9.99** ─────
**1989**
Iphofener Kronsberg Müller-Thurgau
Kab., Wirsching (ROB)
**1988**
Casteller Kirchberg Müller-Thurgau,
Fürstlich Castell'sches Domänenamt
(HAC, WCL)
Casteller Kirchberg Silvaner Trocken,
Fürstlich Castell'sches Domänenamt
(HAC)
Escherndorfer Lump Riesling Kab.,
Gebietswinzergenossenschaft (BYR, GRE)

**1985**
Iphofener Julius Echterberg Silvaner
Spät., Juliusspital (LOE)

───── **c. £42.00** ─────
**1979**
Würzburger Stein Rieslaner TBA,
Juliusspital (LOE)

## BADEN WHITE

───── **Under £5.00** ─────
**Non-vintage**
Baden Dry, Badische Winzerkellerei (BAR,
ROB)
Sainsbury's Baden (SAI)

───── **c. £7.00** ─────
**1988**
Rivaner, Karl Heinz Johner (HAC)

───── **£9.00 to £12.00** ─────
**1986**
Pinot Blanc, Karl Heinz Johner (VIG)
**1988**
Pinot Blanc, Karl Heinz Johner (HAC, BAR)

## BADEN RED

───── **c. £16.00** ─────
**1987**
Pinot Noir, Karl Heinz Johner (HAC)

## GERMAN SPARKLING

───── **Under £6.00** ─────
**Non-vintage**
Henkell Rosé (BO, TES)
Henkell Trocken (BO, SAF, VIC, TES)

───── **£6.00 to £7.99** ─────
**Non-vintage**
Henkell Trocken (WHI, UN, AUG, WRI)

# ITALY

## NORTH-WEST RED

──────── **Under £4.00** ────────
**1991**
Barbera d'Asti Viticoltori dell'Acquese (PIP, VA, WCL, THR)
**1990**
★ Dolcetto d'Acqui Viticoltori dell'Acquese (VIC)
**1988**
Barbera d'Asti Viticoltori dell'Acquese (BAR)

──────── **£4.00 to £4.99** ────────
**1991**
Dolcetto d'Acqui Viticoltori dell'Acquese (AD)
**1989**
Barbera d'Alba Fontanafredda (PEN)
Barbera d'Asti Viticoltori dell'Acquese (GRG)
Dolcetto d'Acqui Viticoltori dell'Acquese (GRG)
**1985**
Spanna del Piemonte, Fiore (BYR)

──────── **£5.00 to £5.99** ────────
**1989**
Barbera Oltrepò Pavese, Castello di Luzzano (GRE)
Barbera Oltrepò Pavese, Fugazza (WHI)
**1988**
Gutturnio Oltrepó Pavese, Fugazza (VA)
Inferno Nino Negri (HOG, GRE)
**1987**
Barolo Terre del Barolo (SAF, MAR)
**1980**
Gattinara Berteletti (HOG)

──────── **£6.00 to £6.99** ────────
**1990**
Dolcetto d'Alba Ascheri (WCL)
**1989**
Dolcetto d'Alba Priavino, Voerzio (OD)
★ Ronco di Mompiano Pasolini (WCL)
**1988**
Dolcetto d'Alba Cassiano, Prunotto (BYR)
**1987**
Barolo Ascheri (SOM)
★ Franciacorta Rosso Cá del Bosco (ROB)
**1986**
Barolo Terre del Barolo (BYR)

**1985**
Barbaresco Gallina di Neive, Bruno Giacosa (BYR)
Barbera d'Asti Guasti Clemente (HOG)
Barolo Aliberti (PIP, BY)
Barolo Fontanafredda (BYR, AUG)
Ghemme Brugo (LAY)
**1982**
★ Barolo Riserva Fontanafredda (OD)
Gattinara Riserva Nervi (LAY)

──────── **£7.00 to £7.99** ────────
**1991**
Dolcetto d'Alba Corsini, Mascarello (WCL)
**1990**
Dolcetto d'Alba Bruno Giacosa (AD)
Dolcetto d'Alba Giacomo Conterno (VA)
**1989**
Barbera d'Alba Altare (WCL)
**1987**
Barolo Oddero (ROB)
**1986**
Barolo Ascheri (GRG)
Barolo Riserva Borgogno (ASD)
**1985**
Barbaresco Fontanafredda (PEN)
Barbaresco la Spinona (BYR)
Barolo Fontanafredda (WHI)
Ghemme Brugo (BU)
**1981**
Barolo Riserva Borgogno (CH)
**1978**
★ Barbaresco Marchesi di Barolo (HOG)
Barolo Marchesi di Barolo (HOG)

──────── **£8.00 to £9.99** ────────
**1990**
Dolcetto d'Alba Rossana Ceretto (BYR)
Nebbiolo d'Alba San Rocco, Mascarello (WCL)
**1989**
Barbera d'Alba Conca Tre Pile, Aldo Conterno (WCL)
Freisa delle Langhe Vajra (WCL)
Freisa Selve di Moirana, Scarpa (AD)
Grignolino d'Asti Briccorosa, Scarpa (AD)
Nebbiolo d'Alba San Rocco, Mascarello (ROB)
**1988**
Barbaresco Santo Stefano, Castello di Neive (VA)
Barolo Ascheri (WCL)
Nebbiolo delle Langhe Vajra (WCL)

**1987**
Barbaresco Sori Paytin, Pasquero (WCL)
Barolo Riserva Borgogno (WHI)
**1986**
Barolo Fontanafredda (GRG)
**1985**
Barbera Vigneto Piana, Ceretto (BYR)
**1984**
Barbaresco Nicolello (NI)
**1983**
★ Barbaresco Gallina di Nieve, Bruno
  Giacosa (RAE)
**1979**
Barolo Riserva Speciale Maria Feyles (RAE)
**1978**
Barolo Riserva Marchesi di Barolo (HOG)
**1976**
Barbaresco Sori Paytin, Pasquero (WCL)

───────── £10.00 to £12.49 ─────────
**1987**
Barolo la Serra di la Morra, Voerzio (OD)
Barolo Zonchetta, Ceretto (BYR)
**1986**
Barbaresco Sori Paytin, Pasquero (GRG)
**1985**
Barolo Montanello, Monchiero (WCL)
Barolo Prunotto (BYR)
Barolo Riserva Borgogno (LAY, ROB, PE)
Sfursat Nino Negri (GRE)
**1984**
Barolo Zonchera Ceretto (NI)
**1982**
Barolo Ascheri (WHI)
Barolo Bricco Boschis Riserva San
  Giuseppe, Cavallotto (VA)
Barolo San Giuseppe, Cavallotto (BO)
**1978**
Barolo Bricco Boschis Riserva San
  Giuseppe, Cavallotto (HOG)
Barolo Fontanafredda (HOG)

───────── £12.50 to £14.99 ─────────
**1988**
Barbaresco Sori Paytin, Pasquero (WS)
Dolcetto d'Alba Vignabajla, Gaja (OD)
**1987**
★ Barolo Prunotto (WS)
Maurizio Zanella, Ca' del Bosco (WCL)
**1986**
Barolo Marcenasco, Renato Ratti (PE)
**1985**
Barolo Contratto (BAR)
Barolo Soriginestra, Fantino (WCL)
Nebbiolo Il Favot, Aldo Conterno (WCL)
**1982**
Barbaresco Bruno Giacosa (HOG)
Carema Ferrando (WCL)
**1979**
Barolo Montanello, Monchiero (WCL)
**1978**
Barbaresco Masseria, Vietti (HOG)
★ Barolo Pio Cesare (HOG)

───────── £15.00 to £19.99 ─────────
**1987**
Barbera d'Alba Vignarey, Gaja (VA)
Barolo Bussia Soprana, Aldo Conterno (PIP,
  WCL)
Barolo Sandrone (WW)
**1986**
Barolo Bussia, Prunotto (BYR)
Barolo Bussia Soprana, Aldo Conterno
  (ROB, TAN, WCL)
Barolo Monprivato, Mascarello (SOM, WCL)
**1985**
Barbaresco Marcarini, Mascarello (WCL)
Barolo Bricco Rocche Brunate, Ceretto
  (HAG, NI)
Barolo Bussia Soprana, Aldo Conterno
  (WCL)
**1984**
Barolo Monprivato, Mascarello (YF)
Maurizio Zanella, Ca' del Bosco (VA)
**1982**
Barolo Conca, Renato Ratti (AD)
Barolo Gattinera, Fontanafredda (VA)
Barolo Lazzarito, Fontanafredda (HOG, VA)
Barolo Montanello, Monchiero (WCL)
Barolo Riserva Giacomo Conterno (VA)
**1978**
Barolo Gattinera, Fontanafredda (HOG, BO)
Barolo Montanello, Monchiero (WCL)
**1967**
Barolo Borgogno (WCL)
**1964**
Barolo Borgogno (WCL)

─────── £20.00 to £29.99 ───────

**1988**
Barbera d'Alba Altare (WCL)
Maurizio Zanella, Ca' del Bosco (VA)
**1986**
Barbaresco Costa Russi, Gaja (OD)
Barbaresco Sori Tildin, Gaja (OD)
Barolo Bricco Rocche Brunate, Ceretto
  (BYR, WR, BOT)
**1985**
Barolo Giacomo Conterno (VA)
Barolo Monprivato, Mascarello (WCL, REI)
**1984**
★ Darmagi Gaja (VA)
**1978**
Barbaresco Vigneto Monticchio, Produttori
  (WCL)
Barolo Borgogno (VA)
**1974**
Barbaresco Bricco Asili, Ceretto (WCL)
Barolo Montanello, Monchiero (WCL)
**1971**
Barolo Borgogno (VA)
Barolo Mascarello (WCL)
Barolo Riserva Borgogno (GRE)
**1970**
Barolo Montanello, Monchiero (WCL)
**1969**
Barolo Mascarello (WCL)
Barolo Montanello, Monchiero (WCL)
**1961**
Barolo Borgogno (VA)
Barolo Riserva Borgogno (GRE)
**1947**
Barolo Borgogno (WCL)

─────── £30.00 to £39.99 ───────

**1988**
Pinero Ca' del Bosco (WCL)
**1987**
Pinero Ca' del Bosco (WCL)
**1986**
Darmagi Gaja (VA)
**1982**
Barbaresco Gaja (VA)
**1974**
Barolo Monfortino, Giacomo Conterno
  (WCL)
**1971**
Barolo Ceretto (WCL)
Barolo Pio Cesare (WCL)
**1970**
Barbaresco Vigneto Montefico, Ceretto
  (WCL)
Barolo Zonchetta, Ceretto (WCL)

─────── £40.00 to £49.99 ───────

**1988**
Barbaresco Costa Russi, Gaja (WW)
Barbaresco Sori San Lorenzo, Gaja (WW)
**1983**
Barbaresco Sori Tildin, Gaja (VA)
**1978**
Barbaresco Gaja (VA, HAG)
**1968**
Barolo Giacomo Conterno (WCL)
**1964**
Barolo Bussia, Prunotto (WCL)
Barolo Prunotto (WCL)
**1961**
Barolo Pio Cesare (WCL)
Barolo Riserva Borgogno (VIG)
**1952**
Barolo Riserva Borgogno (VIG)
**1947**
Barolo Borgogno (VA)

─────── £50.00 to £60.00 ───────

**1978**
Barbaresco Costa Russi, Gaja (REI)
**1970**
Barolo Zonchetta, Ceretto (REI)

─────── c. £70.00 ───────

**1964**
Barbaresco Gaja (WCL)

─────── c. £124.00 ───────

**1961**
Barbaresco Gaja (VA, HAG)

### NORTH-WEST WHITE

─────── Under £5.00 ───────

**1991**
Chardonnay del Piemonte Viticoltori
  dell'Acquese (VIC, VA, WCL)
★ Moscato d'Asti Viticoltori dell'Acquese
  (WCL)
**1990**
Chardonnay del Piemonte Viticoltori
  dell'Acquese (GA, HAG)
Moscato d'Asti Chiarlo (WAI)

─────── £5.00 to £5.99 ───────

**1991**
Moscato d'Asti Ascheri (WCL)
Moscato d'Asti Chiarlo (NI)
**1990**
★ Gavi Fontanafredda (BYR)
Gavi la Chiara (VA)

─────── **£6.00 to £7.99** ───────

**1991**
Favorita Deltetto (WCL)
Moscato d'Asti la Spinetta, Rivetti (AD)
**1990**
★ Favorita Malvira (AD)
Mompiano Bianco Pasolini (WCL)

─────── **£8.00 to £9.99** ───────

**1991**
Arneis del Piemonte Renesio, Damonte (AD)
★ Arneis del Piemonte San Michel,
   Deltetto (WCL)
**1990**
Arneis Blange Ceretto (BYR)
Arneis del Montebertotto, Castello di Neive
   (VA)

─────── **c. £14.50** ───────

**1988**
Pio di Lei, Pio Cesare (VA)

─────── **£20.00 to £30.00** ───────

**1989**
Chardonnay Ca' del Bosco (ROB, VA, WCL)
Chardonnay Rossj Bass, Gaja (VA)

## NORTH-WEST SPARKLING

─────── **Under £5.00** ───────

**Non-vintage**
Asda Asti Spumante (ASD)
Asda Moscato Spumante (ASD)
Gancia Spumante (HOG)
Sainsbury's Asti Spumante (SAI)
Tesco Asti Spumante (TES)

─────── **£5.00 to £6.99** ───────

**Non-vintage**
Asti Spumante Fontanafredda (BYR, VA)
Asti Spumante Martini (BYR, GA, HOG, ASD,
   HAG, WAI, SAF, TES, BO, THR, WRI, AUG, VIN,
   TAN, UN, DAV, BO, EL)

─────── **c. £14.00** ───────

**1988**
Mompiano Spumante Brut Pasolini (WCL)

─────── **c. £20.00** ───────

**Non-vintage**
Franciacorta Brut, Ca' del Bosco (VA)

─────── **c. £39.00** ───────

**1983**
Franciacorta Brut, Ca' del Bosco (VA)

## NORTH-EAST RED

─────── **Under £3.00** ───────

**Non-vintage**
Asda Valpolicella (ASD)
Sainsbury's Bardolino Classico (SAI)
Victoria Wine Valpolicella (VIC)
**1991**
Waitrose Valpolicella Classico (WAI)

─────── **£3.00 to £3.99** ───────

**Non-vintage**
Merlot del Piave Bianchi Kunkler (THR)
**1990**
Valpolicella Classico Negarine (SAI)
**1989**
Valpolicella Tadiello (YF)
**1988**
Valpolicella Classico Boscaini (SAF)
★ Valpolicella Classico Masi (OD)

─────── **£4.00 to £4.99** ───────

**1991**
Bardolino Portalupi (VA, AD)
**1990**
Bardolino Classico Ca' Bordenis (MAJ)
Cabernet Franc di Aquileia, Ca' Bolani (BYR)
Teroldego Rotaliano Gaierhof (WAI)
Valpolicella Classico Allegrini (BAR)
Valpolicella Classico Superiore Masi (PIP)
**1989**
Bardolino Classico Superiore Masi (BYR,
   PIP)
★ Bardolino Classico Superiore Rizzardi
   (HOG, GRE)
★ Cabernet Franc di Aquileia, C'a Bolani
   (BYR)
Valpolicella Classico Allegrini (GRG)
Valpolicella Classico Castello d'Illasi, Santi
   (HOG)
Valpolicella Classico Superiore Masi (BYR,
   BY)
Valpolicella Classico Superiore Rizzardi
   (HOG, VA)
Valpolicella Classico Superiore Zenato
   (THR)

**1988**
Bardolino Classico Superiore Boscaini
(WHI)
Bardolino Classico Superiore Masi (BYR)
Valpolicella Classico Boscaini (WHI)
Valpolicella Classico Superiore Masi (BYR)
Valpolicella Classico Superiore Valverde,
Tedeschi (AD)
Valpolicella Classico Tedeschi (LAY)
**1985**
Merlot Grave del Friuli Collavini (WHI)
Valpolicella Classico Masi (AUG)

───────── **£5.00 to £5.99** ─────────
**1991**
Marzemino del Trentino Letrari (WS)
Valpolicella Classico Allegrini (WCL)
**1990**
Bardolino Classico Ca' Bordenis (TAN)
Bardolino Classico Superiore Bertani (LAY)
**1989**
Bardolino Portalupi (PE)
Maso Lodron Letrari (WS)
★ Valpolicella Classico Castello d'Illasi,
Santi (TAN)
**1988**
Cabernet Grave del Friuli, Collavini (VA)
Lagrein Dunkel Viticoltori Alto Adige (VA)
Refosco Grave del Friuli Collavini (VA)

───────── **£6.00 to £6.99** ─────────
**1990**
Molinara Quintarelli (BIB)
**1987**
Valpolicella Valpantena Bertani (LAY)
**1986**
★ Campo Fiorin Masi (VA, PIP, BYR)

───────── **£7.00 to £7.99** ─────────
**1988**
Cabernet Riserva, Lageder (WCL)
Pinot Nero Collio Felluga (BYR)
Teroldego Rotaliano Vigneto Pini, Zeni (VA)
**1987**
Castello Guerrieri (HOG)
**1986**
Valpolicella Classico Masi (BO)
Venegazzù della Casa White Label,
Loredan-Gasparini (BYR)
**1985**
Merlot Collio Collavini (VIC)
Recioto Amarone Negrar (EL)
**1983**
Recioto Amarone Negrar (WHI)
★ Recioto Amarone Riserva Tommasi (CH)

───────── **£8.00 to £9.99** ─────────
**1989**
Lagrein Dunkel Riserva Tiefenbrunner
(AD)
**1988**
Valpolicella Classico la Grola, Allegrini
(WCL)
Valpolicella Classico Palazzo della Torre,
Allegrini (WCL)
Venegazzù della Casa White Label,
Loredan-Gasparini (GRE)
**1987**
Recioto Amarone Montresor (HOG)
Venegazzù della Casa Loredan-Gasparini
(VIC, ROB)
**1986**
Palazzo della Torre, Allegrini (VA)
Venegazzù della Casa Loredan-Gasparini
(VA, TAN)
**1985**
Recioto Amarone Tommasi (LOR)
Valpolicella Classico Quintarelli (OD)
★ Valpolicella Classico Superiore
Quintarelli (AD)
Valpolicella Monte Cà Paletta, Quintarelli
(RAE)
**1983**
Recioto Amarone Boscaini (VIC)
Recioto Amarone Sartori (HAH)

───────── **£10.00 to £12.99** ─────────
**1988**
Recioto Amarone Tedeschi (TAN)
Recioto Classico della Valpolicella Allegrini
(WCL)
**1987**
Venegazzù della Casa Black Label,
Loredan-Gasparini (BYR)
**1986**
Recioto Amarone Tedeschi (ROB, LAY)
Venegazzù della Casa Black Label,
Loredan-Gasparini (BYR)
**1985**
Recioto Amarone Bolla (VA)
Recioto Amarone Fabiano (GRE)
Recioto Amarone Masi (BYR)
**1983**
Recioto Amarone Masi (BYR)
**1981**
Recioto Amarone Fabiano (GRE)

───────── **£13.00 to £14.99** ─────────
**1989**
Cabernet Sauvignon Puiatti (WCL)
Pinot Nero Puiatti (WCL)

**1986**
Cabernet Grai (BIB)
**1985**
Recioto Amarone Tedeschi (AD)
**1978**
Recioto Amarone Quintarelli (AS)

─────── **£15.00 to £18.99** ───────
**1988**
Recioto Amarone Mezzanella, Masi (PIP)
**1984**
Recioto Amarone Mazzano, Masi (BYR)
**1983**
Recioto Amarone Fieramonte, Allegrini
  (VA, WCL)
Recioto Amarone Mezzanella, Masi (BYR)
Recioto Amarone Vaio Armaron, Alighieri
  (PIP)
Recioto Amarone Vaio Armaron, Masi (BYR)
**1981**
Recioto Amarone Mazzano, Masi (BYR)
Recioto Amarone Mezzanella, Masi (BYR)
**1980**
Recioto Amarone Vaio Armaron, Masi (BYR)

─────── **£20.00 to £29.99** ───────
**1985**
La Poja, Allegrini (WCL)
Recioto Amarone Mazzano, Masi (VA)
**1983**
La Poja, Allegrini (VA, AD)
**1980**
Recioto Amandorlato Monte Ca' Paletta
  (AD)

─────── **£30.00 to £35.00** ───────
**1983**
Recioto della Valpolicella Quintarelli (WCL)
**1979**
Nebbiolo Recioto della Valpolicella Classico
  Quintarelli (AD)

## NORTH-EAST WHITE

─────── **Under £3.00** ───────
**Non-vintage**
Asda Soave (ASD)
Sainsbury's Soave (SAI)
Sainsbury's Verduzzo del Piave (SAI)
Tesco Soave (TES)

─────── **£3.00 to £3.99** ───────
**1991**
Soave Classico Santi (BYR)
**1990**
Bianco di Custoza Pasqua (SAI)
Bianco di Custoza Tommasi (LOR)
Chardonnay Ca' Donini (BO)
Lugana Tommasi (LOR)
Pinot Grigio Ca' Donini (VIC)
Pinot Grigio Ca'vit (ROB)
Soave Classico Boscaini (SAF)
Soave Classico Masi (BYR)
★ Soave Classico Monte Tenda, Tedeschi
  (OD)
Soave Classico Santi (BYR)
Soave Classico Superiore Tommasi (LOR)
**1988**
Chardonnay Ca' Donini (AUG)
★ Chardonnay Lageder (AUG)

─────── **£4.00 to £4.99** ───────
**1991**
Asda Chardonnay Alto Adige (ASD)
Soave Classico Superiore Masi (PIP)
★ Soave Classico Zenato (ASD, DAV)
Tocai di San Martino, Zenato (DAV)
**1990**
Chardonnay Lageder (GRG)
Chardonnay Tiefenbrunner (BYR)
Pinot Grigio Ca' Donini (BAR)
Pinot Grigio Grave de Friuli, Collavini (SAI)
Pinot Grigio Tiefenbrunner (TES)
Sainsbury's Chardonnay Alto Adige (SAI)
Soave Classico Boscaini (WHI)
Soave Classico Tedeschi (LAY)
Soave Classico Zenato (WAI)
Tocai Friulano di Aquileia, Ca' Bolani (SAI)
**1989**
Bianco di Custoza Sartori (BO)
Bianco di Custoza Zenato (ASD)
Chardonnay Ca' Donini (WHI)
Chardonnay Tiefenbrunner (BO)
Pinot Grigio Ca' Donini (WHI)
Soave Classico Masi (AUG)
Soave Classico Superiore Sartori (UN)
Tocai Friulano di Aquileia, Ca' Bolani (BYR)

**1988**
Chardonnay Tiefenbrunner (BYR)
Soave Classico Col Baraca, Masi (AUG)
Tocai Friulano di Aquileia, Ca' Bolani (BYR)

——————— **£5.00 to £5.99** ———————
**1991**
Lugana di San Benedetto, Zenato (DAV)
Pinot Grigio Lageder (PIP)
**1990**
Chardonnay Tiefenbrunner (WHI)
Gewürztraminer Tiefenbrunner (BYR, VA, AD)
Pinot Bianco Tiefenbrunner (AD)
Pinot Grigio Lageder (GRG)
Pinot Grigio Santa Margherita (VA)
Pinot Grigio Tiefenbrunner (BYR)
Soave Classico Anselmi (OD)
Soave Classico Superiore Anselmi (VA)
**1989**
Chardonnay Tiefenbrunner (WHI)
Gewürztraminer Tiefenbrunner (BYR)
Lugana Ca dei Frati, Dal Cero (VA)
Pinot Bianco Tiefenbrunner (VA)
Pinot Grigio Tiefenbrunner (BYR, WHI)
Soave Classico Pieropan (BO, GRE)
Soave Classico Superiore Anselmi (BY)

——————— **£6.00 to £7.99** ———————
**1991**
Chardonnay EnoFriulia (PIP)
Soave Classico Col Baraca, Masi (PIP)
**1990**
★ Breganze di Breganze, Maculan (PIP)
★ Chardonnay Vinattieri (BY)
Lugana Ca dei Frati, Dal Cero (WCL, HIC, LAY)
Pinot Bianco del Collio, Felluga (BYR)
Pinot Grigio Sortesele (BAR)
Soave Classico Monte Carbonara, Tessari (AD)
Soave Classico Superiore Pieropan (BAR)
Soave Classico Vigneto Calvarino, Pieropan (WCL)
Tocai Friulano Collio, Schiopetto (BAR)
Vinattieri Bianco (BIB)
**1989**
Pinot Grigio Collio, Puiatti (SOM)
Pinot Grigio Lageder (HIC)
Soave Classico Monte Carbonare, Di Suavia (BIB)
Soave Classico Pieropan (GRG)
Soave Classico Vigneto Calvarino, Pieropan (GRG)
Venegazzù Pinot Grigio Loredan-Gasparini (GRG)

**1988**
Sauvignon Collio, Puiatti (SOM)

——————— **£8.00 to £9.99** ———————
**1990**
Pinot Grigio Collio, Felluga (BYR)
Soave Classico Capitel Foscarino, Anselmi (VA)
Soave Classico Pieropan (HIC)
Soave Classico Vigneto la Rocca, Pieropan (WCL)
**1989**
Pinot Bianco Collio, Puiatti (YF)
Pinot Grigio Collio, Felluga (VA)
Soave Classico Superiore Masi (REI)
**1988**
★ Recioto di Soave Capitelli, Anselmi (OD)
**1986**
Gewürztraminer Grai (BIB)
Pinot Bianco Grai (BIB)

——————— **£10.00 to £11.99** ———————
**1991**
Chardonnay Collio, Puiatti (WCL)
Pinot Grigio Collio, Puiatti (WCL)
Sauvignon Collio, Puiatti (WCL)
**1990**
Chardonnay Collio, Puiatti (WCL)
Pinot Bianco Collio, Puiatti (THR, WCL)
Pinot Grigio Collio, Puiatti (BAR)
Ribolla Collio, Puiatti (WCL)
**1988**
Vendemmia Tardiva Pojer e Sandri ½ Bottle (WCL)

——————— **£12.00 to £15.99** ———————
**1989**
Chardonnay Jermann (REI)
Recioto di Soave le Colombare, Pieropan (WCL)
Tocai Collio Schiopetto (VA)
**1988**
Chardonnay Jermann (VIG)
Chardonnay Löwengang, Lageder (WCL)
**1987**
Chardonnay Faye, Pojer e Sandri (WCL)
Recioto di Soave Capitelli, Anselmi (BY)

——————— **£16.00 to £19.99** ———————
**1989**
Recioto di Soave Capitelli, Anselmi (VA)
Vintage Tunina, Jermann (VA)
**1988**
Torcolato Vino Liquoroso Maculan (PIP, VA, AD)

**1987**
Tunina Jermann (GRG, BO)
**1983**
Vin de la Fabriseria Tedeschi (AD)

## NORTH-EAST ROSÉ

——————— c. £4.50 ———————
**1991**
Bardolino Chiaretto, Portalupi (VA)

## NORTH-EAST SPARKLING

——————— Under £7.50 ———————
**Non-vintage**
Prosecco di Conegliano Carpenè Malvolti
(HOG, VA, WCL)

——————— £11.00 to £15.00 ———————
**Non-vintage**
Berlucchi Brut (VA)
Ferrari Brut (VA)

## CENTRAL RED

——————— Under £4.00 ———————
**1990**
★ Chianti Rufina Villa di Vetrice (SOM, WCL)
Rosso Cònero San Lorenzo, Umani Ronchi (NI, WAI)
Victoria Wine Chianti (VIC)
Waitrose Chianti (WAI)

——————— £4.00 to £4.99 ———————
**1990**
Chianti Classico Castello Vicchiomaggio (VIC)
Chianti Classico Rocca delle Macie (WAI, SAF)
★ Parrina Rosso La Parrina (WCL)
★ Santa Cristina, Antinori (GRE, MAJ, LAY, VIC)
**1989**
Chianti Classico Aziano, Ruffino (HOG)
Chianti Classico Rocca delle Macie (BYR, WAI, NI, SAF, MAJ, BO)
Chianti Classico Ruffino (VA)
Chianti Classico Viticcio Landini (LOR)
Chianti Rufina Tenuta di Remole, Frescobaldi (HOG)
Parrina Rosso La Parrina (BAR)
★ Rosso di Montalcino Campo ai Sassi, Frescobaldi (WAI)
Santa Cristina, Antinori (BYR, VIC)

**1988**
Chianti Classico Rocca delle Macie (AUG)
Chianti Rufina Riserva Tenuta di Remole, Frescobaldi (AMI)
Chianti Rufina Villa di Vetrice Riserva (WCL)
Rosso Cònero Marchetti (SOM)
Sainsbury's Chianti Classico (SAI)
**1987**
Montefalco Rosso d'Arquata Adanti (OD)
Rosso di Montalcino Villa Banfi (AUG)
**1986**
★ Chianti Classico Castello dei Rampolla (CH)
**1985**
Chianti Rufina Villa di Monte (TES)

——————— £5.00 to £5.99 ———————
**1990**
Chianti Classico San Jacopo, Vicchiomaggio (PEN)
Chianti Rufina Riserva Tenuta di Remole, Frescobaldi (VA)
Rosso Cònero Marchetti (VA)
Santa Cristina, Antinori (BUT, LO, AN)
**1989**
Barco Reale Capezzana (SOM)
★ Chianti Classico Felsina Berardenga (SOM)
Chianti Classico la Lellera, Matta (IR, WHI)
Chianti Classico San Felice (HOG, GRE, VA)
Chianti Rufina Selvapiana (GRG, WCL)
**1988**
Chianti Classico Castello Vicchiomaggio (CH)
Montefalco Rosso d'Arquata Adanti (VA)
Rosso Cònero San Lorenzo, Umani Ronchi (GRE, SAI)
Rosso di Montalcino Campo ai Sassi, Frescobaldi (AMI)
Santa Cristina, Antinori (CB)
★ Vino Nobile di Montepulciano le Casalte (WS)
**1987**
Rosso Cònero San Lorenzo, Umani Ronchi (VA, NI)
Santa Cristina, Antinori (BUT)
**1986**
Rosso Cònero San Lorenzo, Umani Ronchi (GRE, BO, THR)
**1985**
Chianti Classico Brolio (BYR)
Chianti Classico Riserva Villa Cerna (BYR)
Chianti Rufina Villa di Vetrice (BAR)
**1983**
★ Chianti Classico Monsanto (RAE)

## ——— £6.00 to £6.99 ———

**1990**
Carmignano Barco Reale, Capezzana (WCL)
Chianti Classico Felsina Berardenga (WCL)
Palazzo Altesi, Altesino (BAR)
**1989**
Chianti Classico Badia a Coltibuono (ROB)
Chianti Classico Felsina Berardenga (WW)
Chianti Classico Fontodi (WR, BOT)
Chianti Classico Isole e Olena (GRG, WCL)
Rosso di Montalcino Altesino (SOM)
**1988**
★ Brusco dei Barbi Fattoria dei Barbi (BYR)
Chianti Classico Castello di San Polo in
    Rosso (AD)
★ Chianti Classico Isole e Olena (SOM)
Chianti Classico Villa Antinori (BYR)
★ Rubesco Torgiano Lungarotti (ROB)
★ Vino Nobile di Montepulciano Poliziano
    (PIP)
**1987**
Chianti Classico Riserva Ducale, Ruffino
    (HOG)
Chianti Classico Riserva Rocca delle Macie
    (BYR, BAR)
Chianti Classico Riserva Villa Antinori
    (GRE, LAY, VA)
Chianti Classico Villa Antinori (BYR)
Chianti Rufina Riserva Castello di
    Nipozzano (GRE)
Rosso di Montalcino Altesino (GRG)
Rubesco Torgiano Lungarotti (ROB)
Vino Nobile di Montepulciano Bigi (BYR)
**1986**
Carmignano Villa Capezzana (WR, BOT)
Chianti Classico Riserva Rocca delle Macie
    (BYR)
Vino Nobile di Montepulciano Bigi (BYR,
    GRG)
Vino Nobile di Montepulciano Cerro (HOG)
**1985**
Chianti Rufina Riserva Villa di Vetrice (AD,
    WCL)
**1983**
Chianti Classico Riserva Castello dei
    Rampolla (BU)
**1982**
★ Chianti Classico Riserva Montagliari
    (GE)
**1981**
Chianti Classico Riserva Pagliarese (BU)
**1980**
Chianti Rufina Riserva Selvapiana (WCL)
**1979**
Chianti Rufina Riserva Villa di Monte (TES)

## ——— £7.00 to £7.99 ———

**1990**
Chianti Classico Felsina Berardenga (HAG)
Rosso di Montalcino Altesino (WCL)
Rosso di Montalcino il Poggione (AD)
**1989**
Chianti Classico Castello di Cacchiano
    (WCL, BAR)
Chianti Classico Castello di Volpaia (AD,
    WCL)
Chianti Classico Isole e Olena (HAH)
Ser Gioveto, Rocca delle Macie (GRE, MAJ)
**1988**
★ Carmignano Ambra (WW)
Chianti Classico Castello dei Rampolla
    (AN)
Chianti Classico Villa Cafaggio (WRI)
Ser Gioveto, Rocca delle Macie (BO, VA)
**1987**
Chianti Classico Castello di Volpaia (NI,
    HAG)
Chianti Classico Riserva Antinori (LO)
Chianti Classico Riserva Rocca delle Macie
    (VIG)
Chianti Classico Riserva Villa Antinori
    (AN)
Chianti Classico Riserva Villa Banfi (PIP)
Chianti Rufina Castello di Nipozzano (VA)
Chianti Rufina Riserva Castello di
    Nipozzano (WHI, ROB)
Rubesco Torgiano Lungarotti (HAH, TAN)
Sagrantino di Montefalco, Adanti (VA)
Vino Nobile di Montepulciano Bigi (VA)
Vino Nobile di Montepulciano Poliziano
    (VA)
Vino Nobile di Montepulciano Riserva, Bigi
    (GRE)
**1986**
Carmignano Villa Capezzana (BAR)
Chianti Classico Riserva la Lellera, Matta
    (IR)
Chianti Rufina Riserva Selvapiana (YF)
Pomino Rosso Frescobaldi (CV)
Vino Nobile di Montepulciano Bigi (PEN)
Vino Nobile di Montepulciano Cerro (VIC)
**1985**
Chianti Classico Riserva di Fizzano, Rocca
    delle Macie (BYR)
Rubesco Torgiano Lungarotti (REI)
**1982**
Cabernet Sauvignon di Miralduolo,
    Lungarotti (VA)
**1981**
Cabernet Sauvignon di Miralduolo,
    Lungarotti (LAY)

--------------- £8.00 to £9.99 ---------------

**1990**

Brusco dei Barbi Fattoria dei Barbi (VIG)
Chianti Classico Fontodi (WCL)
Chianti Classico Peppoli, Antinori (THR)

**1989**

Chianti Classico Peppoli, Antinori (GRE, VA, LAY, WCL)
Rosso di Montalcino Talenti (BIB)

**1988**

Chianti Classico Castello di Cacchiano (WCL, BER)
Chianti Classico Peppoli, Antinori (BYR)
Chianti Classico Riserva Castello di Volpaia (AD)
★ Chianti Rufina Riserva Selvapiana (WCL)
Pomino Rosso Frescobaldi (VA, ROB)
Prunaio di Viticcio Landini (LOR)
Ser Gioveto, Rocca delle Macie (NI, VIC, BAR)
Vino Nobile di Montepulciano le Casalte (AD, LAY, THR, BAR, REI)

**1987**

Chianti Classico Riserva Antinori (THR)
Chianti Classico Riserva di Fizzano, Rocca delle Macie (GRE)
Ghiaie della Furba, Capezzana (OD)
Palazzo Altesi, Altesino (SOM)
Vino Nobile di Montepulciano Bigi (VIG)

**1986**

Chianti Classico Riserva Badia a Coltibuono (AD)
Chianti Classico Riserva di Fizzano, Rocca delle Macie (GA, VA, MAJ, VIG)
Chianti Classico Riserva Felsina Berardenga (WW)
Chianti Classico Riserva Monsanto (RAE)
Chianti Rufina Riserva Castello di Nipozzano (BER)
Vino Nobile di Montepulciano Baiocchi (WRI)

**1985**

Chianti Classico Riserva Brolio (BYR)

--------------- £10.00 to £14.99 ---------------

**1990**

Chianti Classico Riecine (WCL)

**1989**

Cepparello, Isole e Olena (WCL)

**1988**

★ Cepparello, Isole e Olena (SOM, AD, VA)
Chianti Classico Riserva Peppoli (TAN)
Palazzo Altesi, Altesino (WCL)
Quercia Grande, Capaccia (OD)
Vino Nobile di Montepulciano Bindella (BIB)

**1987**

Alte d'Altesi, Altesino (WCL)
Balifico Castello di Volpaia (AD)
Chianti Classico Riserva Castello di Volpaia (ROB)
Chianti Classico Riserva Vigneto Rancia, Felsina Berardenga (WCL)
Coltassala Castello di Volpaia (AD)
Grifi Avignonesi (WCL, WAI)
Quercia Grande, Capaccia (VA)

**1986**

Balifico Castello di Volpaia (REI)
Brunello di Montalcino Castelgiocondo (VA)

Brunello di Montalcino Villa Banfi (PIP)
Chianti Classico Riserva Marchese Antinori (BYR, HIC)
Chianti Rufina Riserva Selvapiana (GRG)
Coltassala Castello di Volpaia (REI, HAG)
Fontalloro, Felsina Berardenga (WCL)
Vinattieri Rosso Secondo (BY)

**1985**

★ Balifico Castello di Volpaia (BUT)
Brunello di Montalcino Altesino (SOM)
Brunello di Montalcino Castelgiocondo (CV, HOG, GRE, UN)
Brunello di Montalcino Fattoria dei Barbi (HOG)
★ Brunello di Montalcino il Poggione (RAE, AD)
Ca' del Pazzo Caparzo (GRE, VA, AMI)
Carmignano Riserva Villa Capezzana (SOM, GRG, WCL, TAN)
Chianti Classico Riserva Fontodi (WCL)
Nipozzano Cuvée Montesodi, Frescobaldi (CV)
Sangioveto Badia a Coltibuono (AD)
Vinattieri Rosso (BIB)

**1984**

Brunello di Montalcino Villa Banfi (BY)

**1983**

Brunello di Montalcino il Poggione (HAG)
Carmignano Riserva Villa Capezzana (YF)
Chianti Classico Riserva Rocca delle Macie (BUT)
Sangioveto Badia a Coltibuono (VA)

**1982**
Chianti Classico Riserva Monsanto (RAE)
**1981**
Brunello di Montalcino Fattoria dei Barbi
   (GRE)
Chianti Classico Riserva Monsanto (RAE)
San Giorgio Lungarotti (VA)
**1980**
Brunello di Montalcino Fattoria dei Barbi
   (GRE)
Chianti Classico Riserva Castello
   Vicchiomaggio (WRI)
Rubesco Torgiano Riserva Lungarotti (VA)
**1979**
Tinscvil Riserva (RAE)
**1977**
Brunello di Montalcino Fattoria dei Barbi
   (HOG)

─────── **£15.00 to £19.99** ───────
**1990**
Syrah Isole e Olena (WCL)
**1988**
Cabernet Sauvignon Isole e Olena (WCL)
Cepparello, Isole e Olena (REI, CB)
Chianti Classico Riserva Riecine (WCL)
Flaccianello della Pieve, Fontodi (WCL)
Ghiaie della Furba, Capezzana (WCL)
I Sodi di San Niccolò, Castellare (AD)
**1987**
Brunello di Montalcino Altesino (WCL)
Le Pergole Torte, Monte Vertine (WAI)
I Sodi di San Niccolò, Castellare (VA)
Tignanello Antinori (BYR, VA, WCL, LAY, AN,
   TAN)
**1986**
Brunello di Montalcino Barbi (VIG)
Brunello di Montalcino il Poggione (BYR)
Brunello di Montalcino Pertimali (WW)
Brunello di Montalcino Poggio Antico (ROB)
Brunello di Montalcino Talenti (BIB)
Cabreo Predicato di Biturica Ruffino (VA,
   REI)
Chianti Rufina Montesodi, Frescobaldi
   (WCL)
Le Pergole Torte, Monte Vertine (WAI)
Mormoreto Predicato di Biturica,
   Frescobaldi (WCL, AMI)
Tignanello Antinori (HAH, HAG, BO, BER)
**1985**
Brunello di Montalcino Poggio Antico (OD)
Chianti Classico Riserva Castello di
   Cacchiano (WCL)
Chianti Rufina Montesodi, Frescobaldi (VA,
   WHI)

Chianti Rufina Riserva Montesodi,
   Frescobaldi (AMI)
Sangioveto Grosso, Monsanto (RAE)
Tignanello Antinori (HOG, GRE, BUT)
**1981**
Tignanello Antinori (BUT)
**1974**
Chianti Classico Riserva Monsanto (RAE)

─────── **£20.00 to £24.99** ───────
**1989**
Ornellaia, Antinori (WCL)
**1988**
I Sodi di San Niccolò, Castellare (AMI)
**1986**
Brunello di Montalcino Montosoli, Altesino
   (WCL)
Sassicaia Incisa della Rocchetta (SOM)
Tignanello Antinori (ROB, CB, YF)
**1985**
Le Pergole Torte, Monte Vertine (REI)

─────── **£25.00 to £29.99** ───────
**1987**
Sassicaia Incisa della Rocchetta (WCL, VA,
   REI, ROB, HAG, TAN)
**1986**
Sammarco Castello dei Rampolla (WCL)
Sassicaia Incisa della Rocchetta (LAY)
**1985**
Sassicaia Incisa della Rocchetta (BUT)

─────── **£30.00 to £39.99** ───────
**1988**
Sassicaia Incisa della Rocchetta (ROB, FA,
   WS, BUT)
**1986**
Sassicaia Incisa della Rocchetta (GRF, FA,
   YF, VIG, BUT)
Solaia Antinori (LAY)
**1985**
Sammarco Castello dei Rampolla (AN)
Solaia Antinori (BUT)
**1984**
Sassicaia Incisa della Rocchetta (VA, AD, FA)
**1982**
Sassicaia Incisa della Rocchetta (BUT)
**1973**
Brunello di Montalcino Barbi (VIG)
**1970**
Brunello di Montalcino Fattoria dei Barbi
   (BO)
**1964**
Chianti Classico Riserva Badia a
   Coltibuono (REI)

**1962**
Chianti Classico Riserva Montagliari (WS)
**1958**
Chianti Classico Riserva Badia a
 Coltibuono (REI)

─────────── £40.00 to £49.99 ───────────
**1986**
Solaia Antinori (WCL, ROB, CB)

─────────── £55.00 to £90.00 ───────────
**1978**
Solaia Antinori (YF)
**1977**
Brunello di Montalcino Biondi-Santi (VA)
**1976**
Sassicaia Incisa della Rocchetta (BUT)

─────────── £105.00 to £125.00 ───────────
**1975**
Brunello di Montalcino Biondi-Santi (VA)
**1971**
Brunello di Montalcino Biondi-Santi (VA)

## CENTRAL WHITE

─────────── Under £4.00 ───────────
**Non-vintage**
Sainsbury's Orvieto Secco (SAI)
**1990**
Frascati Gotto d'Oro (BO)
Frascati Superiore Colli di Catone (OD)
Frascati Superiore Monteporzio (HOG)
Orvieto Secco le Valette (HOG)
Orvieto Secco Ruffino (HOG)
Tesco Frascati (TES)
**1988**
Marino Superiore Gotto d'Oro (BO)
Orvieto Secco Cecchi (CH)

─────────── £4.00 to £4.99 ───────────
**Non-vintage**
Sainsbury's Frascati Secco (SAI)
**1991**
Est! Est!! Est!!! di Montefiascone, Bigi
 (PEN)
Frascati Superiore Fontana Candida (SAF)
Frascati Superiore Gotto d'Oro (THR, LAY)
Frascati Superiore Monteporzio (BY)
Galestro Antinori (VA, THR)
Orvieto Classico Abboccato Antinori (GRE,
 LAY, THR)
Orvieto Classico Antinori (DAV)
Orvieto Classico Secco Antinori (LAY, THR)
Orvieto Secco Antinori (LO)

**1990**
Bianco d'Arquata Adanti (VA)
Est! Est!! Est!!! di Montefiascone, Bigi (BYR)
Frascati Superiore Fontana Candida (BYR,
 MAJ)
Galestro Antinori (BYR)
Orvieto Classico Abboccato Antinori (HOG,
 ROB)
Orvieto Classico Amabile Bigi (BYR)
Orvieto Classico Secco Antinori (HOG, GRE,
 BYR, WS)
Orvieto Classico Secco Bigi (BYR)
Verdicchio Classico Bianchi (BYR, BO)
Vernaccia di San Gimignano la Torre (HOG)
**1989**
Frascati Superiore Colli di Catone (AUG)
Galestro Frescobaldi (CV)
Orvieto Classico Amabile Bigi (WHI)
Orvieto Classico Secco Bigi (WHI, GRG)
**1988**
Frascati Superiore Colli di Catone (CH)
Frascati Superiore Fontana Candida (AUG)
Orvieto Classico Amabile Bigi (CH)
Verdicchio dei Castelli di Jesi Classico,
 Garofoli (BYR)

─────────── £5.00 to £6.99 ───────────
**1991**
Bianco Villa Antinori (LAY, TAN)
Borro Lastricato Selvapiana (WCL)
Frascati Superiore Colli di Catone (PIP)
Frascati Superiore Satinata, Colle di
 Catone (WCL)
Galestro Antinori (LO)
Orvieto Classico Vigneto Torricella, Bigi
 (VA)
★ Verdicchio dei Castelli di Jesi Classico,
 Casal di Serra (VA)
★ Vernaccia di San Gimignano Teruzzi e
 Puthod (PIP, WCL)
**1990**
Bianco Villa Antinori (THR, HAH)
Frascati Colli di Catone (VA)
Frascati Superiore Colli di Catone (ROB)
Galestro Antinori (AN)
Orvieto Classico Abboccato Antinori (VIC)
Orvieto Classico Vigneto Torricella, Bigi
 (BYR, OD, AD)
Pomino Frescobaldi (VA)
Verdicchio dei Castelli di Jesi Classico,
 Casal di Serra (MAJ, SAI, BAR, VIC)
Verdicchio dei Castelli di Jesi Classico,
 Fazi-Battaglia (WS, PE, TAN)
Vernaccia di San Gimignano Teruzzi e
 Puthod (GRG, BAR, ROB)

**1989**
Borro della Sala, Antinori (GRE)
Castello della Sala, Antinori (BYR)
Pomino Frescobaldi (GRE)
Verdicchio dei Castelli di Jesi Classico,
   Fazi-Battaglia (HAH)
Vernaccia di San Gimignano la Torre (WRI)
**1988**
Orvieto Classico Abboccato Antinori (PEN)

─────── £7.00 to £8.99 ───────
**1991**
Borro della Sala, Antinori (WCL)
★ Vernaccia di San Gimignano
   Montenidoli (AD, BIB)
**1990**
Borro della Sala, Antinori (AN, PIP)
Chardonnay Villa di Capezzana (WCL)
**1988**
★ Chardonnay Villa di Capezzana (GRG)

─────── £9.00 to £10.99 ───────
**1989**
Chardonnay Villa di Capezzana (YF)
Frascati Colle Gaio, Colli di Catone (VA)
**1988**
Il Marzocco, Avignonesi (WAI)
Trebianco Castello dei Rampolla (AN)
Vergena Sauvignon Blanc, Frescobaldi (CV)
**1987**
Pomino il Benefizio, Frescobaldi (CV, AD,
   AMI)
**1985**
Pomino il Benefizio, Frescobaldi (GRE)
Vin Santo Antinori (GRE)

─────── £11.00 to £14.99 ───────
**1990**
Chardonnay Isole e Olena (WCL)
Frascati Colle Gaio, Colli di Catone (WCL)
Vernaccia di San Gimignano Teruzzi e
   Puthod (VA)
**1989**
Chardonnay I Sistri, Felsina Berardenga
   (GRG)
Il Marzocco, Avignonesi (SAI)
Vernaccia di San Gimignano Terre di Tufo,
   Teruzzi e Puthod (REI)
**1988**
Pomino il Benefizio, Frescobaldi (PIP, VA)
**1986**
Orvieto Classico Muffa Nobile, Berberani
   (WCL)
**1985**
Vin Santo Selvapiana (WCL)

─────── £15.00 to £19.99 ───────
**1990**
Cervaro della Sala, Antinori (WCL)
**1989**
Cervaro della Sala, Antinori (LAY)
**1988**
Cervaro della Sala, Antinori (VA)
Orvieto Classico Pourriture Noble,
   Decugnano dei Barbi (AN)
**1986**
Cervaro della Sala, Antinori (YF)
**1983**
Orvieto Classico Pourriture Noble,
   Decugnano dei Barbi (VIG)

## CENTRAL SPARKLING

─────── Under £4.00 ───────
**Non-vintage**
Lambrusco Amabile Luigi Gavioli (HOG, VA)
Lambrusco Bianco Ca' de Medici (WAI)
Lambrusco Bianco del Colle (BYR)
Lambrusco Bianco San Prospero (AUG)
Lambrusco Ca' de Medici (WAI)
Lambrusco di Sorbara Cavicchioli (OD)
Lambrusco di Sorbara Cesari (PEN)
Lambrusco di Sorbara, il Poggio (CH)
Lambrusco Grasparossa di Castelvetro
   (WAI)
Lambrusco San Prospero (GRE)
**1989**
Lambrusco Gavioli (VA)

## SOUTHERN RED

─────── Under £4.00 ───────
**1991**
Montepulciano d'Abruzzo Bianchi (VA)
Montepulciano d'Abruzzo Tollo (PIP)
**1990**
Cellaro Rosso C.S. di Sambuca (WCL, BAR)
Monica di Sardegna, C.S. di Dolianova
   (WCL)
Montepulciano d'Abruzzo Umani Ronchi
   (NI)
Settesoli Rosso (VA)
**1989**
Cellaro Rosso C.S. di Sambuca (SOM)
★ Cirò Classico Librandi (ASD)
Settesoli Rosso (HOG)
**1987**
Cellaro Rosso C.S. di Sambuca (VIC, GRG)
Montepulciano d'Abruzzo Tollo (AUG)
Montepulciano d'Abruzzo Umani Ronchi
   (GRG)

──────── £4.00 to £5.99 ────────
**Non-vintage**
Corvo Rosso Duca di Salaparuta (BO, UN)
**1990**
★ Montepulciano d'Abruzzo Illuminati
  (HOG, WAI, VA)
Montepulciano d'Abruzzo Umani Ronchi
  (VIC)
**1989**
Corvo Rosso Duca di Salaparuta (HOG, GRE,
  VA, PIP)
**1988**
Cellaro Rosso C.S. di Sambuca (YF)
**1987**
Montepulciano d'Abruzzo Riserva Colle
  Secco (VA)

──────── £6.00 to £8.99 ────────
**1987**
Aglianico del Vulture, Fratelli d'Angelo
  (ROB, VA, TAN)
Ramitello Di Majo Norante (WCL)

──────── £10.00 to £11.99 ────────
**1987**
Taurasi Mastroberardino (VA)
**1977**
Rosso Brindisi Patriglione, Taurino (VA,
  WCL)

──────── c. £20.00 ────────
**1985**
Montepulciano d'Abruzzo Valentini (WCL)

## SOUTHERN WHITE

──────── Under £4.00 ────────
**1991**
Cellaro Bianco C.S. di Sambuca (WCL)
★ Vermentino di Sardegna C.S. di
  Dolianova (WCL)
**1990**
Settesoli Bianco (HOG, VA, ROB)
**1987**
Cellaro Bianco C.S. di Sambuca (VIC)

┌─────────────────────────┐
│ *Please remember that*  │
│ ***Webster's** is a price* │
│ *GUIDE and not a price* │
│ *LIST. It is not meant to* │
│ *replace up-to-date*    │
│ *merchant's lists.*     │
└─────────────────────────┘

──────── £4.00 to £5.99 ────────
**Non-vintage**
Corvo Bianco Duca di Salaparuta (BO, UN)
**1990**
Corvo Bianco Duca di Salaparuta (HOG,
  GRE, VA)
Preludio No. 1 Torrebianco (GRE)
Sauvignon di Puglia, Vigna al Monte (GRE)
**1989**
Cellaro Bianco C.S. di Sambuca (YF)
Preludio No. 1 Torrebianco (HOG)
**1988**
Corvo Bianco Duca di Salaparuta (CH)
Corvo Colomba Platino Bianco (HOG)

──────── £6.00 to £7.99 ────────
**1990**
Regaleali Bianco (ROB, PE)
Regaleali Conte Tasca d'Almerita (VA)

──────── £14.50 to £16.99 ────────
**1989**
Fiano di Avellino Mastroberardino (VA)
**1987**
Trebbiano d'Abruzzo Valentini (WCL)

## SOUTHERN ROSÉ

──────── Under £4.00 ────────
**1989**
Cellaro Rosato C.S. di Sambuca (GRG)

## SOUTHERN FORTIFIED

──────── Under £8.00 ────────
**Non-vintage**
★ Josephine Dore de Bartoli (WCL, VA)

──────── £10.00 to £11.99 ────────
**Non-vintage**
★ Vecchio Samperi 10-year-old, de Bartoli
  (WCL)
★ Marsala Vigna la Miccia, de Bartoli
  (TAN, VA, WCL)

──────── £17.00 to £19.99 ────────
**Non-vintage**
Il Marsala 20-year-old de Bartoli (VA, WCL)
Moscato Passito di Pantelleria Bukkuram,
  de Bartoli (VA, WCL)

──────── c. £22.50 ────────
**Non-vintage**
Vecchio Samperi 30-year-old, de Bartoli
  (WCL)

# RIOJA

## RED

### ———— Under £5.00 ————

**1990**
Rivarey (VIC)
**1989**
El Coto (DAV)
**1988**
★ Berberana Carta de Plata (GRE, BE, TES)
CVNE (CV, MAJ, WHI)
CVNE Viña Real (WHI)
El Coto Crianza (BU)
**1987**
Berberana Carta de Oro (BYR)
Campo Viejo (AUG, GRG, WHI, BYR)
CVNE Viña Real (CV, WHI, MAJ)
★ Marqués de Cáceres (LO, CV, WHI, WCL)
Sainsbury's Rioja (SAI)
Siglo Saco (GRE)
**1986**
★ La Rioja Alta Viña Alberdi (SOM)
Marqués de Cáceres (HOG, LO, CV, WHI, GRE)
Paternina Banda Azul (CH)
Siglo Saco (NI, MOR)
**1985**
Berberana Carta de Oro (GRG)
Campo Viejo (WHI)
Campo Viejo Reserva (AUG)
La Rioja Alta Viña Alberdi (ASK)
Marqués de Cáceres (AUG)
Olarra Añares (GE)
**1983**
Domecq Domain (HOG)

### ———— £5.00 to £5.99 ————

**Non-vintage**
Domecq Domain (UN)
**1988**
Berón (PE)
CVNE (LAY, AN, CB)
**1987**
Berberana Carta de Oro (MOR, UN, GRE)
Berón (WHI)
CVNE Viña Real (CH, BYR, ROB)
Faustino V Reserva (GRE, BYR)
La Rioja Alta Viña Alberdi (WAI)
**1986**
El Coto Crianza (ROB)
Faustino V Reserva (BYR)
Marqués de Cáceres (BO, EL, MOR, BYR, TAN, HAH, LAY, AN, DAV, VIN, BER)
Marqués de Riscal Reserva (CH)

**1985**
Berberana Reserva (BYR)
Beronia Reserva (HOG)
Campo Viejo Reserva (WHI, BYR)
Coto de Imaz Reserva (DAV)
Domecq Domain Reserva (THR)
★ Faustino V Reserva (WHI)
**1984**
★ Bodegas Riojanas Monte Real Reserva (MAJ)
**1983**
Campo Viejo Reserva (WHI)
Domecq Domain Reserva (BO)
Faustino V Reserva (WHI)

### ———— £6.00 to £6.99 ————

**1988**
Marqués de Riscal (BYR)
**1987**
Faustino V Reserva (MOR)
La Rioja Alta Viña Alberdi (ASK, THR, ROB)
Marqués de Riscal (BYR, GRE)
Marqués de Riscal Reserva (MOR)
Muga (BYR)
**1986**
Marqués de Riscal (VIC)
Marqués de Riscal Reserva (PEN)
Muga (BYR)
**1985**
Beronia Reserva (BYR, OD, RAE)
Bilbainas Viña Pomal (MOR)
CVNE Reserva (CV, MAJ)
CVNE Viña Real Reserva (MAJ)
Marqués de Cáceres Reserva (LO)
**1983**
Berberana Reserva (GRE)
Campo Viejo Reserva (GRG)
**1982**
Siglo Gran Reserva (NI)
Viña Herminia (GE)
**1981**
Campo Viejo Gran Reserva (AUG)
CVNE Viña Real Reserva (LOR)
**1980**
Siglo Saco Gran Reserva (GRE)
**1966**
★ Bodegas Riojanas Monte Real (BUT)

### ———— £7.00 to £7.99 ————

**1987**
Marqués de Riscal (TAN, PE)
Muga (MOR)

★ Remelluri Reserva (WW)
**1986**
Contino Reserva (PIP)
Marqués de Murrieta (GRE, DAV)
Remelluri (TAN)
**1985**
Contino Reserva (LOR, CV)
CVNE Imperial Reserva (LOR, CV, PIP)
CVNE Viña Real Reserva (PIP, CV, BYR)
Marqués de Cáceres Reserva (BYR, LAY)
Marqués de Murrieta (HOG, DAV)
**1984**
★ Contino Reserva (CV)
**1983**
Marqués de Riscal (UN)
**1981**
Campo Viejo Gran Reserva (GA)
CVNE Imperial Reserva (CV)
CVNE Viña Real Reserva (BEK, CV)
Marqués de Cáceres Reserva (WHI)
**1980**
Paternina Gran Reserva (BYR)
**1978**
Olarra Añares Gran Reserva (GE)

————— **£8.00 to £9.99** —————

**1987**
Marqués de Murrieta (BYR)
**1986**
Contino Reserva (BY, MOR, LAY, THR, EL, BIB)
CVNE Imperial Reserva (BYR)
Marqués de Murrieta Reserva (ROB)
Marqués de Murrieta Castillo Ygay Gran
  Reserva (LAY)
Remelluri Reserva (YF)
**1985**
Contino Reserva (PEN, AMI, REI, AD)
Coto de Imaz Gran Reserva (DAV)
CVNE Imperial Gran Reserva (LAY, PIP,
  BYR, PEN, MOR)
CVNE Imperial Reserva (HAG, AD, ROB)
CVNE Viña Real Gran Reserva (PIP, BY,
  BYR, MOR)
Faustino I Gran Reserva (GRE, BYR, WHI)
La Rioja Alta Viña Ardanza Reserva (ASK,
  MOR, AD, LAY)
Marqués de Murrieta (WCL, WHI, AMI, TAN)
Marqués de Murrieta Reserva (NI, THR, AD,
  WRI, BIB, WS, ROB)
Muga Reserva (BYR)
**1984**
★ Marqués de Murrieta Ygay Reserva
  (BUT)
**1983**
La Rioja Alta Viña Arana Reserva (BYR)

★ La Rioja Alta Viña Ardanza Reserva
  (HOG, BYR)
**1982**
CVNE Imperial Gran Reserva (CV)
CVNE Imperial Reserva (LOR, HAG)
CVNE Viña Real Gran Reserva (CV, PIP,
  HAG)
CVNE Viña Real Reserva (HAG, MOR)
Faustino I Gran Reserva (HOG, BYR, MOR)
La Rioja Alta Viña Arana Reserva (BYR)
**1981**
Contino Reserva (CV)
CVNE Viña Real Gran Reserva (CV)
La Rioja Alta Viña Arana (HOG)
Marqués de Cáceres Gran Reserva (WHI)
Marqués de Cáceres Reserva (PEN, CV, BO)
**1980**
Berberana Gran Reserva (BY, DAV, GRG,
  PEN, GRE, BAR)
Campo Viejo Gran Reserva (WHI, MOR, GRG)
**1978**
Beronia Gran Reserva (BYR)
★ CVNE Viña Real Gran Reserva (CV)
Marqués de Cáceres Reserva (MOR)
**1975**
Beronia Gran Reserva (BYR)
Bodegas Riojanas Monte Real Gran
  Reserva (MOR, MAJ)
Bodegas Riojanas Viña Albina Gran
  Reserva (MOR)
★ Marqués de Cáceres Gran Reserva (CV)

————— **£10.00 to £14.99** —————

**1985**
CVNE Imperial Gran Reserva (TAN, VIG)
La Rioja Alta Viña Ardanza Reserva (WR,
  BOT)
López de Heredia Viña Tondonia (TAN)
**1983**
La Rioja Alta Viña Ardanza Reserva (VIG)
Marqués de Murrieta (GRE)
**1982**
Conde de la Salceda Gran Reserva (TAN)
CVNE Imperial Gran Reserva (LOR, PIP,
  HAG, YF)
CVNE Imperial Reserva (VIN, CB, VIG)
CVNE Viña Real Gran Reserva (ROB)
Faustino I Gran Reserva (UN)

> *Stars (★) indicate wines
> selected by the editors as
> particularly good value
> in their class.*

**1981**
★ La Rioja Alta Reserva 904 Gran Reserva
(SOM, HOG, BYR, ASK, MOR, LAY, WR, BOT)
Marqués de Cáceres Gran Reserva (BYR,
HAH, VIN)
Muga Gran Reserva (BYR)
**1978**
Berberana Gran Reserva (BYR, PEN, GRE)
Beronia Gran Reserva (BIB)
La Rioja Alta Reserva 904 (BYR)
**1975**
Berberana Gran Reserva (MOR, PEN, HAG,
GRG, BE, TES)
CVNE Imperial Gran Reserva (CV)
Marqués de Cáceres Gran Reserva (BER)
**1973**
Berberana Gran Reserva (PEN)
Lagunilla Gran Reserva (BUT)

─────── **£15.00 to £19.99** ───────
**1981**
La Rioja Alta Reserva 904 Gran Reserva
(PE, AMI, CB)
**1978**
La Rioja Alta Reserva 904 Gran Reserva
(VIG)
Marqués de Murrieta Gran Reserva (WCL,
AD, NI, BIB)
**1976**
López de Heredia Viña Tondonia Gran
Reserva (MOR)
**1975**
Marqués de Murrieta Gran Reserva
(MOR)
**1973**
Faustino I Gran Reserva (BUT)

─────── **£20.00 to £24.99** ───────
**1978**
Marqués de Murrieta Gran Reserva (CB)
**1976**
López de Heredia Viña Tondonia Gran
Reserva (TAN)
**1973**
López de Heredia Viña Tondonia Gran
Reserva (MOR)
**1970**
Marqués de Murrieta (GRE)

─────── **£25.00 to £29.99** ───────
**1973**
Marqués de Riscal Gran Reserva (BUT)
**1971**
Bodegas Riojanas Monte Real Gran
Reserva (VIG)

─────── **£30.00 to £39.99** ───────
**1970**
Marqués de Murrieta Gran Reserva (CB)
La Rioja Alta Reserva 890 Gran Reserva
(REI)
Solar de Samaniego Gran Reserva (VIG)

─────── **£40.00 to £59.99** ───────
**1968**
Marqués de Murrieta Castillo Ygay Gran
Reserva (AD, ROB)
Marqués de Murrieta Gran Reserva (MOR)
**1964**
Bodegas Riojanas Monte Real Gran
Reserva (VIG)
**1950**
Bodegas Riojanas Monte Real Gran
Reserva (VIG)
**1942**
Marqués de Murrieta Castillo Ygay Gran
Reserva (NI, BUT)

─────── **£80.00 to £99.99** ───────
**1952**
Marqués de Murrieta Castillo Ygay Gran
Reserva (AD, MOR)

## WHITE

─────── **Under £4.00** ───────
**Non-vintage**
Tesco White Rioja (TES)
**1991**
Marqués de Cáceres (LO, VIC)
**1990**
Marqués de Cáceres (HOG, CV, WHI, GRE)
Sainsbury's Rioja Seco (SAI)
**1989**
Marqués de Cáceres (WHI)
**1988**
Marqués de Cáceres (AUG)
**1985**
La Rioja Alta Viña Leonora (ASK)

─────── £4.00 to £4.99 ───────

**1991**
Marqués de Cáceres (WCL)
**1990**
El Coto (DAV)
Faustino V (BYR)
Marqués de Cáceres (ROB, BYR, HAH, LAY, AD, MOR, TAN, DAV)
**1989**
Berberana Carta de Plata (MOR)
CVNE Monopole (PIP)
Faustino V (BYR)
Marqués de Cáceres (BO, BYR, EL, AV)
Paternina Banda Dorada (BYR)
**1988**
Siglo Saco (MOR)

─────── £5.00 to £5.99 ───────

**1990**
Faustino V (MOR)
Marqués de Cáceres (AN, VIN, BER)
**1989**
CVNE Monopole (CV, MAJ, MOR)
**1988**
CVNE Monopole (CV, PEN, LAY, BEK)
**1987**
CVNE Monopole (PE)
**1985**
CVNE Reserva (CV, PIP, PEN, WAI)

─────── £6.00 to £7.99 ───────

**1988**
CVNE Monopole (TAN)
**1987**
CVNE Monopole (CB)
**1986**
Bodegas Riojanas Monte Real (AD)
Marqués de Murrieta (DAV)
**1985**
CVNE Reserva (MOR, WS, YF, BER)
Marqués de Murrieta (GRE, HOG)

─────── £8.00 to £10.99 ───────

**Non-vintage**
Marqués de Murrieta (UN)
**1987**
Marqués de Murrieta (BYR)
**1986**
Marqués de Murrieta (BYR)
Marqués de Murrieta Reserva (PEN)
**1985**
Marqués de Murrieta (WCL, WHI, NI, MOR, AV, TAN)
Marqués de Murrieta Reserva (VIC, BO, THR, AD, AMI, ROB, WRI, BIB)

─────── £11.00 to £13.99 ───────

**1985**
López de Heredia Tondonia Reserva (MOR)
**1976**
Marqués de Murrieta Reserva (BE, TES)

─────── £25.00 to £29.99 ───────

**1974**
Bodegas Riojanas Monte Real (VIG)
**1970**
Marqués de Murrieta Ygay Gran Reserva (GRE, AD)

─────── £30.00 to £49.99 ───────

**1971**
Bodegas Riojanas Monte Real (VIG)
**1970**
Marqués de Murrieta Ygay Gran Reserva (BIB)
**1966**
Bodegas Riojanas Monte Real (VIG)
**1962**
Marqués de Murrieta Ygay Gran Reserva (MOR)
**1948**
Marqués de Murrieta (VIG)

## ROSÉ

─────── Under £4.00 ───────

**1990**
Marqués de Cáceres Rosado (LO)
**1989**
Marqués de Cáceres Rosado (HOG)
**1988**
Marqués de Cáceres Rosado (CV)

─────── £4.00 to £4.99 ───────

**1989**
Marqués de Cáceres Rosado (BO, BYR)

─────── £7.00 to £8.99 ───────

**1989**
Marqués de Murrieta Rosado (BYR)
**1985**
Marqués de Murrieta Rosado (ROB)

# OTHER SPANISH TABLE WINES

## RED

--------- Under £3.00 ---------
**Non-vintage**
★ Don Darias (SAF, TES)
Don Hugo, Alto Ebro (WAI)
Sainsbury's Navarra (SAI)
**1991**
Sainsbury's La Mancha (SAI)
**1990**
Condestable Jumilla (MOR)

--------- £3.00 to £3.99 ---------
**1989**
Monte Ory (AD)
René Barbier (CV)
**1988**
Condé de Caralt (MOR, WCL)
René Barbier (CV)
**1987**
Sainsbury's Valdepeñas (SAI)
**1986**
Felix Solis Viña Albali Gran Reserva (ASD)
★ Felix Solis Viña Albali Reserva (THR)
Torres Tres Torres (CH)
**1983**
Señorio de los Llanos Reserva (BYR)

--------- £4.00 to £4.99 ---------
**1989**
Condé de Caralt (YF)
Gran Colegiata (AD)
Torres Coronas (WHI, PEN, CV)
Torres Tres Torres (BYR, WHI)
**1988**
Ochoa Tempranillo (HOG)
★ Raimat Abadia (BYR, TES, SAI)
★ Torres Coronas (HOG, BYR, GRE, TES, WHI, LO, MOR, CV, LAY, DAV)
Torres Tres Torres (BYR, GRE, MOR, PEN)
**1987**
Colegiata (LOR)
Gran Colegiata (OD)
**1986**
Torres Coronas (ASD, CH, MAJ)
Torres Gran Sangredetoro (HOG)
**1985**
Condé de Caralt Reserva (MOR)
**1983**
Marius Tinto Reserva Almansa, Piqueras (EL)
René Barbier Reserva (WHI, CV)

**1982**
René Barbier Reserva (CV)
**1978**
Señorio de los Llanos Gran Reserva (BYR)

--------- £5.00 to £5.99 ---------
**1989**
Torres Las Torres (CV, BYR)
★ Torres Viña las Corres, Merlot (HOG)
**1988**
Ochoa Tempranillo (BO, CV, MOR, EL, BOT, WR, WCL)
Raimat Tempranillo (VIC, OD)
Torres Coronas (PE, VIC, UN)
**1987**
Gran Colegiata (PE)
Ochoa Cabernet Sauvignon (HOG)
Raimat Abadia (BO)
Torres Gran Sangredetoro (BYR, WHI, BE, TES)
Torres Viña Magdala (BYR, GRE)
**1986**
Colegiata (GRE)
Gran Colegiata (BO)
Torres Gran Sangredetoro (BYR, GRE, MOR, TES, BE)
Torres Viña Magdala (BYR, MOR)
**1985**
Colegiata (LAY)
Ochoa Reserva (HOG, CV)
Torres Coronas (AUG)
**1983**
Señorio de los Llanos (BO)
**1975**
★ Castillo de Tiebas Reserva (PEN)

--------- £6.00 to £6.99 ---------
**1989**
Raimat Tempranillo (GA, THR)
Torres Las Torres (BE, LO, ROB, PEN)
Torres Viña Magdala (WHI, PEN)
**1988**
Raimat Merlot (BYR, SAF, OD, GRE)
Raimat Tempranillo (SAF, MOR, GRE)
**1987**
Ochoa Cabernet Sauvignon (CV, MAJ)
Raimat Abadia Reserva (HIC)
Raimat Cabernet Sauvignon (TES, VIC)
Torres Gran Coronas (MOR, BYR, BE, TES)
Torres Gran Sangredetoro (HIC, ROB)
Torres Viña Magdala (WHI, BE, TES, LO, WR, BOT)

**1986**
★ Priorato Extra, Barril (WCL)
Raimat Cabernet Sauvignon (BYR)
Torres Gran Coronas (HOG, BYR, RAE, GRE, TES, BE)
**1985**
Torres Gran Sangredetoro (WRI)
**1983**
Jean León Cabernet Sauvignon (SOM)
**1982**
Ochoa Reserva (PE)
**1978**
Castillo de Tiebas Reserva (WRI)

──────── £7.00 to £7.99 ────────
**1987**
Raimat Cabernet Sauvignon (GRE)
Torres Gran Coronas (LO, CV, WCL, DAV)
**1986**
Torres Gran Coronas (WHI, WHI, SAI)
**1985**
Cavas Hill Gran Toc Reserva (ROB)
Torres Gran Coronas (BO, PEN, THR, CH)
**1983**
Torres Viña Magdala (GRE)
**1982**
Ochoa Reserva (TAN)

──────── £8.00 to £9.99 ────────
**1989**
Pesquera, Fernandez (NI)
**1988**
★ Pesquera, Fernandez (OD, WW)
**1986**
Marqués de Griñon Cabernet Sauvignon (BYR, CB, BAR, GRE)
Ribera del Duero Crianza (TAN)
Toro, Farina (TAN)
**1985**
Marqués de Griñon Cabernet Sauvignon (CV)
Mauro (DAV)
**1980**
Jean León Cabernet Sauvignon (LAY, WCL)

──────── £10.00 to £14.99 ────────
**1990**
Torres Mas Borras Pinot Noir (BYR)
**1989**
Pesquera, Fernandez (ROB)
Torres Mas Borras Pinot Noir (BYR, WHI)
**1988**
Pesquera, Fernandez (TAN)
Torres Mas Borras Pinot Noir (HOG, GRE, PEN, WHI, CV, ROB)

**1987**
Marqués de Griñon Crianza (WR, BOT)
Pesquera, Fernandez (WCL, REI, PE)
**1986**
Marqués de Griñon Cabernet Sauvignon (WRI, YF)
**1985**
Pesquera, Fernandez (NI)
**1983**
Jean León Cabernet Sauvignon (ROB)
**1982**
Jean León Cabernet Sauvignon (BYR, PE)
**1981**
Jean León Cabernet Sauvignon (MOR)
**1979**
Jean León Cabernet Sauvignon (REI)

──────── £15.00 to £19.99 ────────
**1987**
Vega Sicilia 3rd year (LAY)
**1986**
Vega Sicilia 3rd year (BYR)
Vega Sicilia Valbuena 3rd year (ASK)
**1985**
Ribera del Duero Protos Gran Reserva (BYR)
Torres Mas La Plana (HOG, GRE, CV, WRI, LO, MOR)
Vega Sicilia 3rd year (BYR, NI)
Vega Sicilia Valbuena 3rd year (ASK, PEN)
**1983**
Torres Gran Coronas Black Label (GRE, RAE)
**1982**
Torres Gran Coronas Black Label (OD)

──────── £20.00 to £29.99 ────────
**Non-vintage**
Torres Gran Coronas Black Label (PEN)
**1986**
Vega Sicilia 3rd year (ROB)
**1985**
Vega Sicilia 3rd year (ROB)
**1983**
Torres Gran Coronas Black Label (LO)
**1976**
Vega Sicilia Unico (NI)
**1973**
Vega Sicilia Unico (NI)

──────── £30.00 to £39.99 ────────
**1980**
Vega Sicilia Valbuena 5th year (MOR)
**1976**
Vega Sicilia Unico (BO, GRE)

**1965**
Vega Sicilia Unico (NI)
**1962**
Vega Sicilia Unico (NI)

─────── £40.00 to £59.99 ───────
**1980**
Vega Sicilia Unico (MOR)
**1975**
Torres Gran Coronas Black Label (VIG)
Vega Sicilia Unico (ASK, TAN, FA, REI, MOR, AMI, ROB)

─────── £60.00 to £89.00 ───────
**1970**
Torres Gran Coronas Black Label (VIG)
**1968**
Vega Sicilia Unico (FA, ROB)
**1966**
Vega Sicilia Unico (REI)

## WHITE

─────── Under £3.00 ───────
**Non-vintage**
Castillo de Liria (WAI, VIC)
★ Moscatel de Valencia Castillo de Liria (WAI)
Safeway Moscatel de Valencia (SAF)
Sainsbury's Moscatel de Valencia (SAI)
Tesco Spanish Dry White Wine (TES)

─────── £3.00 to £3.99 ───────
**Non-vintage**
★ Co-op. del Ribeiro Pazo Ribeiro Blanco (WCL)
Los Llanos Armonioso (WCL)
Moscatel de Valencia Castillo de Liria (BO, TAN, GRG, AUG)
**1991**
Condé de Caralt (WCL)
**1990**
Torres Viña Sol (HOG)
**1987**
Condé de Caralt (MOR)

─────── £4.00 to £4.99 ───────
**Non-vintage**
Barbadillo Castillo de San Diego (WCL)
Torres Moscatel Malvasia de Oro (BYR)
**1991**
Torres San Valentin (WHI)
★ Torres Viña Esmeralda (BYR, WHI, BE, TES, WCL)
Torres Viña Sol (WHI, TES, BE)

**1990**
Barbadillo Castillo de San Diego (CV, PE)
Marqués de Alella (MOR)
Torres Gran Viña Sol (BYR)
Torres San Valentin (BYR, WHI)
Torres Viña Esmeralda (BYR, GRE, MOR, WHI, LO)
Torres Viña Sol (BYR, GRE, WHI, MOR, TES, LO, PE, LAY, DAV, TAN, THR)
**1989**
Marqués de Riscal Blanco Rueda (MOR)
Torres Gran Viña Sol (MOR, BYR, GRE)
Torres San Valentin (BYR)
Torres Viña Esmeralda (HOG, PEN)
Torres Viña Sol (BYR, GRE, AUG)
**1988**
Torres Viña Esmeralda (CH)
Torres Viña Sol (CH)

─────── £5.00 to £6.99 ───────
**1991**
Torres Viña Esmeralda (CV, WRI, ROB, DAV)
**1990**
Marqués de Alella (TAN)
Raimat Chardonnay (BYR)
Torres Gran Viña Sol (WHI, HAG, LO, TES, BE, CV, TAN, AN)
Torres Viña Esmeralda (CV, PE, AN, THR, TAN, VIC, ROB)
Torres Viña Sol (AN)
**1989**
Raimat Chardonnay (BO)
Torres Gran Viña Sol (CV, PE, HIC)
**1986**
Torres Gran Viña Sol (RAE)

─────── £7.00 to £9.99 ───────
**1991**
Torres Gran Viña Sol Castell de Fransola (WHI)
**1990**
Marqués de Griñon (BYR)
Rias Baixas Lagar de Cervera (THR, TAN, ROB)
Torres Gran Viña Sol Castell de Fransola (BYR, WHI, GRE, LO, TAN, ROB)
**1989**
Marqués de Griñon (WRI)
Raimat Chardonnay (VIC)
Torres Gran Viña Sol Castell de Fransola (BYR, GRE)
**1988**
Marqués de Griñon (BYR)
**1987**
Torres Gran Viña Sol Reserva (CH)

────────── £13.00 to £15.99 ──────────
**1988**
Jean León Chardonnay (BYR)
**1987**
Jean León Chardonnay (BYR)
**1986**
Jean León Chardonnay (MOR)

────────── £16.00 to £19.99 ──────────
**1990**
Torres Milmanda Chardonnay (CV)
**1989**
Torres Milmanda Chardonnay (GRE, BYR)
**1988**
Torres Milmanda Chardonnay (GRE, BYR)
**1987**
Torres Milmanda Chardonnay (REI)

────────── c. £32.50 ──────────
**1977**
Torres Viña Sol (CB)

## ROSÉ

────────── Under £5.00 ──────────
**1990**
Condestable Jumilla (MOR)
Torres de Casta Rosado (BYR, TES, BE, LO)
**1989**
Torres de Casta Rosado (BYR, LO, AN)

## SPARKLING

────────── Under £6.00 ──────────
**Non-vintage**
Castellblanch Brut Zero (HOG)
Castellblanch Cristal Seco (WAI, AUG)
Condé de Caralt Blanc de Blancs (MOR)
Condé de Caralt Brut (MOR)
Condé de Caralt Semi-seco (MOR, BYR)
Freixenet Brut Rosé (CV, PIP)
Freixenet Carta Nevada (CV, PIP, WHI)
Freixenet Cordon Negro Brut (HOG)
Jean Perico Brut (HOG)
Mont Marçal Brut (GRG)
Sainsbury's Cava Spanish Sparkling Wine
  (SAI)
Segura Viudas Brut (HOG)
**1989**
Condé de Caralt Brut (BYR)
**1988**
Castellblanch Brut Zero (THR)
Condé de Caralt Brut (BYR)
**1987**
Codorníu Brut (SAF)

────────── £6.00 to £6.99 ──────────
**Non-vintage**
Codorníu Brut Première Cuvée (VIC)
Condé de Caralt Rosado (BYR)
Freixenet Cordon Negro Brut (GRG, WHI,
  LAY, BYR, VIC, EL, AUG, DAV)
Marqués de Monistrol Brut (BO, AUG, UN,
  PE)
Marqués de Monistrol Rosé Brut (THR, AUG,
  PE)
**1988**
Freixenet Brut Nature (LOR)
Freixenet Cordon Negro Brut (CV, MOR,
  MAJ, PEN, ROB)
**1987**
Freixenet Brut Nature (MOR)
Freixenet Cordon Negro Brut (PIP, THR)
**1986**
Freixenet Cordon Negro Brut (TAN)

────────── £7.00 to £7.99 ──────────
**Non-vintage**
★ Raimat Chardonnay Brut (GA, BYR, VIC,
  THR)
**1989**
Codorníu Brut (MOR)

────────── £8.00 to £9.99 ──────────
**Non-vintage**
Raimat Chardonnay Brut (BO)
**1987**
Codorníu Chardonnay Brut (VIC, AUG)
**1986**
Codorníu Chardonnay Brut (THR)

## FORTIFIED

────────── Under £4.00 ──────────
**Non-vintage**
Bodegas Alvear Montilla Cream (LAY)
Bodegas Alvear Montilla Medium Dry (TAN,
  LAY)
Bodegas Alvear Montilla Pale Dry (TAN,
  LAY)
Sainsbury's Moscatel de Málaga 1/2 bottle
  (SAI)

────────── £5.00 to £7.99 ──────────
**Non-vintage**
★ Málaga Solera 1885 Scholtz (WAI, HOG)

────────── £8.00 to £9.99 ──────────
**Non-vintage**
Málaga Lagrima 10 años Scholtz (GRE, TAN)
Málaga Solera 1885 Scholtz (GRE, PE, ROB)

# SHERRY

### DRY

────── **Under £5.00** ──────

Elegante, Gonzalez Byass (HOG, WHI, WAI, THR, TES, AUG, DAV)
Fino Bertola (HOG)
Fino de Sanlúcar, Barbadillo (PIP)
Fino Quinta Osborne (BO)
Harvey's Luncheon Dry (HOG, WRI)
Harvey's Palo Cortado (MAR)
★ Lustau Fino (MAJ)
★ Manzanilla de Sanlúcar, Barbadillo (OD, GE, THR, PIP, HAG, BAR)
Valdespino Fino (WCL, PEN, AS)
Waitrose Fino Sherry (WAI)

────── **£5.00 to £6.99** ──────

Amontillado Napoleon, Hidalgo (HAG, NI, WW, AD)
Don Zoilo Very Old Fino (HOG)
★ Don Zoilo Pale Dry Manzanilla (HOG)
Elegante, Gonzalez Byass (UN, AN)
Fino de Balbaina, Barbadillo (PIP, BAR, HIC, CB)
Fino de Sanlúcar, Barbadillo (BIB)
Fino Hidalgo (VIN, NI, HAH)
Fino Superior Miraflores, Hidalgo (WS)
★ la Gitana Manzanilla, Hidalgo (HOG, WW, HAH, WAI)
Harvey's Luncheon Dry (BO, CH, WHI, HA, THR, HAG, UN, AN)
la Ina, Domecq (HOG, WHI, WAI, WRI, DAV, HAH, YF, CH)
Inocente Fino, Valdespino (VIN, WS, HOG)
Lustau Dry Oloroso (HIG)
Lustau Fino (HIG)
Lustau Palo Cortado (HIG)
Manzanilla de Sanlúcar, Barbadillo (CV, PEN, ROB, HIC, CB, BIB, AN)
Manzanilla Pasada Solear, Barbadillo (PIP, PE, CV, ROB, WS)

Manzanilla Pastora, Barbadillo (HAY)
Oloroso Especial, Hidalgo (WW)
Ostra Manzanilla (LAY)
San Patricio Fino, Garvey (HOG, WHI, CV, PEN, ROB, HAG, WS, WRI)
Tio Mateo Fino, Palomino & Vergara (HA)
Tio Pepe, Gonzalez Byass (HOG, WRI, BO, WHI, WAI, HAH, TES, OD, AUG, THR, DAV, UN, YF, CH, ROB)

────── **£7.00 to £8.99** ──────

Don Zoilo Finest Fino (GRG)
Don Zoilo Pale Dry Manzanilla (GRG, REI)
Don Zoilo Very Old Fino (HAG)
Dos Cortados Old Dry Oloroso, Williams & Humbert (HOG)
Fino Especial, Hidalgo (TAN)
Harvey's Luncheon Dry (YF)
Harvey's Palo Cortado (HOG)
la Ina, Domecq (UN, EL, ROB, AN)
Inocente Fino, Valdespino (AS, WRI, WCL, ROB, TW, BIB)
Jerez Cortado, Hidalgo (WW, TAN, AD, LAY)
Manzanilla Pasada de Sanlúcar, Hidalgo (TAN)
Manzanilla Pasada Solear, Barbadillo (HIC, BIB)
Oloroso Dry, Hidalgo (TAN, AD)
Oloroso Especial, Hidalgo (LAY)
Palo Cortado, Valdespino (WCL)
San Patricio Fino, Garvey (AN)
Tio Diego Amontillado, Valdespino (WCL)
★ Tio Guillermo Amontillado, Garvey (CV)
Tio Pepe, Gonzalez Byass (EL, AN)

────── **£9.00 to £11.99** ──────

Amontillado Almacenista, Lustau (HOG, PEN)
Don Zoilo Finest Old Amontillado (GRG, HAG, ROB)
Don Zoilo Pale Dry Manzanilla (VIG)
Don Zoilo Very Old Fino (VIG, BAR, AN)
Harvey's Fine Old Amontillado (HA)
Harvey's Palo Cortado (HA)
Manzanilla Pasada Almacenista, Lustau (HOG)
Oloroso Muy Viejo Almacenista, Lustau (HOG, PEN)
Oloroso Seco Barbadillo (PIP)
★ Palo Cortado, Barbadillo (PIP)
Palo Cortado del Carrascal, Valdespino (ROB, PE, BIB)

Palo Cortado, Don Beningo (HIC)
Pemartin Fino Solera 1820 (TW)
Pemartin Manzanilla Solera 1820 (TW)
Principe Amontillado, Barbadillo (THR)
Principe Manzanilla, Barbadillo (THR)

───────── £14.00 to £19.99 ─────────
Amontillado del Duque, Gonzalez Byass
   (RAE, HOG, OD, THR, REI, PE, VIN)
Coliseo Amontillado, Valdespino (WCL)

## MEDIUM

───────── £4.00 to £4.99 ─────────
Amontillado de Sanlúcar, Barbadillo (PIP)
Amontillado Lustau (OD, MAJ)
Amontillado Martial, Valdespino (HAH)
Amontillado Valdespino (AS, ROB)
Caballero Amontillado, Gonzalez Byass
   (TES)
Concha Amontillado, Gonzalez Byass (HOG,
   WHI, AUG, TES, WAI)
Harvey's Club Amontillado (BO, HOG, WAI,
   TES)
The Society's Medium Dry (WS)
Tanners Medium Sherry (TAN)
Waitrose Amontillado Sherry (WAI)

───────── £5.00 to £6.99 ─────────
Amontillado de Sanlúcar, Barbadillo (HAG,
   HAY, BAR, HIC, AN, BIB)
Concha Amontillado, Gonzalez Byass (AN)
Dry Sack, Williams & Humbert (HOG, WHI,
   WRI)
Harvey's Club Amontillado (WRI, THR, WHI,
   AUG, HAH, HA, YF, DAV, OD, HAG, UN, CH,
   AN)
Sandeman Amontillado (ROB)

───────── c. £10.00 ─────────
Sandeman Royal Esmeralda (HOG)

───────── £11.00 to £14.99 ─────────
★ Apostoles Oloroso, Gonzalez Byass (RAE,
   OD, HOG)
Oloroso Muy Viejo Almacenista, Lustau
   (PEN)
Sandeman Royal Esmeralda (REI)

┌─────────────────────────┐
│ **Webster's** *is an annual* │
│ *publication. We welcome* │
│ *your suggestions for next* │
│ *year's edition.* │
└─────────────────────────┘

───────── £16.00 to £19.99 ─────────
Apostoles Oloroso, Gonzalez Byass (REI, PE,
VIN)

## SWEET

───────── Under £5.00 ─────────
Bertola Cream (HOG)
Croft Original Pale Cream (WAI)
The Society's Cream (WS)
Tanners Cream Sherry (TAN)

───────── £5.00 to £6.99 ─────────
Croft Original Pale Cream (BO, THR, HOG,
   UN, WHI, TES, WRI, AUG, DAV, CH, OD, HAG,
   EL, YF, VIN)
Don Zoilo Rich Old Cream (HOG)
Double Century Oloroso (UN)
Harvey's Bristol Cream (THR, OD, WAI, TES,
   BO, HOG, CH, AUG, UN, DAV, HA, WHI, WRI,
   HAH, YF)
Harvey's Copper Beech (BO, HA)

───────── £7.00 to £9.99 ─────────
Don Zoilo Rich Old Cream (HAG)
Harvey's Bristol Cream (HAG, EL, AN)
★ Lustau's Old East India (HOG)
Pedro Ximenez Barbadillo (PIP)
Sanlúcar Cream, Barbadillo (HIC, BAR)
**1983**
Harvey's Bristol Cream (HA)

───────── c. £10.00 ─────────
Sandeman Royal Corregidor Oloroso (HOG)

───────── £12.00 to £14.99 ─────────
★ Matusalem Oloroso, Gonzalez Byass
   (RAE, HOG, THR)
Sandeman Royal Corregidor Oloroso (REI)

───────── £15.00 to £19.99 ─────────
Matusalem Oloroso, Gonzalez Byass (OD,
PE, VIN, ROB)

# PORTUGUESE TABLE WINES

## RED

──────── **Under £3.00** ────────
**Non-vintage**
Quinta de Cardiga Ribatejo (TES)
★ Sainsbury's Arruda (SAI)
**1987**
Bairrada Dom Ferraz (WAI)
Sainsbury's Dão (SAI)
Tesco Bairrada (TES)

──────── **£3.00 to £3.99** ────────
**1989**
Dão Terras Altas, J.M. da Fonseca (BYR)
★ Periquita J.M. da Fonseca (MAJ)
**1987**
Bairrada J.M. da Fonseca (BYR)
Bairrada Reserva Caves Aliança (MAJ)
Bairrada Reserva Dom Ferraz (THR)
Dão Dom Ferraz (VIC)
Dão Reserva Dom Ferraz (THR, WCL)
★ Dão Terras Altas, J.M. da Fonseca (BO, WHI)
Periquita J.M. da Fonseca (BYR)
Tesco Dão (TES)
**1986**
Dão Terras Altas, J.M. da Fonseca (GRE)
★ Pasmados J.M. da Fonseca (WAI)
Quinta de Santo Amaro, João Pires (WHI)
**1985**
Bairrada Dom Ferraz (AUG)
Dão Dom Ferraz (AUG, UN)
Dão Grão Vasco (GRG)
Dão Reserva Caves Dom Teodosio (BU)
Quinta de Santo Amaro, João Pires (WHI)
Tesco Douro (TES)
**1982**
★ Dão Grão Vasco Garrafeira (GRG)

──────── **£4.00 to £4.99** ────────
**1988**
Dão Grão Vasco (PE)
João Pires Meia Pipa (OD, THR)
★ Tinto da Anfora João Pires (WAI, OD, BYR, MAJ)
**1987**
Periquita J.M. da Fonseca (WHI, GRE, PE)
Tinto da Anfora João Pires (WAI, BYR, WCL)
**1986**
Quinta da Camarate, J.M. da Fonseca (BYR)
Tinto Velho Reguengos (TES, BYR)

**1985**
Bairrada Reserva Caves Aliança (PEN)
Pasmados J.M. da Fonseca (BYR)
Quinta da Camarate, J.M. da Fonseca (BYR)
**1984**
Cavenal Reserva Caves Nacionais (BOT)
Pasmados J.M. da Fonseca (BYR, GRE, WRI, WR)
**1983**
Beira Mar Reserva, da Silva (WCL)
**1980**
Bairrada Frei João (GE)
★ Romeira Garrafeira (SAI)

──────── **£5.00 to £5.99** ────────
**1988**
★ Quinta da Bacalhoa (SAI)
**1987**
Quinta da Camarate, J.M. da Fonseca (ASK)
Tinto da Anfora João Pires (WHI, CV, THR, WRI, LAY, AD)

**1986**
Quinta da Camarate, J.M. da Fonseca
  (WHI, WCL, AD, PE, PIP, TAN)
Tinto Velho Reguengos (WRI, ROB)
**1985**
Quinta da Camarate, J.M. da Fonseca
  (WHI, GRE)
Tinto Velho Reguengos (WRI)
**1983**
Dão Grão Vasco Reserva (GRG)
Garrafeira J.M. da Fonseca (BYR)
**1982**
Casal da Azenha, da Silva (GRG)
Garrafeira Particular Caves Aliança (MAJ)
Periquita Reserva J.M. da Fonseca (ASK)
**1980**
Garrafeira Caves Velhas (WCL)
**1979**
Garrafeira da Silva (UN)

--------- £6.00 to £7.99 ---------
**1982**
Garrafeira J.M. da Fonseca (WHI, ASK ROB, TAN)
**1980**
Casal da Azenha, da Silva (VIN)
**1979**
Garrafeira Particular da Silva (VIN)
**1975**
★ Bairrada Frei João (ASK)

--------- £9.00 to £11.99 ---------
**1988**
Bairrada Luis Pato (BOT, WR)
**1985**
Quinta da Côtto, Champalimaud (TAN)
**1967**
Dão Reserva Caves São João (ASK)

--------- c. £19.00 ---------
**1983**
Barca Velha, Ferreira (OD)

## WHITE

--------- Under £3.00 ---------
**Non-vintage**
Sainsbury's Vinho Verde (SAI)
**1991**
Bairrada Caves Aliança (GA, MAJ)

--------- £3.00 to £3.99 ---------
**Non-vintage**
Vinho Verde Aveleda (BYR)
Vinho Verde Casal Garcia (PEN, AUG)
Vinho Verde Casalinho (ASK, HOG)
Vinho Verde Gazela (OD, GRE)
**1990**
Dão Dom Ferraz (WCL)
Dão Terras Altas J.M. da Fonseca (BYR)
**1989**
Dão Terras Altas J.M. da Fonseca (BYR, BO, GRE)
**1988**
Dão Grão Vasco (GRG)
**1987**
Dão Porto dos Cavaleiros (ASK)
★ Dry Palmela Moscato, João Pires (ASK)
**1986**
★ Planalto Reserva (GRG)

--------- £4.00 to £4.99 ---------
**Non-vintage**
Vinho Verde Aveleda (HAG, CH, YF, WHI)
Vinho Verde Dom Ferraz (VIN)
Vinho Verde Gazela (TAN, DAV, BO, EL)

**1991**
João Pires Branco (SAI)
Vinho Verde Aveleda (PIP)
**1990**
Dão Grão Vasco (PE)
Dry Palmela Moscato, João Pires (BYR)
Vinho Verde Aveleda (ROB)
**1989**
Dry Palmela Moscato, João Pires (OD, BYR)
João Pires Branco (GRE)
João Pires Catarina (OD)

--------- £5.00 to £5.99 ---------
**Non-vintage**
Vinho Verde Aveleda (AV)
**1991**
João Pires Branco (ASK, DAV, PIP)
**1990**
João Pires Branco (WHI)
**1989**
Dão Grão Vasco (AV)
Dry Palmela Moscato João Pires (BO)
João Pires Branco (WHI)
**1988**
João Pires Branco (CV)

## ROSÉ

--------- Under £4.00 ---------
**Non-vintage**
Mateus Rosé (SAI, WAI, ASD, GA)

--------- £4.00 to £4.99 ---------
**Non-vintage**
Mateus Rosé (HOG, BO, TES, WHI, AUG, VIC, THR, CH, DAV, VIN)

## FORTIFIED

--------- Under £7.00 ---------
**1988**
Moscatel de Setúbal J.M. da Fonseca (BYR)
**1987**
Moscatel de Setúbal J.M. da Fonseca (BYR)
**1985**
Moscatel de Setúbal J.M. da Fonseca (WHI)
**1984**
Moscatel de Setúbal J.M. da Fonseca (GRE)
**1981**
Moscatel de Setúbal Caves Palmela (ASK)

--------- £12.00 to £15.99 ---------
**Non-vintage**
★ Moscatel de Setúbal 20-year-old J.M. da Fonseca (GRE, TAN)

# PORT

--------- **Under £6.00** ---------

**Non-vintage**

★ Croft Fine Ruby (GRG)

Quinta do Noval Old Coronation Ruby
(HOG)

Waitrose Fine Ruby (WAI)

Waitrose Fine Tawny (WAI)

--------- **£6.00 to £6.99** ---------

**Non-vintage**

Cockburn's Fine Ruby (HOG, BO, WAI, WHI,
HA, AUG, THR)

Cockburn's Fine Tawny (HOG, HA)

Cockburn's Fine White (HA)

Graham Ruby (NI)

Sandeman Fine Old Ruby (THR)

Sandeman Tawny (THR)

Smith Woodhouse Fine Tawny (UN, WCL)

Smith Woodhouse Ruby (UN, DAV, WCL)

Taylor Special Ruby (HAH)

Taylor Special Tawny (HAH)

Waitrose Vintage Character (WAI)

Warre's Ruby (AUG, WHI)

Warre's Tawny (WHI)

--------- **£7.00 to £8.99** ---------

**Non-vintage**

Churchill Dry White (CV, IR, THR, WW)

Churchill's Finest Vintage Character (LOR,
IR, CV, ASK, WW, PIP)

Cockburn's Fine Ruby (HAG, VIC, DAV, UN,
EL)

Cockburn's Fine Tawny (HAG, VIC, UN)

Cockburn's Special Reserve (HOG, BO, WAI,
AUG, WHI, CH, HA, THR, YF, VIC, UN, OD)

Dow's Fine Ruby (ROB, AN)

Dow's Fine Tawny (ROB, AN)

Dow's No. 1 White (PEN)

Dow's Vintage Character (HOG)

Fonseca Bin 27 (HOG, GRG, WAI, CH, WCL,
GRE)

★ Quinta do Noval Late Bottled (HOG, WHI,
PEN, WAI, AUG, GRE, TAN, WRI)

Ramos-Pinto Vintage Character (HAH)

Sandeman Fine Old Ruby (EL)

Sandeman Fine Old White (EL)

Sandeman Founder's Reserve (OD, THR)

Sandeman Tawny (OD)

Warre's Warrior (AUG, WHI, GE)

**1985**

Dow's Late Bottled (WAI)

Graham Late Bottled (NI, HOG, LO, GRE)

Taylor Late Bottled (HOG)

**1982**

★ Cockburn's Late Bottled (WHI)

--------- **£9.00 to £11.99** ---------

**Non-vintage**

Churchill Dry White (TAN, BO)

Churchill's Crusted Port Bottled 1986 (CV,
LOR, IR, HIG)

Churchill's Crusted Port Bottled 1985 (HAY)

Churchill's Finest Vintage Character (HAY,
NA, HIC, BAR, MV, VIN)

Cockburn's 10-year-old Tawny (WAI, WHI)

Cockburn's Special Reserve (EL)

Croft Late Bottled (THR)

Dow's Crusted Port bottled 1978 (PEN)

Dow's Vintage Character (PEN, HAG, WRI,
AN)

★ Fonseca 10-year-old Tawny (CH, HOG, GRG)

Fonseca Bin 27 (YF, BE, TES, VIC, NA, LO,
HAH, HAG, WRI, ROB, AN, VIN)

Graham 10-year-old Tawny (NI, MAJ, BIB)

Graham Late Bottled (THR)

★ Quinta da Ervamoira 10-year-old Tawny
(GRE)

Quinta do Noval 10-year-old Tawny (WHI)

Quinta do Noval Late Bottled (UN, ROB)

Sandeman (VIC)

Sandeman Founder's Reserve (UN)

Tanners Crusted (TAN)

Taylor Chip Dry White Port (GRE, HAG, DAV)

Taylor Late Bottled (VIC)

Warre's 10-year-old Tawny (GE, WHI)

Warre's Late Bottled (CV)

Warre's Nimrod Old Tawny (AUG)

Warre's Warrior (PEN)

Wellington Wood Port (BER)

**1985**

Dow's Late Bottled (AN, AV)

Fonseca Late Bottled (HIG)

Graham Late Bottled (BO, TAN)

★ Ramos-Pinto Late Bottled (GRE, BEK)

Taylor Late Bottled (WAI, TES, THR, ROB)

**1983**

Croft Late Bottled (MAR)

Offley Forrester Late Bottled (THR)

Royal Oporto (HUN)

Smith Woodhouse (PIP)

**1982**

Graham Late Bottled (YF, BIB)

★ Quinta da Eira Velha (ROB, HA)

Sandeman (WY)

**1980**
Royal Oporto (TES)
Warre (WY)
**1979**
★ Warre's Quinta da Cavadinha (HIC)
**1977**
Feuerheerd (FA)

─────── **£12.00 to £14.99** ───────
**Non-vintage**
Cockburn's 10-year-old Tawny (THR, HA, VIC)
Dow's 10-year-old Tawny (HAG, AN, ROB, YF)
Dow's Boardroom Tawny (HOG)
Fonseca 10-year-old Tawny (WCL, PIP, HIG, REI)
Graham 10-year-old Tawny (GRE, YF)
Sandeman 10-year-old Royal Tawny (OD)
Taylor 10-year-old Tawny (WHI, LAY, MAJ, GRE, PEN, DAV, UN, WRI)
**1983**
Churchill's Quinta do Agua Alta (HAY)
Gould Campbell (LOE)
Offley Boa Vista (WHI, LOE)
Royal Oporto (WRI, TW)
**1982**
Churchill (HAH)
**1980**
Delaforce Quinta da Corte (CB)
Fonseca (WY, BIB, BU)
Graham (BIB)
Warre (BIB)
**1977**
Royal Oporto (GRG)

─────── **£15.00 to £19.99** ───────
**Non-vintage**
Cockburn's 20-year-old Tawny (WHI, BO, HA)
Dow's Vintage Character (BUT)
Fonseca (BUT)
Fonseca 20-year-old (GRG)
Graham 20-year-old Tawny (NI)
Martinez 20-year-old Tawny (HIC)
★ Sandeman 20-year-old Tawny (OD, WAI, THR)
Taylor 10-year-old Tawny (TAN, VIN)
Warre's 10-year-old Tawny (AV)
William Pickering Finest 20-year-old Tawny (BER)
**1985**
Churchill (BUT, LAY, CH)
Cockburn (BIB, YF, HA)
Dow (BIB, BUT, LOE, CH, BO)
Fonseca (BIB, BO)
Graham (WY, BUT, BO, BAR, GRE)
Offley Boa Vista (VIG)
Quinta do Noval (BUT, LOE)

Sandeman (BIB)
Smith Woodhouse (LOE)
★ Taylor (BUT)
Warre (BIB, BUT, LOE, CH)
**1983**
Cockburn (HOG, YF, HA)
Dow (BUT, HOG, LAY)
Fonseca (BUT, BIB, HOG, MV, YF)
Graham (BIB, BO, MAJ, BUT, YF)
Quarles Harris (VIG)
Smith Woodhouse (HAG, PEN, UN)
★ Warre (BUT, BIB, BO, HOG, THR, ROB, LAY)

**1982**
Churchill (LAY, BER, TW, WW)
Martinez (AD)
Quinta do Noval (HAG, HOG, AD, CH, VIC)
Royal Oporto (UN)
Warre's Quinta da Cavadinha (CV, WAI, WHI, LAY, PIP, OD, TAN, WCL, ROB)
**1980**
★ Dow (ROB, BYR, DAV, BER)
Gould Campbell (BER)
Graham (BO, BYR, DAV, NI, ROB)
Taylor (WY, CV, WHI, GRE, LAY, DAV)
Warre (TAN, CV, ROB, BYR, LAY, PEN, DAV, VIG)
**1979**
Graham Malvedos (GRE, WHI, HAH, LAY, TAN)
**1978**
Taylor Quinta de Vargellas (GRE, LAY, HAH, WRI, DAV, ROB, VIC, OD, YF, TAN)
**1977**
Gould Campbell (GRG)
★ Warre (BIB)
**1975**
Cockburn (BUT)
Croft (BIB, TAN)
Delaforce (BER)
Graham (BIB)
**1970**
Cockburn (FA)
Martinez (BUT)
Royal Oporto (BIB)

Sandeman (FA)
Smith Woodhouse (BIB)
★ Warre (FA)

——————— £20.00 to £24.99 ———————
**Non-vintage**
Dow's 20-year-old Tawny (HAG, AN)
Fonseca 20-year-old Tawny (BAR, PIP)
Graham 20-year-old Tawny (GRE, YF)
Quinta da Bom Retiro 20-year-old Tawny
  (BEK)
Quinta do Noval 20-year-old Tawny (WHI)
Taylor 20-year-old Tawny (WHI, LAY, GRE,
  YF, ROB, EL, UN, PEN)
**1985**
Croft (VIG, TAN)
Dow (LAY, VIC, ROB, DAV, WHI, HUN, BYR)
Fonseca (VIC, DAV, BYR, LOR)
Graham (GE, VIC, VIG, DAV, HUN, BYR)
Warre (MV, LAY, DAV, WHI, ROB, VIC)
**1983**
Cockburn (BUT, DAV, VIC)
Dow (TAN, DAV, AD)
Fonseca (DAV, LOR, VIC, THR, BYR)
Graham (VIG, ROB, DAV, UN, VIC, THR)
Taylor (ROB, DAV, YF, VIC)
Warre (DAV, UN, AD, VIC, AUG, BYR)
**1982**
Croft (VIG, DAV, UN)
Sandeman (TAN, UN)
**1980**
Fonseca (VIG, BER, VIC)
Graham (BER, VIG, VIC, YF)
Taylor (THR, BER, VIG, ROB)
Warre (UN, AUG, VIC)
**1977**
Delaforce (GRG)
Fonseca (BIB)
Gould Campbell (BER)
Graham (FA, BIB)
Offley Boa Vista (VIC)
Quarles Harris (BUT, BER, AD)
Smith Woodhouse (ROB)
**1975**
Cockburn (BU, BER, YF)
Croft (BU, BER, DAV, BYR, GRG)
Dow (BER, PEN, THR, LAY, GRG)
Fonseca (BER, BUT, GRG)
Graham (NI, DAV, BER, GRG, UN)
Martinez (AD)
Quinta do Noval (BU, VIC, ROB)
Sandeman (BER)
Taylor (BUT, BER)
Warre (CV, NI, AD, DAV, BER, VIC, PEN, WHI,
  AUG, THR, BYR)

**1970**
Croft (WY)
Dow (FA)
Graham (BIB)
Quinta do Noval (BIB)
**1966**
★ Dow (FA)
Rebello Valente (BU)
Sandeman (FA)

——————— £25.00 to £29.99 ———————
**1977**
Croft (WHI)
Dow (BUT, LAY)
Fonseca (LOR)
Graham (GRE)
Sandeman (BER)
Taylor (BIB, WY)
Warre (MV, GE, TAN, NI, LAY)
**1975**
Dow (AUG)
Quinta do Noval (AUG)
Sandeman (AUG)
Taylor (DAV, AUG)
Warre (ROB)
**1970**
Croft (BIB, WHI, DAV)
Delaforce (BER)
Dow (BUT, BIB)
Fonseca (FA, BIB)
Graham (FA, BUT)
Rebello Valente (VIC)
Sandeman (BIB, BER)
Taylor (WY, BIB, FA)
**1966**
Delaforce (BER)
Gould Campbell (BER)
Offley Boa Vista (BER)
Smith Woodhouse (REI)

——————— £30.00 to £39.99 ———————
**Non-vintage**
Fonseca 30-year-old Tawny (BAR)
**1977**
Croft (BER, CB, DAV)
Dow (BO, BYR, PEN, BER, DAV, VIC)
Fonseca (MV, BER, BYR, VIC, AD)
Graham (BUT, BO, GRG, DAV, BYR, VIC)
Taylor (AD, DAV, WHI)
Warre (BYR, PEN, WHI, AUG, BER, ROB, BO, UN,
  DAV, HUN, HAG, THR, VIC)
**1970**
Dow (BER, DAV, CB, ROB)
Fonseca (DAV, GE, GRG, BER, LOR, BYR, BAR, CB)
Graham (AUG, DAV, HAG, LAY, BAR, BO)

Quinta do Noval (BER, VIG)
Taylor (DAV, BAR, WHI)
Warre (CV, TAN, BER, MV, DAV, LAY, ROB, THR)
**1966**
Croft (WY, WHI, DAV)
Fonseca (BIB, FA)
Graham (DAV)
Quinta do Noval (DAV, WHI)
Taylor (FA, BUT, DAV)
Warre (GRG)
**1963**
Cockburn (WY)
Croft (WY)
Martinez (HA)
Quinta do Noval (FA)
Rebello Valente (BER)
**1960**
Cockburn (HA, BUT, DAV, GRG)

——————— £40.00 to £49.99 ———————
**Non-vintage**
Fonseca 40-year-old Tawny (GRG, BAR)
**1977**
Taylor (UN, TAN, GRG, ROB, BO)
**1970**
Taylor (CB, BO, HUN, ROB, TAN, YF, VIG)
**1963**
Croft (BIB, MV, HUN)
Offley Boa Vista (ROB)
Quinta do Noval (MV, BU)
Sandeman (BIB)
Warre (BIB, BUT, NI, BAR)

——————— £50.00 to £74.99 ———————
**Non-vintage**
Taylor 40-year-old Tawny (GRE, UN, PEN, VIN)
**1970**
Fonseca (VIN)
**1966**
Graham (ROB)
**1963**
Dow (DAV)
Fonseca (FA, BIB, GRG, DAV, BUT)
Graham (FA, DAV, WS)
Sandeman (TW, DAV)
Taylor (FA, BAR, BIB, BU, DAV)
Warre (ROB, DAV)

——————— £75.00 to £99.99 ———————
**1963**
Dow (ROB)
Taylor (HAG, REI, YF, ROB)
**1955**
Fonseca (GRG)
Taylor (WY, FA)

**1945**
Ferreira (BIB)
**1942**
Rebello Valente (BU)
**1935**
Cockburn (WY)
**1933**
Calem (VIG)
**1924**
Dow (WY)
Warre (WY)
**1922**
Warre (FA)
**1920**
Sandeman (FA)

——————— £100.00 to £139.99 ———————
**1948**
Taylor (FA)
**1935**
Graham (WY)
**1927**
Warre (WY)
**1920**
Dow (WY)
Warre (WY)
**1908**
Mackenzie (FA)
**1904**
Cockburn (FA)

——————— £140.00 to £179.99 ———————
**1948**
Graham (FA)
**1945**
Quinta do Noval (BUT)
Croft (WY, HUN)
**1927**
Cockburn (WY)
Croft (WY)
Dow (WY)
**1912**
Cockburn (WY)

——————— £180.00 to £235.00 ———————
**1945**
Dow (YF)
**1935**
Taylor (FA)
**1924**
Taylor (WY)

——————— c. £305.00 ———————
**1945**
Taylor (YF)

# MADEIRA

## Under £7.99

**Non-vintage**
Bual Blandy (HOG, NI)
Bual Justino Henriques (CH)
Bual Old Trinity House Rutherford &
  Miles (GRG, HAH, TES, BE, ROB)
Malmsey Blandy (HOG, NI, HAH, WAI, GRE,
  DAV)
Malmsey Cossart Gordon (CV)
Malmsey Justino Henriques (CH)
Rainwater Good Company Cossart Gordon
  (CH)
Sercial Blandy (HOG, NI, GRE)
Sercial Cossart Gordon (HAH, CV)
Sercial Old Custom House Rutherford &
  Miles (GRG, ROB)
Verdelho Blandy (HOG, GRE)

## £8.00 to £9.99

**Non-vintage**
5-year-old Bual Cossart Gordon (IR, CV)
5-year-old Malmsey Cossart Gordon (IR,
  HOG)
★ 5-year-old Sercial Cossart Gordon (IR)
Bual Blandy (OD, VIN)
Bual Cossart Gordon (BAR, HIC, WCL)
Bual Henriques & Henriques (HAG)
Bual Old Trinity House Rutherford &
  Miles (TAN)
Finest Old Malmsey Cossart Gordon (HAY)
Malmsey Blandy (THR, VIN)
Malmsey Cossart Gordon (AV, WCL)
Malmsey Henriques & Henriques (HAG)
Rainwater Good Company Cossart Gordon
  (IR, AV, PEN, AD)
Sercial Cossart Gordon (BAR, AV, WCL)
Sercial Henriques & Henriques (HAG)
Sercial Old Custom House Rutherford &
  Miles (TAN)

## £10.00 to £14.99

**Non-vintage**
10-year-old Malmsey Blandy (HOG, NI, WAI,
  THR, GRE, ROB)
★ 10-year-old Malmsey Cossart Gordon
  (GRE)
5-year-old Bual Cossart Gordon (HIC, GRE)
5-year-old Malmsey Cossart Gordon (GRE)
5-year-old Sercial Cossart Gordon (GRE)
Finest Old Bual Cossart Gordon (PIP)
Finest Old Malmsey Cossart Gordon (PIP)

## £15.00 to £19.99

10-year-old Malmsey Cossart Gordon (HIC,
  CV)
10-year-old Verdelho Cossart Gordon (HIC,
  CV)
★ Very Old Bual Duo Centenary
  Celebration Cossart Gordon (CH, HAH)
★ Very Old Sercial Duo Centenary
  Celebration Cossart Gordon (HAH)

## £20.00 to £49.99

**Non-vintage**
Very Old Bual Duo Centenary Celebration
  Cossart Gordon (AD)
Very Old Sercial Duo Centenary
  Celebration Cossart Gordon (AD)
**1954**
Bual Henriques & Henriques (GRE)
**1950**
Sercial Rutherford & Miles (GRE)
**1934**
Malmsey Henriques & Henriques (GRE)

## £50.00 to £75.00

**1964**
Malmsey Blandy (VIG)
**1950**
Sercial Cossart Gordon (HA)
Sercial Leacock (VIG)
**1933**
Malmsey Cossart Gordon (HA)

## £95.00 to £120.00

**1931**
Verdelho Blandy (VIG)
**1920**
Bual Blandy (VIG)
**1907**
Bual Blandy (VIG)

## £135.00 to £155.00

**1930**
Malmsey Quinta do Serrado (AD)
**1927**
Bual Quinta do Serrado (AD)

> Stars (★) indicate wines
> selected by the editors as
> particularly good value
> in their class.

# UNITED STATES

## CALIFORNIA RED

─────── **Under £4.00** ───────

**Non-vintage**
E&J Gallo Dry Reserve (GA, SAF, BO, PE)
E&J Gallo Zinfandel (BO, PE)
Franzia Cabernet Sauvignon (VIC)
Sainsbury's Zinfandel (SAI)
**1989**
Mountain View Pinot Noir (WAI)

─────── **£4.00 to £5.99** ───────

**1989**
Fetzer Zinfandel (WHI, CV)
Robert Mondavi Cabernet Sauvignon (THR, HAH, VIC)
Robert Mondavi Woodbridge Cabernet Sauvignon (WHI)
Stratford Cabernet Sauvignon (MAJ)
**1988**
Beringer Zinfandel (VIC)
Inglenook Zinfandel (VIC)
La Crema Pinot Noir (CH)
**1987**
Fetzer Zinfandel (BO, CV)
Glen Ellen Cabernet Sauvignon (AUG)
Wente Bros Cabernet Sauvignon (WAI)

─────── **£6.00 to £7.99** ───────

**1990**
★ Saintsbury Garnet Pinot Noir (BIB)
**1989**
Carneros Creek Pinot Noir (ROB)
Hawk Crest Cabernet Sauvignon (WW, IR, ASK)
**1988**
Beaulieu Beautour Cabernet Sauvignon (SAI)
Buena Vista Zinfandel (WCL)
Clos du Bois Merlot (AMI)
Firestone Merlot (HOG, CH, AMI, BYR, WHI)
Hawk Crest Cabernet Sauvignon (IR, BO)
Laurel Glen Cabernet Sauvignon (WW)
★ Ridge Paso Robles Zinfandel (HOG)
**1987**
Beringer Cabernet Sauvignon (GA)
Clos du Val Zinfandel (SOM)
Firestone Cabernet Sauvignon (HOG, WHI)
La Crema Pinot Noir (SAI)
Pedroncelli Cabernet Sauvignon (LAY)
Robert Mondavi Woodbridge Cabernet Sauvignon (BER)

**1986**
Dry Creek Cabernet Sauvignon (HOG)
Firestone Ambassador's Vineyard Merlot (HAG)
Firestone Pinot Noir (HOG, AMI)
Hawk Crest Cabernet Sauvignon (ASK, YF)
Lohr Cabernet Sauvignon (BU)
Sterling Cabernet Sauvignon (OD)
**1985**
Edna Valley Pinot Noir (CV)
Wente Bros Cabernet Sauvignon (GE)

─────── **£8.00 to £9.99** ───────

**1990**
★ Saintsbury Pinot Noir (AD, BIB)
**1989**
Clos du Bois Merlot (WHI, WCL)
il Podere Nebbiolo San Olivos (WCL)
★ Ojai Syrah (AD)
Ridge Geyserville Zinfandel (GRE, BYR)
Ridge Paso Robles Zinfandel (SAF, AMI)
Saintsbury Pinot Noir (WS)
**1988**
Buena Vista Cabernet Sauvignon (WCL)
Clos du Bois Cabernet Sauvignon (WHI)
Clos du Bois Merlot (BYR, WHI, NI, PE, BAR)
Clos du Val Merlot (SOM)
Newton Cabernet Sauvignon (AN)
Saintsbury Pinot Noir (RAE)
**1987**
Alexander Valley Cabernet Sauvignon (BYR, AV)
Clos du Val Pinot Noir (REI)
Franciscan Cabernet Sauvignon (PEN)
Newton Merlot (AN)
Ridge Paso Robles Zinfandel (GE)
Shafer Merlot (BYR)
**1986**
Renaissance Cabernet Sauvignon (AD)
★ Robert Mondavi Pinot Noir (CV)
Sanford Pinot Noir (SOM, HOG)
Schug Cellars Pinot Noir (VIG)
Simi Cabernet Sauvignon (SOM, LAY)
**1985**
Beaulieu Beautour Cabernet Sauvignon (BO)
Fetzer Zinfandel (BYR)
Rutherford Hill Cabernet Sauvignon (HOG)
**1984**
★ Robert Mondavi Cabernet Sauvignon Reserve (CH)
**1982**
Clos du Val Cabernet Sauvignon (CHA)

——— £10.00 to £11.99 ———

**1990**
★ Au Bon Climat Pinot Noir (MV)
**1989**
Calera Jensen Pinot Noir (AMI, PIP)
Cuvaison Merlot/Zinfandel (BY)
Newton Merlot (WCL, HAU)
**1988**
Acacia Iuno Pinot Noir (SAF, THR)
Dry Creek Zinfandel (HAH)
Joseph Phelps Cabernet Sauvignon (BYR)
Robert Mondavi Pinot Noir (BYR)
Sanford Pinot Noir (BYR, WHI, WCL)
Stag's Leap Cabernet Sauvignon (WW)
**1987**
Clos du Val Merlot (CHA)
Newton Cabernet Sauvignon (AN)
Ridge Geyserville Zinfandel (GE)
Robert Mondavi Cabernet Sauvignon (ROB)
Rutherford Hill Merlot (AV)
★ Simi Cabernet Sauvignon (CB)
**1986**
Clos du Val Cabernet Sauvignon (REI)
Iron Horse Cabernet Sauvignon (AMI)
★ Newton Cabernet Sauvignon (WCL, HAU)
Ridge York Creek Cabernet Sauvignon (GRE)
Robert Mondavi Cabernet Sauvignon (HOG)
Trefethen Cabernet Sauvignon (AMI)
**1985**
Clos du Val Cabernet Sauvignon (CHA)
Dry Creek Cabernet Sauvignon (YF)
Freemark Abbey Cabernet Sauvignon (AV)
Shafer Cabernet Sauvignon (ROB)

——— £12.00 to £14.99 ———

**1988**
Au Bon Climat Pinot Noir (BUT)
Cuvaison Cabernet Sauvignon (BY)
Matanzas Creek Merlot (BAR)
**1987**
Carmenet Cabernet Sauvignon (BYR)
Laurel Glen Cabernet Sauvignon (BAR)
Robert Mondavi Oakville Cabernet
  Sauvignon (NI)
Stag's Leap Cabernet Sauvignon (IR)
**1986**
Carmenet Cabernet Sauvignon (SOM, PIP)
Freemark Abbey Cabernet Bosche (AV)
Freemark Abbey Cabernet Sycamore (AV)
Newton Merlot (BER)
**1985**
Ridge York Creek Cabernet Sauvignon
  (BYR)
**1983**
Stag's Leap Cabernet Sauvignon (BYR)

——— £15.00 to £19.99 ———

**1987**
Sterling Cabernet Sauvignon Reserve (OD)
**1986**
Chalone Pinot Noir (AMI)
Robert Mondavi Pinot Noir Reserve (WHI,
  AMI)
**1985**
Jordan Cabernet Sauvignon (PEN)
Trefethen Cabernet Sauvignon (VIG)
**1982**
Acacia St Clair Pinot Noir (BUT)
Jekel Cabernet Sauvignon Private Reserve
  (BUT)
**1980**
Grgich Zinfandel (BUT)
Ridge York Creek Cabernet Sauvignon (AD)
Robert Mondavi Cabernet Sauvignon
  Reserve (HOG, WHI, GRE)
**1976**
Firestone Pinot Noir (BUT)

——— £20.00 to £29.99 ———

**1988**
Philip Togni Cabernet Sauvignon (WW)
Robert Mondavi Cabernet Sauvignon
  Reserve (BER)
**1987**
Robert Mondavi Cabernet Sauvignon
  Reserve (NI)
**1985**
Mount Eden Cabernet Sauvignon (WW)
**1982**
Robert Mondavi Cabernet Sauvignon (BYR)
Robert Mondavi Cabernet Sauvignon
  Reserve (AMI)
**1980**
Ridge Monte Bello Cabernet Sauvignon
  (VIG, AMI, BUT)
**1978**
Jekel Cabernet Sauvignon (BUT)

——— £30.00 to £39.99 ———

**1987**
Mondavi/Rothschild Opus One (LAY, GRE)
**1983**
Mondavi/Rothschild Opus One (RAE)
**1982**
Heitz Martha's Vineyard Cabernet
  Sauvignon (GRE)
**1981**
Mondavi/Rothschild Opus One (HOG)
**1978**
Ridge Monte Bello Cabernet Sauvignon
  (AD)

─────────── £40.00 to £49.99 ───────────

**1985**
Mondavi/Rothschild Opus One (BUT, HAH, WHI)
**1977**
Heitz Bella Oaks Cabernet Sauvignon (GRG)
Heitz Martha's Vineyard Cabernet Sauvignon (GRG)
**1976**
Heitz Martha's Vineyard Cabernet Sauvignon (AD)

─────────── £50.00 to £69.99 ───────────

**1985**
Heitz Martha's Vineyard Cabernet Sauvignon (BUT)
**1974**
Mayacamas Late Harvest Zinfandel (VIG)

## CALIFORNIA WHITE

─────────── Under £4.00 ───────────

**Non-vintage**
E&J Gallo Chenin Blanc (PE)
E&J Gallo French Colombard (THR, SAF, BO, GA, PE)
E&J Gallo Sauvignon Blanc (PE, SAF, BO)
Sainsbury's Chardonnay (SAI)
**1990**
E&J Gallo Chenin Blanc (THR, DAV)
E&J Gallo Sauvignon Blanc (SAI)
**1989**
E&J Gallo Chenin Blanc (AUG, BO, UN)
E&J Gallo French Colombard (AUG)
E&J Gallo Sauvignon Blanc (GRG, THR)
Glen Ellen Chardonnay (VIC)

─────────── £4.00 to £5.99 ───────────

**Non-vintage**
Dry Creek Chenin Blanc (THR)
**1990**
Dry Creek Chenin Blanc (GRE, BYR)
Firestone Riesling (BYR)
Glen Ellen Chardonnay (GRE, WHI)
**1989**
Christian Bros Chenin Blanc (BYR)
Firestone Riesling (BYR)
Quady Essensia Orange Muscat 1/2 bottle (BYR)
Robert Mondavi Sauvignon Blanc (THR, HAH)
Robert Mondavi Woodbridge Sauvignon Blanc (WHI)
Wente Bros Chardonnay (HOG)

**1988**
Christian Bros Chenin Blanc (BYR)
Firestone Selected Harvest Johannisberg Riesling 1/2 bottle (GRE)
Quady Essensia Orange Muscat 1 1/2 bottle (PEN)
Renaissance Riesling (AD)
Robert Mondavi Woodbridge Sauvignon Blanc (AMI)
Sterling Sauvignon Blanc (OD)
Stratford Winery Chardonnay (MAJ)
William Wheeler Sauvignon Blanc (HOG)

─────────── £6.00 to £7.99 ───────────

**Non-vintage**
Trefethen Eshcol (BYR, WHI, AD)
**1991**
Firestone Chardonnay (SAI)
**1990**
Clos du Bois Chardonnay (DAV)
Clos du Bois Sauvignon Blanc (GRE, BYR)
Hawk Crest Chardonnay (ASK, BO)
Robert Mondavi Moscato d'Oro (WHI)
Sanford Sauvignon Blanc (SOM)
Simi Sauvignon Blanc (LAY)
**1989**
Clos du Bois Sauvignon Blanc (GRE, BYR, BOT, WR)
Dry Creek Chardonnay (HOG)
Dry Creek Fumé Blanc (CV)
Mark West Gewurztraminer (NI)
Monticello Chardonnay (HOG, AMI)
Pedroncelli Chardonnay (LAY)
Quady Essensia Orange Muscat 1/2 bottle (WHI, BY, HAL, ROB, WRI)
Sanford Chardonnay (SOM)
Simi Sauvignon Blanc (BYR, SOM, REI)
Stag's Leap Sauvignon Blanc (WW, ASK)
**1988**
Dry Creek Fumé Blanc (HOG, HAG)
Rutherford Hill Chardonnay (BYR)
Sanford Sauvignon Blanc (HOG)
Sterling Chardonnay (OD)
**1987**
Robert Mondavi Fumé Blanc (AD)
Robert Mondavi Oakville Reserve Chardonnay (NI)
Rutherford Hill Chardonnay (HOG, BYR, GRG)
**1986**
Robert Mondavi Oakville Fumé Blanc Reserve (NI)
**1983**
Renaissance Botrytis Sauvignon 1/2 bottle (AD)

─────── £8.00 to £9.99 ───────

**1990**
Alexander Valley Chardonnay (HAH)
Buena Vista Chardonnay (WCL)
Chateau St-Jean Fumé Blanc (PIP)
Matanzas Creek Sauvignon Blanc (HAH)
★ Saintsbury Chardonnay (AD, BIB)
**1989**
Clos du Bois Chardonnay (BYR, THR, WHI, AD)
Edna Valley Chardonnay (CV)
Grgich Hills Fumé Blanc (EL)
Mark West Late Harvest Gewurztraminer (HAG)
★ Simi Chardonnay (SOM, LAY)
Simi Sonoma Chardonnay (REI)
**1988**
★ Edna Valley Chardonnay (HOG)
Swanson Chardonnay (HOG, BYR, PEN)
William Wheeler Sonoma Chardonnay (BYR)
**1987**
Robert Mondavi Oakville Chardonnay (WHI)
Robert Mondavi Oakville Fumé Blanc Reserve (WHI)
Sanford Chardonnay (HOG)
Shafer Chardonnay (GRG, WRI)

─────── £10.00 to £11.99 ───────

**1990**
Au Bon Climat Chardonnay (MV)
Clos du Val Chardonnay (REI)
Frogs Leap Chardonnay (LAY)
Philip Togni Sauvignon Blanc (WW)
Qupe Chardonnay (MV, OD)
Sonoma-Cutrer Chardonnay (AV)
**1989**
Cuvaison Chardonnay (BY)
Newton Chardonnay (AN)
**1988**
Cuvaison Chardonnay (BY)
Freemark Abbey Chardonnay (AV)
Rutherford Hill Jaeger Chardonnay (AV)
Simi Chardonnay (TAN)
Sonoma-Cutrer Chardonnay (WRI)
★ Sonoma-Cutrer les Pierres Chardonnay (HOG)
Stag's Leap Chardonnay (WW)
**1987**
Trefethen Chardonnay (AD)
**1986**
Jordan Chardonnay (LAY)
Robert Mondavi Chardonnay (BYR)
Robert Mondavi Oakville Fumé Blanc (BER)

─────── £12.00 to £14.99 ───────

**1990**
Saintsbury Reserve Chardonnay (AD)
**1989**
Grgich Hills Chardonnay (EL)
**1988**
Acacia Chardonnay (AMI)
Chalone Chardonnay (SOM)
Matanzas Creek Chardonnay (HAH, BAR)
Sanford Chardonnay (NI)
**1987**
Robert Mondavi Chardonnay (TAN)
Saintsbury Reserve Chardonnay (BUT)
Sonoma-Cutrer les Pierres Chardonnay (BYR, PEN, GRG)
**1986**
Iron Horse Chardonnay (BER)
**1985**
Clos du Bois Calcaire Chardonnay (GRG)
**1983**
Robert Mondavi Sauvignon Blanc Botrytis ¹/₂ bottle (HAL)
**1976**
Cuvaison Chardonnay (VIG)

─────── £15.00 to £20.00 ───────

**1989**
Chalone Pinot Blanc (VIG)
Far Niente Chardonnay (AV)
**1987**
Robert Mondavi Chardonnay Reserve (AMI, BYR, AD)
Simi Reserve Chardonnay (LAY)
**1986**
Robert Mondavi Chardonnay Reserve (BYR)
**1983**
Joseph Phelps Johannisberg Riesling Selected Late Harvest ¹/₂ bottle (HAL)
**1978**
Firestone Selected Harvest Johannisberg Riesling Ambassador's Vineyard (VIG)

## CALIFORNIA ROSÉ

─────── Under £5.00 ───────

**Non-vintage**
E&J Gallo White Grenache (SAF, VIC)
E&J Gallo White Zinfandel (PE)
**1989**
E&J Gallo White Grenache (GRG)

─────── £5.00 to £5.99 ───────

**1990**
Robert Mondavi White Zinfandel (WHI, ROB, NI)

## CALIFORNIA SPARKLING

──────── **Under £15.00** ────────
**1986**
Schramsberg Blanc de Blancs (AD, ROB)
**1984**
Schramsberg Blanc de Noirs (AD)

──────── **c. £15.00** ────────
**1987**
Iron Horse Brut (AD)

## OTHER USA RED

──────── **Under £7.00** ────────
**Non-vintage**
Cameron Pinot Noir (BIB)
**1988**
Columbia Pinot Noir (ASD)
Covey Run Lemberger (HE)
**1987**
Elk Cove Estate Pinot Noir (WW, HE)
**1986**
Covey Run Cabernet Sauvignon (HE)
Texas Vineyards Ivanhoe Red (HE)

──────── **£7.00 to £8.99** ────────
**1988**
Columbia Pinot Noir (NA)
**1986**
Columbia Pinot Noir (VIG, PEN)

──────── **£9.00 to £10.99** ────────
**1989**
Adelsheim Pinot Noir (WW)
**1988**
Château Ste-Michelle Cabernet Sauvignon (WRI)
Ponzi Pinot Noir (WW)
**1987**
Llano Estacado Cabernet Sauvignon (HE)
**1986**
Elk Cove Estate Pinot Noir (HE)

──────── **£12.00 to £15.99** ────────
**1989**
Eyrie Vineyard Pinot Noir (BYR)
**1988**
Cameron Pinot Noir Reserve (BIB)
Eyrie Vineyard Pinot Meunier (WW)
**1986**
Ponzi Pinot Noir (BYR)
**1985**
Rose Creek Mercer Ranch Cabernet Sauvignon (ASK)

## OTHER USA WHITE

──────── **Under £6.00** ────────
**1991**
Sainsbury's Washington State Sauvignon Blanc (SAI)
**1990**
Hogue Cellars Fumé Blanc (CV)
Snoqualmie Semillon (WW)
**1988**
Columbia Gewurztraminer (BYR, PEN)
Cordier Sauvignon Blanc (GRG)
Fall Creek Emerald Riesling (HE)
Salishan Chenin Blanc (WW)
**1987**
Covey Run Aligoté (HE)
Eyrie Muscat Ottonel (WW)
**1986**
Texas Vineyards Johannisberg Riesling (HE)
**1985**
Llano Estacado Dry Chenin Blanc (HE)
Texas Vineyards Ivanhoe Blanc (HE)

──────── **£6.00 to £7.99** ────────
**1989**
Stewart Chardonnay (WW)
**1988**
Columbia Chardonnay (PEN)
Eyrie Pinot Gris (WW)
Snoqualmie Semillon (ASK, YF)
**1987**
Salishan Chardonnay (WW)
Salishan Chenin Blanc (YF)

──────── **£8.00 to £10.99** ────────
**1988**
Llano Estacado Chardonnay (HE)
**1987**
Elk Cove Estate Chardonnay Estate (HE)
Rose Creek Chardonnay (ASK)

──────── **£11.00 to £14.99** ────────
**1988**
Eyrie Vineyard Chardonnay (WW)
**1987**
Cameron Chardonnay (BIB)
Covey Run Riesling Ice Wine 1/2 bottle (HE)

> *In each price band wines
> are listed in vintage order.
> Within each vintage they
> are listed in A-Z order.*

# AUSTRALIA

## RED

**Non-vintage**
Sainsbury's Shiraz/Cabernet Sauvignon (SAI)
**1991**
Penfolds Dalwood Shiraz/Cabernet Sauvignon (WCL)
**1990**
Berri Cabernet Sauvignon/Shiraz (ASD, WAI)
Hardy Collection Cabernet Sauvignon/Shiraz (PEN)
Orlando Jacob's Creek Red (GA, THR, NA, AUS, WCL, DAV)
★ Penfolds Cabernet Sauvignon/Shiraz Bin 389 (OD)
Tollana Cabernet Sauvignon/Shiraz (THR, WHI)
**1989**
Penfolds Dalwood Shiraz/Cabernet Sauvignon (SOM, HOG, ROB)
Seaview Cabernet Sauvignon (GA)
**1988**
Orlando Jacob's Creek Red (HOG)
★ Rosemount Cabernet Sauvignon (BO)
**1987**
Orlando Jacob's Creek Red (AUG)

**1990**
Brown Bros Milawa Cabernet Sauvignon (DAV)
Leasingham Cabernet Sauvignon/Malbec Bin 56 (MAJ)
Penfolds Koonunga Hill Cabernet Sauvignon/Shiraz (DAV, WHI, THR)
Penfolds Shiraz/Mataro Bin 2 (SOM)
Rosemount Diamond Reserve Cabernet Sauvignon/Shiraz (LO, NI)
Rosemount Diamond Reserve Dry Red (WHI)
**1989**
Krondorf Shiraz/Cabernet Sauvignon (AUS)
Mildara Cabernet Sauvignon/Merlot (VIC)
Orlando Cabernet Sauvignon (SAI, WCL, GRE)
Penfolds Dalwood Shiraz (BYR)
★ Penfolds Koonunga Hill Cabernet Sauvignon/Shiraz (SOM, HOG, AUS, OD, BYR, SAF, MAJ, WHI, WAI, VIC, THR, DAV)

Rosemount Diamond Reserve Cabernet Sauvignon/Shiraz (CHA)
Rosemount Diamond Reserve Dry Red (CV)
Tyrrells Long Flat Red (PIP)
**1988**
Basedow Shiraz (BIB)
Brown Bros Shiraz (GRG)
Nottage Hill Cabernet Sauvignon Limited Reserve (PEN)
Orlando Cabernet Sauvignon (HOG, OD)
Penfolds Dalwood Shiraz (BYR)
Penfolds Kalimna Shiraz Bin 28 (BYR, AUS)
Seaview Cabernet Sauvignon (CH, BYR)
Wyndham's Shiraz Bin 555 (MAJ)
★ Yalumba Oxford Landing Cabernet Sauvignon/Shiraz (AUS)
Yalumba Shiraz (SOM)
**1987**
Berri Cabernet Sauvignon (GA)
Berri Cabernet Sauvignon/Shiraz (HAG)
Lindeman Shiraz Bin 50 (GRG)
Orlando RF Cabernet Sauvignon (SAF, AUS)
Penfolds Coonawarra Shiraz Bin 128 (SOM)
**1986**
Lindeman Cabernet Sauvignon Bin 45 (AUG)
Penfolds Dalwood Shiraz/Cabernet Sauvignon (CH)
Saltram Mamre Brook Cabernet Sauvignon (KA)
**1985**
★ Penfolds Kalimna Shiraz Bin 28 (OD)
★ Rouge Homme Shiraz/Cabernet Sauvignon (BYR)

**1990**
David Wynn Cabernet Sauvignon (WCL, HAU, NA, AD)
David Wynn Pinot Noir (WCL, HAU, NA)
Tisdall Cabernet Sauvignon/Merlot (NA)
★ Wynns Shiraz (WCL)
**1989**
Brown Bros Shiraz (CH, PIP, THR)
Hardy Bird Series Cabernet Sauvignon (VIN)
Penfolds Coonawarra Shiraz Bin 128 (IR, GRG)
Penfolds Koonunga Hill Cabernet Sauvignon/Shiraz (IR, BAR, WCL, UN)
Rosemount Cabernet Sauvignon (SAF, GRE, THR, NI)

Rosemount Hunter Valley Shiraz (WHI, WCL)

Rosemount Pinot Noir (OD, GRE, WHI, NI)

Thomas Mitchell Cabernet Sauvignon/Shiraz (WRI)

Wyndham's Shiraz Bin 555 (DAV, DAV)

Wynns Ovens Valley Shiraz (BYR)

**1988**

Basedow Cabernet Sauvignon (BIB)

Brown Bros Cabernet Sauvignon (BY, BYR)

Brown Bros Shiraz (BYR, WHI, PEN, TES, BE, AUS, MAJ)

Brown Bros Shiraz/Cabernet Sauvignon (WHI)

Krondorf Shiraz/Cabernet Sauvignon (BYR)

Leasingham Cabernet Sauvignon/Shiraz Bin 68 (ROB)

Lindeman Cabernet Sauvignon Bin 45 (WHI)

Lindeman Shiraz Bin 50 (WHI)

Orlando RF Cabernet Sauvignon (WHI, BYR)

Penfolds Coonawarra Shiraz Bin 128 (HOG, WHI, CH, IR, ROB)

Penfolds Kalimna Shiraz Bin 28 (HOG, IR)

Peter Lehmann Shiraz (BYR)

Peter Lehmann Shiraz/Cabernet Sauvignon (BYR)

Rosemount Coonawarra Shiraz (BYR)

Rosemount Giants Creek Pinot Noir (BYR)

Rosemount Pinot Noir (GRE, CHA)

Rosemount Shiraz (CV, CHA, AUS)

Rouge Homme Shiraz/Cabernet Sauvignon (WHI, GRG, AUS, WRI)

★ Taltarni Shiraz (SOM)

Wolf Blass Cabernet Sauvignon (GRE)

★ Wolf Blass Yellow Label Cabernet Sauvignon (BYR)

Wyndham's Cabernet Sauvignon Bin 444 (BYR, WHI)

Wyndham's Pinot Noir Bin 333 (BYR)

Wynns Coonawarra Cabernet Sauvignon (THR)

Yalumba Cabernet Sauvignon/Shiraz (YF)

**1987**

Brown Bros Cabernet Sauvignon (WHI)

Lake's Folly Cabernet Sauvignon (LAY)

Peter Lehmann Shiraz (AUS)

Rothbury Shiraz (SOM)

**1986**

Hill-Smith Cabernet Sauvignon (LO, BYR)

Hill-Smith Shiraz (BYR)

Rouge Homme Shiraz/Cabernet Sauvignon (GRE, BR, WHI, AV, WRI, ROB)

**1984**

★ Idyll Cabernet Sauvignon/Shiraz (HOG)

─────── **£6.00 to £7.99** ───────

**1991**

★ Coldstream Hills Pinot Noir (CV)

Schinus Molle Pinot Noir (AD)

Taltarni Cabernet Sauvignon (BO)

**1990**

Coldstream Hills Cabernet Sauvignon (CV)

Hollicks Coonawarra Cabernet Sauvignon/Merlot (AUS)

Hunter Estate Cabernet Sauvignon (NA)

Mitchell Peppertree Shiraz (LAY)

Rosemount Cabernet Sauvignon (VIC, UN)

Rosemount Show Reserve Cabernet Sauvignon (THR)

Schinus Molle Cabernet Sauvignon (HAU, AD)

**1989**

Balgownie Shiraz (RAE)

★ Cape Mentelle Shiraz (CV)

Chateau Tahbilk Shiraz (BYR)

Jamiesons Run Coonawarra Red (WHI, DAV, AUS)

Mildara Cabernet Sauvignon (BE, TES, AUS)

Orlando RF Cabernet Sauvignon (TAN)

Pikes Polish Hill Cabernet Sauvignon (HAU)

Rothbury Shiraz (WCL)

Tim Adams Shiraz (BO, BAR)

Wolf Blass Cabernet Sauvignon (WHI)

**1988**

Bowen Shiraz (BO)

Brown Bros Cabernet Sauvignon (PEN, PIP, GRG, AD, AUS, WRI, PE)

Brown Bros Koombahla Cabernet Sauvignon (BE, TES, BYR, GRE, HAG, PIP, AUS)

Brown Bros Meadow Creek Cabernet Sauvignon/Shiraz (PIP)

Brown Bros Shiraz (WRI, PE)

Campbells Shiraz (PIP, VIG)

Chateau Tahbilk Cabernet Sauvignon (BYR, HAG, WCL)

★ Hungerford Hill Coonawarra Cabernet Sauvignon (CB)

Knappstein Cabernet Sauvignon (OD)

Penfolds Cabernet Sauvignon/Shiraz Bin 389 (OD, MAJ, GRG, IR, AUS, WCL)

Rosemount Diamond Reserve Cabernet Sauvignon/Shiraz (BYR)

Rosemount Hunter Valley Shiraz (BUT)

★ Rosemount Show Reserve Cabernet Sauvignon (GRE)

Rothbury Estate Syrah (BYR)

Taltarni Merlot (BYR, AN)

Taltarni Shiraz (WHI, BO, BR, AN, REI, SAF)

**1987**
Brown Bros Koombahla Cabernet Sauvignon (WHI)
Brown Bros Meadow Creek Cabernet Sauvignon/Shiraz (BY, GRE)
Chateau Tahbilk Cabernet Sauvignon (GRE)
Hunter Estate Cabernet Sauvignon (YF, PEN)
Knappstein Cabernet Sauvignon/Merlot (GRG)
Lindeman Shiraz Bin 50 (BUT)
Orlando St Hugo Red (AUS)
Penfolds Cabernet Sauvignon/Shiraz Bin 389 (HOG, WHI, IR, CH, DAV, SOM)
Penfolds Shiraz/Mataro Bin 2 (YF)
Taltarni Shiraz (OD)
Tisdall Cabernet Sauvignon/Merlot (GRG)
Wolf Blass Cabernet Sauvignon (AUS)
**1986**
Brown Bros Koombahla Shiraz (WHI)
Orlando St Hugo Cabernet Sauvignon (HOG, CV, SAI)
Penfolds Cabernet Sauvignon/Shiraz Bin 389 (THR)
Penfolds Eden Valley Cabernet Sauvignon (OD, SOM)
Petersons Cabernet Sauvignon (BEK)
Rosemount Show Reserve Cabernet Sauvignon (AUS)
Taltarni Cabernet Sauvignon (BYR, WHI)
Taltarni Merlot (WHI, TAN, REI)
Wynns Cabernet Sauvignon (BYR, AUS)
**1985**
Penfolds Cabernet Sauvignon Bin 222 (HOG, SAF)
Saltram Mamre Brook Cabernet Sauvignon (BYR)
**1982**
Taltarni Shiraz (CV)

─────── **£8.00 to £9.99** ───────
**1990**
Cape Mentelle Shiraz (AD)
Dromana Estate Cabernet/Merlot (NA)
Dromana Estate Pinot Noir (NA, BEK, HAU)
Moss Wood Cabernet Sauvignon (CV)
★ Mountadam Pinot Noir (OD)
St Hallets Old Block Shiraz (AUS)
**1989**
Dromana Estate Cabernet/Merlot (HAU)
Moss Wood Cabernet Sauvignon (BYR)
Mount Edelstone Shiraz (AUS, WCL)
Penley Estate Coonawarra Cabernet Sauvignon/Shiraz (AUS, AUS)

**1988**
Cape Mentelle Cabernet Sauvignon (BYR, CV)
Cape Mentelle Shiraz (RAE, BUT, VIG)
Eileen Hardy Shiraz (OD)
Geoff Merrill Cabernet Sauvignon (AUS)
Lindeman St George Cabernet Sauvignon (AUS)
Orlando St Hugo Cabernet Sauvignon (WCL)
★ Petaluma Coonawarra Cabernet Sauvignon (OD)
Pike Cabernet Sauvignon (ROB)
Plantagenet Shiraz (KA)
Rockford Basket Press Shiraz (WCL, AUS)
Rouge Homme Cabernet Sauvignon (BYR)
**1987**
Balgownie Pinot Noir (RAE)
Lake's Folly Cabernet Sauvignon (LAY)
Lindeman Limestone Ridge Shiraz/Cabernet Sauvignon (GRG)
Petersons Shiraz (BYR)
Rosemount Show Reserve Cabernet Sauvignon (CHA)
**1986**
Balgownie Cabernet Sauvignon (RAE)
Jim Barry Cabernet Sauvignon (TAN)
Knappstein Cabernet Sauvignon (GRG)
Lindeman Pyrus (GRG)
Saltram Mamre Brook Cabernet Sauvignon (AUS)
Stonyfell Metala Shiraz/Cabernet Sauvignon (AUS)
Wolf Blass President's Selection Cabernet Sauvignon (BYR, GRE, WHI, AUS)
**1985**
Penfolds Eden Valley Cabernet Sauvignon (DAV)
Wynns Cabernet Sauvignon (TAN)
**1984**
Redgate Cabernet Sauvignon (RAE)
**1981**
Adams & Wray Shiraz (BIB)
**1980**
Idyll Cabernet Sauvignon/Shiraz (HOG)
Wynns Coonawarra Cabernet Sauvignon (VIC)

─────── **£10.00 to £11.99** ───────
**1990**
Moss Wood Pinot Noir (AD)
Mountadam Pinot Noir (HAU, HIC, NA, WCL)
**1989**
Cape Mentelle Cabernet Sauvignon (TAN, NA, BAR)

**1988**

★ Cyril Henschke Cabernet Sauvignon
(WCL, AUS, LAY)
Dalwhinnie Cabernet Sauvignon (BO)
Moss Wood Cabernet Sauvignon (RAE, HAG)
Mountadam Cabernet Sauvignon (HAU)
Rosemount Giants Creek Pinot Noir (BYR)
Rosemount Kirri Billi Cabernet Sauvignon
(BYR)
Rosemount Kirri Billi Merlot (BYR)

**1987**

Geoff Merrill Cabernet Sauvignon (BYR)
★ Lake's Folly Cabernet Sauvignon (AUS)
Petaluma Cabernet Sauvignon/Merlot
(BYR, ROB)
Petaluma Coonawarra Cabernet
Sauvignon (WCL)
Tyrrells Pinot Noir (AV)
Wolf Blass President's Selection Cabernet
Sauvignon (VIC)

**1986**

Penfolds St-Henri Cabernet
Sauvignon/Shiraz (AUS, IR, BYR)

**1985**

Rouge Homme Cabernet Sauvignon (WHI,
AV, WRI, ROB)

**1978**

Brown Bros Family Reserve Cabernet
Sauvignon (BY, WHI)

——————— £12.00 to £13.99 ———————

**1989**

Yarra Yering Dry Red No.1 (Cabernet) (MV)

**1988**

Dromana Estate Cabernet/Merlot (BUT)
Penfolds Magill Shiraz (THR)

**1987**

Penfolds Magill Shiraz (SAF)

**1986**

Chateau Xanadu Cabernet Sauvignon (BR)
Yarra Yering Dry Red No.1 (Cabernet) (BER)

**1980**

Brown Bros Family Reserve Cabernet
Sauvignon (PIP)

——————— £14.00 to £15.99 ———————

**1989**

Penfolds Cabernet Sauvignon Bin 707
(THR)
Yarra Yering Cabernet Sauvignon (BO)

**1988**

Lindeman Limestone Ridge
Shiraz/Cabernet Sauvignon (BYR)

**1987**

Lindeman St George Cabernet Sauvignon
(BYR)
Penfolds Cabernet Sauvignon Bin 707 (OD)
Vasse Felix Cabernet Sauvignon (BO)

**1986**

Lindeman Pyrus (AUS)
Penfolds Magill Shiraz (WHI, AD, IR)

**1985**

Lindeman Pyrus (WHI)
Penfolds Magill Shiraz (HOG)
Wolf Blass Black Label Cabernet
Sauvignon (GRE)

**1981**

Chateau Tahbilk Cabernet Sauvignon (VIG)

——————— £16.00 to £19.99 ———————

**1986**

Penfolds Cabernet Sauvignon Bin 707
(SOM, HOG, WHI, IR, BO)

**1982**

Vasse Felix Cabernet Sauvignon (VIG)

**1976**

Rouge Homme Shiraz/Cabernet Sauvignon
(BR, AV)

——————— £20.00 to £29.99 ———————

**1989**

Yarra Yering Pinot Noir (BO)

**1987**

Yarra Yering Pinot Noir (BO)

**1986**

Penfolds Grange Shiraz Bin 95 (THR, AUS,
WCL, ROB)

**1984**

Lindeman St George Cabernet Sauvignon
(VIG)

**1983**

Penfolds Grange Shiraz Bin 95 (GRG, SOM,
OD, BU)

**1982**

Penfolds Grange Shiraz Bin 95 (HOG)

**1980**

Penfolds Grange Shiraz Bin 95 (BO)

**1978**

Lindeman St George Cabernet Sauvignon
(VIG)

——————— £30.00 to £39.99 ———————
**1983**
Penfolds Grange Shiraz Bin 95 (IR, FA, VIG,
   BER)
**1981**
Penfolds Grange Shiraz Bin 95 (IR, BER)
**1976**
Wynns Cabernet Sauvignon (BUT)

——————— c. £51.00 ———————
**1978**
Wynns Cabernet Sauvignon (BUT)

——————— c. £84.00 ———————
**1978**
Penfolds Grange Shiraz Bin 95 (BUT)

## WHITE

——————— Under £4.00 ———————
**1991**
★ Hill-Smith Old Triangle Riesling (BYR,
   WAI, GRE, ASD)
Orlando Jacob's Creek
   Semillon/Chardonnay (HOG, NA, AUS, DAV,
   WCL)
Orlando Jacob's Creek White (GA, BO, LO,
   DAV)

——————— £4.00 to £4.99 ———————
**1991**
Hardy Bird Series
   Gewurztraminer/Riesling (SAF, AUG)
Leasingham Chardonnay (MAJ)
Lindeman Chardonnay Bin 65 (THR, GRG)
Orlando RF Chardonnay (OD, NA, WCL)
Penfolds Koonunga Hill
   Semillon/Chardonnay (HOG, OD, WCL, THR,
   DAV)
Penfolds Semillon/Chardonnay (WHI, GRG)
Rosemount Diamond Reserve
   Semillon/Sauvignon Blanc (CV)
Rosemount Semillon/Chardonnay (NA)
Seaview Chardonnay (CH)
Tyrrells Long Flat White (AD, AUS)
Wynns Rhine Riesling (VIC)
★ Yalumba Oxford Landing Chardonnay
   (HUN)

┌─────────────────────────────┐
│   *Stars (★) indicate wines* │
│   *selected by the editors as* │
│   *particularly good value* │
│   *in their class.* │
└─────────────────────────────┘

**1990**
Basedow Semillon (BIB, AUS, WCL)
David Wynn Riesling (HAU)
Houghton Supreme Chenin
   Blanc/Muscadelle (WAI, PEN)
Lindeman Chardonnay Bin 65 (OD)
Nottage Hill Chardonnay (PEN)
Orlando Jacob's Creek White (BYR)
★ Orlando RF Chardonnay (HOG)
Penfolds Chardonnay (WCL)
Peter Lehmann Semillon (AUS)
Rosemount Diamond Reserve
   Semillon/Sauvignon Blanc (CV, WHI, LO,
   BO, NI)
Rosemount Sauvignon Blanc (BYR)
Rosemount Semillon/Chardonnay (WCL,
   BYR)
Seaview Chardonnay (BU, BYR)
**1989**
★ Lindeman Chardonnay Bin 65 (AUG)
Orlando RF Chardonnay (CV, SAF, GA, AUS)
Wyndham's Chardonnay Bin 222 (MAJ)
Wynns Rhine Riesling (BYR)
**1988**
Penfolds Gewurztraminer/Riesling Bin 202
   (CH)
Rouge Homme Estate Dry White (GRG)
**1987**
Rosemount Diamond Reserve Dry White
   (TES)

——————— £5.00 to £5.99 ———————
**1991**
Allandale Sutherland Chardonnay (AUS)
Lindeman Semillon/Chardonnay Bin 77
   (GRG)
Mildara Chardonnay (VIC)
Rosemount Chardonnay (CV, OD, LO, NI)
Rosemount Fumé Blanc (THR)
★ Rothbury Chardonnay (MAJ)
Rothbury Homestead Semillon (CV, WCL)
**1990**
Basedow Chardonnay (BIB)
Brown Bros Dry Muscat (AD)
David Wynn Chardonnay (WCL, HAU, NA,
   AD)
Krondorf Semillon (AUS)
Leasingham Semillon (ASD)
Pewsey Vale Riesling (ROB, WCL)
★ Rosemount Chardonnay (CV, BYR, SAF,
   WHI, DAV, AUS)
★ Tim Adams Semillon (BO)
Tisdall Chardonnay (PIP, NA)
Wolf Blass Chardonnay (GRE)
Yalumba Chardonnay (YF)

**1989**
Basedow Semillon (BO)
Brown Bros Dry Muscat (BYR, BY, PEN, WHI, PIP, HAG, GRE, THR, BO, GRG, MAJ, ROB, TAN)
Hardy Bird Series Gewurztraminer/Riesling (BER)
★ Mitchelton Wood-Matured Marsanne (WAI, MAJ)
Penfolds Semillon/Chardonnay (THR)
Peter Lehmann Semillon (BYR)
Rosemount Fumé Blanc (BYR, VIC, AUS, GRE, WHI, NI, CHA)
Rosemount Semillon (DAV)
Rosemount Wood-Matured Semillon (WHI, WCL)
Wyndham Estate Oak-aged Chardonnay (MAJ, WHI)
**1988**
Houghton Gold Reserve Chardonnay (WAI)
Houghton Gold Reserve Verdelho (WAI, CV, PEN)
Hunter Valley Semillon (NA)
Lehmann Semillon/Chardonnay (AUS)
Lindeman Semillon/Chardonnay Bin 77 (WHI)
Orlando RF Chardonnay (AUG)
Rosemount Chardonnay (TES)
Rosemount Semillon/Chardonnay (CHA)
**1987**
Hill-Smith Semillon (LO, HAG)
**1985**
Brown Bros Semillon (ASK)

——————— £6.00 to £7.99 ———————
**1991**
Cape Mentelle Semillon/Sauvignon Blanc (WCL)
Jamiesons Run Chardonnay (VIC, AUS)
Mildara Chardonnay (TAN)
Penfolds Chardonnay (OD, THR, WHI, IR)
Rosemount Show Reserve Chardonnay (THR)
Rothbury Brokenback Chardonnay (LAY)
Schinus Molle Sauvignon (HAU, AD, ROB)
★ Shaw & Smith Sauvignon Blanc (WCL)
Wynns Chardonnay (VIC)
**1990**
Bridgewater Mill Chardonnay (NA, AUS)
Brown Bros Sauvignon Blanc (BYR, THR)
★ Coldstream Hills Chardonnay (WHI, CV)
Hardy Collection Chardonnay (SAF)
Henschke Semillon (LAY, WCL, AUS)
Hill-Smith Chardonnay (LO)
Hunter Estate Wood-matured Chardonnay (ASD)

Jamiesons Run Chardonnay (BE, TES, VIC)
Knappstein Chardonnay (OD)
Montrose Show Reserve Chardonnay (PIP)
Moss Wood Semillon (BYR)
★ Petaluma Rhine Riesling (AUS)
Pikes Polish Hill River Sauvignon Blanc (HAU)
Rosemount Chardonnay (IR, VIC, WRI, BUT, AN, UN, YF)
Rosemount Fumé Blanc (BO)
Rosemount Show Reserve Chardonnay (BYR, WAI, WCL, SAF)
Schinus Molle Chardonnay (WCL, HAU, AD, BAR)
Schinus Molle Sauvignon (HIC)
Wolf Blass Chardonnay (WHI, LO, VIC, AUS)
**1989**
Brown Bros Chardonnay (PIP, PE)
Brown Bros Finest Reserve Victorian Muscat (TAN)
Brown Bros Sauvignon Blanc (BYR, PIP, WHI, AUS)
Brown Bros Semillon (AD, GRE)
Cape Mentelle Semillon/Sauvignon Blanc (BYR, CV, WW)
Krondorf Chardonnay (VIC, AUS)
Lindeman Semillon/Chardonnay Bin 77 (UN)
Mitchelton Wood-Matured Marsanne (WRI)
Pewsey Vale Riesling (YF, BER)
Rockford Semillon (AUS)
Rosemount Show Reserve Chardonnay (HUN, OD, WHI, GRE)
Rosemount Show Reserve Semillon (BYR)
Rothbury Chardonnay (BER)
Rouge Homme Chardonnay (BYR)
Schinus Molle Sauvignon (BUT)
Wirra Wirra Chardonnay (BYR)
Wolf Blass Chardonnay (SAF, BY, PIP, WRI)
Wyndham's Chardonnay Bin 222 (TAN)
**1988**
Brown Bros Semillon (PIP, GRG, THR)
Hill-Smith Chardonnay (BYR)
Hunter Estate Chardonnay (PEN)
Rosemount Semillon (AUG)
Rosemount Show Reserve Chardonnay (CH)
Rosemount Show Reserve Semillon (BYR, WHI)
Rothbury Reserve Chadonnay (NA)
Tisdall Chardonnay (GRG)
Tolleys Pedare Barossa Chardonnay Select Harvest (ASK)
Yalumba Chardonnay (BU)
**1987**
Brown Bros Semillon (BY, WHI, AUS, PE, ROB)

**1986**
Lindeman Padthaway Chardonnay (TES)
Orlando St Hilary Chardonnay (HOG, WCL)
Petersons Semillon (BEK)
Rosemount Show Reserve Semillon (BUT)
**1984**
McWilliams Chardonnay (AUS)
Redgate Riesling (RAE)

─────── £8.00 to £9.99 ───────
**1991**
Cape Mentelle Semillon/Sauvignon Blanc
  (HAG, NA, DAV, BAR, BUT)
Moss Wood Semillon (ROB)
Shaw & Smith Sauvignon Blanc (MV, AD,
  GRG, ROB, BAR)
**1990**
Balgownie Chardonnay (VIG)
Bridgewater Mill Chardonnay (VIG)
Cape Mentelle Chardonnay (BYR, CV)
Cape Mentelle Semillon/Sauvignon Blanc
  (TAN, AD, HA)
★ Dromana Estate Chardonnay (OD, WCL,
  NA, HAU, BEK)
Moss Wood Wooded Semillon (RAE, DAV, MV)
Mountadam Chardonnay (OD)
Petaluma Chardonnay (OD)
Shaw & Smith Chardonnay (LAY, GRG, WCL,
  BAR, AUS)
Wirra Wirra Sauvignon Blanc (AUS)
**1989**
Eileen Hardy Reserve Chardonnay (CV)
Hunter Valley Semillon (TAN)
Jamiesons Run Chardonnay (BER)
Moss Wood Semillon (RAE, HAG)
Wynns Chardonnay (BYR)

**1988**
Hunter Estate Wood-matured Chardonnay
  (VIN)
Knappstein Chardonnay (GRG, BYR)
Len Evans Chardonnay (AN)
Montrose Show Reserve Chardonnay (BYR)
Petaluma Rhine Riesling (GRG)
Rockford Semillon (WCL)
Rouge Homme Chardonnay (AUS)
Wynns Chardonnay (BO)

**1985**
Jeffrey Grosset Chardonnay (BO)
Quelltaler Estate Wood-Aged Semillon
  (BER)

─────── £10.00 to £12.99 ───────
**1991**
Moss Wood Chardonnay (AD, BAR, DAV)
**1990**
Cape Mentelle Chardonnay (ROB, HA, BUT)
Lindeman Padthaway Chardonnay (BYR)
Moss Wood Chardonnay (BYR, DAV, RAE)
Mountadam Chardonnay (BAR, HAU, AD, NA,
  WCL, AUS)
Pipers Brook Chardonnay (BYR, WW, PEN,
  AD, ROB, AUS)
Tyrrells Vat 47 Chardonnay (AV)
**1989**
Best's Chardonnay (VIG)
Cape Mentelle Chardonnay (BO, YF, AD, WW,
  MV, BUT)
Lakes Folly Chardonnay (LAY)
Petaluma Chardonnay (BYR, NI, WCL, VIG)
Pikes Polish Hill River Sauvignon Blanc
  (BUT)
Tyrrells Vat 47 Chardonnay (AUS)
**1988**
Eileen Hardy Reserve Chardonnay (SAF)
Petaluma Chardonnay (BYR, GRE, ROB, AUS,
  AMI)
Yarra Burn Chardonnay (TAN)
**1987**
Geoff Merrill Chardonnay (BYR)
Lindeman Padthaway Chardonnay (BUT)
Petaluma Chardonnay (GRG)
Rosemount Giants Creek Chardonnay
  (WHI, CHA, THR)
**1986**
Hunter Valley Semillon (BUT)
Rosemount Whites Creek Semillon (WHI,
  CHA)
Tyrrells Vat 47 Chardonnay (BYR)

─────── £13.00 to £15.99 ───────
**1989**
Cape Mentelle Chardonnay (CB)
Pipers Brook Chardonnay (AV)
Tarra Warra Chardonnay (VIG)
**1988**
Rosemount Roxburgh Chardonnay (BYR,
  GRE, WHI, WCL, CHA)
**1987**
Tarra Warra Chardonnay (BYR)
**1984**
Rosemount Chardonnay (BUT)

——— £16.00 to £17.99 ———

**1986**
Chateau Xanadu Chardonnay (BR)
**1985**
Rothbury Chardonnay (BUT)

## SPARKLING

——— Under £6.00 ———

**Non-vintage**
★ Angas Brut (SOM, WAI, MAJ, AUS, BAR)
Angas Brut Rosé (WAI, AUS, MAJ, BO, BAR)
Seaview (GRG, WAI, WHI, BYR, AUS, AUG, BO, LO)
**1988**
Schinus Molle Chardonnay/Pinot Noir (OD)

——— £6.00 to £7.99 ———

**Non-vintage**
Taltarni Brut (AD, AUS)
Taltarni Brut Taché (AUS)
**1989**
Taltarni Brut (WHI)
Taltarni Brut Taché (WHI)
Yellowglen Brut (PEN)
**1987**
Seaview (GRG)

——— £8.00 to £9.99 ———

**Non-vintage**
Schinus Molle Chardonnay/Pinot Noir (HAU)
**1987**
Yalumba D (AD)

——— £10.00 to £11.99 ———

**Non-vintage**
★ Croser (OD)
Yalumba D (OD)
**1988**
Croser (ROB, NA)

——— £13.00 to £15.99 ———

**Non-vintage**
Croser (AUS)
**1989**
Mountadam Chardonnay/Pinot Noir (HAU)

## SWEET & FORTIFIED

——— Under £7.99 ———

**Non-vintage**
Chateau Reynella 10-year-old Tawny (WAI)
Yalumba Museum Release Rutherglen Muscat (AUS)

**1991**
Brown Bros Orange Muscat & Flora ¹/₂ bottle (GRG, BY, WHI, BYR, PIP, AD)
**1990**
Brown Bros Muscat Late Picked (PIP)
Brown Bros Orange Muscat & Flora ¹/₂ bottle (WHI, RAE, WRI, PE, TAN, HAL)
Petaluma Botrytis Affected Riesling ¹/₂ bottle (BYR)
**1989**
Brown Bros Muscat Late Picked (PEN, WHI, GRE, WRI, BO, MAJ, PE)
Brown Bros Orange Muscat & Flora (AUS)
Brown Bros Orange Muscat & Flora ¹/₂ bottle (GRE, THR, BE, TES)
**1988**
Brown Bros Orange Muscat & Flora ¹/₂ bottle (PEN, CH)
**1982**
Brown Bros Noble Late Harvest Riesling (RAE)
Brown Bros Noble Late Harvest Riesling ¹/₂ bottle (WHI, BY, GRE, PEN, WRI, AUS)

——— £8.00 to £9.99 ———

**Non-vintage**
Bleasedale 6-year-old Verdello (BAR)
Campbells Rutherglen Liqueur Muscat (CH)
Chambers Rosewood Liqueur Muscat (RAE)
★ Morris Liqueur Muscat (CV, GRE, WCL)
Stanton & Killeen Liqueur Muscat (AUS, RAE)
**1990**
Mountadam Noble Riesling ¹/₂ bottle (HAU)
**1988**
Petaluma Botrytis Affected Riesling ¹/₂ bottle (AD)

——— £10.00 to £12.99 ———

**Non-vintage**
Baileys Founder Liqueur Muscat (AUS)
Brown Bros Liqueur Muscat (BY, GRG)
Chambers Old Liqueur Muscat (VIG)

——— £14.00 to £16.99 ———

**Non-vintage**
Bleasedale 16-year-old Verdello (BAR)
Campbells Rutherglen Liqueur Muscat (VIG)
Chambers Special Liqueur Muscat (BO)

——— c. £37.00 ———

**Non-vintage**
Chambers Old Liqueur Muscat (BO)

# NEW ZEALAND

## RED

### Under £5.00

**1990**
Montana Marlborough Cabernet
Sauvignon (ASD, VIC)
**1989**
Cooks Cabernet Sauvignon (WHI, DAV, KA)
Montana Marlborough Cabernet
Sauvignon (BYR, PIP, VIC, GRE)
**1988**
Montana Marlborough Cabernet
Sauvignon (BYR, THR)

### £5.00 to £6.99

**1990**
★ Martinborough Pinot Noir (LAY)
Nobilo Pinotage (BYR)
Villa Maria Cabernet Sauvignon (VIC)
**1989**
Babich Pinot Noir (HOG, WHI)
Stoneleigh Cabernet Sauvignon (WHI, KA)
Villa Maria Cabernet Sauvignon (VIC)
**1988**
Cooks Hawke's Bay Cabernet Sauvignon
(BYR)
Mission Cabernet Sauvignon/Merlot (KA)
Nobilo Pinot Noir (BYR)
Stoneleigh Cabernet Sauvignon (WHI, TES,
HAH)
Villa Maria Cabernet Sauvignon (GRE)
**1987**
Nobilo Pinotage (HOG, GRE, WHI, WRI, GRG,
AV)
Stoneleigh Cabernet Sauvignon (GRE, BYR)
**1986**
Nobilo Pinotage (WRI)
Stoneleigh Cabernet Sauvignon (PEN)

### £7.00 to £8.99

**1990**
Pask Cabernet Sauvignon (LAY)
Redwood Valley Estate Cabernet
Sauvignon (FIZ, GRE)
**1989**
Matua Valley Cabernet Sauvignon (LOE, NI,
FIZ)
Redwood Valley Estate Cabernet
Sauvignon (CH, KA)
**1988**
Brookfield's Cabernet Sauvignon (KA)
Nobilo Cabernet Sauvignon (BYR)

**1987**
Kumeu River Merlot/Cabernet Sauvignon
(BO)
Matua Valley Cabernet Sauvignon (BO)
★ St-Nesbit Cabernet Sauvignon (LAY)
**1986**
Nobilo Cabernet Sauvignon (BYR)

### £9.00 to £10.99

**1991**
Martinborough Pinot Noir (HAU)
**1990**
Cloudy Bay Cabernet Sauvignon/Merlot
(WRI, RAE, WCL, LAY, VIG)
Coleraine Cabernet Sauvignon/Malbec
(DAV)
Ngatarawa Cabernet/Merlot (FIZ)
**1989**
Delegats Proprietor's Reserve Chardonnay
(BYR)
Hunter Pinot Noir (KA)
**1988**
Cloudy Bay Cabernet Sauvignon/Merlot
(CV, BUT)
Hunter Pinot Noir (YF)
St-Helena Pinot Noir (THR)
**1987**
Cloudy Bay Cabernet Sauvignon/Merlot
(CV)
**1986**
Coopers Creek Cabernet Sauvignon/Merlot
(BYR)

### £11.00 to £12.99

**1988**
Martinborough Pinot Noir (BUT)
**1986**
Matua Valley Cabernet Sauvignon (YF)

### £13.00 to £14.99

**1990**
Stonyridge Larose Cabernet (FIZ)
**1989**
Te Mata Çoleraine Cabernet
Sauvignon/Merlot (BYR)
**1988**
Te Mata Coleraine Cabernet
Sauvignon/Merlot (BYR)

### c. £21.50

**1988**
Stonyridge Larose Cabernet (YF)

## WHITE

───────── **Under £5.00** ─────────

**Non-vintage**
Cooks Riesling/Chenin Blanc (BO)
Nobilo White Cloud (BYR)
**1991**
Cooks Chardonnay (KA)
Cooks Hawke's Bay Sauvignon Blanc (AS)
Cooks Sauvignon Blanc (LO, GRE, WHI, KA)
Delegat's Hawke's Bay Sauvignon Blanc (NA)
Delegat's Sauvignon Blanc (HOG, SAI)
Montana Marlborough Chardonnay (VIC, THR)
★ Montana Marlborough Sauvignon Blanc (VIC, THR)
Villa Maria Sauvignon Blanc (WAI)
**1990**
Cooks Chardonnay (LO, WHI, KA, DAV, WAI)
Cooks Chenin Blanc (WHI, KA, CH, DAV)
Cooks Hawke's Bay Chardonnay (AS)
Cooks Sauvignon Blanc (WHI, THR, DAV)
Cooks Semillon (WHI, KA, DAV)
Delegat's Hawke's Bay Sauvignon Blanc (NA)
Delegat's Sauvignon Blanc (CV)
★ Matua Valley Late Harvest Muscat ½ bottle (NI)
Montana Marlborough Chardonnay (HOG, BYR, OD, SAF, TES, AUG, GRE, ASD)
Montana Marlborough Sauvignon Blanc (HOG, GRE, SAF, OD, AUG, THR)
Nobilo White Cloud (GRG, WHI, PEN, AV)
**1989**
Cooks Chardonnay (TES)
Cooks Chenin Blanc (TES, IR)
Cooks Riesling/Chenin Blanc (KA, AUG)
Cooks Semillon (THR)
Delegat's Sauvignon Blanc (ASD)
Montana Marlborough Chardonnay (TES)

───────── **£5.00 to £5.99** ─────────

**1991**
Babich Sauvignon Blanc (WHI, CV)
Babich Semillon/Chardonnay (WHI, PEN)
★ Collards Chenin Blanc (BIB)
Collards Marlborough Sauvignon Blanc (WCL, BIB)
Coopers Creek Chardonnay (ASK)
Coopers Creek Marlborough Sauvignon Blanc (ASK)
Delegat's Chardonnay (HOG)
Matua Valley Brownlie Sauvignon (NI)
Selaks Sauvignon Blanc (GRG)

**1990**
Aotea Sauvignon Blanc (KA, FIZ, ROB)
Babich Sauvignon Blanc (BYR, HOG)
Babich Semillon/Chardonnay (BYR, WRI)
Cooks Hawke's Bay Sauvignon Blanc (GA)
Delegat's Hawke's Bay Chardonnay (NA)
Matua Valley Brownlie Sauvignon (LOE, OD)
Mills Reef Gewürztraminer (HOG)
Morton Estate Sauvignon Blanc (BEK, BYR)
★ Redwood Valley Late Harvest Rhine Riesling ½ bottle (FIZ)
Stoneleigh Sauvignon Blanc (GRE, WHI)
**1989**
Babich Sauvignon Blanc (BYR)
Cooks Hawke's Bay Chardonnay (BYR)
Delegat's Chardonnay (CV)
Matua Valley Late Harvest Gewürztraminer ½ bottle (FIZ)
Nobilo Gewürztraminer (BYR)
**1988**
Nobilo Gewürztraminer (BYR)
Selaks Semillon (GRG)
**1987**
Mission Semillon/Sauvignon Blanc (KA)
Stoneleigh Rhine Riesling (WHI, PEN)

───────── **£6.00 to £6.99** ─────────

**1991**
Collards Gisborne Chardonnay (WCL, BIB)
Collards Sauvignon Blanc (AD)
Ngatarawa Sauvignon Blanc (HOG, FIZ)
Selaks Kumeu Estate Sauvignon Blanc (AD)
Stoneleigh Sauvignon Blanc (THR)
Vidal Sauvignon Blanc (HOG, FIZ)
**1990**
Babich Chardonnay (CV, WHI, DAV, WRI, HAY)
Delegat's Chardonnay (BYR)
Nobilo Marlborough Sauvignon Blanc (AV)
Nobilo Sauvignon Blanc (CH, LOR)
Redwood Valley Sauvignon Blanc (HOG)
Selaks Sauvignon Blanc (OD, PE)
Stoneleigh Chardonnay (KA)

**1989**
Babich Chardonnay (HOG)
Morton Estate Chardonnay (BEK)
Nobilo Gisborne Chardonnay (BYR)
Nobilo Marlborough Sauvignon Blanc (BYR)
Selaks Chardonnay (RAE, GRG)
Stoneleigh Chardonnay (WHI, GRE, HAH)
Villa Maria Sauvignon Blanc (KA)
**1988**
Nobilo Gisborne Chardonnay (BYR, LOR)
Stoneleigh Chardonnay (PEN)
Stoneleigh Sauvignon Blanc (GA)

─────── £7.00 to £8.99 ───────
**1991**
★ Cloudy Bay Sauvignon Blanc (BYR, CV,
 BO, BUT, LAY, REI, KA)
Esk Valley Sauvignon Blanc (BAR)
Hunters Sauvignon Blanc (IR, PIP, BAR, KA)
Matua Valley Sauvignon Blanc (AD)
**1990**
Collards Hawke's Bay Chardonnay (BIB)
Hunters Chardonnay (BYR)
Hunters Sauvignon Blanc (BYR, LO)
★ Martinborough Vineyards Chardonnay
 (WCL)
Mills Reef Chardonnay (HOG)
Morton Estate Chardonnay (BYR)
Ngatarawa Chardonnay (HOG, FIZ)
Redwood Valley Chardonnay (HOG, FIZ)
Redwood Valley Wood-Aged Sauvignon
 Blanc (FIZ, ROB)
Rongopai Te Kauwhata Chardonnay (PIP)
Selaks Chardonnay (BYR, PE)
Selaks Sauvignon Blanc/Semillon (BYR)
★ Te Mata Castle Hill Sauvignon Blanc
 (BYR, LAY, WS, WRI)
Vidal Chardonnay (HOG, FIZ)
**1989**
Brookfield's Sauvignon Blanc (KA)
Coopers Creek Chardonnay (WHI)
Corbans Fumé Blanc (BOT, KA)
Delegat's Reserve Chardonnay (PIP)
Hunters Gewürztraminer (YF)
Hunters Sauvignon Blanc (BYR)
Mission Chardonnay (FIZ, KA)
Nelson Chardonnay (WR)
Nobilo Dixon Chardonnay (BYR)
Vidal Chardonnay (KA)
★ Villa Maria Chardonnay (KA)
**1988**
Hunters Wood-aged Sauvignon Blanc (CV)
Nobilo Dixon Chardonnay (BYR, GRE)
Redwood Valley Sauvignon Blanc (KA)
Selaks Sauvignon Blanc (IR)

**1987**
Ngatarawa Chardonnay (KA)
Selaks Sauvignon Blanc/Semillon (BO)
Selaks Semillon (AD)
**1986**
Selaks Chardonnay (BO)

─────── £9.00 to £10.99 ───────
**1991**
Hunters Chardonnay (IR)
Mills Reef Chardonnay (FIZ)
**1990**
★ Babich Irongate Chardonnay (WHI)
Cloudy Bay Chardonnay (CV, BO, BUT, AD,
 WRI, WCL)
Hunters Chardonnay (LO, DAV, PIP)
Martinborough Vineyards Chardonnay (OD,
 PIP, ROB, BAR, BUT)
Matua Valley Chardonnay (ASK)
Millton Gisborne Chardonnay (SAF)
**1989**
Giesen Chardonnay (KA)
Nobilo Dixon Chardonnay (AV, PE)
Vidal Hawke's Bay Chardonnay (YF)
**1988**
Delegat's Reserve Chardonnay (BYR)
Redwood Valley Chardonnay (HA)

─────── £11.00 to £13.99 ───────
**1990**
Cloudy Bay Sauvignon Blanc (YF)
Elston Chardonnay (BOT, WR)
Kumeu River Chardonnay (FA, BYR)
Te Mata Elston Chardonnay (BYR, LAY, GRG)
**1989**
Cloudy Bay Chardonnay (YF)
Te Mata Elston Chardonnay (BYR)
Vidal Reserve Chardonnay (FIZ, HOG)
**1988**
Kumeu River Noble Dry Sauvignon (GRG,
 AD)

─────── £14.00 to £17.99 ───────
**1989**
Kumeu River Chardonnay (GRG, UN)

## SPARKLING

─────── Under £8.00 ───────
**Non-vintage**
Lindauer Brut (BYR, WHI, AUG, ROB, BAR)

─────── c. £11.00 ───────
**Non-vintage**
★ Deutz Marlborough Cuvée (AUG)

# UNITED KINGDOM

## WHITE

――――――― **Under £5.00** ―――――――
**1990**
Hambledon (HAC)
Pilton Manor Vintage Selection (WRI)
★ Tenterden (DAV)
**1989**
Biddenden Huxelrebe (HAC)
★ Carr Taylor Reichensteiner (HAC)
Elmham Park Müller-Thurgau (BO)
Lamberhurst Priory Müller-Thurgau (GRE)
Lamberhurst Priory Seyval Blanc (GRE,
  PEN, VIC)
New Hall Huxelrebe (GRG)
Pilton Manor Vintage Selection (WRI, HAC)
Saxon Valley (DAV)
★ Three Choirs Medium Dry (BO)
Wraxall (EL)
**1988**
Headcorn Schönburger (HAC)
Meon Valley Seyval Blanc (HAC)
**1987**
Lamberhurst Priory Reichensteiner (PEN)
Westbury Müller-Thurgau/Seyval (HAC)
**1986**
Lamberhurst Priory Müller-Thurgau (PEN)
Tenterden (DAV)

――――――― **£5.00 to £5.99** ―――――――
**1991**
★ Adgestone (BYR)
**1990**
Carr Taylor Kerner & Huxelrebe (WHI)
Carr Taylor Reichensteiner (WHI)
**1989**
Astley Severn Vale (TAN)
Biddenden Ortega (HAC, GRG)
Carr Taylor Schönburger (WHI)
Croffta (CV)
★ Nutbourne Manor Schönburger (HAC)
Pilton Manor Huxelrebe (WRI)
Wraxall Müller-Thurgau/Seyval Blanc (AV)
**1988**
Conghurst (HAC)
Headcorn Seyval Blanc (HAC)
Lamberhurst Priory Seyval Blanc (WRI)
Nutbourne Manor Huxelrebe (HAC)
Wake Court (HIC)
**1986**
Penshurst Ehrenfelser (HAC)
Pulham Vineyards Magdalen Rivaner (YF)

――――――― **£6.00 to £7.99** ―――――――
**1989**
Breaky Bottom Müller-Thurgau (HAC)
★ Breaky Bottom Seyval Blanc (HAC)
Chiltern Valley, Old Luxter's Reserve (YF,
  IR)
Lamberhurst Schönburger (BER)
Pilton Manor Seyval Blanc (HAC)
Staple St-James Huxelrebe (BER)
Wootton Schönburger (AV)
**1988**
Barkham Manor Medium Dry (CB)
Pilton Manor Huxelrebe (HAC)
**1987**
Adgestone (HAG)
Pilton Manor Müller-Thurgau (HA, AV)
**1983**
Elmham Park Dry (HAC)

――――――― **£8.00 to £9.99** ―――――――
**1990**
Thames Valley Fumé Blanc (BIB)
**1989**
Thames Valley Fumé Blanc (HAC)
**1988**
Lamberhurst Schönburger (PEN)

## RED

――――――― **Under £6.00** ―――――――
**1989**
Biddenden Red (HAC)
**1987**
Meonwara (HAC)
**1986**
Westbury Pinot Noir (HAC)

――――――― **c. £7.50** ―――――――
**1989**
Thames Valley Dry Red (HAC)

## SPARKLING

――――――― **Under £9.00** ―――――――
**Non-vintage**
Meon Valley Sparkling (HAC)
**1989**
★ Rock Lodge Impresario Brut (HAC)

――――――― **c. £10.50** ―――――――
**Non-vintage**
Carr Taylor (HAC)

# BULGARIA

## RED

### ———— Under £3.00 ————

**Non-vintage**

Bulgarian Cabernet Sauvignon (SAI, TES, VIC)

Bulgarian Cabernet Sauvignon/Merlot (ASD, BO, DAV, UN)

Bulgarian Merlot/Gamza (WAI, BO)

★ Burgas Cabernet Sauvignon/Merlot (WIW)

Mehana Red (WIW, PE)

Pavlikeni Cabernet Sauvignon/Merlot (WIW, OD, BYR, VIC, THR, BU, PE)

Petrich Cabernet Sauvignon/Melnik (WIW, MAJ)

Russe Cabernet Sauvignon/Cinsault (WIW, SAI, TES, THR, ROB)

Suhindol Merlot/Gamza (BYR, GRE)

**1989**

Bulgarian Cabernet Sauvignon (WHI)

Bulgarian Merlot (WHI)

Burgas Cabernet Sauvignon/Merlot (WIW)

Haskovo Merlot (WIW)

Russe Cabernet Sauvignon/Cinsault (WIW)

★ Svichtov Cabernet Sauvignon (WIW)

**1988**

Bulgarian Cabernet Sauvignon (CV, MAJ, ASD, WAI)

Bulgarian Merlot (CV, ASD, GRE)

Burgas Cabernet Sauvignon/Merlot (WIW)

Haskovo Merlot (WIW)

Plovdiv Cabernet Sauvignon (WIW)

Russe Cabernet Sauvignon (MAJ)

Russe Cabernet Sauvignon/Cinsault (WIW)

★ Suhindol Cabernet Sauvignon (WIW)

Suhindol Merlot/Gamza (WIW)

**1987**

Damianitza Melnik Reserve (WIW)

★ Oriahovitza Cabernet Sauvignon Reserve (WIW)

Plovdiv Cabernet Sauvignon (WIW)

Stambolovo Merlot Reserve (WIW)

**1986**

Bulgarian Cabernet Sauvignon (CH, OD)

Bulgarian Merlot (OD)

★ Plovdiv Cabernet Sauvignon (CV)

Suhindol Cabernet Sauvignon (WIW, GRG)

**1985**

★ Damianitza Melnik Reserve (WIW)

Haskovo Merlot (BYR)

Stambolovo Merlot Reserve (WIW)

Suhindol Cabernet Sauvignon (BYR, AUG)

Suhindol Cabernet Sauvignon Reserve (WIW)

**1984**

Damianitza Melnik Reserve (WIW)

### ———— £3.00 to £3.99 ————

**Non-vintage**

Bulgarian Cabernet Sauvignon (LAY, PE)

**1988**

Bulgarian Cabernet Sauvignon (DAV)

Bulgarian Merlot (DAV, UN)

Korten, Cabernet Sauvignon (WIW)

Svichtov Cabernet Sauvignon (TAN)

**1987**

Plovdiv Cabernet Sauvignon (THR)

Sakar Merlot (WIW)

Sakar Mountain Cabernet Sauvignon (WHI)

**1986**

Bulgarian Cabernet Sauvignon (BO, UN)

Damianitza Melnik Reserve (THR)

★ Mavrud Asenovgrad (GRE)

Oriahovitza Cabernet Sauvignon (ASD)

Plovdiv Cabernet Sauvignon (BYR, DAV)

★ Sakar Mountain Cabernet Sauvignon (WIW, TES, WHI)

Suhindol Cabernet Sauvignon (LO, GRE, IR, THR)

**1985**

Assenovgrad Mavrud (WIW)

Haskovo Merlot (AUG, TAN)

Mavrud Asenovgrad (WAI)

Oriahovitza Cabernet Sauvignon (MAJ, VIC, GRE, THR, DAV)

Oriahovitza Cabernet Sauvignon/Merlot (CV, WIW)

Oriahovitza Cabernet Sauvignon Reserve (CV, BU, ROB)

Sakar Mountain Cabernet Sauvignon (OD, GRG, GRE, DAV)

Stambolovo Merlot Reserve (CV, LO, GA)
Suhindol Cabernet Sauvignon Reserve
  (SAF, SAI)
Svichtov Cabernet Sauvignon (MAR)
Vinenka Cabernet Sauvignon (WIW)
**1984**
Assenovgrad Mavrud (CV, BYR)
Damianitza Melnik Reserve (TES, BYR, MAJ)
Oriahovitza Cabernet Sauvignon (BYR, DAV)
Sakar Mountain Cabernet Sauvignon (BYR)
Stambolovo Merlot Reserve (GRG, BYR, AUG)
**1983**
Assenovgrad Mavrud (BYR)
Damianitza Melnik Reserve (BYR)
Oriahovitza Cabernet Sauvignon (BYR,
  AUG)
Sakar Mountain Cabernet Sauvignon (BYR)
Stambolovo Merlot Reserve (BYR)

—————— £4.00 to £4.99 ——————
**1986**
Stambolovo Merlot Special Reserve (WIW)
**1985**
Oriahovitza Cabernet Sauvignon (PE)
Svichtov Cabernet Sauvignon (BYR, WHI,
  GRE, THR)
**1984**
Oriahovitza Cabernet Sauvignon (UN, TAN)
Oriahovitza Cabernet Sauvignon/Merlot
  (BYR)
Sakar Merlot (THR)
Suhindol Gamza (BYR)
Svichtov Cabernet Sauvignon (WIW)
**1983**
Mavrud Asenovgrad (PE)
Oriahovitza Cabernet Sauvignon (AV)

—————— £5.00 to £5.99 ——————
**1991**
Bulgarian Reserve Cabernet Sauvignon
  (BO)
**1989**
Bulgarian Cabernet Sauvignon (WHI)
**1986**
Stambolovo Merlot Special Reserve (CV)
**1983**
Svichtov Cabernet Sauvignon (WIW)
**1982**
Svichtov Cabernet Sauvignon (WIW)

## WHITE

—————— Under £3.00 ——————
**Non-vintage**
Bulgarian Chardonnay (CH)

Bulgarian Muscat/Ugni Blanc (ASD, WAI,
  BO, DAV)
Bulgarian Riesling (CV, ASD, WHI, OD)
Bulgarian Riesling/Misket (GA, SAI, BO)
Bulgarian Sauvignon Blanc (CV, WHI, OD,
  GRE)
Burgas Muscat/Ugni Blanc (WIW, MAJ, LO,
  BYR, OD, GRE, AUG, BU, UN)
Mehana White (PE)
★ Preslav Chardonnay (MAR)
Russe Welsch-Rizling/Misket (WIW)
**1990**
Burgas Muscat/Ugni Blanc (VIC)
**1989**
★ Khan Krum Chardonnay (WIW)
**1988**
Khan Krum Chardonnay (WIW)

—————— £3.00 to £3.99 ——————
**Non-vintage**
Balkan Crown Brut (WIW)
Khan Krum Chardonnay (LAY)
**1991**
★ Novi Pazar Chardonnay (WIW)
**1990**
Novi Pazar Chardonnay (WIW)
**1989**
Khan Krum Chardonnay (WHI, ASD)
Novi Pazar Chardonnay (CV, WIW)
**1988**
Khan Krum Chardonnay (WHI, GRE, BO,
  DAV)
Khan Krum Special Reserve Chardonnay
  (CV, LO, MAJ)
**1987**
Khan Krum Chardonnay (BYR)
Khan Krum Special Reserve Chardonnay
  (LO, THR, GRG)
**1986**
Khan Krum Chardonnay (AUG)

—————— £4.00 to £4.99 ——————
**Non-vintage**
Balkan Crown Brut (BU)
Burgas Muscat/Ugni Blanc (CV)
**1989**
Novi Pazar Chardonnay (WHI)
**1988**
Khan Krum Chardonnay (PE, UN, TAN)
Khan Krum Special Reserve Chardonnay
  (ROB)
**1987**
Khan Krum Special Reserve Chardonnay
  (WIW)
Novi Pazar Chardonnay (BYR)

# SOUTH AFRICA

## RED

─────────── **Under £4.00** ───────────
**Non-vintage**
KWV Cabernet Sauvignon (BO)
KWV Shiraz (BO)
**1990**
Drostdy Hof Rouge Select (BYR, NA)
Pinotage Culemborg Paarl (WAI)
**1989**
Drostdy Hof Rouge Select (BYR)
KWV Cabernet Sauvignon (HOG, PEN, CAP,
  GRE)
KWV Paarl Cinsaut (HOG, BYR, CAP)
KWV Pinotage (HOG, PEN, CAP, GRE)
KWV Roodeberg (CAP, VIC)
KWV Shiraz (HOG)
**1988**
KWV Cabernet Sauvignon (WHI)
KWV Paarl Cinsaut (BYR)
KWV Pinotage (WHI)
KWV Roodeberg (HOG, WAI, BYR, WHI, GRE)
KWV Shiraz (PEN)
**1986**
KWV Cabernet Sauvignon (BYR, CH)
KWV Roodeberg (PEN)
KWV Shiraz (BYR)

─────────── **£4.00 to £4.99** ───────────
**1989**
Fairview Pinotage (CAP)
KWV Cabernet Sauvignon (UN, PE)
KWV Shiraz (CAP, UN)
Nederburg Paarl Cabernet Sauvignon (BYR)
Nederburg Pinotage (BYR)
Rustenberg Cabernet Sauvignon/Cinsault
  (BU)
**1988**
Nederburg Paarl Cabernet Sauvignon
  (BYR)
Nederburg Pinotage (BYR)
**1987**
★ Backsberg Pinotage (CAP)
Diemersdal (CAP, BO)
**1986**
Nederburg Edelrood (HOG)
Nederburg Pinotage (HOG)

─────────── **£5.00 to £5.99** ───────────
**1989**
Backsberg Cabernet Sauvignon (HOG)
★ Rustenberg Dry Red (IR, AV)

**1988**
Delheim Pinotage (BU)
Zonnebloem Cabernet Sauvignon (GRE)
**1987**
Allesverloren Tinta Barocca (BYR)
Backsberg Cabernet Sauvignon (KA)
Groot Constantia Pinotage (ASK)
★ Hamilton Russell Pinot Noir (HOG)
Nederburg Baronne (CAP, WHI)
Nederburg Edelrood (CAP)
Nederburg Pinotage (WHI)
Stellenryk Cabernet Sauvignon (WAI)
Zonnebloem Shiraz (GRE)
**1986**
Allesverloren Tinta Barocca (BYR)
Fairview Pinotage (WRI)
Groot Constantia Pinotage (CAP)
Nederburg Baronne (CAP, WHI)
Nederburg Pinotage (CAP, WHI)
Stellenryk Cabernet Sauvignon (WAI)

─────────── **£6.00 to £7.99** ───────────
**1990**
★ Kanonkop Pinotage (DAV)
**1989**
Hamilton Russell Pinot Noir (CV, PIP, BU)
Kanonkop Pinotage (SOM, ASK)
**1988**
Backsberg Cabernet Sauvignon (BUT)
Delheim Pinotage (PIP, YF)
Hamilton Russell Pinot Noir (GRE, CV, CH)
★ Rustenberg Cabernet Sauvignon (GRE)
Rustenberg Dry Red (BAR)
**1987**
Backsberg Shiraz (CAP)
Hamilton Russell Pinot Noir (LOR, WHI)
Meerendal Pinotage (CAP)
Zandvliet Shiraz (BYR)
**1986**
Groot Constantia Heerenrood (CAP)
Zandvliet Shiraz (BYR)
Zonnebloem Cabernet Sauvignon (CAP, WRI)
Zonnebloem Pinotage (CAP)

─────────── **£8.00 to £9.99** ───────────
**1987**
Kanonkop Pinotage (WRI, CAP)
Rustenberg Cabernet Sauvignon (IR, BYR)
**1986**
Blaauwklippen Cabernet Sauvignon (BUT)
Meerlust Cabernet Sauvignon (BYR)
Meerlust Rubicon (BYR, NA, CAP)

## WHITE

──────── Under £4.00 ────────

**1991**
★ KWV Chenin Blanc (BO, HOG, WAI, ASK, GRE, VIC)
KWV Riesling (HOG)
KWV Sauvignon Blanc (HOG, PEN, WAI, VIC)
**1990**
KWV Cape Bouquet (ASK, HOG, BYR, CAP, WHI, KA)
KWV Chenin Blanc (BYR, WHI, CAP, KA)
KWV Riesling (WHI, CAP)
KWV Sauvignon Blanc (BYR, WHI, GRE)
KWV Steen (HOG, BYR, WHI, CAP)
KWV Steen Special Late Harvest (HOG, CAP)
**1989**
KWV Cape Foret (PEN, CAP)
KWV Chenin Blanc (PEN)
KWV Riesling (PEN)
KWV Steen (PEN)
**1988**
KWV Cape Bouquet (CH)
KWV Chenin Blanc (CH)
KWV Riesling (GRE)
KWV Steen (CH)

──────── £4.00 to £5.99 ────────

**Non-vintage**
KWV Muscat de Montal (CAP, PEN)
**1991**
★ Backsberg Sauvignon Blanc (CAP)
Nederburg Stein (IR)
**1990**
Backsberg Sauvignon Blanc (HOG)
Groot Constantia Weisser Riesling (ASK, KA)
Hamilton Russell Chardonnay (HOG)
★ Klein Constantia Sauvignon Blanc (CV)
Nederburg Paarl Riesling (CAP)
Nederburg Stein (IR)
**1989**
Backsberg Sauvignon Blanc (CAP, BUT)
Klein Constantia Sauvignon Blanc (HOG, CV)
Koopmanskloof Blanc de Marbonne (CAP)
KWV Steen Special Late Harvest (HIC)
Nederburg Stein (CAP)
l'Ormarins Sauvignon Blanc (NA)
Uitkyk Carlsheim (CAP)
de Wetshof Rhine Riesling (CAP)
**1988**
KWV Laborie (CAP)
Uitkyk Carlsheim (HOG)

──────── £6.00 to £7.99 ────────

**1991**
★ Hamilton Russell Chardonnay (CV, ROB, BU, CH)
**1989**
le Bonheur Sauvignon Blanc (CAP)
Hamilton Russell Chardonnay (BYR, LOR, WHI)
**1988**
Klein Constantia Sauvignon Blanc (BUT)
KWV Noble Late Harvest (BYR)
l'Ormarins Sauvignon Blanc (IR)

──────── £8.00 to £9.99 ────────

**1989**
de Wetshof Chardonnay (CAP)
**1987**
de Wetshof Chardonnay (HOG)

## ROSÉ

──────── £4.00 to £5.99 ────────

**1990**
KWV Cabernet Sauvignon Blanc de Noir (CAP)
Nederburg Rosé (CAP, WHI)

## SPARKLING

──────── £5.00 to £6.99 ────────

**Non-vintage**
KWV Mousseux Blanc Cuvée Brut (CAP)
Nederburg Premiere Cuvée Brut (BYR, CAP)
**1989**
Laborie Blanc de Noir (PEN)

──────── c. £8.50 ────────

**1988**
JC Le Roux Sauvignon Blanc (CAP)

## FORTIFIED

──────── Under £4.00 ────────

**Non-vintage**
Cavendish Cape Medium Dry (WAI)
Mymering Pale Extra Dry (HOG, HAG, CAP)
Onzerust Medium (HOG, HAG, CAP)
Renasula Pale Dry (HAG, CAP)

──────── £4.00 to £6.99 ────────

**Non-vintage**
Cavendish Cape Extra Dry (CAP)
Cavendish Fine Old Ruby (HOG, CAP)
**1963**
Cavendish Vintage (HOG, CAP)

# OTHER WINE REGIONS

## ARGENTINA

─────── **Under £4.00** ───────
**Non-vintage**
★ Estancia Torrontes (GRG)
**1987**
Andean Malbec (GRG)

─────── **c. £6.50** ───────
**1983**
Mendoza Cabernet Sauvignon (BO)

## AUSTRIA

─────── **£3.50 to £4.99** ───────
**1990**
★ Grüner Veltliner Lenz Moser Selection
(WAI, PEN, ROB)

## CANADA

─────── **Under £6.00** ───────
**1988**
Inniskillin Riesling (PEN)
**1987**
Inniskillin Maréchal Foch Red (BAR, GRE,
PEN, AV)

─────── **£6.00 to £6.99** ───────
**1988**
Inniskillin Chardonnay (PEN, GRE)

─────── **£7.00 to £10.99** ───────
**1987**
Inniskillin Chardonnay Reserve (VIG)
Inniskillin Pinot Noir Reserve (AV)

## CHILE RED

─────── **Under £4.00** ───────
**1989**
Concha y Toro Cabernet Sauvignon (WAI,
NI)
Undurraga Cabernet Sauvignon (BYR, IR)
**1988**
Concha y Toro Cabernet Sauvignon (NI)
Concha y Toro Cabernet Sauvignon/Merlot
(NI)
★ Errázuriz Panquehue Cabernet
Sauvignon (BYR)
★ Montes Cabernet Sauvignon (BYR)
Santa Helena Merlot (GRG)

**1987**
Caliterra Cabernet Sauvignon (SAI)
Concha y Toro Cabernet Sauvignon (WAI,
GRE)
Concha y Toro Merlot (BYR, NI)
Santa Helena Cabernet Sauvignon (GRG)
Santa Helena Cabernet Sauvignon/Malbec
(GRG)
Undurraga Cabernet Sauvignon (PEN)
★ Viña Linderos Cabernet Sauvignon
(ASD)

─────── **£4.00 to £4.99** ───────
**1989**
Caliterra Cabernet Sauvignon (BYR)
Errázuriz Panquehue Cabernet Sauvignon
(VIC)
San Pedro Merlot (ROB)
Santa Helena Merlot (DAV)
★ Santa Rita 120 Cabernet Sauvignon
(WRI)
Undurraga Cabernet Sauvignon (WRI, BU,
AV, AD)
Undurraga Pinot Noir (IR, GRE)
★ Villa Montes Cabernet Sauvignon (LO,
HAU, BAR)
**1988**
Caliterra Cabernet Sauvignon (CV, BYR)
Cousiño Macul Don Luis Red (NI)
★ Los Vascos Cabernet Sauvignon (WHI,
LAY)
Torres Cabernet Sauvignon (CV)
**1987**
Concha y Toro Casillero del Diablo (BYR,
GRE)
Cousiño Macul Cabernet Sauvignon (BYR)
Montes Cabernet Sauvignon (GRG)
Undurraga Cabernet Sauvignon Reserve
Selection (GRE, BYR, IR)
**1985**
★ Santa Helena Seleccion del Directorio
Cabernet Sauvignon (GRG)

─────── **£5.00 to £5.99** ───────
**1988**
★ Marqués de Casa Concha Cabernet
Sauvignon (GRE)
**1987**
Cousiño Macul Antiguas Reservas
Cabernet Sauvignon (GRE)
Santa Helena Seleccion del Directorio
Cabernet Sauvignon (DAV)

─────── £6.00 to £7.99 ───────

**1988**
★ Santa Rita Cabernet Sauvignon
  Medalla Real (BIB)
**1987**
Montes Alpha Cabernet Sauvignon (GRG,
  BYR, DAV, BAR, TES)
Santa Rita Cabernet Sauvignon Reserva
  (ROB)

─────── £8.00 to £9.99 ───────

**1988**
Montes Alpha Cabernet Sauvignon (WRI,
  ROB)
**1987**
Santa Rita Cabernet Sauvignon Medalla
  Real (YF)

## CHILE WHITE

─────── Under £4.00 ───────

**1991**
Caliterra Sauvignon Blanc (BAR)
★ Santa Rita 120 Sauvignon Blanc (BIB,
  WHI)
Undurraga Sauvignon Blanc (PEN, IR)
★ Villa Montes Sauvignon Blanc (DAV)
**1990**
Caliterra Sauvignon Blanc (WHI)
Concha y Toro Chardonnay (NI, BYR, GRE)
Concha y Toro Sauvignon Blanc/Semillon
  (BYR, GRE, NI)
Santa Helena Sauvignon Blanc/Semillon
  (BYR)
**1989**
Santa Helena Fumé Blanc (GRG)

─────── £4.00 to £4.99 ───────

**1992**
★ Undurraga Sauvignon Blanc (AV)
**1991**
★ Torres Sauvignon Blanc (TAN)
Undurraga Chardonnay (BYR, IR)
**1990**
Cousiño Macul Chardonnay (BO, BYR, GRE)
Errázuriz Panquehue Chardonnay (BYR)
Torres Gewürztraminer (CV)
Undurraga Chardonnay (BYR)
**1989**
Concha y Toro Sauvignon Blanc/Semillon
  (TAN)
Torres Bellaterra Sauvignon Blanc (CV)
Villa Montes Sauvignon Blanc (GRE)
**1988**
Santa Rita 120 Sauvignon Blanc (AUG)

─────── £5.00 to £5.99 ───────

**1991**
Montes Chardonnay (HAU, DAV)
Santa Rita Chardonnay Medalla Real (SAI)
**1990**
Domaine Caperana Gewürztraminer (BOD)
Marqués de Casa Concha Chardonnay
  (GRE)
Torres Bellaterra Sauvignon Blanc (PE)
**1989**
Cousiño Macul Chardonnay (HIC)
Torres Gewürztraminer (BYR)
Torres Santa Digna Sauvignon Blanc (BYR)

─────── £6.00 to £7.99 ───────

**1990**
Montes Chardonnay (ROB)
Santa Rita Chardonnay Medalla Real (WHI,
  YF, BAR)
Santa Rita Sauvignon Blanc Reserva (TAN)
**1989**
Santa Helena Sauvignon Blanc/Semillon
  (GRG)

## CYPRUS

─────── Under £4.50 ───────

**Non-vintage**
Aphrodite Keo White (BYR, WHI, UN)
Othello Keo Red (GRG, WHI, UN)

## CZECHOSLOVAKIA

─────── Under £3.00 ───────

**Non-vintage**
Gewürztraminer (THR)
**1990**
Nitra, Irsay Oliver (ASD)

## GREECE RED

─────── Under £4.00 ───────

**Non-vintage**
★ Mavrodaphne Patras, Kourtaki (WAI)
**1987**
Naoussa Boutari (BYR)
Nemea, Boutari (BYR)
Nemea, Kouros (BO)

─────── £4.00 to £5.99 ───────

**1985**
★ Château Carras Côtes de Meliton (CV,
  WS)
**1981**
Château Carras Côtes de Meliton (BO)

## GREECE WHITE

──────── **Under £4.00** ────────
**Non-vintage**
Demestica Achaia Clauss (GRG)
Retsina Kourtaki (WAI, VIC, AUG, BO, OD, THR)
Retsina Metaxas (GRG, DAV, PE)
**1990**
Santorini, Boutari (BYR)
**1988**
Patras, Kouros (WAI, BO)
**1987**
Patras, Kouros (AUG)

──────── **£4.00 to £5.99** ────────
**Non-vintage**
★ Samos Muscat (OD)
Samos Nectar 10-year-old (WCL)
**1990**
Domaine Carras Côtes de Meliton (WCL)
**1987**
Cephalonia Gentilini (BIB)
**1985**
Domaine Carras Côtes de Meliton (THR)

## HUNGARY WHITE

──────── **Under £3.00** ────────
**Non-vintage**
Hungarian Chardonnay (BYR, WHI, OD)
Hungarian Gewürztraminer (BYR, WHI)
Hungarian Sauvignon Blanc (BYR, WHI)
Safeway Nagyrède Chardonnay (SAF)
Safeway Nagyrède Dry Muscat (SAF)
**1990**
Dunavár Pinot Blanc (ASD)
Hungarian Chardonnay (WIW)
Hungarian Gewürztraminer (WIW, BU)
Hungarian Sauvignon Blanc (WIW)
Nagyréde Pinot Blanc (AUG)
Pecs Olasz Rizling (WIW)

──────── **£3.00 to £4.99** ────────
**1991**
Gyöngyös Chardonnay (MAJ)
Gyöngyös Sauvignon Blanc (MAJ)
**1986**
Tokaji Aszú 3 Putts ½ litre (WIW)
Tokaji Szamorodni Sweet ½ litre (WIW)
**1984**
Tokaji Szamorodni Dry ½ litre (WIW, BU)
**1981**
Tokaji Szamorodni Dry ½ litre (CH)
Tokaji Szamorodni Sweet ½ litre (CH)

──────── **£5.00 to £6.99** ────────
**Non-vintage**
Tokaji Aszú 3 Putts ½ litre (LAY, PE)
**1988**
Tokaji Aszú 3 Putts ½ litre (GRE)
**1983**
Tokaji Szamorodni Dry ½ litre Schlumberger (ROB)
**1982**
★ Tokaji Aszú 5 Putts ½ litre (OD)

──────── **£7.00 to £9.99** ────────
**1981**
Tokaji Aszú 3 Putts ½ litre Schlumberger (BO, LAY, ROB)
Tokaji Aszú 4 Putts ½ litre (HAG)
Tokaji Aszú 5 Putts ½ litre Schlumberger (GRE, LAY)

──────── **£45.00 to £70.00** ────────
**1963**
Tokaji Aszú Muskotalyos ½ litre (AD)
**1957**
Tokaji Aszú 6 Putts ½ litre (AD)
Tokaji Aszú Essencia ½ litre (GRE)

## HUNGARY RED

──────── **Under £3.00** ────────
**Non-vintage**
Hungarian Cabernet Sauvignon (WIW, BYR, WHI, OD)
Hungarian Merlot (BYR, WHI, OD)
Hungarian Pinot Noir (BYR, WHI, OD)
Villany Merlot (WIW)
**1991**
Nagyréde Cabernet Sauvignon Rosé (VIC)
Villany Cabernet Sauvignon (SAF, ASD)
Villany Merlot (ASD)
**1989**
Hungarian Merlot (WIW)
Sopron, Cabernet Franc (WIW)

──────── **£3.00 to £4.99** ────────
**Non-vintage**
Eger Bull's Blood (GA, PE)
**1990**
Kiskórös Cabernet Sauvignon (UN)
**1987**
Eger Bull's Blood (BO, ASD)
**1985**
Eger Bull's Blood (AUG)
**1983**
Hungarian Cabernet Sauvignon (WIW)
Villany Cabernet Sauvignon (WIW)

## ISRAEL

——————— £5.00 to £6.99 ———————
**Non-vintage**
Palwin No. 4 (SAF)
**1991**
Yarden Cabernet Sauvignon White
  Harvest (WRI)
**1990**
★ Yarden Chardonnay (SAF)
**1988**
Gamla Galilee Cabernet Sauvignon (WRI)
**1987**
Gamla Galilee Cabernet Sauvignon (WRI,
  ROB)

## LEBANON RED

——————— Under £7.99 ———————
**1986**
Château Musar (THR)
**1985**
★ Château Musar (GA, GRE, CHA, LO, VIC,
  PEN, BO, NI, NA, AD, HAU)
**1983**
Château Musar (GA, BYR, MAJ, NI, GRE, WHI,
  CHA, WRI, IR, LAY, YF, TAN, UN, HAU, ROB)
**1982**
Château Musar (CV, BYR, BUT, HAG, WHI,
  AUG, GRE)
**1981**
Château Musar (GE, CV, CHA, GRE)

——————— £8.00 to £9.99 ———————
**1980**
Château Musar (GE, CHA, HAG)

——————— £10.00 to £14.99 ———————
**1978**
Château Musar (GE, CHA, ROB, AMI, VIG)

## LUXEMBOURG

——————— c. £6.50 ———————
**Non-vintage**
Cuvée de l'Ecusson Brut (EL)

## MOLDOVA

——————— £4.50 to £7.00 ———————
**1987**
Kodru, Krikora Winery (VIG, BAR)
**1986**
Directors' Reserve Cuvée Kamrat
  Koshushny Winery (AN, AD, VIG)

## ROMANIA

——————— Under £3.50 ———————
**Non-vintage**
Feteasca Neagra Cabernet Sauvignon (ASD)
Pinot Noir Dealul Mare (PE)
★ Sainsbury's Romanian Pinot Noir (SAI)
**1990**
Romanian Sauvignon Blanc (GRE)
**1988**
Romanian Merlot (LO, GRE)
**1986**
Classic Pinot Noir (GRE)
Romanian Cabernet Sauvignon (LO)
Romanian Merlot (BYR)
Romanian Pinot Noir (BYR, LO)
Romanian Sauvignon Blanc (BYR)
Tamaioasa, Pietroasele (sweet) (SAF, TES)
**1985**
Romanian Cabernet Sauvignon (BYR)
Romanian Merlot (CH)
Romanian Pinot Noir (CH, BU)

## SWITZERLAND

——————— £8.50 to £10.50 ———————
**1990**
Dôle Romane Orsat Gamay (EL)
**1987**
Domaine de la Bolliattaz, Villette (WHITE)
  (TAN)

## YUGOSLAVIA WHITE

——————— Under £4.00 ———————
**Non-vintage**
Lutomer Laski Rizling (BO, ASD, THR, UN)
Tesco Laski Rizling (TES)

## YUGOSLAVIA RED

——————— Under £4.00 ———————
**1989**
★ Vranac (SAF)
**1988**
Milion Merlot (WAI)
**1987**
Slovin Cabernet Sauvignon (WHI)

## ZIMBABWE

——————— Under £3.50 ———————
**Non-vintage**
Flame Lily Premium Dry White (GRG)
Flame Lily Red (GRG)

# MERCHANT DIRECTORY

Abbreviations used in the Merchant Directory are as follows. **Credit cards** Access (AC), American Express (AE), Diners Club (DC), Visa/Barclaycard (V). The following services are available where indicated: **C** cellarage, **EP** *en primeur* offers, **G** glass hire/loan, **M** mail order, **T** tastings and talks.

## ADNAMS (AD)

The Crown, High Street, Southwold, Suffolk IP18 6DP (0502) 724222
**Hours** Mail order dept Mon–Fri 9–5, The Cellar and Kitchen Store (Southwold collection) Mon–Sat 10–6.30 (Jan only, Mon–Fri 10–5, Sat 10–6.30);
The Wine Shop, South Green, Southwold, Suffolk IP18 6EW (0502) 722138
**Hours** Mon–Sat 10–7.15;
The Grapevine, 109 Unthank Road, Norwich NR2 2PE (0603) 613998
**Hours** Mon–Sat 9–9.
**Credit cards** AC V.
**Discounts** £3 per case if collected (off mail-order price).
**Delivery** £5 1 case, free 2 or more cases mainland UK.
**Minimum order** 1 mixed case.
**C EP G M T**
*Very go-ahead and comprehensive list, giving one of the widest selections in the country, as well as particularly reliable basic wines, all backed up by the highly readable and often controversial comments of wine director Simon Loftus. The list, in fact, is well worth having just for the read. Adnams are increasingly interested in stocking organically-made wines, and in actively encouraging producers to move in an organic direction, minimizing vineyard and cellar treatments. Loftus' love of the unusual doesn't mean that quality is neglected. Sampler cases aid choice – try Rhône, Burgundy or Antipodean and feel confident of a varied but representative selection.*

## LES AMIS DU VIN (AMI)

51 Chiltern Street, London W1M 1HQ, 071-487 3419
**Hours** Mon–Fri 10.30–7, Sat 10.30–5;
The Winery, 4 Clifton Road, London W9 1SS, 071-286 6475
**Hours** Mon–Fri 10.30–8.30, Sat 10–6.30; mail order dept 081-451 0469 (24 hour).
**Credit cards** AC AE DC V.
**Discounts** 5% unsplit cases for non-members, 10% for members (5% per bottle).
**Delivery** Free 2 or more cases worth over £75, otherwise £5 per order.
**Minimum order** 1 mixed case.
**C EP G M T**
*Two London shops, one called The Winery, the other Les Amis du Vin. Long on French wine, especially Champagne, though the New World section is strong thanks to sister wholesale company Geoffrey Roberts Associates, which imports a huge range of top names from California and elsewhere. The list also contains snippets of gossip – did you know that Olivier Leflaive of Burgundy lived in Paris in his youth 'discovering and promoting unknown rock musicians'? Classic names feature in the list: Guigal, Huet, Château de Beaucastel, Opus One.*

The codes given in brackets on these pages beside the merchants' names are those by which the merchants are listed in the price guides (pages 246-397). They are also listed on page 246.

## ANDRÉ SIMON (AN)

20 Midland Road, London NW1 2AD,
071-388 5008, fax 071-383 7419
**Hours** Mon–Fri 9.30–6.30; 14 Davies
Street, London W1Y 1LJ, 071-499
9144, fax 071-495 2002
**Hours** Mon–Fri 9.30–8, Sat 9.30–7;
50 – 52 Elizabeth Street, London
SW1W 9PB, 071-730 8108
**Hours** Mon–Fri 9.30–6.30, Sat 10–2;
21 Motcomb Street, London SW1X
8LB, 071-235 3723.
**Credit cards** AC AE V.
**Discounts** on cases and single bottles.
**Delivery** Free in central London and
on orders over £100 elsewhere UK.
**C EP G T**
*Chairman and buyer Graham Chidgey
sprinkles the wine list with his own
slightly eccentric brand of tasting note:
'Delightful Wines for the Daily
Exercise of the Corkscrew' runs one
heading. Strong on France, with a
good range of New World wines.*

## ASDA (ASD)

Asda House, Southbank, Great Wilson
Street, Leeds LS11 5AD (0532)
435435, fax (0532) 418666
**Hours** Mon–Fri 9–8, Sat 8.30–8, open
most bank hols.
**Credit cards** AC V. **T**
*The Asda range is broadening and
includes a Fine Wine Section as well
as catering for modern preoccupations
– Asda now sell an 'Organic Claret'.*

## ASHLEY SCOTT (AS)

PO Box 28, The Highway, Hawarden,
Deeside, Clwyd CH5 3RY (0244)
520655
**Hours** 24-hr answerphone.
**Discounts** 5% unsplit case.
**Delivery** Free in north Wales,
Cheshire, Lancs, Merseyside.
**Minimum order** 1 mixed case.
**G M T**

*The mainly French list is augmented
by small selection from Italy, Spain,
Germany, Australia and even less
well-beaten tracks such as England,
Chile and Bulgaria. But the list lets
itself down by omitting producer
names and by being virtually
description-free. This is a club, not a
shop, with a 24-hour answering
machine.*

## ASKHAM WINES (ASK)

Newark, Notts NG22 0RP telephone &
fax (077 783) 659
**Hours** Mon–Fri 9–5.30, Sat 9–12.
**Discounts** By arrangement.
**Delivery** Free for orders over £50 UK
mainland.
**Minimum order** 1 mixed case.
**G M T**
*The fairly brief but accessible list is
put together by headmaster-cum-wine
merchant Andrew Brownridge. The
emphasis on good French producers
(Turckheim in Alsace, Billecart-
Salmon in Champagne) is carried
through to other selections, so Spain is
represented by Vega Sicilia, CVNE,
and Rioja Alta, New Zealand by
Delegat's.*

## AUGUSTUS BARNETT (AUG)

3 The Maltings, Wetmore Road,
Burton-on-Trent, Staffs DE14 1SE
(0283) 512550, fax (0283) 67544
**Hours** Variable, most 10–10 daily.
**Credit cards** AC AE V.
**Discounts** For large orders.
**Delivery** By arrangement at some
branches.
**G M T**
*A chain undergoing a revival, wines
from all corners of the world,
including Chile, Portugal, Australia,
New Zealand, USA, Spain, Italy and
regional France. Augustus Barnett has
559 branches distributed throughout
the UK.*

## AUSTRALIAN WINE CENTRE (AUS)

'Down Under', South Australia House, 50 Strand, London WC2N 5LW
071-925 0751, fax 071-839 9021
**Hours** Mon–Fri 10–7, Sat 10–4.
**Credit cards** AC AE V.
**Discounts** 5% 1 case cash, collected.
**Delivery** Free anywhere in UK for orders over £75, otherwise £5 charge.
**G M T**
*Over 500 including older vintages: buy your old Grange here. Also mail order: The Australian Wine Club (free membership). Every May it holds a tasting of over 350 wines.*

## AVERY'S (AV)

7 Park Street, Bristol BS1 5NG
(0272) 214141, fax (0272) 221729
**Hours** Mon–Sat 9–6.
**Credit cards** AC V.
**Discounts** By negotiation.
**Delivery** Free 2 cases or more, otherwise £5.50 per consignment.
**C E P G M T**
*One of the real old-fashioned, long-established merchants, surviving better than many. Specializes in Burgundies (Remoissenet), clarets, Madeira and port, but classic though that may sound, Avery's were one of the first to do much exploring of New World regions. The line-up now has Undurraga of Chile and Inniskillin of Canada. The mail-order side is strong.*

## BARNES WINE SHOP (BAR)

51 High Street, Barnes, London SW13 9LN, 081-878 8643
**Hours** Mon–Sat 9.30–8.30, Sun 12–2.
**Credit cards** AC V.
**Discounts** 5% mixed case, larger discounts negotiable.
**Delivery** Free in London.
**Minimum order** 1 mixed case or magnum (for delivery).
**C EP G M T**

*Very reliable operation with wines chosen by ex-Cullen's wine wizard James Rogers. It is strong in Australia, New Zealand, fine wines and bin ends.*

## BEDFORD FINE WINES (BE)

Faulkner's Farm, The Marsh, Carlton, Bedford MK43 7JU, (0234) 721153, fax (0234) 721145
**Hours** Office hours or by arrangement.
**Discounts** On preferred wines.
**Delivery** Free in Bedford, Luton and St Albans areas, £80 minimum order.
**Minimum order** 1 mixed case.
**EP G M T**
*The strengths of the list are in claret, including older vintages going back to 1970. Alongside some good choices (Turckheim from Alsace), there are some less exciting ones from France's less classic areas. Spain is Torres and a few Riojas, but there are delicious dessert wines from Andrew Quady in the US and Nobilo from New Zealand.*

## BERKMANN WINE CELLARS (BEK)

12 Brewery Road, London N7 9NH, 071-609 4711
**Hours** Mon–Fri 9–5.30, Sat 10–2. Closed: Bank holiday weekends.
**Credit cards** AC V.
**Discounts** £2 per case collected; £1 per mixed case collected.
**Delivery** Free in London and 20 miles around East Grinstead; elsewhere £4.50 1 case, £3.50 2 cases, free 3 cases.
**Minimum order** 1 mixed case.
**C EP G M T**
*Berkmann is the wholesale side, Le Nez Rouge the retail side. All the names are well chosen: Champagne is Bruno Paillard, Muscadet is Sauvion, Alsace is Muré and of course Beaujolais is Duboeuf. Small but select choices from elsewhere, including CVNE and Rioja Alta from Spain, Morton Estate from New Zealand.*

## BERRY BROS & RUDD (BER)

3 St James's Street, London SW1A
1EG, 071-396 9666, fax 071-396 9600
**Hours** Mon–Fri 9.30–5; The Wine
Shop, Hamilton Close, Houndmills,
Basingstoke, Hants RG21 2YB (0256)
23566
**Hours** Mon–Fri 9–5, Sat 9–1.
**Credit cards** AC DC V.
**Discounts** 3–7.5% according to
quantity.
**Delivery** Free 1 case or more.
**C E P G M T**
*At the same address in St James's for
over two and half centuries. The shop
is worth a visit, though not to browse:
it's so traditional there are no wines on
show. Claret, Burgundy and Vintage
port are the strong points, though
Burgundy is mostly négociants, with a
good selection of Rhine, Mosel – their
list reminds one that German wine
used to be more expensive than white
Burgundy – and New World.*

## BIBENDUM (BIB)

113 Regents Park Road, London NW1
8UR, 071-722 5577
**Hours** Mon–Sat 10–8.
**Credit cards** AC AE V.
**Delivery** Free London, northern
England; rest £5.45 up to 5 cases.
**Minimum order** 1 mixed case.
**C E P G M T**
*A strong Fine Wine list supplements
the main list and there are always
offers and tastings. The Rhône,
Oregon, Portugal, Australia and Italy
are all full of excitement.*

## BOOTHS FINE WINES (BO)

4–6 Fishergate, Preston, Lancs PR1
3LJ (0772) 51701
**Hours** Mon–Fri 9–5.
**Credit cards** AC V.  **G T**
*20 shops in the north-west. Strong on
France but a good showing in the New
World.*

## BORDEAUX DIRECT (BOD)

New Aquitaine House, Paddock Road, Reading, Berks RG4 0JY (0734) 481718, fax (0734) 461493; **Hours** Mon–Fri 10.30–7 (Thu till 8), Sat 9–6; 24-hr answerphone; mail order Mon–Fri 9–8, Sat & Sun 10–5. **Credit cards** AC AE DC V. **Discounts** Special offers. **Delivery** Free for orders over £50. **G EP M T**

*The original 'direct from the vineyard' company. Mostly mail order, but there are six shops in the Thames Valley, offering a particularly good range of French country wines, also well-priced drinking from Chile, Eastern Europe and Spain. Sister company to the Sunday Times Wine Club.*

## BORG CASTEL (BOR)

Samlesbury Mill, Goosefoot Lane, Samlesbury Bottoms, Preston, Lancs PR5 0RN (025 485) 2128 **Hours** Mon–Fri 10–5, Thu 7–9.30pm, first Sun of month 12–4. **Discounts** 6 or more cases. **Delivery** Free 1 case or more within 30 mile radius. **C G M T**

*On this fairly priced list most is from France and Germany. A good range from the Rhône and the Loire, and Alsace is represented by the reliable co-op at Turckheim.*

## BOTTOMS UP (BOT)

Sefton House, 42 Church Road, Welwyn Garden City, Herts AL8 6PJ (0707) 328244, fax (0707) 371398. **Credit cards** AC V. **Discounts** 5% mixed case. **G T**

*Now owned by Thresher, Bottoms Up shops are intended to be the largest outlets of the chain, with the most comprehensive range.*

## BROAD STREET WINE CO (BR)

Emscote Mill, Wharf Street, Warwick CV34 5LB (0926) 493951, fax (0926) 495345 **Hours** Mon–Fri 9–6, Sat 9–1. **Credit cards** AC V. **Delivery** Free 6 or more cases. **Minimum order** 1 mixed case. **C G M T**

*Largest collection in the UK of vintage cognacs. Older vintages of Burgundy, Claret and Loire. Some of the choices are refreshingly individual – there are wines from Cloudy Bay and Rongopai from New Zealand. Also good Rhônes.*

## BUTE WINES (BUT)

Mount Stuart, Rothesay, Isle of Bute PA20 9LR (0700) 502730, fax (0700) 505313; 2 Cottesmore Gardens, London W8 5PR 071-937 1629 **Delivery:** £7 1 case, £9 2 cases, £10 3 cases, £11 4 cases, free 5 cases. **Minumum order:** 1 mixed case, or £250 for delivery outside Central London, Glasgow, Edinburgh, Bute. **EP M T**

*No shop at either address, but stock is held in Bute and London. Much emphasis on classic names, including that of its owner, the Marchioness of Bute. Half a dozen top Alsace producers are represented in depth, but Italy concentrates on just a few famous wines from Piedmont and Tuscany. There's a decent sprinkling of New World, and Bordeaux is strongest of all. Quirky wines include a rosé Meursault from Roulot and the Massandra wines from the Crimea in years from 1891.*

## BUTLERS WINE CELLAR (BU)

247 Queens Park Road, Brighton BN2 2XJ (0273) 698724, fax (0273) 622761 **Hours** Tues, Wed 9-5.30,Thurs-Sat 9-7.

**Credit cards** AC, V.
**Delivery** free locally for a case or more; free anywhere in mainland England and Wales, some parts of Scotland, for 3 cases or more. Otherwise £4.50 for 1 bottle, £6.75 for 2-12 bottles; £8.50 for 13-24 bottles; £10 for 25 to 35 bottles.
**G M**
*Bin-ends are the mainstay of this shop – and what bin ends. Lots are very old indeed – Geoffrey Butler makes a speciality of anniversary years – but not all are terrifically expensive. A 1947 Meursault Charmes, Vandermeulen, at £22.50 would have made a wonderful 45th birthday present for somebody. There's a rapid turnover, of course, and a new list comes out every six weeks. There's also the sort of wine for drinking, not giving: the list starts idiosyncratically with R for Romania and Russia and finishes with B for Belgian Beers. In between there's a quirky, always good and often excellent range from just about everywhere, with plenty under a tenner.*

## ANTHONY BYRNE (BY)

88 High Street, Ramsey, Huntingdon, Cambs PE17 1BS (0487) 814555, fax (0487) 814962
**Hours** Mon–Sat 9–5.30.
**Credit cards** AC V.
**Discounts** 5% mixed case, 10% unsplit case.
**Delivery** £6 less than 5 cases, free 5 or more cases.
**C EP M T**
*Beaujolais is Cellier de Samson, and there is a wide choice of Burgundy growers. Elsewhere choices are carefully made – Italy is represented by Maculan, Anselmi and Masi, the Rhône by Guigal, Australia by the delectable Delatite. An excellent list, with some real treasures – Château Gilette in Sauternes, for example.*

## D. BYRNE (BYR)

Victoria Buildings, 12 King Street, Clitheroe, Lancashire BB7 2EP (0200) 23152
**Hours:** Mon-Sat 8.30-6, Thu-Fri, -8.
**Discounts:** £1 off a mixed case, £1.20 off an unmixed case, 5% on orders over £300.
**Delivery:** free locally.
**C EP G T**
*It's hard to think of anything that this shop doesn't have. You want demi-sec Veuve Clicquot in halves? You want a choice of six Amarone? You want Trousseau from the Jura? It's all here, plus hundreds of others. Excellent on all parts of France including the South; Germany, Australia, South America, New Zealand, South Africa, good on Spain (though no sherry) and Italy. Good prices too.*

## CAPE PROVINCE WINES (CAP)

1 The Broadway, Kingston Road, Staines, Middx TW18 1AT (0784) 451860/455244, fax (0784) 469267
**Hours** Mon–Sat 9–9, Sun 12–1.
**Credit cards** AC V.
**Delivery** Locally and London £4.75; UK mainland varies with quantity.
**Minimum order** 6 bottles.
**G M T**
*Specialists in South Africa, whose list may broaden as the political situation loosens up.*

## CELTIC VINTNER (CV)

73 Derwen Fawr Road, Sketty, Swansea SA2 8DR (0792) 206661, fax (0792) 296671
**Hours** Mon–Fri 8–5.30, other by arrangement.
**Discounts** Negotiable.
**Delivery** Free South Wales, elsewhere at cost.
**Minimum order** 1 mixed case.
**C EP G T**

*An informative and stimulating list. Balance is the key; with Spain for instance you don't just get Torres (which would be no hardship), you get CVNE and Réné Barbier as well. Burgundy looks interesting, and there are quite a few half bottles.*

## CHAPLIN & SON (CH)

35 Rowlands Road, Worthing, Sussex BN11 3JJ (0903) 235888, fax (0903) 823062
**Hours** Mon–Sat 8.45–5.30 (Fri till 6).
**Credit cards** AC V.
**Discounts** 5% mixed case.
**Delivery** Free within 7 mile radius, 1 mixed case or more.
**C G M T**
*A bit of everything in this list – claret, Burgundy, Australia, Italy and so on. Not everything is thrilling – the Rhône and Loire for example – but more adventurously there are wines from New Zealand and Washington State.*

## CHÂTEAUX WINES (CHA)

11 Church Street, Bishop's Lydeard, Taunton, Somerset TA4 3AT telephone & fax (0454) 613959. Mail/phone orders only.
**Hours** Mon–Fri 9–5.30, Sat 9–12.30.
**Credit cards** AC V.
**Discounts** Negotiable.
**Delivery** Free 1 case or more UK mainland.
**Minimum order** 1 case (usually mixed).
**C E P M T**
*Concentrates on Lebanese Château Musar including older vintages, Australian, Californian and Laurent Perrier fizz, Domaine Ampeau Burgundies, and excellent single domaine cru Beaujolais. It's a short list of decent producers rather than hugely varied, but there are oddities like red Coteaux Champenois, from Laurent Perrier, of course. Châteaux Wines have no shop; everything is mail order.*

## CORNEY & BARROW (CB)

12 Helmet Row, London EC1V 3QJ,
071-251 4051; 194 Kensington Park
Road, London W11, 071-221 5122; 118
Moorgate, London EC2, 071-638 3125;
31 Rutland Square, Edinburgh EH1
2BW, 031-228 2233; Belvoir House,
High Street, Newmarket CB8 8OH
(0638) 662068
**Hours** Mon–Fri 9–5.30; 24-hr
answerphone.
**Credit cards** AC V.
**Delivery** Free London 2 cases or
more, elsewhere 3 cases or more.
**C EP G MT**
*Importer of Château Pétrus, which
gives you some clue to the rest of the
list – excellent, and pricy. All the
Moueix wines are here, plus a range of
petits châteaux. There's also a
glittering cast of Burgundy producers
and Australia is represented by
Penfolds Grange, Italy by the
Supertuscan Sassicaia.*

## DAVISONS (DAV)

7 Aberdeen Road, Croydon, Surrey
CR0 1EQ, 081-681 3222, fax 081-760
0390
**Hours** Mon–Sat 10–2, 5–10.
**Credit cards** AC V.
**Discounts** 8.5% mixed case.
**Delivery** Free locally.
**EP G T**
*Strong on claret, petits châteaux,
Burgundy and vintage ports bought en
primeur. The strengths have always
been in the classic areas, but these are
now joined by wines from Australia,
Chile, Spain and Portugal. Often very
good prices.*

## ELDRIDGE, POPE (EL)

Weymouth Avenue, Dorchester,
Dorset DT1 1QT (0305) 251251; mail
order (0800) 378757
**Hours** Mon–Sat 9–5.30.

**Credit cards** AC V.
**Discounts** On application.
**Delivery** £5 for less than 2 cases (24
bottles), free 2 cases or more.
**C G M T**
*Informative, all-embracing, high
quality list with many rarities – port,
for instance, back to 1927– but also
spreading outside the classic European
areas to good effect. There are now
nine shops plus four J.B. Reynier Wine
Libraries which turn into wine bars at
midday – a great way to taste before
you buy, and very good value indeed.
A mix of the traditional – the house
fizz is called 'The Chairman's
Elegantly Dry Champagne' – with the
modern; one shop is a 'drive-in'!*

## FARR VINTNERS (FA)

19 Sussex Street, London SW1V 4RR
071-828 1960, fax 071-828 3500
**Credit cards** AC, V.
**Discounts** On orders of 10 cases or
more.
**Delivery** £8 London; £3.50 per case,
minimum £10.50 Home Counties;
£3.75 per case, minimum £11.25 per
case rest of England and Wales;
£5.60 per case, minimum £16.80
Scotland, or give 48 hours notice of
collection.
**Minimum order** £200 plus VAT.
*Farr Vintners are fine wine brokers;
they have no shop and their wines are
held at Trapps Cellars, 68-74 Tooley
Street, London SE1. This is not the
place to come for a bottle of Aussie
Chardonnay for supper. It is, however,
the place for a splendid selection of
seriously fine wines from classic areas
plus some less classic – New Zealand,
Tokaji, the Crimea. Vintages go back
to the turn of the century. They pride
themselves on the provenance and
condition of all the wines they sell, but
as Stephen Browett says in his Ideal
Cellar on page 17, they are far from
intimidating.*

## FINE WINES OF NEW ZEALAND (FIZ)

PO Box 476, London NW5 2NZ, 071-482 0093, fax 071-267 8400
**Hours** Mon–Sat 9–5.
**Discounts** 2 cases or more.
**Delivery** £9 mixed case except for special offers.
**Minimum order** 1 mixed case.
**M T**
*Small, quality-minded outfit with wines from every wine-producing area in New Zealand. One of the best ambassadors for New Zealand around; pioneered many successful names here. New this year are a Méthode Champenoise fizz from Vidal (other Vidal wines are already on the list) plus names like Ata Rangi and Rippon. Look out too for the delicious Matua Valley Pinot Noir Blanc, and their Late Harvest Gewürztraminer, in half bottles.*

## GATEWAY (GA)

Gateway House, Hawkfield Business Park, Whitchurch Lane, Bristol BS14 0TJ (0272) 359359
**Hours** Mon-Sat 9-6, late opening Friday all stores, some have longer hours.
**Delivery** from Keynsham and Bath stores only, £1 on orders of £20 to £50, free over £50.
**Credit cards** AC, V, T.
*675 stores throughout the UK, about 40 of which have the full list. A further 60-70 have the full list excluding the finer Wine Rack range. The smallest stores have only a very basic range – Aviemore, for example, doubles as the local post office. The Wine Rack range includes Chablis from the local (very good) co-op, Château Bastor Lamontagne Sauternes, a von Kesselstatt Mosel and some good Aussies. On the rest of the list, look for petit château clarets and things like Chateau Musar and Gyöngyös Estate.*

## GELSTON CASTLE (GE)

Castle Douglas, Scotland DC7 1QE (0556) 3012, fax (0556) 4183
**Hours** Mon-Fri 9.00-7.00.
**Delivery** 1 case or more free within 25 miles of Castle Douglas; £4 per case, minimum £8 per delivery rest of mainland UK; free on orders over £150.
**Minimum order** None, but mixed cases carry surcharge of £4 per case, unless they comprise two unmixed half dozens.
**C M T**
*A traditional, knowledgeable, occasionally didactic list from which it would be all too tempting to spend a great deal of money. Not because the wines are overpriced but because it contains so many of the best things in life: lots of brilliant German wines, everyday and fine clarets, plus Rhônes and Burgundies. There's not a huge amount from the New World and very little from Italy, Spain and Portugal, though the fortifieds are better. There's a small but nicely varied list of half bottles.*

## PETER GREEN (GRE)

37A-B Warrender Park Road, Edinburgh EH9 1HJ, 031-229 5925
**Hours** Mon–Fri 9.30–6.30, Sat 9.30–7.
**Discounts** 5% most unsplit cases.
**Delivery** £6 1 case; £4 each additional case.
**G M T**
*Imaginative list of wines from all round the world, with some particularly good buys in France. Increasingly interesting ranges from Portugal and Italy. New this year are a couple of good red Loires, and some more Madeiras, plus more from Australia and New Zealand. Good selection of half bottles. Hold an annual tasting, usually in October.*

## GROG BLOSSOM (GRG)

**Head Office:** 48 King St, Royston, Herts SG8 9BA (0763) 247201, fax (0763) 244601
**Shops:** 66 Notting Hill Gate, London W11 3HT, 071-792 3834; 253 West End Lane, London NW6 1XN, 071-794 7808; 160 High Road, East Finchley, London N2 9AS, 081-883 3588
**Hours** variable; open until 10pm daily.
**Credit cards** AC V.
**Discounts** 5% mixed case.
**G T**
*This is a small chain of London shops – good selections especially from Italy (the good Viticoltori dell'Acquese wines) and Australia (Lindemans, Penfolds, etc.). They also boast a range of 'over 250 beers'.*

## HALVES (HAL)

Wood Yard, off Corve Street, Ludlow, Shropshire SY8 2PX (0584) 877866, fax (0584) 877677.
**Discounts** £2.35 per delivery of 2 cases or more to a single address; 4% on all unmixed cases.
**Delivery** free to mainland UK.
**Minimum order** 1 case of 24 half bottles.
**M**
*You can guess this merchant's speciality by its name: Halves sells only those, and since its launch in 1990 has set about breaking the vicious circle by which we couldn't buy half bottles because nobody much sold them, and nobody much sold them because we didn't buy them. Well, now's our chance. Tim Jackson stocks over 200 different wines in half bottles (see his ideal cellar on page 25) and has just about everything from Alsace to New Zealand, via various unpredictable stops in Cahors and Sicily. He's particularly strong on dessert wines from all over the world; ports, too, for those who want a glass but not a hangover. Prices are proportionately slightly higher than for bottles.*

## HARCOURT FINE WINE (HAC)

3 Harcourt Street, Marylebone, London W1H 1DS, 071-723 7202, answerphone 071-724 5009, fax 071-723 8085
**Hours** Mon–Fri 9.30–6.30, Sat 10–5.
**Credit cards** AC AE V.
**Discounts** 5% mixed case, additional for larger quantities.
**Delivery** Per bottle or per case, free 3 or more cases in London.
**G M T**
*Once known as the English Wine Shop and still stockists of a wide range of English wine. Other specialities are Calvados and Armagnac, plus Germany, reflecting the preoccupations of the buyers. Good range of English wine from 1989.*

## GERARD HARRIS (HAG)

2 Green End Street, Aston Clinton, Aylesbury, Bucks HP22 5HP (0296) 631041, fax (0296) 631250
**Hours** Tue–Sat 9.30–8.
**Credit cards** AC AE V.
**Discounts** 10% mixed case.
**Delivery** Free locally 1 case or more.
**Minimum order** 1 mixed case for delivery, no minimum in shop.
**E P G M T**
*Strong points are Bordeaux and Germany; other countries and regions are well covered.*

## ROGER HARRIS (HAW)

Loke Farm, Weston Longville, Norfolk NR9 5LG (0603) 880171/2, fax (0603) 880291
**Hours** Mon–Fri 9–5.
**Credit cards** AC AE DC V.
**Discounts** 2 cases £1 per case, 5 cases or more £1.50 per case.
**Delivery** Free UK mainland.
**Minimum order** 1 mixed case.
**M T**
*What the Sunday colour supplements would call 'the Specialists' Specialist' – Beaujolais utterly dominates the list and the working life of Roger Harris. Only Champagne, some Mâconnais and a little Coteaux du Lyonnais get a look-in besides. A high-quality list.*

## JOHN HARVEY (HA)

31 Denmark Street, Bristol BS1 5DQ (0272) 268882, fax (0272) 253380
**Hours** Mon–Fri 9.30–6, Sat 9.30–1;
16 The Hard, Portsmouth PO1 3DT telephone & fax (0705) 825567
**Hours** Mon–Fri by arrangement.
**Credit cards** AC AE DC V.
**Discounts** £2 per case for 2–5 cases, £3 for 6–10 cases, £3.50 over 11 cases.
**Delivery** Free 1 case or more UK mainland, £5 less than 1 case.
**C EP M T**

*Sherry (Harvey's), port (Cockburn's), and claret (close association with Château Latour) are the strengths. Regular en primeur offers for claret and Burgundy. Germany and New World wines provide some variation on the classic British sideboard tray.*

## RICHARD HARVEY (HAY)

Bucknowle House, Bucknowle, Wareham, Dorset BH20 5PQ (0929) 480352, fax (0929) 481275
**Hours** By arrangement.
**Discounts** 5% 6 cases or more.
**Delivery** Free within 30 miles for 3 or more cases.
**Minimum order** 1 case.
**C EP G M T**
*It's an appointment-only set-up, but worth it for the wine – every producer listed is a top quality producer – Barbadillo for sherry, Babich for New Zealand, Rivetti for Moscato and Volpaia for Chianti Classico. Prices look good, too.*

## HAUGHTON FINE WINES (HAU)

Chorley Green Lane, Chorley, Nantwich, Cheshire CW5 8JR (0270 74) 537/(0836 597) 961, fax (0270 74) 233
**Hours** Mon–Fri 9–5.30, Sat 10.30–12.30; 24-hr answerphone.
**Credit cards** AC V.
**Discounts** For quantity orders.
**Delivery** Free on UK mainland. Single case supplement £3.
**Minimum order** 1 mixed case.
**G M T**
*Strong on Australian wines, French wines, with a selection of 'tasting cases' for newcomers. In 1992 Northern Wine Merchant of the Year and Wine List of the Year. The varied, informative list is worth getting for the wonderfully refreshing, chatty opinions of the owners. They import a great deal themselves, and have an eye for winners.*

## HAYNES HANSON & CLARK (HAH)

17 Lettice Street, London SW6 4EH,
071-736 7878
**Hours** Mon–Thu 9–7, Fri 9–6;
36 Kensington Church Street, London
W8 4BX, 071-937 4650
**Hours** Mon–Sat 9.30–7.
**Discounts** 10% unsplit case.
**Delivery** Free central London,
elsewhere 5 cases or more.
**Minimum order** Warehouse only 1
case.
**EP G M T**
*A considerable range of first-class
quality wine, with Burgundy the
consuming speciality. Equally
carefully chosen Californians and also
some good Australians.*

## DOUGLAS HENN-MACRAE (HE)

81 Mackenders Lane, Eccles,
Aylesford, Kent ME20 7JA
(0622) 710952
**Hours** Mail order and phone
enquiries only (Mon–Sat to 10pm).
**Credit cards** AC V.
**Discounts** Subject to quantity.
**Delivery** Free 5 cases UK mainland;
otherwise £6 plus VAT per order.
**Minimum order** 1 case.
**M T**
*Instead of roaming around the world,
concentrates on just two areas –
Germany and the US. Some fine-
quality drinking – excellent Rieslings
and increasingly good Texans.*

---

*All the companies listed in the Merchant
Directory have wines featured in the Price
Guides (pages 246–397).
Abbreviations used in the Directory are as
follows: **Credit Cards** Access (AC),
American Express (AE), Diners Club (DC),
Visa/Barclaycard (V).
The following services are available where
indicated: **C** cellarage, **EP** en primeur
offers, **G** glass hire/loan, **M** mail order,
**T** tastings and talks.*

---

## HICKS & DON (HIC)

Blandford St Mary, Dorset DT11 9LS
(0258) 456040, fax (0258) 450147;
Head office: Park House, Elmham,
Dereham, Norfolk NR20 5JY
(0362) 668571/281
**Hours** Mon–Fri 8.30–5.
**Credit cards** AC V.
**Discounts** Negotiable.
**Delivery** 1–2 cases £3 per
consignment, 3 cases & over free UK
mainland.
**Minimum order** 1 mixed case.
**C EP G M T**
*Strong on opening offers of claret,
Burgundy, cru Beaujolais, port and
the Rhône. New this year are quite a
lot of Australians and some good
Germans. Sherries are as strong as
ever – all are from that excellent
Sanlúcar house, Barbadillo. It's a
well-chosen list, and prices are often
good. They also have their own
English wine, Elmham Park.*

## HIGH BRECK VINTNERS (HIG)

Bentworth House, Bentworth, Nr
Alton, Hants GU34 5RB (0420) 62218,
fax (0420) 63827
**Hours** Mon–Fri 9.30–5.30. Other
times by arrangement.
**Credit cards** AC V.
**Delivery** £6 for 1–3 cases, free larger
quantities.
**Minimum order** 1 mixed case.
**EP G M T**
*Pretty catholic selection from
interesting French producers,
particularly Alsace, Bordeaux and the
Loire – nice Germans from Deinhard,
Italian from Antinori and a reasonable
sprinkling of wines specially selected
from other areas, including Australia
and Spain. There are some new wines
from Costières du Nîmes, which used
to be called Costières du Gard, this
year: estates by the names of Château
de Campuget and Domaine l'Amarine.*

## J.E. HOGG (HOG)

61 Cumberland Street, Edinburgh
EH3 6RA, 031-556 4025
**Hours** Mon–Tue, Thu–Fri 9–1,
2.30–6; Wed, Sat 9–1.
**Delivery** Free 12 or more bottles
within Edinburgh.
**G T**
*Claret buyer's delight. Mature
Bordeaux and Burgundy are excellent,
as are malt whiskies, but the list is
also expanding into other areas – Chile
and New Zealand, for example.*

## HUNGERFORD WINE (HUN)

Unit 3, Station Yard, Hungerford,
Berks RG17 0DY (0488) 683238,
fax (0488) 684919
**Hours** Mon–Fri 9–5.30, Sat 9.30–5.
**Credit cards** AC AE V.
**Discounts** 5% case.
**Delivery** Free within 15 mile radius 1
case, elsewhere 5 cases or more.
**C EP G M T**
*The ebullient Nick Davies has a list of
over 1000 wines. Very good value en
primeur offers for Bordeaux, Rhône,
Port and Burgundy.*

## IRVINE ROBERTSON (IR)

10/11 North Leith Sands, Edinburgh
EH6 4ER (031) 553-3521; in
association with Graham MacHarg
Fine Wines, Fowberry Tower, Wooler,
Northumberland NE71 6ER
(06685) 274
**Hours** Mon–Fri 9–5.30.
**Discounts** On 5 cases or more.
**Delivery** Free locally, elsewhere 3
cases or more.
**Minimum order** 1 mixed case.
**G M T**
*Remarkably good range of first class
stuff worldwide. You'd expect good
claret and Burgundy from an ex-
Justerini & Brooks man, but they're
also excellent on New World.*

## J.C. KARN & SON (KA)

7 Lansdown Place, Cheltenham, Glos
GL50 2HU (0242) 513265
**Hours** Mon–Fri 9.30–6, Sat 9.30–1.30.
**Credit cards** AC V.
**Discounts** 5% mixed case.
**Delivery** Free in Glos. **G M T**
*Personally selected list, particularly
good on New Zealand; also strong in
the Loire, especially domaine wines
from Touraine.*

## LAY & WHEELER (LAY)

Head office and shop: 6 Culver Street
West, Colchester, Essex CO1 1JA
(0206) 764446, fax (0206) 564488
**Hours** Mon–Sat 8.30–5.30;
Wine Market, Gosbeck's Road, Shrub
End, Colchester, Essex CO2 9JT
(0206) 764446 **Hours** Mon–Sat 8–8.
**Credit cards** AC V. **Discounts** 1½%
4–11 cases, 3% 12 cases or more.
**Delivery** Free locally 1 case,
elsewhere 2 cases or more.
**C EP G M T**
*Colchester wine merchants with one of
the most comprehensive lists in the
country, with some of the best
producers in each region. The claret is
particularly good, but the others take a
lot of beating. Huge range displaying
knowledge, depth and erudition, but
don't be put off, it just means you can
feel tremendous confidence in the
choices. Half bottles for the unsure;
magnums for the decisive. Regular
wine workshops and tastings.*

## O.W. LOEB (LOE)

64 Southwark Bridge Road, London
SE1 0AS 071-928 7750, fax 071-928
1855
**Hours** Mon-Fri 9-5.30 for collection.
**Delivery** free Central London,
elsewhere 6 cases and over.
**Minimum order** 1 case.
**C EP M T**

*No shop, so they need prior warning of collection, and they don't go out of their way to lure private customers. But ask nicely and you could get access to their astonishingly good list of traditional areas, especially Germany, Bordeaux, Burgundy, Alsace and Rhône. Some California and Australia, too.*

## LONDON WINE (LO)

Chelsea Wharf, 15 Lots Road, London SW10 0QF, 071-351 6856
**Hours** Mon–Fri 9–9, Sat 10–7, Sun 12.00–3.00.
**Credit cards** AC AE DC V.
**Discounts** On very large orders.
**Delivery** Free locally.
**Minimum order** 1 mixed case.
**EP G M T**
*Revitalized warehouse operation with an increasingly good selection of whatever wines are in vogue at the present time. Fine wine investment advice, wine exchange, sale or return service. Short but sound list – Duboeuf, Cavit, etc.*

## LORNE HOUSE VINTNERS (LOR)

Unit 5, Hewitts Industrial Estate, Elmbridge Road, Cranleigh, Surrey GU6 8LW (0483) 271445, fax (0483) 268401
**Hours** Mon–Fri 9–5.30, Sat 9–1.
**Discounts** Negotiable.
**Delivery** Free 2 cases or more within

25 miles central London, or £5 per consignment.
**Minimum order** 1 mixed case.
**G M T**
*The mainly French list offers a decent range of wines from all over the country; there are also clutches of wines from Germany, Spain and California. A 'Shipping Club' gives you a chance to receive advance information on special deals, and offers a ten per cent discount for pre-payment.*

## MAJESTIC (MAJ)

Odhams Trading Estate, St Albans Road, Watford, Herts WD2 5RE (0923) 816999, fax (0923) 819105; 23 branches in London; also in Acocks Green, Amersham, Birmingham, Bletchley, Bristol, Cambridge, Croydon, Gloucester, Guildford, Ipswich, Maidenhead, Northampton, Norwich, Oxford, Poole, Reading, St Albans, Salisbury, Stockport, Swindon, Taunton
**Hours** Mon–Sat 10–8, Sun 10–6.
**Credit cards** AC AE DC V.
**Delivery** Free locally.
**Minimum order** 1 mixed case.
**EP G M T**
*Still no longer quite the force it used to be, with smaller selections despite keen prices. However, it seems to be improving again after last year's low, and has been take over by Wizard Wine Warehouses.*

## MARKS & SPENCER (MAR)

Michael House, Baker Street, London
W1A 1DN, 071-935 4422; 264 licensed
stores all over the country
**Hours** Variable.
**Discounts** 12 bottles for the price
of 11.
**M**
*M&S has shaken off its 'reliable rather
than exciting' tag, but is currently a
little less sparky than it was a couple
of years ago. Expanding list of 200
wines, 40 of which are vintage
selection. Good second wines and
bargains like declassified Chablis.*

## MORENO WINES (MOR)

11 Marylands Road, London W9 2DU,
071-286 0678, fax 071-286 0513
**Hours** Mon–Fri 9–9, Sun 12–2;
2 Norfolk Place, London W2 1QN,
071-706 3055
**Hours** Mon–Fri 9–8, Sat 10–8.
**Credit cards** AC V.
**Discounts** 5% mixed case.
**Delivery** Free locally, elsewhere 4
cases or more.
**G M T**
*Moreno undoubtedly has the largest
range of Spanish wines in the country.
Over 500 wines from all the main
regions and some lesser known ones.
Riojas, Penedés, Navarra, Cariñena,
Galicia, Priorato and others, including
such treats as Vega Sicilia, Bodegas
Riojanas and CVNE, and Albariño for
when you're feeling rich, plus a fine
selection of sherries, brandies and
liqueurs. Also some wines from Chile
and Portugal.*

> The codes given in brackets on these
> pages beside the merchants' names
> are those by which the merchants are
> listed in the price guides (pages 246–397).
> They are also listed on page 246.

## MORRIS & VERDIN (MV)

28 Churton Street, London SW1V
2LP, 071-630 8888
**Hours** Mon–Fri 9.30–5.30, Sat 9–1.
**Discounts** On 5 cases or more.
**Delivery** Free central London and
Oxford, elsewhere free for 5 cases or
more.
**Minimum order** 1 mixed case.
**C EP G M T**
*Imaginative list, majoring on
Burgundy and including names like
Rion, Bachelet, Ponsot. Also Alsace
from Ostertag, Au Bon Climat and
Bonny Doon from California,
selections from Australia and New
Zealand. An increasing choice of
French country wines.*

## THE NADDER WINE CO (NA)

Hussars House, 2, Netherhampton
Road, Harnham, Salisbury, Wiltshire
SP2 8HE (0722) 325418; fax (0722)
716488
**Hours:** Mon-Fri 9-7, Sat 10-3.
**Minimum order:** 1 case.
Delivery:free in central London,
Salisbury area or orders of £50 or
over. Otherwise £6 for 1 case; £3.60
per case, 2-4 cases, £1.90 per case, 5-9
cases, UK mainland and Isle of Wight.
10 or more cases free.
**Credit cards:** AC, V.
**Discounts:** 2.5% on orders over £100;
5% on orders over £500, except for
credit cards.
**G M T**
*There's quite a lot of scope here if you
want mid-level claret, and there's
plenty from Australia, including the
excellent Mountadam, Petaluma and
Dromana Estate wines. There's also
Columbia Winery from Washington
State and some good South Africans.
Ports look interesting. Nadder will
buy ex-cellars for private customers for
orders of ten cases per area or more, at
a low mark up.*

## JAMES NICHOLSON (NI)

27A Killyeagh Street, Crossgar, Co.
Down, Northern Ireland BT30 9DG
(0396) 830091, fax (0396) 830028
**Hours** Mon–Sat 10–7.
**Credit cards:** AC, DC, V.
**Discounts** 5–10% per mixed case.
**Delivery** Free UK for 1 case or more.
**Minimum order** 1 mixed case.
**C EP G M T**
*A pretty comprehensive list of lots of
famous names – Mondavi, Rosemount,
Château Musar, Cousino Macul,
Jaboulet, Duboeuf and so on. New this
year is a Condrieu from the Rhône, a
couple of Bandols and some excellent
additions from Spain (Pesquera, Vega
Sicilia), Germany (Willi Haag, Rainer
Lingenfelder), Italy (Sassicaia, Rocca
della Macie) and Alsace (Schlumberger).
Also lots of good halves – Rhône,
Burgundy, Musar, claret and dessert
wines from New Zealand.*

## ODDBINS (OD)

31-33 Weir Road, London SW19 8UG,
081-944 4400
**Hours** Mon–Sat 9–9, Sun 12–2 and
7–9 except Scotland. Closed:
Christmas.
**Credit cards** AC AE V.
**Discounts** 5% split case wine, 7 bottles
Champagne and sparkling wine for
the price of 6 (if £5.99 or above).
**Delivery** Available locally for most
shops. Free with reasonable order.
**G T**
*Imaginative wine ranges put Oddbins
way ahead of the rest of the High
Street pack. Good value wines from
Italy, sparkling wines for every budget
from Australia, sound and inexpensive
Skalli wines from southern France.
Add to this malt whiskies, excellent
ports and a wide range of beers. The
staff are generally better informed
than at most chains. En Primeur offers
may be by the bottle, paying on receipt.*

## THOS. PEATLING (PE)

Westgate House, Bury St Edmunds,
Suffolk IP33 1QS (0284) 755948,
fax (0284) 705795
**Hours** Variable.
**Credit cards** AC AE V.
**Discounts** 5% mixed case.
**Delivery** Free within East Anglia,
elsewhere 5 or more cases.
**C EP G M T**
*Strong Peatling points have always
been clarets, and especially petits
châteaux, but the New World wines
are getting better all the time.
Peatlings also includes the former
Ostlers, the Australian specialists.*

## PETER DOMINIC (PD)

Sefton House, 42 Church Road,
Welwyn Garden City, Herts AL8 6PJ
(0707) 328244, fax (0707) 371398
**Hours** Mon–Sat 9–10 (some 10.30),
Sun 12–3, 7–10. Closed Sun in
Scotland.
**Credit cards** AC V.
**Discounts** Available on quantity.
**Delivery** Free local, selected
branches only.
*The Dominic chain was bought by
Thresher in October 1991 and
currently all Peter Dominic stores are
being converted to Threshers: Wine
Rack, Thresher Wine Shops or Drinks
Stores from Thresher. Most stores have
now been re-named but some will still
be called Peter Dominic until 1993.*

---

*All the companies listed in the Merchant
Directory have wines featured in the Price
Guides (pages 246–397).
Abbreviations used in the Directory are as
follows: **Credit Cards** Access (AC),
American Express (AE), Diners Club (DC),
Visa/Barclaycard (V).
The following services are available where
indicated: **C** cellarage, **EP** en primeur
offers, **G** glass hire/loan, **M** mail order,
**T** tastings and talks.*

## PENISTONE COURT (PEN)

The Railway Station, Penistone,
South Yorkshire S30 6HG
(0226) 766037, fax (0226) 767310
**Hours** Mon-Fri 9-6, Sat 10-3.
**Delivery** free locally, UK mainland
at cost for 1 case or over.
**G**
*A sound list that covers all the major
areas, though with a tendency to rely
on just one or two major producers in
each. The printed list often fails to list
a producer at all, and quotes prices ex-
VAT. In spite of these drawbacks it is
worth investigating, with California
wines from Renaissance and Quady,
good Spanish and Antipodean and
the hard-to-find Roederer Rich
Champagne, to keep out the Yorkshire
chill. They also sell Lamberhurst
Vineyards fruit liqueurs – English
flavours like plum and pear and
raspberry and the rather less English
orange.*

## CHRISTOPHER PIPER (PIP)

1 Silver Street, Ottery St Mary,
Devon EX11 1DB (0404) 814139,
fax (0404) 812100
**Hours** Mon–Sat 9–6.
**Credit cards** AC V.
**Discounts** 5% mixed case, 10% 3
cases or more.
**Delivery** Free in south-west 4 or
more cases, elsewhere 6 or more cases.
**Minimum order** 1 mixed case.
**C EP G M T**
*Chris Piper is one of the very few
English merchants who is also a wine
producer in France at Brouilly
(Château des Tours). Specializes in
domaine-bottled wines and works very
closely with producers, especially in
Burgundy and the Rhône. Wines are
well-chosen throughout the list, and
even though the prices may not be the
lowest there are treats like George
Goulet Champagne, sweet white Loires
and Barbadillo sherries.*

## RAEBURN FINE WINES (RAE)

23 Comely Bank Road, Edinburgh
EH4 1DS, telephone & fax 031-332
5166
**Hours** Mon–Sat 9–6.
**Credit cards** AC V.
**Discounts** 5% unsplit case, 2.5%
mixed case.
**Delivery** Price negotiable, all areas
covered.
**C EP G M T**
*An amazing list for range and quality;
stocked in a cramped and crowded
shop, but never mind with this sort of
selection. Many of the world's greatest
wines are hiding on the shelves.*

## REID WINES (REI)

The Mill, Marsh Lane, Hallatrow, Nr
Bristol BS18 5EB (0761) 452645,
fax (0761) 453642
**Hours** Mon–Fri 9–5.30.
**Credit cards** AC V.
**Delivery** Free within 25 miles of
Hallatrow (Bristol).
**C EP G M T**
*Good selection of top quality wines
from all the classic areas of Europe
and from some of the new wine areas
of the world; also many fine and rare
wines and a witty wine list.*

## ROBERSON (ROB)

348 Kensington High Street, London
W14 8NS 071-371 2121, fax 071-371
4010
**Hours** Mon-Sat 10-8, Sun 12-3.
**Credit cards** AC, V, AE.
**Delivery** free locally for one case
or more.
**G T**
*This new shop (opened November
1991) aims to be the best in London
and so far it seems to be well on its
way. It stocks around 1000 wines and
over 150 spirits and liqueurs: with
that sort of range, it can hardly fail to
be mouthwatering. In addition they
will hunt for anniversary bottles for
you. Everything is displayed in a most
untraditional manner: salvaged scrap
metal provides the decor and the
wines are all displayed lying down.
Manager Chris Donaldson MW is ex-
Harrods, ex-Sherry-Lehmann in New
York and ex-Alexis-Lichine in
Bordeaux; also ex-the rather pricy
Buckinghams. Robersons, however,
aims to compete on price. Donaldson
reckons he can maintain the high
standards he's set himself; he deserves
to succeed.*

## SAFEWAY (SAF)

6 Millington Road, Hayes, Middx UB3
4AY, 081-848 8744
**Hours** Mon–Sat 8–8 (Fri till 9). Sun
10–4 (selected stores).
**Credit cards** AC V.
**G**
*The surprise supermarket success story
of the 1980s. After years of underachieving, Safeway is dramatically
back in the leading pack of High Street
wine cellars. As well as filling shelves
with organic produce, Safeway extend
this area of concern to wine,
sponsoring an annual organic wine
fair and tasting, and stocking a good
range of organic wine. Increasingly
good French country wines, Eastern
Europe, New World, sound Italians
and port and sherry in half bottles.*

## SAINSBURY (SAI)

Stamford House, Stamford Street,
London SE1 9LL, 071-921 6000.
Main branches: Bath, Cambridge,
Cardiff, Chester, Cobham, Crayford
(Kent), Derby, Guildford, Leeds,
Leicester, London (Camden, Chiswick,
Cromwell Road, Fulham, Hampton,
Harringay, Ladbroke Grove, Nine
Elms, Pinner, Wandsworth), Oxford,
Milton Keynes, Norwich, Nottingham,

Plymouth, Sheffield, Shirley (nr Solihull), York. Savacentres: Basildon, Edinburgh, London Colney, Meadowhall (Sheffield), Merton (south-west London), Oldbury, Reading, Washington (Tyne & Wear)
**Hours** Variable, many open late.
*The country's largest wine retailer. Increasingly imaginative list enlivened by a vintage selection of fine wines available from 238 main stores with the widest selection of 400 wines available in 50 branches and 9 Savacentres.*

## SOMMELIER WINE CO (SOM)

23 St George's Esplanade, St Peter Port, Guernsey, Channel Islands (0481) 721677, fax (0481) 716818
**Hours** Tues-Thurs 10-5.50, Fri 10-6, Sat 9-5.30, answerphone out of hours.
**Delivery** free for 6 unmixed bottles or more
**Discounts** 5% on unmixed cases.
**Credit cards** AC, V at Grapevine shop only.
**G T**
*Thoughtfully-chosen list, strong on France, Italy, California and Australia. There's not necessarily a huge selection of some thing, but there's generally something to interest – a sweet Pacherenc de Vic Bilh, for example, from south-west France. Plenty of French country wines from growers and co-ops rather than big négociants, and a helpful list, with guidance on when to drink.*

## SUNDAY TIMES WINE CLUB (WIC)

New Aquitaine House, Paddock Road, Reading, Berks RG4 0JY
(0734) 481713, fax (0734) 471928
**Hours** Mail order, 24-hr answerphone.
**Credit cards** AC AE DC V.
**Discounts** On special offers.
**Delivery** Free orders over £50.
**EP M T**

*Associate company is Bordeaux Direct. Membership fee is £5 per annum, for which you receive news of the constantly changing list, the regular magazine 'Wine Times', plus news of special mixed case selections.The club also runs an annual festival in London.*

## TANNERS (TAN)

26 Wyle Cop, Shrewsbury, Shropshire SY1 1XD (0743) 232400
**Hours** Mon–Sat 9–5.30.
**Credit cards** AC V.
**Discounts** On 6 unsplit cases or more and cash collection.
**Delivery** Free local delivery for orders of one case or more, otherwise £6 per order, and nationally for orders under £75.
**EP G M T**
*Wide-ranging and adventurously chosen list – good on classic areas like Burgundy (Domaine Dujac, Pousse d'Or, Lafon) and claret, but also the New World. Terrific things from everywhere, in fact – try Champalimaud's Quinta da Cotto from Portugal, the excellent Quinta de Agua Alta port from Churchills, Château Carras from Greece and even not one but three Swiss wines.*

## TESCO (TES)

Delamare Road, Cheshunt, Herts EN8 9SL (0992) 32222. 362 licensed branches
**Hours** Variable. Open Sunday in Scotland.
**Credit cards** AC V.
*An ever-improving list; wines from all over the world. Now catching up with Sainsbury's in terms of sales. Good on Italy (including less common, good value names like Montepulciano d'Abruzzo, Lugana) and Germany, also sound French country wines and Bordeaux reds.*

## THRESHER (THR)

Sefton House, 42 Church Road,
Welwyn Garden City, Herts AL8 6PJ
(0707) 328244, fax (0707) 371398
**Hours** Mon–Sat 9–10 (some 10.30),
Sun 12–3, 7–10. Closed Sun in
Scotland.
**Credit cards** AC V.
**Discounts** Available on quantity.
**Delivery** Free local, selected branches.
*Two different shop fascia* – **Thresher
Wine Shops** *and* **Drink Stores from
Threshers.** *Now owns Peter Dominic,
Bottoms Up, Wine Rack as well as
Thresher shops themselves. Strong on
clarets, including a good choice of
second wines, an expanding range of
Alsace wines (wonderful Zind-
Humbrecht), plus an increasingly good
selection of French country wines.
Australia, New Zealand and
California all on the up.*

## T. & W. WINES (TW)

51 King Street, Thetford, Norfolk IP24
2AU (0842) 765646
**Hours** Mon–Fri 9.30–5.30, Sat
9.30–1.00.
**Credit cards** AC AE DC V.
**Delivery** Free 4 cases or more UK
mainland.  **C EP G M**
*Good people to hunt out old and rare
wines. Specialists in half bottles (older
vintages in halves, too) as well as
Californian (Dunn Vineyards, Flora
Springs, Silver Oak) and Alsace wines.*

## UNWINS (UN)

Birchwood House, Victoria Road,
Dartford, Kent DA1 5AJ
(0322) 272711/7; 300 specialist off-
licences throughout the south-east of
England
**Hours** 10–10.
**Credit cards** AC AE DC V.
**Discounts** 10% mixed case.
**G M T**

*All the world's major wine-producing
areas are covered by this family run
company, though you may need to see
the list rather than the shelves to find
such items as Classed Growths.*

## VALVONA & CROLLA (VA)

19 Elm Row, Edinburgh EH7 4AA,
031-556 6066
**Hours** Mon–Sat 8.30–6. Closed: 1–7
Jan.
**Credit cards** AC V.
**Discounts** 5% mixed case.
**Delivery** Locally free for orders over
£25. Mail order £6.90 per case, £3 for
orders of more than 4 cases, free for 7
or more.
**G M T**
*One of the best selections of Italian
wine in the UK – regular special offers.
Wines from every corner of Italy from
Sicily to the Alto Adige, and from the
pricy stars (Gaja and Biondi-Santi) to
the easily affordable (Montepulciano
d'Abruzzo). A real treasure trove of a
store.*

## VICTORIA WINE (VIC)

Brook House, Chertsey Road, Woking,
Surrey GU21 5BE (048371) 5066.
Over 800 branches throughout Great
Britain
**Hours** Variable, usually Mon–Sat 9–6
(high street), 10–10 (local shops); Sun
12–3, 7–10.
**Credit cards** AC AE V.
**Discounts** 10% mixed case.
**G T**
*The experiments with new images –
Gare du Vin and South of the
Bordeaux – now set aside, the 820
branches of Victoria Wine have been
concentrating on their own wine list
with notable success. Plenty of good
drinking under a fiver, an expanding
shelf of South American wines, as well
as representatives from Europe's
traditional wine regions.*

## LA VIGNERONNE (VIG)

105 Old Brompton Road, London SW7 3LE, 071-589 6113
**Hours** Mon–Fri 10–9, Sat 10–8, Sun closed.
**Credit cards** AC AE DC V.
**Discounts** 5% mixed case collected.
**Delivery** Free locally, Greater London £2.50, mainland England & Wales £5. Scotland £7.50 for under £100 in value; Greater London £1, mainland England & Wales £3.50, Scotland £5 for £100–£250; over £250 free.
**C EP G M T**
*Fascinating list, strong on classic and Southern French – also the place for exceptional Alsace wines, Provençal rarities, outstanding Californians and Aussies. Come here for variety, top quality at all levels, old vintages and wines you've never heard of – for all this, and knowledgeable service, you must expect to pay.*

## VINTAGE WINES (VIN)

116 Derby Road, Nottingham NG1 5FB (0602) 476565/419614
**Hours** Mon–Fri 9–5.15, Sat 9–1.
**Credit cards** AC V.
**Discounts** 10% mixed case.
**Delivery** Free within 60 miles.
**G M T**
*Useful merchant with a traditional taste who takes particular care with his house wines.*

## WAITROSE (WAI)

Doncastle Road, Southern Industrial Area, Bracknell, Berks RG12 4YA (0344) 424680. 100 licensed shops.
**Hours** Mon–Tue 9–6, Wed 9–8, Thu 8.30–8, Fri 8.30–9, Sat 8.30–5.30.
**Discounts** 5% for over £100 of wine or any whole case of wine. **G**
*An incredibly good range of wines from all round the world, always at competitive prices.*

## WHITESIDES OF CLITHEROE (WHI)

Shawbridge Street, Clitheroe, Lancs
BB7 1NA (0200) 22281, fax (0200)
27129
**Hours** Mon–Sat 9–5.30; 39 The
Grove, Ilkley, North Yorks LS29 9NJ
telephone and fax (0943) 816015
**Hours** Mon–Sat 9.30–6.
**Credit cards** AC V
**Discounts** Dependent on amount, 5%
unmixed case.
**G M T**
*A good all-round selection. The list is
at its happiest in France's classic
regions, but there are also familiar
names from Germany, Italy and Spain.*

## WINDRUSH WINES (WW)

The Barracks, Cecily Hill, Cirencester,
Glos GL7 2EF (0285) 650466,
fax (0285) 654280
**Hours** Mon–Fri 9–6; 3 Market Place,
Cirencester, Glos GL7 2PE
(0285) 650466
**Hours** Mon–Sat 9–5.30.
**Credit cards** AC V.
**Discounts** In bond and ex-cellar
terms available.
**Delivery** Free locally, elsewhere
£5.00 for up to 2 cases, free for 3.
**Minimum order** 1 mixed case.
**C EP G M T**
*Specialists in fine single-estate wines.
While the emphasis lies on France,
they have also established a reputation
for the best wines from California and
the Pacific North-West. The list is
unusual but stimulating, with Pinot
Noir from Old World and New
obviously a preoccupation, and choice
names appearing from Germany,
Tuscany and Piedmont.*

## WINE RACK (WR)

Sefton House, 42 Church Street,
Welwyn Garden City, Herts AL8 6PJ
(0707) 328244, fax (0707) 371398

**Hours** Mon–Sat 9–10 (some 10.30),
Sun 12–3, 7–10.
**Credit cards** AC AE V.
**Discounts** Available on quantity.
**Delivery** Free local, selected shops.
*Part of Threshers; but smarter and
with a wider range. Eighty stores
across the country.*

## WINE SOCIETY (WS)

Gunnels Wood Road, Stevenage, Herts
SG1 2BG (0438) 741177, fax (0438)
741392
**Hours** Mon–Fri 9–5; showroom
Mon–Fri 9–6 Sat 9–1.
**Credit cards** AC V.
**Discounts** £1 per case 5–9 cases, £2
per case 10 or more cases.
**Delivery** Free 1 case or more UK
mainland and Northern Ireland.
**C EP G M T**
*You have to be a member to buy wines
from this non-profit-making co-
operative, but lifetime membership is
very reasonable at £20.They offer an
outstanding range of classic wines.
France is the backbone, but there are
also good Germans, plus sound
drinking from Italy, Spain and
Portugal on the well-organized list.
Good own-label sherries too, and the
list rounds off with such useful items
as glasses, corkscrews and even
decanter driers.*

## WINECELLARS (WCL)

153–155 Wandsworth High Street,
London SW18 4JB, 081-871 2668
**Hours** Mon–Fri 10.30–8.30 Sat
10–8.30; The Market 213-215 Upper
Street, London N1 1RL, 071-359 5386
**Hours** daily 9–9.
**Credit cards** AC V.
**Discounts** 10% mixed case.
**Delivery** Free within M25 boundary,
2 cases UK mainland.
**Minimum order** 1 mixed case.
**C G M T**

*One of the most exciting ranges of wine in London is to be found at Britain's leading Italian specialist. Each year the list gets bigger and better – it was always a good read but it's now good to look at too and includes books, coffee, even pasta flour and wonderful olive oil. Regular tastings including many non-Italian subjects.*

## WINES OF WESTHORPE (WIW)

Marchington, Staffs ST14 8NX (0283) 820285, fax (0283) 820631
**Hours** Mon–Fri and most weekends 8–6.30.
**Credit cards** AC V.
**Discounts** £2.40 5–10 cases, £3 11–15 cases
**Delivery** Free on UK mainland.
**Minimum order** 1 mixed case.
**M T**
*The Eastern European experts with a good range of Bulgarian and Hungarian wines, and a very promising new Chilean range. Also Australians.*

## WRIGHT WINE CO (WRI)

The Old Smithy, Raikes Road, Skipton, N. Yorks BD23 1NP (0756) 700886
**Hours** Mon–Sat 9–6, including bank holidays.
**Discounts** Wholesale price unsplit case, 5% mixed case.
**Delivery** Free within 30 miles.
**G**
*Large selection of brandies, malt whiskies, liqueurs. Interesting wines from the New World. You'll find a small clutch of wines from Israel and England in there too.*

## PETER WYLIE FINE WINES (WY)

Plymtree Manor, Plymtree, Cullompton, Devon EX15 2LE (088 47) 555, fax (088 47) 557

**Hours** Mon–Fri 9–6.
**Discounts** Unsplit case.
**Delivery** London 3 or more cases free; 1–2 cases and UK mainland £8 for 1 case then £6 per case.
**C M**
*Claret and Sauternes are the specialities, followed by Burgundy, Champagne and port. Madeira features too. There are plenty of older vintages for the buff to wallow in; in fact mature wines are a speciality, and they describe themselves as 'the UK's largest mature wine holder'.*

## YAPP BROTHERS (YAP)

The Old Brewery, Mere, Wilts BA12 6DY (0747) 860423, fax (0747) 860929
**Hours** Mon– Fri 9–5, Sat 9–1.
**Credit cards** AC V.
**Discounts** On 5 or more cases.
**Delivery** £3 for 1 case, free more than 1 case.
**C EP G M T**
*The specialities are the Rhône and the Loire, but that doesn't prevent Robin Yapp from adding in some Champagne, a little Alsace, Provence and even some fish soup if it takes his fancy.*

## YORKSHIRE FINE WINES (YF)

Nun Monkton, Sweethills, York YO5 8ET (0423) 330131
**Hours** Mon–Fri 9–5.
**Credit cards** AC V.
**Discounts** By negotiation.
**Delivery** Free in northern England and within M25; elsewhere 5 or more cases.
**Minimum order** 1 mixed case.
**C G M T**
*Have been take over by Bibendum in London, which has brought prices for YF's wines down to less stratospheric levels. The list now essentially reflects Bibendum's, which can't be bad.*

# REGIONAL DIRECTORY

## LONDON

| | |
|---|---|
| Les Amis du Vin | AMI |
| André Simon | AN |
| Australian Wine Centre | AUS |
| Barnes Wine Shop | BAR |
| Berkmann Wine Cellars | BEK |
| Berry Bros & Rudd | BER |
| Bibendum | BIB |
| Bottoms Up | BOT |
| Corney & Barrow | CB |
| Davisons | DAV |
| Farr Vintners | FA |
| Fine Wines of NZ | FIZ |
| Grog Blossom | GRG |
| Harcourt Fine Wines | HAC |
| Haynes Hanson & Clark | HAH |
| O W Loeb | LOE |
| London Wine | LO |
| Moreno Wines | MOR |
| Morris & Verdin | MV |
| Roberson | ROB |
| Unwins | UN |
| La Vigneronne | VIG |
| Winecellars | WCL |

## SOUTH-EAST AND HOME COUNTIES

| | |
|---|---|
| Bedford Fine Wines | BE |
| Berry Bros & Rudd | BER |
| Bordeaux Direct | BOD |
| Bottoms Up | BOT |
| Butlers Wine Cellar | BU |
| Cape Province Wines | CAP |
| Chaplin & Son | CH |
| Gerard Harris | HAG |
| Douglas Henn-Macrae | HE |
| High Breck Vintners | HIG |
| Hungerford Wine Company | HUN |
| Lorne House Vintners | LOR |
| Reid Wines | REI |
| Unwins | UN |
| Upper Crust | UP |

| | |
|---|---|
| The Sunday Times Wine Club | WIC |
| Wine Society | WS |

## WEST AND SOUTH-WEST

| | |
|---|---|
| Averys | AV |
| Bottoms Up | BOT |
| Châteaux Wines | CHA |
| Eldridge, Pope & Co | EL |
| Halves | HAL |
| John Harvey & Sons | HA |
| Richard Harvey Wines | HAY |
| Hicks & Don | HIC |
| J.C. Karn | KA |
| Nadder Wine | NA |
| Christopher Piper | PIP |
| Reid Wines | REI |
| Windrush Wines | WW |
| Peter Wylie | WYL |
| Yapp Brothers | YAP |

## EAST ANGLIA

| | |
|---|---|
| Adnams | AD |
| Anthony Byrne | BY |
| Roger Harris Wines | HAW |
| Hicks & Don | HIC |
| Lay & Wheeler | LAY |
| Thos. Peatling | PE |
| T. & W. Wines | TW |

## MIDLANDS

| | |
|---|---|
| Askham Wines | ASK |
| Broad Street Wine Co. | BR |
| Tanners | TAN |
| Vintage Wines | VIN |
| Wines of Westhorpe | WIW |

## NORTH

| | |
|---|---|
| Booths | BO |
| Borg Castel | BOR |
| D Byrne | BYR |
| George Dutton & Son | WIL |

| | |
|---|---|
| Haughton Fine Wines | HAU |
| Penistone Court Fine Wines | PEN |
| Whitesides of Clitheroe | WHI |
| Wright Wine Company | WRI |
| Yorkshire Fine Wines | YF |

## WALES

| | |
|---|---|
| Ashley Scott | AS |
| Celtic Vintner | CV |

## SCOTLAND

| | |
|---|---|
| Bute Wines | BUT |
| Corney & Barrow | CB |
| Gelston Castle | GE |
| Peter Green | GRE |
| J.E. Hogg | HOG |
| Irvine Robertson Wines | IR |
| Raeburn Fine Wines | RAE |
| Valvona & Crolla | VA |

## CHANNEL ISLANDS

| | |
|---|---|
| Sommelier Wines | SOM |

## NORTHERN IRELAND

| | |
|---|---|
| James Nicholson | NI |

## COUNTRYWIDE

| | |
|---|---|
| ASDA | ASD |
| Augustus Barnett | AUG |
| Gateway | GA |
| Majestic | MAJ |
| Marks & Spencer | MAR |
| Oddbins | OD |
| Peter Dominic | PD |
| Safeway | SAF |
| Sainsbury | SAI |
| Tesco | TES |
| Thresher | THR |
| Victoria Wine | VIC |
| Waitrose | WAI |
| Wine Rack | WR |

**Oz Clarke's Wine Guide** *is an annual publication: we welcome any suggestions you may have for the 1994 edition.* Send them to Webster's , Axe and Bottle Court, 70 Newcomen Street, London SE1 1YT.

# INDEX

# ACKNOWLEDGEMENTS

Our thanks go to the following (members of the trade and others) who have generously put information and expertise at the disposal of the guide: Anthony Hanson MW, Haynes Hanson & Clark; Jasper Morris MW, Morris & Verdin; Margaret Bridgeman, Halewood Vintners; Food & Wine from France; Wink Lorch; Wines from Spain. We'd also like to thank all those who sent us their wine lists, and everyone who kindly supplied wines for our tasting.